Other Kaplan Books Relating to College Admissions

Access America's Guide to Studying in the USA
SAT 1998
ACT 1998
ACT In-a-Week
The College Catalog
Parent's Guide to College Admissions
SAT II Math 1998
SAT II Writing 1998
SAT In-a-Week
SAT Math Workbook
SAT or ACT? Test Your Best
SAT Verbal Workbook
Scholarships 1998
You Can Afford College
Yale Daily News Guide to Succeeding in College

THE ROAD TO COLLEGE

Selection • Admission • Financial Aid

Steven Frank, R. Fred Zuker, Alice Murphey
and
the Staff of Kaplan Educational Centers

Foreword by Marcy Hamilton

Simon & Schuster

Kaplan Books
Published by
Kaplan Educational Centers and Simon & Schuster
1230 Avenue of the Americas
New York, New York 10020

Copyright © 1997 by Kaplan Educational Centers

All rights reserved. No part of this book may be reproduced or transmitted in any form or by any means, electronic or mechanical, including photocopying, recording, or by information storage and retrieval system, without the written permission of the Publisher, except where permitted by law.

Kaplan® is a registered trademark of Kaplan Educational Centers.

For all references in this book, SAT is a registered trademark of the College Board, which does not endorse or sponsor this book.

For all references in this book, ACT is a registered trademark of the American College Testing Program, which does not endorse or sponsor this book.

Manufactured in the United States of America
Published Simultaneously in Canada

June 1998

10 9 8 7 6 5 4 3 2 1

Contributors to School Profiles: Shane Christensen, David Gosse, Timothy Nolan, and Keith Yazmir

Special thanks are extended to Linda Volpano and Sara Pearl.

ISBN 0-684-84166-5
ISSN 1087-7894

Project Editor: Richard Christiano
Production Coordinator: Gerard Capistrano
Production Editor: Maude Spekes
Graphic Design: Bola Famuyiwa
Cover Design: Amy McHenry
Assistant Managing Editor: Brent Gallenberger
Managing Editor: Kiernan McGuire
Executive Editor: Del Franz

CONTENTS

A Special Note for International Students i
Foreword v
How to Use This Book xi

SECTION I: COLLEGE SELECTION, by Steven Frank 1
Have Map, Will Travel 3
Your Personal Advisor 7
Academic Shrines 49
Small Wonders 109
Budget Ivies 131
Value Marts 155
All-Around Gems 179
Buried Treasures 201
Separate Quarters 225
HBCUs 245
Briefcase Factories 255
Specialty Shops 273
Houses of Faith 291
Cultural Meccas 303
Travel Agencies 325
Global Villages 337
Alternative Havens 351
Scenic Routes 365
Serious Fun 381
Go State! 397
Sports Powerhouses 419

SECTION II: ADMISSIONS, by R. Fred Zuker 445
Applying to College 447
When to Apply 451
How to Apply 457
Essays That Work 483
Recommendations 493
Interviews and Campus Visits 501
How to Make Your Final Decision 513

SECTION III: FINANCIAL AID, by Alice Murphey 519
Introduction to Financial Aid 521
Paying for College 523
An Inside Look at the Financial Aid Application Process 535

SECTION IV: ACCESSIBLE ACADEMICS 559
Especially for Persons with Disabilities 561

Index of Schools Profiled 593

A Special Note for International Students

Approximately 500,000 international students pursued academic degrees at the undergraduate, graduate, or professional school level at U.S. universities during the 1995–96 academic year, according to the Institute of International Education's *Open Doors* report. Almost 50 percent of these students were studying for a bachelor's or first university degree. This trend of pursuing higher education in the United States is expected to continue well into the next century. Business, management, engineering, and the physical and life sciences are particularly popular majors for students coming to the United States from other countries.

If you are not from the United States, but are considering attending a U.S. college or university, here's what you'll need to get started:

- If English is not your first language, start there. You'll probably need to take the Test of English as a Foreign Language (TOEFL) and the Test of Written English (TWE), or show some other evidence that you are fully proficient in English in order to complete an academic degree program. Colleges and universities in the United States will differ on what they consider to be an acceptable TOEFL score. A minimum TOEFL score of 550 or better is often expected by the more prestigious and competitive institutions. Because American undergraduate programs require all students to take a certain number of general education courses, all students, even math and computer science students, need to be able to communicate well in spoken and written English.

- You may also need to take the Scholastic Assessment Test (SAT) or the American College Test (ACT). Many undergraduate institutions in the United States require both the SAT and TOEFL of international students.

- There are over 2,700 accredited colleges and universities in the United States, so selecting the correct undergraduate school can be a confusing task for anyone. You will need to get help from a good advisor or at least a good college guide that explains the different types of programs and gives you some information on how to choose wisely. Since admission to many undergraduate programs is quite competitive, you may also want to select three or four colleges and complete applications for each school.

- You should begin the application process at least a year in advance. An increasing number of schools accept applications year round. In any case, find out the application deadlines and plan accordingly. Although September (the fall semester) is the traditional time to begin university study in the United States, at most schools you can also enter in January (the spring semester).

- Finally, you will need to obtain an I-20 Certificate of Eligibility in order to obtain an F-1 Student Visa to study in the United States. This you will request from the university. The school will send you the I-20 document once you have been accepted.

For an overview of the undergraduate admissions process, see the appendix on college admissions in this book. For details about the admissions requirements, curriculum, and other vital information on top colleges and universities, see Kaplan's Road to College.

Kaplan's Access America™ Program

If you need more help with the complex process of undergraduate school admissions and information about the variety of programs available, you may be interested in Kaplan's Access America program.

Kaplan created Access America to assist students and professionals from outside the United States who want to enter the U.S. university system. The program was designed for students who have received the bulk of their primary and secondary education outside the United States in a language other than English. Access America also has programs for obtaining professional certification in the United States. Here's a brief description of some of the help available through Access America.

The TOEFL Plus Program

At the heart of the Access America program is the intensive TOEFL Plus Academic English program. This comprehensive English course prepares students to achieve a high level of proficiency in English in order to successfully complete an academic degree. The TOEFL Plus course combines personalized instruction with guided self-study to help students gain this proficiency in a short time. Certificates of Achievement in English are awarded to certify each student's level of proficiency.

Undergraduate School/SAT Preparation

If your goal is to complete a bachelor of arts (B.A.) or bachelor of science (B.S.) degree in the United States, Kaplan will help you prepare for the SAT or ACT, while helping you understand the American system of education.

Applying to Access America

To get more information, or to apply for admission to any of Kaplan's programs for international students or professionals, you can write to us at:

Kaplan Educational Centers
International Admissions Department
888 Seventh Avenue, New York, NY 10106

Or call us at 1-800-522-7770 from within the United States, or 01-212-262-4980 outside the United States. Our fax number is 01-212-957-1654. Our E-mail address is world@kaplan.com. You can also get more information or even apply through the Internet at http://www.kaplan.com/intl.

About the Authors

Alice Murphey is the former Director of Financial Aid at the New York University Stern School of Business/Graduate Division. While at Stern, she worked closely with the Admissions Office personnel in the integration of the admission and financial aid process for entering students. Prior to her tenure at NYU, she held financial aid positions at the University of Souther California and Fordham University. She is currently the Assistant Director of Financial Aid for Systems Management at the City University of New York.

Steven Frank is a professional writer and college instructor. He is also the author of *A+ Term Papers* and *The Everything Study Book*. He received his BA with honors from Cornell University and his MA from New York University. He lives and works in New York City.

R. Fred Zuker has worked in admissions at public and private colleges (Duke University, Tulane University, and Pomona College) for more than 25 years. He holds and M.Ed. in guidance counseling and a Ph.D. is in counseling psychology from Duke University.

Brain-addled by so many choices and under the gun to choose a college, high school senior Timmy Wentworth decides to go for broke and hope for the best.

Foreword

Destination: COLLEGE

For many years, books of this nature were merely concerned with "getting in." As a college counselor, it's my hope that my counselees not just get in, but stay in, be happy, and graduate in considerably less than a decade. My wish for the family is that parents can afford to pay the price for educating their kids, and that these kids might consider returning the favor by footing the bills for their parents' extended and peaceful old age.

WHERE DO I GO? HOW DO I GET THERE?

Going to the wrong school can be very costly—educationally, emotionally, and financially. Transferring can be a nightmare; you can lose credits, friends, and sleep. How do you avoid this predicament? You should begin by not letting anyone else determine what it is you're looking for in a college. Look inside yourself and understand who you are first. This, of course, isn't easy because most high school students are works-in-progress. Even if you know all the right questions to ask yourself, the answers to those questions may not be instantly apparent.

The Road to College proposes to help you look at who you are and what you might want in a college. It's a workbook, so do the work. It will give you insight, and you'll begin to be a prudent buyer of your own education. You should also find out what your parents might want you to do and what they can afford. Most parents are flexible when it comes to your future; they ultimately want your happiness. You, however, need to know what will make you happy so you can make a strong case for it when you get to that important conversation. Remember this phrase: "It's not about just getting in. I want to stay in, be happy, and graduate."

What are your educational hopes, dreams, fantasies? How realistic are your goals? What are your interests, and do your skills and/or talents match them? What does drive your ambitions? Is it money, power, pres-

Expensive Lesson

Kim sat in my office holding back the tears. The local JC was full of middle-aged, reentry women and next-career men. Classmates her own age seemed to be in a "holding pattern." There was little sense of camaraderie because most of the students were commuters. Somehow this wasn't what she had in mind when she envisioned college life. Actually, Kim hadn't envisioned anything much at all during her high school career. Had she given more thought to her future when she was in high school, Kim might have avoided this difficult situation.

Reality Check

John loved to draw but recognized that he had no discernible talent. Art school wasn't for him. Taking art courses as electives or even majoring in art history or arts management would be just the thing.

Finding the Perfect Fit

Peter was a prodigy. Destined for the Ivy League, he came to me to help distill all the brochures coming in the mail. Gifted kids don't always have an easy time of it, and Peter's parents wanted him to be happy above all else. The top schools all share the luster of prestige, but they are very different from one another. A talented musician, Peter was planning to major in astrophysics. We spent hours talking, identifying the intangibles as well as the knowns. He wanted a school where he could temper his scientific side with some artistic pursuits, especially a place where he could sing a cappella. Princeton seemed to be the perfect fit, and they said "yes." Peter will be very happy there indeed.

tige, learning for learning's sake, doing good? Be truthful. If you see yourself driving a Porsche, wheeling and dealing and delegating, don't major in Minor British Poets. What are your politics? Colleges can and should be a forum for ideas. What are yours? If you are vocal and very liberal, you certainly wouldn't be comfortable at a conservative college. What's your learning style? If you learn by doing, you'll be miserable at Mega-State, attending classes taught by a "sage on the stage." Instead, find schools that offer work/study, externships, and study-abroad programs. Are you a cooperative or competitive learner? Whether you're a team player or a self-starter may well determine whether you can handle a pressure-cooker school. Core requirements and school calendars should also influence your school choices. And if you can't handle people telling you what you must do to get your degree, there are plenty of schools offering alternative ways to educate you.

Look, too, at your own high school experience. What kind of school do you attend? Have you been happy there? What would you change about it to make it a better place for you to thrive? Take that information with you when you look at colleges. Visualize the "Perfect U. for You," even though that place may not actually exist.

Lastly, what is your parents' economic situation? After all, they'll pay for some or all of your college and should have some say in the matter. How committed would you be to an expensive, private college if aid were not a possibility and you had to work your way through? Both the process and politics of financial aid and economic necessity have made the 1990s a much different educational climate than the '80s.

Talk to recent grads and listen to what they have to say about their college choices. If they could do it again, what would they do differently and why? Most of all, ask questions, first of yourself, and then of others.

This book wants to help you own the process of college selection, admissions, and financial aid. The idea is to find a set of schools that are appropriate to your very special and individual needs. Spend as much time researching your "safety school" as you do that "reach." You'll be amazed how stress-relieving a visit to a safety can be, if you love the school and don't think of it as settling for sixth best. You also won't upset your family by threatening suicide if you don't get into your number-one choice.

Viable is the key word here. It's a buyer's market! Pick schools that are viable to you, and you'll get into these with ease. The rule is: "Choose; don't be chosen."

DESTINATION: COLLEGE

This book also presents a whole bunch of schools that might meet your needs given who you are. Remember, except for a few highly selective schools, most schools will take you if they feel you're an appropriate applicant. This means if they think they can educate you, make you happy, and get you out in a decent amount of time with a diploma, they will accept you.

OKAY—THE "GETTING IN" PART

While there are no magic potions around to woo the deans of Undergraduate Admissions at Stanford or Swarthmore, here are some insider tips on how the system works and how to work the system. Listen up!

1. Pump up your stats! Your GPA, rank in class, and standardized test scores (ACT, SAT I, and SAT IIs—formerly called Achievement Tests) are the "givens" in your college admissions profile.

2. Give your academic life the priority. Study hard. Take a challenging course load; consult with your high school counselors about the courses and credits needed to get into college, especially if you're heading for your state's university system where the numbers really count.

3. Prepare for the standardized tests. Nobody likes the SAT I, SAT IIs, or ACT, but they're the only tools admissions officers have to compare your performance against the teens at other schools across the country. Take a course if you can afford it—Kaplan courses do work!—or study at least 30 hours on your own. Timing, strategy, skills, and stamina are all necessary for success. A good score can maximize the number of schools that will find you an attractive candidate for admissions. Don't take the tests "for practice." Plan a test-taking calendar and complete all tests early enough to send scores to colleges in a timely way. If you're applying early decision, note that you'll have even earlier deadlines.

4. Don't be a walking "activity list." Joining every club is not the way to impress admissions officers. Your after-school and summer activities do count, but only to the extent that they validate your true self. If you like business, develop a hobby into a moneymaker. Do you love sports and helping others? Try a job shadowing at a physical therapy office. If you become an interesting person, admissions officers will find you interesting.

Money Matters

Theresa wanted to study premed, but she also hoped to find a really small liberal arts college where she could study music and learn science in a broad-based core curriculum. An excellent Chinese American student, Theresa also needed financial aid. Several colleges came across with generous offers. I have counseled her to look carefully at the details of her award letters so that she and her family can make an informed decision.

The Long Run

Bob, another of my counselees, is a very bright business major. He picked Notre Dame, even though he knew he'd never start on the football team. An excellent high school linebacker, Bob recognized that his athletic skills did not quite measure up to his passion for the sport, so he based his decision on where to attend college on longer-term ambitions.

5. Realize that the admissions process for selective schools can be particularly frustrating. Competition is quite fierce and often seems to be unfair. All applicants have stellar "stats." Princeton, for example, drafts a freshman class of 1,130 each year and receives 16,000 applications, of which more than 2,000 are valedictorians of their high school graduating classes. At this level of competition, my advice for getting in would be the same as for any school: Follow the basic strategies outlined in the Admissions section of this book.

I always caution my counselees that it's never wise to read the last page first, so I encourage you to begin the process of college selection now. Turn the page. *The Road to College* will help you travel toward a successful college life.

Marcy Hamilton has a private practice in college admissions counseling called Op/Ed — Opportunities through Education — in Mill Valley, California. A member of Phi Beta Kappa and a former Institute of International Education Fellow, University of London, Regents' Fellow, UC-Berkeley, and high school English Department Chair, she especially enjoys writing on education in the 1990s. She is a member of the Western Association of College Admissions Counselors and Northern California Educational Consultants, as well as the American Counseling Association and American College Counseling Association. She often gives seminars on such topics as "Taking the Stress Out of the College Admissions Process" and "Making Your Summer Count For College Admissions."

10 Things You Can Do Right Now to Make Sure You Choose the Right College

1. **Start thinking seriously about what you really want and need in a college.**
   Who are you? What are your educational goals? Do you want to go to college in a specific region of the country, at a small school or a large school, at a school in the heart of the city, or in the middle of nowhere? What type of intellectual and social environment are you looking for? These are the types of questions that you need to ask yourself before deciding where to spend the next four years of your life.

2. **Research. Research. Research.**
   If you picked up this book, you probably haven't decided exactly where you want to go to college. The best way to make an informed decision is to get informed. Learn as much as you can about the schools that interest you. Read college guide books, ask college graduates about their college experience, talk to college students, visit nearby colleges to get a sense of what colleges are like and how they differ. In other words, get as much information from as many different sources and perspectives as you can. Your ultimate goal is to come up with a list of colleges that are a good fit for you and that seem likely to accept a student like you.

3. **Talk to your high school guidance counselor.**
   Guidance counselors know a great deal about the college admissions process, and they've got lots of resources that you can use to learn more about specific colleges and financial aid.

4. **Decide whether you want to apply for early admission.**
   If you're certain that there's one college that you really want to attend above all the rest, you might want to consider applying for early admission at that school (if the school has that option). If early admission is right for you, you'll have to get all the parts of your application ready earlier than you will for regular admission.

5. **Search for essay topics.**
   Many colleges require applicants to include personal essays with their applications. Start thinking about what you would write to reveal the real you to college admissions committees.

6. **Cultivate your recommendation writers.**
   Many colleges also ask applicants to provide recommendations. Make a list of people who know you well and who can write an effective recommendation for you. Let them know well in advance that you'll be asking them for a recommendation.

7. **Determine what standardized tests you need to take.**
   Do you need to take the SAT or the ACT—or both? Do the schools you're thinking about applying to require applicants to take any SAT II Subject Tests? Do you plan to take any Advanced Placement Tests? Prepare for these tests; scoring even slightly higher can make a big difference.

8. **Don't blow off your senior year.**
   Grades from your first semester will be considered by colleges. You don't want them to think that you're goofing off or slipping academically.

9. **Start thinking about how you're going to pay for college.**
   Once you get into a college, you'll have to pay for it. Talk with your parents about your family's finances. Explore all financial aid options, especially scholarships for which you may qualify.

10. **Read this book!**
    The Road to College should be the cornerstone of your efforts to get into the college or university of your choice.

How to Use This Book

The Road to College is more than just your normal college guide. It doesn't merely give you loads of information about a bunch of colleges and leave it up to you to wade through hundreds and hundreds of pages to find what you're looking for. This book takes a more personalized, direct, and fun approach. It will help you discover what's really important to you so you can make smart decisions about your future. It will help you figure out exactly what you want in a college or university and which schools are right for you. And it will give you useful advice on how to improve your chances of getting into those schools and how to pay for your education once you're there.

Here's how to use the various components of this book.

STEP ONE: COMPLETE THE WORKBOOK QUESTIONNAIRE

We designed the workbook questionnaire, which is located at the beginning of the Selection section, to help you think about the major issues that you'll confront in making your decision about where to go to college. After answering questions about yourself and your preferences, you'll be able to make a list of the things that are most important to you and your education. Yes, we know that filling out a questionnaire can be a pain. But making the right decision requires time, effort, and some serious thinking. To make this process easier and less time-consuming, we've included copies of the worksheets in the back of the book. That way, you can write down your responses on a separate sheet of paper—without having to flip pages back and forth. Trust us on this: Spending a little time now taking a close look at yourself will make a big difference in how much you'll enjoy your college experience.

Step Two:
Find the Schools That Are a Good Fit for You

By using your answers to the workbook questions, you'll be able to narrow your search to the schools that best match up with your wants and needs. In the second part of the Selection section, we've grouped colleges and universities into various categories, such as Academic Shrines, Sports Powerhouses, and Buried Treasures. In each category, we profile the schools that best fit the category and suggest other schools that you should investigate. Of course, if you want to read through all of the categories, go right ahead..

Step Three:
Learn How to Improve Your Chances of Getting Into the Schools of Your Choice

In the Admissions section, you'll learn the best approaches to taking control of the admissions process: how to develop an effective application strategy, how to write great essays, how to get super recommendations, and how to breeze through interviews. Kaplan's admissions expert will also give you insight into how admissions committees make their decisions, what to look for when making campus visits, and what their decisions mean.

Step Four:
Get the Lowdown on Financial Aid

For many students, paying for their education is a major issue that affects what school they choose to attend. In the Financial Aid section, you'll learn the differences between various types of aid, how the financial aid process will work, and how to negotiate aid packages.

* * * * *

The road to college might seem long and winding, and the choice of destinations may seem endless. But with the proper approach, you'll end up in the right place.

COLLEGE SELECTION

BY STEVEN FRANK

"Hello, Dean Smithers! I'm Kip Whitney, Susan's college-search advisor. Before the campus tour commences, I'd like to ask you a few questions...."

Introduction

Have Map, Will Travel

There are basically two types of people in the world, and if you've ever taken a long car trip and gotten lost, you're well acquainted with both. The first type is the one who insists he or she knows the way and, should the car make a wrong turn, continues driving around aimlessly as it gets closer and closer to nightfall. The second type is the one who pulls out a road map from the glove compartment and quickly finds the correct route to the highway. This type of person is soon on the road again, traveling to the right destination, happily singing "One Hundred Bottles of Beer on the Wall." The first type, though, usually winds up on some dark, deserted road and gets abducted by aliens or ambushed by street toughs. Well, at least that's what happens in bad movies.

Believe it or not, the same principles apply to trying to find a college. Of course, you're not likely to be abducted by aliens, but you can wind up pretty lost. After all, there are hundreds of colleges and universities in the country. How are you going to find the one that's right for you? You could apply to all of them, but at $20 or so a pop just to apply, that's going to get pretty expensive, not to mention all those application essays you'll have to write. You can be a bit smarter and consult a college guide book. But if you've been to the bookstore or library, you've seen that there are just about as many college guides as there are colleges. These books are filled with all sorts of interesting facts about the schools, but they're missing something very important: you. They're not written with your specific interests and needs in mind. Most of these books list schools in alphabetical order or by state, and you've still got to plow through them hoping to hit upon the right ones, a process not unlike driving in circles on a dark and stormy night.

Wouldn't it be great if there were some kind of road map that could point you in the right direction? Well, there is. You're holding it in your hands. This College Selection section is designed to help you come up with a list of schools that serve as suitable destinations for you. You won't have to wander around aimlessly, or trudge through college guides, to find your way. Instead, you'll have a set path to follow that will lead you to the colleges that are right for you.

Travel Companion

Each college applicant has his or her own path, which is paved with individual decisions. This book is designed as a road map to help you find your way.

This Selection section consists of two parts. The first part is a workbook designed to help you pinpoint exactly what factors are important to you when it comes to choosing the right school. You may, at this point, only have a vague idea about what kind of school you think you'd like to attend. It's important, though, to get an exact sense of your priorities before you begin hunting for possible destinations. That way, you'll be certain to apply to schools that are best suited to you.

Based on you responses in the workbook, we'll recommend chapters in the second part of the section for you to turn to. Each chapter groups together certain schools that share common traits. We've profiled a selection of those schools in each chapter to give you a sense of what those schools are like and a feel for the range of schools within that category. Of course, you can jump from chapter to chapter as well. You're the one in control of this interactive guide.

After reading the school profiles, you should be able to come up with a list of possible schools that are suited to your interests and needs. Some of them may be schools you always thought you'd like to check out. Some may be ones you've never considered before but, based on some of the priorities you identify, you realize now are worth looking into. Some may even be ones you've never heard of before. There are an awful lot of schools out there, and one that's perfect for you may be one you've never come across before. We hope that you make some great discoveries as you read.

Keep in mind that *The Road to College* is designed to help point you in the right direction for your big college search. We haven't filled this book with lots of facts and figures about all the schools. Although we have profiled some of the schools to give you an idea of the kinds of schools out there, these descriptions aren't the final word on the schools. We strongly suggest that, after coming up with a list of schools here, you then do some further investigation. The more sources you check out, the more information you'll receive, and the better informed your decision will be.

GET THE FACTS
Learn as much as you can about the colleges that interest you. Here are some suggestions for continuing your college search:

Get information from the schools. We've provided addresses and phone numbers for college admissions offices in the back of the book. If you think you're interested in a school, contact the admissions office and request more information. Keep in mind that the brochures you receive will be heavy on the propaganda—not every day is going to be filled with sunshine, and not all students are going to be cheerfully studying away in the library—but they'll give you a lot of basic information about the school.

Visit or talk to students. If you're seriously considering a school, we strongly recommend you go for a visit. You'll learn much more about the school by being there than you ever could from a brochure, no matter how glossy the photographs. You can tour the campus and get a feel for the place, as well as talk to students and teachers. Many schools make it possible for you to stay in a dormitory with a student; this is an excellent way to get a sense of what being a student there is really like. Contact the admissions office to find out about what you can do when you visit. Of course, sometimes it may not be feasible to visit because of the distance and cost of traveling. You can still talk to students, though. Admissions offices usually keep phone numbers on file of students who will be able to talk to you and answer your questions.

Check out books and magazines. There are tons of college guides, and you may want to flip through several of them. Any one opinion is going to be too narrow. The more viewpoints you get, the better. Some of the guides we suggest are:

US News and World Report College Issue: That's the issue with all those rankings. While this magazine may give you a sense of which schools are generally considered hot schools now, keep in mind that ratings are in a sense very subjective. What's going to be a number-one school for some may not be a number one school for you.

The Insider's Guide to the Colleges (St. Martin's Press): A guide written by students for students, the *Insider's Guide* will offer you a credible, inside look at many schools.

Fiske Guide to Colleges (Times Books): Compiled and written by a former education editor for the *New York Times*, the *Fiske Guide* has extensive, detailed takes on various colleges, including assessments of each one's strengths and weaknesses.

The College Catalog (Kaplan Books): Provides essential information, such as tuition, acceptance rates, student body demographics, and programs, for over 1,000 four-year schools in the United States. Includes career advice and a guide for disabled students.

Surf the Internet. The information highway is jam-packed with material of all kinds about different schools. You can access various information services, including Kaplan's World Wide Web site (http://www.kaplan.com), our America Online site (Keyword "Kaplan"), and the sites of most colleges and universities.

When you've narrowed down your list to the schools that you want to apply to, read the Admissions section in this book. It will show you how to maximize your chances of admission and, once the acceptance letters start rolling in, how to decide which school to attend.

That's it for now, so let's hit the road!

Your Personal Advisor

As you answer the questions about yourself on the following pages, you'll find that there are key issues you need to think about when searching for a school. You may have a gut instinct about some of these issues. Before you start answering the questions in the workbook, though, we want you to think very carefully about how you feel about these topics. What seems to be an important issue to you right now may not be, upon deeper reflection, such a big deal. As you start to think about some of these issues, you may find you feel very differently than you had assumed.

Here are some of the key issues you should consider:

SIZE: BIG POND OR LITTLE POND?

We often think of schools as either huge universities or small colleges. Actually, there's a tremendous range of sizes between those extremities. A school's size will actually depend a lot on you and how you see yourself fitting in. For example, you may have gone to a very small high school or lived in a tiny town, in which case many colleges are going to seem very large. On the other hand, if your high school was huge, or if you lived in a major city, you may feel perfectly at home at a big school and think of others as too small.

In general, though, schools can be divided into larger and smaller categories depending primarily upon the size of the student population. Before you settle on a size that's right for you, you should know that there are several areas in which these types of schools particularly differ.

It's A Small World After All

Here are a dozen schools with fewer than a thousand students:

Agnes Scott College

Antioch College

Bard College

Bennington College

Claremont McKenna College

Goucher College

Harvey Mudd College

Knox College

Mills College

New College of the University of South Florida

St. John's College

Wabash College

Land Of The Giants

Here are 14 schools that have more than 35,000 students (including grad students):

University of Arizona

Arizona State University

University of Florida

Indiana University

University of Illinois—Urbana/Champaign

University of Michigan

Michigan State University

University of Minnesota

Ohio State University

Penn State University

Purdue University

University of Texas—Austin

Texas A&M University

University of Wisconsin—Madison

Course Offerings and Student-Faculty Ratio

This is one of the major distinctions between small and large schools. Most large schools have extensive course offerings; in addition to required classes, you'll have the opportunity to choose from all kinds of different and unusual courses. Many of your courses, however, will probably be extremely large lecture classes, sometimes numbering hundreds of students, in which you won't have much chance to participate actively in the class. You also won't have much individual contact with your professors, and it may even be hard for you to meet regularly with your own advisor. Your introductory classes might be taught by graduate student teaching assistants (TAs) rather than professors. You can almost always get help when you need it, but you'll have to take the initiative by going to see your professor during office hours or seeking out advising services. Even at large schools, you'll probably get to take some smaller classes or seminars, either at higher levels or through special programs.

At smaller schools there will be more limited course offerings and fewer majors and departments. Most classes, however, will be pretty small, often limited to 20 students or fewer. Rather than centering on the professor's lecture, these classes will often be discussion-oriented, enabling you to take on a more active role. As a result, you'll also have a great deal of contact with professors, who will usually get to know you by name.

Resources

The primary advantage of large schools over smaller ones is usually the amount and quality of resources available to students. For example, large schools will often have several libraries with extensive collections. This can make a big difference when you start doing research for your coursework; it's nice to be able to go to a library on campus and find all the sources you need right there. In addition to the libraries, large schools will often have extensive laboratory and computer facilities, as well as more sporting complexes, student activities, housing arrangements, dining halls, and various modes of entertainment. While there may be fewer resources at a small school, you're much more likely to get your hands on the ones that are there. In fact, some smaller schools have cutting-edge, state-of-the-art facilities that undergraduates are able to use, even in their first semesters.

Name or Number

While you might find more resources at a large school, you're also going to come up against Big School Bureaucracy. The more students there are, the more procedures there are to follow and the longer the lines and waiting. Expect to fight your way through a regular swamp of red tape, especially when it comes time to register for courses. At a smaller school, there are usually fewer bureaucratic procedures to follow. You can often take care of school business quickly by seeing a single person rather than having to fill out many forms. And administrators in departments might even know you by name rather than by I.D. number.

Social Scene

The size of the student population at a school can have a large effect on the social atmosphere. At a large school, you'll have the opportunity to meet many other people, not only when you first arrive, but throughout your entire time at school. But you'll also be continually surrounded by strange faces, which can make the school feel somewhat cold and impersonal. At a large school, there's going to be a lot more going on at all times—more movies, concerts, sporting activities, parties. There's also going to be more clubs, organizations, and extracurricular activities you can choose to become involved with. But there will be more competition for leadership positions as well. Some find this kind of atmosphere exciting, others overwhelming. It depends on your own personality. If you're an independent person who feels comfortable making a niche for yourself, you'll probably feel fine at a big school. If you are shy, you might want to go to a smaller school.

At small schools, it's much easier to meet other people. It can be quite comforting to see the same faces on a regular basis, making the school feel more like a small community. The downside is that things can feel too close for comfort. You might find that being surrounded by the same people and doing the same things becomes boring. Then there's the gossip factor. A small school can be a regular *Melrose Place* when it comes to everybody knowing everyone else's business. While small schools may offer fewer extracurricular activities and organizations, you do have a much greater chance to hold a major position in them.

It's All Relative

As you think about the differences between small and large schools, keep in mind that this is all relative. Even at large schools, you'll usually have opportunities to take small classes and seminars, either at higher levels or in special programs. There are also ways to make a large school feel smaller. You can, for example, try to make a niche for yourself by becoming involved with some organization or activity. These groups often provide smaller circles of friends who can offer you support within the larger university. At the same time, there are ways to make a small school seem larger. Many small schools, for example, are affiliated with other schools who group together as part of some system or consortium. Students at these schools are able to take courses and utilize the facilities at the other schools within the same consortium, which greatly increases the opportunities and resources available to them.

LOCATION: BEACH OR BLIZZARD?

When thinking about the location of a particular school, several related factors arise. Some people don't care where in the country they live for four years, but for others it can be very important. Different regions of the United States have their own identities that affect the school's atmosphere in more profound ways than whether students say "soda" or "pop." You may want to stay in the same region where you grew up, or you may be interested in testing out another part of the country.

A school's climate can actually be an important consideration for many people. There are those who love experiencing the change of seasons and the snow, especially skiers and people who grew up in warm climates. Keep in mind, though, the thrill of the first snowfall wears off around mid-February, when you're plodding through six-foot snow drifts just to get to your first class of the day. Warm climate schools, especially ones by the beach, have their obvious advantages. But how often are you going to hit the books if you're also working on your tan? In all seriousness, for some, weather can adversely affect their ability to work at school; if you become depressed by a cold, dark winter or easily distracted by constant sunshine, you should think about which climate may be more suited to your personality.

Home or Home Away from Home?

Some people choose to go to school relatively close to home, usually because they want to be near family, friends, or lovers. Others want to get as far away as possible. Living near home can save on travel expenses and cut down on long-distance phone bills. If you choose to live at home, you can save even more money, not to mention the home-cooked

---

State Of Education

Here are some public universities that have well-regarded undergraduate programs:

University of California—Berkeley

University of California—Los Angeles

Georgia Institute of Technology

University of Illinois—Urbana/Champaign

Miami University (Ohio)

University of Michigan—Ann Arbor

New College of the University of South Florida

University of North Carolina—Chapel Hill

University of Texas—Austin

University of Virginia

College of William and Mary

University of Wisconsin—Madison

meals. For many, though, college marks the first opportunity to live on their own, free from the watchful eyes of concerned parents. If, however, you go to school too close to home, your opportunities to become truly independent are much more limited. You might consider going to a school far enough away that your parents won't drop in for surprise visits, but close enough that you can travel back and forth by car or train.

SETTING:
CITY SLICKER OR COUNTRY COUSIN?

The city, as they say, never sleeps. Whether this is a good thing, though, depends on your own personality. You may be the type who craves the 24-hour excitement of big-city life, where there's always something going on. If you attend school in a city, you'll have any number of cultural activities, not to mention cuisines, to choose from. But you'll also have pollution, crowds, and noise. A lot of noise. If you've never lived in a city and you're thinking of going to a city school, try to imagine exactly what it will be like to live in an urban area. The glamour and excitement of a city can quickly wear off when you are trying to study to the sounds of car horns and sirens 24 hours a day. How comfortable will you feel walking to classes on crowded city streets, surrounded by strangers and smog? Crime is also, unfortunately, a consideration in going to a city school. The schools take extra precautions to ensure students are safe on campus, such as having safety patrols, emergency phones around campus, and check points to enter buildings. Still, if you venture off the campus, you need to be more "street smart" and watch out for possibly dangerous situations.

Colleges located in rural locations, on the other hand, are more like those scenic campuses you see in movies. You can live in beautiful, peaceful collegiate surroundings, which can make it easier to work and study. The natural settings also make the schools ideally suited for outdoor sports, such as hiking, swimming, skiing, and camping. The cost of living at rural colleges is usually much less expensive than in cities. Rural colleges, naturally, are also much more isolated than city schools. Big cities are accessible through any number of modes of transportation, so you can get to and from school with ease. When you attend a rural school, you may often find yourself stuck there for long periods of time.

Moo U.

Here are a dozen schools located in small towns or rural settings:

Antioch College

Carleton College

Colby College

Cornell College

Davidson College

Denison University

Kenyon College

Middlebury College

University of the South

Southwestern University

Williams College

University of Wyoming

THE ROAD TO COLLEGE

Opposites Detract

Here are some single-gender schools:

Women Only

Bryn Mawr College

Scripps College

Smith College

Spelman College

Wellesley College

Men Only

Hampden-Sydney College

Morehouse College

Virginia Military Institute

Wabash College

Top Dollar

Here are 10 colleges that have tuitions exceeding $18,000:

Bates College

Bennington College

Boston University

Duke University

Hampshire College

Harvard University

Middlebury College

Pepperdine University

Tulane University

College of Wooster

LIVING ARRANGEMENTS: HOW SUITE IS IT?

There are now a variety of housing opportunities available at different schools. Some schools can guarantee you on-campus housing for your entire education; others guarantee housing only for the first year, after which you'll have to find your own place to live. As you consider schools, you might want to look closely at the building in which you'll be living. Dormitory styles can vary dramatically. Some schools have relatively new dorms, but others have housing dating back several decades that might be somewhat rundown. Don't think that the dormitory will look as warm and comfy as it does in the school's brochure; try to investigate the housing yourself or talk to students attending the school to find out exactly what the housing situation is like.

You might be given a chance to choose which building you want, but it will probably be determined by a lottery in which upper-class students get priority. There are also a variety of rooming arrangements available. Single rooms obviously provide for greater privacy, but there probably won't be very many available. Additionally, if you live in a single room, especially during your first year, you miss out on the opportunity to make friends with roommates. Many college dormitories now have suites in which a group of students share several rooms, including some kind of common area and kitchen.

Coed or Separate Quarters?

Most colleges in the country are now coed. Housing arrangements at these schools might include some single-sex dorms, but most are now also coed, sometimes by floor, sometimes by room. Depending on your personality, you may or may not feel comfortable in a coed dorm, in which case you should check to be certain there are single-sex ones available. You might also look into a single-sex college. Many single-sex colleges still exist in the United States, and many of them are among the top schools in the country. You may not have considered one of these schools before, but they do have certain advantages. Students particularly praise the unique sense of community they find and extra support they receive in these environments. The downside for most students is the social limitations. At some single-sex schools, however, you still have opportunity to mix with the other half. Many are affiliated with some other school where you can cross-register and socialize with other students.

COST: MONEY MATTERS

How much you can afford to pay for your education is obviously a major factor in determining where you apply. As you narrow down your list of schools, you should talk with your parents or some other advisor about your financial situation. How much of your education can be paid for by family members? How much are you going to be responsible for yourself? If money is not a concern, then you can freely pick and choose colleges, without having to worry.

If your budget is somewhat limited, you will probably need to focus your search on colleges you can afford. Don't worry, though, there are many ways to get a good education and still save money. For example, state-funded public schools cost much less than private ones, and many have excellent reputations. You also don't necessarily have to eliminate certain schools from your list because the tuition is too high. Instead, you should begin to investigate the many forms of financial aid that are available. Most schools offer some kind of financial aid that you might apply for, including various scholarships and work-study opportunities. You can also consider taking out a loan; keep in mind, though, that what you receive now, you'll have to pay off later, plus interest. You might also investigate different kinds of national scholarships that are available. The guidance office at your high school should be able to provide information about this for you.

In addition to tuition, you should also be aware of such factors as the room and board expenses and cost of living in different places. Sometimes the tuition might be low, but it costs a fortune for housing and even more to live off campus. At other schools, the tuition may at first seem high, but then you'll discover it includes room and board and is actually lower than comparable schools. You also might want to factor in the travel costs of going back and forth from school and home. They can add up if you're going to school far away.

REPUTATION: WHAT'S IN A NAME?

Like it or not, we live in a world in which people are impressed by names. This applies not only to the clothes you wear or the car you drive, but also to the school you attend. Going to a big-name school with national recognition is something that will impress many people—and not just your relatives. Everyone from potential employers to graduate school admissions officers to blind dates will be impressed if you graduate from a famous school. But be forewarned that not all reputations are earned. Some schools may be riding on the coattails of their past glory, but their quality has actually gone downhill. You might get a much better education at a school with a lesser reputation. The bottom line is this: Don't let a school's name blind you to its actual strengths and weaknesses.

Where the Elite Go to Meet

One of the things you'll find yourself with when you graduate, besides a diploma and perhaps a large debt, is a group of friends and acquaintances. College is an ideal place to form connections with other people who can help you throughout your life, both professionally and socially. Alumni from certain elite colleges are particularly known for looking out for their own. If it's particularly important to you to make social and professional connections, you might want to investigate these schools. Many schools also have particularly strong and active alumni networks, enabling you to maintain connections with people from your school throughout your life.

ACADEMIC MATTERS:
RESEARCH OR STUDENT CENTERED?

Some schools place greater importance on their undergraduates than others. At more research-oriented institutions, professors are given tenure based on the quality of their own work and, therefore, make their research their priority. While these institutions attract prominent faculty members, these professors may not always be accessible to the students. There might be celebrity professors on the faculty, but it won't make a difference to you if you never actually see them. Other schools are much more oriented to undergraduate education. At these schools, the professors are required to teach more classes and usually make themselves frequently available to students. The quality of their teaching will also most likely be superior.

What's Your Major?

You may already be set on a particular major or program of study, particularly if you've chosen a career for yourself. If this is the case, you should look at the schools that have the top departments or programs in your field. However, you should also be aware that many people, once they get to school, change their minds. You may find, once you begin taking courses, that you don't like your chosen field nearly as much as you thought you would. You may even discover a subject you like better. That's why, as you're looking at schools, you should think about how easy or difficult it would be to change a major or program. Some schools make it much easier to change majors or transfer than others. You might want to go to a school that has a range of strong academic offerings so that if you change your mind you won't necessarily have to transfer to another school. You might also consider getting a liberal arts degree, no matter what profession or career you're considering. More and more employers and graduate programs are looking for students with strong backgrounds in several areas. If you currently have a particular career in mind, you might ask some people in the field what kind of undergraduate degree is most relevant.

Is It Off to Work You Go?

If you plan to get a job right out of school, you might want to look into the school's job placement record. Some schools take a very active interest in ensuring their students get jobs, which can make it much easier for you when you graduate. Many schools now have career centers which, in addition to a library of job search materials and guides, offer seminars in such subjects as résumé writing and interview skills. They also have on-staff consultants who can help you plan your job search. The career center might be affiliated with various school alumni and put you in touch with people currently working in your intended field. You should also look into what kind of recruitment program a school offers. Certain schools are "courted" by various companies and corporations on a regular basis; representatives from those companies will come to interview students at the school. With the help of a good career center, you might graduate from school with a job offer already under your belt.

STUDENT LIFE: SOCIAL SCENES

You are going to be spending a significant amount of time going to college; chances are you won't spend the whole time studying. Depending on the school, there are all kinds of different social atmospheres, ranging from regular dens of iniquity where illegal substances flow freely to more conservative campuses where quiet get-togethers are the norm. It's important that you choose a school where you'll feel comfortable, both at work and at play. Even at a specific school, you'll find a number of different crowds with whom you can hang out. You might, though, want to consider the general social atmosphere at a school before going. The best way to judge this might be by visiting and staying overnight with a student.

Many people, in addition to their studies, become involved in some kind of extracurricular activity or organization. You might, for example, play for a sports team, either as a serious athlete on the school team or in more informal intramural games. You might join a particular club or political organization depending on your personal interests. These organizations offer ideal places to mingle and make friends. If you're currently involved in some activity you enjoy, you should be able to find a school where you can continue to do it. You might, though, also be interested in becoming involved with something completely new, even if you don't have any idea now what that might be. As you investigate schools, you might want to look at the range of activities that are available. These activities not only contribute to your social life, they're also the kinds of things that employers and graduate school admissions officers look for on résumés.

Is It All Greek to You?

Many students decide to "Go Greek" and join a fraternity or sorority. A fraternity or sorority can provide you with an exciting and extremely active social life, not to mention a place to live, eat, and hang out. The social options range from small, house-only events like dinners and formal dances to huge, blowout bashes open to the entire campus. Most fraternities and sororities do more than throw a steady stream of parties; you can also become involved in various facets of the house, such as participating in house government, playing on the house's intramural team, or conducting volunteer work and community service. Different houses tend to have different personalities, and you might find ones more suited to yours. Then again, Greek life may not be at all for you. Just be aware that Greek life can dominate the social scene at certain schools; you might want to consider how comfortable you'll be going to such a school if you don't join a house. Make certain there are other social opportunities and activities that interest you.

Diversity Issues

At some schools, the majority of the students will come from a similar background, in terms of race, culture, class, and/or geographic region. Sometimes, the student body at a school will also share the same politics and general values. Other schools have very diverse student populations that represent all different cultures, ethnic groups, classes, and regions, as well as political views and beliefs. What type of school you attend is, of course, up to you and depends on your own personality, interests, and needs. You may feel most comfortable at a school where many of the students are like you and share your values, or you may want to go to a

A Rich Heritage

Here are a dozen historically African American colleges:

Clark College

Fisk University

Florida A&M University

Grambling State University

Howard University

Lincoln University

Morehouse College

North Carolina A&T State University

Spelman College

Tuskegee University

Virginia Union University

Wilberforce University

school where you have the chance to meet and interact with different kinds of people. Keep in mind that at schools with diverse populations you can still find students who share your background and interests, but you'll also have the chance to meet others, which can be a valuable experience. Certain schools take extra measures to foster interaction between different groups and to make certain that all students feel at home. They might have special administrators or deans whose specific duties involve protecting the rights of all students and/or easing tensions between groups. Students at many schools often form their own cultural or political associations to make certain that their voices are heard in campus affairs and that their rights are protected. If these issues are important to you, you can investigate whether such groups are currently present at your possible destinations.

ACCESSIBLE ACADEMICS: HANDY OR HANDICAPPING?

While "doing your homework" is important for anyone choosing a college, it's particularly critical if you're a student with a disability—you'll have a unique set of logistics to work out relating to your disability. Here are just a few issues to consider in your college search.

Smaller schools can provide more individualized instruction, but it'll be harder to preserve your confidentiality as a student with a disability at a smaller school. Bigger schools offer greater diversity and the opportunity to blend in with campus life. They usually have greater resources to provide reasonable accommodations, but they may be more bureaucratic and impersonal.

Schools in the south and west usually offer lower state disability benefits and are less likely than schools in the northeast and midwest to be accessible via mass transportation. But schools in the south and west are more likely to have newer, more accessible facilities and to be situated in places that are warm, flat, and dry.

Living away from home will help you develop key independent living and self-advocacy skills. But you'll have to work out your personal care and accessible housing on top of the challenges that all new college students face. As a commuter, you can draw on the support network you already have in place, but you'll have to negotiate transportation to and from campus.

Tens of thousands of students with disabilities succeed in college each year. Check the "Worksheets, Forms, and Resources" section for organizations that can help you find the assistance you need to achieve your educational goals.

Step One

Go through the following list and in the first column check off each one that applies to you. You can do this relatively quickly; it takes only about 10 minutes. Don't put much thought into this yet, just go with your gut reaction.

Step Two

After you've checked off all the statements that apply to you, go to those responses you've checked. In the second column, rate how important this particular issue is to you on a scale from 1 to 10 (1 being the least important and 10 being most important). This will probably take more time because you'll want to think a bit about your answers.

SIZE, STUDENT POPULATION

I want to go to a large college. ❑ _____

I want to go to a small college. ❑ _____

I want to go to a medium-sized college. ❑ _____

LOCATION

I want to go to school in a certain region,
state, or location. ❑ _____

I want to go to school close to home. ❑ _____

I want to be able to get away from school
without a hassle. ❑ _____

I want to go to a school located around a

central campus. ❏ _____

I want to go to school in a big city. ❏ _____

I want to go to school near a big city
but not in one. ❏ _____

I want to go to school in a small town. ❏ _____

It's important to me to be surrounded
by nature, to be able to lie outside on the
grass and to see trees. ❏ _____

It's important to me to have a lot of
activities going on outside the school. ❏ _____

I need peace and quiet. ❏ _____

LIVING ARRANGEMENTS

I want to live at home. ❏ _____

I want to live on campus the entire time. ❏ _____

I want to live on campus a few years then move. ❏ _____

I want to live off campus the entire time. ❏ _____

I want to live in a suite
(with a kitchen, bathroom, etcetera). ❏ _____

I want to have a car at school. ❏ _____

I want to live in a single-sex dorm. ❏ _____

I want to live in a coed dorm. ❏ _____

I want to have a single room;
I need lots of privacy. ❏ _____

I'd like a single room, but as part of a
suite I share with other people. ❏ _____

I don't mind sharing a room. ❏ _____

I have to live in a very clean, very nice
room and dorm. ❏ _____

I want to have many housing options. ❏ _____

I don't much care where I live as long as
I have a roof over my head. ❏ _____

I want to have many dining options;
I hate having to eat the same thing all the time. ❏ _____

I have to have really good food. ❏ _____

FINANCES

Money is not a problem for me; I can go to
whichever school I want. ❏ _____

Cost is a moderate consideration for me;
I want to go to the best school I can afford. ❏ _____

Cost is a major consideration for me;
I want to go to the most reasonably
priced school I can. ❏ _____

I'm putting myself through school. ❏ _____

I'm depending on financial aid/loans to
help me pay tuition. ❏ _____

I need an on-campus job to help pay for
school and expenses. ❏ _____

My family will be contributing a large
amount to fund my education. ❏ _____

I don't want to build up a lot of debt that
I'll have to pay off after I graduate. ❏ _____

REPUTATION

I want to go to a really famous school
with nationwide name recognition. ❏ _____

I want to attend a school with name
recognition within a particular region. ❏ _____

I want to study with famous professors and faculty. ❏ _____

I want to go to a good school where I can
be most happy; the school's name isn't
that important to me. ❏ _____

ACADEMICS

I'm an above-average student, and my education
is very important to me. I want to get into a
top-rated school. ❏ _____

I'm an average student. I want to get the
best-quality education I can get. ❏ _____

I'm not a great student, but I want to get a
college degree at the best school I can. ❏ _____

I'm a serious student. The quality of my
education is very important to me. ❏ _____

I'm a hard worker. I can handle stress and pressure. ❏ _____

I don't want to have a heavy workload. I want
to enjoy my free time. ❏ _____

I want to go to a school that has only undergraduates. ❏ _____

I want to go to a large research university. ❏ _____

I'd like to be able to get plenty of advice or support
whenever I feel I need it. ❏ _____

I'm pretty self-reliant; if I need help, I'll find it. ❏ _____

I want my professors to know me by name. ❏ _____

I don't want to have to hunt down my professor if I have a question or problem. ❏ _____

It's important to me to be able to use state-of-the-art facilities and resources. ❏ _____

It's important to me to have access to many facilities. ❏ _____

I think the quality of the library is very important. ❏ _____

TYPE OF STUDY

It's important to me to receive a strong background in a wide range of subjects. ❏ _____

I prefer a smaller academic program where I'm known by name. ❏ _____

It's important to me that I have the opportunity to study in small classes and seminars. ❏ _____

It's important to me that I have many courses and programs from which to choose. ❏ _____

I want to have freedom and independence in what I study; I don't want many restrictions and requirements. ❏ _____

I want to have some guidelines and direction to keep me on track. ❏ _____

I'm not certain what I want to major in; I want to be able to study several subjects before I decide. ❏ _____

I know exactly what I want to major in; I want to go to a school that has a strong department or program in this subject. ❏ _____

I'm planning on going on to graduate school in
a particular field; I want an undergraduate
program that will help me prepare for it. ❑ _____

I'm planning on going on to professional school
(medical, law, or business); I want an undergraduate program that will help me prepare for it. ❑ _____

SPECIAL OPTIONS/OPPORTUNITIES

I'm hoping to get a dual degree. ❑ _____

I'm hoping to get an accelerated professional degree. ❑ _____

I want to gain real-world working experience
while I'm an undergraduate. ❑ _____

I want a working internship in my chosen field
to gain experience before I graduate. ❑ _____

I want to study abroad for a semester or a year. ❑ _____

I want to study for a semester or a year at another
school within the United States. ❑ _____

I want the chance to work on special projects
and to conduct my own independent research. ❑ _____

SOCIAL SCENE

I'm a party animal; I want to go to a college
like the one in *Animal House*. ❑ _____

I like to have a lot of friends; I want to be able to
meet a lot of people. ❑ _____

I'd prefer to make a few close friends than have
lots of acquaintances. ❑ _____

I want to go to a school with a lot going on,
but not necessarily a party school. ❏ _____

I get bored easily. I need a lot of excitement. ❏ _____

I like to have a sense of community and to be in a
friendly environment where most people know
one another. ❏ _____

I feel having fun is just as important as studying.
I want to have a good time while I'm in school. ❏ _____

NETWORKING

It's important to me to meet people in college
who can help me with my career or social life. ❏ _____

It's important to me to find a job right after
college; I want to go to a school with helpful
career services and a high job placement record. ❏ _____

INTERESTS

I want to do fun things outside of class, and I'd
like a lot of choices of activities to participate in. ❏ _____

I want to hold a major position in whatever club
I join, or become very involved in some activity
without much competition from other students. ❏ _____

I'm a varsity athlete, and I want to play on a
top-ranked college team. ❏ _____

I'm a decent athlete, and I really want to be on a
top-ranked team in any capacity. ❏ _____

I'm a decent athlete and I love to play; I'd prefer
to play actively in Division II or III rather than
be on a top-ranked team and not be able to play. ❏ _____

I love to watch sports and want to be able to
see top-ranked teams play. ❏ _____

I love to play sports for fun and want to be able to play on an intramural team. ❏ _____

I love to do different health, fitness, and recreational activities, and I want to go to a school with excellent facilities. ❏ _____

I love being out of doors and want to go to a school with lots of outdoor activities. ❏ _____

I love going to museums and galleries, and I want the chance to go as often as possible. ❏ _____

I love going to see theatrical or dance productions, and I try to go as often as possible. ❏ _____

I love going to classical music concerts, and I want to be able to go often. ❏ _____

I love going to popular music concerts, and I want to be able to go often. ❏ _____

It's important to me to stay in touch with whatever's hot (to be up on the latest trends in art, music, styles). ❏ _____

I'm a serious performer (actor, dancer, or musician), and I want to be able to perform in a professional-level company. ❏ _____

I enjoy performing (acting, dancing, playing an instrument), and I would like to perform just for fun. ❏ _____

I want to join a particular club or organization that meets my specific interests or needs. ❏ _____

I want to join a fraternity or sorority. ❏ _____

I want to become involved with campus government. ❏ _____

I want to be involved in politics and political issues. ❏ _____

I want to do volunteer work or community
service. ❑ _____

DIVERSITY/VALUES/ACCESSIBILITY

I need the following assistive services to accommodate
my disability: _____. ❑ _____

I'm a member of a particular ethnic group, culture,
or nationality, and I want to attend a school
where I'll feel comfortable. ❑ _____

Diversity is very important to me; I want to be
around people from different backgrounds
and cultures. ❑ _____

I want to attend a school with a large international
population. ❑ _____

I'm gay, lesbian, or bisexual, and I want to attend
a school where I can be out and comfortable. ❑ _____

As part of my education, I want to have a lot of
interesting experiences, in and out of the class. ❑ _____

As part of my education, I want to be exposed
to many new ideas and points of view. ❑ _____

I have a lot of opinions that I want to be able
to express freely. ❑ _____

I want the freedom to do my own thing. ❑ _____

I like knowing there are other people like me
whom I can hang out with. ❑ _____

I consider myself a liberal and want to be around
people who share my views. ❑ _____

I consider myself conservative and want to be
around people who share my views. ❑ _____

I'm not certain what my views are; I'm hoping I'll find out. ❏ _____

I believe in a pretty traditional, straightforward approach to education; this is the kind of education I want. ❏ _____

I don't want a traditional education; I'm really open to new theories and ideas and a more experimental approach to learning. ❏ _____

I want to go to a school that upholds my religious values. ❏ _____

I want to go to a school that has many members of my faith. ❏ _____

HEY! Remember to go back and rate how important the issues you checked off are to you (Step Two).

Step Three

In the space below, record all of the items you checked off on the checklist in Step One under the numerical value you assigned to them. DO THIS SECTION IN PENCIL BECAUSE YOU WILL BE MAKING CHANGES TO YOUR LISTS.

10s:

_____
_____
_____
_____

9s:

_____
_____
_____
_____

8s:

_____
_____
_____
_____

7s:

_____
_____
_____
_____

6s:

_____
_____
_____
_____

5s:

_____
_____
_____
_____

4s:

_____
_____
_____

3s:

_____
_____
_____
_____

2s:

_____
_____
_____
_____

1s:

_____
_____
_____
_____

Step Four

Now go back to each number in Step Three for which you listed more than one issue. Look over these issues and try to place them in order of importance, with the most important ones on top. You may need to do some heavy thinking about this, but try your best.

THE ROAD TO COLLEGE

Step Five

Starting at the top of the chart in Step Three, copy each statement—in order, beginning with the 10s—in the space below.

Issue List (from Most Important to Least):

1. _____
2. _____
3. _____
4. _____
5. _____
6. _____
7. _____
8. _____
9. _____
10. _____

Step Six

You've just created your priority list—the top ten issues for you in terms of the kind of school you want. This list will help narrow down the schools that you should start to investigate. The other issues you checked off are obviously important, too. Keep those in mind as you read about various schools and come closer to a decision.

For now, keep that top ten list in hand and read the brief descriptions of the categories of schools we discuss in the following chapters of the book. Based on many of the factors you've identified as important to you in the workbook, you should be able to check off which chapters will most interest you and that you'll want to read about. There's a list for you to write down these categories at the end of the category descriptions.

Some of the priorities you've listed above might be relevant to all the categories; each one, for example, will have schools that range in size and location, including city, suburban, and rural locations.

Some of your priorities might take precedence over all the others and immediately narrow down your focus; for example, if you know with absolute, 100 percent certainty, that you want a particular location, or major, or type of school, this might form the basis for your search, regardless of the categories we've included.

Of course, feel free to read any parts of the book you'd like. You never know where you'll find a school that interests you, even if it's one you've never heard of or considered before. And one final comment: If you have a disability, you will need to contact schools individually to determine if they can meet your needs for accessibility, assistance, and support. Aside from your disability issues, your top ten school priorities are a great place to begin your college search.

Descriptions of Categories:

Academic Shrines

These are the top-ranked, most-selective undergraduate colleges and universities in the country with the best overall reputations.

Look here if you listed any of the following statements in your priority list:

- I'm an above-average student, and I want to attend a top-rated school.

- I want to attend a top school with nationwide name recognition.

- I want to study with famous professors and faculty.

- I want to receive a strong background in a wide range of subjects.

- I want to attend a school with state-of-the-art facilities and resources.

- Money is not a problem for me; I can go to whichever school I choose.

- It's important to me that I have many courses and programs from which to choose.

- It's important to me to meet people in college who can help me with my career or social life.

- I'm planning on going to graduate school in a particular field; I want an undergraduate program that will help me prepare for it.

- I'm planning on going to professional school; I want an undergraduate program that will help me prepare for it.

- I'm a serious student. The quality of my education is very important to me.

- I'm a hard worker. I can handle stress and pressure.

Small Wonders

The schools here are smaller, liberal arts colleges with excellent reputations for their academic programs.

Look here if you listed any of these statements in your priority list:

- I want to go to a small college.

- I am an above-average student, and I want to attend a top-rated school.

- I am an average student; I want the best-quality education I can get.

- I want to study with famous professors and faculty.

- I want to receive a strong background in a wide range of subjects.

- I prefer a smaller program where I will be known by name.

- It's important to me that I have the opportunity to study in small classes and seminars.

- I want to hold a major position in whatever club I join, or become very involved in some activity without much competition from other students.

- I want to play a sport or perform just for fun.

- I'd like to get plenty of advice or support whenever I need it.

- I want my professors to know me by name.

- I don't want to hunt down my professors if I have a question or problem.

- I'd prefer to have a few close friends than lots of acquaintances.

- I'm a serious student. The quality of my education is very important to me.

- I'm a hard worker. I can handle stress and pressure.

Budget Ivies

These are larger schools and universities that offer excellent academic programs at lower prices than the top schools.

Look here if you listed any of these statements in your priority list:

- I want to go to a medium-sized or large college.

- I want to go to a large, research university.

- Cost is a moderate consideration for me; I want to go to the best school I can afford.

- I'm an above-average student, and I want to attend a top-rated school.

- I'm an average student; I want the best quality education I can get.

- I'm a serious student. The quality of my education is very important to me.

- I want to study with famous professors and faculty.

- I want to attend a school with state-of-the-art facilities and resources.

- It's important to me that I have many courses and programs from which to choose.

- I want to do fun things outside of class, and I'd like a lot of choices of activities.

- I want to play a sport or perform for fun.

- I want to go to a school with a lot going on, but not necessarily a party school.

- I like to have a lot of friends; I want to be able to meet a lot of people.

Value Marts

The schools listed here have the lowest price tags; you can receive a good education at very low cost. Of course, if money is at all a consideration for you, you'll want to check out this chapter. But keep in mind that virtually all schools offer a variety of financial aid packages and that there are various forms of scholarships. You should, therefore, check out the schools in the other sections and apply for financial aid. You might get in to one of these schools and receive a package that makes it affordable for you to attend. You should also find out about scholarships and other awards that are available.

Look here if you listed any of these statements in your priority list:

- Cost is a major consideration for me; I want to go to the most reasonably priced school I can.

- Cost is a moderate consideration for me; I want to go to the best school I can afford.

- I'm putting myself through school.

- I need a job to help me pay for school and expenses.

- I don't want to build up a lot of debt that I'll have to pay off when I graduate.

- I want to go to a school where I can be most happy; the school's name isn't that important to me.

- I want to go to a school close to home or I want to live at home.

- I'm not a great student, but I want to get a college degree at the best school I can.

- I'm an average student. I want the best-quality education I can get.

All-Around Gems

These schools are generally good in almost all areas and provide high-quality academic programs and facilities. All of them are probably worth checking out for just about anybody.

Buried Treasures

The schools here aren't very well known, particularly outside their region, but they have excellent programs and facilities.

Look here if you listed any of these statements in your priority list:

- I want to go to a school where I can be most happy; the school's name isn't that important to me.

- Cost is a major consideration for me; I want to go to the most reasonably priced school I can.

- Cost is a moderate consideration for me; I want to go to the best school I can afford.

- It's important to me to receive a strong background in a wide range of subjects.

- I want to hold a major position in whatever club I join, or become very involved in some activity without much competition from other students.

- I want to play a sport or perform just for fun.

- I'd like to get plenty of advice or support whenever I need it.

- I want my professors to know me by name.

- I don't want to hunt down my professors if I have a question or problem.

- I'd prefer to make a few close friends than have lots of acquaintances.

- I want to attend a school with name recognition within a particular region.

- I want to go to a small or moderate-sized school.

Separate Quarters

These are the nation's best all-male and all-female colleges.

Look here if you listed any of these statements in your priority list:

- I want to live in a single-sex dormitory.

- I like to have a sense of community and to be in a friendly environment where most people know one another.

- I want to go to a small or medium-sized college.

- I'd prefer to make a few close friends than have lots of acquaintances.

HBCUs

These are historically black colleges and universities: schools where African American students can study and socialize in the context of their heritage.

Look here if you listed any of these statements in your priority list:

- I'm a member of a particular ethnic group, culture, or nationality, and I want to attend a school where I'll feel comfortable.

- I like knowing there are other people like me whom I can hang out with.

- I like to have a sense of community and to be in a friendly environment where most people know one another.

- It's important to me to meet people in college who can help me with my career or social life.

- I prefer a smaller academic program where I'm known by name

Briefcase Factories

These schools are where many of the doctors, lawyers, and business executives of tomorrow are trained today.

Look here if you listed any of these statements in your priority list:

- I'm planning on going to professional school (medical, law, or business school); I want an undergraduate program that will help me prepare for it.

- I'm hoping to get an accelerated professional degree.

- I want to have some guidelines and direction to keep me on track.

- I want the opportunity to use state-of-the-art facilities and resources.

- It's important to me to meet people in college who can help me with my career.

- I want the chance to work on special projects and to conduct my own independent research.

Specialty Shops

These schools focus their attentions in very specific fields and programs for which they're very well known.

Look here if you included any of these statements in your priority list:

- I know exactly what I want to major in; I want to go to a school that has a strong department or program in this subject.

- I'm planning on going to graduate school in a particular field. I want an undergraduate program that will help me prepare for it.

- I want to have some guidelines and direction to keep me on track.

- I want the opportunity to use state-of-the-art facilities and resources.

- It's important to me to find a job right after college; I want to go to a school with helpful career services and a high job-placement record.

- It's important to me to meet people in college who can help me with my career.

- I want to gain real-world working experience while I'm an undergraduate.

- I want a working internship in my chosen field to gain experience before I graduate.

- I want the chance to work on special projects and to conduct my own independent research.

- I'm an above-average or average student.

Houses of Faith

These are schools that maintain strong religious affiliations.

Look here if you listed any of these statements in your priority list:

- I want to go to a school that upholds my religious values.

- I want to go to a school that has many members of my faith.

- I like to have a sense of community and to be in a friendly environment where most people know one another.

- I like knowing there are other people like me whom I can hang out with.

Cultural Meccas

These schools are located in the cultural capitals of the country, usually in big cities where there's large numbers of cultural and social offerings.

Look here if you listed any of these statements in your priority list:

- I want to go to a school in a big city.

- I love going to museums, galleries, theatre and dance performances, classical music concerts, and popular music concerts, and I want to be able to go often.

- It's important to me to stay in touch with whatever's hot (to be up on the latest trends in art, music, styles).

- I want to go to a school near a big city but not in one.

- I want to go to a large or medium-sized college.

- I want to be able to get away from school without a hassle.

- It's important to me to have a lot of activities going on outside the school.

- I get bored pretty easily; I need a lot of excitement.

- I'm pretty self-reliant; if I need help, I'll go out and find it.

- I want to get real-world experience while I'm an undergraduate.

- Diversity is very important to me; I want to be around people from different backgrounds and cultures.

- As part of my education, I want to be exposed to many new ideas and points of view.

- I want a working internship in my chosen field before I graduate.

- I like to have a lot of friends; I want to be able to meet a lot of people.

- Money is not a problem for me; I can go to whichever school I want.

- Cost is a moderate consideration for me.

- I want to attend a school with name recognition within a particular region.

Travel Agencies

These schools have extensive study-abroad programs that most students take advantage of.

Look here if you listed in your priority list:

- I want to study abroad.

- I want to go to a school with a large international population.

- As part of my education, I want to have a lot of interesting experiences, in and out of the class.

- As part of my education, I want to be exposed to many new ideas and points of view.

Global Villages

These schools have particularly diverse student bodies and provide nurturing environments for people of different backgrounds, cultures, religions, ethnicities, and sexual orientations, as well as top academic programs in a diverse range of fields and disciplines.

Look here if you listed in your priority list:

- Diversity is very important to me; I want to be around people from different backgrounds and cultures.

- As part of my education, I want to be exposed to many new ideas and points of view.

- I'm a member of a particular ethnic group, culture, or nationality, and I want to attend a school where I'll feel comfortable.

- I'm gay, lesbian, or bisexual, and I want to attend a school where I can be out and comfortable.

- I want to go to a school with a large international population.

- I want to study abroad.

- I have a lot of opinions that I want to be able to express freely.

- I'm not certain what my views are; I'm hoping I'll find out.

- As part of my education, I want to have a lot of interesting experiences, in and out of the class.

Alternative Havens

These schools take a nontraditional approach to education and appeal to less mainstream students who want something different.

Look here if you listed any of these statements in your priority list:

- I don't want a traditional education; I'm really open to new theories and ideas and a more experimental approach to learning.

- I'm pretty self-reliant; if I need help, I'll go out and find it.

- I want to have freedom and independence in what I study; I don't want many restrictions and requirements.

- I want the chance to work on special projects and to conduct my own independent research.

- As part of my education, I want to be exposed to many new ideas and points of view.

- I want the freedom to do my own thing.

Scenic Routes

These schools are the most scenic campuses around the country, surrounded by breathtaking natural scenery that's ideal for outdoor sports and activities.

Look here if you listed any of these statements in your priority list:

- I want to go to a school in a particular region, state, or location.

- I want to go to a school located around a central campus.

- It's important to me to be surrounded by nature, to be able to lie outside on the grass and to see trees.

- I need peace and quiet.

- It's important to me that I live in a nice room or dorm.

- I love to play sports for fun and want to be able to play on an intramural team.

- I love to do different health, fitness, and recreational activities, and I want to go to a school with excellent facilities.

- I love being out of doors, and I want to go to a school with lots of outdoor activities.

- I like to have a sense of community and to be in a friendly environment where most people know one another.

- I want to have a car at school.

Serious Fun

A category that speaks for itself.

Look here if you listed any of these statements in your priority list:

- I'm a party animal.

- I like to have a lot of friends; I want to be able to meet a lot of people.

- I want to join a fraternity or sorority.

- I'm a varsity athlete, and I want to play on a top-ranked college team.

- I'm a decent athlete, and I really want to be on a top-ranked team.

- I love to watch sports.

- I love to play sports for fun, and I want to be able to play on an intramural team.

- I want to do fun things outside of class, and I'd like a lot of choices of activities to participate in.

- I don't want a heavy workload. I want to have plenty of free time to enjoy myself.

Go State!

These are large, state universities with lots of options, people, and opportunities.

Look here if you listed these statements in your priority list:

- I want to go to a large research university.

- It's important to me to have access to many facilities.

- I love to watch sports and want to be able to see top-ranked teams play.

- Cost is a major consideration for me; I want to go to the most reasonably priced school I can.

- It's important to me that I have many courses and programs from which to choose.

- I want to have many housing options.

- Diversity is important to me: I want to be around people from different backgrounds and cultures.

- I want to attend a school with name recognition within a particular region.

Sports Powerhouses

These schools have the top sports programs and teams in the country.

Look here if you listed these statements in your priority list:

- I'm a varsity athlete, and I want to play on a top-ranked college team.

- I'm a decent athlete, and I really want to be on a top-ranked team in any capacity.

- I love to watch sports and want to be able to see top-ranked teams play.

- I am a party animal.

- I love to play sports for fun and want to be able to play on an intramural team.

- I love to do different health, fitness, and recreational activities and want to go to a school with excellent facilities.

- I like to have a lot of friends; I want to be able to meet a lot of people.

- I want to do fun things outside of class, and I'd like a lot of choices of activities to participate in.

THE ROAD TO COLLEGE

List of Chapters to Read

1. _____
2. _____
3. _____
4. _____
5. _____
6. _____
7. _____
8. _____
9. _____
10. _____
11. _____
12. _____
13. _____
14. _____
15. _____
16. _____
17. _____

Key to Icons

The symbols appearing at the beginning of each school's profile are to be interpreted as follows:

School Size

Icon denotes undergraduate enrollment.

🏛 = under 1,000 students

🏛🏛 = 1,001–5,000 students

🏛🏛🏛 = 5,001–10,000 students

🏛🏛🏛🏛 = 10,001–14,999 students

🏛🏛🏛🏛🏛 = 15,000 students or over

Tuition

Icon denotes in-state tuition when both in-state and out-of-state tuition are provided.

$ = under $1,000

$$ = $1,000–$4,999

$$$ = $5,000–$9,999

$$$$ = $10,000–$14,999

$$$$$ = $15,000 and over

Selectivity

★ = accepts 81% or more of applicants

★★ = accepts 61–80% of applicants

★★★ = accepts 41–60% of applicants

★★★★ = accepts 21–40% of applicants

★★★★★ = accepts 20% or less of applicants

Academic Shrines

The schools in this section are the chart toppers, the ones everybody's family is just dying for them to get into. If these schools have hallowed reputations, it's because they've earned them. Students come to these schools to get an education, and the schools do their part to make certain they get it, providing an exceptional number of outstanding academic programs that run the gamut from traditional liberal arts and sciences to more unusual fields of studies, and extensive facilities and resources of the highest quality. Of course, these stellar reputations also mean these schools are just about the toughest to get into; those admitted are usually in the top five percent of their high school classes and score 1300 and higher on their SATs.

When it comes to the admissions procedure, top-flight grades and test scores won't make you stand out from the rest; they're just factors that keep you in the running. Assuming you have the right numbers, whether or not you get into one of these schools will depend on how you distinguish yourself in other areas. These schools are looking for students who, besides excelling in their courses, can make a substantial contribution in some way. Those involved with interesting extracurricular activities, clubs, organizations, or who have special talents have an edge. By the same token, a masterful essay or impressive interview might be the thing to get you in. Keep in mind that, no matter how many explanations admissions officers give, the whole process is still rather mysterious; there's no real way to tell, beyond these factors, what will be that one thing to win over a committee. In general, if you have the grades, and want to go to one of these schools, it's worth a shot.

Once you get into an Academic Shrine, you can expect to work hard. Very hard. Students going to these schools talk of studying at least three or four hours a day, and that's after a full day of classes. Large portions of the weekend will usually be spent at the library as well. Some of the schools can be real pressure cookers and ruthlessly competitive; there have been stories about students tearing out articles from books in the libraries to keep others from reading them! For the most part, though, the schools attract the kind of highly motivated students who put far more pressure on themselves than they do on their peers. In fact, as these schools attract the best and the brightest, students often stimulate one another intellectually, inside and outside the classroom.

Going to one of these Academic Shrines means you're going to study a lot, so it's especially important that you find an atmosphere where you'll feel comfortable. While all these schools are top-rated, they're not all alike by any means. Each one, as admissions officers will no doubt proudly tell you, has its own distinct look and personality.

One main way to distinguish between them is to separate the smaller liberal arts and sciences colleges from the larger universities. Each type of school has its advantages and disadvantages that appeal to different kinds of students.

We'll start by looking at some of the top liberal arts colleges. These schools, catering almost exclusively to undergraduates, specialize in providing general liberal arts and science degrees, which means they usually have strong departments across the board. Many of them have also created specialized programs and subject areas that make them unique. Interdisciplinary studies — programs that combine several traditional studies in a particular field, such as American studies, women's studies, and various cultural studies — have particularly become the rage at different colleges. Most schools have made it a point to develop several of these programs.

Probably the biggest asset these liberal arts schools have in common is the amount of interaction students have with their professors. In general, the professors at these schools are there to teach; even full professors will teach introductory classes. Because class sizes are generally kept small, usually between 15 and 20 students, professors often get to know students by name. As the classes are usually more discussion- than lecture-oriented, students participate more actively in the class. If you're the type that likes to hide in the back of a big lecture hall, safe from ever having to say a word, you probably won't want to go to one of these schools unless you're willing to change your ways. Professors at these schools are also easily found outside of class. They don't flee from campus the second class ends. It's not uncommon for students to dine with their professors or get together for informal discussions over coffee.

Academic Shrines

These schools also tend to have very small student populations (1,300 to 2,000), which fosters a sense of community. However, the size can be a plus or a minus. Some find the community can be too close for comfort. It can become a drag to see the same exact people day after day, and there's a certain lack of privacy when everybody on campus knows everybody else's business.

A major complaint many students have is the slim pickings when it comes to the social scene at these schools. While many of these schools have gorgeous, picture-perfect campuses (you know, grassy knolls, bubbling brooks, frolicking squirrels), they are also pretty isolated. As a result, students usually have to find their fun on campus, where there won't necessarily be much going on. The schools provide on-campus entertainment, usually in the form of movies and visiting entertainment groups, but this only goes so far. Students try to make their own fun, usually in the form of small dorm parties, which tend to center on some form of alcohol. In recent years, though, schools have become much more strict about their alcohol policies, so even this form of entertainment isn't as wild as it once was.

Everybody gets to know everyone else pretty quickly, which doesn't exactly make for ideal dating conditions. The close-knit atmosphere seems to breed either intense relationships that last for years or platonic friendships, but little in the way of casual dating.

At the same time, the small campus atmosphere is one in which close friendships form quickly and remain that way for years. Despite some of these drawbacks, most students seem extremely happy at their chosen liberal arts colleges. They know that they're receiving a top education in a truly collegiate setting.

THE LIBERAL ARTS COLLEGES

AMHERST COLLEGE IN AMHERST, MASSACHUSETTS

Admissions Address: Office of Admission, Box 2231, Amherst College, P.O. Box 5000, Amherst, MA 01002-5000
Web Address: www.amherst.edu/
Phone: (413) 542-2328

Amherst College

$$$$$
★★★★★

Setting: Suburban
# of Undergraduates: 408
Tuition: $22,680
Room and Board: $5,600
# of Students Applied: 4,836
   Admitted: 943   Enrolled: 408
Lowest 25% of Freshmen Scored
   At or Below: SAT Verbal: 570
   SAT Math: 640
Highest 25% of Freshmen
   Scored At or Above: SAT
   Verbal: 690   SAT Math: 730
Required Admissions Test: either
   SAT I or ACT; three SAT II tests
H.S. Rank, Top 10%: 81%

When most people imagine what a top-rated liberal arts college should be, they picture everything Amherst offers: exceptional academics, intimate teaching arrangements, a student body with an insatiable intellectual thirst, and a picture-postcard, New England collegiate setting.

As befits a school with such a sharp focus on individual study and motivation, classes at Amherst are exceptionally small, even by liberal arts college standards. Students have a great deal of interaction with their professors, and department chairs and top professors teach all levels of classes, including freshman ones. The faculty make it a point to be accessible, and as one student put it, "there's almost as much learning going on in one-on-one meetings with faculty as there is in the classroom. There's a huge emphasis here placed on student/instructor interaction."

Amherst pioneered the interdisciplinary American studies program (a program that examines American literature, history, politics, culture, etc.), and it remains one of the most popular majors on campus, as well as political science, economics, and the premed program. As students also have the options of designing their own major, interdisciplinary programs are also hot. Beside the American studies program, two of the best are international studies and women's studies.

If you're looking for a strong, structured curriculum, Amherst is not the place. However, for highly motivated students with an independent streak and intellectual thirst, it's Nirvana. The only school-wide required class is "Introduction to Liberal Studies." This seminar, led by two professors from different disciplines, helps the students develop their analytical skills in several different fields. But with all this academic freedom comes its corresponding responsibility: the workload here is one of the heaviest in the nation. This is the result of several factors: the emphasis placed on individual study and personalized discipline areas, the challenging instructional style of the faculty, and the peer pressure brought on by being in an environment of highly-motivated students.

Amherst's standing as one of the Five-College Consortium—an affiliation that includes UMass—Amherst, Smith, Hampshire, and Mount Holyoke—substantially increases the number and kinds of courses and programs students may enroll in. If you don't find what you're looking for at Amherst, you're encouraged to attend a class at one of these other fine schools.

Amherst not only offers one of the top liberal arts educations in the country, it's also one of the most scenic campuses you'll see. The 1,000-acre campus, which includes a wildlife preserve and forest, is situated on a hill overlooking the town of Amherst. It's spectacular in the fall, when the many trees on campus turn stunning shades of gold and brown.

"The housing gets better as time in school goes on," one student told us. Most of the students live on campus in dorms that range in style from singles to suites to converted fraternity houses. A brand new Campus Center offers a place for students to hang out over coffee or a game of pool.

As opposed to its once-WASPy reputation, you'll find a diverse student body at Amherst, and, befitting a northeast liberal arts school, diversity is celebrated and tolerance emphasized.

In 1994 and again in 1995, Amherst was ranked the top liberal arts college in the country by *U.S. News & World Report*, which may have helped fuel a recent significant increase in the number of applicants, and competition to get into Amherst was already intense. Students here are not only extremely intelligent but have a genuine interest in working hard to expand their knowledge.

Students at Amherst work hard and work a lot; even a large portion of the weekend is spent studying. When it comes to socializing, it seems they sometimes have to put the same kind of effort they put into their studies into finding fun. The school is located about 90 miles from Boston—a bit too far for frequent road trips. The town of Amherst, one of those quaint New England towns, doesn't offer much in the way of excitement, so students tend to stick around campus. "Get used to seeing the same faces around," says one student. Fraternities and sororities, often the focus of a campus social scene, were abolished in the mid-1980s. Today, the campus social life centers on small dorm parties where, as one student reported, "Eight hundred people congregate in the common room and try to get to the keg—so no one ever gets there, they just get pushed."

THE ROAD TO COLLEGE

Clusters of dorms called "demes" sponsor their own parties and activities, and there are several school-wide social events, the most popular one being Casino Night. Particularly at a small campus, though, these small get-togethers can become tired. "The social scene is pretty pathetic," one student complained. Another said the off-campus life was "underutilized—with no official fraternities or organized party structure, you could be lost" when looking for something to do.

If social opportunities are few, there are, however, a healthy number of extracurricular activities and organizations on campus, including several student written newspapers and journals, various music, dance and theater companies, political and professional clubs, and a host of a cappella singing groups. Because of the school's relatively small size, students are able to become actively involved in these groups. Additionally, if students can't find fun on campus, they are free to participate in the activities at the other schools in the Five-College Consortium. Athletics are very popular, with decent varsity teams in soccer, baseball, basketball, and lacrosse, and their intramural program draws many students. The school's location particularly lends itself to outdoor sports and activities, including hiking, biking, and jogging.

With its superb academic offerings and highly rated faculty, it's no wonder that among the nation's top liberal arts colleges, Amherst is currently one of the hottest.

BOWDOIN COLLEGE IN BRUNSWICK, MAINE

Admissions Address: Admissions Office, 5000 College Station, Brunswick, ME 04011-8450
Phone: (207) 725-3100 (207) 725-3000
Web Address: www.bowdoin.edu/

Bowdoin is one of the few top schools that doesn't require SAT or ACT scores in the admissions process, an option about one-third of those who are eventually accepted decide to take them up on. The administration claims that they're much more interested in examining the whole student than test scores. And the focus on independent study and opportunity that's available at Bowdoin backs that up.

Bowdoin students rave about the opportunities for independent study, and about 80 percent are involved with some form of individualized work: either a custom major or for-credit research project not connected with any course but under a professor's (or department's) guidance. As

ACADEMIC SHRINES

you would expect, this requires an active and accessible faculty, something Bowdoin has in abundance. Most, if not all, are there when you need them. "There may be a couple of visiting professors who aren't always around when you'd like, but they are the exception, rather than the rule," said one Bowdoin student. Bowdoin students have opportunities for many different kinds of academic experiences, including renowned interdisciplinary programs from Asian Studies to Arctic Studies, and inexpensive study abroad from Beijing to India. Utilizing cutting-edge facilities and resources, Bowdoin's science departments are excellent, particularly in chemistry (the school is known for its microscale labs), biology, and environmental studies. With high enrollments, government, history, and economics are also strong, popular departments.

Bowdoin students are smart and devoted to their studies; a great deal plan on going to graduate- or medical school. Yet, there's a markedly relaxed atmosphere free of cutthroat competition, perhaps a result of the days not too long ago when Bowdoin didn't give students grades.

Visit the Bowdoin campus, surrounded by spectacular Maine wilderness, and you might feel you've stepped into a beer commercial—complete with mountain views, pine tree groves, and icy streams. The school's location makes it a haven for outdoor lovers, who can go canoeing, hiking, and rock climbing in the region.

The school's endowment has been put into heavy-duty construction. Recent additions include a major science complex and a library extension, with special study sections. Two new dorms were opened in August 1996 and more are planned. The different forms of housing include a 16-story dormitory that's one of the tallest buildings in Maine, coed suites sharing a common living room, luxurious on-campus apartments for fortunate upperclassmen, and special-interest living houses. The students meet and eat in one of two dining halls serving four-star quality food, including the occasional Maine lobster. Fraternities exist, but are taking no new pledges to obey an administration edict that all close by May 2000.

At this small, rural college there's a real sense of community among most students, who get along pretty easily. But there isn't much diversity, and this is a common complaint. The administration is trying to solve this problem through recruiting, but as one student said, "it's Maine, what do you expect?" But another said, "I wish I could tell you that the diversity problem has been solved. But really, it hasn't." A vast majority of the stu-

---

Bowdoin College

$$$$$
★★★★

Setting: Small town
# of Undergraduates: 1,574
Men: 49.2% **Women:** 50.8%

Tuition: $22,460
Room and Board: $6,115
# of Students Applied: 4,435
  Admitted: 1,264 **Enrolled:** 443
Required Admissions Test: None
Lowest 25% of Freshmen Scored At or Below: SAT Verbal: 630 SAT Math: 640
Highest 25% of Freshmen Scored At or Above: SAT Verbal: 730 SAT Math: 720
H.S. Rank, Top 10%: 85%
Top 25%: 97%
Top 50%: 100%
Avg. Score of Applicants Admitted: SAT Verbal: 690 SAT Math: 680
Most Popular Majors (% of Student Body): Government (15.9%), Biology (14.4%), English (13.6%), Environmental Science (10.2%), History (9.9%)

dents come from upper-class New England, prep school backgrounds. "I don't like the homogeneity here. There have been problems with women's status and minority status in the past few years," a history major reported.

Since the nearest city, Portland, is a half an hour away, most of the social activities are to be found on campus. Bowdoin's large athletic center provides the opportunity to become involved in a number of indoor sports and physical activities. Hockey is the number-one sport, and students crowd the rink to watch Bowdoin's ECAC Eastern Division winning team the Polar Bears.

Along with its academics, Bowdoin's size and the opportunities it presents for outgoing students are its biggest strengths. As one sophomore raved, "The best thing here is that it's a small college atmosphere that gives you the chance to be involved with an incredible number of activities."

Carleton College

$$$$$
★★★

Setting: rural
# of Undergraduates: 1,867
Men: 48.4% **Women:** 51.6%
Tuition: $20,988
Room and Board: $4,290
# of Students Applied: 2,962
   Admitted: 1,467 **Enrolled:** 475
Required Admissions Test: either SAT or ACT
Lowest 25% of Freshmen Scored At or Below: SAT Verbal: 620 SAT Math: 630 ACT Comp.: 28
Highest 25% of Freshmen Scored At or Above: SAT Verbal: 740 SAT Math: 720 ACT Comp.: 31
H.S. Rank, Top 10%: 67%
Top 25%: 94%
Top 50%: 100%
Most Popular Majors (% of Student Body): Biology (13.1%), English (8.8%), Political Science (7.7%), Psychology (7.5%), History (7.3%)

CARLETON COLLEGE IN NORTHFIELD, MINNESOTA

Admissions Address: Admissions Office, 100 South College Street, Northfield, MN 55057
Phone: (507) 646-4190 (800) 995-2275
Web Address: www.carleton.edu/

Carleton's location in Minnesota has made it one of the better-kept secrets in the country, but probably not for long. As more people learn about Carleton's exceptional academics, the school's popularity will no doubt increase.

Carleton students receive solid liberal arts backgrounds. The extensive general education requirements includes courses in art and literature, history, philosophy, social science, math, natural science and physical education, as well as at least one course in a non-Western culture. To graduate, seniors complete a comprehensive examination or complete an independent project within their chosen field. Carleton's special offerings include self-designed majors, several interesting off-campus study programs, such as geological study in Death Valley, and various interdisciplinary and cultural studies departments, including African, Asian, Latin American, and American studies programs. The sciences, especially chemistry, and various departments in the humanities, such as English, history, and performing arts, are all considered quite good.

ACADEMIC SHRINES

The classes are generally small and intense, making a large part of the Carleton education center on discussion rather than large lectures. The faculty is rated among the best in the nation, and, as one "Carl" said, they didn't get that way by being softies. They're tough, but they're there, and there a lot. Readily spotted around campus, faculty members meet with students outside of class for extra help or informal discussions over meals and coffee. Says one freshman, "This is an open academic environment. The students and the faculty are friendly and open. The professors are always willing to help students out." The intensity is increased by the difficult, but "doable" workload, and Carleton's trimester schedule (each term lasting 10 weeks) means exams and deadlines creep up frequently.

Students say the facilities are generally nice and particularly praise the computer accessibility. The housing is guaranteed for four years, and there's a variety of options. The college owns ten off-campus "theme" houses for students sharing a common interest, from foreign languages to love of the outdoors.

Visit in the fall and spring and you'll probably find students comfortably lounging around outside or tossing a Frisbee. That casual atmosphere, however, masks the intense, and sometimes stressful, environment. Then comes the Minnesota winter, and suddenly everything is buried under mounds of snow and buffeted by subzero temperatures. Many of the school's buildings are connected by underground tunnels, which, while it may protect students from the cold, can also make them feel stir-crazy after a few months of being cooped up.

Nonetheless, the vast majority of students feel lucky to be there. Everyone knows everyone else, and the first-name basis that students and profs are on helps take the edge off. You'll meet students from all over the country, though the majority are from the Midwest. Almost all are involved either with intramural sports, the over 100 extracurricular activities, and/or the community. There's not a lot of diversity on the campus, but the administration is sensitive to this and is making efforts to recruit more minorities.

Carleton's isolated location could be hard to love if you're not a nature lover or into cows, but "Carls" really do love the place. And they know how to have a good time. Students sometimes make road trips to the Twin Cities (only by bus; cars aren't allowed on campus) or hit a few of the restaurants and bars in the nearby town of Northfield, which it shares with neighbor St. Olaf College, with whom students frequently socialize. On campus, a student activities group called "Co-op" organizes social activities and events, such as movies and concerts, but going to parties is still probably the most popular student activity, we hear. A majority of the students play some kind of intramural sport, from hockey to volleyball to softball. The school is in a particularly ideal location for those who like hiking and cross-country skiing. The brutal winter may force students into close confines with one another, but if anything, it helps increase the unmistakable bond between them. Year-round, Carleton students seem to enjoy their work, enjoy their play, and enjoy hanging out together.

DAVIDSON COLLEGE IN DAVIDSON, NORTH CAROLINA

Admissions Address: Admissions Office, 405 N. Main Street, P.O. Box 1737, Davidson, NC 28036
Phone: (704) 892-2230 (800) 768-0380
Web Address: www.davidson.edu

Davidson College

$$$$$
★★★★

Setting: Suburban/Small Town
# of Undergraduates: 1,613
Men: 51.2% **Women:** 48.8%
Tuition: $20,595
Room and Board: $5,918
# of Students Applied: 2,830
  Admitted: 1,062 **Enrolled:** 442
Required Admissions Test: SAT I or ACT
Recommended: SAT II
Lowest 25% of Freshmen Scored At or Below: SAT Verbal: 610 SAT Math: 630 ACT Comp.: 26
Highest 25% of Freshmen Scored At or Above: SAT Verbal: 700 SAT Math: 710 ACT Comp.: 30
H.S. Rank, Top 10%: 76%
Top 25%: 89%
Top 50%: 100%
Avg. Score of Applicants Admitted: SAT Verbal: 657 SAT Math: 664 ACT Comp.: 28
Most Popular Majors (% of Student Body): History (17%), English (15%), Biology (14%), Political Science (10%), Psychology (9%)

Although not widely known outside the southeast, Davidson is a top liberal arts school that is gaining more widespread recognition—with good reason. While aspiring to provide its students with the same high level education of an Ivy League school, Davidson is a bit less competitive and not as expensive as many comparable schools. As one student described it, "for better or worse, we are a family."

Academics at Davidson also have a distinctive international flair. The international studies program is one of the most renowned in the country, and the school's foreign language departments are highly acclaimed. The student body includes a number of international students. At the same time, many Davidson students opt to check out other countries in one of the school's overseas programs.

Interdisciplinary studies are also quite good at Davidson, including such acclaimed and innovative programs as gender studies, medical humanities, and a humanities program that takes a nontraditional, broad approach to the study of Western civilization. Students are generally encouraged to pursue their own interests through independent studies and double majors.

The extensive core requirements include courses in literature, history, natural sciences, math, social sciences, fine art, philosophy, writing, foreign language, and a class on non-Western thought. Because of Davidson's Presbyterian affiliation, one course in religion is also required.

Students have wonderful things to say about their professors, who teach frequently, and seem to enjoy teaching. "Davidson's greatest resource is the faculty; we know our professors and we truly enjoy talking to them," said one student. Most report professors giving out their home numbers and enjoying meeting with students over coffee at the cafes in the town of Davidson. Classes are small, and the profs really want to hear what the students have to day. Most Davidson students welcome the chance to voice their views. Although the courses are difficult and demand lots of study time, students do have free time to pursue other interests.

The beautiful campus, with its sprawling lawns and heavily wooded areas, is extremely safe, making for a peaceful collegiate atmosphere. The library, while not as well stocked as at other top-notch liberal arts schools, does provide a central location for students to study and socialize, although the student center makes a more comfortable place for hanging out. The school has been making many improvements, the most recent being a $9.1 million Visual Arts Center, providing exhibition space for student and professional work. Dormitories vary in style, including highly coveted apartment-like arrangements and university-owned houses; all freshman live and eat together.

Most of the students are from the South and tend to come from upper middle-class, conservative backgrounds. Many are also religious. This combination creates a distinctive atmosphere that some describe as "typically Southern": friendly and warm to some, homogeneous and "claustrophobic" to others. By all accounts the student body is tight, and that can be a help or a hindrance. But by and large students are friendly, respectful of one another, and concerned about honesty and moral issues.

The social life on campus centers on the eating clubs and fraternities, which draw well over half the student population. Located at Patterson Court, the ten eating clubs are a unique facet of Davidson life. Each one, with its own dining room and cook, not only provides a place for members to eat, but also hosts special events and parties. Each club is also required to have parties open to the entire school.

Athletics are very popular, particularly outdoor sports. The school has facilities on a nearby lake, so students can go water skiing and sailing. A new athletic center has really expanded the recreational facilities. The soccer team, the Wildcats, is a top-rated team, and Davidson students come out in droves to cheer them on, helping fuel a sense of school pride. Many students play some kind of intramural sport, the most popular one being a variation on touch football called flickerball.

THE ROAD TO COLLEGE

For Davidson students, friendly peers and a community environment make Davidson as comfortable a place to live and work as their own hometowns. As one student said, "Davidson isn't for everyone, but most students I know wouldn't trade a Davidson education for any other."

GRINNELL COLLEGE IN GRINNELL, IOWA

Admissions Address: Office of Admission, P.O. Box 805, Grinnell, IA 50112-0807
Phone: (515) 269-3600 (800) 247-0113
Web Address: www.grin.edu

Dedicated teachers, top-rated liberal arts programs, a safe, congenial Midwestern location, a self-governing student body, and a more affordable price tag all recommend Grinnell, another well-kept secret in the upper echelon of liberal arts schools.

There's no core curriculum at Grinnell. Working closely with their faculty advisors, students are encouraged to pursue their own academic interests. Students may receive additional credit for most courses by conducting independent projects. The only college-wide requirement is an intense writing tutorial; students choose from a wide range of tutorials for which they meet regularly with a professor who's also a faculty advisor. While students are pursuing their own academic interests, they receive a great deal of support and mentoring. The professors care about their students and often take the time to work with them on an individual basis. "They'll make office hours whenever you need to see them, and some will even meet you at their houses," said one student.

Classes are generally limited to 20 people, and they are, by all reports, pretty tough. There isn't too much of a social scene, as most free time is spent studying. Students rate the workload extremely difficult, but not competitive. The pressure comes from their own desire to do their best, and as a result many of the undergraduates feel the student body come together as a community.

However, not all feel that way. Many students cited Grinnell's attempts to draw a more diverse student body to the school through grants and other forms of aid, which has lead to multicultural study and cultural understanding. But more than one source reports that this has also lead to a rise in racial tension on campus. "There have been some minor tensions among students of different backgrounds over these issues," said one junior. These differences have been a concern for the student body's

---

Grinnell College

$ $ $ $ $
★★

Setting: Rural
# of Undergraduates: 1,307
Men: 44.9% **Women:** 55.1%
Tuition: $17,142
Room and Board: $5,152
# of Students Applied: 1,820
  Admitted: 1,323 **Enrolled:** 355
Required Admissions Test: Either SAT or ACT, TOEFL (for international students)
Lowest 25% of Freshmen Scored At or Below: SAT Verbal: 630 SAT Math: 600 ACT Comp.: 28
Highest 25% of Freshmen Scored At or Above: SAT Verbal: 740 SAT Math: 710 ACT Comp.: 31
H.S. Rank, Top 10%: 62%
Top 25%: 89%
Top 50%: 98%
Avg. Score of Applicants Admitted: SAT Verbal: 669 SAT Math: 656 ACT Comp.: 29
Most Popular Majors (% of Student Body): Biology (12%), Economics (10%), Anthropology (10%), History (8%), English (7%)

"self-governance" policy, but they have also brought a cloud of tension to the campus.

The "self-governance" policy allows students to deal with issues that affect them directly, such as the racial problems, drugs, and alcohol. At least one student described it as "the best thing about Grinnell." Another student admired the responsibility entrusted to the students by the administration: "It's good training for the outside world." But others seem to think it makes the administration indifferent. "The administration and board of trustees can seem inflexible and unresponsive to student desires, especially for cultural space," said one student.

For a small school, there's plenty going on to keep students busy beyond their classes. Harris Hall, with a theater, movie theater, and dance space, provides a site for school-sponsored special events, including weekly concerts and dances. There are several movies, concerts, and performances each week, and all on-campus events are free. Students who shy away from official events can usually find an informal party or go to a local bar to hang out. A number of extracurricular activities and organizations, with a range of social and politically oriented groups, also enable students to become involved in activities outside their studies. There are some sporting events, but "most people aren't into it," a student reports. Students do, though, enjoy hanging out around the campus and playing informal games. Grinnell is far from a major city (Des Moines and Iowa City are each well over an hour away), and although some may find that sticking around campus gets boring, most students don't mind it.

Despite the problems with the different student groups, and a sometimes indifferent administration, most students seem to like Grinnell. The friendly, Midwestern atmosphere and beautiful campus all lend to an environment for learning and enjoying student life.

HAVERFORD COLLEGE IN HAVERFORD, PENNSYLVANIA

Admissions Address: Admissions Office, 370 Lancaster Avenue, Haverford, PA 19041-1392
Phone: (610) 896-1350
Web Address: www.haverford.edu/

"Do you mean Harvard?" is how people often respond when they first hear of this excellent, but relatively unknown, college. Haverford may not have the big name cachet of that school in Massachusetts, but it's

Haverford College

$$\$\$\$\$\$$$
★★★★

Setting: Suburban
# of Undergraduates: 1,137
Men: 48.4% **Women:** 51.6%
Tuition: $21,534
Room and Board: $7,070
# of Students Applied: 2,812
   Admitted: 975   **Enrolled:** 313
Required Admissions Test: Either SAT or ACT
Lowest 25% of Freshmen Scored At or Below: SAT Verbal: 630
SAT Math: 630
Highest 25% of Freshmen Scored At or Above: SAT Verbal: 730   SAT Math: 720
H.S. Rank, Top 10%: 79%
Top 25%: 96%
Top 50%: 100%
Most Popular Majors (% of Student Body): Biology (14%), History (12%), English (9%), Sociology (9%), Economics (8%)

---

nevertheless one of the best liberal arts schools in the country. Its small student population and scenic campus make for an idyllic collegiate experience.

Small class size—"What's a lecture hall?" students wryly respond—fosters a great deal of interaction with faculty, whom students praise as one of the school's major assets. Every class is taught by a professor (there are no TAs or graduate assistants), and students report that even in freshman-level classes, professors go out of their way to get to know students. The instructors at Haverford genuinely care about their teaching, not just their own research, and devote much of their time to working closely with students. Students often form personal relationships with professors, who get to know them by name. Even the administration is much more personalized than at other schools; at Haverford, the students are treated as people by other people.

Haverford offers a strong, general liberal arts program. The requirements include three courses each in humanities, social sciences, and natural sciences, as well as a foreign language, freshman writing seminar, and a course on "social justice." To fulfill their majors, most students complete a special project or thesis during their senior year, which gives them a chance to work closely with a chosen faculty advisor. Students also have the option to design their own majors or enroll in a dual major. English and biology are the most popular majors.

"Fords," as Haverford students are known, are extremely intelligent (many come from the top of their high school classes), lending the school a distinctively intellectual atmosphere. They take great pride in their programs and are encouraged to take the lead in their studies, rather than being given a prescribed course of study. "Haverford gives us the opportunity to care about our work," says one student. As a result, they are highly self-motivated with a great intellectual thirst, and this pervades the atmosphere on campus.

"I think the school attracts a student body with a strong sense of social justice. It's certainly hard to leave without feeling some sense of obligation to give back to your community," says one Ford. Regardless of the workload, nearly everyone finds time to volunteer for local organizations. Several students have even started their own organizations, some of which have grown to Philadelphia and beyond.

In addition to the academic rigor, the school's character is dominated by its honor code. It's fully student-run and covers not only academics, but social interaction as well. According to the code, students schedule and monitor their own exams as well as set and enforce many of the campus regulations; the student-run Honor Council hears all complaints and determines the proper disciplinary measures for those who break the code. While the code is not for everyone, many Fords feel the code makes Haverford unique and "lets you be treated like an adult. The code teaches you that what you say has merit, but also teaches you to give merit to others." The code lends to the strong sense of community and is, according to one student, "as responsible for my intellectual and personal growth as any course I took."

The school's close ties with nearby Bryn Mawr also make Haverford unique; many think of them as two parts of the same school. The two schools have complete academic cooperation. Students can take courses and even major at either school. Haverford students can also eat meals or even live at Bryn Mawr, which is connected by a shuttle bus that runs frequently. They also have the option of taking courses at Swarthmore and the University of Pennsylvania, meaning despite its small size, there's not much you can't find if you really look and make an effort.

Haverford has a working arboretum, and with its 19th-century stone buildings, clusters of trees, woods, and grassy knolls, the school has a serene natural beauty that makes it a peaceful setting in which to work and study. But visit on a spring day when the quad is filled with Frisbees and sunbathers, and you'll be surprised anyone ever gets any work done.

The small size provides a friendly atmosphere in which it's relatively easy not only to make friends but to form close bonds that last throughout college and long after graduation. Freshmen arrive a week early for an orientation program called "Customs Week" and become part of a "customs group" of fellow first-years that creates a sense of family right from the start.

The small campus unfortunately also limits the social scene significantly. Students say that the social scene is not boring, but the small community is limiting. "Fords are like onions, they have layers, and the more you hang out with them, the more you see," said one student. Most agree the social scene is what you make of it, and if you know what you want to do, you can do it. The school tends to be rather quiet, during the week as well as on weekends. Although the student activity fund pays for student-run parties, many students surprisingly don't take advantage of this opportunity. "If you're looking for a party school, keep looking," said one student of the low-key social scene. Most of the social life on campus involves casual hanging out in dormitory common rooms. Still the lack of a fraternity system is a plus, according to some, because it eliminates the exclusivity of parties. Although it receives mixed reviews from students for its design, the new student center provides a much-needed space for hanging out.

For those who look, though, there are activities to be found beyond small get-togethers. There are excellent movie and concert series on both the Bryn Mawr and Haverford campuses, which are free. There's also a number of clubs and extracurricular programs, including music and performance groups, and students are able to hold leadership positions without much competition. Although the school isn't known for its sports teams, many students participate in intramural sports (Haverford does have the distinction of having the leading varsity cricket team in the United States). Its track team is a steady Division III contender, and its women's lacrosse team is also strong. Additionally, there are several special events that take place each year, including a formal winter ball, proceeds of which go to charity, and Haverfest, a large all-school party with live music. When students are in need of more excitement, Philadelphia is only a 20-minute train ride away; nevertheless, most students tend to stay on campus.

The dormitories are in good condition; almost everyone has a single room, and most are in suite arrangements that share a common living room area. The housing policy is another example of how Haverford treats its students like adults. Men and women can share a suite with a common living room and bathroom. (There are single-sex floors and bathrooms for those who prefer them.) There's only one dining hall, which may offer a chance to socialize, but the quality of the food has improved, most students report, from the days when students would head over to Bryn Mawr to eat. Diversity is currently a big issues on the campus with, interestingly enough, the students taking the lead and pressuring the administration to make greater strides in this area. There are student organizations and support groups for students of color, women, and gay and bisexual students, and most students report tolerance, if a certain amount of self-separation between groups. Haverford used to be an all-male school, and the number of women enrolled has only recently caught up to the number of men enrolled; however, when considered along with the Bryn Mawr population, women outnumber men almost two to one. In general, students are extremely open and tolerant, as well as rather liberal and politically active.

As most Fords know, the school began as a Quaker institution. Certain Quaker values, such as strong community and hard work, continue to flourish, making Haverford one of the best academic environments in which to receive a liberal arts education today.

MIDDLEBURY COLLEGE IN MIDDLEBURY, VERMONT

Admissions Address: Office of Admissions, The Emma Willard House, Middlebury, VT 05753-6002
Phone: (802) 443-3000
Web Address: www.middlebury.edu/

Some students may get nervous when the first thing they hear about a school is, "Oh, the skiing is great!" But while the idea of paying $27,000 a year to hit the slopes and learn to slalom may be appealing to some, others should relax. There's a lot of first-rate learning going on here, too.

While its location in the middle of Vermont ski country does make it a heavenly choice for winter sports buffs, Middlebury College offers its students an excellent liberal arts education, with a special focus on international issues. The foreign language programs—including Chinese, French, German, Italian, Spanish, Russian—are all considered superb, and most students study at least one language intensely, even if it's not required. In the summer, the school offers special immersion programs in which students eat, breathe, and sleep in a foreign language. Students put their newly acquired language skills to good use; more than half the students opt to study abroad in one of Middlebury's many overseas programs. There's also several interdisciplinary programs with an international bent, including international studies, international politics, and a unique Northern Studies program that combines study of the biological, human, and physical systems within the Northern Hemisphere.

The general requirements include courses in several academic areas, as well as two years of a foreign language or culture. Writing is an important part of the curriculum; all first-year students are required to take a Writing Seminar, chosen from a range of topics. During an additional January term, more casual than the fall and spring semesters, students take more nontraditional courses, hang out, and ski.

Classes stay small, and most professors encourage discussion over straight lecture. Most students report that they feel the faculty care deeply about them, and none complained that professors didn't spend enough time with them. "However much you need, they give," reported

Middlebury College

$$$$$
★★★★

Setting: Rural
# of Undergraduates: 2,097
Men: 48.7% Women: 51.3%
Tuition: $29,340
# of Students Applied: 4,599
  Admitted: 1,337   Enrolled: 519
Required Admissions Test: 3 SAT II Tests, 3 AP Tests, 3 Int'l Baccalaureate Subsidiaries, ACT
Lowest 25% of Freshmen Scored At or Below: SAT Verbal: 660
  SAT Math: 650   ACT Comp.: 27
Highest 25% of Freshmen Scored At or Above: SAT Verbal: 730   SAT Math: 710
  ACT Comp.: 31
H.S. Rank, Top 10%: 66%
Top 25%: 85%
Top 50%: 97%
Avg. Score of Applicants Admitted: SAT Verbal: 680
  SAT Math: 660   ACT Comp.: 28
Most Popular Majors (% of Student Body): History (10%), English (8%), Economics (6%), International Relations (6%), Biology, Political Science (6%)

one. And when the warm weather does hit, many take the classes outside, "to soak up learning and sunshine in equal amounts."

Because Middlebury has the unique feature of including room and board in the price of tuition, few students live off campus. Residence halls are grouped together to form one of five Commons. Each Commons, run by an elected student council and a faculty associate, has its own activity fund and sponsors special events, including parties and local field trips.

One thing that seems to scream out to students about the student body is the lack of diversity. "When I first got here, I saw an isolated campus with a lot of rich, white people," said one student. The administration is making efforts in this area by broadening recruiting and financial aid, but the above description seems to still be accurate—the vast majority of students are white, upper-middle-class, and from the northeast. But within that, there's a range of political views, from the conservative yacht-club crowd to "raging liberals." But the relaxed atmosphere among the students allows for all to get along; it's a friendly group. And the gender balance is even—unusual at colleges in Middlebury's league—and there is a strong commitment to women's studies at the faculty, administration, and student levels.

As previously mentioned, the campus is pretty isolated, which, when the winter hits, can leave social offerings wanting. Students reported to us that they party on campus quite a bit, but there are many who also hang out in the dorms or head to the Gamut Room, the on-campus coffeehouse that is run by students and often features live entertainment (usually by other students). But other on-campus activities include concerts, movies, and dances.

And, of course, there are the slopes. As has been said, Middlebury is a dream location for winter sports lovers. The winters are long, and there's lots of snowfall, but with several first-rate ski slopes nearby, students don't seem to mind. Even if you're not a skier, there's skating, kayaking, swimming, hiking, and hockey. The Winter Carnival, one of Middlebury's most popular social events, transforms the school into a winter wonderland, as everyone plays in the snow and enjoys ice-sculpture contests, ice skating, ski races, and a formal dance.

With all these activities, its laid-back student body, and its scenic locale, most students are quite happy studying in this snowy paradise.

OBERLIN COLLEGE IN OBERLIN, OHIO

Admissions Address: Admissions Office, Carnegie Building, 101 North Professor St., Oberlin, OH 44074
Phone: (216) 775-8411 (800) 622-OBIE
Web Address: www.oberlin.edu

Oberlin College's combination of top academic departments, a world-renowned music conservatory, and an eclectic student population makes it a first-rate liberal arts college with several special features.

As one student said, "Obies" are always contemplating the implications of . . . well, everything. Students hold "speak outs" on the steps of the student union, and recent topics have included everything from federal financial aid cuts to drug policy to the sexist graffiti showing up around campus to coed dorms. Students feel this spirit makes Oberlin vibrant, exciting, stimulating—and sometimes exhausting.

An Oberlin senior tells us, "The professors are really helpful when it comes to classwork, and they are eager to get to know students on a personal level. Some professors have picnics and parties at their houses." Students work extremely hard, often studying for several hours a day. However, pressure is primarily of the self-motivated kind and there's not much competition.

Students in Oberlin's College of Arts and Sciences and Conservatory of Music, which attracts top musicians intent on a professional career, live and eat together and share the same facilities. For the ambitious, it's possible to study within both schools and earn a dual B.A./B.M. degree. At Oberlin's College of Arts and Sciences, the sciences are as cultivated as the arts, and biology and chemistry are as strong as English and art history. A high percentage of students go on to medical school or graduate school.

In both schools the course load is demanding. Liberal arts students, in addition to nine required courses in three academic areas—humanities, natural sciences, social sciences—also take courses in cultural diversity and demonstrate writing and quantitative proficiency. The Experimental College (known as EXCO) with its unusual, nontraditional courses in everything from pop culture to pottery, is one way students escape the core course grind. Three required January terms provide additional opportunities for exploration: Students pursue special interests or flex their creative muscles through independent projects and special course offerings.

Oberlin College
$$$$$
★★

Setting: Rural
# of Undergraduates: 2,797
Men: 41.8% **Women:** 58.2%
Tuition: $22,282
Room and Board: $6,358
# of Students Applied: 3,863
   Admitted: 2,507 **Enrolled:** 671
Required Admissions Test: SAT or ACT
Lowest 25% of Freshmen Scored At or Below: SAT Verbal: 620
   SAT Math: 580 ACT Comp.: 25
Highest 25% of Freshmen Scored At or Above: SAT Verbal: 720 SAT Math: 680
   ACT Comp.: 30
H.S. Rank, Top 10%: 47%
Top 25%: 79%
Top 50%: 99%
Avg. Score of Applicants Admitted: SAT Verbal: 633
   SAT Math: 670 ACT Comp.: 28
Average GPA of Applicants Admitted: 3.46
Most Popular Majors (% of Student Body): English (17%), History (10%), Politics (10%), Biology (8%), Psychology (6%)

As mentioned, Oberlin's diverse student body is loud but quite tolerant. The speak-outs, part protest and part discussion, occur several times a year, and students enthusiastically take part. "They take theory out of the classroom and make it emotional," said one student. Another reported that Obies are perpetually drained from living in constant dialogue. But this student quickly added that the stimulation and tolerance skills picked up on campus will shape him for a lifetime. Oberlin has a history of leading the way among liberal arts schools in recruiting minorities, and was the first co-ed college in the country. There is also a large and active gay and lesbian population.

The spacious 440-acre campus accommodates a student population that's a bit larger than at other liberal arts colleges. Oberlin provides a number of outstanding facilities, particularly its four exceptionally well-stocked libraries—although the Mudd Library is known as much for its socializing as for its resources—as well as high-tech science laboratories, a computing center, and an art museum whose elegant design rivals the works inside it. The choice of living arrangements includes several special interest theme houses and student run co-ops.

In addition to all the musicians on campus studying at the conservatory, many other Obies are creatively inclined. As at schools across the country, Oberlin has seen an increase in conservative views, but most students continue to be liberal. It's a place where a number of opinions are freely voiced and everyone is respected.

Surrounded by farmland in all directions, the town of Oberlin is small and unexciting and can, students say, be "gloomy." However, relations between the town and the school are good, and many students do volunteer work or conduct internships in town. While it can be bitter cold in winter, the Oberlin campus manages to be a mini-cultural mecca within Ohio, as it should, given the presence of a prestigious conservatory on campus. There are frequent concerts, dance performances, and plays on campus, some by student groups, others by professional visitors. For social activities, most students tend to stay on campus, unless they venture into Cleveland, where people like to go to "The Flats," an area with several bars and music clubs.

ACADEMIC SHRINES

POMONA COLLEGE IN CLAREMONT, CALIFORNIA

Admissions Address: Admissions Office, 333 North College Way, Claremont, CA 91711
Phone: (909) 621-8134
Web Address: www.pomona.edu/

If you think all top liberal arts colleges are those New Englandy campuses with golden fall foliage and gargoyle-laden Gothic buildings, check out Pomona College. Offering a liberal arts education equal to the top Northeast liberal arts schools, Pomona is located in Southern California—and that means palm trees and sunshine. The Spanish-style architecture contributes to the school's Western look and feel and provides plenty of lovely courtyards and gardens.

Pomona College is also unique because it is part of the Claremont school system, made up of five small colleges (along with Claremont McKenna, Harvey Mudd, Pitzer, and Scripps), each with its own academic focus and character. As the school's publicity materials point out, going to Pomona gives students the best of all worlds: a small campus community with all the benefits of a large research university. Students can freely register for courses at the other schools and take part in social and extracurricular events together. There are even some interdisciplinary courses team-taught by teachers from all five schools, which enable students to examine subjects across the academic boundaries of the different schools. The five schools share many facilities and services, such as computer and science labs, a health center, and sporting complexes. Combined, the libraries contain an exceptional number of sources.

At Pomona, the classes, mostly seminars, are very small. "The professors are the best thing about Pomona," raves one senior. "They're very easy to speak with. Because classes are so small there's a lot of individualized instruction. Some undergraduates get the chance to do independent studies or research with their professors," she said.

Pomona's departments are strong in almost all subject areas. The broad distribution requirements include study within several academic areas, including humanities, social sciences, natural sciences, writing, and a foreign language. During their freshman year, students choose a seminar in a single subject area to help them develop critical thinking and writing skills. To graduate, students either take a comprehensive examination or complete a senior project with the help of a faculty member.

Students report that the workload is "hard, but doable." While the courses are demanding, many students adopt that stereotypical laid-back,

---

Pomona College
$$$$$
★★★★

Setting: Suburban
# of Undergraduates: 1,515
   Men: 52.2% Women: 47.8%
Tuition: $20,500
Room and Board: $8,180
# of Students Applied: 3,439
   Admitted: 1,168 Enrolled: 399
Required Admissions Test: either SAT or ACT
Recommended: SAT II (writing test plus two others)
Lowest 25% of Freshmen Scored At or Below: SAT Verbal: 650 SAT Math: 670 ACT Comp.: 29
Highest 25% of Freshmen Scored At or Above: SAT Verbal: 750 SAT Math: 740 ACT Comp.: 32
H.S. Rank, Top 10%: 83%
Top 25%: 96%
Top 50%: 100%
Avg. Score of Applicants Admitted: SAT Verbal: 708 SAT Math: 708 ACT Comp.: 31
Most Popular Majors (% of Student Body): Economics (9%), Psychology (8%), Biology (8%), Politics (7%), International Relations (5%)

West Coast attitude. You'll almost always find students hanging around on lawns and in courtyards, barbecuing, tossing a Frisbee, and even studying outside.

Although the college isn't far from Los Angeles, and students can easily take a bus to hang out at UCLA, the campus is the social center for students. The nearby town of Claremont isn't exactly a college town; you might find expensive shops and boutiques, but no divey bars and restaurants that attract students. But students find plenty to keep them busy, especially since the Claremont system expands the number of possibilities. There's always something going on at one of the schools, including large parties for students from all five schools. One thing most Pomona students like about their school is the strong focus on life outside the classroom. Whatever your interest, you'll find some way to explore and express it on campus.

On campus, most of the social life centers on the dormitories, which are in good condition. Most of the students choose to live on campus during all four years of their Pomona educations. A new student union in the works should also create a prime socializing spot.

When asked if Pomona students deserve their reputation for being a little pretentious, she responded, "I wish I could say that wasn't true." But she also reported that "we're all pretty smart people," which provides an atmosphere that helps students stay motivated and focused. Many plan to go on to graduate school in academic subject areas. A substantial number of students come from California (about 40 percent of the student body), but the school is steadily attracting more students from across the country. And why shouldn't it? With superior academics, sunny weather, and a casual, friendly student body, there's plenty at Pomona to call students westward.

SWARTHMORE COLLEGE IN SWARTHMORE, PENNSYLVANIA

Admissions Address: Office of Admissions, 500 College Avenue, Swarthmore, PA 19081-1397
Phone: (610) 328-8300
Web Address: www.swarthmore.edu/

In 1996, Swarthmore was rated the number-one liberal arts college in America by *U.S. News & World Report*. The accompanying article cited Swarthmore's attention to student needs and concerns, and its fostering

ACADEMIC SHRINES

of an atmosphere in which undergraduates not only receive a top-notch education but find a confidence within themselves that shows them they are highly skilled, intelligent, special people. And the faculty and administrators go out of their way to broadcast that message.

Swarthmore's small student population particularly cultivates a feeling of being immersed in a closely knit, highly intellectual community. Students work closely with fellow students as well as the faculty. The professors, who teach all the classes, even for freshmen, are extremely involved with their students' educations. Many students have stories of profs holding their final seminar classes over dinner in their homes. But they also demand a lot from their students in return. Classes are described by some as "intense" and "challenging," by others as "a real pressure cooker." And this seems to be exactly what Swarthmore's highly motivated students are looking for.

Almost all departments and programs are first-rate, from English to engineering to the performing arts. Swarthmore's core curriculum doesn't have many rigid requirements (there are no special requirements for freshmen), leaving students a certain amount of freedom in planning their schedules. Incoming students will probably be happy to learn that freshmen are graded on a pass/fail basis for their first semester to help them get used to the school's rigorous academics. The course offerings are a bit limited, and it can be tough to get into certain courses. However, students can cross-register with nearby Haverford, Bryn Mawr, and University of Pennsylvania, which all have their own excellent academic offerings.

For the extremely well-motivated, or "masochistic," Swarthmore offers a special program called the External Examination Program, particularly recommended for those looking to continue with their educations upon graduating. These students take eight seminars, with very limited enrollments, during their last two years, but don't take any exams until the end of senior year, when they're subjected to a difficult comprehensive written and oral examination. It's not for everyone, but the ones who participate in it find it very rewarding, and given the student makeup, an opportunity to push the outer limits is always welcome.

While this special program is particularly tough, the everyday classes aren't exactly a breeze. The school expects a lot from its students, but the "Swatties," as Swarthmore students call themselves, probably expect even more from themselves. "People take pride in their work. They don't compete with each other, but there's a common endeavor to work," one student reports.

Swarthmore College

$$$$$
★★★★

Setting: Suburban
# of Undergraduates: 1,435
Men: 45.6% **Women:** 54.4%
Tuition: $20,846
Room and Board: $7,176
# of Students Applied: 4,001
  Admitted: 1,206 **Enrolled:** 411
Required Admissions Test: Either SAT or ACT plus 3 SAT IIs including Writing; Math IIC for engineering
Lowest 25% of Freshmen Scored At or Below: SAT Verbal: 630 SAT Math: 630
Highest 25% of Freshmen Scored At or Above: SAT Verbal: 760 SAT Math: 730
H.S. Rank, Top 10%: 82%
Top 25%: 97%
Top 50%: 100%
Avg. Score of Applicants Admitted: SAT Verbal: 689 SAT Math: 673
Most Popular Majors (% of Student Body): Biology (13%), Economics (13%), Political Science (11%), English Literature (10%), Sociology/Anthropology (7%)

In general, Swatties tend to be politically aware, leaning toward the left, and many participate in volunteer groups. "We have an international reputation of being very liberal, active, and worldly. People are open to all cultures," says one student. Another mentioned how Swatties don't seek to just tolerate but "understand and appreciate what makes people different." The small community makes much of this possible. Says another student, "If we have problems in the community, we resolve them in the community. There's almost no hierarchy. Students get really involved with the school."

The small community has its positives, but it has its negatives as well. "Our community makes it possible to maintain a rumor mill whose efficiency rivals the Internet." Although located in a suburban environment, the campus is as green and appealing as any rural liberal arts college. "It's a lovely suburban campus," a student reports. The horticultural society labels all the trees on campus which, unlike on an urban campus, is no small feat here. The dormitories and food are considered fine, although not outstanding. Most freshman live in double rooms, and there are a variety of arrangements available for upperclassmen, the majority of whom live on campus all four years.

Most of the on-campus fun revolves around school-sponsored events like concerts, parties, dances, and movies, which are all free for students. The school does have its wackier special events too, including the McCabe Mile, an 18-lap race through—no kidding—the basement of the library; the Crum Regatta, a student boat race on the campus' Crum Creek; and an all-day, live music festival.

If students get tired of the campus social scene, they have the advantage of being only 20 minutes away by train from Philadelphia, so when they crave a culture fix or a cheesesteak sandwich, help is nearby.

VASSAR COLLEGE IN POUGHKEEPSIE, NEW YORK

Admissions Address: Office of Admission, Vassar College, Box 10, 124 Raymond Ave, Poughkeepsie, NY 12601
Phone: (914) 437-7300 (800) 827-7270
Web Address: www.vassar.edu/

Vassar gives its students a high degree of independence, and encourages students to use it. Consequently, the school attracts free-thinking students and those who will be motivated to, as one student said, "find a space to grow and excel." Many students design their own majors.

ACADEMIC SHRINES

Liberal arts departments are highly rated across the board. English and performing arts are especially well regarded and have large enrollments, but sciences, especially biology, and Vassar's unique cognitive science major, are steadily gaining in reputation.

The classes are kept small, usually between 10 and 15 students, and this has a good side and a bad side, we hear. While students welcome the small classes because they foster discussion (the focus of many classes), the enforced small size can make it difficult to get the classes students need or want, a situation at least one student described as "irritating." Administrators and professors, who live on campus, are very accessible ("amazingly so," says one student). "My professors are always around," said another student, "and always willing and interested to discuss whatever's on my mind." It's not uncommon for students to be on a first-name basis with faculty or to have dinner at professors' houses. The workload is "definitely challenging," but "people don't study a ton," reports one student.

One of the school's key assets is its dynamic and diverse student body, which includes various ethnic and cultural groups and a large gay population. The school recently opened a new Intercultural Center, which houses the Asian Students Alliance, the Black Students Union, and Poder Latino. "People are very individualistic," says one student. "We're a really diverse community as far as interests and activities." Musicians, actors, writers, and artists abound; they consider the school a haven for their creativity and lifestyles. Some are put off by the "people-in-black" crowd, but most Vassar students revel in the diverse group who, as one student said, "share the desire to discuss, explore, and learn from one another."

Vassar was an all-female school until 1968, and female students outnumber men, altering the traditional balance found at most colleges (except at all-female schools). Some find this a plus, others a big minus, for reasons you can probably guess. The school's female majority parallels a high number of women administrators and professors.

At one time a sprawling farm, the 1,000-acre campus has beautiful foliage and even a few lakes. Vassar's many superb facilities include a gorgeous Gothic-style library, a college art gallery, science laboratories with the latest equipment, and several theaters and performance spaces. All four class years are housed together in above-average, spacious dormitories; freshmen usually live in doubles, but it's not hard to get a single after your first year. Serving the entire Vassar community, the All

Vassar College

$$$$$
★★★

Setting: Suburban
# of Undergraduates: 2,245
Men: 37.8% **Women:** 62.2%
Tuition: $21,780
Room and Board: $6,470
# of Students Applied: 4,037
  Admitted: 1,954 **Enrolled:** 618
Required Admissions Test: either SAT or ACT
Lowest 25% of Freshmen Scored At or Below: SAT Verbal: 630 SAT Math: 600 ACT Comp.: 25
Highest 25% of Freshmen Scored At or Above: SAT Verbal: 710 SAT Math: 670 ACT Comp.: 29
H.S. Rank, Top 10%: 59%
Top 25%: 87%
Top 50%: 99%
Avg. Score of Applicants Admitted: SAT Verbal: 682 SAT Math: 656 ACT Comp.: 29
Average GPA of Applicants Admitted: 3.93
Most Popular Majors (% of Student Body): English (16%), Psychology (8%), History (7%), Political Science (6%), Art History (5%)

73

Campus Dining Center, with spectacular views and less than spectacular food, is an ideal place for socializing with friends and faculty.

Poughkeepsie, Vassar's hometown, was described by one student as a city that "leaves much to be desired" and in many reports, the feeling is mutual. Poughkeepsie is a blue-collar town (though until recently IBM was a major presence), and it has little to do with the school. While the Mid-Hudson Civic Center does draw name concerts, and there are small theater groups around, there's usually not too much to do in town. While many students do work and volunteer in the city, but they stick close to campus for fun. There is also a train to New York; the trip is between ninety minutes and two hours, but for a day trip it's doable, and perfectly suited to the urban tastes of the Vassar student body.

Vassar isn't known for its athletic teams and sporting events. However, extracurricular activities are an important part of students' lives. Many students are part of artistic or performing groups, so students have no shortage of cultural events on campus. Students hang out in their dorms or at a campus coffeehouse.

Matthew's Mug is the college pub, which students report is low-key during the week, when it has jazz music and poetry readings, but turns into a dance club on weekends. There are several traditional events each year, including spring and fall formals, and Founder's Day, with rides, live bands, and a big picnic.

Vassar is a great school for tolerance and freedom, both scholarly and social, as well as academic excellence.

WILLIAMS COLLEGE IN WILLIAMSTOWN, MASSACHUSETTS

Admissions Address: Admissions Office, P.O. Box 487, Williamstown, MA 01267
Phone: (413) 597-2211
Web Address: www.williams.edu/

It shouldn't be surprising to find that Williams and Amherst are archrivals, given how alike they are. Both schools provide students with exceptional liberal arts educations at picture-perfect New England campuses. Yet Williams has its own distinctive features, including unusual academic offerings and a location ideal for winter sports and outdoor recreation.

ACADEMIC SHRINES

If Amherst's wide-open curriculum structure is not to your liking, Williams's might be. The set college-wide curriculum requires students to take several courses in major areas, including languages and arts, social sciences, science, mathematics, and non-Western civilization, as Williams, like most schools, has been trying to establish a more multicultural base. Students looking for established structure will feel more at home, as will students looking for a more well-rounded background.

But there is room for self-designed study at Williams, and one way students achieve is by taking advantage of the required winter term. Most students devote it to completing special projects or studying something a bit off the beaten path, which makes it a nice break from the rigors of the academic year. There's also an unusual program called Free University in which students teach each other a variety of subjects, from cooking various cultural cuisines to dance.

Williams classes are kept small, often numbering only 15 students. Students praise their professors and the amount of interaction they have with them. Says one student, "The professors are here because they have a genuine desire to teach. They are accessible and they are genuinely interested in the welfare of their students." In case classes of 15 are still too large, students can also enroll in tutorials in which they meet regularly with a professor once a week to discuss their independent research in different subjects.

Williamstown, in the heart of the Berkshires, is strikingly beautiful and tiny. With the school buildings right in the middle of town, the environment provides all the advantages and disadvantages of small-town life: it is pretty, is friendly, sits atop a hill, and looks out onto breathtaking scenery. It is also small, with a very limited number of social choices, and it is in New England, which means long, cold winters that one student described as "lasting from October to May." While the nearby skiing, sledding, and skating are excellent, if you're not into winter participatory sports you might be stuck for different things to do on the weekend after you've tried all the different sandwiches at Papa Charlie's. If you are into skiing, however, the slopes are close enough so that you can be gliding down the mountain on a study break.

One genuine attraction at Williamstown is the annual Theater Festival, where A-list Broadway and Hollywood stars come up for the summer, and theater students can intern on tech crews at mainstage productions and audition for the smaller ones. It is remarkable to see this sleepy Berkshire town turn into a bustling theater mecca every summer, and many students do stick around for it.

Williams College

$$$$$
★★★★

Setting: Small town
# of Undergraduates: 1,961
Men: 51.2% **Women:** 48.8%
Tuition: $21,759
Room and Board: $6,140
# of Students Applied: 5,063
  Admitted: 1,232 **Enrolled:** 554
Required Admissions Test: either SAT or ACT
Lowest 25% of Freshmen Scored At or Below: SAT Verbal: 650 SAT Math: 660 ACT Comp.: 28
Highest 25% of Freshmen Scored At or Above: SAT Verbal: 770 SAT Math: 750 ACT Comp.: 32
H.S. Rank, Top 10%: 83%
Top 25%: 96%
Top 50%: 100%
Most Popular Majors (% of Student Body): History (17%), Biology (15%), English (15%), Economics (11%), Political Science (9%)

The dormitories, ranging from older renovated buildings to more modern styles, are in good condition, which is fortunate since, come winter, you'll be spending a lot of time there. Incoming students can expect to gain the infamous "freshman fifteen" as the food is considered better here than at most colleges. Most of the social scene is centered in the dorms, leaving some students looking for an "alternative to the keg scene."

Williams has been trying to create a diverse atmosphere of well-rounded students. The student body already includes a 25 percent minority population, and the school is actively trying to recruit more; also a recently formed commission is working on improving race relations. Most students are liberal-minded, and many are active in volunteer organizations or political groups.

More rural than Amherst, Williams is several hours from most cities, and you might start to feel you're more likely to run into a cow than a large party. Still, the school does offer a great deal of activities for students willing to find them and become involved; in addition to many of the standard activity groups, there are several campus music and theater groups, and with the Festival, opportunities are around. Sports are also huge. As one student reports, "Athletics are huge. I would venture to say over half the students compete in some level of athletics." Popular intercollegiate team sports include hockey, skiing, swimming and football, while broomball is the intramural sport of choice. A recently built athletic center provides space for a range of activities, including indoor courts and weight rooms.

For the student who wants a sound mind and body, Williams is ideal; where else can you receive a first-rate liberal arts education while skiing to your heart's content after class?

The Universities

Brown University in Providence, Rhode Island

Admissions Address: College Admissions Office, Box 1876, Providence, RI 02912
Phone: (401) 863-2378
Web Address: www.brown.edu/

Brown University is a little different from its Ivy brothers. To begin with, there is no core curriculum or any forced requirements. Students claim this is Brown's biggest selling point: the most nontraditional and flexible curriculum in the Ivy League, designed to give students complete freedom in their academic pursuits. Students can freely pick and choose courses that interest them from Brown's extensive and often unusual course offerings. As one student raved, "You can take anything you want, and you can take anything pass/fail!"

The point behind this is to encourage Brown students to focus completely on learning and indulging their academic and intellectual curiosities. Students create their own structure and order based on self-imposed limits, but sometimes, as one student put it, "the responsibility of the independence is overwhelming." Still, others find the challenge exciting and invigorating.

Students need to pass only 30 courses to graduate—which means they never need to take more than four courses a semester—leaving time for study as well as to pursue other interests. Brown also has, as mentioned, an atypical grading policy, with two options: A, B, C, No Credit (without any pluses or minuses) or Satisfactory/No Credit. Be warned, though, that too many "no credits" does get noticed by the higher-ups.

While Brown's curriculum gives students academic freedom, it makes demands on them in return. Students are expected to do their work and show up to class ready to participate. While the students work hard, the workload isn't overwhelming. "Bs aren't hard to come by," said one student. The lack of structure, however, isn't for everyone because it requires enormous self-discipline and motivation. Brown does provide an extensive system of advising that helps students stay somewhat on track. The Curricular Advisory Program places freshmen in seminars taught by their first-year academic advisors, giving freshmen much-needed support right from the beginning. During following years, students can meet with a number of advisors and counselors as the need arises.

Brown University

$$$$$
★★★★★

Setting: Urban
# of Undergraduates: 5,500
Tuition: $22,270
Room and Board: $6,538
# of Students Applied: 15,012
 Admitted: 2,856 Enrolled: 1,510
Required Admissions Test: SAT I; some departments require ACT, SAT II
H.S. Rank, Top 10%: 28%

English, literature, history and economics are popular majors, and because of Brown's prestigious medical school, many people major in biology and chemistry. Students are also able to design their own majors and create their own interdisciplinary programs. Brown has been working to increase the quality and expand the range of its programs, departments, and facilities. Recent additions include the Center for Information Technology, with its state-of-the-art science facilities, and the Center for Race and Ethnicity. Students also have the option of cross-registration at the Rhode Island School of Design.

Although Brown has extensive course offerings, the more popular classes can be difficult to get into and may take several semesters of trying. While some introductory courses will certainly be large lectures, students also take a number of seminars, particularly at higher levels. Some courses and most discussion sections are taught by graduate TAs, but Brown students generally praise the interaction they have with their professors. Professors are "into teaching" and readily available for help, said one student.

The intellectual atmosphere and emphasis on individual freedom that distinguishes Brown's academics also characterizes the student body. Theater, art, and politics are most students' main interests, not necessarily in that order. Students come from a variety of cultures and backgrounds and tend to be liberal and socially conscious; gay rights, feminism, multiculturalism, and the environment are among the many hot topics on campus. One of the most popular organizations on campus is the Brown Community Outreach volunteer program. The general atmosphere on campus is a tolerant one in which students can display their individuality in whatever way they choose. While political correctness has become much maligned at some schools, Brown students genuinely value diversity and individual freedom.

A separate entity from the city of Providence, outside its gates, Brown's relatively small campus does not have the sprawling lawns, gentle hills, and glorious foliage of the more scenic New England campuses. It does, though, have a certain charm, primarily due to its eclectic mixture of buildings separated by patches of grass and trees. The school has recently been on a renovation kick, and several dormitories, the theater complex, and the student center have all been newly improved. Students do most of their studying and research in Brown's well-stocked John D. Rockefeller Library (known by students as "The Rock," rather than "The John") or science library (called "Sci Li"). Most freshmen live in double rooms on one of two campuses with slightly different personalities. Many dormitories have been renovated and, if somewhat generic looking, are in decent condition.

The social life at Brown reflects the diversity of the students. Students especially enjoy attending the many fine cultural events on campus including music and dance concerts, theater, and movies. The Brown campus provides plenty of places for students to hang out—a favorite Brown activity—including snack bars where you can use your dining card if you've missed a meal, and an on-campus pub/dance club called The Underground. Although there aren't many fraternities or sororities, one student said "there are a lot of frat parties" for those who want them.

While Providence has a reputation as a blue-collar town, there is evidence that is changing, and a new Civic Center and an attempt to lure NFL and NBA games to the city is underway. The city is promoting itself as a college town, with Brown, Providence College, and URI all in the immediate area. Downtown Providence is a 10-minute walk, and students often head there for movies and dining options. Thayer Street, just off campus, is also popular, with inexpensive stores, eateries, bars, and an art house movie theater. Boston is only 45 minutes away and is a popular road trip that Brown students frequently undertake.

But it's not the location or the campus that draw most students to Brown; it's the nonrestrictive academic environment and, to a large extent, the other students. As one said, "The people you meet here are so interesting. It makes every day really exciting."

COLUMBIA UNIVERSITY IN NEW YORK, NEW YORK

Admissions Address: Office of Undergraduate Admissions, 1130 Amsterdam Avenue, MC 2807, New York, NY 10027
Phone: (212) 854-2522
Web Address: www.columbia.edu/

All the Ivies have something special about them that sets them apart from the rest of the League. For Columbia, it's the college town in which it's set—New York City.

Students who come to Columbia do so mostly because, while they could have gone to Brown or Penn or other top-flight universities, they wanted the activity, culture, and excitement of the Big Apple coupled with their Ivy League education.

Columbia College

$$$
★★★★★

Setting: Urban
Tuition: $20,884
Room and Board: $7,160
# of Students Applied: 10,247
Admitted: 2,145 **Enrolled:** 975
Required Admissions Test: either SAT or ACT; three SAT II subject tests (one must be Writing)
SAT Scores, Middle 50% of Entering Class: SAT Verbal ranging from 640–750, SAT Math ranging from 640–730
H.S. Rank, Top 10%: 84%

Columbia has one of the best liberal arts and engineering programs of the Ivies, not to mention the nation, and one reason is the core curriculum, which is strict and heavy with requirements. There are two undergraduate schools: Columbia College, home of the arts and sciences division, and the School of Engineering and Applied Science. English, history, political science, biology, and chemistry are all popular majors, as is prejournalism, since most Columbia undergrads are preparing for further education, either medical school, law school, or Columbia's acclaimed School of Journalism.

But no matter what major you choose, you have to go through the core curriculum. Unlike Brown, which allows students to design their own program, or Princeton, which has only broad institutional requirements, Columbia students are required to take courses in literature humanities, art humanities, music humanities, contemporary civilization, non-Western culture, several semesters of science, as well as freshmen writing seminars. Even though all students are required to take these courses, Columbia manages to keep the classes small and discussion oriented. Students immerse themselves in these classes, and many say that they are the most valuable they take at Columbia. At least one student that, "far from just training me for a chosen profession, these classes expanded my mind and taught me to think in wholly new and exciting ways." The core courses do absorb a lot of credits, though; some students are less happy about that than others.

Columbia draws an A-list faculty, many of whom live in New York and are lured to the campus. This can make for some incredible opportunities (former New York mayor David Dinkins teaches poli-sci courses here) though it can make reaching profs outside of class a chore. One student said that "those looking for a nurturing environment" should look elsewhere. Likewise, advising is not readily available, we hear. "If you see your faculty advisor more than once after orientation, you're lucky." Others say that if you're willing, you can get close to your advisor. "You have to be determined and make the effort," said one.

Columbia's bureaucracy is, by all reports, a nightmare. One student dryly noted, "It has an upside: I've gained valuable skills in working within a complex system to get what I want and need." This could be the biggest truth at Columbia: strong, self-sufficient, determined students rise above the challenges and thrive.

Columbia's small campus at 116th Street and Broadway centers primarily on the large, central quadrangle, lined by academic buildings with the large, main library at its head. The quality of the dormitories varies, we hear and most students live in the dorms for all four years since rents are . . . well, this *is* New York. There's also been some concern about the neighborhood. Columbia sits on the edge of Harlem in Morningside Heights, and there have, in the past, been instances of the white, wealthy student body rubbing up against the neighborhood folks the wrong way. Many students, though, say the problems with the neighborhood are way overrated. "There are restaurants and shops in the area where I go all the time," said one student. Another added, "whenever I go a few blocks off-campus to get a bite, the people are always friendly. I don't see a problem."

What most students suggest is being "street smart," which means being aware of yourself and your surroundings. "Know where you are, don't be naive, but don't be defensive, either. Do that, and you'll be fine," said one student.

Most Columbia students learn the city quickly, and learn it well. Some, though, can find the pull of Manhattan a distraction. "It's always a temptation to blow off studying to head downtown," said one student. Another said the pace, bustle, and atmosphere of New York can add to the stress of the school for the uninitiated. "Know you're going to be in New York when you come," said one student, "because if you think otherwise, you won't be able to deal."

Columbia's student body is as diverse as the city itself, and much more diverse than at any other Ivy League school. While there have been reports of students being cliquish and staying in their racial, ethnic, or economic groups, many students see the diversity as a huge asset Columbia has over the other Ivies: "The classes teach you to open your mind, and that is reinforced, even challenged, by the diversity of the student body." Students, like the city they study in, tend to be liberal, and many are politically active.

Columbia's sports are on a rebound, particularly the football team, which is now a power in the Ivy League after years of consistent losing, and as the team has improved, students fill Baker Field at the top of Manhattan to cheer on the Lions. Other teams, such as the soccer, baseball, and fencing teams, also do well. Columbia does have good sports facilities for those who want them, and there's a thriving intramural program.

The fraternities, while not the focal point of the Columbia social scene, do throw parties. Most students socialize in small, dormitory get-togethers or head out with friends to nearby bars and coffeehouses just outside the campus. On weekends, students have what one called "a mass exodus from the 116th Street subway station" to other parts of the city, particularly to bars, clubs, and cafes on the Upper West Side or downtown in the East Village. While living in a big city can be stressful, most students take advantage of New York for all it's worth. The school itself organizes many cultural activities in the city, including museum, theater, and concert trips. "Going to Columbia is like going to a school with hundreds of museums, art galleries, movies, radio stations, theaters, dance clubs, and restaurants," said one happy student.

One student summed up Columbia this way: "It's sink or swim, but once you learn how to swim, you will know how to do it in any pool." After all, you'll have learned in the biggest pool of all.

CORNELL UNIVERSITY IN ITHACA, NEW YORK

Admissions Address: Admissions Office, 410 Thurston Avenue, Ithaca, NY 14850-2488
Phone: (607) 255-5241
Web Address: www.cornell.edu/

Ezra Cornell wanted an "institution where anyone may find instruction in any study." And at his extraordinary university, that's exactly what you'll find.

Cornell has seven undergraduate schools, but three are unique among Ivy schools. The agriculture and life sciences school, human ecology school, and school of industrial and labor relations, are funded by New York State, so New Yorkers can attend for just above SUNY tuition. It's an incredible bargain that sets Cornell apart, but also increases enrollment (currently the highest in the Ivy League). The four private schools and the schools of hotel management, engineering, and arts and sciences are considered among the best in their fields in the nation.

Each school has its own admission and core requirements, as well as its own administration, but all students live together, and share many other facilities. Students can take courses in any of the seven schools as well. This greatly increases Cornell's course offerings. Wine tasting in the hotel school, for example, is a popular course for all Cornell seniors. Many of the more popular lectures can be large, but they're usually broken down into smaller sections that meet regularly with a TA. There are also a number of smaller classes and seminars.

Academic Shrines

Cornell's size and reach make it ripe with opportunities, but they also bring a downside. For one thing, it's "intimidating" said one student; "12,000 or so undergraduates at an Ivy League school can be culture shock," said another. Forming relationships with the faculty can be another challenge. "It takes time to find your way," said one student. "But once you do, you find professors who you can count on." Many advisors are assigned great numbers of students and, as a result, cannot spend much time with each one. Another problem: enough red tape to make the federal government blush.

There's a popular saying among students that it may be easier to get into Cornell than other Ivies, but it's the hardest one to stay in. Cornell courses are incredibly demanding, and students work harder than most of their Ivy League counterparts. "The workload varies from field to field," said one student, but on most nights, you'll find the library study rooms filled with anxious students.

These all feed into what most students say is the biggest problem with Cornell: stress. "Let's face it, you're taking very demanding courses at a huge school where the winter starts in October and runs to April. It can make you buggy." About ten years ago, the problem became so acute that the administration stepped in and created new facilities, such as the athletic center and performing arts center, to help students chill out. Still, everyone gripes about the weather, particularly when it "ithacates" (i.e., rains and sleets simultaneously—something that seems to happen constantly in the winter).

Weather aside, Cornell boasts perhaps the most beautiful campus among the Ivies, if not the nation. "This place could be a vacation spot," was the kind of praise we heard from students. Spread out over 745 acres, Cornell's academic buildings are surrounded by sprawling lawns, wooded hills, and sparkling streams. Ithaca is known for its many gorges, and several are located right on the Cornell campus. When the weather is right, students head for a gorge to sun themselves on rocks and swim in the rushing water.

The campus centers on the impressive central Arts Quad, and the dorms are clustered on the noisier West Campus, whose older, renovated dormitories mainly attracts first-year students, and the quieter North Campus, which with newer dormitories and more single rooms, draws many upperclassmen.

Cornell University

$$$$$
★★★★

Setting: Rural
# of Undergraduates: 13,512
Men: 52.7% **Women:** 47.3%
Tuition: $21,840
Room and Board: $7,110
# of Students Applied: 21,004
  Admitted: 6,878 **Enrolled:** 3,084
Required Admissions Test: SAT
Recommended: None
Lowest 25% of Freshmen Scored At or Below: SAT Verbal: 600 SAT Math: 640
Highest 25% of Freshmen Scored At or Above: SAT Verbal: 700 SAT Math: 730
H.S. Rank, Top 10%: 81%
Top 25%: 94%
Top 50%: 100%
Avg. Score of Applicants Admitted: SAT Verbal: 600 SAT Math: 640
Most Popular Majors (% of Student Body): Engineering (17%), Agricultural Studies (14%), Biological Sciences (11%), Business (11%), History (9%)

The food at Cornell merits special mention. It's rated among the best in the nation. Students choose from a number of dining plans that offer a great deal of choice as to where, when, and what they eat. Several times a year, staffs from the country's best restaurants prepare their signature dishes for students. Cornell's own dairies make homemade ice cream, served every night.

Cornell's many first-rate facilities include a distinguished art museum designed by I. M. Pei, a sleek Performing Arts Center with several theaters and dance studios, and a new sports center with its own rock-climbing wall.

The large student population includes students from all over the country and the world, although, due to the state-funded colleges, there's a large percentage of students from New York. The state-funding and the financial aid programs also allows Cornell to have a economically diverse student body, as opposed to other Ivies. While this and the 25 percent minority population help to keep Cornell one of the most diverse schools, it also bring with it some self-segregation and cliquishness. "Students generally want to be with other students of similar experience," said one student. "I'm glad to know people of different backgrounds, but often students from wealthier backgrounds don't have a lot to identify with students from more middle- or working-class families." Political viewpoints range; what they have in common is they're all pretty vocal. "The good part about that is most students listen as well as talk," said one student.

While Cornell students work hard, they have a surprisingly active social life. The Greek system is a large one here and draws an enormous percentage of the students, who live and eat in the many stately houses that surround the campus. The fraternities and sororities are a central aspect of the Cornell social scene, as one student said, "they play a prominent role in social life." There are large parties just about any weekend, many open to all students.

If you don't go Greek there is the bar scene, or hanging out with friends. "The local bar scene is pretty big," said one student. "If you're not at the frats, that's usually the place to go." But others paint a broader picture. "This school is so big there's a niche for everybody. If you push and make the effort, you'll find your way." Students who don't live in the dorms or in fraternity houses mostly move off campus to Collegetown, adjacent to Cornell's campus, where there are affordable apartments, inexpensive restaurants, several popular bars, and coffeehouses.

ACADEMIC SHRINES

Cornell has hundreds of extracurricular activities, clubs, and organizations that, as one student said, "make the place more manageable." On-campus cultural activities include plays, lectures, and readings. Cornell Cinema screens several movies each night of the week, including cult classics and foreign films. The Concert Commission brings several high-profile rock bands to campus each year.

The extensive sports facilities enable Cornell students to satisfy their phys ed requirements in anything from scuba diving to bowling. There are also many intramural competitions, with frats or groups playing against each other. Hockey is easily the most popular intercollegiate sport, and the annual Cornell-Harvard game is the highlight of the season. Students sleep out to buy season tickets and pack Cornell's indoor ice rink to cheer on the Big Red hockey team. Football games also draw many students, who enjoy a number of pregame tailgate parties, and the strong lacrosse team has a vocal following.

New York City is about five hours away by car. Binghamton and Syracuse are closer but don't offer much except other schools. Ithaca itself, though, is a small, cosmopolitan town with a number of fine art galleries, movie theaters, and restaurants. The Finger Lakes region is home to beautiful state parks and wineries.

It may at times feel isolated, but Cornell has so much happening academically and socially that students will be far from bored. And they'll certainly get plenty of exercise.

DUKE UNIVERSITY IN DURHAM, NORTH CAROLINA

Admissions Address: Admissions Office, 2138 Campus Drive Box 90586, Durham, NC 27708-0586
Phone: (919) 684-3214
Web Address: www.duke.edu/duke.html

"Harvard. The Duke of the North."

That's about how Duke students feel about their school, their education, and the constant comparisons they "endure" with the Ivy League. Duke students don't like the Ivies and, as a part of their intense school pride, don't consider them competition. And with top-notch academics, campuses, and sports teams, it's easy to see where Blue Devil pride comes from.

THE ROAD TO COLLEGE

Duke University

$$$$$
★★★★

Setting: Suburban
# of Undergraduates: 6,207
Men: 52.3% **Women:** 47.7%
Tuition: $21,550
Room and Board: $6,853
# of Students Applied: 12,814
   Admitted: 4,077 **Enrolled:** 1,653
Required Admissions Test: Either SAT or ACT
Lowest 25% of Freshmen Scored At or Below: SAT Verbal: 640 SAT Math: 650 ACT Comp.: 28
Highest 25% of Freshmen Scored At or Above: SAT Verbal: 730 SAT Math: 740 ACT Comp.: 32
H.S. Rank, Top 10%: 84%
Top 25%: 95%
Top 50%: 100%
Most Popular Majors (% of Student Body): Biology (15%), English (9%), Psychology (9%), History (8%), Economics (8%)

Few schools are a powerhouse in so many different areas. "We have an unbelievable combination of top-quality sports and top-quality academics," enthused one student. All students reported that support of the sports teams (basketball, football, soccer, tennis, etc.) is a huge component of being a Duke undergraduate.

Duke's two undergraduate schools, the School of Engineering and the Trinity College of Arts and Sciences, are both considered excellent. The humanities, particularly history and English, and the sciences, especially biology and chemistry, are particularly popular among undergraduates. The prestigious Terry Sanford Institute of Policy Science is one of the few such programs in the country in which undergraduates can study public policy. General distribution requirements include courses in five of six general areas: arts and literature, civilizations, foreign languages, natural sciences, quantitative reasoning, social sciences, and a writing seminar.

Duke students are extremely driven, and one claimed that fellow students are "career and goal oriented from when they get off the bus." There is a substantial workload at Duke, and students spend a lot of their time studying, but most students reported the competition as "more internal than external." "You are pushed within yourself to do the best you can at everything," said one student. While some students report that the competition among the sizeable premed community is more intense, most report that the campus is "too laid-back" to support too much cutthroat competition among students. This, too, is a point of prideful comparison between Duke students and their Ivy brethren. While the faculty is top-notch in their fields, opinions vary as to the quality of their teaching. "It really depends on your area," said one student. An English major we spoke to said that she had only one class taught by a TA. Others, some in the sciences, report that there are "profs more interested in their research." Like most big schools, the rule of thumb is to ask around and focus on the better teachers. "They are here," said one student, "in abundance." Another student reported that at least once a semester she goes to dinner with one of her professors, unusual at a school Duke's size. Duke students also have the option to take large classes or small seminars, so there are plenty of ways around the shortcomings of the system.

Duke's campus is one of its great strengths; "it is absolutely gorgeous," said one student, a sentiment echoed by all we spoke to. "The campus is one of the reasons the students are relaxed," said one student. "The climate is very temperate, and the campus is so big, it is easy to find some

ACADEMIC SHRINES

space to yourself when you need it." The campus is divided in to the West and the East. West Campus is where many of Duke's Gothic stone buildings are. It is also the more socially active of the two, since it houses the fraternities and the Bryan Student Center. The East campus has more of the lovely Georgian architecture the school is known for, and houses all first-year students, though there are dormitories on both campuses. The style and personalities of the dormitories varies depending on which cluster they're located in. There are several popular theme dormitories and special interest houses (for arts, foreign languages, etcetera). Students enjoy a range of eating options all over the campuses, which are divided by a large wood and connected by shuttle buses and, with Duke's temperate weather conditions, stays green for much of the year. With its expansive lawns and heavily wooded areas, the campus is ideal for biking and jogging, Frisbee games, and lounging around—activities students take advantage of all year.

Duke is not cheap, in any sense. Tuition, room, and fees are all at or near the top of the scale, and there's no way around them, a gripe shared by students and their parents alike. Students and families can take solace in the fact that they can see their money being spent all over campus. Duke invests heavily in its campus, which includes state-of-the-art science facilities and an extensive library system.

Durham is a blue-collar town that isn't popular with students and not thought of as "real safe." While many students participate in volunteer programs that bring them into Durham, and a few venture into town in search of bars, most stay on campus. The campus itself is kept secure; the school provides an escort service and emergency phones.

The typical Duke student is often thought of as white, affluent, and conservative, and many students say that's not far off the mark. One student listed her pet peeve as the school being "too conservative," and another felt the student body broke on economic lines: "We could use some children of cops or firemen here. Just once, I'd like to hear one of my classmates say his parents worked for a living." Indeed, there appears to be a division of students along class and racial lines. There is a 20 percent minority population and "many, many international students." While one students said that Duke was "not a southern school like University of North Carolina is, because of the draw of students," another reported that she and her friends felt a "plantation mentality—most of the students are white, most of the service staff are black. You can fill in the picture." A third reported that minority students would have to break the ice with white students, "because the white students don't feel they have to approach them."

Student report they are most comfortable with other students of the same background and experience, be they racial or economic. Politically, though, students are informed, but as in all things, "laid-back."

One place the Duke community comes together as a whole is at Cameron Indoor Stadium. Duke students, as states, are really into their sports, and men's basketball games are an event, and the "Cameron Crazies" turn up the heat on the Blue Devils' opponents, elevating cheering to an art form. Additionally, intramural sports are extremely popular, with almost everyone participating in some sport or other.

The Greeks are also huge on campus, and fraternity parties dominate the social scene. Nearly half of both men and women belong to the system, although the sororities don't live together. The administration heavily polices alcohol on campus, but students report that those who want it can find it. Other socializing on campus takes place at dorm room parties, the on-campus pub, or the Bryan Student Center, which has snack bars, theaters, a game room, and space for special events. Some seniors head off campus for the local bar scene, which is "pretty weak," a student says.

For those who aren't into sports and don't opt for Greek life, it can be difficult to find a niche. Still, it's not impossible, especially with the hundreds of clubs and extracurricular activities that often form their own social networks. Those tired of partying or attending sports events can also choose from a number of events and cultural activities on campus, including movies, theater, and musical concerts. And everyone can enjoy the warm weather on the beautiful campus.

Duke students love Duke. At least one reported being "so glad" she came to Duke because "you feel you are part of something great. It's a real campus experience on a beautiful campus."

HARVARD UNIVERSITY
IN CAMBRIDGE, MASSACHUSETTS

Admissions Address: Admissions Office, Byerly Hall, 8 Garden Street, Cambridge, MA 02138
Phone: (617) 495-1551
Web Address: www.fas.harvard.edu/

How do you appraise Harvard? After all, it's Harvard. It's the oldest and most prestigious school in the country (probably one of the five most in the world), and Harvard's alumni include world leaders, Nobel Prize

ACADEMIC SHRINES

winners, presidents, poets, giants of business and industry—pretty heavy-duty company. Small wonder it could also be the toughest school in the country to get into (straight As and 1600 SATs have been turned down or put on the waiting list). Chances are, you probably won't get in.

But what if you do? You're going to opt for another school over Harvard? We don't think so.

This is the conundrum of Harvard. It's so big and well renowned that its academics are above reproach, the value of its education ultrapowerful, and questions of student life and comfort versus those of other schools are almost irrelevant. After all, Harvard is your ticket to the world. With its unprecedented reputation and strong alumni network, the Harvard name can open doors for you wherever you go.

But just what is it like to be an undergraduate at Harvard? Exciting, invigorating, frustrating, ultimately very rewarding, and tough as hell.

The academic departments and programs are outstanding in almost all areas, from the standard liberal arts and sciences—anthropology, English, economics, history, classics, government—to many fine cultural and interdisciplinary studies programs, such as African American studies and Eastern studies. Students also have the option to petition for independent fields of study.

The curriculum is set up to give students a broad background of knowledge before heading into their major. Expository writing and quantitative reasoning are required courses, and proficiency in a foreign language is also a must. You'll also take eight core courses in such fields as literature and arts, history, or sciences. You'll have to declare a concentration at the end of your first year, but it's not written in stone.

You can compare the quality of classes at Harvard to temperamental divas: if they're going to be this difficult, they'd better be good. And, of course, they are. Even the classes taught by the B-level Harvard faculty are going to give you a brilliant academic experience, and the professors below the A-level are still well-enowned, respected, and equally brilliant ("B-level at Harvard is A-level at most other schools," said one undergraduate). But classes can be enormous, and even at the large class size, you can have trouble getting the courses you need (not to mention the courses you want). And at least one student described the advising as "subpar." Another student put it this way, "Survival of the fittest is the rule." You may have to beg, plead, and hustle to work your way into the

Harvard and Radcliffe Colleges

$$$$$
★★★★★

Setting: Urban
# of Undergraduates: 6,633
Men: 54.8% **Women:** 45.2%
Tuition: $19,770
Room and Board: $6,995
# of Students Applied: 18,183
   Admitted: 2,074 **Enrolled:** 1,617
Required Admissions Test: Either SAT or ACT, plus 3 SAT IIs
Lowest 25% of Freshmen Scored At or Below: SAT Verbal: 700 SAT Math: 690 ACT Comp.: 30
Highest 25% of Freshmen Scored At or Above: SAT Verbal: 790 SAT Math: 790 ACT Comp.: 34
H.S. Rank, Top 10%: 90%
Top 25%: 98%
Top 50%: 100%
Most Popular Majors (% of Student Body): Economics (11.8%), Biology (8.47%), Government (8.43%), English (7.63%), Biochemistry (6.2%)

upper-level courses taught by the noted faculty. And you may have to settle for a B-level prof (not a big sacrifice) or a graduate assistant or TA (which is a real dice roll). When you stop to think about how much of your GPA is going to be dependent on a TA, who is teaching his or her first seminar (and who may be only a few years older than you) you could be excused for wondering if you were motivated by a genuine desire to attend Harvard or simply masochism.

But where else can you hear Stephen Jay Gould lecture on evolution, Henry Louis Gates talk about race in America, or learn sociology from Lawrence Bobo? This is a big part of what Harvard is all about. Because of the faculty's status, there are opportunities available here that aren't available anywhere else.

Make no mistake, professors are there to do their own research, which is why they're famous in the first place. That means you won't get the same kind of daily, individualized attention as at a liberal arts college. Still, professors are required to hold office hours, and some of the lesser-renowned professors are preferred by many students, as they are much more down-to-earth. "Don't expect the professors to know you by name," warns one student. There are, however, those exceptions to the rule; some professors do make an effort to get to know students and take time to work closely with them. A relationship with an upperclassman can be a valuable tool to making your way through the faculty choices.

The student body can be just as high-caliber. "My freshman class of 20 students had two Westinghouse science winners, an all-American athlete, a world-class musician, and the granddaughter of a famous professor—and me. Pretty fast company." Harvard students range in personality, background, and experience, and there are high percentages of minority and international students. Politically, there's an equal share of conservatives and liberals (although most students are, as one says, "pretty apathetic"). All of them, though, are extremely intelligent and articulate. Stress and competition run high; one student said Harvard "constantly has the feel of a rat race." Another said that attending means, for most students, encountering failure for the first time. Again, survival of the fittest. Students work hard and push themselves to excel, but most get along with one another.

Like most buildings at Harvard, the residential halls and dorms are old but elegant. They have been brought into the 20th century, though, through renovations and the additions of computer hook-ups to Harvard's computer network. The housing system helps make the large

ACADEMIC SHRINES

university more manageable. Most freshmen are clustered together in a large building around Harvard Yard. After the first year, those who want to remain on campus, as most do, live in one of several "houses" arranged in quadrangle formations. Each house holds about 400 students and has its own dining room, library, and special facilities. Housing assignments are determined by lottery, but students can sign up with as many as 20 friends. The houses provide a home base for the Harvard student's social life. Living for three years with the same group of people makes it easier to forge friendships.

Because of all the studying required of the students, the social scene is a tame one. Students, when they take time off from the books, often prefer to go to a movie or a concert rather than a wild party. "Some go to bars or student events, but in all, it's pretty quiet," one student observed. Cambridge was described by one student as being the "perfect college town," and by another as a place "you wouldn't want to walk around in by yourself at night." Two facts, though, are above argument: the campus is beautiful, and Harvard's ultraendowment provides the resources to keep it that way. Harvard regularly attracts impressive lecturers, guest speakers, and performers, and there's always a concert, play, or special program to attend. Because of their heavy schedules, most students tend to commit themselves to only one or two of Harvard's 200-plus activities and organizations, but they then become deeply involved with them. There aren't fraternities or sororities, but there are several social clubs that are reportedly very selective—and gender exclusive. Fortunately, they don't dominate the social scene at Harvard by a long stretch.

There is a wide range of sporting activities available. Crew, football against rival Yale, and hockey are particularly popular spectator events. The Head of the Charles, a crew race up the Charles River, in addition to drawing large crowds of spectators, is also Harvard's big social event, with more parties and partying than usual taking place before, during, and after the race.

If you go to Harvard, there's no question you'll work like a dog. But there's also no doubt you'll have an unparalleled, exceptional academic experience. The kick out of just being at Harvard goes a long way. "There's a tremendous heritage here," says one proud student. "You can take a class in a building that's 180 years old." It's the toughest school you'll ever love.

THE ROAD TO COLLEGE

MASSACHUSETTS INSTITUTE OF TECHNOLOGY
IN CAMBRIDGE, MASSACHUSETTS

Admissions Address: Admissions Office, 77 Massachusetts Avenue, Cambridge, MA 02139
Web Address: web.mit.edu/

Massachusetts Institute of Technology

$$$$$
★★★★

Setting: Urban
# of Undergraduates: 4,429
Men: 61% Women: 39%
Tuition: $22,000
Room and Board: $6,350
# of Students Applied: 8,000
   Admitted: 1,950 Enrolled: 1,071
Required Admissions Test: 3 SAT IIs (Math, Science, and one of the following: English composition, History, or Writing)
H.S. Rank, Top 10%: 94%
Top 25%: 100%
Top 50%: 100%
Avg. Score of Applicants
   Admitted: SAT Verbal: 630
   SAT Math: 760 ACT Comp.: 31
Average GPA of Applicants
   Admitted: 3.91
Most Popular Majors:
   Engineering, Sciences, Humanities and Social Science

One student described MIT as a school that's "better to be from than at," but from what we hear that's a minority opinion. Most would agree with one MIT sophomore who summed up his and his fellow student's lives at "the Tech" this way: "We work hard and we play hard."

MIT's strengths are it's facilities and faculty, and the administration commits huge sums of grant money to keeping those up. As a result, MIT's research facilities are the gold standard to the world. At the same time, its faculty includes some of the world's most brilliant minds, several of them Nobel Prize winners. Where MIT is of real value to undergrads is that they actually get to interact with the world-class faculty and get their hands dirty in the labs. More than being allowed to do so, they're expected to. "A-list faculty don't shy from teaching undergraduates, even at the freshman level," said one student. "You're given the whole set of tools, and are expected to work your butt off with them."

Drawn from the tops of their high school classes, MIT students are among the most intelligent in the country, often receiving close to perfect scores on their SATs. Many MIT graduates go on to make major contributions in science and technology, as well as in business and politics. Engineering and the sciences are obviously the standouts at MIT; the departments of electrical engineering, computer science, and aerospace, in particular, are considered the cream of the crop.

The core curriculum, called the General Institute Requirement, makes certain students don't become tech zombies by requiring study in several academic areas, including an eight-course humanities, arts, and social science requirement, science and math electives, as well as writing and physical education. Although overshadowed by their science and technology counterparts, many of MIT's other departments—especially in economics, political science and linguistics—are also outstanding.

Once only the ambitious students took advantage of MIT's program to earn combined bachelor's and master's degrees in five years, but it is now becoming standard, we hear. "It's pretty much expected," said one student, "and, in many cases, part of the curriculum." MIT also offers students a number of innovative academic options to broaden their educational experience, including the chance to cross-register at Wellesley or

Harvard, or study abroad. The Independent Activities Period in January provides many students with a break from the rigors of their normal routine, as they take up some subject or project outside of their field of study. With the Undergraduate Research Opportunities Program, students earn credit by doing research and often get to work one-on-one with big names on the faculty in the process.

The teaching quality at MIT varies significantly, students report, and class size can be a problem. Large lectures can makes it difficult for students to form relationships with the professor. However, as one student told us, "there are some professors students adore; they are ranked up there with God. In general, most professors care about their classes." There are five large lecture halls at MIT and classes there can number 400 or so, but most classes fall in the 15 to 20 range, especially as students work into their major. But large class size can deter students in using the facilities, as well. "How do you get a 200-person class around a lab table?" Likewise, there are advisors and other help for students available, but you have to seek it out. "There are no alarm bells going off if you're falling behind, until you're in too deep," said one student. "If you know you need help, you have to go out and get it. But it's there."

When asked about the campus, one student said bluntly, "It's ugly!" It is industrial in appearance, with buildings made of brown brick and rooms with exposed pipe, but at least one student called it a "point of pride." The building's contents are generally more impressive than their exteriors. The scientific and technological facilities are all outstanding. "Whenever a student comes to visit, we show them Athena, the MIT computer network, which is the largest anywhere," a student told us. He also pointed out that all of MIT's facilities, science- and nonscience-related, are excellent, including a spacious sports center and an enormous library system.

Most students opt to live on campus or in fraternity houses. The Greeks are a force on campus, and one student called it "unusual" that MIT relies on the frats for housing. But frats here are different from those at other schools. "There's no hazing or wild orgies," said one student, "which is either regrettable or good." Students can choose from several dormitories that range in style, quality, and, most significantly, in personality. Students with common academic and social interests tend to stick together.

Freshmen are graded only on a pass/fail basis, and failing grades don't show up on their transcripts, which does help them adjust to the difficulty of MIT courses. MIT is no picnic, for freshmen or anyone else, and stress and pressure run high. All MIT students work incredibly hard, slaving away long hours in the lab or on endless problem sets. The intense workload and high-pressure environment, however, seems to draw students together, and when asked if there's a strong sense of camaraderie, one student responded, "Yes! It's us versus them!" MIT students bond over their hard work and goals.

The MIT student body includes a substantial number of minority students, who make up about half the student body. There was a time when men far outnumbered women, but that is changing by all reports; MIT is now about 42 percent women. And MIT students are not the stereotypical geeks and nerds you might imagine, as evidenced by the broad spectrum of clubs and activities in which many are engaged. Students may not have all that much free time beyond their studies, but as one student said, "you make time to have fun." And there's plenty to do: join a fraternity or sorority, play for a band, become involved with a musical group, work for the TV station or radio, write for a publication, or play on an intramural or intercollegiate team, among others. They also freely take advantage of the offerings in Cambridge and Boston.

The opportunities MIT presents, many out of reach for undergraduates at most other schools, and the exceptional preparation it provides for the future, make all the pressure and work somehow worth it.

PRINCETON UNIVERSITY IN PRINCETON, NEW JERSEY

Admissions Address: Office of Admission, Princeton, NJ 08544-0430
Phone: (609) 258-3060
Web Address: www.princeton.edu/

A group of students sits around a professor's spacious study, alongside a fireplace, their books open on their laps as they discuss King Lear or the War of 1812, the snow falling to the ground outside the bay window. This kind of idyllic, intimate study atmosphere, while rare at many large research universities, is not at all uncommon at Princeton. With only about 4,500 undergraduates, Princeton comes close to giving undergraduates the individual attention of top liberal arts colleges, but the setting is unmistakably Ivy League. Walking around the beautiful Princeton campus, you can feel the tradition and prestige practically oozing off the ivy-covered Gothic buildings.

Academic Shrines

Several distinctive facets of the Princeton curriculum ensure that undergraduates receive individual attention and the chance to participate actively in their courses. All lectures are broken down into smaller precepts, which are discussion groups led most often by graduate TAs, but occasionally by faculty members. Additionally, there are a number of freshman seminars for first-year students led by professors. "Of any major research institution, Princeton places the biggest emphasis on their undergraduates," said one Princetonian. "They are a true priority here."

Although there are broad distribution requirements designed to provide students with a general liberal arts background, students are given a certain amount of freedom in their studies, particularly through two required junior papers and a senior thesis. These independent projects, conducted outside of the classroom, are an opportunity for students to delve into a topic of interest as well as a chance to work closely with a professor who serves as advisor.

There are some complaints about the work, and the schedule, which packs a full semester into just 12 weeks, and also holds first-semester exams after winter break. "A real pain," said one student. While almost all liberal arts departments are strong—philosophy and history have especially high enrollments—Princeton also has an outstanding engineering program. The renowned Woodrow Wilson School of Public and International Affairs ("Woody Woo," to those in the know) is difficult to get into but provides students with an exceptional educational experience.

One of the most original aspects of student life at Princeton is the housing. During their freshman and sophomore years, students are housed in one of several "colleges," each with its own dining hall. This provides a sense of community and makes it easier to make friends, particularly during those first difficult months adjusting to college life. On the downside, the system separates the first-years from the upperclassmen.

For those first few years, the underclassmen anxiously await joining an "eating club," an essential aspect of Princeton life. Lined up along Prospect Street, and run independent of the administration, the eating clubs began as a means of offering students alternatives to university dining and have become the equivalent of fraternities. Students eat in their chosen club (though they continue to live in their dorms), which also forms the center of their social lives through special events and parties. Today, they're all coed, although two became so only following a court order. The clubs range in personality, from ones for jocks to ones for the

---

Princeton University

$$$$$
★★★★★

Setting: Small town, suburban
# of Undergraduates: 4,609
Men: 53.9% **Women:** 46.1%
Tuition: $22,920
Room and Board: $6,515
# of Students Applied: 14,869
  Admitted: 1,712 **Enrolled:** 1,130
Required Admissions Test: Either SAT or ACT
Lowest 25% of Freshmen Scored At or Below: SAT Verbal: 670 SAT Math: 680 ACT Comp.: 660
Highest 25% of Freshmen Scored At or Above: SAT Verbal: 770 SAT Math: 780 ACT Comp.: 740
H.S. Rank, Top 10%: 91%
Top 25%: 100%
Top 50%: 100%
Most Popular Majors (% of Student Body): History (11%), Economics (9%), Politics (8.5%), English (8%), Molecular Biology (7%)

artistically inclined. Students join one at the end of sophomore year; most clubs choose their candidates based on a lottery system, although a few of the more elitist ones make selections during a process called "bicker."

While most students consider the eating club a central part of their Princeton experience, there are those who criticize the way it limits social lives. "Centering the social life on 12 eating clubs tends to limit diversity," says one student. Another lists their pet peeve of Princeton as the "cliquishness that occurs, mostly as a result of the eating clubs. You can become known by that group." The eating clubs do suggest the tendency among Princeton students to cluster together in small groups according to similar interests. "The main drawback here," a sophomore reports, "is that there is a lot of underlying pressure to conform to what you see." Another student weighs in with, "Whether it's the eating club, or being an athlete, or joining a religious or social organization, you become known by that group really quickly." There are other options: Some choose to live off campus or in a recently built hall with high-quality rooming options. There are also a handful of fraternities, although they don't have the same kind of influence on social life as the eating clubs. And the school is trying to change the cliquishness of the atmosphere, but as one student said, "I don't know how successful they are."

Although the university is strict in its alcohol policy, drinking is still apparently a major part of the social life. For those students who don't want to party, the social activity takes the form of cultural events on campus, particularly movies or concerts. The acclaimed McCarter Theater, just off campus, draws top playwrights, directors, and performers; productions originating here sometimes make it to New York.

At intercollegiate games, other schools have been known to taunt, "Princeton's in New Jersey." Both the campus and the town, however, are picture-postcard beautiful. The town of Princeton, just outside the gates, is a quiet and peaceful small town. It doesn't offer much entertainment for students, who shy away from the expensive boutiques and shops. If students do wander into town, it's to go biking, hang out in one of the small parks, or perhaps eat in one of the many restaurants. Students who want more of a culture fix have an easy escape route: New York City and Philadelphia are each an hour away by train.

While many of the students come from conservative upbringings, they tend not to be conservative politically. In fact, one student said, "I think the campus is actually split fifty-fifty. There seems to be a lot of everything here. I know most Ivies are a little to the right, but Princeton seems

ACADEMIC SHRINES

to cut right down the middle." Students are also smart and extremely driven, doing what it takes to excel, in classes and in their chosen extracurricular activities. As one student pointed out, "the workload here is difficult, but Princeton students are very capable of pulling it off."

STANFORD UNIVERSITY IN PALO ALTO, CALIFORNIA

Admissions Address: Undergraduate Admissions, Old Union, Stanford, CA 94305-3005
Phone: (415) 723-2091
Web Address: www.stanford.edu/

If Duke is the Ivy League school of the South, then Stanford can certainly lay claim to being the Ivy League school of the West Coast. Stanford's academics and research facilities are on par with the Ivies and the top liberal arts colleges of the Northeast. But you won't find any Gothic ivy-covered stone buildings here, not to mention oppressive winters. Stanford's sprawling 8,180-acre campus, known as "The Farm" by students, is distinctively western in style, layout, and attitude.

The school's main strengths are in the sciences and engineering, due in part to the high-tech facilities Stanford provides. Humanities programs are also excellent, though lately there has been a lot of talk on the Stanford campus about the sciences and engineering programs getting a disproportionate amount of attention. Regardless, the economics, English, and American studies are among the most popular majors. For those students who don't want to be pigeonholed into arts or sciences, the school encourages them to create their own interdisciplinary majors under the guidance of a faculty advisor.

Additionally, Stanford's broad and extensive distribution requirements ensure that students study across disciplines and fields. In addition to freshman English and a course called "Culture, Ideas, and Values," students take one course each in literature and arts; philosophical, social, and religious thought; human development, behavior, and language; social processes and institutions; mathematical sciences; natural sciences; and technology and applied sciences.

The academic year is divided into quarters. On the upside, this calendar lends a certain variety to students' course loads each year. On the downside, though, it means heavy material crammed into a short time span, with papers and exams creeping up on unsuspecting students all too frequently.

Stanford University

$$$$$
★★★★★

Setting: Suburban
# of Undergraduates: 6,354
Men: 50.4% Women: 49.6%
Tuition: $20,490
Room and Board: $7,340
# of Students Applied: 16,359
  Admitted: 2,634 Enrolled: 1,614
Required Admissions Test: either SAT or ACT
H.S. Rank, Top 10%: 87%
Top 25%: 97%
Top 50%: 100%
Avg. Score of Applicants
  Admitted: SAT Verbal: 703
  SAT Math: 709 ACT Comp.: 32
Most Popular Majors: Economics, English, Engineering

97

Freshman classes can be big—especially in the big majors. And with the bigger classes can come more demands on the professor's time. However, by the time students reach their junior or senior years and are working in their majors, most classes average around ten students. Stanford's reputation as a renowned research institution attracts top names in their fields and provides them with cutting-edge equipment and facilities. One student gripe, though, is that the school cares more for the research conducted by the faculty than undergraduate education, and that many professors don't put much into their teaching—and even less into their advising. It does seem that the administration has been sensitive to this issue and have been taking steps to change the situation by requiring instructors to teach more small seminars for freshmen and sophomores. "The profs care," reported one student. "It can sometimes be an effort to get to them, but most are responsive." Another reported, "I've never had a teacher who I felt didn't give a hoot." At least one student also reported that the "world-class facilities are a plus, but can also be a bit intimidating, especially for new students."

Stanford's beautiful campus features Spanish-style courtyards amidst lush gardens and palm trees. While the last big quake did wield its share of destruction, Stanford doesn't hold back its funding when it comes to building. If students and parents turn pale at Stanford's costs, at least they can see the money being spent. Renovations are always underway, and new buildings are going up everywhere, including a fancy new residence hall and sports complex. The dormitories vary in style and personality, including all kinds of theme houses and special interest houses, many with their own dining facilities.

Like its Ivy League counterparts, Stanford attracts extremely smart and outgoing students, most of whom were in the top five percent of their high school classes. While most students pick up a mellow California attitude, many students report that they've heard that the place was more mellow in the '80s. Students work extremely hard, though they're not necessarily overworked. In most majors there's more cooperation than competition, but in the engineering program it can be cutthroat. Although many students are "pretty apathetic" when it comes to political issues, "the school's general feel is liberal," one student says. Their generally laid-back attitude makes Stanford students especially accepting of most lifestyles and viewpoints. There's a significantly high minority population (between 40 and 50 percent), and little tension exists among different groups.

ACADEMIC SHRINES

Dorm and frat parties comprise most of the Stanford social scene, with some students going into Palo Alto to eat at some of the less expensive places (the few that there are). On the weekends, students attend casual dorm parties that, while not exactly wild bashes, provide a chance to relax and hang out. Some men and women join the Greek system, but it doesn't dominate the socializing opportunities on campus. Since Stanford has such a large student population, most people fall into and hang out with a particular group, often determined by where they live or a particular extracurricular activity or organization. Stanford does have an enormous range of extracurricular programs and clubs, many of an ethnic, cultural, or political nature.

Most students love to go into San Francisco, about an hour to the north, and many don't get there as much as they would like to. Stanford's location is great for students looking for outdoor activities, with beaches to the west and mountains, for hiking and skiing, about four hours to the east.

Stanford's varsity teams continually win championships across the board—basketball, baseball, swimming, and tennis, just to name a few. Games are well attended by the student body, and none more popular than the "Big Game," when Stanford's football team takes on rival Cal—Berkeley. The game is both school tradition and social event, especially when the offbeat, occasionally raunchy Stanford marching band takes the field.

For those not on a varsity team, Stanford's superb sports facilities, including tennis, handball, racquetball, and squash courts, swimming pools, a golf course, and sailing facilities, make it possible to play or do whatever sport or physical activity you want. "Most people are busy," said one student.

Other than the occasional earthquake, there's little to disrupt the generally peaceful and mellow collegiate setting at Stanford, where students pursue their studies under blue skies and palm trees all year long.

THE ROAD TO COLLEGE

UNIVERSITY OF CHICAGO IN CHICAGO, ILLINOIS

Admissions Address: Admissions Office, 1116 East 59th Street, Chicago, IL 60637
Phone: (773) 702-8650
Web Address: www.uchicago.edu/

University of Chicago

$$$$$
★★★

Setting: Urban
# of Undergraduates: 3,515
Men: 54.1% Women: 45.9%
Tuition: $20,970
Room and Board: $7,275
# of Students Applied: 5,472
    Admitted: 3,165 Enrolled: 980
Required Admissions Test: either SAT or ACT
Lowest 25% of Freshmen Scored At or Below: SAT Verbal: 640 SAT Math: 640 ACT Comp.: 27
Highest 25% of Freshmen Scored At or Above: SAT Verbal: 740 SAT Math: 730 ACT Comp.: 32
H.S. Rank, Top 10%: 77%
Top 25%: 92%
Top 50%: 100%
Most Popular Majors (% of Student Body): Economics (19%), Biology (10%), English (8.5%), Psychology (6%), Political Science (5.5%)

The University of Chicago is dedicated to the pursuit of ideas, and draws the kind of student who takes great pride and draws great energy from that premise. Many consider Chicago (the school, not the city) to be the birthplace of high academic theory, and it is where high theory continues to thrive.

While graduate students outnumber the undergrads, there are no second-class citizens at Chicago. Undergrads have the same access to state-of-the-art facilities and world-class faculty (including several Nobel Prize winners). They can also enroll in graduate courses. At least one student reported that "there is really no line between graduate and undergraduate students in terms of what they can and cannot do on the campus." This can be an A-1 opportunity, or an intimidating and overwhelming proposition, depending on who you are.

Chicago's stiff core curriculum, known as the Common Core program, takes up half of the credits required for graduation, and shows just how serious an academic institution this is. Students take required sequences in humanities, social sciences, physical sciences, biological sciences, foreign language, and in math, art, or music. There's also a requirement in civilization, which includes study of a Western or non-Western culture. There is some flexibility in choosing subject matter for the requirements, and exemptions are possible. But students are expected to perform as well and work as hard in these courses as they would in the courses in their major.

While almost all of the traditional liberal arts departments are strong, Chicago also has a number of acclaimed interdisciplinary programs, such as Asian studies and Near Eastern studies, and many esoteric, theory-oriented fields, such as its highly touted program in social thought. Qualified students can receive a combination B.A./M.D. in eight years.

Chicago has a reputation for being an academic pressure cooker in which students study long, long hours. "Professors have very high expectations," said one student. "Academic pressure can be intense." The student body seems to thrive in this environment rather than wilt, even under a quarter system that crams a semester's worth of work into 10 weeks. Students don't mind spending time engaged in study and research, and many go on to make it a career.

Academic Shrines

Classes at Chicago are generally small and seminar oriented, adding to the stress and intensity as well as to the quality of the academic experience. "Be prepared to work and contribute," said one student. As we mentioned, the faculty is world class. And as with larger schools of Chicago's caliber, teacher's classroom conduct can be hit or miss. The majority live in Hyde Park and are therefore accessible, but that doesn't mean they're nice people. "Profs can be jerks, but they can be nice guys as well," said one student, "and that's not any different from other schools." Most report the professors are very accessible, even if some are arrogant and condescending.

The campus itself functions as its own, self-contained entity, with "big trees and spacious quadrangles," a student says. Most buildings are Gothic, gray stone structures, including the remarkable Rockefeller Memorial Chapel. Many campus buildings are stunners, such as Frank Lloyd Wright's Robie House, which itself attracts tourists to the campus. One side of the campus borders Lake Michigan, where there are parks and a beach, and students can bike and swim. There's an enormous grass expanse called the Midway Plaisance, a remnant of the Chicago World's Fair, on which special events and some intramural sports are held. In the winter, a section is filled with water and frozen for ice skating.

The school's many exceptional facilities include the fantastic Regenstein library, known by students as "The Reg." The monolith-like building design "isn't oppressively modern; it's pretty cool," a student told us, and "you'll find everything you could possibly need." Housing can be sketchy, though. "A fair number of upperclassmen take apartments off-campus to escape the dorm system," said one student. Another said that while "some are nice, some are definitely below standard." One of the favorite dorms is Shoreland Hall, a converted hotel with spacious rooms that have incredible views of the lake.

Because most students are so devoted to their studies, which occupy a great deal of their time, the social life at Chicago is not exactly booming, but it's apparently improving. There are many forms of entertainment on campus, including visiting lecturers and speakers, student and professional performances, and a student-run movie theater. The campus has its own cultural venues, including a professional theater in residence (The Court Theatre) that puts on classic works, two art galleries, and an excellent archaeological museum with a fascinating collection, called the Oriental Institute. The Greeks provide some social life, but not a substantial part and what they do offer is, in the words of one student, "for a limited audience."

Chicago's location in the Hyde Park area of the South Side has its ups and downs, as well. Most students have great things to say about Hyde Park, and many play down the disadvantages, such as the surrounding area's reputation as a high-crime area. "The crime rate is relatively low, really," said one student. Another said that the area is safe, especially compared to other urban schools: "You wouldn't want to have a picnic there, but that doesn't mean it poses a threat." Hyde Park is itself an integrated, interesting community that most students have great things to say about. "It's very historic; there are all these beautiful, old mansions. It also has excellent food, including authentic Chicago pizza places," says one fan of the area. There is also one South Side blues club left, the Checkerboard, that students frequent, and it's "the real McCoy," as opposed to the more commercial, touristy ones downtown.

Students can also head to other sections of Chicago, although it's not entirely easy to do so. Having a car can be a big advantage. Chicago recently installed a U of C express bus that takes students downtown and to the North Side. It's cheaper than the commuter trains and safer than the El, which, to its credit, does provide freedom from a fixed itinerary. However they go, students do make it to the downtown and Lincoln Park sections of Chicago, both rich in cultural and social venues.

Chicago students love going to the University. "I love the energy of the place, I love Hyde Park, and my fellow students," said one student. While most students have some complaints and peeves about their particular programs or departments, most place a high value on the education they receive at Chicago and the way it develops them as intellectuals.

WESLEYAN UNIVERSITY IN MIDDLETOWN, CONNECTICUT

Admissions Address: Admissions Office, Wesleyan University, Middletown, CT 06457
Phone: (860) 685-3000
Web Address: www.wesleyan.edu/

Like its liberal-arts college brethren, Wesleyan students rave about their school's wide choice of academic offerings, its strong and encouraging faculty, and its open curriculum that has "no requirements, only expectations." But in addition to these, Wesleyan students take great pride in their independence, their drive, and their passions for learning.

ACADEMIC SHRINES

Academic and social freedom are central to the Wesleyan educational experience. The school attracts diverse, progressive students who value their own individuality. As one senior told us, "The best thing about Wesleyan is the students. It's a bunch of people who weren't cool in seventh grade, but at Wesleyan, can be free to be themselves. It's very liberating."

The faculty is willing to work with the students on just about anything, from "molecular biology to postmodern fiction." If you have a passion and a plan, you will find a professor who will provide the guidance. Student-designed majors are common, as are private tutorials. The undergraduate is the focus, and the undergrads at Wesleyan are not only serious about their studies, but study in general. "Undergrads here are too driven to be content with a school that's a degree factory," said one student.

Wesleyan offers an especially high number and large variety of academic programs, including interdisciplinary programs, such as their reputable American studies program, and three special programs students must formally apply to: the College of Letters, the College of Social Science, and Science in Society. All three programs require a great deal of hard work, but that doesn't faze the Wesleyan students (in fact, they thrive on it). It does give students an unparalleled, highly concentrated education in specific areas. In the unlikely event students can't find a course they want here, they can easily go elsewhere, due to Wesleyan's status as part of the Twelve College exchange. Once past the introductory course, most classes are under thirty people, and most students work so closely with faculty in individual instruction that class size is rarely complained about.

What students do complain about is the bureaucracy, which was likened by one student to that of a small country. In contrast to the individualized instruction of the faculty, and the celebration of individualism in the student body, the registrar, bursar, and other administrative offices can do more to make you "feel like a number" than anything else on campus. One student pointed out that it could look worse by contrast with the rest of the campus, but most we talked to said it was the one thing they would change about Wesleyan if they could.

The spirit of academic freedom and sense of intellectual inquiry in the classroom is just as evident in the Wesleyan community at large. Wesleyan students are open to many different viewpoints and experiences; most feel that part of the Wesleyan education is to be found in

Wesleyan University

$$$$$
★★★★

Setting: Suburban
# of Undergraduates: 2,725
Men: 48.7% **Women:** 51.3%
Tuition: $22,230
Room and Board: $6,210
# of Students Applied: 6,100
   Admitted: 1,960   **Enrolled:** 739
Required Admissions Test: Either SAT or ACT
Lowest 25% of Freshmen Scored At or Below: SAT Verbal: 610 SAT Math: 610
Highest 25% of Freshmen Scored At or Above: SAT Verbal: 720   SAT Math: 700
H.S. Rank, Top 10%: 63%
Top 50%: 99%
Avg. Score of Applicants Admitted: SAT Verbal: 670 SAT Math: 660   ACT Comp.: 29
Average GPA of Applicants Admitted: 3.75
Most Popular Majors (% of Student Body): English (13%), Government (10%), Economics (8%), Psychology (7%), History (6%)

interactions with one's peers. The school is extremely diverse, with about a 25 to 30 percent minority population and a large (and well-supported) gay and lesbian population. And unlike some other liberal-arts schools in Wesleyan's league, different groups mix well and interact freely. "We don't have enough leftover energy to put up fronts," said one student. "The common goal here is learning. With that bond, connections are easy and encouraged. You want to learn everything about everyone."

Brownstone Row, with its ivy-covered buildings, defines the collegiate atmosphere of the campus. Featuring a wide range of architectural styles, the relatively small Wesleyan campus offers the top facilities of a large university, including particularly well-stocked libraries and a sleek new athletic center. Most students live on campus in buildings that range from townhouses to university-owned apartments to special interest houses. The dormitories vary in style and personality, ranging from wild party houses to more community-like special interest houses. There's one main dining hall and two smaller ones, but students generally don't give the food a thumbs-up.

Although Wesleyan is located in the midst of Middletown, the two are separate entities. There seems to be a divide between the students and the mostly blue-collar town, but no one reports any hostility. "We just keep to ourselves," said one student, which may make life easy, but does limit social opportunities to the campus. The nearby cities of Hartford and New Haven do have their share of clubs (especially around Yale) but not much else in the way of culture. For that students usually head for New York or Boston, each about two hours away. But for a school of its size, there's plenty going on on campus. Movies and concerts are offered on campus, and there are frequent dorm parties and lots of places to hang out. There's a particularly high number of extracurricular activities, clubs, and organizations, including many politically oriented groups as well as several theater, dance, and music groups.

Wesleyan is a school whose students truly care about learning in the purest sense, from their classes, teachers, and each other. As one student said, "it will not hamper those with great initiative, nor will it coddle those who lack it."

ACADEMIC SHRINES

YALE UNIVERSITY IN NEW HAVEN, CONNECTICUT

Admissions Address: Office of Undergraduate Admissions, P.O. Box 208234, New Haven, CT 06520-8234
Phone: (203) 432-9316 (203) 432-9300
Web Address: www.yale.edu/

Harvard and Yale, Yale and Harvard. They are almost always mentioned in the same breath. And there's little wonder why. They make up a sort of "Ivy League's Ivy League." Both have prestigious reputations, based in large part on the schools' renowned alumni and acclaimed faculty.

If Yale doesn't have quite the same revered history as Harvard, it does focus much more on undergraduate education than most universities, including Harvard. Its ranking as the number-one university in America in 1996 by U.S. News & World Report confirms that. (By the way, Harvard was third.) Your first classes may number hundreds of students, but by the time you're done, you will have been in many seminar classes taught by the school's finest faculty. Additionally, students often find professors approachable and willing to give extra help.

Yalies list the school's wide array of options as one of it's greatest strengths, and, indeed, Yale gives its students a great deal of freedom in their academic pursuits. There aren't rigid distribution requirements, and, if they're ambitious enough, freshmen can enroll in upper- level seminars. Additionally, Yalies are given the chance to pick and choose which courses they take; rather than a formal preregistration, students go shopping for courses during the first two weeks and then sign up for the ones that interest them most.

Yale's best and most popular departments include the humanities, particularly English and history, as well as certain sciences, particularly molecular biophysics and biochemistry. Yale is especially known for its reputable theater and music programs, whose presence help cultivate a large artistic and bohemian student community on campus. These programs also guarantee there will always be professional-quality plays, concerts, and performances presented on campus.

The unique and intensive Directed Studies Program brings together studies in history, literature, and philosophy. Those who get accepted are completely immersed in their subject area, writing long weekly papers. While the workload is close to impossible, the courses are seminar sized, and the students work closely with one another and their professors. When they finish the program, students feel like experts in their fields.

Yale University

$$$$$
★★★★★

Setting: Urban
# of Undergraduates: 5,296
Men: 51.4% **Women:** 48.6%
Tuition: $22,200
Room and Board: $6,680
# of Students Applied: 12,952
   Admitted: 2,371 **Enrolled:** 1,409
Required Admissions Test: either SAT or ACT
Recommended: SAT I and/or subject tests required for some depts.
H.S. Rank, Top 10%: 95%
Top 25%: 100%
Most Popular Majors (% of Student Body): History (12.2%), English (9.1%), Biology (8.7%), Economics (7.3%), Political Science (7%)

105

There may not be many requirements at Yale, but there certainly is work. Yale students are required to take 36 courses to graduate, compared to the 32 of other Ivy League schools (including at least three credits each in four distribution areas). And it is tough. Workload is heavy, pressure is intense, and if you don't keep up, you get left behind quickly. Needless to say, stress can be high, although the pressure, many report, is self-inflicted rather than the result of cutthroat competition.

It also helps if you're confident and maybe even a little aggressive. "Quieter students may get lost in the crowd," said one student. "There are lots of superachievers here, and that's an easy crowd to get lost in." Another Yalie claimed that "Yale is really what you make of it, and like it or not, the environment favors glib, confident, aggressive people who can charm professors and classmates."

Just as much of the Yale education comes from interactions and discussions among students outside of their classes as it does from lectures inside the classroom. The student body is made up of all kinds and types, and this mix lends a certain energy and spark to the school. Minority students make up a little more than 30 percent of the student body. There's also a large gay and lesbian population. Students tend to be much more liberal than at some of the other Ivies, although there is also a solid and apparently growing conservative population. Many students become involved with political issues and causes, or conduct volunteer work and community service. They are also tolerant and, more than other Ivies, fun. "My classmates are really a happy bunch," said one student. "They really like to have fun."

A large part of student life at Yale centers on the residential college in which a student is housed. Incoming freshman are assigned to one of 12 "colleges," each with its own dining room and library, as well as other facilities such as laundry rooms, computer labs, and game rooms. Each has its own administration, headed by a dean and faculty affiliate, and hosts a number of events, ranging from special lectures and discussion groups to parties and performances. Most freshmen spend their first year at Old College but eat at their assigned college, which makes the transition into their residential college easier and enables them to socialize with upperclassmen. Although some students complain that the college system can limit one's social life, the colleges foster close friendships and provide a niche within the much larger university.

The Yale campus features typical Ivy League-style Gothic academic buildings, as well as more contemporary structures. As with Harvard,

ACADEMIC SHRINES

Yale's facilities are excellent, particularly the enormous and extensive library system, and the gargantuan Payne Whitney Gymnasium, the largest in North America.

If there's one downside to Yale, and many say it's a big one, it's the location. New Haven is not too attractive and not particularly safe. New Haven does have its restaurants and culture, and even one or two great clubs (Toad's Place is particularly famous, where many top rock-and-roll acts got their start) and the city is steadily improving due to a major urban renewal plan. However, New Haven, at present, is no Boston or New York, and the fact that most students prefer to take the two-hour road trip to those cities rather than venture into New Haven is telling.

If you stay on campus, though, there's no shortage of things to do. Yale is particularly known for its many theater and performance groups, ranging from the acclaimed Yale Repertory to many a cappella groups, including the world famous Yale Whiffenpoofs. Additionally, Yale has hundreds of organizations and clubs, many of a political nature, as well as a host of extracurricular activities. "There are scores of student organizations, from neoconservative debating societies to social action groups," said one student. If you're not into a formal activity or club, there's certain to be a hot guest lecturer, debate, performance, or discussion group going on somewhere around campus.

Yale has a few fraternities, but they aren't a major part of the social scene. There's also a number of exclusive social clubs that are more notable for various rumors about bizarre rituals than the influence they have on school life. Most students are happy to hang out with friends in their residential colleges, attend small room parties, or go to movies and concerts on campus. Some students frequent nearby bars, music clubs, and cafes, including the ritzy Mory's, a venerable Yale institution.

Sports are also popular (especially anything against Harvard), and several varsity sporting teams are strong, especially hockey, soccer, lacrosse, and tennis. The teams are also well supported. If you want it, and if you can take it, Yale truly has much to offer. Student here want to make a difference in the world, and if they can get through the rigors, they leave well equipped to do it.

THE ROAD TO COLLEGE

ALSO, CHECK OUT THESE SCHOOLS

Bryn Mawr College
California Institute of Technology
Dartmouth College
Johns Hopkins University
Northwestern University
University of Pennsylvania
Rice University
Smith College
University of Virginia
Wellesley College

Small Wonders

All over the country, there's some pretty heavy thinking going on at pretty small campuses. In fact, it's partly because these schools are undersized that we call them Small Wonders. With enrollments averaging only about 1,500 to 2,000 students, these schools enable students to study within an intimate and stimulating academic environment.

The schools in this chapter are small liberal arts colleges where the focus is on undergraduate education. The small student populations ensure that most class sizes are kept at a minimum, averaging about 15 to 20. These schools have only a few huge lectures in which you can hide behind other students when the teacher asks a question. Instead, in discussion-oriented seminars, you'll usually have to take on a more active role; you'll not only have to be prepared to answer questions, you'll have to take part in most class discussions on a regular basis. In the process, you'll get to test out your thoughts and opinions in public and learn how to present your ideas coherently and convincingly. And it's a lot less likely you'll be able to zone out while some professor drones on.

The workload at these schools is going to be intense. You'll have to spend many hours each week keeping up with the reading so you can be prepared for your classes. Students at these schools, though, say they don't much mind the work, as they find their studies challenging. Learning new things excites them. The intellectual discussions of the classroom often carry over to debates at dinner or over coffee with fellow students and faculty.

Students at Small Wonders generally rate the quality of the faculty one of their college's greatest assets. At these schools a professor's teaching ability is usually more important than the amount of work that he or she has published. Professors are committed to their teaching duties and their students, who are their number one priority. Due to the small class sizes, professors are able to get to know their students very well, usually by name. The atmospheres at these schools encourages a certain easygoing informality between students and faculty. It's not uncommon for professors to meet with students over coffee or a meal.

The small enrollment also fosters a sense of closeness and community among students at these schools. It's easy to make friends in a close-knit environment, where you'll always be surrounded by familiar faces. Some students do, though, find it becomes a bit too close for comfort, especially when things like how your date went or how you slept through a psych exam are known by the entire student body within minutes. While some students like the sense of community at their schools, they also pointed out how there is also a lack of diversity among the student body.

Many Small Wonders are located in out-of-the-way locales, which contributes to the sense that you're there to become totally immersed in your studying. That's not necessarily as painful as it sounds. While remote, these campuses are among the country's most beautiful. The tranquil natural surroundings and stately collegiate settings lend themselves to deep contemplation. At the same time, as students often put the same motivation into having fun as they do their studies, many Small Wonders also have a surprisingly decent social scene.

The heavy workload will make its demands, but in turn, you'll receive an exceptional liberal arts education. Additionally, you'll be supported in your efforts in many ways; you'll be using first-rate facilities, without competing with many other students or graduates. You'll have the encouragement and advice of caring professors. And you'll have close friendship with students who share your interests and academic ideals.

BUCKNELL UNIVERSITY IN LEWISBURG, PENNSYLVANIA

Admissions Address: Office of Admisssions, Lewisburg, PA 17837
Phone: (717) 524-1101
Web Address: www.bucknell.edu/

"The 'Bucknell Bubble' lives on," said one Bucknell undergrad when asked about her school. "That can sound like a negative thing, but it's actually really good. We love it."

The "Bucknell Bubble" refers to the secluded atmosphere at Bucknell University, where about 3,000 undergraduates work and play. It's three and one-half hours from any city of any size, so there's little room for outside distraction. And those who live under the Bubble like that just fine. "This place really is a country club, or a retreat center," said one student. "It is a great place to get focus."

There are two undergraduate schools at Bucknell: the College of Engineering and the College of Arts and Sciences. Bucknell's academics are strong in almost all areas, both sciences and humanities. Many students go on to graduate school or professional school within a year of graduation, and those courses that pave the way for law, business, and medical school are particularly popular.

The requirements in both colleges are rigorous, providing students with a solid liberal arts background before they concentrate in a specific field. In the College of Arts and Sciences, students must take four humanities courses, two social sciences courses, and three courses in natural science and mathematics. Freshmen take a special seminar that helps foster their critical thinking across academic fields. Seniors are required to complete a Capstone project to graduate. It could be a thesis, internship, or independent project. In the College of Engineering, all first-year students take the same course load, helping to develop a sense of camaraderie.

The class sizes are kept to a minimum, although popular introductory courses might be somewhat larger. There are five classes for which over 100 students are allowed to sign up, but other than that, groups are small. Even large lab courses will break into smaller groups, though these groups are often taught by a TA.

Students report that they receive a great deal of attention from professors, who go out of their way to help them with their studies and projects. "They are always approachable," said one student. Another reports that the profs are "always around. You don't have to hunt them down." This accessibility is another advantage of bubble life: Where else are they going to go? "I once was trying to crack a chemistry problem late at night," one student tells, "and I called my professor at around ten in the evening. Not only was she not put off that I called, she was excited! And she was excited when I solved the problem. That's typical of how I interact with my professors," one student told.

Bucknell has many top-notch facilities to support students in their work. Science majors benefit from state-of-the-art laboratories and equipment in a recently built science center, and music and performing arts students take advantage of the Weis Center for Performing Arts. The Bertrand

---

Bucknell University

$$$$$
★★★

Setting: Small town in rural area
# of Undergraduates: 3,339
Men: 50.2% **Women:** 49.8%
Tuition: $21,080
Room and Board: $5,200
# of Students Applied: 7,364
  Admitted: 3,628 **Enrolled:** 895
Required Admissions Test: Either SAT or ACT
Lowest 25% of Freshmen Scored At or Below: SAT Verbal: 580 SAT Math: 600
Highest 25% of Freshmen Scored At or Above: SAT Verbal: 650 SAT Math: 660
Average ACT Score of Applicants Accepted: ACT 26.7
H.S. Rank, Top 10%: 53%
Top 25%: 85%
Top 50%: 99%
Average GPA of Applicants Admitted: 3.40
Most Popular Majors (% of Student Body): Engineering (12%), Business Administration (11%), Biology (10%), Economics (9%), English (7%)

Library, also recently renovated, has an impressive collection of resources.

The school offers a rich variety of living arrangements. Freshmen must live in the dorms but can select from five different housing options, each of which is oriented around common academic interests (arts, environmental, humanities, international, and social justice). Students live together and take common seminars in their chosen area for the first year.

After the first year, student can go Greek if they wish; roughly half the eligible students do. Bucknell students take their studying seriously, but also take their leisure time seriously as well. The houses host many all-campus parties, and any weekend (and many weeknights) there's certain to be some kind of party going on somewhere. Students also enjoy hanging out in their dormitories, at the Bison student center, or at the on-campus cafe. To augment the parties, there are many extracurricular activities, on-campus performances, concerts and movies, as well as visiting lecturers and performers, all of which keep students well entertained. "There's always something going on," said one student. "If you're bored, it's your own fault."

The stereotypical Bucknell student has been described as "preppie," and students we talked to were hard put to argue with that. "Pretty white, pretty well off," said one student. However, it is a high priority of the administration to increase diversity through recruitment and financial aid. Most students would like to see the stereotype change: "You'd like to meet some different kinds of people," said one student.

While the "Bucknell Bubble" may have its limitations, it does provide an ideal "think tank" atmosphere in which most students thrive, particularly academically.

CLAREMONT McKENNA COLLEGE IN CLAREMONT, CALIFORNIA

Admissions Address: Admissions Office, 890 Columbia Avenue, Claremont, CA 91711-6425
Phone: (909) 621-8088 (909) 621-8000
Web Address: www.mckenna.edu/

With only about 1,000 undergraduates, Claremont McKenna College (CMC) is a place where you can easily recognize all your fellow students "by name if not by face," and where professors will all know you. The

SMALL WONDERS

school's broad liberal arts curriculum is designed, as the school's brochure states, "to educate leaders in management, the professions, and public affairs." The curriculum primarily focuses on economics, government, and international relations. Upon graduation, high numbers go on to professional schools (11 percent to law, 7 percent to business, 7 percent to medical schools) or hold some type of leadership position. The school's science departments and facilities are also reputedly excellent. The distribution requirements include courses in calculus, English, humanities, social sciences, natural sciences, and a senior thesis.

Professors, who teach all classes (no TAs here), receive high praise from their students for their attention and concern. "The professors make an effort to get to know their students. They also have high expectations. Because classes are so small and the professors know you, they expect quality work," one student told us.

CMC can be as large or as small as students want to make it. While the McKenna campus is a compact 50 acres, it is part of the much larger Claremont system, which makes it feel much bigger. Students can freely take advantage of the facilities at the four other colleges in the Claremont system (Pomona, Scripps, Pitzer, and Harvey Mudd), which a student rates as "excellent." Students can become involved with clubs and activities that draw on all five schools, and attend social events and parties at the other schools.

Socializing also benefits from the Claremont system. If there is one complaint that CMC students have, it is regarding the social life. One student reported that the place can get "claustrophobic," and another said that the need to "get out and away from Claremont" can be a strong, if only occasional one. Trouble is, there's no place really to go that isn't an ordeal of a trip (Los Angeles is close, but not real close). The center of social life seems to be the dorms, where student party and hang out.

There are organizations and clubs to draw students. "It takes a little initiative, but you can get involved with campus life," reports one student. There are also many cultural events, and athletics are extremely popular. About one-third of the student population plays for one of CMC's Division III varsity teams; most others are deeply involved in the school's extensive intramural program.

McKenna students are housed in one of three quads, each with its own personality ranging from loud and raucous to sedate. A significant portion of the students come from California, and although the school isn't

---

Claremont McKenna College

$$$$$
★★★★

Setting: Suburban
# of Undergraduates: 954
Men: 56.9% Women: 43.1%
Tuition: $18,320
Room and Board: $6,510
# of Students Applied: 2,611
  Admitted: 762 Enrolled: 246
Required Admissions Test: SAT
Recommended: ACT
Lowest 25% of Freshmen Scored At or Below: SAT Verbal: 620
  SAT Math: 630 ACT Comp.: 27
Highest 25% of Freshmen Scored At or Above: SAT Verbal: 710 SAT Math: 720
  ACT Comp.: 31
H.S. Rank, Top 10%: 71%
Top 25%: 95%
Top 50%: 100%
Avg. Score of Applicants Admitted: SAT Verbal: 670
  SAT Math: 680 ACT Comp.: 29
Average GPA of Applicants Admitted: 3.88
Most Popular Majors (% of Student Body): Economics (28%), Government (15%), Biology (10%), Psychology (8%), Literature (7%)

as well known in the East, it does attract students from across the country and throughout the world. "There's a whole range of students here in terms of conservatives and liberals, although conservative voices are louder," a student reports.

As one happy CMC student raved, "In general, this is a great school!"

COLBY COLLEGE IN WATERVILLE, MAINE

Admissions Address: Admissions Office, 4800 Mayflower Hill, Lunder House, Waterville, ME 04901-8848
Phone: (207) 872-3168 (800) 723-3032
Web Address: www.colby.edu/

Colby College

$$$$$
★★★★

Setting: Suburban
# of Undergraduates: 1,764
Men: 47.7% **Women:** 52.3%
Tuition: $21,260
Room and Board: $5,710
# of Students Applied: 4,601
  Admitted: 1,432 **Enrolled:** 466
Required Admissions Test: Either SAT or ACT
Lowest 25% of Freshmen Scored At or Below: SAT Verbal: 620 SAT Math: 620 ACT Comp.: 26
Highest 25% of Freshmen Scored At or Above: SAT Verbal: 700 SAT Math: 700 ACT Comp.: 30
H.S. Rank, Top 10%: 61%
Top 25%: 90%
Top 50%: 99%
Avg. Score of Applicants Admitted: SAT Verbal: 660 SAT Math: 660 ACT Comp.: 28
Most Popular Majors (% of Student Body): English (11%), Biology (11%), Economics (7%), Government (7%), Psychology (5%)

In the woods of rural Maine, the liberal arts are alive and well at Colby College, where students enthusiastically take up their studies while enjoying a campus rich in spectacular natural scenery.

The broad core curriculum includes courses in several key areas, including historical studies, arts, literature, natural science, social science, quantitative reasoning, and human diversity—a course on non-Western culture—as well as writing, foreign language, and physical education requirements. While the courses themselves are tough, students can fulfill the requirements relatively easily, leaving time to pursue their own academic interests or fields in greater depth.

Colby's unique "Jan Plan" was the first of its kind in the Northeast, until it became all the rage at many other schools. Students devote the month of January to taking up something that interests them but that they may not necessarily have room for in their schedules during the fall and spring semesters—say, learning to play the harpsichord or speaking Russian. They can complete independent projects with faculty members, fulfill internships, or take special courses on or off campus; many professors lead field trips and study groups overseas. When students tire of the Maine outdoors activities, they can escape to any number of countries around the world through Colby's extensive study-abroad program.

The spirit of independent work carries through to the regular classes, where one student loved the small class size: "It makes it easy to pursue personal interests and work closely with faculty." The profs are by all reports accessible and sincerely interested in students' goals and concerns.

While the student body is not very diverse, the administration has of late shown sensitivity to this concern of students by building the new Pugh Multicultural Center. Although political views range, the students are generally tolerant and concerned about a variety of issues, including minority rights, women's rights, free speech, and the environment.

Many students rate the social scene as exciting, but recent administrative efforts to curb drinking on campus seem to have backfired. "It wasn't that bad to begin with," said one student, and another reported that the attempts to rewrite the alcohol policy "has exacerbated the problem." Waterville is small, quaint, and not terribly exciting, but Portland and the coast are about an hour away in one direction, the mountains about the same in the other direction. But still, much of the social life centers on the residential commons in which students are housed. The food is "above average," but many students find the single meal-plan offering restrictive. Many faculty members drop in at the Commons, eating meals and mingling with students. The Commons system makes an already close community even closer, providing a family-like atmosphere in which friendships are quickly and easily formed. Also providing a place to get together with friends is the school's large student center, with a game room, TV lounge, lecture and performance space, a coffee house, and "The Spa" grill.

The school's rural location, rather than limiting the amount of social and extracurricular activities, greatly increases them. The Maine wilderness is perfect for outdoor sports, including skiing, white-water rafting, and even ice skating on Colby's own pond. While many students mentioned that for the unprepared, the winter can be harsh. But rather than complain about the winter, students manage to enjoy it. The Winter Carnival is reportedly a favorite social event among students. Sports of all kinds are popular at Colby. In fact, the athletic complex—which houses an ice-hockey rink, track, and weight room, among other things—is one of the largest in New England.

For those in search of less physically demanding activities, there's also a host of extracurricular activities and clubs, including the radio station, the newspaper, community service organizations, and several performing groups. Then again, there's also the Outing Club, for those who find their fun in physically exerting outdoor adventures.

CONNECTICUT COLLEGE IN NEW LONDON, CONNECTICUT

Admissions Address: Admissions Office, 270 Mohegan Avenue, New London, CT 06320-4196
Phone: (860) 439-2200
Web Address: camel.conncoll.edu/

Connecticut College

$$$$$
★★★

Setting: Suburban
# of Undergraduates: 1,682
Men: 42.7% **Women:** 57.3%
Tuition: $28,475
# of Students Applied: 3,444
   Admitted: 1,474   **Enrolled:** 450
Required Admissions Test: SAT II or ACT
Lowest 25% of Freshmen Scored At or Below: SAT Verbal: 600 SAT Math: 580
Highest 25% of Freshmen Scored At or Above: SAT Verbal: 690 SAT Math: 670
H.S. Rank, Top 10%: 44%
Top 25%: 94%
Top 50%: 100%
Avg. Score of Applicants Admitted: SAT Verbal: 636 SAT Math: 621 ACT Comp.: 25
Most Popular Majors (% of Student Body): Psychology (15%), English (11%), Government (8%), History (8%), Economics (7%)

"No, I don't go to the University of Connecticut." This could be the most common complaint heard by Connecticut College undergraduates. And, given the small size of the school, the beautiful campus, and the liberal arts education that ranks with the best in the nation, it's one of the few complaints you're likely to hear.

Connecticut has exceptional academic programs set in a comfortable environment. Conn's academics are first-rate in almost all departments, from the arts to the sciences. The core requirements include courses in eight areas in addition to standard courses in sciences and humanities. Like the best of the Ivies, students select from within such specific fields as philosophical and religious studies, and quantitative disciplines and logic. Freshmen may enroll in an intensive writing program that combines study from several fields.

The student body is small, creating a comfortable, warm, mutually enriching environment for students and faculty. As with the top liberal arts schools, tales of students being invited to professors' homes for dinner are common. Class sizes are kept small, enabling students to interact with their professors and one another in a challenging environment that's not limited to the classroom. The professors, who teach all classes, are, according to one student, "very well educated. They have high standards and challenge our intellect."

The Honor Code gives students control over their own educations, including being able to schedule and monitor their own final exams. Students are therefore treated as responsible and mature individuals. At the same time, the Honor Code fosters trust and respect among students who are responsible for one another as well as for themselves. One student said that being able to take self-scheduled exams under the Honor Code was "what Connecticut was all about."

For a school of its size, Conn's facilities, including a new science center and a well-stocked library, are impressive. "Basically, we have everything we need," a student says. After their freshman year, most students can get a single in Conn's comfortable dormitories. The Crozier-Williams student center—with a bar, snack shop, game room, and coffeehouse—

provides a great hangout for students who want to relax and take a break far from their books. Overlooking the Atlantic Ocean, the Conn campus stretches out over 700 acres, a large portion taken up by an arboretum, instilling a natural beauty that can also calm the nerves and reduce stress.

Students study about three to four hours a night and are reportedly very concerned about their grades. But starting on Thursday nights, things get "very lively" for the weekend, we hear. There's usually a selection of dorm-sponsored parties, and the Student Activity Committee organizes campus-wide social activities including dances. The theater and dance departments, and other student groups, produce quality plays and performances on campus.

The industrial town of New London offers little to appeal to students, who tend to remain on campus for their fun. Some quickly tire of being stuck on campus with the same people and the same social options every weekend. Those who want additional activity can become involved in an extracurricular activity—perhaps writing for the newspaper, or joining a band, or playing on one of the many intramural teams—all of which help students enjoy a life beyond the classroom. If they're in desperate need of a break from the Conn scene, New York and Boston (each about two hours away) are popular road trips.

If you attend Connecticut, get used to white preppies; they make up a majority of the population. More than one student listed the lack of diversity as a pet peeve. "It's primarily a homogeneous campus," said another student. However, just below this surface lies a variety of interests and viewpoints. Students tend to be liberal and concerned about a variety of issues, including minority rights, women's rights, and the environment. Many are also active in community service. But, as a junior told us, students "center their lives on their academics."

It can get frustrating, said one student, to attend a school that has to sing its own praises the loudest. But this same student said that she wouldn't trade her Connecticut experience, and found it exciting to be attending Connecticut just as its reputation is beginning to grow.

GETTYSBURG COLLEGE IN GETTYSBURG, PENNSYLVANIA

Admissions Address: Dean of Admissions, Eisenhower House, Gettysburg, PA 17325-1484
Phone: (800) 431-0803 (717) 337-6100
Web Address: www.gettysburg.edu/

Gettysburg College

$$$$$
★★

Setting: Rural
# of Undergraduates: 2,100
Men: 49.3% **Women:** 50.7%
Tuition: $20,744
Room and Board: $4,760
# of Students Applied: 3,680
   Admitted: 2,495 **Enrolled:** 605
Required Admissions Test: Either SAT or ACT
Lowest 25% of Freshmen Scored At or Below: SAT Verbal: 560 SAT Math: 560 ACT Comp.: 24
Highest 25% of Freshmen Scored At or Above: SAT Verbal: 640 SAT Math: 640 ACT Comp.: 28
H.S. Rank, Top 10%: 40%
Top 25%: 77%
Top 50%: 95%
Avg. Score of Applicants Admitted: SAT Verbal: 540 SAT Math: 600 ACT Comp.: 26
Average GPA of Applicants Admitted: 3.40
Most Popular Majors (% of Student Body): Business Administration/Management (19%), Political Science (10%), Psychology (10%), History (8%), English (8%)

Located right near Cemetery Ridge, where the tide of the Civil War turned, the beautiful Gettysburg campus is literally surrounded by history—in fact, one of the campus' oldest buildings was used as a hospital during the battle. So it should come as no surprise that history is one of the most popular majors here, but by no means the extent of the great programs available.

The school is committed to instilling its student body with a strong liberal arts background. The curriculum has been restructured so that distribution requirements fall under three broad areas to which students can apply courses: humanities, social science, and natural science. There are courses on non-Western civilizations as part of the social science requirement.

In their small classes, students get to know their professors, who are "friendly and accessible," a student reports. Students are encouraged to undertake independent research projects, with the help and guidance of faculty advisors, and upon graduation, Gettysburg College students have decent acceptance rates at professional schools (7 percent of the student body goes on to law school; 5 percent to business school; and 6 percent to medical school).

Gettysburg began as a Lutheran school, and its religious affiliation still carries an impact. Many students are somewhat religious and concerned about moral issues and values. A number are involved in community service activities or religious clubs. The school's honor code is taken with the utmost seriousness by students, who view it as a moral guidepost.

The stereotypical Gettysburg students are white, upper or middle class, and conservative in their values and political views, but like most stereotypes, this is not entirely accurate. The students here are "not all that conservative," reports one student, while another reports that you'll get "lots of everything, politically" out of the student body. And while they are keenly aware of issues of the outside world, students are not necessarily all that politically active. Similarly, the school has been working on drawing a more diverse student population. These include the construction of a Cultural Resource Center on campus, as well as forming committees of African American and Asian American students. Financial aid, which is reported to be "good" by students, is also helping with this endeavor.

The most popular major is management, followed by history, and the science majors are considered the toughest. For those who don't have their noses in books, the "workload leaves enough time for socializing," a student reported. The nearby town of Gettysburg primarily attracts tourists, which leads most students to stick close to campus for socializing. Social life is dominated by the Greeks: Many of the students belong to one of the 11 fraternities or 5 sororities. The school has also been working on non-Greek social events, but "the Greeks are the campus leaders," said one student.

There are other things to do if you're not in the Greek system. Students hang out on campus at the student center and the Junction, an on-campus club that shows movies, hosts student bands, and, occasionally, other forms of entertainment. There is also a new branch of the Junction called the Coffeehouse, which is nonalcoholic. The Student Senate sponsors day trips to Washington, Baltimore and New York, and there are at least two concerts a year by name acts on campus. "This is not a suitcase school," said one student, "everybody's here on the weekends." For students who want physical activity beyond a bike ride or jog on the battlefield can take advantage of the athletic facility which is highly rated by students.

Gettysburg students are proud of their school, and feel that it delivers on its promise of creating a community of learning, discovery, and exploration through liberal arts education.

HAMILTON COLLEGE IN CLINTON, NEW YORK

Admissions Address: Office of Admissions, Clinton, NY 13323
Phone: (315) 859-4421 (800) 843-2655
Web Address: www.hamilton.edu/

One of the best things about Hamilton, a student tells us, is how committed the professors are to their students. The professors here aren't likely to disappear after class or hole up in their offices. "Many make it a point to eat regularly in the cafeteria," we hear. "Most know your name. It just feels very natural for them to speak to you."

Hamilton College

$$$$$
★★★

Setting: Rural
# of Undergraduates: 1,684
Men: 53.9% Women: 46.1%
Tuition: $21,700
Room and Board: $5,450
# of Students Applied: 4,045
  Admitted: 1,774 Enrolled: 499
Required Admissions Test: Either SAT or ACT
Lowest 25% of Freshmen Scored At or Below: SAT Verbal: 580 SAT Math: 580
Highest 25% of Freshmen Scored At or Above: SAT Verbal: 680 SAT Math: 670
H.S. Rank, Top 10%: 46%
Top 25%: 72%
Top 50%: 98%
Avg. Score of Applicants Admitted: SAT Verbal: 628 SAT Math: 626
Most Popular Majors (% of Student Body): English (11%), Economics (10%), Government (8%), Psychology (8%)

Class sizes are also kept at a minimum, around 15 students, giving the students a chance to voice their opinions and participate actively in their studies. The distribution requirements include courses in several major areas: writing, arts, history, social sciences, science and mathematics, humanities, and courses in cultural diversity and ethics.

Surrounded by acres of Hamilton-owned woodland, the campus is divided into two sections: the Hamilton campus with its ivy-covered stone buildings, and the more modern Kirkland campus, formerly an all-women's college that merged with Hamilton. The dormitories, which range in style and arrangement, including a number of special-interest houses, are in first-rate condition. A new student center located between the campuses provides a central socializing spot and a tasty diner popular with students.

While minorities comprise less than a fifth of the minority population, the overall student body is somewhat homogenous in terms of class and background. Many students are from upper-class and upper-middle-class backgrounds. Politically, the conservative and liberal factions are equally vocal, and most students fall somewhere in between. However, according to at least one student, the student body as a whole tends to split along economic lines. "I don't think the students from the less well-off families feel they have a lot in common with those from wealthier backgrounds," said one student, "and vice versa."

While students from urban or suburban settings may feel Hamilton is isolated, other do not. Many students are from upstate New York, and a more rural feeling is pretty natural. Others feel that "your nights will often be spent doing the same things you did the night before." Some seniors venture into Clinton to bars, but most students remain on campus, where the social life centers on the fraternities, which often throw parties for the entire campus. The school makes an effort to provide additional activities, one student tells us, by sponsoring special events and cultural performances by guest artists, and there are often movies, plays, and concerts on campus. There are many music groups on campus, both official and student run. Athletics are also big. Most students play on one team or another (varsity or intramural) and all enjoy using the new fitness center. The men's basketball and hockey teams have good records and draw many enthusiastic—and rowdy—student fans to their games. At a hockey game you can see the Hamilton spirit at its finest, as students throw oranges at the opposing team's goalie, an old Hamilton tradition.

SMALL WONDERS

KENYON COLLEGE IN GAMBIER, OHIO

Admissions Address: Office of Admissions, Gambier, OH 43022
Phone: (614) 427-5776
Web Address: www.kenyon.edu

Your first impression of Kenyon College could very well be, as one student said, "it's in the middle of nowhere." But it may take only one walk around the campus to make you realize it's the center of everything, including first-rate learning.

With only about 1,500 students, undergrads at Kenyon feel a strong sense of community, even family. "It doesn't take long to fall into that mind set," said one student. Class sizes average about 15, enabling students to interact a great deal with one another and their professors. Students become "very close" to their professors, most of whom live within a few miles of campus.

While it may be located in an out-of-the-way locale, Kenyon is far from unknown. In academic circles, it's associated with the renowned literary journal, The Kenyon Review. Kenyon's academic strengths range from its traditional liberal arts offerings, English having the largest enrollment, to several excellent interdisciplinary programs, including the International Studies Program, an in-depth comparative study of Western and non-Western cultures, and the Integrated Program in Humane Studies, which combines the academic study of literature, politics, and history. Drama, music, and the arts also thrive here, as you'd expect upon hearing that Paul Newman is a Kenyon graduate.

The breathtaking campus is spread out over 800 sprawling, heavily wooded acres, where 19th century academic halls and residences lie alongside more modern buildings. Housing is, by all reports, excellent. There are modern buildings and three historic dormitories that are open to all students, regardless of their year. All are both "incredibly beautiful" as well as "very well maintained." The computer services also receive raves; students can hook up their personal computers to the school's network from their rooms or any other building on campus. The administration is making efforts to increase the diversity of the student body; the minority population currently makes up about 12 percent of the students. Students generally get along rather easily and are tolerant of different views and lifestyles. As a matter of fact, one student pointed to a recent independent poll that rated Kenyon's student body "one of the five happiest in the nation."

Kenyon College

$$$$$
★★

Setting: Rural
# of Undergraduates: 1,547
Men: 46.2% Women: 53.8%
Tuition: $22,200
Room and Board: $3,990
# of Students Applied: 2,474
   Admitted: 1,645 Enrolled: 445
Required Admissions Test: SAT, ACT, or TOEFL
Lowest 25% of Freshmen Scored At or Below: SAT Verbal: 610 SAT Math: 580 ACT Comp.: 26
Highest 25% of Freshmen Scored At or Above: SAT Verbal: 720 SAT Math: 680 ACT Comp.: 31
H.S. Rank, Top 10%: 52%
Top 25%: 74%
Top 50%: 100%
Avg. Score of Applicants Admitted: SAT Verbal: 663 SAT Math: 628 ACT Comp.: 29
Average GPA of Applicants Admitted: 3.50
Most Popular Majors (% of Student Body): English (21%), History (12%), Psychology (10%), Poltical Science (7%), Economics (6%)

Winter in the middle of Ohio is not a treat, but most of the students at Kenyon don't let it get them down. "There's too much you can do," said one student. Another added, "When you come here, you know what to expect. So you deal with it." Most students take advantage of Kenyon's Ernst Athletic-Recreation-Convocation Center, which has a pool, several racquet courts, and an exercise area. "I can jog in the fall and spring, and use the pool in the winter," said another student. "You have to throw yourself into what's available here," said another. Those who look will find plenty. There are frequent parties, though by no means are the less rowdy students out of the loop. "My biggest challenge on Friday night is deciding what to do," said one student. The Gund Commons hosts dances and concerts and provides a place to eat, play pool, and hang out. There are also movies, lectures, presentations, and special events, and the on-campus Bolton Theatre presents several professional-quality student productions each year.

Many students play on an athletic team, and men's soccer, women's tennis, and swimming are particularly strong. Other popular activities are the newspaper, literary publications, the radio station, student bands, performance groups, and several environmental groups. Some may consider Kenyon to be in the middle of nowhere, but when you examine the many social opportunities and the breadth of academic offerings, it's at the center of the collegiate map.

REED COLLEGE IN PORTLAND, OREGON

Admissions Address: Office of Admission, 3203 Southeast Woodstock Boulevard, Portland, OR 97202-8199
Phone: (503) 777-7511 (800) 547-4750
Web Address: www.reed.edu

Known as a liberal, highly progressive school, Reed College lives up to its reputation, both in terms of its academics and its student body. Students are given tremendous freedom, academically and socially, and they value their individuality. Highly motivated nonconformists thrive here. Those who are not can get direction on the campus, but may need to seek it out. There is a chance you could feel lost if you're not a go-getter. Reed treats its curriculum like an honors program in which all students are given almost total responsibility for the direction of their studies.

Classes are taught primarily according to what Reed calls "the conference method of teaching," in which small classes numbering between 10 and 20 students function as discussion sessions with the professor serving as facilitator. That means students have to come to class well read and ready to discuss the material and other issues. And they do come prepared. "That's what makes it fun," said one student. "If you're not ready, you're not going to be able to participate." Students speak highly of the help they receive from their professors. "The professors are great. They are both committed to their students and committed to research. It's the best of both worlds, especially when the professors have the undergraduate help with their research." Another student praised professors for "taking the students seriously, without being condescending."

Grades are de-emphasized by the administration and students alike. Students do not receive grades unless they ask for them, though grades are recorded. Students do, though, get extensive feedback from their professors. No grades doesn't mean the students don't work. Reed students are very serious about their own studies. As one student told us, "People study a lot, some for several hours a night."

The core requirements give students a sampling from a number of areas—including literature and the arts, history, social science, psychology, natural science, mathematics, foreign language, linguistics, and an interdisciplinary course in the humanities—before they dive into their chosen field. Students must pass a somewhat grueling qualifying examination in their field during junior year, followed by a substantial project or paper senior year. A senior described this project as being "similar to a master's dissertation, and some students do publish." One student told us that a favorite school tradition is the Thesis Parade, when the seniors march from the library to the administrative building, accompanied by a brass band, to turn in their papers.

The responsibility students take for their own educations, plus the challenging nature of their courses apparently makes them highly qualified for graduate school; impressive numbers of Reed students are accepted at graduate schools and go on to receive their doctorates.

The freedom of the curriculum attracts a progressive student body. As one student told us, "All of the people who sat in the corner and wore black in high school come here." While one student described the student body as "liberal intellectually," politically the school is not as far to the left as it has been in the past. "There's a range of political views," said another student. There is little diversity, though the minority population has been growing, but most students agree it could be better still. Students value individuality, in whatever shape it comes. "We have pretty odd senses of humor," says a Reed sophomore.

Reed College

$$$$$

Setting: Suburban
# of Undergraduates: 1,248
Men: 46.9% Women: 53.1%
Tuition: $22,180
Room and Board: $6,200
# of Students Applied: 2,086
  Admitted: 1,585 Enrolled: 363
Required Admissions Test: SAT
Lowest 25% of Freshmen Scored At or Below: SAT Verbal: 630
  SAT Math: 600
Highest 25% of Freshmen Scored At or Above: SAT
  Verbal: 720 SAT Math: 690
H.S. Rank, Top 10%: 47%
Top 25%: 78%
Top 50%: 97%
Avg. Score of Applicants Admitted: SAT Verbal: 673
  SAT Math: 645 ACT Comp.: 29
Average GPA of Applicants Admitted: 3.70
Most Popular Majors (% of Student Body): English (13%), Psychology (9%), Biology (9%), History (9%), Political Science (6%)

The social atmosphere reflects the individuality of the students. "The social scene is pretty fragmented," one student said. Since the 1960s, when the school had a communelike atmosphere, Reed has had a reputation for being a school for hippies and potheads. While that reputation has changed significantly since the days of free love, it's not hard to find those trying to keep the spirit alive. But you'll also find groups of students and individuals engaged in a variety of social and extracurricular activities. Reed recently received a special endowment, the Gray Fund, to promote cultural activities on campus, as well as outdoor facilities, such as skiing, kayaking, and canoeing, which also "helps to bring together students and faculty outside the classroom," a student reported. Some students attend small get-togethers and parties, while others head into Portland, which is described as "a wonderful, safe, friendly city" with its many cafes, coffeehouses, and bars.

Some students become involved with extracurricular activities or clubs, many politically oriented, while others are happy to hang out with friends and have heated intellectual discussions or listen to music. Doing volunteer work, especially at the campus' wildlife preserve, is one of the most popular student activities. There are a few events that attract larger crowds, especially the Renaissance Fair held at the end of the year when, as a sophomore described, "there are bands and a feast, games, and mazes. It's really fun, and it helps us blow off the end-of-the-year stress."

Reed students consider themselves true intellectuals, striving to live a "life of the mind" as one student said. The college teaches students to think. It's intense, there's little competition between students, but individually, they drive themselves hard. "It's difficult here, but worthwhile," one student said. "But if you can graduate from Reed, you can do anything!"

RHODES COLLEGE IN MEMPHIS, TENNESSEE

Admissions Address: Office of Admissions, 2000 North Parkway, Memphis, TN 38112-1690
Phone: (901) 843-3700 (800) 844-5969
Web Address: www.rhodes.edu

Rhodes is a small, southern college with a closely knit, community-like atmosphere, yet it's only minutes away from the excitement and cultural activity of Memphis. You don't need to leave campus to enjoy the school's physical location, though; the campus itself is considered one of the nation's most beautiful. Sprawling lawns and wooded areas surround the stately Gothic academic buildings, several of which are listed in the National Register of Historic Places. The small student population helps maintain the reputation of Rhodes as a friendly, easygoing campus, where most students readily recognize one another and greet each other with a smile.

Traditional liberal arts programs are generally excellent, especially in the sciences, as are the school's many interdisciplinary programs, including urban studies, American studies, Asian studies, and women's studies. Rhodes boasts of a high acceptance rate of its students by graduate and professional schools (40 percent go to graduate school, 7 percent go on to medical school, 8 percent to law school, and 5 percent to business school), many the best in the nation. The liberal arts requirements are broad, as students take courses in four key areas: humanities, social sciences, natural sciences and mathematics, and fine arts. Students are also required to take a four-course interdisciplinary program combining elements of Western history, philosophy, and religion.

Rhodes attracts bright students, often in the top 10 percent of their classes, and draws students from all over the country. But the majority of students are from the South and from middle- and upper-class families. Consequently, the student body is rather homogeneous in terms of ethnicity and socioeconomic background. While most students share conservative values, they are "middle of the road" politically, we hear. Either way, there's much tolerance among the student body. The dormitories continue to be single sex, a vestige of the school's Presbyterian affiliation.

Social life at Rhodes is divided between ventures into the city—where museums, theaters, blues bars, restaurants, and cultural venues abound—and the active campus social scene. The Greeks draw about half of the students, but they are by no means the only source of social life. There are over 100 different groups on campus, from outdoor clubs to Habitat for Humanity. "There's always a lot going on," said one student. The Greeks, in addition to throwing big parties, help make the intramurals program especially active. Additional social activities are organized by the school-funded Social Commission.

One of the most important aspects (one student said "the most important aspect") of life at Rhodes is the honor system. It is a student-run system that investigates charges of lying, cheating, and stealing, and can result in expulsion if the student is found guilty of the charge. The honor system results in an extremely safe campus: "I can be studying and leave my

Rhodes College

$$$$$

Setting: urban
# of Undergraduates: 1,382
Men: 45.2% **Women:** 54.8%
Tuition: $15,920
Room and Board: $4,912
# of Students Applied: 2,205
   Admitted: 1,646 **Enrolled:** 375
Required Admissions Test: SAT or ACT
Lowest 25% of Freshmen Scored At or Below: SAT Verbal: 590 SAT Math: 590 ACT Comp.: 26
Highest 25% of Freshmen Scored At or Above: SAT Verbal: 690 SAT Math: 680 ACT Comp.: 30
H.S. Rank, Top 10%: 61%
Top 25%: 83%
Top 50%: 99%
Average GPA of Applicants Admitted: 3.62
Most Popular Majors (% of Student Body): Biology (18%), English (12%), Business Administration (11%), Political Science (9%), International Studies (8%)

books and things and go to dinner and come back, and my stuff will be right where I left it," said one student, and locked doors are rare. Rhodes students truly love the honor code, they can't overemphasize its importance to them, and people we spoke to said it was, "incredibly empowering" to be entrusted with so much responsibility by the administration.

WASHINGTON & LEE UNIVERSITY
IN LEXINGTON, VIRGINIA

Admissions Address: Office of Admissions, Lexington, VA 24450
Phone: (540) 463-8710
Web Address: www.wlu.edu

If ever there was a school that was in the heart of the South and had the South in its heart, it's Washington and Lee University. What else would you expect of a school founded by Robert E. Lee?

The liberal arts department is strong in all areas, including economics, English, and journalism, but the standout department is (big surprise) history, what with Lee's tomb and many other historic sites right on the campus. There are also other choices in other schools of W&L. Students intent on professional careers often enroll in the School of Commerce, Economics, and Politics, which provides them with an educational background impressive to many prospective employers. A number of W&L graduates are themselves highly successful professionals with powerful positions.

Whatever field they choose, W&L students receive well-rounded educations. The broad requirements include proficiency in foreign language and English composition, and several courses in literature, fine arts, science and mathematics, social sciences, as well as five courses in physical education.

The course load requires heavy-duty studying. As one student told us, "It's a tough school," but the competition is not really amongst students. "We do drive ourselves hard," he said. Students aren't alone in their efforts though, because they receive constant support and guidance from their professors. The quality of the teaching is one of the school's greatest strengths, students report. Class sizes average 15, and classes are always taught by full-time faculty. "The faculty is very dedicated," said one student, and another added, "They're wonderful! They go out of their way to take care of the students."

Washington and Lee University

$$$$$
★★★★

Setting: Rural
# of Undergraduates: 1,618
Men: 59% Women: 41%
Tuition: $15,280
Room and Board: $5,360
# of Students Applied: 3,440
  Admitted: 1,074 Enrolled: 435
Required Admissions Test: either SAT or ACT
Lowest 25% of Freshmen Scored At or Below: SAT Verbal: 570 SAT Math: 630 ACT Comp.: 28
Highest 25% of Freshmen Scored At or Above: SAT Verbal: 660 SAT Math: 710 ACT Comp.: 30
H.S. Rank, Top 10%: 74%
Top 50%: 100%
Avg. Score of Applicants Admitted: SAT Verbal: 660 SAT Math: 675 ACT Comp.: 28
Most Popular Majors (% of Student Body): History (13%), Economics (10%), Biology (8%), English (7%), Business Administration (7%)

SMALL WONDERS

W&L is on a rather unusual trimester schedule consisting of fall and winter terms of 12 weeks, followed by a 6-week spring term. During the spring term, students take only one or two courses, very often in a non-traditional field, or use the time for study abroad or internships. The lighter course load enables students to take advantage of the warm spring weather on their beautiful campus when it's at its finest.

While the tuition is less expensive than at many top liberal arts colleges, the school's facilities are comparable. Located in the Shenandoah Valley, this picture-perfect, quintessentially collegiate campus has ivy-covered red brick buildings, complete with white columns and more than its fair share of historic landmarks. The housing is generally good, and there's enough to go around. In fact, anyone who wants a single can get one without having to gamble on some convoluted lottery system. Many upperclassmen, however, opt to live off campus, in fraternity houses or apartments.

Lee himself established the honor code while he was president of the university, and the current crop of W&L students take this code very seriously. More than one student described it as "the best thing about W&L." The school's honor code is completely student run, and punishment for lying, stealing, or cheating is nothing less than expulsion from school. "The honor system works, period," said one student. "It allows students the freedom of take-home exams and 24-hour access to buildings." Apparently the code is successful; most students trust their neighbors enough to keep their doors unlocked at all hours. Contributing to this sense of community fostered by the code, the "speaking tradition" dictates that everyone say hello to whomever they meet during the day. The code is not to be trifled with. "No one would think of breaching the code," a student affirms.

While students form a close community, the student body is not a diverse one. One student said, "The students here have it pretty rough. They're smart, attractive, motivated and drive Jeep Cherokees." Students are predominantly white, wealthy, and from the South, with a majority being very conservative. But students seem a little sensitive on this subject. "Oh, we have liberals," one student said. Another pointed to the profs: "The faculty is very liberal," he said.

The town of Lexington, while pretty, is also pretty quiet, so students tend to remain on campus where the social scene, while pretty limited, is anything but quiet. W&L parties are so popular, in fact, that they draw students from five all-women's schools in the area. The social scene is dominated by the fraternities, which draw a solid majority of the men, while sororities draw well over half of the women. With all those fraternities and sororities, there are always parties going on—usually big, blow out bashes involving heavy drinking. While the parties keep the social scene rockin' and rollin' year round, those who don't go Greek or tire of constant partying might feel left out. "You've got no place to hide and nowhere to spend Saturday night if you're not Greek or don't drink." Clubs and extracurricular activities provide alternatives, but the social scene is unmistakably one that centers on parties.

Lacrosse is the sport of choice, although football also draws a decent crowd and is fun to attend. Tennis and track are also strong. Many students play on a team in W&L's extensive intramural program. The school's Appalachian Mountain location also makes outdoor sports, such as camping, skiing, rafting, and hiking, popular recreational activities.

The big social event of the year is the Fancy Dress, consisting of several days of parties and dances culminating in a formal ball for which students get decked out to the nines. When you see the students in their formal wear passing through the campus' historic buildings, you might think you've traveled back to the Old South—which can only make Robert E. Lee look down and smile on the school that bears his name.

Also, Check Out These Schools:

Barnard College
Bates College
Bennington College
Birmingham-Southern College
College of the Holy Cross
Colorado College
Earlham College
Franklin and Marshall
Hampshire College
Hampden-Sydney College
Hobart and William Smith Colleges
Kalamazoo College
Knox College
Lewis and Clark College
Macalester College
Mount Holyoke College
Oberlin College

SMALL WONDERS

Pitzer College
St. John's College
St. Olaf College
Sarah Lawrence College
Skidmore College
Trinity College (CT)
University of the South
Wabash College
Washington and Jefferson College

Budget Ivies

It may be true that you get what you pay for, but, as some students have discovered, sometimes you get a lot more. The schools listed in this chapter offer superb academic programs, accomplished faculties, and first-rate facilities at low tuitions. It's no wonder that many students, realizing they don't necessarily have to sacrifice quality for cost, choose these schools over Ivy League schools and elite private colleges.

Most Budget Ivies are able to keep costs down because they're public, rather than private, institutions that receive funding from the state. Tuition is therefore especially low for state residents. Although the tuition might be substantially higher for out-of-state students, it's still a bargain when compared to the steep tuition at many private schools.

As you consider these schools, though, keep in mind that many states have been cutting education budgets, and it's not clear how these cuts will affect the schools. In some cases, courses, programs, and services have already been cut. Before enrolling in any of these schools, you should make certain the school still offers what you expect. For all you know, your chosen field may be wiped out.

Given all these schools do offer, it's not surprising that the competition to get into them can be tough. Because these universities are often the best public institutions in their respective states, their admissions offices are flooded with applications from state residents hoping to get the best there is at the state tuition. Most state-affiliated schools will admit only a small percentage of students from out of state, making it especially difficult for nonresidents to get in. As a result, students attending these schools are usually in the top 10 or even 5 percent of their high school classes, which creates a scholarly, intellectual atmosphere at many campuses.

Most of these schools are large research institutions with undergraduate populations numbering between 10,000 and 20,000 students. Attending a school this size presents its challenges, especially to undergraduates who are not always the center of attention. Overcrowded dorms and classrooms, lecture courses numbering hundreds of students, difficulty getting into popular courses, and miles of red tape are just a few of the problems students voiced complaints about. Some of these factors can make it difficult to graduate within four years, which diminishes the cost-saving benefits.

Most students, however, find the advantages of Budget Ivies far outweigh the disadvantages. These schools offer students an enormous range of academic programs, course offerings, and facilities, and the social opportunities are just as extensive and varied. With such large enrollments, students are likely to find people with whom they share common experiences and interests.

Large schools like these are not for everyone; those in search of a small, secluded community might feel overwhelmed. The students who excel in these environments are the ones who, by being outspoken and a bit pushy, find their way around the problems and make opportunities for themselves. These students find the excitement and energy generated by a large student population, as well as the abundance of choices and opportunities at a big school, incredibly appealing. Of course, the low price makes them more than appealing; these schools are downright irresistible.

COLLEGE OF WILLIAM AND MARY IN WILLIAMSBURG, VIRGINIA

Admissions Address: Admissions Office, P.O. Box 8795, Williamsburg, VA 23187-8795
Phone: (804) 221-4223
Web Address: www.wm.edu/

"There's a reason all the dorms here are named after former presidents like Tyler, Jefferson, and Washington," a W&M biology major told us. "William and Mary has a long history." Over 300 hundred years old, W&M is the second oldest institution of higher learning in the country (you can probably guess which one is the oldest). You can't help but feel an overwhelming sense of history and tradition as you roam the campus, where colonial-style buildings flank beautiful formal gardens. The Wren Building, one proud student informed us, is the oldest building in America in continuous academic use, and it continues to be the center of many William and Mary traditions.

BUDGET IVIES

If there's not enough history on campus, stepping off campus is like traveling back to the 18th century—or at least a Disneyland approximation of it. W&M is located in Colonial Williamsburg, a kind of historical amusement park, which adds to the historical aura surrounding the school, even if it draws flocks of camera-laden tourists.

William and Mary does share certain features with its rival UVA, including a deep connection to Thomas Jefferson, who graduated from W&M before going on to found UVA. Both schools' exceptional academic offerings and reasonable prices attract Virginia's best and brightest as well as a large number of interested out-of-state candidates (about two-thirds are Virginians). According to one student, W&M's size—about 5,000—is fantastic: "It's not too small and not too big. You get the best of both worlds." While William and Mary doesn't offer the extensive academic and social offerings of a larger university, it makes up for it with it's strong feeling of community. As one student puts it, "I don't feel like a number here."

William and Mary was created as a liberal arts college, and traditional arts and sciences remain its primary focus. Biology, English, and government are considered particularly good, as is the history department, which benefits from the school's proximity to major historic sites. In addition to liberal arts, the business school has an excellent reputation, although it's extremely competitive. William and Mary also offers several interdisciplinary programs such as an acclaimed international studies program. Other special offerings include a prestigious honors program and study-abroad options. While people are serious about their academics, one student told us "there's no snobbiness factor here."

W&M attracts faculty who are often well known in their fields yet remain devoted to their teaching. Although there are a few introductory classes with enrollments approaching 200, most classes are small and professors get to know students on an individual basis. "It's not hard to get in touch with professors at all," one student told us. "They're very encouraging and really want to get to know you."

The tuition is exceptionally low for Virginians, and even out-of-staters consider it a good deal "compared to Northern privates." This fact combined with the quality of education makes W&M highly competitive in terms of admissions. Those students who do get accepted are extremely well qualified, most coming from the top five percent of their high school classes. Once they arrive here, students find that the workload is more than challenging. "People study quite a bit; the workload is hard," a stu-

---

College of William and Mary

$$
★★★

Setting: suburban
# of Undergraduates: 5,424
Men: 40.9% **Women:** 59.1%
In-State Tuition: $4,906
Out-of-State Tuition: $14,916
Room and Board: $4,470
# of Students Applied: 7,069
   Admitted: 3,226 **Enrolled:** 1,333
Required Admissions Test: either SAT or ACT
Recommended: SAT II Writing subjects
Lowest 25% of Freshmen Scored At or Below: SAT Verbal: 600 SAT Math: 590 ACT Comp.: 28
Highest 25% of Freshmen Scored At or Above: SAT Verbal: 710 SAT Math: 690 ACT Comp.: 32
H.S. Rank, Top 10%: 74%
Top 25%: 95%
Top 50%: 100%
Avg. Score of Applicants Admitted: SAT Verbal: 655 SAT Math: 638 ACT Comp.: 30
Most Popular Majors (% of Student Body): Business (14%), Government/History (14%), Biology (12%), English (10%), Psychology (9%)

dent told us. Professors have high expectations from their students and can be very tough. One biology major complained of the constant "grade deflation."

Students remain highly focused on their studies and are exceedingly motivated. Part of the school's strong sense of tradition stems from its honor code—the oldest collegiate code in the country—which gives students a great deal of independence, including the right to take unproctored examinations.

Although W&M has a relatively small enrollment, the campus itself spreads out over a large, beautifully landscaped area. Buildings of different age and style are clustered around the campus, surrounded by breathtaking gardens and foliage. Almost everything about W&M is carefully maintained and in excellent condition, from the library to the student housing. Students can choose from one of three main eating centers, the Dining Cafe, the Marketplace, and the University Center for their meals. Housing is guaranteed only for three years, and at least 20 percent of students eventually move off campus, many opting for fraternity and sorority houses.

The school's recent additions include Tercentenary Hall, built in 1993 in celebration of W&M's 300th birthday, and an enormous student center, with places to eat, student organization offices, an auditorium, bookstore, and lounge.

Minorities make up about one-fifth of the student body. Most students are white, upper- or middle-class, and conservative in their values as well as their politics, although "there's definitely a liberal contingency," according to one sophomore. Another student adds that, while the school is "very traditional," it's also "very open minded."

The proximity to Colonial Williamsburg does have its advantages, enhancing the picturesque quality of the campus and providing a number of job opportunities for students. Most students, though, avoid the crowds of tourists who flock through town. As one student puts it, "Williamsburg is no thriving metropolis." Both Richmond, which is an hour away, and Washington, D.C., which is two-and-a-half hours away, provide students with popular weekend road trip destinations. And when the weather is good, Virginia Beach is a quick 45-minute drive.

While the social life at W&M might not be a raging party scene, students do kick back and relax when they've closed the books. A significant number go Greek (about a quarter of both men and women), although not enough to dominate the social activities. The fraternities and sororities keep the social life jumping, though, by hosting parties and other events, many open to the whole campus. In addition to frat parties, students enjoy hanging out at nearby cafes, coffeehouses, and delicatessens.

The sports program at William and Mary, if not on par with some of its main rivals, is good. The football, basketball, and soccer teams have decent records and games draw a fair following of student fans. The athletic complex provides facilities for a large number of sporting activities, including swimming, tennis, racquetball, weight training, and running. Students especially enjoy participating in the school's extensive intramural program, which offers more than 40 sports. The 200-plus clubs and activities include student-written publications, theater and performing groups, and community service organizations.

For a school to endure as long as William and Mary has, it must be doing something right. The idea of establishing a small academic community of intelligent students within a beautiful setting has certainly caught on.

RICE UNIVERSITY IN HOUSTON, TEXAS

Admissions Address: Office of Admission MS 17, 6100 Main Street, Houston, TX 77005
Phone: (713) 527-4036 (800) 527-OWLS
Web Address: www.rice.edu

Thanks to an approximately $2 billion endowment, Rice has been able to provide Ivy League level academics and facilities at a super-bargain price. And as a result of all the positive publicity it's been receiving in recent years, Rice is gaining in prestige and popularity. That means more students applying, making it more competitive to get in.

Most of those who are admitted are among the top 5 percent in their high school classes, giving Rice a smart and career-driven student population. Many go on to graduate school or professional school. Although Rice is primarily known for science and engineering, its humanities departments, particularly history and English, are gaining in reputation. The school is just completing the James A. Baker Institute of Public Policy, which will attract prominent visiting faculty and speakers. Many students are premed, which makes the biology and chemistry classes popular. Rice also has highly rated undergraduate programs in architecture and music. Students are encouraged to combine majors or conduct inde-

Rice University

$$$$
★★★★

Setting: urban
# of Undergraduates: 2,625
Men: 54.5% Women: 45.5%
Tuition: $13,097
Room and Board: $6,200
# of Students Applied: 7,050
   Admitted: 1,727 Enrolled: 671
Required Admissions Test: either SAT I or ACT; SAT II
Lowest 25% of Freshmen Scored At or Below: SAT Verbal: 660 SAT Math: 670 ACT Comp.: 29
Highest 25% of Freshmen Scored At or Above: SAT Verbal: 760 SAT Math: 780 ACT Comp.: 33
H.S. Rank, Top 10%: 88%
Top 25%: 95%
Top 50%: 99%
Most Popular Majors (% of Student Body): Engineering (21.1%), Economics (8%), English (6.9%), Biochemistry (6.3%), History (6%)

pendent studies. Rice's distribution requirements include four courses each in the natural sciences, social sciences, and humanities.

Although Rice is a major research university, the atmosphere for undergraduates tends to resemble that of a small, liberal arts college because of its relatively small undergraduate population. While introductory classes might be large, which can limit the personal attention paid to students, class sizes are generally kept small. The professors, one student affirms, are "very, very approachable. They eat lunch with students, they attend events with students."

Rice's compact campus, with its distinctive Spanish-Mediterranean buildings, is located in a tree-lined suburb of Houston. Facilities are "fine," although the library is "not too hot," says one student. The "brand new, modern" science buildings do receive strong praise. The food in the campus dining halls, on the other hand, does not.

Although about half of the students are native Texans, the school attracts people from all over the country as well as from 30 foreign countries. About one-fifth of the students are from minority populations.

Students are very serious about their studies and future careers, but contrary to what one student calls Rice's "nerdy reputation," they're laid-back about everything else. "People are really friendly here," one senior tells us. "It's not a cutthroat environment." The population tends to be liberal, but not politically active.

Rice students are concerned about their studies, but they also like to have fun when the studying is done. Downtown Houston is only a few miles from Rice's campus, and students can find movies, music, bars, and good restaurants there. Houston also has many cultural venues, including a host of superb art museums and galleries. "Unfortunately, most students don't take advantage of it," one student reports.

Student life revolves around campus and, in particular, the residential colleges. In addition to the low tuition and quality academics, many students consider the residential college housing system one of the school's best assets. First-year students are assigned to a college when they arrive, and they remain affiliated with the college for their entire four years (unless they opt to move off campus, which over half of the students do). The college, therefore, provides a small community in which students form especially close friendships. The colleges function like fraternities, hosting special events and parties (with funding from the school), but without the "cliquishness" and competition of the Greek system. Despite the absence of fraternities and sororities, "partying tends to be pretty drunk and wild," according to one student.

Rice is the smallest NCAA Division I school in the country. Although not typically known for its varsity sports, this may be changing as Rice moves to the Western Athletic Conference "escaping" such football powerhouses as Texas A&M and the University of Texas. Students like participating in intramural sports and most also become involved in at least one of the school's many activities and clubs. Here too, Rice's small size is an advantage, according to one student: "We get tons of opportunities to take responsibility and have an incredible impact on campus life and even academic policy."

Rice also has its sense of humnor of wild and weird events and traditions. One student told us about "Club Baker 13," whose members regularly run buck naked through the colleges covered in shaving cream, and the annual beer-biking race, which, as you might imagine, isn't exactly the Tour de France.

STATE UNIVERSITY OF NEW YORK / BINGHAMTON

Admissions Address: Admissions Office, P.O. Box 6001, Binghamton, NY 13901-6001
Phone: (607) 777-2171
Web Address: www.binghamton.edu/

About half of Binghamton's students graduated in the top 10 percent of their high school classes. These students generally had the grades and test scores to get them into the nation's most competitive private colleges and universities, yet they opt for Binghamton because of its super-low tuition. These students recognize that the tuition might be low at Binghamton but that the academics are still first-rate.

Binghamton's reputable undergraduate colleges include professional schools in engineering, management, and nursing, as well as the acclaimed Harpur College, where liberal arts programs are strong across the board. Biology, chemistry, English, and psychology have particularly large enrollments. Binghamton also offers several good interdisciplinary programs including women's studies; Latin American and Caribbean area studies; Asian and Asian American studies; and philosophy, politics, and law.

SUNY/Binghamton

$$

★★★

Setting: Suburban
# of Undergraduates: 8,913
Men: 47.2% Women: 52.8%
In-State Tuition: $3,400
Out-of-State Tuition: $8,300
Room and Board: $4,814
# of Students Applied: 15,660
   Admitted: 6,573   Enrolled: 1,819
Required Admissions Test: Either SAT or ACT
Recommended: SAT I or ACT
Lowest 25% of Freshmen Scored At or Below: SAT Verbal: 550 SAT Math: 570
Highest 25% of Freshmen Scored At or Above: SAT Verbal: 650   SAT Math: 670
H.S. Rank, Top 10%: 52%
Top 25%: 94%
Top 50%: 99%
Avg. Score of Applicants Enrolled: SAT Verbal: 595 SAT Math: 619
Average GPA of Applicants Enrolled: 3.68
Most Popular Majors (% of Student Body): Management (16%), Psychology/Psychobiology (12%), English (10%), Biology (9%), Philosophy (6%)

A new set of general education requirements has been designed to provide students with a focused liberal arts foundation. Students will be required to take courses in five areas: lab science and mathematics, esthetic perspective, language and communication, creating a global vision, and physical activity and wellness.

Class sizes at the introductory levels can be large and one student complains that "it's difficult to make contact with professors when you first arrive." But students regularly break into smaller discussion sections taught by graduate students. For the most part, professors do the teaching, and class sizes average about 20 students. One student reports that some departments, such as English, are known for having especially approachable professors. While the workload and amount of studying varies with each major, Binghamton students don't seem all that stressed about their work. One candid junior reports, "Let's say that if my parents knew how little I studied, they'd want their money back."

The institutional look of the campus—its functional buildings are arranged in a circular pattern—is alleviated by the beautiful natural surroundings. The campus is heavily wooded, which makes it particularly lovely in the fall and spring when the foliage camouflages some of the uglier concrete and wood buildings. The dormitories are clustered together to form five residential communities, each with its own personality. Many juniors and seniors opt for off-campus housing.

Students are currently concerned about how state cuts from the SUNY budget will affect the school and the tuition. The tuition, though, continues to be reasonable.

More than 90 percent of Binghamton students come from New York State, and more than half come from New York City, Long Island, and Westchester. Unlike many other highly rated public institutions, Binghamton doesn't attract large numbers of applicants from out-of-state. Although mostly New Yorkers, the student body is made up of between 25 and 30 percent minorities. Some students point out that different groups don't necessarily mix although the administration is working "very hard" on issues involving racial, ethnic, and political diversity on campus.

One student complained that college guides "totally misrepresent" the social scene at Binghamton. Contrary to what many books say, there's a pretty active social life, he told us, one that changes each year as different activities and hangouts become popular. In general, he said, "people who live on campus like to go to fraternity parties or dorm parties or local clubs. There's always something to do. The upperclassmen go to State Street where all the bars are." The city of Binghamton, while primarily an industrial, working-class city, does have some restaurants and shopping areas, as well as a few dance clubs, that attract students. Town-gown relations have reportedly improved in recent years, particularly due to students' involvement in several community service and volunteer programs.

On the Binghamton campus, the student union, with several fast-food establishments, a pub, and a game room, is a central hangout. Fraternities and sororities have been attracting more and more students, although they don't have their own houses. The Anderson Center for the Arts serves as a campus cultural center where any number of musical and theatrical events will be held each year.

For New Yorkers looking for a quality education at a reasonable cost, Binghamton should certainly be considered.

UNIVERSITY OF CALIFORNIA/BERKELEY

Admissions Address: Office of Undergraduate Admissions and Relations with Schools, 110 Sproul Hall #5800, Berkeley, CA 94720-5800
Phone: (510) 642-3175 (510) 642-8396
Web Address: www.berkeley.edu/

The University of California System is one of the most acclaimed state school systems in the country. Berkeley (Cal, for short) is not only the system's flagship campus, but it's also one of the most respected and well-known public institutions in the country.

Berkeley's strength is its superb faculty combined with its unique student environment. Berkeley professors consistently earn national and international accolades (including a high number of Nobel Prize winners) and are held in the highest esteem in their fields. And on the Cal campus, as one student attests, "the opportunities to explore and be exposed to new things are literally endless."

Due to the school's size, undergraduates have incredible academic options; they can choose from among more than 100 different majors or design their own. Virtually all of the departments are superb, but the sciences, English, and history have particularly strong reputations. The

University of California/Berkeley

🏛🏛🏛🏛🏛
$$
★★★★

Setting: urban
Total Undergrad Enrollment: 21,176
Men: 52% **Women:** 48%
In-State Tuition: $3,956
Out-of-State Tuition: $12,350
Room and Board: $6,710
# of Students Applied: 25,111
   Admitted: 9,030   **Enrolled:** 3,775
Required Admissions Test: either SAT or ACT; three SAT II subject tests
SAT Scores, Middle 50% of Entering Class: SAT Verbal ranging from 570–700, SAT MATH ranging from 610–730
Average GPA of Applicants Admitted: 3.84

requirements vary by department, but all undergraduates must demonstrate English and writing proficiency and take interdisciplinary courses in American history, institutions, and cultures.

As a very large research institution, Cal presents its challenges for undergraduates, who, even though they number several thousand, are a small part of the Berkeley picture; faculty and graduate research tend to be the top priorities. Undergraduates must grapple with classes numbering hundreds of students and bureaucratic red tape that can be maddening.

Because Berkeley is primarily known as a research institution, where professors must publish to get tenure, the faculty is pretty focused on their own work. This can make it difficult to get personal attention from them, although it's not impossible. Students who don't mind being assertive can gain access to their professors, even the seemingly busier ones. One student said she has found all of her professors to be accessible. "We can E-mail them and call them, as well as visit during office hours," she said.

Despite the problems, undergraduates benefit enormously from Cal's research-oriented academic environment. Berkeley students are able to study and work with brilliant scholars who are well known in their fields. They also take advantage of the school's state-of-the-art facilities, including high-tech laboratories and research equipment in prime condition, and a library system, with more than 20 specialized libraries, that's one of the best stocked in the nation.

Just as central to the Cal experience as the acclaimed faculty is the vibrant and intelligent student population. Berkeley is the most selective school in the California system. About 85 percent of the students come from California, which makes it especially difficult for out-of-state hopefuls. Due to the high admissions standards, Berkeley students are usually among the smartest in their high school classes. They need to be in order to meet the rigorous demands of their courses. "The workload is tough; this is not an easy school," a senior told us. Most students are up to the challenge though; Berkeley students succeed at their courses and a large percentage continue in graduate school.

In the 1960s, Cal earned a reputation as a hippie haven; although times have changed, there is still an aura of '60s radicalism around the campus. Diversity of all kinds is highly valued and evident in just about every aspect of the Berkeley student population, which ranges from artsy bohemians to serious preprofessionals, from screaming liberals to diehard conservatives. As one student told us: "It's not like it was in the '60s, unfortunately. But there's still a liberal residue."

Although Berkeley was one of the first schools to espouse the values of multiculturalism and work actively to diversify its student population and curriculum, recent California state laws have put a halt to the campus' affirmative action activities. Although there's been a slight decline in minority student applications to Cal, African Americans and Hispanics still make up about 20 percent of the student body, while Asian Americans number about 40 percent. There's also a visible and generally accepted gay and lesbian population.

While the campus is still probably more liberal than conservative, one student assured us that there's a wide range of views. Students may have different opinions, but they're all opinionated. The constant exchange of ideas and experiences gives Cal a distinctive energy and buzz. As one freshman raved, "I love how diverse this school is. I've already learned about so many other cultures and customs. I feel like people really respect one another here." To match the diversity of students' experiences and interests, there are hundreds of different clubs and activities, including many ethnically, culturally, and politically oriented organizations. The DARE Project (Diversity Awareness through Resources and Education) encourages freshmen to interact with people of all kinds.

Contributing to the offbeat character of the school are the offbeat characters who wander around campus. A familiar sight to Cal students, faculty, and staff, these oddball personalities stroll around campus espousing some political or personal agenda be it religious ravings, the discordant tones of "our off-key singer," or the angry diatribes of a character affectionately known as the Hate Man.

The large Berkeley campus, unlike its rival Stanford, is more akin to Eastern Ivy League schools in its design. Buildings range in style from ivy-covered stone academic structures to ultra contemporary, all situated around expansive lawns that provide prime suntanning, Frisbee, and outdoor study spots. Housing ranges from recently renovated modern dormitories to older high-rises. As housing is in short supply and only guaranteed for the first year, many students must look off campus for accommodations after freshman year. Options include several student-run co-ops, fraternity and sorority houses, and a wide range of off-campus apartments.

Students at Berkeley are serious about their studies. They do, however, like to relax on weekends. The Greeks provide one mode of social entertainment here, hosting large parties every weekend. They don't, however, dominate the social scene by any means. With such a large student population, there's always a range of informal parties and get-togethers happening both on campus and off. As one student explains, "everyone, and I mean everyone will find a place where they fit in socially." But, considering the schools huge size, he adds "you have to search for it. It takes effort." There's also no shortage of cultural activities, including many plays, special guest lecturers, and concerts in Cal's outstanding Zellerbach Auditorium.

Just outside the campus gates, Berkeley is itself a small city with many cultural and social options. While safety is a concern in some parts of the city, the streets directly adjacent to the campus definitely cater to students. The main strip, Telegraph Avenue, is lined with street vendors hawking tie-dyed T-shirts and homemade jewelry. Students hang out in cafes, ethnic restaurants, small eateries, coffeehouses, bars, bookstores, shops, and music clubs.

Cal students also attend their school's major intercollegiate sporting events, especially football and basketball games. Students camp out for days to get basketball tickets (something the administration is struggling to discourage). The big football rivalry is against Stanford. "There are sing-offs between our school and Stanford, there are pep rallies, and people decorate the whole town with balloons," a student described.

If people are in search of more cultural activity beyond what Berkeley has to offer, there's always that beautiful city across the Bay, San Francisco. As diverse as Berkeley but many times larger, SF is only 20 minutes away on public transportation and offers an easy break from campus life.

Attending a large school like Cal isn't for everyone, but for highly motivated students who are willing to stand up for themselves and seek out opportunities, Berkeley has more than its fair share of rewards. According to one senior: "You can't go wrong coming here. If you take the initiative, the range of opportunities is unbeatable." As a happy freshman told us, if you are "open minded, tolerant, independent, and a hard worker, this is the place for you!"

BUDGET IVIES

UNIVERSITY OF IOWA IN IOWA CITY

Admissions Address: Admissions Office, Calvin Hall, Iowa City, IA 52242-1396
Phone: (319) 335-3847
Web Address: www.uiowa.edu/

As one University of Iowa senior told us, "For the price, students get a thorough, great education here." Indeed, its hard to find such extensive academic offerings at Iowa's low tuition. Many students are on a preprofessional track, and almost all of the preprofessional departments are excellent. One student also told us that "Iowa turns out a lot of fine scholars. This school is best for people who want to go on to graduate school."

Iowa has long been innovative in its academic offerings; it was the first school to offer programs in speech pathology and audiology, and the site of the first Writers Workshop. All of the sciences benefit from the school's outstanding resources, which is one reason the premedicine courses are so popular. The largest of Iowa's 10 colleges is the liberal arts school, whose students must fulfill some pretty stiff general education requirements by taking required courses in nine basic academic fields. Although almost all departments are good, English, which benefits from its association with the prestigious writing programs (ranked tops in the United States), is especially noteworthy and extremely popular.

With an undergraduate enrollment exceeding 15,000, many classes are inevitably filled to overflowing—when students can get into them. As one student pointed out, this can be a problem as many students, trying to fulfill their requirements, aren't able to graduate in four years. Even the largest lectures will break down into small discussion groups, and there are a number of courses that are significantly smaller. Considering the enormous student enrollment, professors are surprisingly accessible and the teaching quality is excellent, students report. Although the school has extensive facilities, including a well-stocked library system, housing is not one of them. A majority of students look for housing off campus, although several students complain that apartment rentals are very expensive.

The student population tends to be liberal, particularly in their generally relaxed and tolerant attitudes. Although the minority population isn't very large (representing less than 10 percent of the student body), students embrace what diversity there is; students from vastly different social backgrounds comfortably intermingle without much tension. About a third of the students are from out of state.

University of Iowa

$$
★

Setting: Small city
# of Undergraduates: 16,263
Men: 46.3% Women: 53.7%
In-State Tuition: $2,566
Out-of-State Tuition: $9,422
Room and Board: $3,688
# of Students Applied: 9,847
   Admitted: 8,431   Enrolled: 3,535
Required Admissions Test: Either SAT or ACT
H.S. Rank, Top 10%: 22%
Top 25%: 52%
Top 50%: 90%
Average GPA of Applicants Admitted: 3.37
Most Popular Majors (% of Student Body): Business (7%), Engineering (6%), Psychology (6%), English (5%), Nursing (4%)

In general, students find their school's location in Iowa City one of its greatest strengths. "In the middle of conservative Iowa, Iowa City is a liberal mecca," an Iowa senior told us. Iowa City certainly has a lot to appeal to a student population, including bars and music clubs that are a major part of the U of I social scene. One student told us that the best thing about Iowa was the bar he hangs out in with his friends. Another student agrees: "The bar scene is the best, especially during football season." Of course, there are always alternatives: "Coffeehouses are becoming huge here. The most popular one, the Java House, was started by a 21-year-old marketing student. People go there to hang or study, and there's sometimes live music and comedy," a journalism major told us.

Beyond the beer and caffeine scenes in town, fraternities and sororities keep the social life active as well although, according to one student, they're not as predominant as at other large schools: "If you're not in a house, it doesn't mean you're missing out on anything." Residence halls also host parties, and the recently renovated student union provides prime socializing space. Interest in the arts brings many cultural groups and special events to campus to provide entertainment. Students also cram into Iowa's enormous football stadium to cheer on the Hawkeyes, now a formidable team. Basketball, wrestling, and field hockey are also competitive. Homecoming is a major social event, complete with floats and a king and queen. Thanks to the school's sporting facilities, students can keep themselves healthy and fit. The annual Riverfest includes a race and bike-a-thon along the Iowa River.

In addition to the reasonable tuition, it's probably just as much this relaxed atmosphere, combined with extensive academic options, powerhouse sports, and a student-friendly location, that make U of I such a popular choice.

UNIVERSITY OF MICHIGAN/ANN ARBOR

Admissions Address: Office of Undergraduate Admissions, 1220 Student Activities Building, 515 E. Jefferson, Ann Arbor, MI 48109-1316
Phone: (313) 764-7433
Web Address: www.umich.edu/

With an undergraduate enrollment of more than 20,000 students and a campus stretching out over 2,665 acres, to call the University of Michigan big is an understatement; it's a town unto itself. A school this size clearly isn't for those searching for a closely knit community in which everybody knows you by name. It's perfect, though, for those who like having plenty of options—academically and socially—and living on a campus where there's always something interesting going on.

Michigan's prestigious undergraduate schools include the School of Music, School of Art and Design, College of Architecture and Urban Planning, and the acclaimed, although extremely difficult, College of Engineering. In the College of Literature, Science, and Art, Michigan's largest school, programs are strong across the board, particularly in English, political science, history, and psychology. Due to its acclaimed medical school and health programs, natural sciences at Michigan are highly regarded. Undergraduate science students are able to use state-of-the-art resources and work with an accomplished faculty of scientists and researchers.

Michigan also offers many special, innovative programs, including a highly selective honors program for incoming freshmen and a seven-year accelerated M.D. program. The Residential College fosters a small college feel, housing about 1,000 students who take eight small core courses together.

Although requirements vary by school, most students fulfill breadth requirements in humanities, natural sciences and math, social sciences, foreign language, and freshman composition. Literature, science, and arts students also take a course on race and ethnicity. These requirements are relatively easy to fulfill, and students have ample room in their schedules to pick and choose from Michigan's huge number of course offerings.

The school's reputation, beautiful campus, and superb research facilities draw professors well known in their respective fields. Getting to meet with them, however, can be a challenge. Classes, especially at the introductory level, are often crammed to overflowing. Popular course fill up quickly, but with some perseverance—and perhaps a little begging—students can sometimes find a way into them.

A common complaint is that a number of classes are taught by graduate students. Since Michigan is a research institution whose professors need to have their work published, some professors are "more interested in research than in teaching." The same student points out that "the upside is that students get an opportunity to conduct hands-on research" along with top faculty members.

Even if a class is taught by a professor, it's likely to be so large that you'll just be a face in the crowd. Students don't, however, need to remain

---

University of Michigan / Ann Arbor

$$$

Setting: Suburban
# of Undergraduates: 22,019
Men: 50.4% **Women:** 49.6%
In-State Tuition: $5,532
Out-of-State Tuition: $17,738
Room and Board: $5,137
# of Students Applied: 19,703
  Admitted: 13,469 **Enrolled:** 5,327
Required Admissions Test: Either SAT or ACT
Lowest 25% of Freshmen Scored At or Below: SAT Verbal: 570 SAT Math: 610 ACT Comp.: 25
Highest 25% of Freshmen Scored At or Above: SAT Verbal: 690 SAT Math: 720 ACT Comp.: 30
H.S. Rank, Top 10%: 69%
Top 25%: 93%
Top 50%: 99%
Average GPA of Applicants Admitted: 3.63
Most Popular Majors (% of Student Body): Psychology (7%), Biology (5%), Business Administration (4%), Mechanical Engineering (4%), English (4%)

anonymous. Those who aren't shy and are willing to seek out professors usually find them more than willing to talk and offer advice. Most professors make themselves accessible outside of class during their office hours. Additionally, in their upper-level classes, students usually receive more individualized attention and form closer bonds with their teachers.

Students have terrific things to say about their enormous campus, with its own galleries, museums, planetarium, botanical gardens, and arboretum. "It's made for students," a senior raved. Divided between the Central Campus and North Campus, the campus architecture runs the gamut from classical to postmodern. The range of facilities is extensive and the quality well above average. The 23 libraries have combined sources in the millions. There are computer facilities all over campus, and students are able to link their personal computers to the university mainframe from their rooms.

The dormitories are clustered in different arrangements that vary in personality, from the louder, more social quads to the sedate ones that appeal more to upperclassmen. Students can also live in on-campus apartments, university-owned coops, and special-interest houses, including one for first-year students from different cultures and backgrounds. Freshmen are guaranteed on-campus housing, but many upperclassmen look for housing elsewhere. There's no shortage of student housing in Ann Arbor, although the rent and the conditions of many apartments are far from ideal.

In its promotional material, Michigan declares its commitment to promoting diversity and building a multicultural community, and the administration has taken specific measures to help realize this goal. There's currently a 20 percent minority population, and, with such a large enrollment, that's not an insubstantial number of students. The student body is diverse in many respects, coming from a variety of social, ethnic, cultural, class, and political backgrounds. Thirty percent come from out of state, which also adds up to a large number of students, although the competition for them to get in is still extremely heavy. One student praised, "the unique thing about Ann Arbor is the wide range of people," which, despite the massive population, "enables everyone to find their own social niche." At Michigan, you'll find a large bohemian crowd lobbying to legalize marijuana alongside a Young Republican set voicing its support for the Contract for America. Politically, though, a student tells us that "the campus is a lot more liberal than most campuses. The most mainstream views are liberal."

Many students tend to stick with a particular group with whom they share a common background. While this does help students find a place for themselves within the larger university, it also indicates a lack of integration among different groups. For those who want the opportunity to meet students from different backgrounds, there are several options, including certain residences as well as hundreds of clubs and extracurricular activities.

Although Michigan students work hard to meet the demands of their rigorous courses, they do enjoy an active social life. The Greek system is popular, drawing about 20 percent of the students. While the Greeks help keep the party lovers partying, they are far from the only social outlet. On a campus of Michigan's size, there's always something going on somewhere, ranging from movies, concerts, and theatrical productions to visiting lecturers and performers. Many students casually hang out in residence halls, or on the central lawn, or at the Union. Students who venture off campus find even more social opportunities. Ann Arbor is a true college town that caters to students, with coffeehouses, cafes, bars, shops, and restaurants that regularly bring students off campus.

In addition to its superior academics, Michigan is a sports powerhouse; the men's football and basketball teams are often championship contenders and have huge student followings. Football Saturdays are major social events; crowds of Michigan students flock to the huge football stadium, which seats 102,000, to cheer on the Wolverines. This enthusiasm for sports carries over to other aspects of student life, including participation in an expansive intramural program and in outdoor recreational activities in the beautiful surrounding areas.

The bottom line is that Michigan is a powerhouse on all levels: the academics, athletics, and social scene.

UNIVERSITY OF NORTH CAROLINA/CHAPEL HILL

Admissions Address: Admissions Office, CB #2200 Jackson Hall, Chapel Hill, NC 27599-2200
Phone: (919) 966-3621
Web Address: adp.unc.edu/sis/admissions/undergrad/html

"We like our sports here," a UNC—Chapel Hill student told us. With several powerhouse teams, particularly football and the NCAA championship–winning basketball team (of which Michael Jordan was once a part), North Carolina fans have plenty to like. But it's not just the sports

UNC/Chapel Hill

$$$$$
★★★★★

Setting: suburban
# of Undergraduates: 14,412
Men: 39.6% **Women:** 60.4
In-State Tuition: $1,386
Out-of-State Tuition: $9,918
Room and Board: $4,600
# of Students Applied: 16,063
  Admitted: 5,570 **Enrolled:** 3,238
Required Admissions Test: Either SAT or ACT
Avg. Score of Applicants
  Admitted: SAT Verbal: 610
  SAT Math: 610 ACT Comp.: 28
Most Popular Majors (% of Student Body): Biology (12.15%), Psychology (8.05%), Business (8.03%), Journalism (5.27%), Political Science (4.72%)

---

that get rave reviews from students. UNC, the oldest public university in the country, has a long history of providing superior academics and excellent facilities in an ideal collegiate environment.

"We rank up there with the Ivy League in terms of educational opportunities," says a UNC junior. UNC's liberal arts departments, especially English, political science and natural sciences, are particularly acclaimed, and the business, premed, and prelaw programs all have high enrollments. General education requirements ensure that all UNC students receive a broad background of knowledge before pursuing more focused areas of study. The school is big, which enables students to select from hundreds of course offerings; the problem, though, is getting into some of them. Class sizes can be as high as 400, but there are many as low as 15 or 20. "We don't have a good professor-to-student ratio," one student complained, "but there are some professors who do care and get to know their students." For the most part, the student has to make the effort to seek out professors when they need help or advice.

The spacious campus, arranged in quadrangle formation, is "pedestrian friendly, with older brick buildings, tree-lined paths, 200-year-old oak trees, lots of azaleas, and open green spaces," according to one student. The beautiful campus and temperate weather cultivate the easygoing, relaxed campus atmosphere. UNC students work hard, but also like to have fun. According to one student, during exam week, one group takes to streaking through the library which, to say the least, helps ease up on some of the tension. For every student hitting the books in the library, you'll find one hanging out on the school's quads. There are several residence halls grouped together into different campuses, but many juniors and seniors opt for off-campus apartments. The school's facilities, as a student tells us, are "great," and include a well-stocked library system, with prime space for studying and socializing, a large student union, and first-rate sports and exercise facilities.

UNC's excellent academics and facilities have made it highly selective, especially for out-of-state hopefuls. In describing the student population, one student told us, "On the whole we're a liberal campus. But we've got a bit of everything." While the majority of the students come from North Carolina (about 80 percent), the students represent a diverse mixture in terms of ethnic, cultural, political, and social backgrounds. One student complained about a "slight problem with self-segregation between ethnic groups" but went on to say that efforts were underway to address this issue.

Almost all of the students, though, share an enthusiasm for North Carolina's powerhouse sports teams, which include football, basketball, lacrosse, and field hockey. The women's soccer team has been the most successful of all, winning the NCAA championships more often than not over the past 20 years. Games are well attended by wildly supportive student fans. Most popular, "of course, is Carolina basketball, which is fantastic," says one student. "(Coach) Dean Smith is God" and, as one might imagine, to get a ticket to one of his games can take some real time and effort.

Students also enjoy an active and varied social life. Fraternities and sororities are popular, but there are many other options for entertainment. Students can attend a number of cultural and musical events; guest performers and groups frequently appear at UNC, and there's a professional repertory company that uses UNC faculty and outside talent to present plays. One student sums it up this way: "Anything you want to do, you can do here."

Students have good things to say about Chapel Hill itself, a "small town with big-city benefits." The main strip, Franklin Street, is lined with bars, cafes, eateries, and live music venues. And like many college towns, a student points out, "it's very progressive." Chapel Hill has become a new hot spot for alternative music. After sports, barhopping is perhaps students' favorite activity. Most UNC graduates agree, as students commonly remark, "it's the southern part of heaven."

UNIVERSITY OF TEXAS/Austin

Admissions Address: Admissions Office, Main Building, Room 7, Austin, TX 78712
Phone: (512) 475-7399
Web Address: www.utexas.edu/student/admissions

Like its home state, the University of Texas at Austin is big. How big, you wonder? About 30,000 undergraduates big. While the large size presents its challenges, it also means that UT has an incredible range of academic and social offerings, including hundreds of majors. And thanks to its high endowment, the school keeps its many resources in stellar condition. In terms of academics, just about anything a student might want to study can be found. The 11 undergraduate schools at UT include schools for business (one of the most popular programs), engineering, education, architecture, communications, biological sciences, and liberal arts. The academics are primarily the reason UT has attracted so many knowledgeable and acclaimed faculty members.

University of Texas/Austin

Setting: Urban
# of Undergraduates: 30,574
Men: 50.6% Women: 49.4%
In-State Tuition: $960
Out-of-State Tuition: $7,380
Room and Board: $3,901
# of Students Applied: 17,263
  Admitted: 10,517 Enrolled: 6,430
Required Admissions Test: Either SAT or ACT
Lowest 25% of Freshmen Scored At or Below: SAT Verbal: 540 SAT Math: 560 ACT Comp.: 22
Highest 25% of Freshmen Scored At or Above: SAT Verbal: 650 SAT Math: 670 ACT Comp.: 28
H.S. Rank, Top 10%: 44%
Top 25%: 79%
Top 50%: 96%
Avg. Score of Applicants Admitted: SAT Verbal: 601 SAT Math: 620 ACT Comp.: 25
Average GPA of Applicants Admitted: 2.70
Most Popular Majors (% of Student Body): Business (13.6%), Engineering (11.3%), Psychology (6.1%), Education (6%), Biology (4.8%)

The requirements vary according to the program, as does the workload. "Liberal arts students study about 4 to 5 hours a week, but engineering students study about 40 to 50 hours a week," an English major told us. The classes, not surprisingly, are often huge lectures; introductory-level classes will number several hundred students, and even upper-level classes can have close to one hundred. The school's size also means it can take some creativity, not to mention aggressive measures, to get into popular courses, to see professors, and to cut through the miles of red tape. Given the number of students they deal with, the professors are surprisingly accessible and generally receive praise from students for their efforts.

University housing can only hold a small percentage of the students; most find apartments close to campus or in downtown Austin. UT attracts such a wide range of types of people and offers so many activities and organizations that students inevitably find a niche for themselves. Within such a large student population, every type of culture, religion, political affiliation, and ethnic group is represented. Less than 10 percent of the student body hails from out of state. In terms of students' politics, one student reports, "Those who aren't apathetic are liberal. On the whole, the campus is quite liberal." In general, students are pretty tolerant and respectful of one another's differences.

There are just as many social offerings at UT as there are academic programs, including hundreds of organizations, clubs, and activities for just about any interest. Intercollegiate and intramural sports are extremely popular; UT's football and basketball teams are national powers, and games regularly draw crowds of adoring student fans. In addition to sports, cultural activities also thrive, from the many student groups who perform on campus to events in the Performing Arts Center, which brings in major music, dance, and theatrical productions on a regular basis. Many students join fraternities or sororities, which come with an instant and active social life, but there's no shortage of other social opportunities. The school traditions, such as drinking tea on the day when Texas won its independence, help foster a sense of community among students.

One of UT's major attractions, though, is the location. Austin is currently one of the more progressive, happening cities in the country that attracts a hip, young population. One student describes it as "an oasis in the desert of Texas, both politically and socially." In addition to the many bars, restaurants, and clubs students like to hang out in, Austin has scads of live music venues; going to scope out up-and-coming bands at local clubs is a major part of UT student life.

A favorite story around campus involves their sizeable endowment. When the Texas State Legislature established the state university system, they donated a sizeable amount of land in East Texas for future use. It soon became clear that this relatively lush area was too valuable as farm and pasture land, so the legislature exchanged it for a barren piece of property in West Texas. Of course oil was discovered not long after, and the University of Texas thrived.

If you're looking for a solid education in a vibrant environment at a bargain price, and you have the discipline to navigate your way through one of the country's biggest university bureaucracies, the University of Texas might be the perfect school for you.

UNIVERSITY OF VIRGINIA IN CHARLOTTESVILLE

Admissions Address: Office of Undergraduate Admission, P.O. Box 9017, Charlottesville, VA 22906
Phone: (804) 982-3200
Web Address: www.virginia.edu/

Considering how firmly Thomas Jefferson believed in education, it should come as no surprise that the school he founded is among the best in the nation. As its founder envisioned, the University of Virginia (UVA) continues to be a place where a solid education can be attained at an affordable price.

One of the clear benefits of attending a large school like UVA is the variety of academic programs, course offerings, and facilities made available to students. There are six undergraduate colleges at UVA, including acclaimed programs in architecture, engineering, and commerce, as well as schools for nursing and education. The College of Arts and Sciences continues to draw the most students; almost all departments are excellent, but English, history, and psychology in particular receive praise. Many students major in preprofessional fields, and high percentages of students go on to law or medical school.

In addition to traditional programs of study, UVA also offers students special academic options and innovative programs, including independent study, self-designed majors, dual majors, interdisciplinary studies, and several prestigious honors programs including the Echols Scholars program in which the top entering first-year students live and study together in an intense, student-driven academic program.

University of Virginia

$$
★★★★

Setting: Suburban
# of Undergraduates: 11,942
Men: 46.9% **Women:** 53.1%
In-State Tuition: $3,832
Out-of-State Tuition: $13,534
Room and Board: $3,962
# of Students Applied: 16,898
  Admitted: 5,650 **Enrolled:** 2,827
Required Admissions Test: Either SAT I or ACT required, SAT I preferred; SAT II required
Lowest 25% of Freshmen Scored At or Below: SAT Verbal: 590 SAT Math: 610 ACT Comp.: 23
Highest 25% of Freshmen Scored At or Above: SAT Verbal: 690 SAT Math: 710 ACT Comp.: 30
H.S. Rank, Top 10%: 79%
Top 25%: 96%
Top 50%: 99%
Avg. Score of Applicants Admitted: SAT Verbal: 660 SAT Math: 668 ACT Comp.: 28
Most Popular Majors (% of Student Body): Commerce (8.6%), Biology (7.1%), Psychology (6.2%), English (6%), History (4.3%)

UVA has relatively flexible area requirements designed to provide students with a broad liberal arts background. Students take courses across academic disciplines including the humanities, social science, mathematics, natural science, and composition, as well as several semesters of a foreign language. Because the requirements are easy to fill, students can devote substantial time to their chosen fields.

The downside to any big school is the overcrowding. Getting into popular courses at UVA can take some perseverance. While introductory classes tend to be very large, upper-level classes are much smaller, providing students with more interaction with professors and peers as well as a challenging, academic environment. "Once you get into the upper levels, there's great interaction with other students and with the professors," says one junior. Overall, students praise the attention they receive from their professors and advisors.

The expansive campus is picture-postcard beautiful and one that would make Thomas Jefferson, the accomplished agrarian, proud. Elements of his original design still stand, including several white-columned, colonial brick buildings and a majestic Rotunda, modeled on the Roman Pantheon. Students love studying and socializing on the Lawn, the central campus green.

The school's facilities are, for the most part, in prime condition. There are several well-stocked libraries, with open-stack policies for heavy studiers and areas conducive to socializing. Another main hangout is Newcomb Hall, which has a game room, movie theater, lounge, and offices for clubs and organizations. The North Ground Recreation Center provides superb sporting and exercise facilities.

While a number of older dormitories bear the same colonial style as the academic halls, recently built dorms have a much more modern look, with suite arrangements rather than single rooms. Housing is mandatory for all first-year students and guaranteed for all second years. About half the students move off campus, often to one of the many fraternity houses.

Because of its exceptional offerings, UVA is a very selective school, especially for out-of-state students. Those who do get in are highly qualified. About two-thirds of the students come from Virginia and many of the rest from the Northeast, although there are students from across the country and from more than 90 foreign countries.

Contrary to many people's perception of the school, there's not a lack of diversity on campus; the minority population currently stands at about 25 percent. While there's been a tradition of self-segregation between groups, students report that this situation seems to be improving. UVA tends to attract students who are conservative in their tastes and values, but there's also a vocal, if not very large, liberal population.

School spirit runs high at UVA, nowhere more so than at sporting events. UVA has a number of powerhouse teams that compete in the tough Atlantic Coast Conference; men's soccer and men's and women's basketball, as well as football, lacrosse, and swimming, have all done exceedingly well. Major sporting events draw crowds of student fans whose formal attire—one of many UVA traditions—doesn't prevent them from raucous cheering.

Dating back to the school's beginnings, UVA's many traditions, including calling one's professors Mr. and Ms. and describing the campus as "the grounds," also contribute to students' affection for their school. Instituted in 1842, the honor system, overseen by a student panel, is also an important part of UVA, fostering a deep commitment and respect among the campus community.

In addition to these many traditions, you'll hear students referring to the Wahoo, a legendary fish who can reportedly outdrink its body weight. The Wahoo is the ideal social role model at a school like UVA, where students are committed to the pursuit of happiness. Much of the partying revolves around the very active Greek system, which draws about 30 percent of the student population. While this percentage does not add up to a majority, some might feel pressure to join although many of the house parties are open to the entire campus. Students who aren't big partiers shouldn't be deterred. "There's no pressure to drink if you don't want to, even at frat parties."

One student complains that the Wahoo actually sends the wrong message: "UVA has a stigma that frat life is all there is on weekends. Actually, there's tons more to do." Indeed, those looking for fun beyond the Greeks can head to the Corner, a strip just off campus with bars, cafes, coffeehouses, and shops. Washington and Richmond, each two hours away, are popular weekend road trips.

On campus, the student-run University Union sponsors special events, movies, concerts, and socials. There are also over 300 clubs, organizations, and extracurricular activities, including newspapers and literary publications, performing groups, community service organizations, and an extensive intramural program.

"Don't be intimidated by UVA's size," advises one student. "It's really easy to dive into life here and find your niche. Because it's a big school, there's really something for everyone." With its solid academics, comfortable atmosphere, and beautiful setting, UVA continues to live up to the ideals of its founding father.

Also, Check Out These Schools:

University of California—Los Angeles
University of California—San Diego
University of Colorado—Boulder
Davidson
Florida State University
Georgia Institute of Technology
University of Illinois—Urbana/Champaign
Indiana University
Macalester College
Mary Washington College
University of Michigan—Ann Arbor
New College of the University of South Florida
Rhodes College
Rutgers University—New Brunswick
St. Olaf College
Southwestern University
SUNY—Albany
SUNY—Buffalo
SUNY—Stony Brook
Texas A&M University
University of Vermont
Wake Forest University
Washington and Lee

VALUE MARTS

Going to college has always been considered a costly venture. For a long time, it was a luxury only affordable for a privileged few. Today, costs continue to be astronomical, leading some parents to begin saving for their children's educations before they've even been conceived. However, as more and more people want—and even expect—to get a college degree, more schools have cropped up with affordable tuitions. At some, you can receive your entire education for less money than a single year at another school. And best of all, you can still get a great education even as you save money.

The best bargains around are often to be found at state-funded university systems, which usually have a number of strong academic programs and high-quality facilities. For in-state residents, the tuition will be exceptionally low, although even out-of-staters may find these schools to be bargains. If you want to save money, you should definitely consider your own state's university. State universities are usually quite expansive, offering a wide range of academic programs that meet the interests and needs of its residents. Some of them will have several campuses located throughout the state, which also differ in appearance and personality. Some campuses are major research centers, while others are considered "second-tier" because they mainly focus on preprofessional fields.

One thing to consider about attending publicly funded schools is the impact of budget cuts. Many states have been instituting severe budget cuts and have more planned in the future. This often means courses, programs, and services are cut, while tuition is raised. Nevertheless, when you compare the tuition with private universities and colleges, these schools remain a bargain.

Saving money does mean having to make some sacrifices. In many cases, less expensive tuition means less facilities and resources, or at least, ones of less outstanding quality. At the same time, though, you might also find some new, state-of-the-art facilities mixed among the more substandard ones. The same holds true for the faculty. Some of the schools hire fewer full-time faculty as a means of cutting costs, so you might not have the same kind of close attention from them as you would at other schools. At the same time, though, you might also find some exceptional teachers if you seek them out.

Keep in mind that if you're looking for savings, you don't necessarily need to limit yourself to schools with low tuitions. You can also investigate scholarship opportunities and the many forms of financial aid available. You might be able to receive enough funding to make many other schools affordable.

As you consider how to save money for your college education, remember that if the final product is damaged, it's no bargain, no matter how low the cost. We hope this chapter will show you that you can save money on tuition without having to sacrifice getting a good education.

COOPER UNION FOR THE ADVANCEMENT OF SCIENCE AND ART IN NEW YORK, NEW YORK

Admissions Address: Admissions Office, 30 Cooper Square, New York, NY 10003
Phone: (212) 353-4120
Web Address: www.cooper.edu

"We are the best-kept secret in New York, and maybe in the college world," said one Cooper Union student. And it's a wonder why. Cooper Union was recently named the number-one engineering school in American by *US News & World Report* (for schools not offering Ph.D. programs), and the last time a student refused admission after acceptance to the architecture school, Rutherford B. Hayes was President (it was 1879). And perhaps the most unbelievable part is: it's tuition free. There are fees, and room and board is expensive, but the overall bill is a fraction of what you'd pay anywhere else for what you receive.

This is not to say Cooper Union is a free ride. It's tough to get in, and it's tough to stay in. Cooper Union has three schools—Architecture, Art, and Engineering. The schools completely focus upon preparing students for professions in these areas. Students are immediately thrust into an intensive program that combines academic study with practical, hands-on projects. Don't even apply if you're unsure of what you want to do—the only flexibility you'll find is in the Engineering School, and there you can switch only to different disciplines of engineering. You have to know what you want and be ready to show you can do it to get into Cooper Union.

It doesn't get any easier upon acceptance. The workload is heavy, and students spend the bulk of their hours committed to school work and projects. Students at Cooper Union bond quickly though, in part because the workload is intense and support is needed, and in part because teamwork is encouraged by the faculty. "You won't make it through here unless you learn to work as a team. They tell you that from day one, and you find out quickly it's true," said one student. "There's no room here for arrogance or timidity. And, frankly, there's no room for it in these fields once you go on to the outside world. In a way, it's the best training."

While students work intensely with those in their program, they have little interaction with those in the other schools through their classes (socially is another matter). All students take a few required courses in humanities and social sciences, which serve as some of the only places in which students from the three schools intermingle. While the facilities of nearby NYU are available to Cooper students (such as the library, athletic center, and student center) cross-registration is an irregular arrangement. "Some semesters it's available, some not," said one student. About one-third of the students are minority students. Over half are from New York, mostly from the five boroughs.

Cooper Union doesn't have a campus so much as a cluster of four buildings, including their new dormitory. Housing is guaranteed only to freshmen, so after your first year you have to either hope there's space available or look for an apartment. Since the school is small, campus social offerings are limited, but students are allowed to participate in NYU's extracurricular activities, and, since getting the word out in the small community is easy, students are always starting their own groups. Cooper Union's location in the East Village, the funky downtown section of New York City, provides social opportunities by the thousand. In fact, Cooper Union students can find movies, restaurants, music clubs, galleries, bars, theaters, and shops within a few blocks of their own campus. St. Mark's Place, the heart of the East Village, is the "main street" of the Cooper Union "campus," and if you like exotic restaurants and shops, you're in luck. "There are 30 nationalities of restaurants in a two-block stretch," said one student.

Cooper Union

$$$
★★★★★

Setting: Urban
# of Undergraduates: 844
Men: 64.8% **Women:** 35.2%
Tuition: $8,300
Room and Board: $5,500
# of Students Applied: 1,962
  Admitted: 286 **Enrolled:** 178
Required Admissions Test: Either SAT or ACT; SAT II in Math, Physics, or Chem for Engineering
Lowest 25% of Freshmen Scored At or Below: SAT Verbal: 600 SAT Math: 700
Highest 25% of Freshmen Scored At or Above: SAT Verbal: 710 SAT Math: 760
H.S. Rank, Top 10%: 66%
Top 25%: 100%
Avg. Score of Applicants Admitted: SAT Verbal: 660 SAT Math: 740
Average GPA of Applicants Admitted: 3.40
Most Popular Majors (% of Student Body): Fine Arts (30%), Architecture (17%), Electrical Engineering (14%), Civil Engineering (13%), Mechanical Engineering (11%)

For a great education at a great price in a great location, Cooper Union is hard to beat. If you're ready for the commitment, willing to do the work, and able to see it through, it could be the perfect choice.

THE CITY UNIVERSITY OF NEW YORK (CUNY)

Like New York City itself, the City University of New York has a richly diverse student population made up of the many different cultural and ethnic groups that call New York City home and bring with them a significant range of academic and professional interests. CUNY's 17 schools, located throughout all five boroughs, meet these interests with a variety of academic offerings, ranging from strong liberal arts departments to more specific preprofessional programs to professional training—at a cost that's affordable for almost everyone.

Many of the schools in the CUNY system have excellent reputations. Accomplished academics and professionals in their fields who live in New York City often teach at these institutions. And graduates of CUNY range from Nobel laureates to published writers to entertainers.

The public higher education system run by the City of New York, CUNY was designed to provide higher education for virtually all New York residents who desire it at an affordable price. The system now includes several two-year community colleges as well as four-year colleges. Admissions standards are generally stricter for the four-year colleges, but also vary depending upon the specific college. The CUNY system offers special programs to help students who aren't yet up to college levels.

The various schools in the system differ in terms of their location, layout, and facilities. They range from the truly urban—a series of large buildings without a central campus—to more traditional campuses.

While each school has its specific academic strengths, almost all of them have core requirements that include basic courses within the arts and sciences; many also now require courses with a multicultural emphasis. Special academic options available at CUNY schools include dual majors, dual degrees, accelerated degrees, engineering co-op programs, internship programs, one-on-one faculty mentorship, cross-registration at other NYC schools, and honors programs.

Students at the different campuses have many common peeves. The biggest is about the administration: Like many city agencies, it's a large, inefficient bureaucracy and is the cause of endless frustration. But one recent alum said that in recent years the schools had become more sensitive to how difficult registration and other processes can be and had taken steps to improve. The quality of the facilities varies greatly: Some are state-of-the-art, like those in many of the media studies departments and education departments, others are genuinely substandard.

Teachers and professors are, for a large school, relatively accessible. All have office hours, and students report that teachers can be relied on to keep to those hours. Many report that instructors give out phone numbers where they can be reached on the first day of the term; some even give out their home numbers. Required classes are crowded, but as students work more into their majors, the classes get smaller and students get closer to their instructors. Budget cuts have also taken their toll, most notably evident in increasing class sizes.

Students are clear, though, about the advantages. A recent graduate told us, "The low tuition was amazing. I felt I got a good education, with a lot of options, and some great teachers. And I saved so much money." Another advantage to the schools, a student told us, is the diverse student population. "I like how there were so many groups of people who brought their viewpoints to the classes," she said.

CUNY students recently made the news when they participated in large-scale protests of proposed budget cuts—a major concern on all CUNY campuses because they threaten to raise tuition while cutting back on faculty and the programs available. The protests not only showed how CUNY students from all different backgrounds manage to bond together as a group for common concerns, but showed they could be effective as well—as a result of the protests, the city restored much of the CUNY budget, and tuition has stayed stable for the past three years.

Almost all of the CUNY schools are commuter schools. Only Hunter College has a residence hall. That means almost all of the students live off campus, and in fact, many continue to live at home because housing in New York City is so expensive. Many of the students have jobs, which means they don't hang out around campus that much. CUNY offers courses at night for the many students who have full-time jobs.

Being a commuter school does affect the social atmosphere. A majority of the students are there to receive their degrees and aren't particularly

---

VALUE MARTS

CUNY/Brooklyn College

$$

★

Setting: Urban
# of Undergraduates: 7,769
Men: 44% **Women:** 56%
In-State Tuition: $3,200
Out-of-State Tuition: $6,800
Room and Board: $1,800
# of Students Applied: 3,598
 Admitted: 2,984 **Enrolled:** 1,376
Recommended Admissions Test:
 Either SAT or ACT
H.S. Rank, Top 10%: 21%
Top 25%: 45%
Top 50%: 81%
Avg. Score of Applicants Admitted: SAT Verbal: 520
 SAT Math: 520

159

THE ROAD TO COLLEGE

CUNY/Hunter College

$$
\text{\$\$}
$$
★★★

Setting: Urban
# of Undergraduates: 8,834
Men: 28.3% **Women:** 71.7%
In-State Tuition: $3,200
Out-of-State Tuition: $6,800
Room and Board: $1,800
# of Students Applied: 6,126
  Admitted: 3,289 **Enrolled:** 1,605
Recommended Admissions Test: Either SAT or ACT
Lowest 25% of Freshmen Scored At or Below: SAT Verbal: 440 SAT Math: 450
Highest 25% of Freshmen Scored At or Above: SAT Verbal: 570 SAT Math: 560
H.S. Rank, Top 10%: 23%
Top 25%: 55%
Top 50%: 84%
Avg. Score of Applicants Admitted: SAT Verbal: 502 SAT Math: 504
Most Popular Majors (% of Student Body): Psychology (18%), Sociology (8%), English (7%), Accounting (6%), Media Studies (4%)

interested in socializing. People do, though, manage to meet one another in such common areas as student centers, study lounges, the libraries, or in one of the many clubs and organizations. While there may not be a central campus social scene, CUNY schools do offer many extracurricular activities and organizations, including intramural and intercollegiate sports teams, volunteer and community service work, student publications and media centers, and many academic, political, religious, and cultural clubs. Some have a few fraternities and sororities. Students are particularly pleased that they can take advantage of New York City's dizzying number of cultural and social venues.

The CUNY system offers a sound education, in some cases an excellent one, with a very Noo Yawk atmosphere. It's probably significant that Jerry Seinfeld—who now, more than anyone, conjures images of the New Yorker—is a CUNY graduate. Like Seinfeld himself, CUNY is virtually inseparable from the Big Apple.

BROOKLYN COLLEGE

Admissions Address: Admissions Office, 1602 James Hall, Brooklyn, NY 11210
Web Address: www.146.245.2.151

Less urban than some of its Manhattan counterparts, this CUNY school, located in the residential Midwood section of Brooklyn, is particularly strong in the preprofessional areas of premedicine, prelaw, and prebusiness. Departments related to these fields are among its best, including biology, chemistry, physics, history, English, and accounting. Its TV/radio program benefits from superb media facilities, and the music school is also highly regarded. While a commuter school, the many hangouts in the neighborhood, as well as the many extracurricular activities, provide the basis for a good social scene.

HUNTER COLLEGE

Admissions Address: Office of Undergraduate Admissions, 695 Park Avenue, New York, NY 10021
Phone: (212) 772-4492
Web Address: www.hunter.cuny.edu

Hunter originated as an all-female teacher's college, and while it is now coed, it remains 70 percent women. It is also 50 percent minority, reflecting the great diversity of the whole CUNY system. Hunter is the closest the CUNY system comes to a traditional liberal arts college, but its professional preparation programs are also excellent and a huge draw for many students. In addition to education, highly rated departments now include English, sciences, economics, urban planning, physical therapy, and social sciences. Premedicine and prelaw are popular majors, and Hunter students have high acceptance rates at graduate schools. Hunter is more competitive than most of the other CUNY schools and has more non-New York residents than most. The main campus is in the affluent Upper East Side of Manhattan, while the downtown campus, primarily for health sciences and nursing, is the site of the only residence hall in the CUNY system, which houses a very small percentage of the students.

QUEENS COLLEGE

Admissions Address: Admissions Office, 65-30 Kissena Boulevard, Flushing, NY 11367
Web Address: www.cuny.edu

Queens College, along with Hunter, has been ranked the highest by *U.S. News & World Report's* College Guide of all the CUNY schools. Its many well-regarded academic programs include anthropology, biology, business, chemistry, computer science, economics, education, and psychology. Queens has a more traditional college campus, with stately academic buildings arranged around a large central quad with a breathtaking view of the Manhattan skyline. The school also has more of an active social scene than many of the others, due to the hundreds of popular clubs and organizations. Free hours during the week, when there are no classes scheduled, enable clubs to meet and students to linger on campus socializing rather than returning home after class.

CUNY/Queens College

$$
★

Setting: Urban
# of Undergraduates: 14,000
Men: 40% **Women:** 60%
In-State Tuition: $3,200
Out-of-State Tuition: $6,800
Room and Board: $1,800
# of Students Applied: 4,633
  Admitted: 3,734   Enrolled: 1,834
Recommended Admissions Test:
  Either SAT or ACT
Avg. Score of Applicants Admitted: SAT Verbal: 450
  SAT Math: 450
Average GPA of Applicants Admitted: 2.84

Service Academies

United States Air Force Academy
in Colorado Springs, Colorado

HQ USAFA/RRS, 2304 Cadet Drive, Suite 200, Colorado Springs, CO 80840-5025
Phone: (719) 333-2520
Web Address: www.usafa.af.mil

United States Coast Guard Academy
in New London, Connecticut

Admissions Address: Admissions Office, 15 Mohegan Avenue, New London, CT 06320-4195
Phone: (860) 444-8501 (800) 883-8724
Web Address: www.dot.gov/dotinfo/uscg

United States Military Academy
in West Point, New York

Admissions Address: Admissions Office, West Point, NY 10996-1797
Phone: (914) 938-4041
Web Address: www.usma.edu/

United States Naval Academy
in Annapolis, Maryland

Admissions Address: Admissions Office, 117 Decatur Road, Annapolis, MD 21402-5017
Phone: (410) 293-4361
Web Address: www.nadn.navy.mil

When one looks at the education received for the price paid (it's free), there could be no bigger college bargain than the service academies of the United States. It is such a good bargain, it's ridiculous. It's so ridiculous, that there has to be a whopper of a catch.

There is. You get your diploma, you belong to the armed services for six years.

Most cadets at the four service academies didn't go there for the free education. The military obligation, the strict admissions standards, the rigorous academic, physical, and mental requirements can all make you forget you're going for free in a hurry. As one cadet said, "I'm at West Point because I always wanted to go to West Point."

United States Air Force Academy

★★★★★

Setting: Suburban
# of Undergraduates: 4,083
Men: 84.2% Women: 15.8%
Tuition: $0
# of Students Applied: 9,165
   Admitted: 1,616   Enrolled: 1,239
Required Admissions Test: Either SAT or ACT
Recommended: PSAT
Lowest 25% of Freshmen Scored
   At or Below: SAT Verbal: 580
   SAT Math: 610
Highest 25% of Freshmen
   Scored At or Above: SAT
   Verbal: 670 SAT Math: 690
Avg. Score of Applicants
   Admitted: SAT Verbal: 626
   SAT Math: 649

VALUE MARTS

The service academies will give you an exceptional, highly respected education—cost free. You, then, are committed to six years of post-graduation service. But you will start with certain significant advantages. After graduating from a military academy, you're given officer status in whatever military branch your academy has trained you to enter. Since the commitment is a long one, prospective students are advised to consider their desired form of service carefully before choosing an academy.

Because these academies are devoted to training cadets to eventually serve as officers, they are highly selective in their admissions standards. To get in, an applicant must be nominated by a member of Congress or meet some other narrow requirements for consideration (for example, a parent's having been awarded the Congressional Medal of Honor). There are also rigorous academic requirements—SAT/ACT scores are quite high—and extensive physical testing. Students who are accepted by the service academies are therefore highly intelligent and have the stamina for both the physical and intellectual challenges that await them.

All of these academies have beautiful campuses, superb facilities, and highly qualified faculties, as well as strong academic programs in many fields. At almost all of them, their best programs are in engineering. However, many other departments are also excellent, particularly in the natural sciences. The political science, history, and government studies departments at all the academies are some of the best in the nation.

Generally, a cadet's first two years are geared toward fulfilling core requirements that often include engineering and computer courses, as well as specific training for the particular branch of the military. The cadet's year begins on July 4, and from the minute you arrive, you're in the service. Summer is when cadets receive their military training. The first-year cadets receive basic training, the same basic training that all soldiers get in boot camp. The grueling basic training is designed to get cadets into prime physical shape.

There are other challenges to your first year. A first-year cadet is given the rank of cadet fourth class, and to upperclassmen there is no lower creature on Earth than a cadet fourth class. At West Point, for example, cadets fourth class are at the beck and call of the cadets first class. This system is encouraged by the administration as a way of orienting new cadets to military life, and while there are occasional abuses, this system usually works. "You have to remember when you were a plebe (cadet fourth class), and it gives you a level of compassion," said a West Point

---

United States Coast Guard Academy

★★★★

Setting: urban
# of Undergraduates: 827
Men: 72.3% **Women:** 27.7%
Tuition: $0
Room and Board: $0
# of Students Applied: 2,511
   Admitted: 537 **Enrolled:** 292
Required Admissions Test: Either SAT I or ACT
Lowest 25% of Freshmen Scored At or Below: SAT Verbal: 510 SAT Math: 600 ACT Comp.: 25
Highest 25% of Freshmen Scored At or Above: SAT Verbal: 600 SAT Math: 680 ACT Comp.: 28
H.S. Rank, Top 10%: 56%
Top 25%: 85%
Top 50%: 100%
Avg. Score of Applicants Admitted: SAT Verbal: 614 SAT Math: 643 ACT Comp.: 26
Average GPA of Applicants Admitted: 3.70
Most Popular Majors (% of Student Body): Management (21%), Marine Science (18%), Government (17%), Naval Architecture and Marine Engineering (11%), Electrical Engineering (10%)

THE ROAD TO COLLEGE

United States Military Academy

★★★★★

Setting: Rural
# of Undergraduates: 4,005
Men: 86.9% Women: 13.1%
# of Students Applied: 12,886
Admitted: 1,566 Enrolled: 1,187
Required Admissions Test: Either SAT or ACT
Lowest 25% of Freshmen Scored At or Below: SAT Verbal: 560 SAT Math: 590 ACT Comp.: 26
Highest 25% of Freshmen Scored At or Above: SAT Verbal: 670 SAT Math: 690 ACT Comp.: 30
H.S. Rank, Top 10%: 56%
Top 25%: 86%
Top 50%: 98%
Avg. Score of Applicants Admitted: SAT Verbal: 624 SAT Math: 649 ACT Comp.: 28
Most Popular Majors (% of Student Body): Systems Engineering (4%), Political Science (4%), Modern History (3.5%), Foreign Language (3.4%), Civil Engineering (3.3%)

upperclassman. "By the time you're a cadet first class you know and believe in the system, and you're less likely to abuse it."

It does get better as you move from year to year. Academically, cadets can move into the majors or areas of concentration after their second year. The military training also gets more specialized and advanced. When they get to be upperclassmen, their summer military training may involve travel to military bases around the world.

The class sizes at these schools are generally kept at a minimum, and the faculty is highly attentive to their students. Faculty members remain on campus for extended periods of time (many are military personnel and live on the campus with their families) and are readily available for guidance. A large portion of each day is devoted to rigorous physical training and exercise. Cadets are regularly tested to ensure they remain in prime physical condition.

Military academies put students on strict regimens from the minute they arrive. Students who need discipline to keep them on track will find it in abundance at these schools. Each day is carefully scheduled, with set hours for classes, physical exercise, extracurricular activities, and study time.

Cadets are usually put into some kind of group, referred to by various names depending on the military branch, such as squadron or company. This group often forms a smaller, closely knit social unit within the academy. The dorm rooms are generally basic doubles, and all of the cadets eat together. Attendance at breakfast and lunch is usually mandatory, though dinner might be more informal. The schools reward the hard physical labor with decent and plentiful food.

Much of a cadet's day is devoted to academic and military exercises, which does limit the social opportunities. Athletics and sports are the primary form of extracurricular activity, largely because exercise is a required part of the program. Intramural and intercollegiate sports enable cadets to get physical activity while enjoying themselves. You probably won't find games at other schools as well attended as at military academies because attendance is strongly encouraged. Games provide cadets the chance to voice their pride in both their school and their military branch. There are other forms of extracurricular activity, including debate and language groups, radio stations, and newspapers.

As in the military, cadets gain privileges as they change rank from their first year to their last (moving from being a cadet fourth class to first class), privileges that include wearing civilian clothing occasionally, and the opportunity to leave the campus during the evenings and weekends.

You shouldn't attend a military academy solely for the tuition break. It's a tough go while you're in school, and that's before the required six-year commitment following graduation. If you're not truly interested in gaining this kind of specific military training and then serving, then you probably won't be able to complete the workload. However, if you do want to serve in the military, and you have the stamina and qualifications, you'll be hard pressed to find a better education at this price.

THE STATE UNIVERSITY OF NEW YORK (SUNY)

The State University of New York, known as SUNY, is the largest university system in the world, providing high-quality education and facilities at an exceptionally low tuition, particularly for New York residents. With more than 60 campuses located around the state, the academic offerings run the gamut, from traditional liberal arts to preprofessional programs to career training. Some campuses are full-fledged universities with many choices, while others are smaller, specialty school with tighter focuses, such as health career training or the performing arts. As the schools differ, so do admission requirements, school style, size, layout, and personality. Many of the schools have highly respected academic reputations.

The student populations at most of these schools include a healthy ethnic and cultural mix, if not a geographic one. Almost all students come from New York state, as the tuition is significantly lower for New York residents. In years past, there was much concern about the effects of state budget cuts on tuition and programs. That seems to have passed, but as with any public school, state funding can blow with the political winds. However, tuition has remained stable, and the low tuition, particularly for New York state residents, still remains a great deal. We've profiled a few SUNY schools to give an indication of their range, but if you're a New Yorker, you will want to investigate the others as well.

Three SUNY schools are profiled in this section, and a profile of SUNY/Binghamton appears in the Budget Ivies section.

United States Naval Academy

$
★★★★★

Setting: Small town
# of Undergraduates: 4,042
Men: 85.4% **Women:** 14.6%
Tuition: $0
# of Students Applied: 9,965
  Admitted: 1,537 **Enrolled:** 1,213
Required Admissions Test: Either SAT or ACT
Lowest 25% of Freshmen Scored At or Below: SAT Verbal: 500 SAT Math: 600
Highest 25% of Freshmen Scored At or Above: SAT Verbal: 620 SAT Math: 700
H.S. Rank, Top 10%: 61%
Top 25%: 85%
Top 50%: 99%
Avg. Score of Applicants Admitted: SAT Verbal: 627 SAT Math: 653
Most Popular Majors (% of Student Body): Systems Engineering (10%), Political Science (10%), Economics (10%), Mechanical Engineering (8%), Oceanography (8%)

SUNY/ALBANY

Admissions Address: Admissions Office, 1400 Washington Avenue, Albany, NY 12222
Phone: (518) 442-5435
Web Address: www.albany.edu/

SUNY/Albany

$$
★★

Setting: Suburban
# of Undergraduates: 9,455
Men: 51.8% Women: 48.2%
In-State Tuition: $3,400
Out-of-State Tuition: $8,300
Room and Board: $5,241
# of Students Applied: 13,678
  Admitted: 8,922   Enrolled: 2,007
Required Admissions Test: either SAT or ACT
Lowest 25% of Freshmen Scored At or Below: SAT Verbal: 500 SAT Math: 510
Highest 25% of Freshmen Scored At or Above: SAT Verbal: 600 SAT Math: 610
H.S. Rank, Top 10%: 13%
Top 25%: 47%
Top 50%: 89%
Avg. Score of Applicants Admitted: SAT Verbal: 552 SAT Math: 562
Most Popular Majors (% of Student Body): English (7%), Psychology (6%), Business Administration (5%), Biology (5%), Sociology (4%)

One of the largest schools within the acclaimed New York state system, SUNY—Albany offers students a variety of academic choices and social opportunities. Within the five undergraduate schools, students can find many different academic programs, including some that are considered the best in the SUNY system.

The business school is generally thought of as Albany's star attraction, and graduates regularly get accepted to top firms. Most Albany students major in accounting or business administration. If you know you want to major in business when you enter as a freshman, you can be admitted directly into the business school. But students who are undecided when they enter and later decide they want to major in business must apply to the business school after their second year. The competition to get in is pretty intense, and students set on careers in business might be disappointed if they don't get accepted and have to search for a new concentration. There are many other strong departments, including English, government, and psychology. The core curriculum includes courses in natural science, social science, fine arts and literature, symbolics, as well as world cultures and writing skills.

As with other large state schools, most freshman-level classes are huge, though they get considerably smaller as you work into your major. The faculty members all have excellent credentials (there are Pulitzer Prize winners on staff, including novelist William Kennedy), but may take some tracking down if you need or want individual instruction. Once you find them, though, most students report that they are helpful, friendly, and concerned.

The main campus is essentially a large quadrangle, with the four dormitories, known as quads, at each corner and the academic buildings in between. Mostly made of concrete, it isn't exactly pretty, but it's certainly functional, as students can easily get from their rooms to class and back. If students are somewhat negative about their campus, they do like the enormous podium and fountain at its center, which provides optimal hanging-out space in a central location. The downtown campus has more traditional collegiate, red-brick residence halls. Because Albany is a large school, the social life tends to be fractured. Students socialize with people in their suites and halls, or with groups sharing common interests.

VALUE MARTS

They all enjoy an active social scene, attending fraternity parties, dormitory parties, or heading to off-campus bars and hangouts. The Greek system attracts about 15 percent of both men and women, and enough extracurricular activities, clubs, and organizations so that students can find just about anything that interests them. Students also benefit from being in Albany, New York's state capital. In addition to providing many internships, particularly for students in government and politics, there's a not insignificant amount of cultural and social opportunities.

SUNY/UNIVERSITY AT BUFFALO

Admissions Address: Admissions Office, 17 Capon Hall, Buffalo, NY 14260
Phone: (716) 645-6411
Web Address: www.buffalo.edu

Buffalo is the largest school in the SUNY system, comprising 11 undergraduate colleges and awarding the largest number of bachelor's degrees of any school in the state. Like any large school, Buffalo's size presents some inherent problems, such as enormous introductory classes, difficulty getting into popular courses, frustrating registration and administrative procedures, and red tape. Recently, though, the administration has helped this problem by installing a telephone registration system. Student we talked to rave about it. "It really makes things easier—it works well and is easy to use. Most students love it!"

The advantage to the school's size, though, is the wealth of academic and social choices. Business, engineering, and premedicine majors are among the school's more well-known and popular programs. Buffalo also has a range of strong liberal arts departments as well as more specific preprofessional training programs, such as its acclaimed programs in physical therapy and architecture. There are many special academic options as well, including internships, accelerated and dual degrees, an honors program, and opportunities for off-campus study.

General education requirements include courses in math and computer science, literature, writing, social sciences, and natural sciences. Graduate TAs teach a lot of these courses, but the students seem satisfied with them. "They teach well and work with the students well," said one student. The school, divided between two campuses, features many modern buildings. Buffalo has added several impressive new buildings and facilities in recent years, including a fine-arts center, sports stadium, and science and math buildings.

SUNY/Buffalo

$$

★★

Setting: Suburban
# of Undergraduates: 13,234
Men: 55.7% Women: 44.3%
In-State Tuition: $3,400
Out-of-State Tuition: $8,300
Room and Board: $5,454
# of Students Applied: 14,100
  Admitted: 9,975 Enrolled: 2,545
Required Admissions Test: either SAT or ACT
Lowest 25% of Freshmen Scored At or Below: SAT Verbal: 500 SAT Math: 520 ACT Comp.: 21
Highest 25% of Freshmen Scored At or Above: SAT Verbal: 600 SAT Math: 630 ACT Comp.: 26
H.S. Rank, Top 10%: 22%
Top 25%: 58%
Top 50%: 97%
Avg. Score of Applicants Admitted: SAT Verbal: 560 SAT Math: 583 ACT Comp.: 24
Average GPA of Applicants Admitted: 3.20
Most Popular Majors: Business Administration, Interdisciplinary/Social Sciences, Psychology, Health Professions, Engineering

The social options at Buffalo are as plentiful and varied as the academic ones. While Buffalo winters are notorious for subzero temperatures, lots of snow and winds whipping off both Lake Erie and Lake Ontario, the school makes a lot of accommodations to the climate. All the buildings are connected by either tunnels or covered bridges, or both. "I never have to go outside to get to class or to another dorm in the winter," said one student. The many social options also help. There are clubs and organizations to meet just about any kind of political or social interest, and the Greek system attracts a number of students. Intramural and intercollegiate sports are both popular and benefit from an enormous sports center. Becoming involved in one of these groups or with an extracurricular activity is one strategy for making the larger university feel a bit smaller.

The city of Buffalo also offers a number of social venues, including several popular bars and hangouts off campus, some shopping, and Buffalo Bills football. Students also rave about the Buffalo theater district, which draws many Broadway shows either in previews or on tour. "You'd be really surprised how good it is," said one student. "Buffalo students love it." Buffalo students also enjoy the city's major claim to fame—eating buckets full of the best wings you'll ever taste.

SUNY/STONY BROOK

Admissions Address: Admissions Office, Stony Brook, NY 11794
Phone: (516) 632-6866
Web Address: www.sunysb.edu/

Because of its top-notch facilities and resources as well as its distinguished faculty, Stony Brook is known primarily as a research institution with particular strengths in the sciences, engineering, and health professions. Most undergraduates, including a high percentage of premed students, major in these fields. Undergraduates benefit from Stony Brook's prominent university hospital and research center, which provides students with research opportunities and practical experience. At the same time, a number of nonscience programs are also considered quite good, ranging from the social sciences, such as psychology, to artistic pursuits such as theater and music.

The Diversified Education Curriculum ensures that all students receive a broad liberal arts background before specializing. Students are required to take courses in 11 general areas, including quantitative rea-

---

SUNY/Stony Brook

🏛🏛🏛
$$
★★★

Setting: Suburban
# of Undergraduates: 9,839
Men: 49.2% **Women:** 50.8%
In-State Tuition: $3,400
Out-of-State Tuition: $8,300
Room and Board: $5,594
# of Students Applied: 12,725
  Admitted: 7,433 Enrolled: 1,770
Required Admissions Test: SAT, SAT II (writing, mathematics, area of choice)
Lowest 25% of Freshmen Scored At or Below: SAT Verbal: 385 SAT Math: 475
Highest 25% of Freshmen Scored At or Above: SAT Verbal: 500 SAT Math: 610
H.S. Rank, Top 10%: 23%
Top 25%: 63%
Top 50%: 95%
Avg. Score of Applicants Admitted: SAT Verbal: 456 SAT Math: 549
Average GPA of Applicants Admitted: 2.96
Most Popular Majors (% of Student Body): Psychology (15%), Biology (6%), Business (6%), English (6%), Biochemistry (6%)

soning, literature, philosophy, fine arts, science and society, and several multidisciplinary and multicultural courses. Special academic options include an honors program, study abroad, internships, and programs designed to provide students with closer interaction with faculty members. One such program has students taking several courses on a common theme with the same professors. Many faculty members are highly committed to their own research. While this doesn't make them the most committed teachers, it does provide students with the opportunity to study and work with experienced researchers. Because Stony Brook does have a large enrollment, many classes are big lectures, particularly in introductory levels and in the sciences. Students who want help or attention from professors will most likely have to seek them out.

About half the students live on campus, while the other half are Long Island residents who commute from home. While the majority of the students come from New York, Stony Brook has a number of international students. The student body also includes a significant minority population, including a particularly large percentage of Asian American students. For students who live on campus, the dormitory, known as one's "college," often forms a center for making friends and socializing. But there are also clubs and organizations for every interest; as one student said, "there's lots and lots to do." Students and administration encourage involvement with the clubs. Every student belongs to at least one, and many start their own. "They make it easy for you," said one student. "Locations are convenient, and schedules are set up in a way that makes it easy to budget your time." Intramural and intercollegiate sports are both becoming more popular as the school has been investing more in its athletic facilities and programs. On weekends, many students head to off-campus dance clubs and bars, but the campus is the social center. "This school used to be a ghost town on weekends," said one student, "but now it's different. The school is always holding dances, mixers, parties, starting on Wednesday and going through to Sunday afternoon." Students can also head for nearby beaches or take the hour-long train trip to New York City.

If there's one pet peeve students have with Stony Brook, it's with cliques. "We have great diversity, but the groups all tend to stick together. If you're from Brooklyn, you hang out with Brooklyn people, if you're from the Five Towns, you're going to be with other people from the island." Students who take it upon themselves to mingle, though, tend to be welcome. "You have to make the effort, though," said one student.

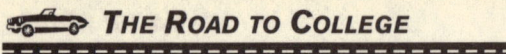

TEXAS A&M UNIVERSITY IN COLLEGE STATION

Admissions Address: Office of Admissions and Records, Texas A&M University, College Station, TX 77843-1265
Phone: (409) 845-3741
Web Address: www.tamu.edu

Texas A&M University

Setting: Suburban
# of Undergraduates: 31,914
Men: 53.6% Women: 46.4
In-State Tuition: $960
Out-of-State Tuition: $7,380
Room and Board: $3,933
# of Students Applied: 15,973
   Admitted: 11,023   Enrolled: 6,387
Required Admissions Test: Either SAT or ACT
Lowest 25% of Freshmen Scored At or Below: SAT Verbal: 520
   SAT Math: 550   ACT Comp.: 23
Highest 25% of Freshmen Scored At or Above: SAT Verbal: 630   SAT Math: 660
   ACT Comp.: 28
H.S. Rank, Top 10%: 47%
Top 25%: 83%
Top 50%: 98%
Avg. Score of Applicants Admitted: SAT Verbal: 578
   SAT Math: 606   ACT Comp.: 25
Most Popular Majors (% of Student Body): Biomed (6.7%), Psychology (3%), Accounting (2.4%), Interdisciplinary (2.4%), Animal Science (2.3%)

It's hard to think of a school with over 40,000 students as homey and comfy, but by all reports, that's exactly what Texas A&M is. To understand this, you have to know the history of the place.

Texas A&M started out as a farmer's school and military academy. Until the late '60s and early '70s, the school was small. Then, when the military requirement was made optional, enrollment increased. The administration at the time then decided to expand the school. Because it was, and is, one of the best values in higher education, the school boomed to its present size. But it never lost its small-campus feeling, even with today's huge enrollment. It is still a great atmosphere that owes more to the Texas hospitality than a huge state school. Despite its size, the student body manages to form a pretty tight community, and it's largely the result of their extraordinary school pride.

Texas A&M is particularly known for its programs in agricultural sciences and engineering. All science and technology courses are good and have large enrollments. The business school is also excellent and draws a substantial number of students. Because of its acclaimed school of Veterinary Medicine, the preveterinary departments are also highly rated. The core curriculum provides students with a broad liberal arts background. Students take required courses in American and Texan history, computers, speech and writing skills, math/logical reasoning, science, social science, humanities, physical education, and foreign language.

Given the school's size, the administration and registration procedures aren't nearly as horrendous as one might expect. Nevertheless class sizes, especially at introductory levels, often number in the hundreds (classes of 300 or more are not uncommon at the freshman levels). They do get significantly smaller once you start working into your major. But, obviously, students aren't necessarily going to have professors who know them by name. TAs teach a number of classes and their teaching abilities vary, depending on their prior experience. There are, however, many professors and TAs whom students like quite a bit; the trick is trying to find them. Asking around for tips on courses and professors is a smart strategy. Students in the honors program study in much smaller classes that provide more interaction with the professors.

VALUE MARTS

To accommodate all those students, the campus is equally enormous, the largest in the nation. With mostly modern buildings, the campus functions like a small city. The facilities are generally in good condition, particularly for the sciences. The school has a hefty endowment (thanks in large part to many wealthy alumni making donations), a large portion of which goes to constructing and expanding facilities. Only about 30 percent of the students are able to live in university housing, but there is no shortage of affordable student apartments off campus. There's a university shuttle bus that gets people around the campus, and it is safe, reliable, and fun according to the students we talked to. There's also a brand-new, state-of-the-art athletic center on campus, as well as a new special events center for marquee basketball games, concerts, and other large gatherings.

Most of the students are Texas natives, although the student body also includes people from all 50 states and more than 100 foreign countries. Students tend to cover the political spectrum—remember, there's a veritable army of undergraduates, so you'll get some of everything. But remember, too, that this is Texas, and liberal and conservative may not mean what they mean at an East Coast school.

A tremendous school pride helps unite this enormous student body, especially when it comes to intercollegiate sports. The intercollegiate teams, particularly in basketball, baseball, and football, are followed with fanatic devotion by students. Large numbers crowd the games and launch into carefully choreographed school cheers. Texas A&M is a school rich in traditions, many of which revolve around the sporting events. One of the biggest events of the year is the supersized bonfire before the football game against in-state archrival, the University of Texas. When students aren't attending intercollegiate games, chances are they're playing intramural games. Texas A&M has an excellent and extensive intramural program, with hundreds of teams competing in sports of all kinds.

Although most students share an interest in sports, other extracurricular and social activities are popular. There are about 700 clubs and organizations, as well as a few hundred social and cultural events each year, to keep students entertained. The Greek system attracts about 10 percent of the students. The Corps of Cadets, a prestigious military training group well known on the Texas A&M campus that traces its roots to the school's early days as a military academy, also draws students. When it comes to the campus social scene, parties and social events come in droves. Many students head for off-campus bars and dance clubs. College Station, as you might guess from its name, is a city that caters to the school and has street after street of shops, restaurants, and cafes popular among students. In the unlikely event that they tire of the campus and surrounding areas, students can take road trips to Houston, Austin, and Dallas.

THE UNIVERSITY OF CALIFORNIA

The nine campuses of the University of California system are as diverse as California itself. At how many places can you go to the beach and get a great tan, then go to the mountains for world-class skiing—in the same week? And how many college systems allow you to study everything from viticulture in the heart of the wine country to marine biology near the depths of the Pacific.

UC runs the gamut, from traditional arts and sciences departments to preprofessional programs to more unusual academic offerings. Each school has it strong suit, for which it is well known. Campuses also differ markedly in atmosphere, from the laid-back attitude at San Diego to the academically intense Berkeley. Likewise, admissions standards also vary and, depending on the campus and the course of study chosen, can be quite competitive.

Like most publicly funded schools in the country, UC has been subject to the political rumbles of budget cuts and subsequent tuition hikes and program cutbacks. But all of the students we talked to said that despite some belt tightening at the state level a few years back, there has been no noticeable difference at most of the campuses. "We've been able to weather the storm pretty well," said one UC student, but, as always when politicians are concerned, stay tuned. Nonetheless, UC continues to offer students strong academic programs and high-quality facilities at a comparatively low tuition.

While the UC schools have a reputation for being research oriented at the expense of undergraduates, most we talked to felt the exact opposite was true. Depending on the school you attend, faculty can be attentive, accessible, and in many cases, willing to include the undergraduates in their research, an invaluable learning experience that is unusual for school of the UC caliber. And students have access to cutting-edge facilities and resources. Several of the campuses have very large enrollments, which can present challenges, including large introductory classes and messy registration procedures (though telephone registration is gaining widespread use throughout the system).

Profiles of UC's **Davis, San Diego,** and **Santa Cruz** campuses appear in this section. There are also UC profiles in the following sections:

Berkeley: Budget Ivies

Santa Barbara: Serious Fun

Los Angeles: Sports Powerhouses

Most UC students are California natives. However, a number of out-of-staters and international students enroll either in the better-known schools or for special, hard-to-find programs such as viticulture and marine biology. While not geographically diverse, most of the schools have a healthy cultural and ethnic mix, including large populations of Asian American and Hispanic students. The students generally enjoy an active and highly varied social life since the schools have hundreds of clubs, organizations, and extracurricular activities that reflect their diverse experiences and interests. Many students also take advantage of their school's surrounding regions, whether to check out the city lights or to head for California's spectacular beaches and mountains.

UNIVERSITY OF CALIFORNIA/DAVIS

Admissions Address: Admissions Office, Davis, CA 95616-8678
Phone: (916) 752-2971 (916) 752-4840
Web Address: www.ucdavis.edu/

The third-largest school in the UC system, Davis is one of the top research institutions in the nation, with many unique programs. One student we talked to was majoring in viticulture, the science and art of wine production. It's one of only two schools in the country offering this major, and it's location in the heart of the beautiful California wine country makes it the American mecca for this science. UC is known for offering unusual programs that take advantage of California's diversity and geography.

While originally an agricultural school, Davis also has a full slate of academic offerings, including psychology, English, international studies, and political science. But the strongest programs are in the sciences, such as biology, biochemistry, and agriculture, and engineering.

While requirements vary considerably depending upon the program, the general curriculum includes courses in the areas of civilization and culture, contemporary societies, and nature and the environment. The workload in many of these programs is pretty intense. Davis is on a quarter system, which means students have more examinations and more frequent due dates for assignments, creating some additional stress. Faculty members are very involved with research, but they find the time to be accessible and attentive to the undergraduate, by all reports. The beautiful campus is expansive and, as one student said, "better than it looks when you drive by—you have to really ride around to see how beautiful

---

University of California/Davis

$$$
★★

Setting: Suburban
# of Undergraduates: 10,697
Men: 73.8% **Women:** 82.7
In-State Tuition: $4,230
Out-of-State Tuition: $8,394
Room and Board: $5,468
# of Students Applied: 18,587
  Admitted: 13,659 **Enrolled:** 3,697
Required Admissions Test: Either SAT or ACT
Lowest 25% of Freshmen Scored At or Below: SAT Verbal: 503 SAT Math: 545 ACT Comp.: 21
Highest 25% of Freshmen Scored At or Above: SAT Verbal: 620 SAT Math: 680 ACT Comp.: 26
H.S. Rank, Top 10%: 95%
Top 25%: 100%
Top 50%: 100%
Avg. Score of Applicants Admitted: SAT Verbal: 589 SAT Math: 622 ACT Comp.: 25
Average GPA of Applicants Admitted: 8.79
Most Popular Majors (% of Student Body): Biological Sciences (8.9%), Biochemistry (4.9%), Psychology (3.7%), Computer Science (3.5%), Human Development (2.9%)

it is." Most students do this by bicycle, in part out of concern for the environment, but mostly, as one student said, "jut because it's the easiest way to get around."

The social scene at Davis is active but laid-back, with lots of on-campus activities to keep students busy, including the popular Whole Earth Festival and various cultural festivals. Davis itself is a pretty, quiet town ("almost too quiet" said one student) that does have its share of restaurants, movie theaters, and student hangouts. Students who have access to a car can also make the hour-long trip to San Francisco for more cultural and social options. The beaches and mountains are also an option, albeit distant ones.

While most students are politically aware and tend to be liberal, the relaxed attitude of the student body prevails over any political passions. As a way to make the larger university feel smaller, many Davis students become active in the numerous clubs, organizations, and extracurricular activities. Most of the time, though, students are more than happy with the peace and quiet of their own idyllic campus.

UNIVERSITY OF CALIFORNIA/SAN DIEGO

Admissions Address: Office of Admissions and Outreach, 9500 Gilman Drive, Dept. 0337, La Jolla, CA 92093-0337
Phone: (619) 534-4831
Web Address: www.admissions.ucsd.edu/

"Oxford on the Pacific"—that's the model UCSD sets for itself. While Oxford never saw this much sunshine in all its years (not to mention palm trees), the British university is the model for UCSD's academic structure. The university is actually made up of five colleges, each with its own requirements, curriculum, academic emphasis, and character. The colleges enable students to experience a more intimate academic community in which they form tight circles of friends and colleagues, even though they're part of a large research institution. And it works, by all reports.

UCSD is known as an exceptional research institution, particularly strong in the sciences and engineering. The faculty, which includes several Nobel laureates, are accomplished scientists and researchers. While some students reported that this high-powered faculty does not necessarily correlate to teaching excellence, others disagree (and disagree strongly). Many students enjoy having the opportunity to work with accomplished faculty members on research, and the difference of opinion regarding teaching quality depend on whether or not students put in the necessary time and effort to sniff out the premiere teachers. UCSD students consider themselves serious academics, scientists, and researchers, and their work proves it. A high percentage go on to earn Ph.Ds or attend medical school. In addition to the sciences, academics are strong in most areas, from the humanities to social science to the arts. The UCSD campus is also home of the renowned Scripps Institute of Oceanography. Core requirements vary according to the college.

When students aren't studying or conducting research, they can enjoy a variety of social activities. For students who live on campus, their college often serves as a focal point for meeting people. At the same time, there are well over 200 clubs, organizations, and activities that students can become involved with. The Greek system attracts about 10 percent of the students, about half of what it was in the past, so it is not a tremendous social focus.

The college's beautiful location makes it ideal for participating in various outdoor sports and activities. San Diego has temperate weather year-round, and UCSD students know how to enjoy—and even worship—the sun. One of the major campus festivals each year is devoted to the Sun God, whose statue graces the campus. Whether just lying about the campus or participating in recreational activities and sports, from biking and jogging to volleyball, UCSD students enjoy being outside.

UCSD is in La Jolla, which, while being one of the world's most well-known beach resort towns, is "not a college town" in the words of one student. La Jolla is affluent, scenic, and expensive. It doesn't really cater to students, because it doesn't have to. Some UCSD students do get jobs or do volunteer work in the city, but when students go out at night or on weekends, they're more likely to head to other parts of San Diego, such as Mission Beach or even across the border into Mexico. La Jolla's spectacular beaches do function as an outdoor annex to the UCSD campus, given the number of students who head to the beach after class.

University of California/ San Diego

Setting: Urban
# of Undergraduates: 14,623
Men: 50% Women: 50%
In-State Tuition: $4,198
Out-of-State Tuition: $8,984
Room and Board: $6,836
# of Students Applied: 23,685
  Admitted: 11,909 Enrolled: 2,725
Required Admissions Test: either SAT I or ACT; SAT II
Avg. Score of Applicants
  Admitted: SAT Verbal: 593
  SAT Math: 632
Average GPA of Applicants
  Admitted: 3.90
Most Popular Majors: Biology, Psychology, Economics, Political Science, Applied Mechanics and Engineering

UNIVERSITY OF CALIFORNIA/SANTA CRUZ

Admissions Address: Admissions Office, Cook House, 1156 High Street, Santa Cruz, CA 95064
Phone: (408) 459-4008 (408) 459-2131
Web Address: www.ucsc.edu.admissions

University of California/Santa Cruz

$$

Setting: Suburban
# of Undergraduates: 8,629
Men: 40.2% Women: 59.8%
In-State Tuition: $3,799
Out-of-State Tuition: $8,057
Room and Board: $6,429
# of Students Applied: 11,400
  Admitted: 9,479 Enrolled: 1,997
Required Admissions Test: SAT I, SAT II
Lowest 25% of Freshmen Scored At or Below: SAT Verbal: 510 SAT Math: 510 ACT Comp.: 20
Highest 25% of Freshmen Scored At or Above: SAT Verbal: 630 SAT Math: 630 ACT Comp.: 26
H.S. Rank, Top 10%: 94%
Top 25%: 100%
Top 50%: 100%
Avg. Score of Applicants Admitted: SAT Verbal: 570 SAT Math: 565 ACT Comp.: 23
Average GPA of Applicants Admitted: 3.49
Most Popular Majors (% of Student Body): Psychology (14%), Literature (8%), Biology (8%), Anthropology (6%), Sociology (6%)

Founded in the radical 1960s, Santa Cruz remains one of the more progressive schools within the UC system, attracting a politically active and socially aware student body. For many years, UCSC sought to de-emphasize competition by doing away with traditional grading in favor of a system that allowed students to opt for a more extensive, narrative evaluation from their professors. While the student body recently voted to go back to traditional grades, it is clear that the faculty members are very attentive to the students at UCSC. Professors go out of their way to get to know students as individuals. To protect this, UCSC has begun capping its enrollment in response to student criticisms that classes have grown too large and profs don't have the time to devote to individual attention that they once had.

While UCSC's strengths are, and have been, in the liberal arts, there has been of late an influx of professionally oriented science programs, including computer science and engineering. There has also been an investment in the music programs. The school just completed the construction of a $30 million New Music Center, with state-of-the-art facilities. Other strong departments include anthropology, literature, English, psychology, political science, visual arts, interdisciplinary programs in women's studies and environmental studies, and ethnic and cultural studies programs. In order to graduate, all students are required to complete a senior thesis or take a comprehensive examination. A high percentage of UCSC students go on to graduate-level study.

The sprawling campus, located between Monterey and San Francisco, is surrounded by beautiful Northern California woods, nature, and wildlife. This setting, in addition to creating a pleasant and serene academic environment, lends itself to various outdoor sports, such as hiking, biking, and camping. Santa Cruz has many state-of-the-art facilities, including recent additions such as marine and earth science labs and visual arts studios.

Students live in one of several residential colleges, which function as smaller communities within the larger university; each college has its own distinctive look and feel. Most students are politically active and are on the far left of the political spectrum, though there are some "mainstream conservatives" on campus as well. UCSC students value individualism and respect other viewpoints. These are students who like to do their own thing, both academically and socially.

Santa Cruz isn't a huge party school; students instead enjoy hanging out in small groups or attending low-key dormitory and apartment parties. The town of Santa Cruz, in addition to its beaches, has a number of popular student hangouts. For most Santa Cruz students, becoming immersed in intense political and philosophical discussions in smoky cafes and coffeehouses is more their speed than suntanning and volleyball.

ALSO, CHECK OUT THESE SCHOOLS:

Arizona State University
Brigham Young University
College of William and Mary
Evergreen State University
University of Florida
Florida State University
Georgia Institute of Technology
University of Hawaii—Manoa
University of Houston
Howard University
University of Illinois—Urbana/Champaign
Indiana University
University of Iowa
University of Massachusetts—Amherst
University of Michigan—Ann Arbor
Morehouse College
New College of the University of South Florida
University of North Carolina—Chapel Hill
Ohio State University
Pennsylvania State University
Rice University
Rutgers University—New Brunswick
SUNY—Binghamton
Temple University
University of Texas—Austin
University of Virginia

All-Around Gems

If there's a formula for a good, all-around school, it's a combination of strong academic programs, quality facilities, dynamic student bodies, and a variety of social and extracurricular activities. The schools in this chapter have gotten that formula just right. We think that these All-Around Gems are worth checking out and adding to your list of choices.

BATES COLLEGE IN LEWISTON, MAINE

Admissions Address: Admissions Office, 23 Campus Avenue, Lewiston, ME 04240
Phone: (207) 786-6000
Web Address: www.bates.edu/

Founded in 1855 by advocates of human freedom and civil rights, Bates was established as an institution of higher learning open to people of any race, religion, nationality, or sex. In fact, it was one of the first coeducational colleges in New England. In 1990, the faculty voted to make submitting standardized test scores as part of the admissions process optional because they felt that test scores don't present the entire picture of a student's individual strengths and potential. As a result, writing samples and personal interviews may hold much greater weight in the selection process. That's just one example of the many ways the school has maintained its ideal as a place where students are treated as individuals in an open, tolerant academic environment.

The school's departments remain strong across the board, although some have substantially larger enrollments and faculties than others. The most popular programs include biology, economics, political science, and psychology. Interdisciplinary studies have grown increasingly popular, too, and neuroscience, East Asian studies, and environmental studies are new majors with increasing enrollments. Many departments have added "sec-

---

Bates College

$$$$$
★★★★

Setting: Suburban
# of Undergraduates: 1,672
Men: 48.1% Women: 51.9%
Tuition: $28,650
# of Students Applied: 3,847
   Admitted: 1,355   Enrolled: 501
Lowest 25% of Freshmen Scored At or Below: SAT Verbal: 610
   SAT Math: 590
Highest 25% of Freshmen Scored At or Above: SAT Verbal: 690   SAT Math: 680
H.S. Rank, Top 10%: 55%
Top 25%: 90%
Top 50%: 100%
Avg. Score of Applicants Admitted: SAT Verbal: 650
   SAT Math: 650

ondary concentrations" that substitute for minors. For all students, the core curriculum includes five courses in the humanities, three in the social sciences, three in the natural sciences, and physical education.

Students also must take two "short terms" before they graduate. The short term is a special five-week period in May when students can take it a bit easier by studying something more offbeat, from a recreational sport to the study of pop culture. Favorite courses are "The Philosophy of Star Trek" and "Beat Poets." Some of the short-term courses involve field trips and more extensive travel. Many students at Bates study abroad at some point.

Although there are a few introductory courses that have around 100 students, most classes contain 20 to 30. These smaller classes focus on discussion and healthy intellectual arguing. Some classes are team taught by three or four professors who challenge students to articulate and rethink their opinions. Bates professors are also extremely harsh graders who make strict demands on students. At the same time, though, they are described by students as friendly and accessible: "While As are nearly impossible to receive, so are Fs. The profs will do everything they can to help you make it through," explained a Bates woman. Working hard for good grades is part of the Bates experience, and students adjust to it. Most Batesies seem intelligent and highly motivated.

An hour from the stunning Maine coastline, Bates's small, beautifully maintained campus has an impressive mixture of old and new structures. As part of a commitment to keeping up with academic trends, the school continually invests its endowment in making improvements and additions to the school's facilities. Recent improvements include a new student center and an impressive social science building. Other additions include the Olin Arts Center, with its own gallery, art studios and theater, a winter sports center with its own ice rink, and "The Village," a residential housing complex consisting of three buildings and a study center. Housing at Bates is generally pretty good and includes some converted Victorian houses that are absolutely charming. Students eat together in the same dining room, The Commons, which contributes to the overall sense of community on campus.

About a tenth of the student body comes from Maine, and a significant portion of the remainder are from other parts of New England, especially Massachusetts. Despite the school's equal-opportunity credo, there is only about a 9 percent minority population. Most students are white and upper-middle class, although some receive financial aid. Batesies are generally tolerant and open to new experiences and viewpoints. Many involve themselves in political organizations and causes.

While students love Bates's pretty campus, the long, long winter is less popular, which may be why students are so willing to spend many hours in the library. Rather than hibernate through the winter, they hit the books. Oh, and they also party—quite a bit, for a small liberal arts school. Partying is how students blow off stress from the stiff workload. Parties start on Wednesday night and last through the weekend. Bates has always discouraged fraternities and sororities, which might have discriminatory practices. When students party, they head to a few large dorm parties or to Frye Street, a strip of large, off-campus student houses that have their own wild party scene. Students say that the school, which treats them as responsible adults, doesn't heavily police parties.

Students don't find much appealing about Lewiston, an old mill town that still has an industrial feel to it. Batesies head into town only for the occasional meal or movie, although there are some students involved in community service and volunteer groups. Beyond the town, though, the gorgeous Maine forest and coastline are perfect for various outdoor activities, such as hiking, camping, mountain biking, and skiing. Almost every Bates student is into playing some sport or activity, either on an intercollegiate or intramural team. Lacrosse, football, and soccer are the most popular spectator sports, especially when games are waged against rival Bowdoin, while men's and women's cross-country track, rugby, and skiing teams also have strong records. During winter, a fun campus event is the "Puddle Jump," when students attempt to navigate around a hole in the frozen campus lake.

Bates is a pressure cooker without the pressure: a school whose teachers are fierce graders but also friendly, whose students work their butts off during the day and party at night. "Students can affect just about anything here, from policy to party," reflects a graduating senior. "Sleep seems optional because, to borrow a cliché, we work and play so hard."

COLGATE UNIVERSITY IN HAMILTON, NEW YORK

Admissions Address: Admissions Office, 13 Oak Drive, Hamilton, NY 13346-1383
Phone: (315) 824-7401
Web Address: www.colgate.edu/

Colgate University

$$$$$
★★★★

Setting: Rural
# of Undergraduates: 2,847
Men: 49.9% Women: 49.4%
Tuition: $22,610
Room and Board: $6,110
# of Students Applied: 6,848
   Admitted: 2,520 Enrolled: 718
Required Admissions Test: Either SAT or ACT
Lowest 25% of Freshmen Scored At or Below: SAT Verbal: 600 SAT Math: 600 ACT Comp.: 26
Highest 25% of Freshmen Scored At or Above: SAT Verbal: 680 SAT Math: 690 ACT Comp.: 30
H.S. Rank, Top 10%: 54%
Top 25%: 88%
Top 50%: 100%
Avg. Score of Applicants Admitted: SAT Verbal: 637 SAT Math: 644 ACT Comp.: 28
Most Popular Majors (% of Student Body): English (13.9%), Political Science (10.1%), History (8.9%), Economics (7.2%), Psychology (6.4%)

Don't let the New York state address fool you—Colgate is about as far away from Manhattan's urban mayhem as you can get. Colgate students love the location for its beauty and accessibility to outdoor sports, as well as for the active party scene they've created for themselves. One junior reflected, "Colgate is very isolated—the nearest city, Syracuse, is one hour away. The university's isolation focuses everyone's attention on campus life and creates a strong sense of community."

Although Colgate bears the university designation, it is still unquestionably a small, liberal arts school that focuses on undergraduates (there's only one graduate department and just a handful of graduate students). The school has many strong courses in traditional liberal arts and science departments; English, economics, history, and political science have large undergraduate enrollments. The core curriculum includes a unique four-course general education requirement, taught by faculty members in various disciplines and fields, that includes the study of Western civilization, non-Western culture, and current issues (especially scientific topics). Additional requirements include two courses each in social sciences, natural sciences, and humanities. Foreign language and physical education are also required, as is passing a swim test (a former donor made this a requirement after his child had drowned).

Students have terrific things to say about the academic environment at Colgate. "I love the small classes because there is so much individualized attention," says one freshman. Even the introductory classes will usually have around 20 to 25 students. Students praise their professors for being incredibly accessible and clearly concerned about their students. Freshmen take seminars with the professor who serves as their advisor until they choose a major and pick a new one. This system provides them with a faculty mentor right from day one.

On-campus housing includes seven coed dormitories which are relatively cramped, and more spacious apartment complexes. Some students move into a selection of special-interest houses, while many more move into fraternity and sorority houses or off-campus apartments. Hamilton is a quiet and peaceful town with not much going on to draw students off campus other than a few bars, restaurants, and a popular coffee shop.

Eighty-five percent of Colgate's student body is white, and many come from an upper-middle-class background, which doesn't create an especially diverse student body. Almost 70 percent come from out of state, although those students are still primarily from the Northeast. With Colgate's small student enrollment, most students can be on friendly terms with one another, and the general atmosphere is laid-back. "It's not a particularly cutthroat environment," says a Colgate sophomore.

Greater selectivity, improved academic programs, and concerted efforts by the administration to diminish, if not eliminate, Colgate's party image have boosted its overall intellectual reputation. Still, students enjoy a very busy, active social life. The Greek system remains a major presence here, with about 40 percent of the men and about 30 percent of the women joining. In the past, some students have criticized the lack of non-Greek social opportunities at Colgate, pointing out that there are limited extracurricular activities. Yet one student said she felt that "a new culture turning away from Greek life is growing stronger, especially among third- and fourth-year students" and that, while there aren't the hundreds of activities that you'll find at a larger school, students are able to become much more involved in the ones available without heavy-duty competition. A new student center has added a much-needed space for students to hang out.

After Greek-related events and parties, sports are the activity of choice for most students. Basketball, soccer, and hockey are the school's best intercollegiate teams. Colgate's extensive athletic facilities enable students to participate in sports of all kinds, even in the dead of winter. Facilities include several athletic centers that, combined, offer students indoor tennis, racquetball, track, exercise and weight equipment, and a pool. That's just indoors. For those who want to venture out, the campus' setting is fantastic for outdoor sports like climbing, biking, hiking, sailing, and camping.

One senior explained his experience at Colgate in the following way: "It's a small school with a unique culture. The classes are good, the social scene is strong, and the athletic facilities are great. You know everyone on campus and grow together with your peers and professors for the four years you spend here."

GEORGIA INSTITUTE OF TECHNOLOGY IN ATLANTA

Admissions Address: Office of Undergraduate Admissions, Atlanta, GA 30332-0320
Phone: (404) 894-4154
Web Address: www.gatech.edu/admissions/undergrad/

Georgia Institute of Technology

$$
★★★

Setting: Urban
# of Undergraduates: 8,743
Men: 72.1% Women: 27.9%
In-State Tuition: $2,235
Out-of-State Tuition: $8,970
Room and Board: $5,700
# of Students Applied: 7,893
Admitted: 4,404 Enrolled: 1,843
Required Admissions Test: either SAT or ACT
Recommended: SAT
Lowest 25% of Freshmen Scored At or Below: SAT Verbal: 580 SAT Math: 630
Highest 25% of Freshmen Scored At or Above: SAT Verbal: 670 SAT Math: 730
Avg. Score of Applicants Admitted: SAT Verbal: 624 SAT Math: 674
Average GPA of Applicants Admitted: 3.60
Most Popular Majors (% of Student Body): Mechanical Engineering (11%), Electrical Engineering (11%), Industrial and Systems Engineering (10%), Management (8%), Civil Engineering (8%)

"The best and worst thing about Georgia Tech is the academics. For engineering majors, especially, classes can be very, very difficult. But this is good because it helps you learn how to handle tough situations and heavy workloads. But if you have poor time-management skills, you won't last here," says a senior mechanical engineering student currently at the Georgia Institute of Technology.

Georgia Tech is primarily known for its acclaimed programs in engineering. The school of Management also now has a large enrollment. While the liberal arts and sciences are not as highly rated, the school's social science programs, particularly in international relations and public policy, are considered quite good. All students in their first year are required to take English, calculus, computer science, social science, and a physical education course. Further distribution requirements include social science, a course in U.S. history, math, science, and humanities. All students must also pass a writing competency examination.

The school's location in Atlanta makes it accessible to a number of internships in various fields. The engineering co-op program, rated best in the country, enables students to receive a great deal of hands-on experience by alternating between semesters in the classrooms and internships. Over one-third of the student body engages in the program. It does add an extra year of school time, but you graduate with impressive experience on your résumé that can make it easier to get a job. In general, only about 30 percent of the students get their degrees in four years, but most do get that diploma in their fifth year (okay, some take six). Georgia Tech enjoys great loyalty from its alumni, which endows the school with substantial funds.

While Georgia Tech's faculty consists of many brilliant, highly experienced researchers, the teaching quality varies greatly. "We have many bright researchers whose teaching skills are wanting. The new teachers are typically excellent; the problem lies with some of the others," says one student. Most professors are considered very tough graders and extremely demanding.

The campus has some very good facilities, particularly those oriented to the engineering programs. Dorms and campus apartments were greatly

ALL-AROUND GEMS

improved to house Olympic athletes in 1996, and students are reaping the benefits. For the summer Olympics, an Aquatic Center, Coliseum, sports complex, and seven new residence halls were built.

More than 25 percent of the student body consists of minority students. About half are natives of Georgia, who are drawn by Tech's very low tuition. Even for out-of-state students, though, the tuition is an excellent bargain for an engineering and technical school of this caliber. Students come from across the country and more than 80 foreign countries. When it comes to political inclinations, a student says, "There's a lot of apathy on campus. You'll never get more than a third of the students to care about a single issue." In general, the student body is conservative and self-absorbed.

That apathy may be a symptom of the heavy workload. The courses and requirements are extremely tough at Georgia Tech. Students reportedly work very hard, and getting As seems virtually impossible. Due to academic demands, most students don't have much time for a social life. Some do manage, however, to take time off and relax, at least on weekends. Because Georgia Tech is an urban campus and because students are so devoted to their studies, there doesn't seem to be a strong sense of campus community. Older students head into Atlanta to cruise the local bar and club scene or to see a play or movie. On campus, students who join a fraternity or sorority—and about 30 percent do—enjoy a more active social life than their peers. The Greeks throw large parties that are often open to the entire campus. The athletic program also creates a degree of social interaction. Georgia Tech's football and basketball teams compete in the tough ACC, and both draw large crowds of student fans to games. A large athletic complex also serves as a center for a thriving intramural program.

NORTHWESTERN UNIVERSITY IN EVANSTON, ILLINOIS

Admissions Address: Admissions Office, 3003 Snelling Avenue N, St. Paul, MN 55113-1598
Phone: (612) 631-5111 (800) 827-6827
Web Address: www.nwc.edu

Northwestern may not measure up to its fellow Big Ten schools in terms of its football and basketball teams, but it does leave many of them in the dust when it comes to academics. As one student proudly told us, "The best thing about Northwestern is the combination of rigorous academics with an active social scene."

Northwestern University

$$$$
★★★★

Setting: suburban
# of Undergraduates: 7,609
Tuition: $19,152
Room and Board: 6,387
# of Students Applied: 15,620
   Admitted: 4,790 **Enrolled:** 1,948
Lowest 25% of Freshmen Scored At or Below: SAT Verbal: 620 SAT Math: 630 ACT 28
Highest 25% of Freshmen Scored At or Above: SAT Verbal: 710 SAT Math: 720 ACT 31
Required Admissions Test: either SAT I or ACT; three SAT II tests

---

The six undergraduate schools—the Medill School of Journalism, the McCormick School of Engineering and Applied Sciences, the School of Education and Social Policy, the School of Music, the School of Speech, and the College of Arts and Sciences—offer a variety of outstanding programs. Northwestern is one of the few universities able to claim that it regularly produces accomplished journalists, film and theater professionals, doctors, and engineers.

The school also offers highly regarded interdisciplinary programs and several special programs, including the Honors Program in Medical Education, which enables qualified students to earn their B.A. and M.D. in seven years. Although requirements vary by school, all six require courses in several basic areas, providing students with an extensive background before proceeding with their more focused studies. Northwestern's quarter system crams four courses into 10 weeks; although this has the advantage of making it relatively easy to fulfill course and major requirements, it also makes for a heavy workload and frequent exams.

With their rigorous schedules, it's not surprising that Northwestern students study a lot and that most can be found in the library after class. Still, some students say the work is "challenging but not overwhelming," and manage to round out their studies with other activities and a social life.

Northwestern has attracted a number of prominent faculty members, who teach courses on all levels including introductory classes and freshman seminars. While lectures tend to be large, upper-division courses may have as few as 10 people. For the most part, students consider the professors friendly and very accessible. "I haven't had a professor yet who I wouldn't feel comfortable talking with one-on-one," says one student.

With prime lakefront property along Lake Michigan, Northwestern's scenic, spacious campus resembles a giant park, with bike and jogging paths and long stretches of lawn for students to lie out along the water—that is, when weather conditions allow. Come winter, when that icy wind kicks off the lake, students won't be singing about the joys of the Windy City, although an occasional brave soul might be seen cross-country skiing across the snowy campus.

Divided between the more social North Campus and the quieter, more comfortable South Campus, the dormitories are generally in good condition, which is fortunate given that students may be confined there for much of the winter. Several residential colleges house students together, many according to common interests such as performing arts, public service, and women's studies.

About 75 percent of the students live on campus; those who don't mostly live in fraternity and sorority houses or in apartments west of campus. About 30 percent of the men and women join fraternities and sororities, and the houses keep the student social life afloat, hosting many large parties that attract Greeks and non-Greeks alike.

The student population is diverse in many respects; students represent a variety of academic interests, ethnic and cultural groups, and political affiliations. While members of these groups tend to stick together, there doesn't seem to be much tension among students. "Everybody seems to get along. I haven't personally seen any discrimination because of race or sexual orientation. Everybody's very tolerant," a student reports.

In addition to attending parties on weekends, students go to many on-campus social events, posted on a rock at the center of campus. Because of Northwestern's strong theater and music programs, there's almost always some kind of interesting student production. While the varsity sports teams are generally known for their losing streaks, students are loyal to the school team and many participate in intramural programs and other sporting activities at Northwestern's first-rate facilities.

Bordering Northwestern lies the suburban town of Evanston which, despite its few stores and restaurants, doesn't cater to the nearby student population. Easily accessible via the El, Chicago's public rail service, Chicago is definitely the place to go in search of big-city culture and excitement. When they want a break from studying, students head into the city to one of several museums, including the Fine Arts Institute with its superb Impressionist and postimpressionist collection, renowned theater companies, blues bars, and restaurants. On those days, students forget about Chicago's bitter winters and sing the praises of the Windy City.

OHIO STATE UNIVERSITY IN COLUMBUS

Admissions Address: Admissions Office, Third Floor Lincoln Tower, 1800 Cannon Dr., Columbus, OH 43210-1200
Phone: (614) 292-3980
Web Address: www.acs.ohio-state.edu

Ohio State University

$$
★

- **Setting:** Urban
- **# of Undergraduates:** 30,274
- **Men:** 52.3% **Women:** 47.7%
- **In-State Tuition:** $3,468
- **Out-of-State Tuition:** $10,335
- **Room and Board:** $4,907
- **# of Students Applied:** 16,645
  - Admitted: 14,194 Enrolled: 5,976
- **Required Admissions Test:** Either SAT or ACT
- **Lowest 25% of Freshmen Scored At or Below:** SAT Verbal: 500 SAT Math: 500 ACT Comp.: 21
- **Highest 25% of Freshmen Scored At or Above:** SAT Verbal: 620 SAT Math: 630 ACT Comp.: 27
- **H.S. Rank, Top 10%:** 24%
- **Top 25%:** 50%
- **Top 50%:** 81%
- **Most Popular Majors (% of Student Body):** Psychology (5%), Communications (4%), Accounting (4%), English (3%), Marketing (3%)

A senior at OSU describes the school as "big but personal." There's no question that the school is big, with about 30,000 undergraduates alone. In addition to the main Columbus location, there are five extended campuses in the state. You might wonder how in the world a school that size can possibly be personal. The answer, this student tells us, is that there are so many people, who come from all kinds of backgrounds, and so many clubs, organizations, and activities, you're bound to fall in with some group who will become your own little community.

"Any program you want to study is offered at OSU," says one student, who apparently is not exaggerating. OSU has 14 undergraduate schools that offer hundreds of majors and thousands of courses, from A (agriculture) to Z (zoology). Preprofessional and career-oriented programs—such as accounting, engineering, and nursing—are particularly strong and have high enrollments. Communications and journalism are two more popular majors.

All students have to fulfill distribution requirements in natural science, social science, art and humanities, as well as writing, foreign language, and social diversity. A special course called University College is required of all freshmen; it introduces them to the campus and university system and gives them the opportunity to meet fellow freshmen.

OSU students inevitably encounter the problems associated with big schools. Many classes are very large, numbering from 200 to 500 people, but they'll usually have a smaller recitation class that meets once a week with a graduate TA. At higher levels, classes will have fewer students, averaging about 30 to 40. The honors program, open to about 2,500 students with high enough GPAs, generally has much smaller classes (10–15 students) taught by professors.

Obviously, these circumstances make it tough to establish close relationships with professors, but it's not impossible. Those who seek out professors can sometimes get to know them very well. As one motivated student explained, "it's up to me to take the initiative and go to my professors' office hours. It's the only way they'll remember my name if I need a recommendation later." Although students criticize the number of courses with TAs, some find they establish good relations with the TAs and rely on them for advice and instruction. Registration and other administrative policies, though, can be bureaucratic hassles; phone registration is on a first-come, first-serve basis and should be taken care of early.

The OSU campus is large enough to qualify as a city in its own right; it has facilities and resources akin to one, including more than 20 libraries. Like a city, it's even divided into older and more modern sections. At its center lies a monstrous oval quad where people study and play Frisbee in warm weather. Only about 20 percent of the students can fit in university housing, but there's a lot of affordable housing nearby. The campus dorms vary in appearance, from luxurious to cramped. Students in the nicer dorms, however, pay a bit more for the extra luxuries.

About 90 percent of the students are Ohio residents, for whom the low tuition is an excellent bargain. Even for out-of-staters, the tuition is comparatively low, given all the academic opportunities and extensive facilities. Fifteen percent of the student population is non-Caucasian. With a total enrollment of over 40,000, virtually every kind of person is represented in the OSU student body.

Students enjoy an active, extremely varied social life. On a campus of this size, there's always something going on somewhere—a party, a visiting lecture, a concert, or play. There are well over 500 clubs and activities that run the gamut of causes and interests, from the school's television, radio, and newspaper, to political and culturally oriented groups. Students also enjoy hanging out and going to parties of all sizes, from small gatherings in rooms to blowouts at apartments and fraternities. "The second you step off campus, you are on High Street, which has tons of fast-food restaurants and shops and bars. That strip is a huge OSU hangout," says one student. Additionally, the Greek system maintains an active social calendar, attracting about 10 percent of the student body.

Despite these divergent interests, enthusiasm over sports seems to unite everyone and gives a boost to the overall social atmosphere at the school. The major spectator sport is football, especially when games are against their archrival, the University of Michigan. "Every football Saturday is a party," says one OSU senior. "There are tons of tailgate parties. The freshmen sit in a special section of the stadium called 'Block O.' It's their job to hold up cards that spell out stuff like OSU. They're expected to help the cheerleaders lead cheers. Hey, if you want to be a part of the game, you need to pull your weight. We were all freshmen. We all had to do it!" The marching band calls themselves TBDBITL, which stands for "The Best Damned Band in the Land." Win or lose, the band marches in the street and the students go wild. "It's just an awesome experience," exclaims one football lover. After football, basketball is a close second in terms of generating enthusiasm among students.

OSU boasts a tremendous athletic program, with more than 30 intercollegiate sports and more than 100 intramural sports and activities. The school's ample facilities keep all of these people tackling, batting, pitching, swimming, dribbling, serving, volleying, and tumbling.

There's no getting around OSU's mammoth size. But many find ways to turn the size to an advantage by seeking out academic and social opportunities. Those who do seem rather happy with their choice. "There's no other college experience—with so many options if you just take the initiative—that beats OSU," says one student proudly.

PENNSYLVANIA STATE UNIVERSITY
IN UNIVERSITY PARK

Admissions Address: Undergraduate Admissions Office, 201 Shields Building, Box 3000, University Park, PA 16804-3000
Phone: (814) 865-5471
Web Address: www.psu.edu/

Many people associate Penn State entirely with its nationally ranked, championship-winning football team. If your only picture of Penn State comes from watching Coach Joe Paterno's teams on TV, you're getting a very small part of the bigger picture that is Penn State. Sure, football is important—it's probably the best sign of how deeply school pride runs here—but you also need to consider the range of academic programs and the party scene that keeps about 30,000 students calling their campus the "Happy Valley."

There are 22 campuses in the Penn State system, but the University Park Campus, the main campus, is the oldest and largest, where most of the programs and facilities are clustered. At the 10 undergraduate schools, students can find programs of all kinds, from agriculture to hotel management. Engineering, communications, and the sciences are generally regarded as the school's strongest areas. While humanities aren't considered as strong, the school is currently revamping many of the humanities departments.

All-Around Gems

Specific requirements vary by program. All students, however, must fulfill the broad general education requirements, which include quantitative and communication skills, natural sciences, arts, humanities and social behavioral sciences, health sciences, and physical education. Students also must enroll in courses that reflect cultural diversity.

Penn State is a big school. That means you can expect mostly large lecture classes, often numbering in the hundreds. When you're sitting in such a big lecture, it may be more difficult to focus your attention, and you'll have to work at staying involved. It's not easy to establish relationships with teachers in this kind of setting. Your professors most likely will not know you by name, but you can try to see them during office hours if you have questions. Most likely, you'll rely on TAs for help with coursework. Luckily, many upper division classes accept no more than 40 students. The quality of teaching varies; some professors focus on their own research at the expense of time for their students. But there are also those professors who care for their students and place a greater emphasis on teaching. If you ask around, you can get good tips from fellow students on who are the better professors. Even though registration is now done by phone, there's still frustration because courses close quickly.

By the way, if you have a high GPA and SAT scores, you'll want to check out Penn State's University Scholars Program. Students who qualify for the program live together and take much smaller, more intense classes in which they are guaranteed more interaction with professors.

So why do students put up with the big-school problems? The answer involves opportunities. Men and women come to Penn State because of the range of academic possibilities. Students say they like the variety of courses and the numerous resources and facilities available to them. They also like the opportunity to meet eclectic people who bring with them a wide range of interests and experiences.

Many students opt to study at one of the branch campuses to experience a different location and a smaller, more manageable environment. The enormous University Park campus, spreading out over 5,000 acres, has the feel of a large village or small town, yet has a certain charm because of its naturally beautiful and serene surroundings. The dormitories on campus hold many students and are pretty crowded. Most freshmen live in East Hall, which isn't the most spacious but has a social atmosphere in which first-year students easily make friends. Many students move off campus to apartments or to fraternity houses. Downtown State College

Penn State / University Park

$$$
★★★

Setting: Suburban
# of Undergraduates: 30,547
Men: 54.6% **Women:** 45.4%
In-State Tuition: $5,434
Out-of-State Tuition: $11,774
Room and Board: $4,170
# of Students Applied: 25,654
  Admitted: 12,676 **Enrolled:** 4,742
Required Admissions Test: Either SAT I or ACT
Lowest 25% of Freshmen Scored At or Below: SAT Verbal: 540 SAT Math: 570
Highest 25% of Freshmen Scored At or Above: SAT Verbal: 641 SAT Math: 670
H.S. Rank, Top 10%: 54%
Top 25%: 90%
Top 50%: 97%
Avg. Score of Applicants Admitted: SAT Verbal: 593 SAT Math: 617
Average GPA of Applicants Admitted: 3.70
Most Popular Majors (% of Student Body): Business (18%), Engineering (15%), Education (7%), Health Sciences (7%), Communications (5%)

caters to students, with restaurants, bars, and shops that are fun and affordable.

Pennsylvanians comprise about 80 percent of the students, drawn by the low tuition, and the rest of the student body comes primarily from the Northeast. There's a 10 percent minority population. Within such a large population, students represent all kinds of backgrounds, groups, and interests. There's never a shortage of people to meet, including those who share interests with you.

Penn State students enjoy an active social scene. Many party heavily, from Wednesday night through the weekend. Ten to 15 percent of the student body joins the Greek system. With 54 national fraternities and 21 sororities to choose from, even the Greek system at Penn State provides students with choices. The Greeks provide many big parties that draw large numbers of students. There's also a local bar scene that's popular among students of legal age. The campus also has many hangout spots, including the Hetzel Union Building (known as "The Hub"), a huge student center with places to socialize and/or eat fast food. With more than 400 clubs and activities—including the school's own radio and television station, a daily newspaper, literary journals, art, theater, and music groups, professional and political clubs, volunteer work, and ethnic and cultural groups—there's no shortage of things to do after class and before the parties. In fact, student involvement in school extracurriculars is increasingly popular.

For most of the students, as well as several hundred visiting alumni and friends, football Saturdays are major social events, from pregame tailgate to postgame parties. But the Penn State athletic program is huge and goes well beyond football. The more than 25 intercollegiate sports include highly-ranked teams in men's basketball and wrestling, and women's basketball, field hockey, and lacrosse teams, just to name a few. There are over 30 intramural sports for men and women. Providing the space and equipment for all of these sports and more, the incredible athletic facilities include three gymnasiums, five pools, two golf courses, and courts and fields galore. A junior comments that, despite Penn State's size, "there's a program suited to each students needs, both academically and socially."

ALL-AROUND GEMS

SKIDMORE COLLEGE IN SARATOGA SPRINGS, NEW YORK

Saratoga Springs, NY 12866
Phone: (518) 584-5000 (518) 584-5000 x2213
Web Address: www.skidmore.edu/

If you visit Skidmore, you'll quickly notice how new everything is and how much more seems to be under construction. For the past 20 years or so, Skidmore has consistently been making changes and additions that keep improving its academic offerings and its overall reputation. Skidmore draws many people to its art, music, and theater departments. Business, English, psychology, and government also have large enrollments.

Central to Skidmore's academic program is its innovative liberal arts core curriculum. The core begins with Liberal Studies I: The Human Experience, a massive course on Western civilization that's team taught by professors from virtually every department and that combines large lectures with discussion groups. Students then take courses in such broad, interdisciplinary fields as Cultural Traditions, Artistic Forms and Critical Concepts, and Science and Human Values. Other requirements are lab science, creative arts, non-Western culture, quantitative reasoning, and foreign language.

It can take up to two years to fulfill these requirements, but the core curriculum provides students with a broad academic background, as well as important analytical and critical skills. Taking a heavily interdisciplinary approach, the core encourages students to bring an open, global perspective to their studies and to make connections between subjects, which is reflective of the academic philosophy at Skidmore in general. It's not uncommon for students to mix academic disciplines. For example, a fine arts student might take a business management course, which would certainly come in handy for any struggling artist.

Special academic opportunities include cross-registering for courses at other schools in the Hudson-Mohawk Consortium, engineering and business co-ops at Clarkson, a Study-in-Washington semester, dual and self-designed majors, study abroad, and the University Without Walls, which gives students credit for real-world and work experiences.

Classes are small, usually no more than 25 students. Students work closely with professors, not only in their discussion-centered classes, but often through special projects. A graduating senior remarked, "professors are the first to admit that they learn just as much from us as we learn from them. They're definitely here to help us."

Skidmore College

$$$$$
★★

Setting: Suburban
# of Undergraduates: 2,170
Men: 40.6% **Women:** 59.4%
Tuition: $20,670
Room and Board: $6,110
# of Students Applied: 4,747
  Admitted: 3,120 **Enrolled:** 705
Required Admissions Test: Either SAT or ACT
Recommended: 3 SAT II subject tests, including writing and a foreign language
Lowest 25% of Freshmen Scored At or Below: SAT Verbal: 660 SAT Math: 650
Highest 25% of Freshmen Scored At or Above: SAT Verbal: 560 SAT Math: 560
H.S. Rank, Top 10%: 34%
Top 25%: 62%
Top 50%: 90%
Avg. Score of Applicants Admitted: SAT Verbal: 611 SAT Math: 602 ACT Comp.: 26
Most Popular Majors (% of Student Body): Psychology (13%), Business (12%), English (12%), Government (7%), Studio Art (7%)

193

The pretty Skidmore campus offers striking views of the Adirondack mountains, plenty of flowers and trees, and its own pond. Because so many buildings and facilities are new, they are often in sparkling condition. Recent renovations include a new library and science center, additions to the sports center, and a teaching museum still underway. Students have nothing but praise for the campus housing, which provides more than the typical college dorm room. Most upperclassmen have their own apartments, but rooms in all of the dorms are generally big and comfortable. The food at Skidmore is said to be better than standard institutional fare.

Although a solid majority of the student body applies from out of state, most still come from the Northeast. Skidmore students are often labeled as wealthy, Northeastern prepsters. The student body is overwhelmingly white. The college has actively been attempting to increase the diversity of its student body in terms of ethnicity and socioeconomic background. Skidmore was an all-female school until it went coed in 1970, and women still outnumber men, but not by many. When it comes to politics, students are "mostly apathetic."

The campus social scene is pretty tame. There's no Greek system, and students tend to hang out in small parties rather than go to large barnburners. There's no football team either, but the tennis and equestrian teams have strong records. The athletic facilities are excellent in terms of enabling students to participate in casual recreational and sports activities. Opportunities for outdoor activities seem endless. The surrounding region, thanks primarily to the beautiful Adirondack mountains, is perfect for hiking, camping, and skiing. In warm weather, students can be seen rollerblading and biking around campus.

Saratoga Springs, known for its race track, is a pleasant, upscale summer resort area. It's also laden with parks, cafes, and bars that are frequented by students, and the Saratoga Performing Arts Center offers several popular productions each year. Skidmore has its own cultural scene; among the school's many clubs and activities, artistic and performing groups abound, including singing groups, band and orchestra, and several high-quality student theater productions. The major campus events, Oktoberfest and Spring Fling, feature live music, often by well-known visiting bands. When students want more excitement than is available to them in Saratoga, they travel to neighboring Albany or take road trips to Boston and New York City. Montreal is also a popular destination.

ALL-AROUND GEMS

WAKE FOREST UNIVERSITY IN WINSTON-SALEM, NORTH CAROLINA

Admissions Address: Admissions Office, P.O. Box 7205 Reynolda Station, Winston-Salem, NC 27109
Phone: (910) 759-5201
Web Address: www.wfu.edu/

If you visit Wake Forest, you might have to remind yourself that it's designated as a university. With a pretty, compact campus and small student population, it has the look and feel of a small liberal arts college. For undergraduates, Wake seems much like a small college because they receive a great deal of personal attention from the faculty. Yet Wake, with four graduate divisions, is also a university, with the faculty and facilities of a major research institution. Undergraduates reap these benefits, which include the chance to study with full professors, even in lower-level courses, and to use superb facilities like the expansive library system with millions of sources.

The two undergraduate divisions are the School of Business, where the accounting program is particularly outstanding, and the College of Arts and Sciences, where biology, English, history, and psychology are generally considered strong and have high enrollments.

Students receive a solid, well-rounded liberal arts education because of the extensive core curriculum that takes about two years to fulfill. The curriculum includes, in addition to English composition and foreign language, three courses each in four basic areas: literature and fine arts; natural sciences, math, and computer science; social and behavioral sciences; and history, religion, and philosophy. A few WFU students petition for the open curriculum, by which they don't have to fulfill the requirements, but it's very difficult to get into the program. Many students like the core requirements because they provide an opportunity to test out different fields before having to settle on a concentration. Many also take advantage of Wake's unique study-abroad semesters in London and Venice. Professors lead semester-long courses in those cities, and students stay in the school's own houses there.

Students say the workload is really tough and requires about three hours of studying a day after class, but they get a great deal of advising and support from their teachers. "There's a lot of academic pressure and it's difficult to land good grades," observes one WFU student. Yet he has great things to say about their interaction with the professors, who often know students by name. "You really get to know each other." The class sizes are small, almost always less than 30 students, which allows stu-

Wake Forest University

$$$$$
★★★

Setting: Suburban
# of Undergraduates: 3,565
Men: 49.5% Women: 50.5%
Tuition: $19,450
Room and Board: $5,450
# of Students Applied: 6,450
   Admitted: 2,715   Enrolled: 936
Required Admissions Test: SAT
Recommended: SAT II subject tests
Lowest 25% of Freshmen Scored At or Below: SAT Verbal: 600 SAT Math: 620
Highest 25% of Freshmen Scored At or Above: SAT Verbal: 690   SAT Math: 700
H.S. Rank, Top 10%: 69%
Top 25%: 94%
Top 50%: 99%
Most Popular Majors (% of Student Body): Psychology (14%), Business (12.8%), Biology (12.2%), Politics (8.4%), English (7.7%)

dents to participate frequently in discussion and to form relationships with professors. These relationships often extend beyond the classroom, as faculty often meet with students to give advice or just to hang out and talk.

Wake undergrads also rave about their "gorgeous" and "immaculate" campus, with its flower gardens, pockets of woods, and stately Georgian brick buildings. "The Main Quad is grand, with Wait Chapel at one end and the impressive administration building at the other. Beautiful ash trees extend in two rows," describes one student. "There are also two fields, and when the weather's nice people lie out and study in the sun." The housing ranges from newer, more comfortable dorms further from the quad, and more cramped ones closer to campus. There are coed and single-sex houses, as well as theme houses for languages and common interests. To encourage students to live on campus, the school does not allow students to return to campus housing once they've moved off campus.

The student body is a very homogeneous one. Most students are white, upper or upper middle class, and from the South or Atlantic states. Students tend to be preppie in appearance and conservative in their tastes. Wake Forest was affiliated with the Baptist movement and attracts a number of students who consider themselves religious. There's about a 10 percent minority population, but one student laments that, "little interaction exists between races here. There's a definite feeling of tension." The school is trying to recruit more minority students and has instituted campus-wide programs on race relations.

The small size of the campus fosters a sense of community, one that is further bolstered by the honor code. Students accept that code with varying degrees of seriousness (cheating and dishonesty still exist), yet it does seem to encourage treating one another with courtesy and respect.

When it comes to the social scene, "this is definitely a Greek-oriented campus," says one student. About 45 to 50 percent of the students join 14 fraternities and 10 sororities. Competition to get into houses is tough. Those who don't make it, or who don't want to rush, need to find some other group or activity, as it's easy to feel like an outsider. Fortunately, there's no shortage of such alternative opportunities, including the school radio station, student government, volunteer organizations, and a variety of clubs. If students don't head to fraternity parties, they hang out in dorms or apartments or at the massive Benson University Center, with a food court, pub, club offices, lounges, a theater, and gym. Many also go to nearby bars, restaurants, and movies. Winston-Salem is a pretty quiet town that, with the exception of a few bars and clubs, doesn't offer much of appeal to students.

Athletics make up a big part of Wake Forest. The school's "country club–like" sports and recreational facilities enable people to take part in a number of activities. Basketball is the main spectator sport, especially when games are waged against UNC—Chapel Hill. Football games also draw a decent following of fans. Although Wake Forest's records go up and down in sports, students continue to be enthusiastic supporters of their teams. "When we win a game, everyone goes to the Quad and toilet papers it!" says one senior. "It's one of our biggest traditions."

UNIVERSITY OF ILLINOIS IN URBANA-CHAMPAIGN

Admissions Address: Office of Admissions, 506 S. Wright St., Urbana, IL 61801
Phone: (217) 333-0302
Web Address: www.uiuc.edu/

Like most of its fellow Big Ten schools, the University of Illinois is a large, state-funded university that offers a wide range of academic programs and social activities, as well as powerhouse athletics.

The 10 undergraduate schools include agriculture, business, communications, education, engineering, fine arts, and liberal arts and sciences. Students apply directly to a specific program. Consequently, most of them come to Illinois already set on a professional school or career path, although those enrolled in liberal arts and sciences may remain undecided. Engineering is generally regarded as the school's top division, especially in electrical and computer engineering. The business school is also extremely popular, particularly in accounting. While requirements vary by college and major, all students must take courses in social sciences, natural sciences, and humanities.

Classes are often large, especially at the introductory levels, which affects the quality of the teaching and the amount of interaction students have with professors. One freshman reports, "Professors who teach large classes do not even know their students exist, but if you are in a small class, they're usually helpful and get to know their students. If you don't like feeling anonymous, it's really important to meet your profs in office hours." All large lectures break down into smaller weekly discussion sections. The amount of work students put into their studies depends main-

---

University of Illinois/Urbana-Champaign

$$

★★

Setting: Urban
# of Undergraduates: 26,349
Men: 52% Women: 48%
In-State Tuition: $3,308
Out-of-State Tuition: $9,924
Room and Board: $5,078
# of Students Applied: 17,250
    Admitted: 12,134   Enrolled: 5,946
Required Admissions Test: Either SAT or ACT
Avg. Score of Applicants
    Admitted: SAT Verbal: 608
    SAT Math: 640 ACT Comp.: 26.7
H.S. Rank, Top 10%: 50%
Top 25%: 79%
Top 50%: 98%
Average GPA of Applicants
    Admitted: 3.53

ly on the individual. "In general, I think people study a lot," says one student. "You need to work hard to get good grades here."

The spread-out campus centers on the scenic Main Quad, which has a large grassy area where, weather permitting, students hang out and study or play hackeysack, football, and Frisbee. At one end of the Quad is the enormous Student Union, with a bowling alley, news stand, reading room, and performance space. At the other end is the large domed amphitheater, which hosts major concerts, plays, and lectures. The Main Library, just off the Quad, is large and has different sections for different fields of study, as well as noisier "study" areas where students socialize as much as they work. An addition to the library was built underground so as not to disrupt the experimental cornfield that has been a part of the school since its beginnings.

Many Illinois students come from the greater Chicago area and the rest of the state; you'll find the city slickers from Chicago interacting with students from the more rural regions of the state for the first time here. Because the student population is so large, students can generally find a group of friends with common backgrounds or interests. There's about a 25 percent minority population, consisting in large part of Asian, students.

Many students become actively involved in some extracurricular activity or club, of which there are hundreds to choose from. Students generally like to hang out and go to parties, either at dorms or fraternities. Because the university Greek system is considered one of the largest in the nation, the Greeks are a major presence on campus, with more than a fifth of the students joining 50 fraternities and 25 sororities. The Greeks ensure that large blowout parties and other social events keep coming throughout the year. The strip of bars and fast-food joints along Green Street, known as Campustown, is also a very popular hangout area for students. Some also head to downtown Champaign for shops, restaurants, and movie theaters. As befits a Big Ten school, students are fanatical about their intercollegiate sports teams, especially in football and basketball. All students enjoy the enormous sports complex and extensive facilities for intramural events and other recreational activities. As one students raves, "it's a big school with infinite opportunities to learn and have fun."

ALSO, CHECK OUT THESE SCHOOLS:

Arizona State University
Boston College
Boston University
Brigham Young University
University of California—Berkeley
University of California—Los Angeles
University of California—San Diego
University of Colorado—Boulder
College of William and Mary
Columbia University
Cornell University
University of Connecticut
DePaul University
Duke University
Emory University
University of Florida
Florida State University
Georgetown University
George Washington University
Harvard University
University of Houston
University of Iowa
Johns Hopkins University
University of Massachusetts—Amherst
University of Miami
University of Michigan—Ann Arbor
University of North Carolina—Chapel Hill
University of Notre Dame
Northwestern University
University of Pennsylvania
University of Pittsburgh
Princeton University
Rice University
Rutgers University—New Brunswick
University of Southern California
Stanford University
Syracuse University
Temple University
Texas A&M University
University of Texas—Austin
Tulane University
Vanderbilt University
University of Vermont
University of Virginia
Yale University

Buried Treasures

We all know, thanks to a certain Elizabethan playwright, that a rose by any other name would still smell as sweet. Would the Bard say the same thing about today's colleges? There's no denying that for some, going to a college with a well-known name is extremely important. Indeed, having "Harvard" or "Yale" on your résumé will most certainly open doors for you upon graduation.

This is a big country, however, and there are a lot of schools in it. Tucked away in various rural locales, towns, suburbs, and even some cities, you'll find some of the nation's best- kept collegiate secrets. While not many people know them by name, these schools still have a great deal to offer: exceptional academic programs, attentive faculty members, superb facilities, beautiful campuses. Some even draw big-name professors who like to keep low profiles.

The obvious disadvantage to going to a more unfamiliar school is that you won't have some employer hire you based on the strength of your college's reputation alone. There are advantages, though, that—depending upon your own situation—make up for it. Because these schools don't have the same kind of widespread popularity, there aren't hordes of students desperately trying to get into them, which increases your chances of being accepted.

The lack of competition to get in characterizes the overall atmosphere at many of these schools even when you get in. Most students we spoke to at these schools told us about the friendly, casual student body, free of cutthroat competition, and the close sense of community they encountered. At the same time, while you may have to pay for a name-brand product, many of these schools are much more reasonable than their more famous counterparts.

The Road to College

By the way, many of these schools are not as unknown as you may think. Within their own regions, these schools often have the same widespread recognition of a Harvard or Yale. If you're planning on looking for a job or going to graduate school in the same area, you won't have to be as concerned that people will raise their eyebrows and say, "Where did you say you graduated from??!" At the same time, as people become more wary of paying huge tuitions and search out quality educations at reasonable prices, many of these schools are gaining more and more attention. The extra publicity ironically raises some concern for students at these schools who worry that increased enrollments will disrupt their quiet, intimate collegiate environment. Publicity has its advantages, though. You might apply to one of these schools now and find that by the time you graduate it's become a hot school.

In addition to any Buried Treasures we've listed, we encourage you to be on the lookout for some of your own. If you concentrate less on the name recognition and examine what schools actually offer, you might find some pretty amazing colleges. They may not be marked with an "X," but those treasures are out there.

DENISON UNIVERSITY IN GRANVILLE, OHIO

Admissions Address: Admissions Office, P.O. Box H, Granville, OH 43023
Phone: (614) 587-6276 (800) DENISON
Web Address: www.denison.edu

Denison was once one of the more infamous party schools, but it seems to be in the midst of an important transition period both socially and academically. During the past few years, the administration has made serious efforts to boost the quality of its faculty and academic programs, rendering the school more competitive, and it has adopted stricter regulations governing campus Greek life. This is not to say that Denison's social scene has evaporated, but it has become more subdued.

The school is small and focuses primarily on undergraduate education. The science and math programs are highly rated and draw many accomplished, knowledgeable faculty members. Students in these majors also benefit from Denison's outstanding research facilities, and, because of the school's small size, undergraduates actually get the opportunity to enjoy them. In the liberal arts, economics, political science, philosophy, history, English, and psychology are all considered strong departments. A number of students do premed or prelaw.

First-year students enroll in special seminars that investigate various modes of communication and inquiry. The seminars are one of the many ways in which students interact closely with their peers and professors. Almost all classes are kept at a civilized size, enabling students to participate more actively than they would in large lectures. A freshman remarked, "The professors are really good here. They go out of their way to help out students," while a senior praised, "The faculty are interested in us as people. They are open and warm. You feel like you can knock on their door at any time." Many students also have opportunities to work closely with professors on their research or on independent projects.

One of the ways in which Denison has bolstered its academic reputation has been by hiring new professors who are carefully screened before receiving a job offer. In fact, the students participate directly in the hiring process: Candidates come speak to the students, and the students are then asked to give their opinions about the prospective teachers to the administration. Undergraduates really seem to appreciate being included in this way, and it gives the professors a great deal of legitimacy once they are hired (as if the students voted for them).

The campus and facilities also receive compliments from students. The picturesque campus, set on a hill above the tiny town of Granville, features colonial brick buildings arranged around carefully manicured greens, accented by nearby woods. The dormitories are divided into three residential quads and housing is guaranteed for all four years. Seniors are given the option to live off campus, in apartments in Newark and Granville.

More than 60 percent of the student body comes from out of state, primarily from the Midwest and the East Coast. There's not much ethnic or socioeconomic diversity; most students are white and from upper-middle- and upper-class backgrounds. However, as part of its drive to improve the school academically, there has been an attempt to increase the diversity of the student population. With its small enrollment, the student body forms a friendly and closely knit community.

The social atmosphere at Denison has been undergoing some changes. The Greeks have become nonresidential, and fraternities have become like dorms, open to everyone. Frat parties have moved off campus, and Greek life no longer dominates the social scene. One undergraduate expressed relief about this, commenting, "Greeks and non-Greeks interact together on campus much more than before."

Denison University

$$$$
★

Setting: Rural
# of Undergraduates: 1,930
Men: 48.9% **Women:** 50.1%
Tuition: $19,310
Room and Board: $5,370
# of Students Applied: 2,569
   Admitted: 2,116   **Enrolled:** 642
Required Admissions Test: Either SAT or ACT
Lowest 25% of Freshmen Scored At or Below: SAT Verbal: 530 SAT Math: 530   ACT Comp.: 22
Highest 25% of Freshmen Scored At or Above: SAT Verbal: 630   SAT Math: 640 ACT Comp.: 28
H.S. Rank, Top 10%: 35%
Top 25%: 65%
Top 50%: 86%
Avg. Score of Applicants Admitted: SAT Verbal: 582 SAT Math: 584   ACT Comp.: 25
Average GPA of Applicants Admitted: 3.10
Most Popular Majors (% of Student Body): English (12.2%), Psychology (11.4%), Economics (11.2%), Communication (8.7%), History (7.8%)

Denison students seem to feel that there's almost "too much to do" when it comes to extracurricular options. The Student Activities Committee, for example, works with a large budget, enabling many bands, comedians, and lecturers to come visit. There are occasionally large parties held outside on the quad, including the "Eastivalia," which one student described as "a celebration of spring," and "the Gala," a big evening event the Friday of Homecoming weekend when bands play, people dance, and chocolate volcanoes are consumed in large quantities.

Most Denison students become involved in various activities, including working for the newspaper or radio station, student government, and volunteer and community service groups. Due to the school's small size, students have a greater chance to hold leadership positions in various clubs and organizations. Many students also participate in intercollegiate and intramural sports. Among the school's highly rated teams are basketball, swimming, men's cross country and track, and women's lacrosse. While Denison's days as a wild and rowdy party school are apparently on the wane, Denison still offers students a fun social atmosphere in the midst of improving academics.

EARLHAM COLLEGE IN RICHMOND, INDIANA

Admissions Address: Admissions Office, Bolling House, 801 National Road West, Richmond, IN 47374-4095
Phone: (765) 983-1600 (800) EARLHAM
Web Address: www.earlham.edu/

Earlham is a small liberal arts school established by the Quakers and, while only a minority of its students actually practice that religion, traditional Quaker values of education and community permeate the college and help make it an idyllic collegiate environment. "We have created an atmosphere based on mutual respect," explained a senior. "Policies are set by the Quaker-oriented 'Community Code' under which teachers and students interact with one another via friendly, open lines of communication." Students report "peer relationships with professors that are on first-name bases."

Earlham is strong in many traditional liberal arts departments, including English, history, psychology, and biology, as well as more unusual, harder-to-find programs such as peace and global studies and Japanese studies, considered one of the best such programs in the country. The extensive general education requirements include courses in humanities, natural sciences, lab sciences, social sciences, religion and philosophy, fine arts, and foreign language. The solid liberal arts background they receive helps a high percentage of Earlham grads gain acceptance at graduate and professional schools.

Earlham is making the transition from a trimester to semester system, leading teachers to reorganize their classes to fit the longer term. A student characterizes the college's academic environment as "work intensive." Students are actively involved participants in their learning, and often work as hard inside the classroom as they do outside. Classes, which often number less than 20 students, are "very discussion-oriented," we hear, so students need to be prepared to speak up.

Surrounded by acres of woods, the Earlham campus is tranquil, yet distinctively collegiate. Most students live on campus in dormitories that have been greatly improved by recent renovations. There are also several university-owned houses, including theme and language homes. Most people praise the Earlham library, impressive for a school of this size. Students come to Earlham from all over to form an interesting and eclectic student body. There's about a 10 percent minority population, with African Americans making up close to 5 percent. One student proclaimed that his fellow students are the school's greatest strength. "Earlham has a very open-minded community, which is progressive, friendly, accepting, and intellectual. We are an intelligent, diverse community," he said.

The school's rural location leaves the campus somewhat isolated. The town of Richmond and the Earlham campus are distinctly separate entities. Students don't often go into town, which isn't particularly student-friendly. But a junior told us that there are more than enough student-led activities to keep everyone busy. "We're an officially dry campus, so many abstinence-minded people come here looking for activities that don't involve drinking," he said. "That's not to say that nobody drinks here, but it's usually done off-campus or in closed and quiet groups." Rather than attending large parties, students go to movies or concerts and performances or simply hang out with groups of friends.

Students are also deeply involved in the campus community either through student government or participation in the college's many clubs and activities. There are more than 60 groups to choose from, which, given the small size of the student body, means they have no shortage of choices. Particularly popular among students are intramural sports, joining student performance groups and bands, and working for volunteer and community service programs. Many students become politically

Earlham College

$$$$$

Setting: Suburban
# of Undergraduates: 977
Men: 43.4%   **Women:** 56.6%
Tuition: $18,056
Room and Board: $4,544
# of Students Applied: 1,180
   Admitted: 976   **Enrolled:** 280
Required Admissions Test: SAT I or ACT
Lowest 25% of Freshmen Scored At or Below: SAT Verbal: 550 SAT Math: 510   ACT Comp.: 22
Highest 25% of Freshmen Scored At or Above: SAT Verbal: 690   SAT Math: 650 ACT Comp.: 29
H.S. Rank, Top 10%: 84%
Top 25%: 100%
Avg. Score of Applicants Admitted: SAT Verbal: 620 SAT Math: 580   ACT Comp.: 26
Average GPA of Applicants Admitted: 3.40

active and join organizations that reflect a variety of liberal political interests and issues.

If people tire of the campus social scene, there are ways to get away. The surrounding forests are ideal for outdoor sports, such as hiking, mountain biking, and jogging. Road trips to other cities, such as Indianapolis, are popular. If students want to get farther away, Earlham has an extensive study-abroad program. About three quarters of the students go overseas at some point, choosing from destinations in Mexico, Africa, South America, Europe, and the Middle East. Back on the Earlham campus, there are several major campus events that bring the entire student body together, including an annual autumn reggae festival and an International Fest, a celebration of the students and their rich ethnic and cultural backgrounds.

FRANKLIN AND MARSHALL COLLEGE
IN LANCASTER, PENNSYLVANIA

Admissions Address: Admissions Office, P.O. Box 3003, Lancaster, PA 17604-3003
Phone: (717) 291-3953
Web Address: www.fandm.edu/

A small liberal arts college in the scenic Pennsylvania Dutch region, Franklin and Marshall has one of the most rigorous and intense academic programs in the country. Students complain about the workload and the difficulty of getting A-level grades but also take pride in their perseverance. Surviving the academic rigors of F&M means they can handle just about anything. Indeed, high percentages go on to academic and career success.

Almost everything about the academic programs at F&M is designed to encourage students to engage actively and intellectually with their studies. The general requirements include courses in many challenging academic areas, such as historical studies, literature, scientific inquiry, social analysis, arts, foreign culture, and systems of knowledge and belief. First-year seminars help students develop communication and critical-thinking tools that become crucial skills in their other courses. All classes are limited in enrollment and emphasize student participation and discussion. Professors, while notoriously tough graders, are "generally attentive and helpful," students report.

Some of the best-known departments are in premed sciences, which benefit from state-of-the-art facilities that undergraduates can use in their

BURIED TREASURES

own research. However, one student warned that while many people begin by studying premed, a lot also wind up changing majors once faced with the difficult science courses. Those who stick with it, though, are more than well prepared for medical school. Business courses, geology, government, and English, are also strong and have high enrollments.

F&M's location, in Pennsylvania's Amish country, provides a safe and serene setting for the picturesque campus. While some of the college's facilities receive criticism, students praise the computer accessibility, including E-mail and online services directly from their rooms. The housing ranges in style and arrangement and includes special-interest and language houses. Some upperclassmen opt to move off campus.

The student body is generally classified as conservative. Efforts by the administration have increased the number of minority and international students, although they still don't represent a large percentage. About 30 percent of the students come from Pennsylvania.

While the Amish country is popular among tourists and visiting parents, the novelty of it quickly wears off for most students, who choose to stick close to campus for social activity (some people make an occasional road trip to Philadelphia, just over an hour away). One student assured us that "there's a lot of opportunity to get involved in extracurricular activities," ranging from a TV and radio station to different types of music, drama, and ethnic groups, but noted that many students don't become involved for fear of detracting from their academics. The Greek system, while not officially recognized by the administration, "dominates much of the social scene," a student said. About 40 percent of the men and 30 percent of the women join fraternities and sororities.

The College Entertainment Committee brings a decent number of entertainers, major bands, and cultural performances to campus each year. In the spring, there's a large live music festival during Spring Arts Weekend. Also, a new sporting facility called the Alumni Sports and Fitness Center has greatly enhanced F&M's recreational and intramural activities. The center includes an Olympic-size pool, track, weight room, and basketball courts.

F&M students work harder than students at most other schools, yet they also manage to enjoy themselves. A departing senior looked back at her college, saying, "Franklin and Marshall, while academically challenging, has left me with many friends and beautiful memories."

Franklin and Marshall College

$$$$$
★★★

Setting: Suburban
# of Undergraduates: 1,763
Men: 52.9% Women: 47.1%
Tuition: $22,664
Room and Board: $4,906
# of Students Applied: 3,729
   Admitted: 2,217   Enrolled: 525
Required Admissions Test: Either SAT or ACT
H.S. Rank, Top 10%: 58%
Top 25%: 88%
Top 50%: 98%
Most Popular Majors (% of Student Body): Political Science (16.7%), Business (12%), English (9.6%), Biology (9.2%), History (8.7%)

GUSTAVUS ADOLPHUS COLLEGE
IN SAINT PETER, MINNESOTA

Admissions Address: Admissions Office, 800 West College Avenue, St. Peter, MN 56082-1498
Phone: (507) 933-7676
Web Address: www.gac.edu/

Gustavus Adolphus College

$$$$$

Setting: Suburban
# of Undergraduates: 2,376
Men: 45.8% **Women:** 57.2%
Tuition: $15,940
Room and Board: $4,010
# of Students Applied: 1,883
   Admitted: 1,565 **Enrolled:** 627
Required Admissions Test: Either SAT or ACT
Lowest 25% of Freshmen Scored At or Below: SAT Verbal: 540 SAT Math: 550 ACT Comp.: 23
Highest 25% of Freshmen Scored At or Above: SAT Verbal: 670 SAT Math: 660 ACT Comp.: 28
H.S. Rank, Top 10%: 37%
Top 25%: 72%
Top 50%: 97%
Avg. Score of Applicants Admitted: SAT Verbal: 610 SAT Math: 615 ACT Comp.: 25
Average GPA of Applicants Admitted: 3.40
Most Popular Majors (% of Student Body): Psychology (13%), Biology (10%), Education (9%), History (6%), Political Science (6%)

You've probably heard that Minnesota winters are, to be polite, rather chilly. Yet students at Gustavus Adolphus—perhaps inspired by their school's namesake, a legendary Swedish ruler used to adverse conditions—mock the cold with their defiant spirits. This is the time that "Gusties" race out to ski, skate, sled, and frolic in the snow, relieving some of the stress induced by challenging academic classes.

While many people may be unfamiliar with the school, it plays host each year to a prestigious Nobel Conference—more evidence of that Swedish influence—that brings renowned scientists and speakers to campus. Sciences are among the school's strengths and provide cutting-edge facilities and resources, including several newly built science centers. Many other departments are also highly regarded, including English, history, psychology, and music.

Before focusing in a specific field, students take up one of two general course loads. Curriculum I, the more traditional one, requires study within basic academic areas, such as humanities, fine arts, math and science, social science, foreign culture, and religion. Sixty students can enroll in Curriculum II, which takes an interdisciplinary approach to liberal arts material. Students also must take three courses that are writing intensive. These stiff requirements make for a demanding, highly stressed academic environment. Classes are small and discussion oriented, requiring that students participate. Students like the fact that their professors get to know them by name and that they often get to work closely with them on special projects. "I'm already on a first-name basis with most of my profs," boasted a freshman.

The school has made many improvements to its facilities in recent years. The Lund Center for athletics and health makes a number of sports and activities popular; in addition to a pool and a weight room, there are racquetball courts, a hockey ice arena, basketball gym, and an indoor track. The dormitories, grouped in two main areas, the North and South End of campus, are reportedly in good condition, and most students live on campus. The school has an extensive study-abroad program, and about 40 percent of the students go abroad at some point.

Gustavus Adolphus's origins as a Lutheran institution are still evident in the student body, made up of a majority of Lutheran students. About 70 percent of the students come from Minnesota, and more than 90 percent are white. Obviously the student body is not the most diverse. Students do, though, form a closely knit, friendly community, smiling and saying hello to people they pass around campus, whether or not they already know them.

Students sometimes journey to St. Paul or Minneapolis for a bit of big-city culture and excitement. For the most part, though, they stick to their own campus and the surrounding areas. The local fraternities and sororities have no national affiliations but they keep the social scene hopping. Students also hang out at various places around campus, such as the large student union, dorm rooms, the library, and an on-campus dance club called The Dive. Thanks to the school's music and theater departments, there are usually a number of student concerts or productions on campus. Several intercollegiate teams that compete in Division III (like basketball) are strong, and games are well attended.

KNOX COLLEGE IN GALESBURG, ILLINOIS

Admissions Address: Admissions Office, Box K-148, Galesburg, IL 61401
Phone: (309) 341-7100 (800) 678-KNOX
Web Address: www.knox.edu

A senior at Knox College raved that "the professors here are just as much my friends as anyone else on campus." With a student enrollment smaller than at many high schools, Knox's close-knit academic environment helps students and faculty enjoy an easygoing, comfortable familiarity with one another.

With a solid, exceptional liberal arts background under their belts, high percentages of Knox graduates are accepted at graduate and professional schools. Many students are on the premed path, and the premedical sciences, enjoying top-notch facilities, are among the school's strongest programs. Advanced premed students have the opportunity to apply for early acceptance at Rush Medical College. Similarly, students in business can apply for early acceptance to the University of Chicago graduate school of business. Other special academic options available at Knox include cooperative programs at several other universities, college honors programs, and study abroad in over 15 countries.

Knox College

$$$$$
★

Setting: Small Town
# of Undergraduates: 1,109
Men: 46.4% **Women:** 53.6%
Tuition: $18,186
Room and Board: $4,896
# of Students Applied: 1,347
  Admitted: 1,098 **Enrolled:** 310
Required Admissions Test: Either SAT or ACT
Lowest 25% of Freshmen Scored At or Below: SAT Verbal: 540 SAT Math: 540 ACT Comp.: 23
Highest 25% of Freshmen Scored At or Above: SAT Verbal: 660 SAT Math: 680 ACT Comp.: 29
H.S. Rank, Top 10%: 39%
Top 25%: 70%
Top 50%: 96%
Most Popular Majors (% of Student Body): Political Science (12%), English (12%), Biology (10%), Psychology (7%), Economics (6%)

Class sizes at Knox are generally limited to 20 students or less and they are always taught by professors. As the classes are small, students are expected to participate a great deal in each class. When all your professors know you, it's hard to hide or fake your way through when called on. "The faculty is receptive to student input and sensitive to how we think and feel," commented a sophomore.

Students like the trimester system for letting them focus on a few courses at a time, but they dislike it for cramming a semester's worth of work into 10 weeks. "It always seems like exams are just around the corner," complained a freshman. "You've definitely got to be on top of your work, and it's easy to get off track." The combination of challenging professors, a heavy workload, and extensive requirements leaves students having to study between three and four hours a night.

The stiff distribution requirements include courses in basic liberal arts subject areas such as humanities, fine arts, social sciences, math, natural sciences, and foreign language proficiency. Many courses emphasize writing skills. During their first year, students enroll in a Freshman Preceptorial in which freshmen work closely together in an interdisciplinary seminar focusing on writing and critical thinking. Students are required to take a second interdisciplinary seminar, called an Advanced Preceptorial, as upperclassmen.

The pretty, easily navigated campus combines the best of old and new; historic and modern structures are side by side in neatly arranged quad formations. Knox's facilities are generally in superb condition. There have been many improvements and additions, including extensive renovations of academic buildings. The housing is particularly impressive; most students live in suite-like arrangements (a new suite-style dorm is being built). With several rooms sharing a large common area that is ideal for hanging out, the suites enable students to form close circles of friends. There are also several special-interest and theme houses.

A majority of the students come from the Midwest, and over half are from Illinois. There's about a 20 percent minority and international student population. In terms of their politics, a sophomore told us, "the student body is about 70 percent liberal, 25 percent apathetic, and five percent conservative," and there is little tension between students.

Smack in the middle of Illinois farmland, Knox's location and the Illinois winters often leave students confined to the campus. Yet one student we spoke to had no trouble listing the various social activities available to her on or near campus. Fraternities and sororities contribute significantly to the social and party scene, but there isn't fierce competition to get into houses. Most parties they throw are open to everyone. Many other extracurricular activities keep students busy, from intramural sports to student theater productions. Knox's athletic facilities, including a field house with an indoor track and tennis courts, allow people to enjoy a number of sports and recreational activities, even during the dark days of winter. Several events draw the entire student body, including Flunk Day, a day each spring when classes are canceled and students celebrate the end of the long winter.

The compact campus and isolated location can be drawbacks. Some students find things become a bit too close for comfort, especially when everyone knows so much about one other. Chicago and St. Louis, each roughly three hours away, provide good weekend escapes. At the same time, though, Knox's intimate academic setting enables students to become active participants in their own educations rather than passive receptors of information. After all, when you're friendly with your professors, intellectual discussion doesn't have to end at the classroom door.

MACALESTER COLLEGE IN ST. PAUL, MINNESOTA

Admissions Address: Admissions Office, 1600 Grand Avenue, St. Paul, MN 55105
Phone: (612) 696-6357 (800) 231-7974
Web Address: www.macalester.edu

Macalester has often been labeled as a liberal, free-thinking institution lost somewhere in the Midwest. When people hear that Macalester is located in Minnesota, they may picture it as completely cut off from all signs of civilization and surrounded by miles of snow-covered farmland. Actually, the campus lies only minutes from the cultural meccas of Minneapolis and St. Paul. Interest in international issues and an especially diverse, progressive student population make Macalester truly cosmopolitan.

Macalester's academics have been getting stronger and stronger in recent years, and the combination of an attentive faculty and small classes leads students to rave about their courses. Students also praise the selection of course offerings: "There is such a wide range of classes, and you can usually get into the ones you want," we hear. If they don't find what they want at "Mac," they have the option of taking courses at one of the other four schools in the Associated Colleges of the Twin Cities: Augsberg, Hamline, St. Catherine, and St. Thomas.

Macalester College

$$$$$
★★★

Setting: Urban
# of Undergraduates: 1,715
Men: 43.4% **Women:** 56.6%
Tuition: $18,630
Room and Board: $5,430
# of Students Applied: 3,132
  Admitted: 1,718 **Enrolled:** 491
Required Admissions Test: Either SAT or ACT
Lowest 25% of Freshmen Scored At or Below: SAT Verbal: 620 SAT Math: 600 ACT Comp.: 27
Highest 25% of Freshmen Scored At or Above: SAT Verbal: 720 SAT Math: 690 ACT Comp.: 31
H.S. Rank, Top 10%: 57%
Top 25%: 92%
Top 50%: 99%
Avg. Score of Applicants Admitted: SAT Verbal: 610 SAT Math: 640 ACT Comp.: 29
Most Popular Majors (% of Student Body): English (11%), Economics (11%), Psychology (10%), History (10%), Biology (9%)

Core requirements include courses in humanities and fine arts, natural science, mathematics, social science, and diversity. During their freshman year students are required to take the First Year Course, a seminar limited to 15 students and taught by their advisor. This enables students to establish personal relationships with their advisors right from day one, making it easier to turn to them in future days for more help and advice. Also, a majority of the freshmen are placed in housing with their peers from the First Year Course. A sophomore reflected on the merits of this system, saying, "I made close friends at Macalester last year because I was living and studying with the same group all year. This made it really easy to get to know them well." The relationship between students and teachers seems to be close at Macalester. As for the workload, students say it depends on what you take, but that "classes definitely become more challenging as you move into your major."

Because the course requirements are relatively easy to fulfill, students have time to pursue their own interests. Many facets of the Macalester education encourage students to explore on their own. Students can pursue independent studies, for example, or design their own majors. During their senior year, Mac students engage in a "capstone" experience that depends on their major; it might involve special courses or projects, independent study, seminars, or a combination of all four.

Macalester claims one of its goals is to promote "multicultural awareness," and there's plenty of evidence this is more than just talk. Minorities account for 15 percent of the students, while 10 percent are international students from more than 80 countries around the world. Interest in international issues is reflected in other aspects of the Macalester experience. International Studies, for example, is one of the strongest and most popular programs. Additionally, a large percentage of students opt for study abroad at some point. Whether abroad or at home, Mac students generally welcome the opportunity to share experiences and views with those from very different backgrounds.

Macalester has long catered to an activist student body, which staged antiwar protests during the 1960s and annual antinuclear "lie down" demonstrations. One junior regretted the lack of passionate protest during her time at Mac, accusing fellow students of being overly comfortable with where they are in the world and waiting apathetically for a hot topic to arise. Still, it would be fair to say that today's Mac students retain their liberalism and concern about a variety of issues, including sexual harassment, gay rights, the environment, and the protection of abortion rights. Students are also respectful of one another's differences, and there's reportedly little discrimination against minorities, gays and lesbians, or women. For what it's worth, nearly half the students are vegetarians or vegans.

Macalester has an especially high endowment (as one student told us, "There's a lot of money here . . . a *lot*."), much of which goes into extensive renovations and additions. The science, computer, and technology facilities have been key beneficiaries of this money in recent years. There's also a newly built library, a gym with a pool, and a student union with a cafeteria and access to many school facilities. Some of the money has also gone into renovating existing dormitories and building a new one, and all rooms are being hardwired so you can easily connect your computer to the school network. Students are required to live on campus their first two years. Upperclassmen covet rooms in Kirk or the few duplexes in the football stadium, which only a select few can enter by lottery. About 30 percent of the students move off campus after their second year.

Because Macalester sits in a residential section halfway between St. Paul and Minneapolis, students can easily venture off campus to a number of cafes, coffeeshops, bookstores, and ethnic restaurants. The campus' proximity to the Twin Cities—both relatively safe and manageable for cities—is appealing to the students. St. Paul, a 15-minute bus ride away, is home to the Ordway Music Center and St. Paul Orchestra, while Minneapolis boasts the Walker Arts Complex and Guthrie Theatre, 15 museums, and a pretty hip music scene. After all, an artist formerly known as Prince got his start here. Heading downtown provides an escape from winter doldrums, a survival skill that is crucial here. As one student succinctly put it, "the winter sucks."

Macalester has no fraternities and kegs have been banned, so students tend to socialize in smaller get-togethers in rooms or at cafes and bars, rather than at big parties. In addition to the cultural offerings in the Twin Cities, there are also on-campus movies, dances, and concerts. Joining one of Macalester's many student clubs or becoming involved in an extracurricular activity, which include performing groups, political organizations, service groups, literary magazines, journals, and a popular radio station, also helps keep students busy through the long winter months.

Sports have become another popular diversion, although that wasn't always the case here. "Some of the past's antiathleticism has faded," comments a progressive student. "We now feel that athletes are people too."

While another student laments, "we have the world's worst football team, with one of the longest losing streaks in college football history," other teams, particularly men's and women's soccer, show some strength. Intramural sports of all kinds, like rugby, skiing, and ultimate Frisbee, are popular, and recent additions to Macalester's athletic facilities offer more opportunities for sports and physical activities.

Come spring, Mac students come out to celebrate the return of the sun in full force with two popular events, the Scottish Country Fair and Springfest, an all-day outdoor party with live bands. "It's really something else, especially after a few beers," says an anonymous student. Watching the crowds of people out enjoying the weather and being around one another, you can see how much Mac students love their school—especially when it's sunny.

Mary Washington College

$$
★★★

Setting: small city
# of Undergraduates: 3,047
Men: 34.3% Women: 65.7
In-State Tuition: $3,556
Out-of-State Tuition: $8,516
Room and Board: $5,080
# of Students Applied: 4,003
   Admitted: 2,219   Enrolled: 736
Required Admissions Test: either SAT or ACT
Recommended: SAT II subject tests
Lowest 25% of Freshmen Scored At or Below: SAT Verbal: 550 SAT Math: 540
Highest 25% of Freshmen Scored At or Above: SAT Verbal: 650 SAT Math: 620
H.S. Rank, Top 10%: 35%
Top 25%: 84%
Top 50%: 98%
Avg. Score of Applicants Admitted: SAT Verbal: 609 SAT Math: 594
Average GPA of Applicants Admitted: 3.53
Most Popular Majors (% of Student Body): Business (13%), English (8.6%), Psychology (8.4%), Biology (8.2%), History (5.4%)

MARY WASHINGTON COLLEGE

Admissions Address: Office of Admissions, 1301 College Avenue, Fredricksburg, VA 22401
Phone: (540) 654-2000 (800) 468-5614
Web Address: www.mwc.edu/

Current students at Mary Washington have expressed concern that their college is becoming too popular, with more and more applicants rushing to get in. As greater numbers of high school seniors learn about this small liberal arts college, with its gorgeous campus, top-rate facilities, and low tuition, enrollment is rapidly increasing and the campus is becoming crowded.

The extensive core curriculum demands much time and work from students. Lower division requirements encompass atypical academic areas with names like Intellectual Frameworks, Modes of Creativity, the Human World, and Abstract Thought. Students also take laboratory science, math, physical education, and must have at least five classes that focus on writing. Those that didn't complete the equivalent of four high school years of foreign language must fulfill a college language requirement as well.

Liberal arts departments are generally strong at Mary Washington, with English and psychology enjoying the largest enrollments. Programs in political and international studies benefit from the school's proximity to Washington, D.C., where internship and work-studies possibilities abound. Additionally, the college's location, surrounded by major historical sights from the Civil War, makes history-related subjects popular. Mary Washington's Center for Historic Preservation is one of the best of its kind.

Class sizes are kept to a minimum and emphasize discussion over lecturing. Faculty members make teaching, rather than research, their number one priority. Students freely consult with professors for advice, often working closely with them on independent projects. The college encourages undergraduates to conduct their own research with the help of faculty members and often assists with special funding schemes.

The immaculate campus looks like a restored colonial village, with brick white-columned buildings lining pathways along a central campus mall. Don't let the older architecture fool you—Mary Washington has been on a recent building spree, investing in renovations and additions. Most facilities are superb, and students have great things to say about their housing. "From what I've seen, even our worst dorms are better than those at other colleges," boasts a freshman. Until recently, on-campus housing was guaranteed for all four years, but with the increased enrollment juniors and seniors are starting to trickle off campus to nearby apartments.

While about three quarters of the students come from Virginia, the rest arrive from more than 30 states and 15 countries. 90 percent of the student body is white. Until 1970, Mary Washington was considered the all-female branch of the University of Virginia, leaving a ratio today of 65 percent women. Most students consider themselves politically and socially conservative, although they're not particularly vocal about their politics. As a whole, students seem to get along harmoniously, and the school honor code fosters an atmosphere of trust and respect.

The town of Fredericksburg, although not much of a college party town, is pretty, clean, and safe. For social activity, students remain on campus or take easy road trips to Richmond or Washington, D.C. Fraternities and sororities don't exist here, so students seeking parties head for off-campus bashes or smaller dormitory parties. While the campus is strictly dry, the Underground coffee house, beneath the admissions building, is another popular student hangout that hosts live music on weekends. A formal dance is held each term in the Campus Center. Students also become involved in various extracurriculars, such as student government, theater production, and music groups. Mary Washington hosts several large and traditional campus events each year that draw the entire student body, like "Grill on the Hill" and Weststock, an outdoor music festival. In spring, numerous dorm-sponsored picnics with great grub and loud bands spring up on the college lawns.

As you can tell, Mary Washington has plenty of activity to keep your calendar booked for academic and social appointments. As a junior pointed out, however, "students need to be very self-motivated here. The school has everything to offer, but it doesn't go out of its way to give it to you. You've got to find what's right for you and create your own agenda."

Occidental College

$$$$$
★★

Setting: Urban
# of Undergraduates: 1,544
Men: 48% Women: 52%
Tuition: $17,666
Room and Board: $6,231
# of Students Applied: 2,085
  Admitted: 1,389 Enrolled: 407
Required Admissions Test: Either SAT or ACT
Mean SAT Verbal: 525
Mean SAT Math: 594
H.S. Rank, Top 10%: 55%
Top 25%: 85%
Top 50%: 100%
Avg. Score of Applicants
  Admitted: SAT Verbal: 643
  SAT Math: 613

OCCIDENTAL COLLEGE IN LOS ANGELES, CALIFORNIA

Admissions Address: Admissions Office, 1600 Campus Road, Los Angeles, CA 90041-3314
Phone: (213) 259-2700 (800) 825-5262
Web Address: www.oxy.edu/

Occidental College is proud of its commitment to what it calls a "total education," which combines strong liberal arts programs and interdisciplinary studies with an unwavering concern for multiculturalism. With a small, diverse student population, Occidental has the atmosphere of an intimate and vibrant academic community. "This is a serious academic college with a closely knit and active student body," summarized a graduating senior.

A variety of academic departments and programs are strong at Oxy, including economics, English, politics, as well as less traditional programs, such as diplomacy, world affairs, and marine biology. Many students are on a professional or graduate school track, and some of the school's strengths are in preprofessional areas, including premed sciences.

The distribution requirements are extensive and can take up about two years to fulfill. The basic core curriculum includes classes in Western and non-Western history, science, math, fine art, and foreign language. Some students have the option for the accelerated Collegium, a more intimate, more intense core program with an interdisciplinary approach to various topics. The stiff core does mean students have less space for electives, but most students appreciate the well-rounded background they receive as a result. Unlike at larger universities, the core courses here are kept relatively small and are always taught by professors, fluctuating between 10 to 20 students. At the upper levels, class sizes will be even smaller, often between 12 to 15 students.

Students are challenged every day in their small classes, where participation and discussion usually take precedence over lecturing. In small classes, students have plenty of interaction with professors, who are generally friendly and extremely attentive to students. Students also form close relationships with their peers. The school is small enough so that everyone knows everyone else—at least by face.

Unlike many schools where concern about multiculturalism is more a matter of talk than action, Occidental's commitment to fostering cultural diversity is evident in many specific ways, including the recent addition of a Cultural Resources Center, which was built to increase the school's cultural resources, programs, and events. Occidental's recruitment and admissions procedures have created a diverse student body with what the administration reports as a nearly 50 percent minority population, with Hispanic students representing the largest minority group, followed by Asian Americans, African Americans, and international students. About half the student population comes from out of state.

Academically, the school encourages the study of non-Western cultures in its core curriculum and offers an interdisciplinary program in Asian studies as well as history and literature courses for different cultures. There are several large student cultural organizations on campus, including the Black Student Alliance, MECHA/ALAS, the Chicano and Latino group, CASA, the Central American Students Association, and The Asian Pacific Alliance, which sponsors several Asian student groups including Chinese, Korean, Filipino, and Vietnamese. Each of these groups organize several campus-wide special events and festivals.

The tree-laden campus, with its Spanish-style architecture, is situated around a central quad, ideal for hanging out and enjoying the California sunshine. Most students live on campus in residence halls divided between upper and lower campus. Residence halls vary in personality but are all small enough that students get to know most people they live with. For many, the residence halls become the focus for their social lives, especially during their first two years at Occidental. Several dorms have special theme floors for students sharing interests in particular issues, cultures, or foreign languages. The Multicultural Hall, housing about 100 residents, fosters intercultural interaction among students, although we hear that students all over campus generally meet and mingle without much difficulty.

The students themselves form a close community. Most are liberal and progressive. They enjoy a relatively casual, but varied, social life. Rather than attending blowout parties, students hang out in small groups in dorms or around the campus. There are a few fraternities and sororities, which draw a small percentage of the student body, and they host parties open to all. Various extracurricular activities are popular, particularly intramural sports, volunteer work and community service, and participation in various politically oriented groups.

While Oxy is itself pretty comfortable and serene, the suburban L.A. neighborhood surrounding it is a little less safe. For a break from the campus social scene, it's crucial to have a car, or at least a friend with one, in order to take advantage of the social offerings of Los Angeles and the surrounding areas. Students enjoy heading to Los Angeles' restaurants, clubs, museums, movie theaters, cultural centers, and beaches. Old Town Pasadena, located only 10 minutes away by car, also draws students to its chic cafés, restaurants, and bars.

SOUTHWESTERN UNIVERSITY
IN GEORGETOWN, TEXAS

Admissions Address: Admissions Office, 1001 E. University, Georgetown, TX 78626
Phone: (512) 863-1200 (800) 252-3166
Web Address: www.southwestern.edu

Although Texas is the site of several well-known, large universities, most people don't realize that the first university in the state was Southwestern University. Unlike its fellow Texas universities whose student populations number in the thousands, SU is home to about 1,200 students, who become immersed in their liberal arts studies within a friendly environment. "The best thing here," a student told us, "is the intimacy of the campus and the ease with which you can make friends."

Southwestern's liberal arts and science departments are strong across the board, from biology and chemistry, to psychology and sociology, to history and music. Many preprofessional programs are also popular, including communications and business. A number of students consider themselves premed or prelaw. The extensive core curriculum includes several courses within broad academic fields such as arts, humanities, social science, natural science, and math. Students are also required to take English composition and a freshman symposium, which provides them with an opportunity to interact closely with fellow first-year students while acclimating themselves to university life. Students must also demonstrate computer literacy. Many students opt to round out their

BURIED TREASURES

educations with a semester abroad in one of SU's many programs, including study in England, France, Korea, and Mexico. Because the student enrollment is small, there's no need for large lecture courses. All classes are kept small, which means that students receive a great deal of personal attention from their professors, who are reportedly committed to helping their students. "While I had 30 to 40 people in classes my freshman year," remembered a sophomore, "they're now a lot smaller, and I know the professors as well as most of my peers."

SU has a large endowment that goes into maintaining its exceptional facilities which, in turn, draw many renowned faculty members. There have been many improvements made to the campus in the past few years, including the addition of a central academic mall and a recreation center. Many more major improvements are in the works. Most students live on campus, where they live and eat in a comfortable, traditionally collegiate environment.

While the student body includes a small Hispanic population, the vast majority are Texans. The students seem quite intelligent and committed to their studies. "Students study here more than any other activity. As soon as classes are over, people start to study," a junior told us.

The school is located in Georgetown ("the other Georgetown," a student lamented), a quiet town with few student hangouts. As a result, students find ways to enjoy an active social life on campus. "Because there is so much stress due to the heavy workload, people need an outlet, so there's a lot of 'adult beverage' drinking," a junior told us. There are also more than 50 activities and clubs, including student publications, music groups of all kinds, and professional, political, and public service groups.

The active Greek system drives much of the campus social scene. In addition to attending fraternity and sorority events and parties, students go to smaller, informal gatherings and attend movies, concerts, and dances on campus. While there are no varsity teams, students do play a number of intramural sports, such as basketball and softball. SU's natural surroundings enable students to participate in outdoor sports such as jogging, hiking, camping, swimming, and biking.

One of the more prestigious events associated with Southwestern is the annual Brown Symposium. Every spring, prominent and renowned speakers visit the campus for a three-day conference on a particular subject. Classes are canceled so that students may reap the academic benefits and attend the conference.

Southwestern University

$$$$
★★

Setting: Suburban
# of Undergraduates: 1,183
Men: 41.9% **Women:** 58.1%
Tuition: $14,000
Room and Board: $4,969–$5,569
# of Students Applied: 1,231
  Admitted: 969 **Enrolled:** 309
Required Admissions Test: Either SAT or ACT
Lowest 25% of Freshmen Scored At or Below: SAT Verbal: 550 SAT Math: 530 ACT Comp.: 23
Highest 25% of Freshmen Scored At or Above: SAT Verbal: 660 SAT Math: 650 ACT Comp.: 29
H.S. Rank, Top 10%: 41%
Top 25%: 73%
Top 50%: 98%
Avg. Score of Applicants Admitted: SAT Verbal: 600 SAT Math: 595 ACT Comp.: 26
Average GPA of Applicants Admitted: 3.40
Most Popular Majors (% of Student Body): Psychology (10.3%), Biology (9.5%), Business (9.5%), History (7.3%), Communications (7.2%)

219

While Georgetown offers little to appeal to students, many like to escape to Austin, just 30 minutes away by car, on weekends. Austin is currently one of the nation's most popular cities among students, with a thriving music and culture scene, as well as the kinds of restaurants, bars, and clubs that cater to young student crowds. Many Southwestern students feel they have the best of both worlds; they can head into a great city when they want to, but then return to a tranquil, intimate campus.

TRINITY COLLEGE IN HARTFORD, CONNECTICUT

Admissions Address: Admissions Office, 300 Summit Street, Hartford, CT 06106-3100
Phone: (860) 297-2180 (860) 297-2000
Web Address: www.trincoll.edu

Trinity College

$$$$$
★★★

Setting: Urban
# of Undergraduates: 1,877
Men: 51% **Women:** 49%
Tuition: $20,450
Room and Board: $6,130
# of Students Applied: 4,000
   Admitted: 1,751 **Enrolled:** 504
Required Admissions Test: Either SAT I or ACT
Recommended: SAT II
Lowest 25% of Freshmen Scored At or Below: SAT Verbal: 590 SAT Math: 580 ACT Comp.: 26
Highest 25% of Freshmen Scored At or Above: SAT Verbal: 670 SAT Math: 660 ACT Comp.: 28
H.S. Rank, Top 10%: 43%
Top 25%: 76%
Top 50%: 97%
Avg. Score of Applicants Admitted: SAT Verbal: 630 SAT Math: 610 ACT Comp.: 27
Most Popular Majors (% of Student Body): English (10%), Economics (10%), History (13%), Psychology (10%)

Trinity College can be defined as a work-hard, play-hard school. At this small liberal arts college, students become immersed in an intense, well-rounded academic program. They apply themselves to their studies, but they're also more than ready to go out and have fun once those books are closed. Liberal arts departments are strong across the board; history, English, political science, philosophy, and psychology are particularly popular. The school's interdisciplinary programs—such as Asian studies, Russian studies, American studies, and women's studies—remain highly regarded.

The core curriculum includes one course each from five distribution areas: arts, humanities, natural sciences, numerical and symbolic reasoning, and social sciences. Students must also fulfill an "integration knowledge" sequence of six related courses that supplement their major field of study with courses from other academic disciplines. The Freshman Seminar, chosen from a range of topics, enables students to work closely with fellow first-years and professors who also serve as their faculty advisors. Students in one seminar live together in the same dorm, fostering an even tighter sense of community (for example, there's a Literature dorm, Science dorm, and Philosophy dorm). The Guided Studies program and Interdisciplinary Science program, for which special applications are required, offer highly qualified first-year students opportunities for intense, multidisciplinary study in the humanities or science.

Qualified students can also devote an entire semester to the study of a single subject area, combining course work and seminars with independent study and research. Students have terrific things to say about the teachers who "are very accessible and friendly." Except for introductory courses, classes are small (usually fewer than 25) which fosters close interaction among peers and professors. Professors almost always know students by name and frequently meet with students over coffee, lunch, or dinner.

A self-contained, separate entity from the city of Hartford, the pretty Trinity campus features Gothic academic structures situated around a tree-lined central quad. While students like their own collegiate-looking campus, they don't find the city itself very appealing. For a long time, town-gown relations were strained, but they now appear to be improving, due in large part to an extensive, highly active student community outreach program. More and more of the men and women of Trinity are volunteering in Hartford to help the homeless and hungry, to clean up pollution, and to tutor disadvantaged children. "It's a rewarding, fantastic trend," comments a sophomore.

Students also like the many work and internship programs made available to them in Hartford. About 65 percent of the students take up an internship and there are hundreds to choose from, including many in state government or at local industries. Students who want experiences further from campus can study abroad in programs all over the world, including Trinity's own Dublin and Rome campuses.

Many of the students are wealthy, white, and from the Northeast; many also come from private schools. The school has a long-standing reputation for attracting the preppie set. The administration, however, is attempting to recruit more minority students and is encouraging efforts aimed at fostering interaction among groups on campus.

While most students study long hours, they are also ready to have fun outside of class and the library. For many students, the weekend begins on Wednesday night and involves early-evening parties sponsored by student government, followed by fraternity and dorm parties or visits to local bars, music and comedy clubs. The Greek system attracts many people and contributes to the active social scene on campus. About 20 percent of the student body joins a house, and many others rely on the fraternities for social activities. The administration is attempting to make the fraternities coed, which has met with mixed reactions and results.

The campus itself has many other social opportunities. Students hang out in the Koeppel Student Center, where there's a popular bistro and an underground coffeehouse that has live music and acts. The Trinity Activities Council invites major bands and performers to campus, and the Arts Center produces plays and dance and music concerts on a regular basis. A student-run movie theatre shows art-house films. Many students become committed to clubs and extracurricular activities; because of the school's small size, it's possible to hold major positions without competition. Sports, both intercollegiate and intramural, receive lots of attention. Basketball, football, and hockey are the spectator sports of choice, and any games against rival Williams draw huge crowds of student supporters. Some students head into Hartford for movies, restaurants, and various cultural venues including the prestigious symphony and Hartford Stage. Boston and New York are both easy road trips.

WOFFORD COLLEGE IN SPARTANBURG, SOUTH CAROLINA

Admissions Address: Admissions Office, 429 North Church Street, Spartansburg, SC 29303-3663
Phone: (864) 597-4180
Web Address: www.wofford.edu/

Wofford College has everything a serious student with a laid-back attitude could want. At Wofford, strong academics, particularly in preprofessional fields, combine with an easygoing Southern atmosphere to create a comfortable environment in which to study. Most Wofford students are preprofessionally minded—a significant number go on to medical, law, and business schools—and programs that prepare students for these fields are among Wofford's best and most popular. Sciences are particularly outstanding, and the school has a high placement rate for medical school. Almost all of Wofford's liberal arts departments are strong, including English, history, philosophy, and religion.

A large portion of each student's credits are devoted to fulfilling extensive core requirements, including courses in science, math, history, philosophy, English, fine arts, foreign language, and a first-year humanities seminar. Additionally, as the school maintains its Methodist affiliation, religious courses are required. During the required interim session in January, students have the opportunity to broaden their educational experiences through independent research and projects or off-campus study.

Classes at Wofford remain small, challenging students to be active participants in their studies. Students work closely with their professors, both inside and outside the classroom, and the profs are praised for being so accessible.

Wofford College

$$$$$

★

Setting: Urban
# of Undergraduates: 1,066
Men: 54.7% Women: 45.3%
Tuition: $15,085
Room and Board: $4,410
# of Students Applied: 1,226
   Admitted: 1,032   Enrolled: 291
Required Admissions Test: Either SAT or ACT
Lowest 25% of Freshmen Scored At or Below: SAT Verbal: 520
   SAT Math: 520   ACT Comp.: 21
Highest 25% of Freshmen Scored At or Above: SAT Verbal: 630   SAT Math: 600
   ACT Comp.: 27
H.S. Rank, Top 10%: 36%
Top 25%: 72%
Top 50%: 97%
Most Popular Majors (% of Student Body): Biology (11%), English (10%), Business Economics (10%), Sociology (9%), Psychology (9%)

BURIED TREASURES

Founded in 1854, Wofford retains the Old World look and feel of its early days, with its beautiful landscape and original buildings still intact. In addition, new buildings, such as the Richardson Physical Activities center with a Nautilus weight room, racquetball courts, and dance studios, have been added, and science facilities are being upgraded with state-of-the-art equipment. The dormitories, both coed and single-sex, vary in quality depending on their age. Even the older and more run-down dorms are said to be friendly and social, and most students chooses to stay in university housing all four years.

The student body consists of mostly upper-middle class whites, conservative politically and socially. African Americans make up 6 percent of the school population, and roughly 70 percent of the students hail from South Carolina.

The college's small size fosters a sense of closeness among the students. Most people here know each other, at least by face if not by name. The social scene is largely dictated by the Greek system, which draws half the students into its national system of fraternities and sororities. On weekends, students head to parties on Fraternity Row or in off-campus apartments. The sports program at Wofford is particularly impressive given its size. Varsity sports were recently bumped up to NCAA Division I and the football team joined the Southern Conference. Like David versus Goliath, Wofford's teams often pummel their bigger rivals.

Wofford's long history and many traditions, along with its friendly collegiate environment and academic programs that lead to professional success, give its students a deep sense of pride. As one senior reflected, "Wofford is a community-oriented college dedicated to our overall growth."

Also, Check Out These Schools:
Antioch College
Birmingham-Southern College
Colorado College
Connecticut College
Evergreen State College
Gettysburg College
Hamilton University
Kalamazoo College
Lewis and Clark College
University of Puget Sound

The Road to College

Rhodes College
St. John's College
St. Olaf College
Skidmore College
Sweet Briar College
Union College
University of the South
Wabash College
Washington and Jefferson College

Separate Quarters

Although many single-sex colleges have gone coed in the last decade, they're not necessarily a dying breed. Not only are a number of single-sex colleges still around, many provide students with first-rate academic experiences and facilities. Contrary to popular belief, single-sex colleges are not strictly separatist institutions, overrun by warden-like administrators with severe rules forbidding members of the opposite sex from stepping foot on campus. Most of the colleges listed in this chapter are closely affiliated with other schools, enabling students to take courses, socialize, and, in some cases, live with members of the opposite sex.

If you haven't considered one of these schools, you may be wondering why anyone would want to go to a single-sex college. Students we spoke to at these schools were quick to point out the many advantages. For starters, these colleges usually offer top-notch academics and a dedicated, attentive faculty. In fact, several all-female colleges listed here are considered among the top ten liberal arts colleges in the nation. Because fewer students tend to apply to these schools, however, they're a bit less competitive than similarly ranked coed schools.

These schools often have prestigious alumni who are eager to give something back to their alma mater. Alumni donations help the schools maintain healthy endowments that are put, among other things, into maintaining facilities of the highest quality. And since there are usually small enrollments, you'll actually get to use some of the most cutting-edge equipment and resources, even during your first year. Alumni from these schools also form a tight network and help fellow schoolmates with career and social opportunities.

The big plus at these schools, as we heard from many students, is becoming part of a close community based on mutual respect and support. Men describe a unique fellowship and camaraderie they enjoy at these schools. Women are particularly drawn to studying within an academic climate free of the biases and obstacles that they still face at other institutions. The faculty at all-female schools tends to have a much higher percentage of women, and the courses are taught with special attention to gender issues.

Of course, a single-sex college is still not going to be for everyone. The main complaint we heard was how the social scene is limited in certain respects, particularly in terms of opportunities to meet and mingle with members of the opposite sex. Those who wish to date members of the opposite sex often might have to take more active measures to meet them. Even students at single-sex colleges who are skeptical at first eventually find much that's appealing about their schools. Students we talked to said that after awhile they couldn't imagine going anywhere else.

The colleges listed here are good schools. As you read more about them, you might find what they do offer far outweighs the social challenges. As one Smith senior told us, it "requires adjustment time," but going to a single-sex college "is a wonderful and valuable experience."

Men's Colleges

HAMPDEN-SYDNEY COLLEGE IN HAMPDEN SYDNEY, VIRGINIA

Admissions Address: Office of Admissions, P.O. Box 667, Hampden-Sydney, VA 23943
Phone: (804) 223-6120 (800) 755-0733
Web Address: www.hsc.edu

When students at Hampden-Sydney talk about things like honor, character, and tradition, they're not throwing around flashy catch phrases or discussing Faulkner. These ideals are a way of life at Hampden-Sydney, just as much today as when the school was founded in 1776. Students revere their honor code, which condemns stealing, cheating, and dishonesty of any kind; those who break the code go before a student court and receive harsh penalties.

Hampden-Sydney caters to the young Southern gentleman; students are primarily wealthy, white Southerners with very conservative and traditional values and ideals. The minority population numbers less than 10

Hampden-Sydney College

$$$$

Setting: Rural
# of Undergraduates: 956
Men: 100%
Tuition: $14,909
Room and Board: $5,383
# of Students Applied: 817
  Admitted: 680 Enrolled: 285
Required Admissions Test: Either SAT or ACT
Recommended: SAT II (Math, English)
Lowest 25% of Freshmen Scored At or Below: SAT Verbal: 520
  SAT Math: 510 ACT Comp.: 21
Highest 25% of Freshmen Scored At or Above: SAT Verbal: 630 SAT Math: 620
  ACT Comp.: 26
H.S. Rank, Top 10%: 17%
Top 25%: 40%
Top 50%: 76%
Avg. Score of Applicants Admitted: SAT Verbal: 587
  SAT Math: 565 ACT Comp.: 24
Average GPA of Applicants Admitted: 3.00
Most Popular Majors (% of Student Body): Economics (32%), History (22%), Political Science (11%), Biology (7%), Psychology (6%)

percent. About half the students are from Virginia. Obviously, this is not a school for everyone; reference to the liberal arts curriculum is about the only time you'll hear mention of the word liberal. Students who fit the profile, though, revel in the fraternity-like atmosphere of the tiny Hampden-Sydney community.

In addition to forming close bonds with their fellow students, students also receive a top liberal arts education. A large portion of the first two years at Hampden-Sydney is spent fulfilling the rigorous distribution requirements, which, in addition to required courses in humanities, social sciences, and natural sciences, include foreign language proficiency and a challenging Rhetoric Program that centers on writing composition and critical thinking. A majority of the students major in fields related to business and go on to attain impressive positions at major companies upon graduation. With a student body numbering only 950, class sizes remain at a minimum. Professors, most of whom live on campus, are always available for one-on-one mentoring.

In addition to academics, athletics and socializing are key components of the Hampden-Sydney experience. Intramural and intercollegiate sports are both strong. Fraternities, which about 40 percent of the students join, regularly throw parties (culminating in a week-long blow-out called Greek Week) that draw women from several surrounding all-female schools.

WABASH COLLEGE IN CRAWFORDSVILLE, INDIANA

Admissions Address: Admissions Office, P.O. Box 352, Crawfordsville, IN 47933-0352
Phone: (765) 361-6225 (800) 345-5385
Web Address: www.wabash.edu

Central to Wabash's philosophy is the "Gentleman's Rule," dictating that all Wabash undergraduates conduct themselves as gentlemen, on and off campus. Wabash prides itself on shaping character and instilling students with a sense of responsibility that earns them respect and guarantees future success.

The preprofessional majors are particularly popular at Wabash, and an impressive number of graduates go on to business, medical, or law school. The stiff Wabash core curriculum, however, ensures that all students first receive a solid liberal arts background. The broad requirements include courses in just about everything: natural sciences and

Wabash College

$$$$$
★★

Setting: urban
# of Undergraduates: 824
Men: 100% **Women:** 0%
Tuition: $15,400
Room and Board: $4,780
# of Students Applied: 945
  Admitted: 651 **Enrolled:** 248
Required Admissions Test: either SAT or ACT
Lowest 25% of Freshmen Scored At or Below: SAT Verbal: 520 SAT Math: 530 ACT Comp.: 25
Highest 25% of Freshmen Scored At or Above: SAT Verbal: 640 SAT Math: 670
H.S. Rank, Top 10%: 36%
Top 25%: 64%
Top 50%: 89%
Avg. Score of Applicants Admitted: SAT Verbal: 577 SAT Math: 598
Average GPA of Applicants Admitted: 3.40
Most Popular Majors (% of Student Body): Psychology (16%), Biology (14%), English (12%), Philosophy (7%), Religion (7%)

math, literature and fine arts, history, philosophy, and religion. Students must also demonstrate proficiency in English composition and a foreign language. Freshmen choose a special tutorial from a list of interesting subjects, and sophomores take an interdisciplinary course in culture and tradition. Before graduating, students must pass a demanding oral and written comprehensive examination. One student referred repeatedly to the "very challenging academics" and "very heavy workload." Fortunately, the environment at Wabash lends itself to this kind of intense academic study. The school's high endowment keeps facilities in prime condition; additions and renovations are commonplace.

Because classes are very small, students are expected to arrive prepared to participate in discussions. Professors usually know all of their students by name and are easily found for extra help or advice. According to one sophomore, "most people have probably eaten a meal or had a beer with their professor." Many students also work closely with professors on independent research projects. Another benefit of Wabash's size is how "extremely easy it is to get involved and assume roles of responsibility," according to one sophomore who himself already held several leadership positions on campus.

Wabash students don't have to worry about too many things distracting them from their studies. The town of Crawfordsville doesn't cater to the students, so most stay on campus during weekends or take road trips to nearby universities—Purdue, Indiana, and DePauw—where they can find a wider range of social activities. On campus, socializing primarily centers on the fraternities; most of Wabash students join one of 10 fraternities, each with its own house. "Being an all-male school," one student explains, "most of the frats work with sororities at DePauw, Butler, and Purdue to throw big parties at least every other weekend."

If they're not partying, Wabash students are probably engaged in some kind of athletic activity; varsity teams have good track records, and there's a well-run intramural sports program. Students' enthusiasm for athletics culminates in the big bout for the Monon Bell waged annually between Wabash and DePauw University. It's one of the nation's oldest and fiercest football rivalries. As one student explains: "If we lose every game in every sport but win that one, it's a winning season." Attending the game, or one of Wabash's many Homecoming events, you'll see how much pride Wabash students take in their school, which they express loudly but never crudely. After all, they are gentlemen.

Men's and Women's Colleges

HOBART AND WILLIAM SMITH COLLEGES IN GENEVA, NEW YORK

Admissions Address: Admissions Office, 629 South Main Street, Geneva, NY 14456
Phone: (315) 781-3472 (800) 245-0100
Web Address: www.hws.edu

Imagine the supportive community of a single-sex college without the social isolation that's so often a complaint. Under Hobart and William Smith Colleges' innovative "coordinate system," students enjoy the best aspects of the single-sex and coed campus experiences. These two colleges (Hobart for him, William Smith for her) each has its own administrations, student governments, and sports programs, but the schools share the same campus, facilities, and courses. There are both single-sex and coed living arrangements.

The academics at HWS are generally well regarded; the school has just redesigned its distribution requirements to give the students a solid exposure across the liberal arts, including the social sciences, natural sciences, humanities and fine arts, and mathematics. To achieve this goal, students are required to graduate with both a major and a minor, one in a single department and one in an interdisciplinary area. The faculty works closely with the students to assure they are achieving the appropriate breadth and depth in their studies. Many students round out their education with a semester abroad or special internships and programs within the United States.

The small, pretty campus is located on Seneca Lake, in the lush Finger Lakes region of New York State. The town of Geneva doesn't provide much excitement for students, and town-gown relations are somewhat strained. The Finger Lakes, however, are perfect for all kinds of outdoor sports, including sailing on the lake, wine tasting at nearby vineyards, and hiking in gorgeous state parks.

Most HWS students come from upper- and middle-class backgrounds and hail from the Northeast, with about half coming from New York State. Although not terribly diverse (minorities make up about 15 percent of the population), the student body is concerned about multiculturalism as well as other topical issues, such as sexism and homophobia. Gender studies and interest in gender issues particularly hold interest for students and form the basis for many special programs and events.

Hobart and William Smith Colleges

$$$$$
★★

Setting: Small Town
# of Undergraduates: 1,785
Men: 48.5% **Women:** 51.5%
Tuition: $20,940
Room and Board: $6,315
# of Students Applied: 2,805
   Admitted: 2,198 **Enrolled:** 535
Required Admissions Test: Either SAT or ACT
Lowest 25% of Freshmen Scored At or Below: SAT Verbal: 540 SAT Math: 530
Highest 25% of Freshmen Scored At or Above: SAT Verbal: 630 SAT Math: 630
H.S. Rank, Top 10%: 28%
Top 25%: 55%
Top 50%: 90%
Average GPA of Applicants Admitted: 3.26
Most Popular Majors (% of Student Body): English (17%), Individual Major (13%), Psychology (13%), Economics (9%), Biology (8%)

Both colleges enjoy a fairly active social life and cross-college events are common. Although there are no sororities at William Smith, fraternities draw about one third of the Hobart men. Despite alcohol regulations, there are frequent parties at fraternities and in residence halls, as well as campus-wide parties, dances, and special events such as the spring folk festival.

Sports are also a major part of student life, especially men's and women's lacrosse; not only do students show up to support the excellent varsity teams, but just about everyone plays lacrosse for fun. The superb athletic facilities at both schools, including indoor tennis and squash courts and an indoor track, make it possible to participate in just about any sport. Students also enjoy boating and sailing on the lake, the second largest of the Finger Lakes. Students admit that the long, cold winters in upstate New York are a drag, but road trips to neighboring colleges in nearby Syracuse, Ithaca, and Rochester help break the doldrums.

Hobart and William Smith Colleges offer an intense academic and social environment in a beautiful setting. If you appreciate the benefits of single-sex education but are intrigued by a dual college environment, this might be the place for you.

Women's Colleges

Barnard College in New York, New York

Admissions Address: Admissions Office, 3009 Broadway, New York, NY 10027-6598
Phone: (212) 854-2037
Web Address: www.barnard.columbia.edu

Barnard might not provide the kind of calm serenity and peaceful natural surroundings as its sister schools in New England, but it has other advantages. Its location in New York City and its close affiliation with neighbor Columbia University give Barnard students seemingly unlimited academic and social offerings.

Barnard students can take as many courses as they like across the street at Columbia, without having to grapple with the infamous Columbia registration process. Courses at Barnard, though, tend to be much smaller, enabling students to work closely with Barnard's prestigious faculty, a high percentage of whom are women. The education at Barnard is excellent and tough. During their first year, students take a writing course and a seminar. Additional requirements include work in foreign languages, lab science, social science, humanities, quantitative reasoning, and physical education. During their senior year, students must complete a senior project or take a comprehensive examination.

While Barnard students are "conscientious about schoolwork, they also have plenty of outside interests," one student tells us. Socially, Barnard women can take part in a number of clubs, organizations, and activities at both campuses, including several coed fraternities, newspapers and literary journals, service organizations, varsity and intramural sports, and singing and theater groups. But the biggest social attraction is undoubtedly New York City itself. Just off campus are a number of bars and cafes that are popular student hangouts, but students also head out to museums, theatres, music clubs, and restaurants all over the city. Common complaints about the limited social offerings at some single-sex colleges—lack of activities, feelings of isolation—are absent here.

Although it enjoys close ties with Columbia, Barnard maintains its own identity in several important ways. First-year students live together in the Barnard Quad, helping them feel part of a close community of women, even while surrounded by an enormous city. This small environment is a "good place for women to grow and gain confidence," according to one student. About 35 percent of the student body are minority students; its dynamic student population, drawn from across the country and around the world, comes from a variety of ethnic, cultural, and social backgrounds.

Barnard students are intelligent, ambitious women who freely voice their political and social concerns. Unlike some all-women's colleges in the Northeast where some student complaint that the PC attitude stifles open discourse, "students at Barnard don't mind conflict when they discuss things." They certainly aren't the type to shy away from the excitement and energy of big city life, which, for the most part, is what has drawn them to Barnard in the first place.

Barnard College

$$$$$
★★★

Setting: Urban
# of Undergraduates: 2,219
Men: 0% **Women:** 100%
Tuition: $20,202
Room and Board: $8,626
# of Students Applied: 3,296
   Admitted: 1,506 **Enrolled:** 576
Required Admissions Test: Either SAT or ACT
Recommended: None
Lowest 25% of Freshmen Scored At or Below: SAT Verbal: 610 SAT Math: 600 ACT Comp.: 26
Highest 25% of Freshmen Scored At or Above: SAT Verbal: 700 SAT Math: 680 ACT Comp.: 29
H.S. Rank, Top 10%: 58%
Top 25%: 97%
Top 50%: 100%
Avg. Score of Applicants Admitted: SAT Verbal: 670 SAT Math: 650
Average GPA of Applicants Admitted: 3.67
Most Popular Majors (% of Student Body): English (14%), Psychology (12%), Political Science (11%), Biological Science (7%), Economics (7%)

BRYN MAWR COLLEGE IN BRYN MAWR, PENNSYLVANIA

Admissions Address: Admissions Office, 101 North Merion Avenue, Bryn Mawr, PA 19010-2899
Phone: (610) 526-5152
Web Address: www.brynmawr.edu

Imagine an all-female college with coed dormitories, and you'll begin to get a sense of just how different Bryn Mawr is. Like Wellesley, Bryn Mawr is a surviving member of the Seven Sisters and one of the nation's top liberal arts colleges. Bryn Mawr's close affiliation to Haverford makes it a unique all-female college. Bryn Mawr women have the option to take courses, eat, and even live at Haverford; "Fords" and "Mawrters" can live together in two coed dormitories. Thus Bryn Mawr offers its students a closely knit, supportive community of women without the isolation that turns some people away from single-sex colleges.

The academic programs are outstanding across the board, from the liberal arts standbys to more unusual, harder-to-find programs, such as the Study of Growth and the Structure of Cities (the only undergraduate Near Eastern archaeology program in the country) and acclaimed interdisciplinary programs in urban studies, women's studies, peace studies, and Hispanic studies. The science programs are generally excellent; about six percent of Bryn Mawr's students go on to medical school.

Bryn Mawr is serious about cultivating a well-rounded, highly educated student body. There are rigorous general liberal arts requirements in several key areas, including courses in lab sciences and quantitative work, as well as English composition, foreign language, and physical education. First-year students take an intense interdisciplinary writing seminar in which they meet regularly with their professors. Students also have the option to design their own majors or to double major. If they can't find a course they want, they're encouraged to cross-register or even major at Haverford, and they can take classes at any of the other schools with which Bryn Mawr is affiliated, including nearby Swarthmore College and the University of Pennsylvania.

Students have great things to say about their teachers, who put a personal interest into their students' educations. "The professors support and encourage each student's creativity. I have felt very empowered to do whatever I want to do academically," one senior in political science told us.

Bryn Mawr attracts bright and motivated women from the tops of their high school classes, making for an intellectual, yet casual, atmosphere.

Bryn Mawr College

$$$$$
★★★

Setting: Suburban
# of Undergraduates: 1,164
Men: 0% **Women:** 100%
Tuition: $21,020
Room and Board: $7,590
# of Students Applied: 1,623
  Admitted: 936 **Enrolled:** 360
Required Admissions Test: Either SAT, ACT, and SAT II
Recommended: SAT
Lowest 25% of Freshmen Scored At or Below: SAT Verbal: 610
  SAT Math: 590
Highest 25% of Freshmen Scored At or Above: SAT Verbal: 710 SAT Math: 660
H.S. Rank, Top 10%: 60%
Top 25%: 90%
Top 50%: 100%
Avg. Score of Applicants Admitted: SAT Verbal: 660
  SAT Math: 620
Most Popular Majors (% of Student Body): English (13%), Biology (11%), Psychology (9%), History (9%), Chemistry (8%)

Mawrters are serious academics, devoted to their studies, as well as generally interested in all kinds of issues and subjects. Like Haverford, Bryn Mawr has an honor code that allows students to schedule their own examinations and monitor themselves. The honor code also helps set the serious academic tone at the school. The students work hard but don't engage in cutthroat competition with one another; each individual places pressure on herself to excel.

One of Bryn Mawr's assets is the diversity of its student body. Students come from all over the country and around the world, and there's a substantial minority population. According to several students, the cultural and ethnic groups interact without tension. Bryn Mawr women are open to new experiences and points of view; you'll find students from vastly different backgrounds interacting frequently and forming close friendships. "It's so amazing how many different kinds of people you can meet here," a student told us. "Where else can you even find practicing witches?" Additionally, the students tend to be politically active and concerned about many issues, particularly feminism, the environment, and multiculturalism.

The beautiful, tree-laden campus is primarily Gothic in appearance. The dormitories, ranging in style from renovated older buildings with fireplaces to more modern structures, mix all four classes together. Housing is guaranteed for all four years, and many juniors and seniors have single rooms. There are four dining rooms, and the food, unlike at Haverford, is first-rate, particularly the vegetarian specialties.

The campus, while scenic, is somewhat isolated, and there isn't a very active social scene. On weekends, the school is quiet; no alcohol is allowed on campus, and students who want a party head over to Haverford or take the quick train trip into Philly. For those students who do stay on campus, there are small, laid-back dorm parties, as well as many cultural activities and events such as movies, concerts, and student dance performances.

Bryn Mawr has several traditions that add color to the school year. Events include Lantern Night, an elaborate initiation for first-year students at which the lamp of knowledge is passed along to them, and a festive May Day celebration. The students are also involved in many sporting activities, and have the option of becoming involved in a wide range of extracurricular activities including campus groups and organizations.

With its small classes, supportive faculty, and extensive resources, Bryn Mawr is a place where, as one student put it, "you can go as far as your intellect will take you."

MOUNT HOLYOKE COLLEGE IN SOUTH HADLEY, MASSACHUSETTS

Admissions Address: Admissions Office, Newhall Center, South Hadley, MA 01075-1488
Phone: (413) 538-2023
Web Address: www.mtholyoke.edu/

Mount Holyoke College

$$$$$
★★

Setting: Suburban
# of Undergraduates: 1,825
Men: 0% **Women:** 100%
Tuition: $22,200
Room and Board: $6,525
# of Students Applied: 2,026
  Admitted: 1,324 **Enrolled:** 482
Required Admissions Test: Either SAT I or ACT I
Recommended: TOEFL, ACT
Lowest 25% of Freshmen Scored At or Below: SAT Verbal: 576 SAT Math: 561
Highest 25% of Freshmen Scored At or Above: SAT Verbal: 683 SAT Math: 677
H.S. Rank, Top 10%: 50%
Top 25%: 92%
Top 50%: 99%
Avg. Score of Applicants Admitted: SAT Verbal: 639 SAT Math: 601 ACT Comp.: 27
Most Popular Majors (% of Student Body): English (13%), Biological Sciences (11%), Psychology (9%), Politics (7%), International Relations (7%)

As the first all-women's college in the United States, Mount Holyoke has a long history of providing a superior liberal arts education with a special commitment to women's issues. MHC maintains its traditional emphasis on academics with a standard core curriculum. Distribution requirements include courses in the basic areas of humanities, social sciences, science and mathematics, as well as a foreign language and physical education. At the same time, MHC's curriculum includes such recent additions as a course in multicultural perspectives and a required minor, in addition to one's major field of study.

Although the humanities and, in particular, political science and international relations, are generally very strong at MHC, the natural sciences are its most noteworthy departments. Science students use the most up-to-date high-tech equipment, including a scanning electron microscope that brings students over from other Five College schools for labs. Thanks in part to MHC's exceptional laboratory sciences, a high number of students go on to receive doctorates in biology and chemistry.

The school's membership in the Five College Consortium—which includes nearby Smith, Amherst, Hampshire, and the University of Massachusetts at Amherst—expands the academic and social opportunities. As one student told us, "we have access to libraries, classes, parties, and can audition at other schools. I go to a small school without the limitations of a small school."

In terms of admissions, Mount Holyoke is slightly less competitive than comparable all-female schools. Once students arrive, however, they find themselves working away at all hours in an intense academic environment. "There's a really high workload, and the professors have really high expectations of us," one student remarks. "But we get exposed to so much." The MHC course load is demanding, but if students feel pressure, it's not from their peers. While MHC's self-motivated students are very driven to succeed, this isn't an everyone-for-herself environment.

The student-run honor code means students must take their studies seriously as no one is going to force them to complete work and take examinations. Fortunately, the attention students receive from their professors helps cut the pressure and anxiety. Professors frequently meet with students at length outside of class to give advice, talk at greater length about issues from class, or just chat. The First Year Tutorial is a special honors program that gives interested students the chance to work one-on-one with a professor on an independent project.

This quintessentially New England liberal arts campus mixes the best of old and new, with ivy-covered brick buildings standing alongside more modern facilities. "The campus is gorgeous," one student raved. "We've got ponds, trees, and everything is spread out. Everything is really well maintained." The dormitories, some older and some modern, mix all four classes and provide a small social unit in which close friendships form easily.

"Lots of students complain about the social life," one student reported. "There's this feeling that because there are no men, there's nothing to do. That's not true! If you take the initiative, rather than just sitting around complaining, you can have fun." School traditions include Founder's Day, when "everyone gets up at dawn and eats ice cream on the grave of the school founder," and "M and Cs, when every night at 9:30 on the dot, a food cart is brought out with milk and cookies. This is where the old cliché of the 'freshman fifteen' originates!" she said.

The beautiful natural surroundings, as well as the tolerant, liberal student population, help create a warm academic atmosphere in which women's issues are an open concern for all. After studying with a supportive community of fellow students and faculty, Mount Holyoke graduates are ready to take on just about any challenge in their future careers.

SMITH COLLEGE IN NORTHAMPTON, MASSACHUSETTS

Admissions Address: Admission Office, 7 College Lane, Northampton, MA 01063
Phone: (413) 585-2500
Web Address: www.smith.edu

Smith College

$$$$$
★★★

Setting: Small City
# of Undergraduates: 2,572
Men: 0% **Women:** 100%
Tuition: $21,360
Room and Board: $7,250
# of Students Applied: 3,131
   Admitted: 1,632   **Enrolled:** 643
Required Admissions Test: Either SAT or ACT
Recommended: SAT II Writing and two of choice
Lowest 25% of Freshmen Scored At or Below: SAT Verbal: 620 SAT Math: 590   ACT Comp.: 26
Highest 25% of Freshmen Scored At or Above: SAT Verbal: 720   SAT Math: 690   ACT Comp.: 30
H.S. Rank, Top 10%: 53%
Top 25%: 85%
Top 50%: 97%
Most Popular Majors (% of Student Body): Government (9.9%), Psychology (8.6%), English (8.5%), Economics (7.7%), Art (7.6%)

Smith's 125-acre campus, designed by Frederick Law Olmstead, features a botanical garden, an arboretum, and Paradise Pond—an ace spot for studying.

Smith's curriculum, or rather lack of one, is one way in which the school strives to instill its students with a sense of independence and provide them with the freedom to discover their own talents and abilities. The honor code, which permits students to schedule their own examinations, fosters students' maturity and self-reliance. Smith women don't have any academic requirements beyond those of their majors; instead, they work closely with faculty advisors to create a course of study that suits their academic goals. The renowned Smith Scholars program allows students to devote one or two years to conducting independent research. Almost all departments are superb.

All this choice, of course, has its downside, because Smith offers about a thousand courses, not including the vast array of classes open to them at other schools in the Five College Consortium. Smithies have the option of taking up to half their classes at Amherst, Hampshire, Mount Holyoke, and the University of Massachusetts at Amherst, which are all connected by shuttle bus.

Taking advantage of small, discussion-oriented classes and caring professors who encourage students to push themselves academically, Smith students immerse themselves in a demanding, yet rewarding, educational environment. The workload, a student told us, is "very, very difficult," but serves as "preparation for anything you choose to do in the future." The intellectual atmosphere of the classroom frequently carries over to informal discussions with professors and fellow students outside of class.

Although many Smithies come from upper-class New England backgrounds, the student body has become more mixed in terms of class, ethnicity, and culture. Students are committed to creating an environment in which differences are valued and respected. The lesbian community, for example, is a visible one and generally accepted. Most students are very liberal, proud to be PC, and outspoken about many topical issues, particularly feminism. Some students complain that this liberal environment isn't conducive to real discourse as it stifles opposing opinion.

Smith isn't a heavy-duty party school; those looking to meet men and date frequently might find things slow on campus until the weekends, when many students travel to parties at nearby school or welcome visitors. But, there are also enough clubs, organizations, and extracurricular activities, as well as on-campus cultural events, to keep everyone but the most diehard party freaks happy.

The town of Northampton provides a beautiful respite from campus life, offering a fine array of restaurants, cafes, movie theaters, and ice cream parlors. Amherst is a short drive away, and students can reach Boston in about three hours.

Smith's unique housing system plays a unique role in students' social lives. Students are assigned to one of 40 houses, each with its own living room, fireplace, piano, dining room, and kitchen. All four classes are housed together, providing a sense of family among the residents. House parties and formals each semester are favorite social events. Smith is also a school rich in tradition, including weekly house teas, candlelit dinners, and the celebration of Mountain Day, when classes are canceled so students can enjoy the beautiful natural surroundings of the Berkshires.

SCRIPPS COLLEGE IN CLAREMONT, CALIFORNIA

Admissions Address: Office of Admission, 1030 Columbia Avenue, Claremont, CA 91711
Phone: (909) 621-8149
Web Address: www.scrippscol.edu

Scripps College is a small, all-women's college within a coed university setting. Scripps is part of the acclaimed Claremont College system, and students can freely take courses, use the facilities, and become involved with social activities at the four other schools—Pomona, Harvey Mudd, Pitzer, and Claremont McKenna.

The academics at Scripps are generally strong, particularly in the humanities, as well as in interdisciplinary programs like women's studies. The core curriculum is a traditional liberal arts one, with courses required in a variety of areas including foreign language, fine arts, social science, natural science, math, writing, as well as intercultural and women's studies requirements. Students must also complete a senior thesis in their field.

Scripps College

$$$$$
★★

Setting: Suburban
# of Undergraduates: 699
Men: 0% **Women:** 100%
Tuition: $18,680
Room and Board: $7,650
# of Students Applied: 944
  Admitted: 725 **Enrolled:** 189
Required Admissions Test: Either SAT or ACT
Recommended: SAT II
Lowest 25% of Freshmen Scored At or Below: SAT Verbal: 590 SAT Math: 560
Highest 25% of Freshmen Scored At or Above: SAT Verbal: 690 SAT Math: 650
Avg. Score of Applicants Admitted: SAT Verbal: 630 SAT Math: 600
Average GPA of Applicants Admitted: 3.49
Most Popular Majors (% of Student Body): English/Literature (15%), Psychology (12%), Int'l Relations/Pol. Studies/Government (8%), Biology/Human Biology (7%), Studio Art (6%)

The classes average about 15 students and are primarily discussion oriented, helping students form and articulate their ideas and opinions. As one student testifies, "the small size of the classes forces you to participate and do the work and really, to understand." In addition to their close interaction with students in classes, professors are easily found around the campus for extra help and guidance.

As for the social life, one student calls it "average, but improving." For social events, many students head over to the other Claremont schools. While some students complain about the lack of social opportunities on their own campus, others praise the separation between their studies and social lives. Although the five Claremont colleges are literally situated one on top of the other, the separations between them are surprisingly distinct. One student advises that "you have to work hard to take advantage of the five colleges."

As an academic home base, the Scripps campus, with Spanish Mediterranean architecture and Southern California greenery—not to mention blue skies and sunny weather—is beautiful. The center of campus social life is the residential houses, each of which is home to about 80 students. They each have a dining hall and common areas and often sponsor their own parties and events.

The majority of students are from California and are generally liberal and outspoken about political issues, particularly feminism and multiculturalism. One student commented, however, that Scripps "wasn't as feminist as I thought it would be. Not at all radical, although certainly not conservative, either." The student body has itself been especially vocal about trying to increase the minority population of the students and staff.

The town of Claremont is an idyllic community within an hour's drive of downtown Los Angeles. Students at Scripps are far from isolated; even if they tire of attending social events at the other Claremont schools, they can easily escape to the beaches, ski resorts, and other California colleges and universities that are in easy distance.

SWEET BRIAR COLLEGE IN SWEET BRIAR, VIRGINIA

Admissions Address: Office of Admissions, P.O. Box B, Sweet Briar, VA 24595-1052
Phone: (804) 381-6142 (800) 381-6142
Web Address: www.sbc.edu

Sweet Briar's exceptionally small undergraduate enrollment brings with it certain obvious advantages, most notably the chance to spend four years studying in an intimate academic environment surrounded by familiar, friendly faces. Classes are so small at Sweet Briar that a class of 30 students is considered overcrowded. The faculty members are dedicated to teaching, and establish relationships with almost all their students that extend beyond the classroom. Although friendly, the professors are demanding; in small classes, each student must be ready to participate actively in discussions. Outside the classroom, "you can't hide, and you're forced to get involved in the community," one student told us.

Sweet Briar's demanding academics help prepare students to go on to professional schools and careers. While the administration is in the process of reviewing the school's extensive core requirements, students must currently take courses in natural and social sciences, art and literature, classical and European history, and non-Western civilization, as well as a first-year English class and one in health and fitness. Students must be able to demonstrate proficiency in a foreign language before graduation, and can expand their academic horizons by studying at one of the other colleges in the Seven College Exchange or participating on one of several study-abroad programs.

With red brick colonial buildings surrounded by acres and acres of woods and the stunning Blue Ridge Mountains in the distance, the campus's idyllic setting is a perfect place in which to engage in deep study and thoughtful contemplation. Almost all the facilities are in prime condition, including the laboratories (with such advanced equipment as a scanning electron microscope), well-stocked libraries, and a dining hall with above-average food. The dormitories mix all four classes together, which helps first-years in getting the lowdown from their "big sisters."

As for the benefits of attending an all-women's college, we'll let this sophomore explain how she sees it: "I wasn't looking at women's colleges at all and I think most Sweet Briar students were like that. And when I arrived, I thought the all-women thing was the worst part about the school. Now I think it's the best. I used to think the stuff about women being around other women making them better leaders was bull, but it's totally not."

Sweet Briar College

$$$$$

Setting: rural
# of Undergraduates: 542
Men: 0% **Women:** 100%
Tuition: $15,420
Room and Board: $6,510
# of Students Applied: 432
  Admitted: 394 **Enrolled:** 152
Required Admissions Test: either SAT or ACT
Recommended: SAT II
Lowest 25% of Freshmen Scored At or Below: SAT Verbal: 510 SAT Math: 490 ACT Comp.: 21
Highest 25% of Freshmen Scored At or Above: SAT Verbal: 640 SAT Math: 590 ACT Comp.: 28
H.S. Rank, Top 10%: 28%
Top 25%: 64%
Top 50%: 86%
Most Popular Majors (% of Student Body): Psychology (12.8%), Biology (10.1%), Art History (7.4%), Political Science (7.4%), Economics (7.4%)

While many Sweet Briar students are white, southern, and wealthy, recent recruitment efforts have brought in more students from other parts of the United States and from around the world. While serious about their studies, students are generally easygoing with one another. Most students, if not active politically, are conservative in their tastes and values.

The school's small size and remote setting to some extent limit the social life. Nevertheless, there are a number of events, activities, and social goings on to keep most students occupied. Sports are popular, including Sweet Briar's acclaimed equestrian program where students can take beginning riding or perfect their advanced skills (alumnae have represented the United States in the Olympics). Students also enjoy other outdoor activities such as canoeing and hiking. Students enjoy hanging out at the main dining hall or nearby restaurants and dance clubs.

When it comes to meeting men, students head out on weekends to parties at nearby colleges like Hampden-Sydney and Washington and Lee; large campus parties and formals also bring the men to Sweet Briar. As one student explains: "We're not a big university, and some new students show up looking for the Animal House experience. Well, they won't find it here, at least not during the week."

Sweet Briar has come a long way since the days it had the reputation of a finishing school for dainty Southern belles hoping to find husbands. With its solid liberal arts departments, attentive faculty and excellent resources, Sweet Briar instills its students with the knowledge, skills, and self-confidence to help them find personal and professional success.

WELLESLEY COLLEGE IN WELLESLEY, MASSACHUSETTS

Admissions Address: Admissions Office, 106 Central Street, Wellesley, MA 02181-8292
Phone: (617) 283-2270
Web Address: www.wellesley.edu/

One of the remaining Seven Sisters, Wellesley is one of the top liberal arts colleges in the country—just ask Hillary Rodham Clinton, one of the school's many prestigious alumnae. Wellesley draws some of the country's most intelligent and motivated women, many of whom go on to impressive professional careers. Graduating from Wellesley means becoming a part of this distinguished group of women who maintain close bonds with one another throughout their lives.

Wellesley offers first-rate departments not only in the humanities, such as English and the arts, but in the sciences as well. Wellesley women have access to cutting-edge science equipment and facilities. Wellesley students take advantage of well-stocked libraries, a newly built theater, a greenhouse, several science and computer centers, an art museum, and a beautiful sports center.

The academic program is tough, but most students find it fulfilling. The rigid liberal arts curriculum includes distribution requirements in the humanities, social sciences, and natural sciences. Students also must take a writing course, a quantitative reasoning course, and at least one course in multicultural issues as well as demonstrate proficiency in a foreign language. There is also a required seminar for first-year students.

Class sizes are kept relatively small and professors are extremely attentive, making themselves available during office hours and for informal meetings; many students find faculty members with whom they can conduct research and special projects. "All professors get to know you," one student remarked. "After class they'll stay and chat with you, and whenever you call them they're available."

Many students engage in independent projects or tutorials in a particular subject of interest. Students may also register at nearby colleges, taking advantage of other schools' strengths, for example, by enrolling in engineering courses at MIT. Wellesley is part of the Twelve College Exchange program, which allows students to enroll for a semester or year at another school (including Amherst, Bowdoin, Dartmouth, Vassar, Wesleyan, Williams, and other top liberal arts colleges). For those who seek educational experiences beyond the United States, studying abroad is also a popular option.

Wellesley students are devoted to their studies, which creates a definite intellectual climate on campus. Students gather at coffee shops, in the student center, and in the dormitories' common living areas to discuss classes, literature, and current events. "People stress out a lot about work," says one junior. "But," she adds, "the pressure is self-inflicted." The students are extremely self-motivated, as evidenced by the school's honor system under which students schedule their own final exams and take them without supervision.

The small, 500-acre campus is among the country's most beautiful, with "typical New England–style" architecture, lovely foliage, and a pretty lake. The dormitories, most of which have been renovated recently, are

---

Wellesley College

$$$$$
★★★★

Setting: suburban
# of Undergraduates: 2,197
Men: 0% **Women:** 100%
Tuition: $21,254
Room and Board: $6,670
# of Students Applied: 3,310
  Admitted: 1,331 **Enrolled:** 597
Required Admissions Test: either SAT or ACT
H.S. Rank, Top 10%: 75%
Top 25%: 94%
Top 50%: 100%
Avg. Score of Applicants
  Admitted: SAT Verbal: 673
  SAT Math: 651 ACT Comp.: 23
Most Popular Majors (% of Student Body): Economics (13.3%), Political Science (10.3%), English (10%), Psychology (10%), Biology (6%)

charming and comfortable; many have common rooms for hanging out. Most students live on campus, and juniors and seniors are guaranteed single rooms. The food is reportedly decent, and the vegetarian dining hall is particularly recommended. The campus is also extremely secure, and students feel comfortable walking on the campus at all hours.

Wellesley social life has two distinct components: on campus and off. "There's definitely not a wild on-campus social life," comments one student. The social scene for those who stick close to home is quiet and, some students complain, can be dull. Others praise how relaxed things are. There's usually some form of entertainment such as movies, plays, and concerts. But, for those who want to party and meet men, Boston, with its hundreds of colleges, is only a half-hour away. Many students head off campus to clubs and parties at neighboring schools, especially Harvard and MIT.

As for extracurricular activities at Wellesley, there's no shortage of clubs and organizations, including several elite "societies" for art, music, literature, and other similar interests. Sports are also extremely popular; if students don't play on a team, they're likely to enjoy some kind of physical activity in the sports center.

Certain Wellesley events and traditions spark pride in the school and bring students closer together. Hoop Rolling is a race run by seniors to determine who will be the first major success; the winner gets tossed into the lake. All first-year students have a "big sister" who shows them the ropes and with whom they attend Flower Sunday, a chapel sing-along in the fall.

Although the small town of Wellesley doesn't offer much in the way of student hangouts, "we spend a lot of time in Boston," one student tells us. Students are quick to take advantage of all the museums, theater, and music, that city has to offer.

The school recruits students from all over the country, as well as from all over the world, making for a geographically diverse student body. The minority population on campus is around 30 percent. This diversity is reflected in the range of viewpoints and attitudes of students, although many tend to be politically liberal (multiculturalism, feminism, and the environment are some of the main areas of concern on campus). In general, students are respectful of one another and there isn't much division. One junior explained how the students are actually Wellesley's primary strength: "A lot of the women here are incredible. They're self-assured, ambitious . . . and they're willing to share what they know."

More than the exceptional academics and beautiful campus, it's the Wellesley environment that seems to win students over. "I picked Wellesley because of the incredibly supportive atmosphere," one student raves. "Everything around here is just perfect!"

HBCUs

Historically black colleges and universities (commonly called HBCUs) have not enjoyed the same fanfare as certain other institutions of higher education, but consider this—almost one-third of all bachelor's degrees and one-fourth of all doctoral degrees earned by African American students are awarded at these schools. Many of these schools date back to the end of the Civil War, and although the odds were against them at the outset, they have since gained prestige by producing many teachers, doctors, attorneys, executives, and other prominent figures of American society. The schools listed in this section are all members of the National Association for Equal Opportunity in Higher Education (NAFEO), which reports that 85 percent of African American physicians, 80 percent of African American federal judges, and 75 percent of African American military officers are graduates of HBCUs.

This category of schools has a sense of purpose more pronounced than any other—the cultivation of talented minds in the context of a common heritage. Low student-to-faculty ratios, personalized advising, challenging academics, and a nurturing environment are typical strong points at these schools. That, in addition to their generally reasonable tuitions and strong alumni networks, makes these schools a very attractive choice for bright students who seek to further their intellectual, social, and spiritual development in a community of others who respect and share the same interests and goals.

Keep in mind that although African American studies are often a prominent part of the curriculum, these are well-rounded schools with different strengths in arts, sciences, foreign languages, business, engineering, premed, and other courses of study. They also have many of the trappings of other types of schools: fraternities and sororities, academic disciplines of all kinds, and partnerships with other colleges and universities that enable access to more resources than one school could provide.

Fisk University

Admissions Address: Admissions Office, 1000 17th Ave N, Nashville, TN 37208
Phone: (615) 329-8866
Web Address: www.fisk.edu

Fisk University

$$$
★★

Setting: Urban
# of Undergraduates: 751
Men: 29.7% Women: 70.3%
Tuition: $7,328
Room and Board: $4,062
# of Students Applied: 1,023
   Admitted: 800   Enrolled: 250
Average GPA of Applicants
   Admitted: 3.10
Most Popular Majors (% of Student Body): Business Administration (21%), Biology (13%), Psychology (13%), English (7%), Political Science (6%)

A small, predominantly African American university opened to a group of former slaves in 1866, Fisk has established an excellent liberal arts and science tradition just north of Nashville. Among its famous alumni are W. E. B. DuBois, one of the founders of the NAACP; Nikki Giovanni, a modern poet and author; and Hazel O'Leary, who serves as Secretary of Energy under the Clinton administration.

Preprofessional degrees, such as business and premed, attract a large percentage of the student body. Fisk also boasts an excellent music department. Core requirements for all students include a freshman orientation class which familiarizes first-years with the university's history, a written and oral communication course, an African American literature class, math, general science, and philosophy. All classes offer an Afrocentric curriculum, focusing on the role blacks have played in each of the fields. More graduates of Fisk go on to receive their doctorate degrees than African American graduates of any other U.S. university.

Students report that classes are easy to enroll in, with introductory classes limited to 40 people and upper divisions holding 8 to 25. The relationship between students and teachers is a "relaxed one," reports a junior. "We're often invited to professors' homes for social gatherings, and most are more than willing to help." Student performance is evaluated under a typical semester system of midterms and finals.

Most students who are not commuting from homes in Nashville live in campus dorms their first two years. Juniors and seniors tend to move off campus to nearby apartments. A sophomore rates many of the school's facilities as old and slightly outdated, although he says Fisk's science facilities are modern. There are few sports programs here, although Fiskites can join intramural teams to play basketball, tag football, and track.

The Greek system plays a tremendous role in uniting the student body by organizing social activities and parties. People also hang out in the student center, with its TV, video games, pool tables, and cafeteria. Extracurriculars like student government, the college radio station, and guest speaker days also bring people together. Numerous seminars are given on racism and its psychological effects; the annual W. E. B.

DuBois Day is organized in the leader's honor to remind students of their common background and objectives. Jubilee Day, held in October, is another campus-wide event honoring the spiritual Jubilee singers who saved a financially strapped Fisk many years ago. As they continue to do even today, the Jubilee singers tour the world and solicit donations for the university; students recall that after hearing the Jubilees, Queen Victoria named Nashville the "City of Music."

Occasionally, students leave their intimate campus, situated on a hill overlooking Nashville, to head for downtown, where they can enjoy the city's many bars, clubs, and music venues. However, social life takes second priority to Fisk's competitive academic environment for most students. As a junior reflected, "we are here to learn, not only about our studies but about ourselves and our history. When we graduate from Fisk, we will leave with strong self-esteem and a great deal of pride for the black community."

HAMPTON UNIVERSITY

Admissions Address: Admissions Office, Hampton, VA 23668
Phone: (757) 727-5328 (800) 624-3328
Web Address: www.cs.hampton.edu

A historic, predominately black college founded in the wake of the Civil War, Hampton University sits on a peninsula surrounded by the Chesapeake Bay. Students praise their beautiful campus for its many trees, older buildings, and strong sense of community.

Men and women from all over the country come to Hampton for a black college experience, with African Americans comprising over 90 percent of the student body (2 percent come from overseas), and with many programs and organizations focused on issues in the black community. The most popular majors here are accounting, biology, and psychology, although business and mass media attract many students as well. Hampton even has its own radio and cable news stations to give media majors first-hand experience.

Classes remain small, with introductory classes usually limited to 50 and upper division classes taking only 8 to 10 people. Students describe a split in relations with teachers; some professors, they say, are supportive and nurturing, while other professors believe that students need to function independently in a "real world" environment. The academic year is

Hampton University

🏛🏛🏛
$$$
★★★

Setting: Urban
# of Undergraduates: 4,219
Men: 37.2%   Women: 62.8%
Tuition: $8,198
Room and Board: $3,878
# of Students Applied: 5,662
   Admitted: 2,948   Enrolled: 923
Required Admissions Test: Either SAT or ACT
Highest 25% of Freshmen Scored At or Above: SAT Verbal: 588   SAT Math: 559   ACT Comp.: 29
H.S. Rank, Top 10%: 24%
Top 25%: 64%
Top 50%: 92%
Avg. Score of Applicants Enrolled: SAT Verbal: 487   SAT Math: 512   ACT Comp.: 20
Average GPA of Applicants Admitted: 2.86
Most Popular Majors (% of Student Body): Biology (11.4%), Psychology (8.8%), Mass Media Arts (7.6%), Business Management (7.4%), English (5.5%)

---

based on the semester system, and phone registration can sometimes make classes difficult to get.

Core requirements for everyone include University 101, providing freshmen with a history of the college; Humanities 1 and 2, interdisciplinary classes encompassing history, science, and art, English; and physical education. Other requirements depend on one's major. Study abroad and a semester in Washington are two options many upper-division Hampton students pursue.

The college's social scene is divided between on-campus activities and Greek life. Fraternities and sororities have sprung up with just about every focus imaginable; in addition to the "Big 8"—the most selective social frats and sororities—Greek honors houses, music houses, and houses associated with students' majors all attract a substantial portion of Hampton's student body. While fraternities throw many big parties, the Student Union Board also hosts on-campus functions, including movie nights and school-sponsored parties. Younger students may also come together in dorms (freshmen are required to live on campus), while older students often congregate in off-campus apartments and houses. About 40 percent of students commute to Hampton. The honors dorms are the most up to date, students say, although many other dorms, both single sex and coed, are in the process of being renovated. Food is served in two cafeterias, described by a freshman as "pretty standard institutional fare."

There are a number of activities students can engage in, and student government, the college radio and TV stations, and community service seem to be among the most attractive options. Many students volunteer in the Hampton Roads community, tutoring disadvantaged children or becoming a Big Brother or Sister. Sports draw much of students' attention as well. The big varsity sports are basketball and football, although students come to games as much to see the powerful Marching Force band as to watch the athletes. Intramural teams encompass nearly every sport, and soccer and track and field are enjoyed year-round. Students can also be found biking and rollerblading around campus in nice weather.

Homecoming weekend and the Black Family Conference are two big annual events that help unite the people of Hampton. During the latter, speakers come to discuss issues concerning the black community; in 1996, the topic was technology and how it affects African Americans. The Convocation Center, which acts as a gym, conference facility, and concert hall, is also a unifying force on campus. Hampton itself is a quiet town of limited interest to young people. Although the school is fairly self-contained, students do enjoy getting away once and a while, perhaps to Virginia Beach, about 45 minutes away, or to Washington, D.C., just over two hours away.

HOWARD UNIVERSITY IN WASHINGTON, D.C.

Admissions Address: Admissions Office, 2400 6th Street Northwest, Washington, DC 20059
Phone: (202) 806-2755 (202) 806-2752
Web Address: www.howard.edu/

Howard is the largest and most renowned predominantly African American university in the United States. Founded in 1867, the school has a long history of providing an exceptional education to a group of intelligent, highly motivated students while fostering a strong sense of unity. Howard's prestigious alumni—who include Jessye Norman, Debbie Allen, Toni Morrison, Thurgood Marshall, and Phylicia Rashad—often go on to achieve career and professional success.

With 10 undergraduate schools, Howard's academic offerings cover a wide range of subject areas. Many students arrive set on a professional career path, and preprofessional programs are among Howard's best and most popular offerings. The business, engineering, and communication schools obtain high enrollments each year. Those studying communications gain important hands-on experience at the university's own radio and cable television stations, and students in all three programs can take advantage of internship and work opportunities available to them in Washington, D.C. Because of Howard's acclaimed medical and dental schools, premedical sciences attract many undergraduates here. In the Arts and Sciences School, political science, history, and psychology are among the many reputable departments.

Although requirements vary by college and program, all students take courses in English, speech, math, and African American history; students in the School of Arts and Sciences must also take a swimming class. As you would expect, the African studies and African American studies programs are excellent, with far more course offerings than at many other schools. In general, though, courses at Howard bring an African American perspective to bear upon the material. Students have good things to say about most professors, who are highly accessible and genuinely concerned about their students' education. The teachers push students to work hard and fulfill their potential. Class sizes vary, with

Howard University

$$$

Setting: Urban
# of Undergraduates: 6,909
Men: 39% Women: 61%
Tuition: $7,700
Room and Board: $4,830
# of Students Applied: 6,510
  Admitted: 3,937 Enrolled: 2,000
Required Admissions Test: Either SAT or ACT
Avg. Score of Applicants
  Admitted: SAT Verbal: 426
  SAT Math: 457 ACT Comp.: 21

general courses filled with as many as 200 students and most upper divisions limited to under 20.

The campus centers around "The Yard," a grassy area where students meet and hang out between classes. In good weather, students can be found reading and relaxing in this campus park, or even listening to music and dancing. University housing can only accommodate about half the student body, although affordable student apartments lie nearby. The urban area surrounding the campus is not particularly safe. Students need to be careful and act with common sense when leaving the school's property.

About ninety percent of the student body is African American. Students come from a wide range of backgrounds, from across the nation and more than 100 foreign countries, bringing a variety of experiences, ideas, and interests that create a dynamic, interesting student body. Most students are politically liberal. They're also very bright and highly supportive of one another's academic and career pursuits.

Students tend to stick to the campus for socializing. Many national African American fraternities and sororities originated at Howard and they maintain a strong, but not dominant, presence on campus. In addition to hosting the occasional party, the fraternities and sororities are also very involved in the campus community, conducting volunteer work and sponsoring special events, such as visits by guest speakers. Students hang out in the Yard, dorm rooms, or at the large student center, where there are offices for the many clubs and organizations. When they want more of a nightlife, students go clubbing in the District. Georgetown and Adams Morgan continue to attract large college crowds, especially on weekends. Intramural and intercollegiate sports are both very popular. Football games are particularly well-attended. Howard's energetic marching band gets the student fans up on their feet and cheering for their team. The homecoming game against rival Morehouse is the highlight of the football season as well as the social event of the year, when students party in full force.

Both on and off the football field, Howard students take great pride in their university. Given the school's long history and prestigious alumni, it's not surprising to hear them say they couldn't imagine studying anywhere else.

MOREHOUSE COLLEGE IN ATLANTA, GEORGIA

Admissions Address: Admissions Office, 830 Westview Drive, SW, Atlanta, GA 30314
Phone: (404) 215-2632
Web Address: www.morehouse.edu

The only predominantly African American, all-male, four-year college in the United States, Morehouse combines first-rate academic programs with a supportive community and attracts exceptional, highly motivated students. Morehouse students are particularly proud of their school's heritage and prestigious reputation; Morehouse's many distinguished alumni include Julian Bond, Spike Lee, and Dr. Martin Luther King Jr.

Students begin their study at "the House" by fulfilling the comprehensive core requirements, which can take up the first two years of study. In addition to taking several courses in the sciences and humanities, students also study African and African American heritage and culture. Preprofessional majors (business, engineering, and premed) are particularly popular, and a high percentage of students go on to graduate or professional schools. Students can also take courses from other colleges that are part of the Atlanta University Center, including the all-female Spelman College, located across the street. In addition to expanding the educational opportunities, this program allows Morehouse students to interact with women on a regular basis.

A successful fund-raising campaign has enabled the school to make major renovations around the campus. Campus housing can accommodate only about half the students, leading many to scramble for affordable off-campus housing that is often a good distance from the campus. Kilgore Center, with such amenities as a TV lounge and pool tables, offers students a central location in which to hang out, as well as quieter spots in which to study.

The social life at Morehouse is a busy one; students attend parties and get-togethers in dormitories or apartments, at which they are able to meet and mix with students from the other colleges in the Atlanta University system. Fraternities have an active presence and, despite the fact that many have tough initiation procedures, draw a sizable percent of the students. The Greeks frequently host special events and parties in conjunction with the Spelman College sororities. Many of the parties take place in one of several Atlanta dance clubs that are popular with students.

Morehouse College

$$$
★★

Setting: Urban
# of Undergraduates: 2,804
Men: 100% **Women:** 00
In-State Tuition: $7,200
Out-of-State Tuition: $7,700
Room and Board: $5,976
# of Students Applied: 2,798
  Admitted: 1,898 **Enrolled:** 771
Required Admissions Test: Either SAT or ACT
Lowest 25% of Freshmen Scored At or Below: SAT Composite Range 680–930
Highest 25% of Freshmen Scored At or Above: SAT Composite Range 1170–1490
Avg. Score of Applicants Admitted: SAT Verbal: 527 SAT Math: 529 ACT Comp.: 22
Average GPA of Applicants Admitted: 3.08
Most Popular Majors (% of Student Body): Business Administration (24%), Biology (13%), Engineering (11%), Psychology (8%), Computer Science (6.4%)

The social event of the year is Homecoming which, in addition to the big football game against rival Howard University, involves various celebrations and formals. Students definitely take advantage of their school's location, on the outskirts of Atlanta. "People head into the city all the time for jobs, movies, restaurants, and to hit the bar and club scene."

SPELMAN COLLEGE

Admissions Address: Admissions Office, 350 Spelman Lane, SW, Atlanta, GA 30314
Phone: (404) 681-3643
Web Address: www.auc.edu/

Spelman College

$$$
★★★★
Setting: Urban
# of Undergraduates: 2,000
Men: 0% Women: 100%
Tuition: $7,452
Room and Board: $5,900
# of Students Applied: 3,722
    Admitted: 1,054 Enrolled: 434
Required Admissions Test: Either SAT or ACT
H.S. Rank, Top 10%: 47%
Top 25%: 85%
Top 50%: 99%
Avg. Score of Applicants
    Admitted: SAT Verbal: 480
    SAT Math: 520 ACT Comp.: 22
Average GPA of Applicants
    Admitted: 3.38

Spelman College is a private, historically black women's college dedicated to academic excellence and service to the community. Founded in 1881 with $100 and 11 former slaves determined to learn to read and write, Spelman today boasts famous and highly successful graduates in all walks of life, from government, law, and business to the arts. Just ask Alice Walker or Marion Wright Edelman, founder of the Children's Defense Fund. If you're looking for a quality education in a supportive environment, Spelman is the place to be.

The school prides itself on its strong academics, offering a wide variety of traditional liberal arts courses. The most popular departments are biology, engineering, psychology, and English. Less traditional offerings include theater, dance, and drama, comparative women's studies, and the five-year dual degree program in engineering. Students also have the option of cross-registering for classes at other Atlanta University Center colleges such as Morehouse or at certain schools in the University Center in Georgia consortium, including Georgia Tech and Georgia State University.

The general education requirements at Spelman are designed to expose students to a broad liberal arts background and include courses in English composition, history, literature, and mathematics. Students have less vigorous requirements in the areas of fine arts, humanities, natural science, and social science. All students must be proficient in a foreign language prior to graduation. Additionally, all first-years take the two-semester survey course, "The African Diaspora and the World."

Spelman's relatively small size contributes to a manageable, student-oriented academic setting. The average class has about 20 students, and 35 is considered large. Students appreciate this aspect of the school: "The classes are challenging and the professors are approachable." However, the option to cross-register at nearby schools significantly broadens the school's more intimate academic boundaries. "You get the individual attention of a small school and the opportunities of a large one."

The social scene at Spelman also benefits from the proximity to other schools in the Atlanta University Center. Morehouse, the only all-male historically black college in the country, is literally across the street; as one student told us, the entire area often feels "just like one big campus." Morehouse fraternities team with Spelman sororities to sponsor events and throw parties, which are frequently held at Atlanta dance clubs. First-year students are even paired with "big brothers" from Morehouse. But Spelman social life is by no means limited to the immediate area. "The social life here is what you make of it," explains a sophomore. With Atlanta right outside your door, the options are literally endless.

Spelman prides itself on having a good balance between academic rigor and social activities. As one student explains, "Anything you can imagine is available: a lot of community service clubs and organizations." The school's long tradition of community service is upheld by an active and committed student body. It's extremely easy to get involved as the school has its own community service program that places students in different service positions.

The campus is relatively small and is arranged in an oval. The academic buildings are clustered in the center while the dorms are arranged around them. One student referred to the setting as "like a park." Although located on the outskirts of Atlanta, the surrounding neighborhood "isn't particularly safe," one student told us. However the entire campus is surrounded by a gate, security is good, and students feel safe. The majority of underclassmen live in the dorms, but many upperclassmen choose to move off campus.

Spelman's committed students, its small size, and its close relationship with its neighboring colleges combine to create a unique learning environment. While the campus community provides many of the benefits of a small school, there isn't the same hand holding that goes on at other small colleges. While the school provides the opportunity, "you really get to make your own way here," explains one student. "No one's going to do it for you—kind of like the real world." And judging from the school's illustrious alumnae, the Spelman experience provides its students with invaluable preparation.

Briefcase Factories

Many professional minded students use their undergraduate degrees as a springboard to prestigious business, law, and graduate schools. Getting into a top professional school or graduate program can be fiercely competitive, and there's no guarantee you'll even be accepted anywhere. You can, however, go with the odds and choose an undergraduate school where high percentages of the graduating students get accepted into graduate programs. We've listed many of those schools here.

Briefcase Factories successfully churn out future doctors, lawyers, and CEOs because they offer particularly highly rated programs in fields related to these professions. For example, strong biology, chemistry, and biochemistry departments often attract high numbers of premed students. History, English, and political science departments are often considered excellent prelaw degrees. Accounting, finance, economics, and management majors set students on the path for M.B.A.s. In addition to outstanding academic programs, Briefcase Factories also provide you with exceptional facilities and opportunities to acquire real-world, hands-on experience in your chosen profession. These experiences impress graduate programs and future employers alike.

Universities that have their own medical, law, or business schools often have the best preprofessional programs because undergraduates are able to utilize the graduate level facilities and have the opportunity to study with esteemed faculty members. However, not all professional boot camps are within large research universities. Many smaller liberal arts colleges, due to their strong overall academic programs, also have high professional school acceptance rates.

Several colleges offer accelerated programs that enable you to receive your undergraduate degree and an M.B.A. or M.D. or J.D. in less time and at a lower cost. You won't have to go through the tedious process of applying to graduate schools and have the security of knowing where you're headed after graduation. These programs are certainly worth investigating. You should keep in mind, however, that the workload in these programs is going to be especially intense. You're also not going to have much room in your schedule for electives and may feel you're missing out on a well-rounded undergraduate education.

Even if you're completely set on a particular career path, keep in mind that people have been known to change their minds. You may discover you're not as much of a lawyer or doctor at heart as you thought, especially when you're actually immersed in the daily grind of the field. Just to play it safe, you might want to check out what other academic programs are offered by these schools and how difficult it might be to change programs in midstream. At some schools, it may be very hard to switch from major to major. It may even be hard to transfer to another college if you haven't had to take core courses required during the first few years at other schools.

Make certain that, in addition to offering the preprofessional programs you want, the college you attend also has social and extracurricular options that appeal to you. You'll most likely have your career for a long time; you'll only be an undergraduate for four or five years. Don't cheat yourself out of the full undergraduate college experience.

BRANDEIS UNIVERSITY IN WALTHAM, MASSACHUSETTS

Admissions Address: Carl and Ruth Shapiro Admissions Center, Box 9110, Waltham, MA 02254-9110
Phone: (617) 736-3500 (800) 622-0622
Web Address: www.brandeis.edu

Brandeis is a major research institution that attracts renowned scholars and researchers, yet it remains highly focused on its undergraduates. Although the faculty might be immersed in their own work, they value their students and give serious priority to their teaching duties. The university makes certain that the faculty members are highly accessible to, and work closely with undergraduates. High percentages of Brandeis students go on to law and medical school, and all Brandeis graduates leave with a solid, well-rounded, liberal arts education.

Brandeis boasts a core curriculum that provides students with greater flexibility in planning their academic programs. Students take a Seminar in Humanistic Inquires, a small class taught by a senior faculty member that touches on various topics and issues. Other requirements include quantitative reasoning, writing, and foreign language. Students are also required to take three related courses that mix academic approaches and disciplines. As they determine the sequence themselves, students are given some freedom to pursue their own interests. Students have room in their schedules to take advantage of Brandeis's range of excellent academic offerings, even when they're immersed in preprofessional fields of study.

The school charges a high tuition and receives a great deal of money in grants and donations. The funding allows the school to maintain cutting-edge facilities, most of which the undergraduates are able to utilize. The campus features an eclectic mix of architectural styles, including several striking modern and contemporary structures. Housing arrangements are equally eclectic in style but of generally high quality. Students have great things to say about both the variety and the quality of the food on campus.

Brandeis was founded as a Jewish university. Even though it doesn't maintain a formal religious affiliation, about two-thirds of the students are Jewish. The student body as a whole includes a mixture of various ethnic, religious, and cultural groups and claims a significant minority population. Most students are actively and proudly liberal, concerned with a variety of political issues and generally open-minded. They form a friendly community of students that performs well without much tension or competition.

Although not a big party school, Brandeis students enjoy an active and varied social life. Brandeis' many clubs and student organizations reflect the range of students' interests, from volunteer and community service programs to underground fraternities (not officially sanctioned by the school) to various political factions and groups. There are several major university events attended by almost the entire student body, including visiting bands and performers.

Students can take advantage of the enormous Gosman Sports and Convocation Center for a number of indoor recreational and athletic activities. The town of Waltham doesn't offer much that appeals to students, but with Boston accessible via commuter rail, it hardly matters. Brandeis students often make the quick train trip to hang out with friends at Boston's many other schools or to take advantage of the city's cultural and social activities.

Brandeis University

$$$$$
★★★

Setting: Suburban
# of Undergraduates: 2,968
Men: 46.3% Women: 53.7%
Tuition: $22,360
Room and Board: $6,970
# of Students Applied: 5,513
    Admitted: 2,913   Enrolled: 770
Required Admissions Test: SAT I and II or ACT
Lowest 25% of Freshmen Scored At or Below: SAT Verbal: 610 SAT Math: 600
Highest 25% of Freshmen Scored At or Above: SAT Verbal: 690   SAT Math: 710
H.S. Rank, Top 10%: 59%
Top 25%: 81%
Top 50%: 98%
Avg. Score of Applicants Admitted: SAT Verbal: 660 SAT Math: 670
Most Popular Majors (% of Student Body): Psychology (5.8%), Economics (5.2%), American Studies (4.7%), Biology (4.7%), Politics (4.2%)

BIRMINGHAM-SOUTHERN COLLEGE IN BIRMINGHAM, ALABAMA

Admissions Address: Admissions Office, 900 Arkadelphia Road, Box 349008, Birmingham, AL 35254
Phone: (205) 226-4696 (800) 523-5793
Web Address: www.bsc.edu/

Birmingham-Southern College

$$$$
★

Setting: Urban
# of Undergraduates: 1,266
Men: 44.1% Women: 55.9%
Tuition: $13,100
Room and Board: $4,960
# of Students Applied: 680
   Admitted: 548   Enrolled: 273
Required Admissions Test: Either SAT or ACT
Lowest 25% of Freshmen Scored At or Below: SAT Verbal: 540 SAT Math: 530   ACT Comp.: 24
Highest 25% of Freshmen Scored At or Above: SAT Verbal: 670   SAT Math: 660   ACT Comp.: 30
H.S. Rank, Top 10%: 57%
Top 25%: 64%
Top 50%: 89%
Avg. Score of Applicants Admitted: SAT Verbal: 598 SAT Math: 588   ACT Comp.: 26
Average GPA of Applicants Admitted: 3.20
Most Popular Majors (% of Student Body): Business Administration (13%), Biology (7%), English (8%), Education (7%), Psychology (6%)

Birmingham-Southern College combines strong liberal arts academics with a small, friendly, collegiate environment—not exactly the typical combination for our Briefcase Factory schools. And yet many of BSC's strongest departments are in preprofessional fields, particularly in the sciences, and an impressive number of BSC graduates go on to law and medical schools. A high percentage also pursue business-related careers. The core curriculum provides students with a solid liberal arts background, as they fulfill basic distribution requirements in the humanities and sciences. Students can devote the January term to independent research, internships, or off-campus study.

There are no huge lecture courses at BSC, so students get to work closely with their professors, who almost always know students by name. It's not uncommon for students to establish relationships with professors that extend beyond the classroom. "I have been spending a lot of time with my biology professor," says a BSC freshman. "He has been teaching here for 30 years. He is so smart, and I really respect him. But he's also down-to-earth."

More than 50 percent of BSC's undergraduates go on to further study within their first two years in the real world. Of the prelaws, a whopping 94 percent got into some law school on first try, and 80 percent of the premeds are back in the dissection lab after their first round of applications.

With such a small enrollment, almost all the students know one another, creating a sense of community. "I was really nervous about meeting new people when I got here," said one student from out-of-state, "but everyone seems very nice, and I've formed some close friendships." And as one of the best liberal arts colleges in the South, BSC attracts some of the brightest students in the region.

Most students come from a similar background and share similar, usually conservative values. "I would say that the biggest complaint is that there is not enough diversity on campus. Everyone is white and upper middle class. There are few minority students," said one junior. There are as many women as men at BSC.

The social life at BSC is clearly dominated by the Greek system, which attracts more than two-thirds of the student population. In addition to Greek-oriented events that draw large numbers, there are other major all-campus events including large outdoor concerts and festivals.

Although prominent, the Greek system isn't the only option for social activity. Independents and Greeks alike become involved in different extracurricular activities, including intramural sporting events and volunteer work and community service. The BSC basketball team always enjoys a high turnout no matter their standings. One student said going to games are extra special events. Birmingham itself is a city with plenty to do in terms of culture and night life, and students take advantage of both.

JOHNS HOPKINS UNIVERSITY IN BALTIMORE, MARYLAND

Admissions Address: Admissions Office, 3400 North Charles Street, Baltimore, MD 21218-2688
Phone: (410) 516-8000 (410) 516-8171
Web Address: www.jhu.edu/

Johns Hopkins is known primarily for its graduate programs, especially its prestigious medical school. However, its small undergraduate population benefits by association with the graduate programs in many ways. Premed students, for example, work with world-famous researchers, use state-of-the-art research facilities, and conduct graduate-level work. This puts them in an ideal position for applying to medical schools, which are often impressed by the breadth of experience that Hopkins undergraduates bring with them.

Hopkins has gained a reputation as a preprofessional powerhouse in other fields as well. The prelaw, business, and engineering programs are all highly acclaimed, have large enrollments, and excellent placement records. The Krieger School of Arts and Sciences has several excellent departments including English, history, art history, anthropology, and psychology, as well as one of the most esteemed writing programs in the country.

As expected, the departments that prepare students for these careers are the most popular and among Hopkins' finest. Living up to the Johns Hopkins reputation, all science programs are superb; biology and chemistry have the largest undergraduate enrollments, while the school's bio-

Johns Hopkins University

$$$$$
★★★★

Setting: Urban
# of Undergraduates: 3,589
Men: 61.5% Women: 38.5%
Tuition: $21,700
Room and Board: $7,355
# of Students Applied: 8,508
   Admitted: 3,407   Enrolled: 1,017
Required Admissions Test: SAT
Recommended: SAT
Lowest 25% of Freshmen Scored
   At or Below: SAT Verbal: 620
   SAT Math: 650
Highest 25% of Freshmen
   Scored At or Above: SAT
   Verbal: 720   SAT Math: 740
H.S. Rank, Top 10%: 76%
Top 25%: 95%
Top 50%: 100%
Avg. Score of Applicants
   Admitted: SAT Verbal: 690
   SAT Math: 710   ACT Comp.: 31
Average GPA of Applicants
   Admitted: 3.80
Most Popular Majors (% of
   Student Body): Biology (16%),
   Biomedical Engineering (14%),
   International Studies (9%),
   Political Science (5.5%),
   Economics (5%)

medical engineering program is world renowned. For the prelaw set, the school offers exceptional programs in political science and international relations, which draw on the resources of Hopkins' acclaimed School of Advanced International Studies in Washington, D.C.

Requirements vary by school and program, and there's no real core curriculum. Most students come to Hopkins already set on a field of study, to which they are devoted from day one. Undergrads must take at least 30 credits outside their major, a policy designed to ensure students gain a broader academic perspective. Communication skills are emphasized through required writing courses.

If you're looking for a place to prepare you for the rigors of graduate life, Hopkins may be the one. The undergraduate administration recently instituted a cash awards program that funds undergraduate research projects. The program is designed to prepare undergrads for the demands and rewards of graduate-level work.

Class sizes vary primarily according to level. As students reach the higher levels, they often work in seminar-sized classes. The professors, many of whom are award-winning scientists and researchers, are devoted to their own research or their graduate students, and can be inaccessible. However, as one undergraduate told us, students who seek out professors will get results. "In my experience, the professors have been really approachable," he said.

Even though the campus is located in a residential section of Baltimore, the surrounding neighborhood can be dangerous, and safety is a concern. The campus itself is a quiet, easy-to-manage, peaceful place with adequate security, and that makes it easier for Hopkins' students to tackle the heavy workload.

Hopkins students are very serious about their studies and future careers. They're also extremely intelligent, most graduating from the top five percent of their high school classes. They are competitive, especially since grading is done on a curve. Contrary to rumors, though, they're not all cutthroats. The lack of an honor system may have contributed to unsavory student reports such as destroying books, refusing to share class notes, and the like.

The dormitories range in quality. Older dorms are "really cramped," according to students, but recently renovated ones are more accommodating. Housing is guaranteed for the first two years, which often sends upperclassmen in search of affordable and livable off-campus pads. Two-thirds of the undergraduate body is male. About 30 percent of the undergraduate population are minority students, most of whom are Asian Americans.

Due to students' commitment to their studies and the heavy workload, there's not much of a social life at Hopkins. "We'll never be known as a party school, that's for sure," one student said. However, the 13 fraternities and three sororities work hard to maintain some form of social activity. For those who want a diversion from their course work, Hopkins does provide alternatives, including on-campus movies, concerts, plays, and performances. There are several campus-wide annual events and festivals that bring together large groups of students and help spark some form of school spirit.

Hopkins' lacrosse team, which has won five Division I national championships, is a big draw on campus. A large part of the student body comes to games to cheer on the Blue Jays. All other Hopkins teams are Division III, but one student told us "they still play well, and they're always fun to watch. It's a good, cheap break from the work."

Baltimore itself is an active city with many cultural and social opportunities for those who take advantage of them. The famed National Aquarium, a terrific art museum, the bars and clubs of the Fell's Point area, excellent restaurants in Little Italy, and the Orioles baseball team at Camden Yards are all centrally located and relatively easily accessible from campus. From Baltimore, it's a short trip by car or train down to Washington, D.C. when students need a little distance from their work.

Yes, Hopkins students are among the most hard working. But their work does pay off, especially when acceptance letters from graduate schools and job offers start pouring in.

TUFTS UNIVERSITY IN MEDFORD, MASSACHUSETTS

Admissions Address: Admissions Office, Tufts University, Medford, MA 02155
Phone: (617) 627-3170
Web Address: www.tufts.edu/

Tufts students are able to take advantage of Boston's cultural and social opportunities, not to mention the work and internship possibilities, thanks to easy access via the T, the city's mass-transit system. At the

Tufts University

$$$$$
★★★★

Setting: Suburban
# of Undergraduates: 4,504
Men: 48.3% **Women:** 51.7%
Tuition: $22,230
Room and Board: $6,838
# of Students Applied: 11,873
  Admitted: 3,749 **Enrolled:** 1,190
Required Admissions Test: Either SAT I or ACT, SAT II required of students who submit SAT I
Lowest 25% of Freshmen Scored At or Below: SAT Verbal: 600 SAT Math: 630 ACT Comp.: 26
Highest 25% of Freshmen Scored At or Above: SAT Verbal: 690 SAT Math: 700 ACT Comp.: 30
H.S. Rank, Top 10%: 63%
Top 25%: 91%
Top 50%: 99%
Most Popular Majors (% of Student Body): Biology (11%), International Relations (9%), English (8%)

---

same time, they can return to the quiet and serenity of their own relaxed, beautiful New England campus.

Once considered a second-tier Ivy League school, Tufts now offers powerhouse academic programs. Benefiting from their affiliation with Tufts' graduate schools, undergraduate programs in preprofessional areas are strong. A high percentage of Tufts students go on to law, medical, and business school.

Popular majors include English, international relations, and political science. Everyone at Tufts, though, receives a solid liberal arts education. The tough core requirements include courses in humanities, arts, social sciences, math, natural sciences, writing, and foreign language, as well as a course in World Civilization. Requirements are slightly different for engineering students.

Tufts offers its students several interesting academic programs and opportunities, including the popular options of designing a major or conducting independent study and an extensive study-abroad program. Particularly innovative and a popular choice among students, the Experimental College has students as well as professors giving instruction in nontraditional, sometimes offbeat subjects, from pop culture to political events.

Class sizes vary, and some courses are taught by graduate teaching assistants. Some students say they like having TAs, who are often younger and easier to talk to than their professors. One student noted that "there are a lot of big-name professors here who aren't around much." However, students report that when they make appointments to see professors, they often find their professors friendly and helpful. For the most part, students work pretty hard. "We get swamped with work," a student complained, but added "as long as you make the effort, you stay on top of it."

Taking advantage of its splendid New England setting, the Tufts campus has a large central green, around which various academic buildings are situated. However, some students say the location is not all that pleasing on the leg muscles when they have to negotiate the New England hills. Many students said that while they like their campus, they also like being able to get into Boston easily and frequently.

Tufts is a costly school, but the money is often put to use in ways that benefit students directly. Improvements include a recent library expansion, the construction of a language and cultural studies center, science and technology center, an arts center, and the addition and renovation of student residence halls.

One student said that the best thing about Tufts was his fellow students, who bring with them a variety of interests and experiences that create a dynamic student community. Students represent a range of political views and are vocal about various issues. A significant number participate in community service and volunteer work. One student did criticize, though, that "People waste their time complaining about things that happen on campus instead of trying to fix the problems." When we asked about the social life, a student said, "There really isn't much of a social scene outside of Greek life." Most students said they are happy that they can easily travel into Cambridge and Boston, where there is social and cultural activity in abundance.

UNION COLLEGE IN SCHENECTADY, NEW YORK

Admissions Address: Admissions Office, Becker Hall, Schenectady, NY 12308
Phone: (518) 388-6112
Web Address: www.union.edu/

When you look at its academic offerings and particularly at its science and research facilities, you might think Union is a large research university. In actuality, it's a small liberal arts college, one of the oldest in the country, with an undergraduate enrollment that's kept to just over 2,000 students. Union College administrators boast their school was the first higher learning institute in the country to have a unified campus plan integrating architecture and landscape design—this is no motley group of buildings converted from other uses.

Union was the first liberal arts school to offer study in engineering, and that discipline remains strong. Social sciences and physical sciences are the most popular courses of study. Union is also known for its strengths in the premedical science departments; students are able to make use of superb laboratories and equipment and are encouraged to conduct their own scientific research. Many of its liberal arts departments are highly regarded; English, history, and political science, are very popular majors as preparation for law school. Ambitious students can receive an M.S. or M.B.A. through Union's accelerated programs. Cooperative programs with local medical law schools also allow students to receive M.D. and J.D. degrees.

Union College

$$$
★★

Setting: Small city
# of Undergraduates: 2,044
Men: 52.8% **Women:** 47.2%
Tuition: $21,945
Room and Board: $6,330
# of Students Applied: 3,474
   Admitted: 1,913 **Enrolled:** 589
Required Admissions Test: SAT I or 3 SAT II subject tests (including Writing) or ACT
Lowest 25% of Freshmen Scored At or Below: SAT Verbal: 560 SAT Math: 570 ACT Comp.: 25
Highest 25% of Freshmen Scored At or Above: SAT Verbal: 640 SAT Math: 650 ACT Comp.: 29
H.S. Rank, Top 10%: 46%
Top 25%: 82%
Top 50%: 99%
Avg. Score of Applicants Admitted: SAT Verbal: 610 SAT Math: 630 ACT Comp.: 23
Most Popular Majors (% of Student Body): Psychology (12.6%), Economics (9.9%), English (8.4%), Biology (8.1%), Political Science (8.1%)

Union's General Education Curriculum includes one course in social or behavioral science, one course in mathematics, and two courses in basic or applied science, as well as a writing-intensive "preceptorial" taken during the first year. Most classes at Union are small (under 20 on the average); students become deeply immersed in their studies and get to work closely with their professors.

Union is one of the few schools to operate on a trimester system, and students generally take three courses a term. While this isn't as stressful as a quarter system, students still have a long academic year in which exams and paper deadlines come up frequently. Students do find ways to ease the tension, often by taking up an internship or gaining work experience off campus. A substantial number of students take advantage of Union's extensive Term Abroad program.

The city of Schenectady isn't a town that appeals to students, who don't venture off campus often. Fortunately, the campus, with its ivy-covered walls, gardens, and woods, is much more scenic and stately than the city outside the walls. Most students live on campus, and there are many housing options, including several special-interest houses.

Union was the first school to have fraternities, and the Greek system remains a prominent part of student life. Fraternities draw about a third of the men and sororities attract substantial numbers of women. Although the college strictly regulates all parties, the Greeks manage to maintain a healthy party scene on campus.

Many students are also interested in sports, particularly in popular intramural sports like soccer and football. The most successful sport in recent years is men's and women's swimming, both of which are nationally-ranked. Varsity football and Division I hockey also have strong records, and the Union's Division III NCAA team keeps the bleachers full.

The student body doesn't have much of a minority population and is made up primarily of upper- and upper-middle-class students from New York and other Northeastern locations. Men outnumber women somewhat, which sometimes sends students on road trips to nearby colleges in order to meet members of the opposite sex. While social options are limited, the academic opportunities and facilities are mostly what bring students to Union, and in that sense, they are far from disappointed.

UNIVERSITY OF THE SOUTH IN SEWANEE, TENNESSEE

Admissions Address: Admissions Office, 735 University Avenue, Sewanee, TN 37383-1000
Phone: (800) 522-2234
Web Address: www.sewanee.edu

The University of the South, known to many as Sewanee, is one of the nation's finest small, liberal arts colleges. Sewanee's emphasis on high-quality academic programs makes students uniquely qualified for a number of fields upon graduation. In fact, the school turns out a large number of Rhodes Scholars. A high percentage also go on to law, medical, veterinary, education, and technical postgraduate programs.

No matter what career they are planning, Sewanee students all receive a solid liberal arts education. The extensive distribution requirements include courses in math and science, literature, social science, fine art, foreign language, philosophy and religion, and physical education.

Because the school is very small, students receive a great deal of individual attention from both the faculty and administration. Most courses have fewer than 20 students, enabling the enrolled to participate actively in class and get to know their professors. The faculty members are devoted to their teaching and are often on friendly terms with their students.

Certain things are taken very seriously at Sewanee. One is the honor code, which condemns dishonesty of any kind, as well as cheating or stealing. Academics are also highly valued and deeply respected. Students dress formally for class to demonstrate their high regard for their peers and teachers, as well as their reverence for academic study. Students with outstanding GPAs become part of the prestigious Order of the Gownsmen.

As you might guess, given its name, most students are Southern. There are students from other states and foreign countries, which makes it geographically (but not necessarily ethnically) diverse. Students we talked to corroborate the stereotype of the undergraduate body as generally conservative in their politics and values. Founded by Episcopalian church leaders and maintaining its church affiliation though 28 Church diocese, the school attracts a number of religious students.

While students are committed to their studies as they are at other Briefcase Factories, Sewanee students aren't as prone to stress about their work. The honor code fosters a sense of respect among students,

---

University of the South

$$$$$

Setting: Small town
# of Undergraduates: 1,241
Men: 49.2% Women: 50.8%
Tuition: $17,730
Room and Board: $4,660
# of Students Applied: 1,837
   Admitted: 1,210 Enrolled: 366
Required Admissions Test: Either SAT or ACT
Lowest 25% of Freshmen Scored At or Below: SAT Verbal: 570 SAT Math: 570 ACT Comp.: 24
Highest 25% of Freshmen Scored At or Above: SAT Verbal: 660 SAT Math: 660 ACT Comp.: 29
H.S. Rank, Top 10%: 52%
Top 25%: 87%
Top 50%: 99%
Avg. Score of Applicants Admitted: SAT Verbal: 617 SAT Math: 613 ACT Comp.: 27
Average GPA of Applicants Admitted: 3.40
Most Popular Majors (% of Student Body): English (19%), History (12%), Psychology (10%), Natural Resources (9%), Economics (8%)

and there's no cutthroat competitiveness. You won't find people tearing out key chapters from books in the library or refusing to share their notes. Students offer one another advice and support, and frequently help one another prepare for examinations. Due to the small size, there's a warm and friendly sense of community.

The campus, one of the most scenic in the nation, is a serene and comfortable environment that helps minimize school-related stress. As you can probably tell from a tradition like the Gownsmen, Sewanee models itself in part on Oxford. If not for the beautiful Tennessee mountains, the impressive Gothic architecture would convince visitors they were visiting Great Britain. The scenic mountains are an asset to the schools beauty; the campus is completely surrounded by breathtaking natural scenery, including a 10,000-acre, university-owned forest that serves as a natural laboratory for many courses. Additionally, Sewanee's location in the mountains is ideal for outdoor sports. Students take breaks from studying to go hiking, kayaking, spelunking, rock climbing, canoeing, and sailing.

Beyond outdoor sports in surrounding areas, most social activities are found on campus rather than in the town. Fraternities and sororities, which draw well over half the student body, host a number of parties and keep the on-campus social scene active. Many students are involved in various political, professional, social service, and religious-oriented clubs and organizations. Intramural sports are also very popular on campus, with involvement is estimated as high as 70% by some students. While the undergraduate body is an approximately equal split between men and women, minorities make up a tiny percentage of the student population.

The school recently acquired Tennessee Williams's estate (his grandfather was a preacher and Sewanee alumni), which includes rights to all of Williams's plays, funding provisions for the annual Sewanee Writer's Conference, and funding for the construction of the Tennessee Williams Center for the Performing Arts.

At the University of the South, you'll find a formal respect, reverence for, and involvement in serious academics. You'll also find a casual, relaxed environment and friendly student body. Together, they make an unusual and appealing combination.

BRIEFCASE FACTORIES

WASHINGTON AND JEFFERSON COLLEGE IN WASHINGTON, PENNSYLVANIA

Admissions Address: Admissions Office, 60 South Lincoln Street, Washington, PA 15301-4801
Phone: (412) 223-6025

With a name like Washington and Jefferson, you can imagine on what kind of presidential standards and academic ideals this college is founded. With an undergraduate enrollment under 1,200, W&J provides students with an exceptional liberal arts education and produces an especially high percentage of doctors, lawyers, and business executives.

One of the nation's oldest colleges, Washington and Jefferson attracts an affluent and elite student body who, once they graduate, become part of a closely knit network of alumni who stay connected socially and professionally.

Students begin with an intensive liberal arts core curriculum including courses in history, philosophy and religion, art and music, language, literature, science and math, economics and business, political science, and biology, as well as freshman English and physical education. Most students consider themselves prelaw or premed, which makes biology, chemistry, English, history, and political science among the school's strongest and most popular programs. Students become deeply involved in their studies as the class sizes are kept at a minimum (almost always fewer than 25 students), requiring a great deal of student attention and participation.

Several sophomores stated the workload is very rigorous. Professors often rely on the Socratic teaching method, meaning students must come to class prepared to be called on by the professor. With such small classes, professors get to know their students by name and form pretty close ties with them.

The intense work pays off for M&J graduates, as 86 percent go on to successful business careers, and 13 percent advance to medical school. The remainder split equally to law school or educational careers.

Given the compact, 35-acre campus, small class sizes, and low undergraduate enrollment, it's not surprising that students feel closely tied to their school community. Students particularly feel attached to their fraternities or sororities, which attract a majority of the students and form the basis of the campus social life, or become involved in athletics. Though not known as a commuter school, some students said they pre-

---

Washington and Jefferson College

$$$$$

Setting: Suburban
# of Undergraduates: 1,103
Men: 53.9% Women: 46.1%
Tuition: $17,700
Room and Board: $4,345
# of Students Applied: 1,227
   Admitted: 1,050 Enrolled: 321
Required Admissions Test: either SAT or ACT
Lowest 25% of Freshmen Scored At or Below: SAT Verbal: 500 SAT Math: 500 ACT Comp.: 24
Highest 25% of Freshmen Scored At or Above: SAT Verbal: 620 SAT Math: 610 ACT Comp.: 27
H.S. Rank, Top 10%: 39%
Top 25%: 64%
Top 50%: 97%
Avg. Score of Applicants Admitted: SAT Verbal: 557 SAT Math: 557 ACT Comp.: 24
Average GPA of Applicants Admitted: 3.40
Most Popular Majors (% of Student Body): Business Administration (18%), Biology (14%), Psychology (10%), English (9%), History (8%)

267

fer to leave campus on weekends to head home. Others visit friends at other colleges or go into Pittsburgh, about 30 minutes away. The university recently added the Olin Fine Arts Center and the Washington & Jefferson Arts Festival to keep students around and to keep the visitors rolling in; both students and patrons are happy with the programs.

For students who shy away from large, research-oriented universities, Washington and Jefferson is an ideal place to get on a preprofessional track in an intimate, collegiate community.

WASHINGTON UNIVERSITY IN ST. LOUIS, MISSOURI

Admissions Address: Admissions Office, Campus Box 1089, One Brookings Drive, St. Louis, MO 63130-4899
Phone: (314) 935-6000 (800) 638-0700
Web Address: www.wustl.edu

Washington University

$$$$$
★★★

Setting: Suburban
# of Undergraduates: 5,033
Men: 51.4% Women: 48.6%
Tuition: $21,000
Room and Board: $6,593
# of Students Applied: 11,276
  Admitted: 5,715 Enrolled: 1,296
Required Admissions Test: Either SAT or ACT
Lowest 25% of Freshmen Scored At or Below: SAT Verbal: 580 SAT Math: 620 ACT Comp.: 27
Highest 25% of Freshmen Scored At or Above: SAT Verbal: 690 SAT Math: 710 ACT Comp.: 31
H.S. Rank, Top 10%: 66%
Top 25%: 92%
Top 50%: 99%
Most Popular Majors (% of Student Body): Engineering (17%), Premedicine (15%), Business (12%), Psychology (11%), English (5%)

When we asked a Washington University sophomore what fields of study her fellow students chose, she said, "Everybody is premed." This was an exaggerated statement, but not by much. A large percentage of Washington University students are in preparation for medical school and an impressive number get in.

However, premed is not the only preprofessional route that's popular here; students can also study in the schools of architecture, business, or engineering. A high percentage also go on to law school.

One advantage Wash U has over many schools oriented toward preprofessional studies is the range of academic fields. Its hard for students to become boxed into an undesirable field of study with five undergraduate schools at Wash U (architecture, business, engineering, fine arts, and arts and sciences), and students are encouraged to take courses in any of them. Changing majors, even from one school to another, isn't difficult.

No matter what their major, all students take the same basic requirements including courses in natural sciences, social sciences, humanities, foreign language, fine arts, or philosophy, as well as freshman writing. Responding to student needs, within the past two years the University initiated a number of new majors and interdisciplinary programs.

A common complaint among students is that professors are involved in their own research or writing and can be inaccessible or remote. One student, however, reported that when she seeks help, she finds her professors available. Some students report that teaching assistants are valuable assets, as they are closer in age to the students, more available, and easier to communicate with. Students do have opportunities to gain experience by working with professors on research projects.

Located in a suburban section of St. Louis, Washington University's Colonial and Gothic buildings and beautiful, flower-lined courtyards make for an idyllic, picture-perfect campus. The facilities, including a number built within the last few years, are generally in excellent condition. Recent construction yielded two new dormitories, and plans for renovation of several existing residence halls are in the works (the students we talked to say the renovations will be welcomed). A number of new academic structures have appeared on campus in recent years, including a law school building, a natural science building, a psychology department building, a School of Social Sciences Building, and several new medical school buildings.

Given its Midwestern location (remember, the school is in Missouri, not Washington state), the student population is surprisingly diverse in terms of geography and ethnicity. Recent efforts by the administration to recruit more students from different backgrounds has led to a minority enrollment rate of about 20%. In terms of politics, students are "largely apathetic," we are told, but there's "a vocal conservative voice."

Students tend to enjoy the social environment. "There is generally a relaxed and friendly atmosphere here. It's not cutthroat. The administration is pretty liberal. Their policy is to treat students like adults unless they prove otherwise," one student said.

The atmosphere may be relaxed, but the workload is anything but. In preparation for graduate or professional schools, students study like fiends, and they're very concerned about their grades. Students say they tend to study a lot, even on weekends. Nevertheless, Wash U has a fair share of social outlets. Intramural sports are popular, and many students gravitate to the school's Division III, nationally ranked volleyball team's games; the team has won the national championship six times in the past seven years.

A sophomore said students go to the on-campus pub on Thursday nights and, if they're not studying on weekends, might head over to the "row," the strip of fraternity houses where "there's always a party." Slightly more than one-quarter of the students actually are involved in the Greek system, but many parties are open to the whole campus. Many students also go to smaller gatherings in dormitories and off-campus apartments. A few major events bring all the students together, including WILD, an outdoor party with a live band, and the annual student-run carnival.

The city of St. Louis is accessible via Metro Link and offers other options, including museums, a trendy section with cafes, coffeehouses, restaurants, and clubs, and, of course, the famous St. Louis Zoo. The campus is near Forest Park, one of the nation's largest urban parks. Between the park, the city itself, and the campus, students are able to relax and even have fun while preparing for their future careers.

Also, Check Out These Schools:

Amherst College
Bowdoin College
Brown University
Bucknell University
University of California—Berkeley
University of California—San Diego
California Institute of Technology
Carleton College
Carnegie Mellon University
University of Chicago
Claremont McKenna College
Colby College
College of the Holy Cross
College of William and Mary
Columbia University
Cornell University
Dartmouth College
Davidson College
Duke University
Emory University
Franklin and Marshall College
Georgetown University
Grinnell College
Harvard University
Haverford College
Howard University
Massachusetts Institute of Technology
Middlebury College
New College of the University of South Florida
New York University
University of North Carolina—Chapel Hill

BRIEFCASE FACTORIES

Northwestern University
Oberlin College
Pomona College
Princeton College
Reed College
Rhodes College
Rice University
Southwestern University
Stanford University
Swarthmore College
University of Texas—Austin
Tulane University
Vanderbilt University
University of Virginia
Wabash College
Washington and Lee University
Wellesley College
Williams College
Yale University

Specialty Shops

Rather than doing several things poorly, do one thing and do it well. That's been the secret behind many a success story, from Olympic gold medal winners to Noble laureates. The schools in this chapter have adopted the same strategy, specializing in a few very specific fields in which they concentrate the bulk of their resources and funding. As a result, they're often considered the top institutions in these areas, becoming known as the place to study these subjects.

As these schools narrow the academic scope to a few select areas, you can become a real expert in your chosen field. You study your field in great depth, gaining not only a general understanding of the subject but also a chance to examine the intricacies and subtleties of your calling. While at other schools you might find limited course offerings and facilities in your chosen major, at these schools you'll receive singular support in your endeavors. The faculty will include leading scholars in the field, as well as qualified professionals who bring with them a wealth of real-world experiences. Very often these schools combine intense academic study with practical, hands-on experience, encouraging you to learn by doing. By the time you graduate, you are uniquely qualified for a professional position.

Specializing in anything means making a serious commitment. Although these schools often offer courses outside their specialty fields, the offerings might be pretty slim. These generally aren't schools where you can dabble and experiment in different subjects before making up your mind about a major. Obviously, you should not go to one of these schools unless you're pretty set on that particular field.

It's also crucial that you truly love what you're studying because you're probably going to devote long hours to it. Becoming a specialist takes time, hard work, and total dedication. The students we talked to at these schools all described the heavy workload and intense pressure of their programs. One of the advantages to going to a specialty school, though, is the opportunity to meet many people who share your interests and can offer emotional support and practical advice.

Babson College

$$$$$
★★★

Setting: Suburban
# of Undergraduates: 1,627
Men: 62.5% **Women:** 37.5%
Tuition: $18,940
Room and Board: $7,800
# of Students Applied: 2,394
   Admitted: 1,084 **Enrolled:** 369
Required Admissions Test: SAT I, SAT II in Writing and Math
Lowest 25% of Freshmen Scored At or Below: SAT Verbal: 500 SAT Math: 560
Highest 25% of Freshmen Scored At or Above: SAT Verbal: 600 SAT Math: 650
H.S. Rank, Top 10%: 25%
Top 25%: 57%
Top 50%: 87%
Most Popular Majors (% of Student Body): Marketing (6%), EPS/Marketing (5%), Accounting (5%), Economics (4%), Finance/Investments (4%)

BABSON COLLEGE IN BABSON PARK, MASSACHUSETTS

Admissions Address: Admissions Office, Mustard Hall, Babson Park, MA 02157-0310
Phone: (617) 239-5522 (800) 488-3696
Web Address: www.babson.edu

To succeed in business today takes dedication, brains, and fierce perseverance. A Babson degree couldn't hurt, either.

Babson students display the intensity of successful future business leaders from the first day they arrive. To enroll at Babson, where business-related fields are the primary focus, is to set yourself firmly on a professional track. The combination of academic programs and real-world experiences at Babson leaves students uniquely qualified to take the professional world by storm.

Business-related majors are obviously the strongest and most popular areas of concentration, with marketing attracting the most students. But the Babson curriculum involves more than number crunching and strategic planning. Although more than one-third of students' credits must be in business-related fields, another third must be in the liberal arts. Several courses stress skills that are key assets in business, such as business writing and information processing. Students round out their schedules with courses in foreign language and culture and have the option of cross-registering at nearby schools, such as Brandeis and Wellesley for more academic variety (or, as one student mentioned, a better chance at a date).

Students have high praise for Babson professors, who bring with them extensive expertise and practical experience. One student told us how the school's size enables students to form friendships not only with each other but also with professors who "are always there for you when you need them." The campus and facilities also receive student kudos.

Course work at Babson is rounded out by opportunities to garner real-world experience. Through the Center for Entrepreneurial Studies, many students practice what they are learning by running their own businesses—and donating their profits to charity. The school's proximity to Boston is a big plus, providing students with a range of internships at major corporations, not to mention supplying a mixed bag of social hangouts and entertainment venues. At the same time, leading Beantown entrepreneurs and CEOs visit the campus to reveal their secrets of success.

Additionally, as so many Babson alumni hold major positions in the business world, excellent job connections come faster than you can say "alma mater." Students preparing to graduate are introduced to the Babson alumni network, and it seems many find successful job placement through contacts fostered through the school.

The workload as an undergraduate, as with any Specialty Shop, is rigorous. A freshman reported, "The workload is pretty rigorous, especially coming from high school. It's much harder than I expected."

Preparing students for the heated world of big business that awaits them, Babson's general atmosphere is a highly competitive one fraught with pressure, particularly when students are after the same internships and job positions. A marketing major told us that even within this competitive environment, there is "a sense of family" because of the small enrollment. She did go on to say that the student body is "unfortunately somewhat segregated. Most are white. And we're generally very conservative."

Students' primary concerns are unquestionably career related, which to some extent puts the social life on the back burner. The ratio of two men to every woman isn't conducive to heavy dating. Many students head off campus in their free time to hang out with friends at Boston's other colleges and universities or to enjoy the city's night life. Campus-wide events include parties, movies, and even a few student musical and dramatic performances. Many students like to play sports and take advantage of Babson's slick athletic complex. Fraternities and sororities draw less than 10 percent of the students; while not a major social influence, they provide a steady stream of social events and parties.

While these activities provide minor diversions, they don't pull students away from their career tracks, to which they are firmly attached. Students recognize that the rigors of Babson are ideal preparations for the challenging work experiences lie ahead.

CALIFORNIA INSTITUTE OF TECHNOLOGY
IN PASADENA

Admissions Address: Office of Admisssions, Mail Code 55-63, Pasadena, CA 91125
Phone: (818) 395-6341
Web Address: www.admissions.caltech.edu/

California Institute of Technology

$$$$$
★★★★

Setting: Suburban
# of Undergraduates: 882
Men: 74.4% **Women:** 25.6%
Tuition: $18,000
Room and Board: $5,700
# of Students Applied: 1,993
  Admitted: 518 **Enrolled:** 216
Required Admissions Test: SAT I and II (Writing, Math IIC and one of the sciences)
Lowest 25% of Freshmen Scored At or Below: SAT Verbal: 690 SAT Math: 740
Highest 25% of Freshmen Scored At or Above: SAT Verbal: 780 SAT Math: 800
H.S. Rank, Top 10%: 98%
Top 25%: 100%
Avg. Score of Applicants Admitted: SAT Verbal: 725 SAT Math: 767
Most Popular Majors: Chemistry, Physics, Engineering & Applied Science, Electrical Engineering, Biology

---

With an undergraduate enrollment of under one thousand, Cal Tech can offer a much more intimate and personalized academic environment than most other science and technical schools without sacrificing top-notch research assets. Students, therefore, have a much greater chance to work closely with Cal Tech's prestigious faculty and to get valuable experience with state-of-the-art resources.

Getting accepted at Cal Tech isn't easy; many students were the brains in their high schools and aced the SATs. Once in, they become immersed in an intensive and demanding program that combines high-level academic study with heavy-duty research, including opportunities to gain practical experience and to conduct independent projects. It's not unheard of for students to publish academic papers before graduation. When they do graduate, Cal Tech students go on to prestigious graduate programs or receive top positions in their chosen fields. "It's very, very challenging," one student said, then quickly added, "but I wouldn't want to be anywhere else."

The majority of students' credits are devoted to their concentrations. The comprehensive core curriculum can also take up to two years to complete, so there's not much room for elective study. Students take required courses in math, physics, and chemistry, several labs, and about 12 courses in humanities and social science, as well as physical education. Students describe their professors as friendly, understanding, and very approachable, although their teaching abilities may vary. Lectures in introductory classes are large, but upper-level courses usually have 20 or fewer students.

Cal Tech is on a quarter system, and each session is crammed. The schedule alone increases the academic pressure as exams and deadlines come up more frequently. The level and amount of work for each class also creates a high-pressure environment. Each class alone can take 15 to 20 hours of work a week.

While students have mounds of work, there's still a laid-back attitude in the air that prevents a cutthroat environment. Freshmen are graded on a pass/fail basis, providing a transition to the tough coursework, and students rely on each other for support. Additionally, collaborative work is often encouraged so that students don't have to feel isolated.

Research was just made a little easier with the opening of the Sherman Fairchild Library of Engineering and Applied Sciences, which offers state-of-the-art information technology including fiber-optic wiring, and a CD-ROM library.

The campus, with its Spanish architecture and courtyards coupled with the temperate California weather, keep students from feeling like they're in a pressure cooker. Most significantly, Cal Tech's honor code reduces competition between students and fosters a sense of camaraderie.

The unique housing system also enables students to become part of a smaller community and form close friendships. Students choose a house that suits their interests and personality and can remain there for as many years as they like (until they graduate). Like a fraternity or sorority, the house will often serve as the focal point for the student's social life.

Almost half the student body is made up of minority and international students. Asian Americans account for about 30% of the students. The men far outnumber the women, which, depending on your point of view, may help or hurt your social chances. However, one student told us, "it can be tough finding dates around campus, but then there are other scenes. After all, this is southern California."

Cal Tech students are far from being workaholic drones. Their notorious pranks, from which no one in the region is safe, indicate their sense of fun as well as their creativity. Other social outlets include informal parties, hanging out on campus or in rooms, and going to movies. Intramural sports and athletics are also very popular, and anyone who wants to play usually can. The accessibility to Los Angeles provides an abundance of social and cultural alternatives to the study grind.

Students at Cal Tech can expect to put in a lot of work hard for four years, knowing that they're setting a standard of excellence for themselves in their academic and professional careers.

CARNEGIE MELLON UNIVERSITY IN PITTSBURGH, PENNSYLVANIA

Admissions Address: Admissions Office, 5000 Forbes Avenue, Pittsburgh, PA 15213-3890
Phone: (412) 268-2082
Web Address: www.cmu.edu/

Carnegie Mellon University

$$$$$
★★★

Setting: Urban
# of Undergraduates: 4,737
Men: 67.7% Women: 32.3%
Tuition: $20,275
Room and Board: $6,225
# of Students Applied: 13,314
   Admitted: 6,218   Enrolled: 1,386
Required Admissions Test: Either SAT or ACT, SAT II Required
Lowest 25% of Freshmen Scored At or Below: SAT Verbal: 600 SAT Math: 660 ACT Comp.: 27
Highest 25% of Freshmen Scored At or Above: SAT Verbal: 710 SAT Math: 750 ACT Comp.: 31
H.S. Rank, Top 10%: 65%
Top 25%: 93%
Top 50%: 100%
Average GPA of Applicants Admitted: 3.70
Most Popular Majors (% of Student Body): Engineering (31%), Business (11%), Comp. Science (8%), Social Science (6%), Architecture (5%)

Andrew Carnegie is one of America's greatest success stories, and the students at his namesake school appear to be set on following his example. Carnegie Mellon students are some of the hardest workers you'll find anywhere. One student told us that it's common for students to study about 30 hours during the week, and then several more hours on the weekend. Most have already decided on a future career upon arrival and set to work immediately, but they're not all on the same path. One of the strengths of Carnegie Mellon lies in its different and specialized areas of engineering and drama—both among the best in the nation. Many other programs in the arts, sciences, and architecture are also excellent.

Carnegie's power is clearly in its academics. As a student told us, "People almost universally acknowledge they're getting a quality education here. We have some of the best professors in the country. Academically speaking, this school is top-notch."

The six undergraduate colleges at Carnegie are the College of Fine Arts, the College of Humanities and Social Sciences, the School of Computer Science, the School of Industrial Management, the Carnegie Institute of Technology, and the Mellon College of Science. Each has its own admissions process and core requirements. Transferring between the schools can be difficult, we're told, but thankfully such an event is a rare given most student's motivation, direction, and serious attention to studies. A recent major added to the academic program was European studies, and a new engineering hall opened last year.

Almost all programs provide students with opportunities for hands-on, practical experience. Engineering, computer, and science students utilize superb facilities as they become immersed in independent projects. In the drama program, students work with experienced theater personnel to put on professional-quality shows. In addition, this spring saw the groundbreaking for the Pernell Center for Performing Arts.

Although teaching assistants handle lower-level and intro classes, most mid- and upper-level courses are taught by accomplished professors. The faculty are generally very supportive of their students. As one student told us, "I get the impression some professors do more research than teaching, but overall they're pretty accessible." Introductory levels are almost always large lectures, but most students are able to take smaller size classes at higher levels.

The Carnegie Mellon campus, located about four miles from downtown Pittsburgh, features an eclectic range of styles that strikes some as interesting and others as ugly. The school's facilities generally cater to its academic strengths; the engineering and science library is a vital resource for those students. Carnegie Mellon ensures all students have computer access through its many computer labs.

Minority and international students compose about 40 pecent of the population, and men outnumber women by about two to one. About 20 percent of the students come from Pennsylvania. The one factor at Carnegie that most distinguishes students is their different academic disciplines; one student told us "the student body gets polarized" between science/engineering students and fine arts students.

No matter who they are, where they come from, or what they study, students all work hard at their courses. A typical morning stroll about campus will reveal bleary-eyed, book-laden students trudging to class after intense all-nighters. The caffeine-dependent workload doesn't accommodate a party atmosphere. As one student moaned, "People spend an awful lot of time working. There are some who spend 30 hours a week on homework. I don't think they do anything for fun here. The social scene is pretty pathetic." However, another student countered this party pooper by stating that "there are some great, fun parts of town within walking distance, and the school borders one of the largest parks in the city."

Yet students also take a strange kind of pride in their ability to survive the laborious academics. Their devotion to their respective studies is something that brings many students closer together, and that camaraderie may help students survive the demanding academics.

Students are guaranteed housing for all four years, a real advantage in a city school. Approximately 70 percent of undergrads live on campus. Some of those who don't are involved in the Greek system. The Greek system is not an overpowering presence, but it does guarantee there will be an active party scene. The arts departments provide frequent professional-quality performances and cultural events on campus, and a new University Center offers students a convenient place to gather.

There are a number of campus activities for students who do want a break from studying. Students can also head into the nearby, upscale Oakland area where there are several hip bars and decent restaurants, or over to the trendy Squirrel Hill or Shady Side sections of town. After major spurts of urban renewal and renovation, Pittsburgh was recently named one of the nation's most livable cities, and now offers many cultural and social options.

Carnegie Mellon students do work hard, but they also take tremendous pride in their work, gaining satisfaction in their preparations for whatever success the future holds.

College of the Atlantic

$$$$$
★★

Setting: Small coastal town
# of Undergraduates: 250
Men: 30.4% **Women:** 69.6%
Tuition: $16,950
Room and Board: $5,075
# of Students Applied: 352
   Admitted: 227 **Enrolled:** 112
Required Admissions Test: None
Recommended: SAT, ACT, SAT II
Lowest 25% of Freshmen Scored At or Below: SAT Verbal: 560 SAT Math: 540
Highest 25% of Freshmen Scored At or Above: SAT Verbal: 700 SAT Math: 680
H.S. Rank, Top 10%: 49%
Top 25%: 76%
Top 50%: 99%
Avg. Score of Applicants Admitted: SAT Verbal: 645 SAT Math: 623 ACT Comp.: 23
Average GPA of Applicants Admitted: 3.67
Most Popular Majors (% of Student Body): Human Ecology (100%)

COLLEGE OF THE ATLANTIC IN BAR HARBOR, MAINE

Admissions Address: Office of Admissions, 105 Eden Street, Bar Harbor, ME 04609-1105
Phone: (207) 288-5015 (800) 528-0025
Web Address: www.coa.edu

Given its name, it's probably no surprise that College of the Atlantic specializes in ecological issues. When you also consider that the breathtaking campus is set on an island in Maine, you can begin to understand just how central the natural environment is to the school.

There is only one major at COA—Human Ecology—but it is investigated and studied by students and faculty from many viewpoints and approaches. The core curriculum includes studies in basic areas, such as environmental science, human studies, and art, as well as writing. All students are also required to take a 10-week internship position. The core program was recently extended to study in the Yucatan, Mexico, and COA now operates on an exchange program with Palacki University in the Czech Republic. The Human Ecology curriculum seems to work well, as the school is celebrating its 25th anniversary this year, with a total of 820 alumni.

Students are given a great deal of academic freedom in planning their programs according to their individual interests, including working on independent projects. With a student population that just peaked at 250 students, close friendships between students (and even with professors) is the norm. Students work closely with their peers and professors in small classes and on special projects. They receive individual evaluations of their work and get grades only if they ask for them. In general, the overall atmosphere is that of a relaxed, cohesive communal retreat.

Students are given a large role in the school administration and campus government, which fosters a strong sense of commitment and responsibility to the school. The very liberal student body is idealistic, intelligent, and generally tolerant. There are twice as many women as men at COA, hailing from 32 states in the nation.

Students are proud of their active role in the Mount Desert Island community service, through local social programs or environmentally related work at the nearby Acadia National Park. Though small, the college is building two new dorms, and is planning a Maine Natural History Museum. There is an active artistic community on the island, and the college recently opened the Blum Art gallery to critical acclaim.

The social scene reflects the casual attitudes of the students and primarily revolves around the school's natural surroundings. While students can feel isolated at times, especially in the midst of the frozen winter months, the outdoor activities and stunning beauty of this natural setting sparks students' deep and lasting affection for their school. One magazine voted COA's students "the happiest in the United States," a title any COA student wears with pride.

EMERSON COLLEGE IN BOSTON, MASSACHUSETTS

Admissions Address: Admissions Office, 100 Beacon Street, Boston, MA 02116-1596
Web Address: www.emerson.edu/

Emerson, a small school nestled in Boston's beautiful Back Bay, specializes in communications and performing arts. One of the best assets is the way Emerson provides its students with classroom, as well as practical, real-world experiences. The school operates its own radio station that is listened to throughout the city as well as a television station for aspiring broadcasters and journalists. The theater department's actors and technical crew hone their craft and showcase their talent at the painstakingly preserved Majestic Theatre, which has turned into a must-attend destination for Boston's many culture vultures. "For my craft," said one student, "I couldn't think of going anywhere else. Emerson really lets me get a head start on my career."

Most classes are very small, providing students with an excellent opportunity to work with teachers who are themselves successful journalists, filmmakers, actors, and advertising executives. Due to the small size of the school, students are able to work closely with these professors.

Emerson College

$$$$$
★★

Setting: Urban
# of Undergraduates: 2,600
Men: 43% **Women:** 57%
Tuition: $16,640
Room and Board: $8,210
# of Students Applied: 1,856
  Admitted: 1,285 Enrolled: 523
Required Admissions Test: Either SAT or ACT
H.S. Rank, Top 10%: 20%
Top 25%: 55%
Top 50%: 80%
Avg. Score of Applicants Admitted: SAT Verbal: 525
  SAT Math: 510
Average GPA of Applicants Admitted: 3.05

Professors know most of their students by name and make themselves available for counsel, often outside of class over coffee or a meal (but don't expect the profs to pick up your lunch, though).

The school occupies a number of converted Victorian houses along Beacon Street, which gives it a quaint, New England look that contributes to the generally relaxed and neighborly feel of the school. Emerson's location in Boston is a real plus, affording internship and work opportunities as well as numerous social and cultural venues. Beacon Hill is the backyard of the school, and the lush greenery of the Boston Commons is the front lawn.

The student body, as might be expected, is an artsy crowd that is accepting of one another's individuality in any form it might take. This is one group of people that was tattooed and pierced before it was mainstream, but the students aren't so busy being trendy that they don't have time to network. Between classes, students hang out on the steep steps of Emerson's administration building at 100 Beacon Street, a meeting place affectionately known as "the Wall." Here students trade ideas for films, short stories, stand-up comedy routines, and music videos.

When they're not in class, internship programs allow Emerson students an excellent hands-on primer for their future careers. Past internships have been successfully negotiated at such companies as Disney and Houghton Mifflin, and a recently initiated Los Angeles internship program sends students out west for their first professional experience.

Because the school is so concentrated in communications, students share many of the same interests and philosophies. Many friendships struck up at "the Wall" turn into business relationships after students graduate and form production companies, theater groups, and advertising and public relations companies. Being amidst all of this creative energy has paid off for many of the school's famous alumni, who include Norman Lear, Jay Leno, Spalding Gray, and Denis Leary.

SPECIALTY SHOPS

HARVEY MUDD COLLEGE IN CLAREMONT, CALIFORNIA

Admissions Address: Admissions Office, 301 East 12th Street, Claremont, CA 91711-5990
Phone: (909) 621-8011
Web Address: www.hmc.edu/

Question: When is a tech school more than a tech school?

Answer: When it's a part of the Claremont College system.

Each of the schools in the Claremont system—which also includes Claremont McKenna, Pitzer, Pomona, and Scripps—has its own academic focus, campus, and faculty. Students at each of these schools can freely cross-register, use facilities, and take part in activities at all five colleges. HMC students, therefore, have many opportunities, academic and social, available to them while being immersed in their own exceptional, highly concentrated technical studies.

Harvey Mudd College is the school for science and engineering in the Claremont system, as well as one of the top schools for those fields in the nation. Undergraduates take up one of six majors: biology, chemistry, computer science, engineering, math, or physics. Engineering by far has the highest enrollment, drawing almost half of the student body.

All students must fulfill extensive requirements, called the Common Core, that take about a year and a half to complete. The Common Core ensures that all students a receive broad, well-rounded educational background. The Core requirements include four semesters of math, three of physics, two of chemistry, and one of computer science, as well as two electives. Students are also required to take about a third of their credits in humanities and social science fields, such as literature, psychology, philosophy, and history; these courses often serve as a welcome change from their more concentrated major studies.

Students can take these courses at other Claremont schools, where they are well-supported. HMC students not only graduate with a well-rounded background, they also know how to swim; physical education courses, and passing a swim test, are required to graduate.

With less than 700 undergraduates, the enrollment is significantly smaller than at most tech schools. That means students have much greater opportunity to work with professors closely and to get their hands on the school's cutting-edge equipment and resources. Professors teach all the classes, which often have fewer than 20 students. In the large lecture

---

Harvey Mudd College

$$$$$
★★★

Setting: Suburban
# of Undergraduates: 643
Men: 75% **Women:** 25%
Tuition: $18,960
Room and Board: $7,520
# of Students Applied: 1,303
   Admitted: 597 **Enrolled:** 177
Required Admissions Test: SAT and SAT II
Lowest 25% of Freshmen Scored At or Below: SAT Verbal: 640 SAT Math: 710
Highest 25% of Freshmen Scored At or Above: SAT Verbal: 740 SAT Math: 780
H.S. Rank, Top 10%: 90%
Top 25%: 100%
Avg. Score of Applicants Admitted: SAT Verbal: 680 SAT Math: 740
Most Popular Majors (% of Student Body): Engineering (43%), Physics (15%), Chemistry (14%), Biology (10%), Computer Science (8%)

283

classes, professors will also lead smaller weekly review sessions. Professors generally take an active interest in their students and are readily available and accessible when students need them. One upper-level student told us there was never a time when he couldn't reach one of his professors.

Many of the programs encourage students to round out their theoretical studies with practical applications. The clinic program provides engineers and computer science students with real world experience by having them work at solving problems for industries and corporations. Many students also conduct independent research and projects, often publishing the results.

About half the students come from out of state, and about 25 percent are minority students, almost all of whom are Asian Americans. There are about three times as many men as women. All of the students, though, are highly intelligent and extremely motivated. They need to be—the course load and work requirements are grueling. Most students take five courses each semester, which require long hours of problem solving, lab work, and preparation outside of class. Rather than becoming competitive with one another, the grueling labors they share foster a sense of camaraderie among the students.

The school has an honor code that creates an atmosphere of mutual trust and respect among students. Their hard work generally pays off, as a substantially high percentage go directly into graduate school, most towards earning a Ph.D. HMC boasts the highest percentage of undergraduate students to earn doctoral degrees in science and technology in the nation. Many students, however, also drop out along the way because they're not able to maintain a high enough GPA.

Because HMC students are so focused on their work, there isn't much of an active social scene on campus. Students report "the area seems pretty quiet, anyway." Those who want other activities have many options, though, particularly within the other Claremont schools. Becoming involved in activities and organizations at the other schools gives students a break from their fellow HMC techies and a chance to mingle with students who have many different interests.

On campus, the socializing centers are the dorms. The dorms bear the same institutional appearance as the rest of the campus, but they're generally comfortable and well maintained. Best of all, dorm rooms are networked to the HMC mainframe. Each dorm hosts various socials and special events, from movie nights to parties. Dorms host the popular "Wednesday Night Prof Thing," where faculty visit the dorms and get involved in social activities and discussions with their students.

Students also hang out at the Muddhole, a student center with lounges, video games, fast food, pool tables, and table tennis. Rather than becoming involved with intercollegiate sports, more students play intramural sports against teams from other Claremont campuses. A sporting event that is entirely a Harvey Mudd tradition, though, is the Five Class competition, a goofy—if not grueling—day of bizarre relay races involving food, mathematical abilities, and occasionally a bit of physical prowess.

THE JUILLIARD SCHOOL IN NEW YORK, NEW YORK

Admissions Address: Admissions Office, 60 Lincoln Center Plaza, New York, NY 10023-6588
Phone: (212) 799-5000, ext. 223

At most schools, admissions are based primarily on grades and standardized test scores. At Juilliard, the decision is based mostly on a sink-or-swim audition—during which either you have it or you don't. Take a look at some of the accomplished alumni—Yitzhak Perlman, Leontyne Price, Kevin Kline, Patti LuPone, just to name a few—and you'll get a sense of the high level of talent that is recruited and cultivated at Juilliard. With its uncompromising admissions standards and tough programs, Juilliard is the finest and most exclusive school in the country devoted entirely to the study of performing arts. Students who graduate from Juilliard are considered uniquely qualified for professional careers in the field.

Students' work within the divisions of music, drama, and dance is not so much a matter of academic study as the actual exercising of their talents. In addition to taking classes in the history and theory of their chosen disciplines, students spend hours each day practicing and working with Juilliard's renowned instructors. They also perform regularly in Juilliard's many professional-quality productions, recitals, and concerts.

The teaching quality varies at Juilliard. Some professors are much better teachers, both coddling and critiquing their students, while other teachers may not demonstrate the same level of concern. No matter the teaching style, though, all students will receive a high level of individualized attention.

The Juilliard School

$$$$
★★★★★

Setting: Urban
# of Undergraduates: 490
Men: 49% **Women:** 51%
Tuition: $13,600
Room and Board: $6,500
# of Students Applied: 1,176
  Admitted: 128 **Enrolled:** 104
Required Admissions Test:
  Audition

In addition to their concentration, students are also required to take two years of humanities classes to guarantee they receive some kind of basic college education. The classes are not as difficult as at liberal arts colleges and universities. Nevertheless, between their academic courses and intensive performance programs, these students work hard.

Juilliard is considered a highly competitive school, and the competition extends well beyond the initial effort to get in. At the same time, the pressure and competitiveness are excellent training for the rigors of the professional world.

The closest Juilliard comes to a campus is the Lincoln Center of Performing Arts, where its main buildings are located. While it may not have a central quad or lawn, the school is positioned in a prime location in terms of the New York cultural and performing arts scene. Students are just steps away from the Metropolitan and New York State opera, the ballet, the theater, and concerts.

Juilliard recently built a residence hall that provides students with comfortable and relatively affordable housing in pricey Manhattan. This addition has also made it possible for students to form friendships more easily with their peers. While a few Juilliard extracurricular activities and events draw students' attention, most turn to New York City for its incomparable cultural options.

Common belief dictates that talent is something people are born with that can't be taught. The students who get accepted at Juilliard are already highly talented. What the Juilliard experience provides is an opportunity for that talent to be cultivated while preparing students more seriously for the professional careers they dream of.

RHODE ISLAND SCHOOL OF DESIGN
IN PROVIDENCE, RHODE ISLAND

Admissions Address: Admissions Office, 2 College Street, Providence, RI 02903
Phone: (401) 454-6300

When we talk to most students about the social lives at their colleges, they are quick to describe the on-campus parties or popular bars. The freshmen we interviewed from the Rhode Island School of Design, however, raved about the frequently attended gallery openings and exhibitions. That's just one indication of how much the school and its students are focused on art and design. RISD (pronounced RIZ-DEE), as the school is referred to, is one of the most renowned schools in the country for art, design, and architecture.

Although the arts are the primary focus, the core curriculum includes courses in several areas that give students a broad background of knowledge. Students take courses in art and architectural history, history and politics, and social science, and are required to take several electives outside their major field of study. Most seniors complete some kind of major project in their field, very often completing a portfolio or putting together an exhibit. Once students select a major, the bulk of their time is divided between academic courses and studio time. Students often exhibit their work and receive feedback from peers and teachers. During the six-week intersessions, students are able to take time off from their intense studio work and experiment with something else that interests them.

Although students are primarily involved in the arts and design, the workload is no less intense than at liberal arts colleges and research-oriented universities. In fact, if you add up the amount of time students spend in their studios, it's probably greater than the number of hours most students hit their books, and often, one student said, more than the time RISD students spend in their dorms. Students practically live in their studios to the point of sleeping there.

The RISD faculty brings a wealth of knowledge and practical experience to their teaching. This enables students to study with masters in the field who have an accurate view of the "real world" beyond the walls of the campus. They can be, at times, brutally critical, a student told us, but she praised how "they are genuinely interested in how you develop."

Just as tech schools offer students cutting-edge laboratories and resources, RISD provides incomparable studio space in which they make furniture, sculpt, and design clothes using top-of-the-line working materials. RISD even has its own art museum with a considerable collection. Students further benefit from the school's affiliation with its neighbor, Brown University, as they can cross-register and use the facilities, including Brown's library system and sports complex.

First-year students quickly bond because they're thrown together in studios and classes and live together in one of four dormitories. Upperclassmen usually move off grounds in search of more affordable housing. During their first year, an intensive Freshmen Foundation pro-

Rhode Island School of Design

$$$$$
★★★

Setting: Urban
# of Undergraduates: 1,818
Men: 42.5% **Women:** 57.5%
Tuition: $18,450
Room and Board: $6,618
# of Students Applied: 1,952
   Admitted: 837 **Enrolled:** 381
Required Admissions Test: Either SAT or ACT
Recommended: SAT
H.S. Rank, Top 10%: 26%
Top 25%: 61%
Top 50%: 84%
Avg. Score of Applicants Admitted: SAT Verbal: 600 SAT Math: 640
Average GPA of Applicants Admitted: 3.20
Most Popular Majors (% of Student Body): Fine Arts (40%), Architecture (14%), Graphic Arts (14%), Industrial Design (11%)

gram introduces students to various artistic fields both in theory and practice. The Foundation allows students to learn from each other, becoming part of a close community of fellow artists and designers where they are able to trade ideas, philosophies, and techniques until the wee hours of the morning. The students are creative and take themselves seriously, which makes them (self-admittedly) an interesting and unusual group. In addition, the school sponsors and exhaustive program that brings almuni back to speak in lectures, seminars, and as guest speakers in classes.

Although there's not a high percentage of minority students, those who are there reportedly don't encounter much prejudice or tension. While not ethnically diverse, the school does attract students from all over the United States and the world. The student population is generally a very liberal, very open-minded group.

The social life at the school is not a raging one. Students become so immersed in their work and projects that they shy away from most activities geared toward large groups of people, preferring instead to attend small informal parties and get-togethers. Although Providence isn't a large city, the proximity Brown and RISD makes allows some college-type music and bar scene activity. For really big parties, Boston is a road trip away.

Providence is an attractive New England city, and much of its beauty is owed to RISD alum who've designed most of the downtown area. The artistic bent of the school also fosters an artistic community around town.

Certain events bring out the whole school community in full force. At the annual Halloween ball, students' artistic talents go into creating imaginative and extravagant costumes. Another event in which the RISD spirit shines in 3D Technicolor is the annual graduation ceremony; graduating seniors design their own caps and gowns—an appropriate testament to the creativity they have nurtured throughout their time at RISD.

RISD is proud of its reputation for turning out so many talented artists and designers. Many at the school, though, believe those who succeed are already artists when they enter, waiting to be refined by the school's rigorous programs. What RISD offers is an important opportunity for artists and designers to fine-tune their talents and abilities, to benefit from the talented faculty's real-world experience, and to interact with fellow serious students.

ALSO, CHECK OUT THESE SCHOOLS:

Architecture
Carnegie Mellon University
Catholic University of America
University of Hawaii—Manoa
University of Houston
Rice University
Syracuse University
University of Texas—Austin
Washington University

Business
Indiana University
Lehigh University
University of Michigan—Ann Arbor
New York University
University of Pennsylvania (Wharton School)
University of Southern California
Southern Methodist University

Engineering
Boston University
Brown University
Bucknell University
Carnegie Mellon University
Columbia University
Cooper Union
Cornell University
Dartmouth College
Duke University
Georgia Institute of Technology
Harvard University
Johns Hopkins University
Lehigh University
Massachusetts Institute of Technology
University of Miami
Northwestern University
University of Notre Dame
Princeton University
Rice University
Stanford University
Swarthmore College
Tufts University
Tulane University

Vanderbilt University
Villanova University
Washington University
Yale University

Fine Arts
Amherst College
Boston University
University of California — Los Angeles
Carnegie Mellon University
Columbia University
DePaul University
Florida State University
Indiana University
University of Miami
University of Michigan — Ann Arbor
Northwestern University
Oberlin College
Skidmore College
Smith College
University of Southern California
Southern Methodist University
Temple University
Washington University
Yale University

Houses of Faith

Many colleges and universities in the United States were founded by religious organizations. Some maintain their affiliation in name only and attract students of various faiths. A large number of schools, however, continue to have strong religious ties, which have a significant impact on the school environment.

Although several of these schools do attract students from other faiths, the vast majority of the student body shares the same religion. They won't, however, necessarily be religious. These schools provide a kind of religious buffet, from which students can pick and choose what they like, becoming involved in religious activities to whatever extent they desire. For those who want it, the schools provide opportunities for students to maintain, or even increase, their spirituality. Religious services are performed on a regular basis, and a number of clergy members are on staff to provide guidance. There will often be several religiously oriented clubs, special events, and community-service organizations.

These schools also have exceptional religious studies courses taught both by scholars and religious leaders. At least a few religious classes are required for students, although there are probably many more available beyond the requirement. These classes enable students to investigate their faith in a much wider, more academic context than they may have previously done. The academic and social environment at these schools encourages students to think about what their faith means to them.

As these schools must conform to the doctrines and beliefs of their respective religions, there will be certain limitations on students that may be problematic. For example, none of these schools will officially recognize gay student groups. There might also be strict regulations regarding interaction between men and women, as well as very stiff alcohol and drug policies. The extent to which students can vocalize political opinions that don't conform to religious views has been a hot issue on many of these campuses.

Another issue at these schools is the general lack of diversity. As most of the student body shares the same religion, it will often be a very homogenous one. On the other hand, the shared religious ties create a sense of kinship and community among the student population.

For all students, college is a time of growth and maturity, a place where they gain greater knowledge of the world and a better understanding of themselves. Religiously affiliated schools add another dimension to students' education—that of spiritual growth. For some, that may be the most significant aspect of their educations.

Boston College

$$$$$
★★★

Setting: Suburban
# of Undergraduates: 8,958
Men: 46.7% **Women:** 53.3%
Tuition: $19,770
Room and Board: $7,770
# of Students Applied: 16,501
  Admitted: 6,750 **Enrolled:** 2,474
Required Admissions Test: Either SAT I and three SAT IIs or ACT
Lowest 25% of Freshmen Scored At or Below: SAT Verbal: 580 SAT Math: 600
Highest 25% of Freshmen Scored At or Above: SAT Verbal: 670 SAT Math: 690
Most Popular Majors (% of Student Body): English (10%), Finance (8%), Psychology (8%), Biology (8%), Political Science (8%)

BOSTON COLLEGE IN CHESTNUT HILL, MASSACHUSETTS

Admissions Address: Office of Undergraduate Admissions, 140 Commonwealth Avenue, Devlin Hall 208, Chestnut Hill, MA 02167-3809
Phone: (617) 552-3100
Web Address: www.bc.edu

The largest Catholic university in the nation, Boston College offers a huge variety of choices in terms of academic and social options, as well as an opportunity for theological study for those who want it.

Boston College's four undergraduate schools indicate the range of programs available. The schools of business, education, and nursing all have excellent reputations, while arts and sciences, the largest school at BC, has strong departments in a number of areas, including English, political science, history, economics, and philosophy. Each school has its own admissions procedures.

The rigid core curriculum reflects the classical Jesuit emphasis on the liberal arts. It can take much of the first two years to complete and includes required courses in several basic academic fields: natural and social science, history, philosophy, theology, literature, math, arts, and cultural diversity. Freshmen take a writing seminar and all students must be proficient in a foreign language to graduate. BC offers many courses that combine religious and secular studies. The innovative and highly respected PULSE program combines community service with the study of theology, ethics, and philosophy. In addition to BC's own extensive course offerings, students can also cross-register at several other schools, including Boston University.

Because of the heavy core curriculum and relatively large enrollment, some of the introductory courses can have hundreds of students. Professors won't necessarily know people by name, and students may have to actively seek out contact with faculty. As happens at most larger schools, as students progress in their major, class sizes reduce. One junior we spoke with said "I've gotten to know a majority of my professors personally."

Students generally praise their professors as being extremely accommodating and supportive when they meet with students. And the faculty includes a significant number of Jesuit teachers who provide special support and guidance.

The expansive campus, located in an upper-class Boston suburb, has a number of high-quality, well-maintained facilities, including the recently constructed theater arts center, sports complex, state-of-the-art chemistry center, and ultramodern O'Neill Library. Residence halls are scattered in several locations around campus. Most first-year students live together in the dorms, while juniors frequently move off campus. Senior year, many students choose to return to BC housing and live in the Mods, blocks of student townhouses complete with yards for barbecues and parties.

Most BC students are white and Irish Catholic, although about one-fifth are ethnic minorities and there are a significant number of non-Catholics. The school is making an effort to increase diversity among the student population.

While, according to one junior, "BC is getting to have a much stronger academic reputation, we still party hard." In fact, BC students seem to enjoy an active social life, although the wild parties won't necessarily be found on campus where alcohol policies are strictly enforced. On weekends, students attend a wide range of parties thrown by everyone from "the sports teams to the Irish Society to the campus newspaper." Many people head off-campus to apartment parties or popular local bars. The school's proximity to Boston greatly enhances entertainment options. Students frequently head to popular hangouts and restaurants in the city or to visit friends at other Boston-area schools.

Organized events such as concerts and movies are also quite popular. The main spectator attraction, however, is unquestionably BC sporting events. Crowds of enthusiastic fans come to watch BC's powerhouse football, hockey, and basketball teams. The tailgating and generally raucous atmosphere that surrounds these events generates a feeling of an all-campus party. One student commented that "the Boston College/Notre Dame game is like the biggest event of people's lives." Intramural sports are also popular campus activities.

BC's wide variety of academic, athletic, and social options combined with its prime location make an attractive package. Factor in the strong sense of community and the friendly environment students find here and it's easy to see why so many people are happy here.

BRIGHAM YOUNG UNIVERSITY IN PROVO, UTAH

Admissions Address: Admissions Office, A-183 ASB, Provo, UT 84602
Phone: (801) 378-2507
Web Address: www.byu.edu/

Founded and run by the Church of Jesus Christ of Latter-Day Saints (a.k.a. the Mormons), Brigham Young attracts Mormon students from all 50 states and from around the world. The school's administration is firmly rooted in the doctrines of the Mormon church, and because most students are themselves very religious, they appreciate how the school accords with their beliefs. Attending church is a central part of campus life, and students are required to take at least seven religious courses. In general, discussion of religious issues and the church pervades life at BYU, even in nonreligious courses and out-of-class interactions.

Before enrolling, all Brigham Young students agree to follow the University Code of Honor, which strictly forbids the use of alcohol, drugs, and tobacco. A dress and grooming code is also mandatory. In addition to these specific rules, the honor code also creates a community-like environment in which students trust and respect one another, which is no mean feat considering there are close to 27,000 undergraduates.

Brigham Young offers courses in 12 undergraduate schools. Most departments are excellent, with business, engineering, and education considered particularly strong. Strict general education requirements are designed to provide students with a broad background in the liberal arts.

HOUSES OF FAITH

Students take courses in such areas as English and writing, foreign language or math, natural sciences, social science, arts and letters, and physical education. Such stiff requirements make the workload somewhat heavy. As one student told us, "Trying to balance the burden and load of required classes and major classes is almost impossible." It's difficult to graduate in only four years. Additionally, many students leave campus to do their missionary work, which further extends their graduation date.

Despite the high work load, the academic environment at BYU remains noncompetitive and supportive. "The atmosphere lends itself to an open forum for learning and discussion. It's a safe, noncompetitive environment. Learning at BYU is a team effort," said one student. Although some courses have hundreds of students in them, most are kept under 30 students and professors are extremely approachable. One senior told us she had "only taken one or two classes where I didn't know my professor personally."

Because of its strong reputation and relatively low, church-subsidized tuition, BYU does attract some non-Mormon students, but the vast majority of BYU students are devout members of the LDS church. Although this contributes to an admitted lack of diversity, the administration is intent on addressing this problem. And, as one student points out, although people may look the same, students come from "extremely diverse backgrounds—socially, economically, geographically. People here have been everywhere and done everything. It's great." The school actively recruits international students, who currently come from more than 100 foreign countries.

With nearly 27,000 undergraduates, campus housing is a crunch, and many students are forced to move off campus, which can be expensive according to some. The campus, like much of the state of Utah, is kept absolutely pristine, from the flawless landscaping to the modern buildings, and it's completely safe. "Overall, our facilities are pretty good," a student said. "The sports programs are pretty big, so the sports facilities are top-notch."

Sports comprise an important part of the social life at BYU, be it participating or watching. Varsity and intramural teams are very popular, and students take full advantage of BYU's extensive facilities that include an indoor track, basketball, volleyball, and racquetball courts, and a swimming pool. BYU has several very strong varsity teams that compete in the Western Atlantic Conference, men's basketball and football being the strongest. BYU fans crowd Cougar Stadium to watch football games

Brigham Young University

$$
★★

Setting: Urban
# of Undergraduates: 26,553
Men: 47.7% Women: 52.3%
In-State Tuition: $2,630
Out-of-State Tuition: $3,950
Room and Board: $3,955
# of Students Applied: 6,817
   Admitted: 5,244   Enrolled: 4,289
Required Admissions Test: ACT
Lowest 25% of Freshmen Scored At or Below: ACT 24
Highest 25% of Freshmen Scored At or Above: ACT 29
Avg. Score of Applicants Admitted: ACT 26.9
H.S. Rank, Top 10%: 53%
Top 25%: 86%
Top 50%: 98%
Average GPA of Applicants Admitted: 3.68
Most Popular Majors (% of Student Body): Business Management (7.3%), Elementary Education (5%), Zoology (4.7%), English (4.3%), Family Science (3.9%)

295

which, after church services, are probably the most highly attended events on campus. Additionally, the school's location lends itself to a number of popular outdoor sports, especially hiking and skiing.

As you can probably guess, the social life at BYU doesn't remind anyone of Animal House. Although there may not be huge keg parties, more sedate campus events such as dances and movies are well attended. "The social scene consists of a lot of dating," a student told us, as many students are already thinking about marriage. Dating also conforms to church and honor code standards, which forbid members of the opposite sex from visiting each other's rooms. Students can also become involved in a number of clubs and organizations, the most popular being community service and volunteer work.

Chances are that, unless you're a Mormon, this isn't the place for you. For Mormon students, however, Brigham Young offers a fantastic opportunity to receive a superb education in an environment singularly supportive of their lifestyle and beliefs.

CATHOLIC UNIVERSITY OF AMERICA IN WASHINGTON, D.C.

Admissions Address: Office of Undergraduate Admissions, Catholic University of America, Washington, DC 20064-0001
Phone: (800) 673-2772 (202) 319-5600
Web Address: www.cua.edu

The Catholic University of America (CUA) is a perfect example of how a strong religious affiliation by no means limits a school's educational possibilities. The official university of the Roman Catholic Church in the United States, Catholic University has first-rate academic programs in such diverse areas as drama, nursing, and politics, to name just a few of the many academic offerings in its six undergraduate schools. The pre-professional programs are among the most popular, and many students go on to graduate and professional schools.

CUA's location in Washington, D.C., makes it truly cosmopolitan and enables students to enjoy an active off-campus social life. In addition to enjoying the District's many cultural offerings, including visits to the Smithsonian and National Gallery, many CUA students head for popular bars and clubs. Washington also offers plenty of internship and work experiences. Being located in the heart of the U. S. capital gives CUA students in the political department an unbeatable advantage.

HOUSES OF FAITH

There are six undergraduate schools at CUA: architecture, engineering, music, nursing, philosophy, and arts and sciences. A rigid liberal arts core curriculum includes courses in philosophy, literature, natural and social sciences, foreign language, and, of course, religion classes taught by clergy.

Students praise the accessibility of their teachers, who are generally friendly and approachable. After introductory level courses, most student's classes will be small and manageable. Some classes are taught by graduate students, but undergraduates will have the opportunity to study with and get to know full professors.

Although CUA is located in a pretty dangerous part of the city, the campus itself is self-contained and secure. As one student says, "the kids who get into trouble are generally just not being smart." Beneath the impressive National Shrine of the Immaculate Conception, the campus is also rather beautiful, with a mixture of Gothic stone and contemporary buildings neatly arranged along tree-lined paths. Students criticize the facilities, the library in particular, as being "substandard" and complain about the lack of a "real serious student gathering place." However, the University does have a 10-year master plan to make capital improvements and is currently renovating dormitories and adding on line connections in every student room.

Although students come mostly from the Middle Atlantic and Northeastern states, they do represent all 50 states as well as about 100 foreign countries. They're predominantly (about 85 percent) white and, not surprisingly, predominantly (about 80 percent) Catholic. As a church-sponsored institution, CUA's administration follows the dictates of the Roman Catholic Church, which does to a certain extent affect student life in significant ways, including strict policies regarding alcohol and dorm room visitors. One student "likes the fact it's a Catholic university and doesn't try to hide from it."

Yet, not all of the students are strictly religious. For some, going to church every so often and taking the required religion courses amount to the entire scope of their personal religious duties. "People from other religions are very accepted," says one senior. For those who want to maintain or strengthen their religious ties, however, there's plenty of opportunity to do so, both in CUA's excellent religious studies courses as well as in a variety of church-related programs and activities. And there are "lots of church options," from liberal to ultratraditional.

Catholic University of America

$$$$$
★★

Setting: suburban
# of Undergraduates: 2,400
Tuition: $15,562
Room and Board: $4,632
# of Students Applied: 2,527
   Admitted: 1,529   **Enrolled:** 570
Required Admissions Test: Either SAT or ACT
Recommended: SAT II
Lowest 25% of Freshmen Scored At or Below: SAT Verbal: 540 SAT Math: 520 ACT Comp.: 23
Highest 25% of Freshmen Scored At or Above: SAT Verbal: 650 SAT Math: 630 ACT Comp.: 28
H.S. Rank, Top 10%: 37%
Top 25%: 62%
Top 50%: 89%
Avg. Score of Applicants Admitted: SAT Verbal: 512 SAT Math: 561 ACT Comp.: 24
Average GPA of Applicants Admitted: 3.32
Most Popular Majors (% of Student Body): Architecture (20%), Nursing (11%), Engineering (11%), Politics (10%)

Although the student body is generally considered conservative, there's still a range of views and values. One student insisted that there are pockets of "absolutely liberal" students who are " by no means apathetic." Regardless of political beliefs, the common religious ties create a generally friendly and closely knit student body. "People enjoy being here," says one student.

On campus, organizations, activities, and events provide opportunities for students beyond the classroom. "Community service is a big thing here," says one senior. Both intramural and intercollegiate sports benefit from the use of a $10 million sports facility. Additionally, because of the acclaimed drama and music programs, there are frequently high-quality student productions on campus.

As for campus social life, one student puts it this way: "Students here are serious about their academics but it's also a party school." She adds that the administration is actually trying to tone things down by enforcing the campus alcohol restrictions more seriously. Another student disagrees, calling the social scene dead. "But," he adds, "the school is located in the middle of Washington, D.C., so there are always things to do in the city." By heading out into the District, CUA students who want it are able to enjoy a pretty active, even wild, social life.

Between its prime location and extensive academic offerings, Catholic University is far from being a secluded religious retreat.

COLLEGE OF THE HOLY CROSS IN WORCESTER, MASSACHUSETTS

Admissions Address: Admissions Office, One College Street, Worcester, MA 01610-2395
Phone: (508) 793-2443 (800) 442-2421
Web Address: www.holycross.edu/

Anyone who attends a Holy Cross varsity football game and sees the crowds of rowdy student fans roaring in support of their team can get a sense of how deeply school spirit runs here. Numbering less than 3,000 undergraduates, the student body at this relatively small, Roman Catholic, Jesuit-affiliated school has a warm sense of community that's bolstered by their common religious ties.

The religious influence of the Jesuits at Holy Cross, while not pervasive, is evident in different ways. The religious studies courses are excellent, and students are required to take at least one course as part of their core curriculum. Most students are Irish Catholic, but they're not necessarily strictly religious. For those who want it, though, there are opportunities to be spiritually active by attending church services and going on retreats with Jesuit teachers.

At the same time, Holy Cross is a very academically oriented college that's strong in many liberal arts subjects. The broad distribution requirements include, in addition to the religious studies requirement, courses in philosophy, art, language and literature, natural science and math, cross-cultural studies, and social science, as well as foreign language proficiency. In addition to traditional liberal arts courses, students can choose from special options including interdisciplinary courses, study-abroad programs, and local internships. And because Holy Cross is a member of the Worcester Consortium for Higher Education, they can also cross-register at ten nearby schools.

Central to Holy Cross's academic strength is that class sizes are kept small to enable students to interact with their professors. Students can't hide at the back of the room and must be prepared to become involved in class discussion and to answer questions.

The workload can be pretty heavy at Holy Cross, but, as one student explains, "it's not at all competitive or cutthroat." And the environment is very supportive: "Students are really down-to-earth and the professors are friendly and approachable."

Although according to one student the administration is "working very hard" to increase campus diversity, most students are still white and from New England. While the stereotypical image of a Holy Cross student as that of a conservative right out of the J. Crew catalogue holds some truth, there's a range of political views and issues represented on campus by different groups.

Holy Cross is set apart from Worcester, an industrial city that, according to one student, "isn't the nicest place in the world." But the campus itself is "beautiful," dotted with trees, flowers, and lawns. The superb facilities include residence halls that range from apartment-style suites to special-interest houses. Many seniors opt for more affordable off-campus housing.

Holy Cross students work hard, but they also like to have fun. Although there are no fraternities or sororities and the alcohol policy is strictly

---

College of the Holy Cross

$$$$$
★★★

Setting: Urban
# of Undergraduates: 2,636
Men: 48.1% **Women:** 51.9%
Tuition: $20,700
Room and Board: $6,900
# of Students Applied: 4,185
   Admitted: 1,897 **Enrolled:** 699
Required Admissions Test: Either SAT or ACT and three SAT II subject tests (one must be Writing)
Lowest 25% of Freshmen Scored At or Below: SAT Verbal: 570 SAT Math: 550
Highest 25% of Freshmen Scored At or Above: SAT Verbal: 650 SAT Math: 650
H.S. Rank, Top 10%: 64%
Top 25%: 90%
Top 50%: 99%
Avg. Score of Applicants Admitted: SAT Verbal: 631 SAT Math: 618
Most Popular Majors (% of Student Body): English (12%), Psychology (9%), History (8%), Economics (7%), Biology (6%)

enforced on campus, it's not hard to find parties in dorm rooms or at off-campus apartments. Many students also head to local bars and hangouts. "Drinking's pretty big here," says one student. "We are predominantly Roman Catholic and have a reputation to keep up."

The city of Worcester doesn't offer all that much that appeals to students other than a few bars, restaurants, and movie theatres. However, the school is about an hour from Boston, making it a popular road trip. On campus, popular events include several formal and semiformal dances and the Spring Weekend, a large outdoor rock concert. Many students also are active in volunteer work and community service.

But at Holy Cross, sports are probably the most popular extracurricular activity. With the extensive range of intramural teams to choose from, almost every student finds some sport to play. The varsity teams have strong records and games are very well attended. And Holy Cross fans will have even more to cheer about as the school plans to begin offering basketball scholarships in the fall of 1998.

With its pretty campus, strong academics, wide range of extracurricular activities, and superior athletics, Holy Cross resembles New England's other fine liberal arts colleges with, of course, the addition of a strong religious affiliation.

YESHIVA UNIVERSITY/STERN COLLEGE IN NEW YORK, NEW YORK

Admissions Address: Admissions Office, 500 West 185th Street, New York, NY 10033-3201
Phone: (212) 960-5277
Web Address: yu1.yu.edu/

Students at Yeshiva University combine intensive study of liberal arts or business subjects with intensive study of Jewish topics and issues. In keeping with the tenets of orthodox Judaism, men and women are separated into two different colleges: Yeshiva College for the men and Stern College for the women. A shuttle bus runs between the two schools for special events and social activities.

Students take half their courses in liberal arts or business, and the other half in Jewish studies. Jewish studies courses are Yeshiva's strength and a main reason students decide to attend. Students study Hebrew language and literature with an esteemed faculty of Jewish scholars. They

HOUSES OF FAITH

also meet and work with distinguished and learned teachers and rabbis to study and discuss central Jewish texts and doctrines. Entering students come from a wide variety of backgrounds. As one student says, "you don't have to already be well-versed in Judaism to come here." Most students, however, do come from an orthodox background and have had prior Jewish education.

The liberal arts departments and the courses offered in Yeshiva's Sy Syms School of Business have good reputations. And the student body itself is a strong educational resource. As one senior points out, "students here are extremely intelligent. About half of them turned down admission to higher ranked schools to come here."

The students who choose to come to Yeshiva "have the need to know about their religion," according to a political science and business double major, "but most don't go on to become rabbis." Most Yeshiva students, in fact, are on a preprofessional track, and the corresponding programs are particularly popular. Many students also take advantage of the opportunity to spend a year studying in Israel.

Most classes are small with highly approachable teachers who know their students by name. "You get lots of attention here," says one senior, "and you have a greater opportunity to participate in campus life." The downside of this small size is the less diverse range of academic offerings than one might find at a larger school. However, for most students this is more than offset by the strong Judaic studies curriculum.

Stern College is in midtown Manhattan, making it easily accessible to any number of popular places. Yeshiva College, far less central, is located in the Washington Heights section of Manhattan, which is not considered one of the safest areas in the city. Campus security, however, is quite good and keeps the campus relatively safe. And while Yeshiva's location is less attractive than Stern's, it benefits from more extensive, better-quality facilities, including a large athletic center.

The combination of liberal arts and religious studies makes for a particularly heavy workload. Students spend long hours in class and then many more hours hitting the books at home. When not studying, students take part in a range of extracurricular activities. Basketball, both at the varsity and intramural levels, is the most popular sport. While Yeshiva and Stern have no fraternities or sororities, there are numerous clubs and organizations, ranging from political action groups to student theater.

Yeshiva University

$$$$

Setting: Urban
# of Undergraduates: 2,086
Men: 57.6% **Women:** 42.4%
Tuition: $14,280
Room and Board: $6,860
# of Students Applied: 1,354
  Admitted: 1,140 **Enrolled:** 788
Required Admissions Test: Either SAT or ACT
Recommended: Any SAT IIs
Lowest 25% of Freshmen Scored At or Below: SAT Verbal: 510 SAT Math: 560
Highest 25% of Freshmen Scored At or Above: SAT Verbal: 630 SAT Math: 680
Avg. Score of Applicants Admitted: SAT Verbal: 557 SAT Math: 634
Average GPA of Applicants Admitted: 3.50
Most Popular Majors (% of Student Body): Psychology (17%), Biology (10%), Accounting (9%)

As would befit a school in New York City, there is no one center for social life. While many students live on campus, others live elsewhere in the city and head home right after class. "Some people just study all the time," says one senior. "Others hit the bars every chance they get." The big night to go out is Thursday as many students spend the Sabbath off-campus with friends or relatives. Many students also take advantage of New York City's museums, plays, and concerts.

A student summed up the Yeshiva experience best: "It's an intense education filled with long days. But if people are interested in really broadening their Judaic understanding and getting a good secular education, it's a great place!"

Also, Check Out These Schools:

Brandeis University
DePaul University
Earlham College
Georgetown University
Gustavus Adolphus College
University of Notre Dame
St. Olaf College
Villanova University
Wofford College

Cultural Meccas

For many students, a college social life spent mostly going to local parties and attending the occasional concert or play is enough to sustain them. True culture vultures, however, hunger for much more. Not content waiting for cultural events to come to them, they go where the culture is, attending one of the schools we've listed here.

Most often, cultural meccas are located within major cities. Of course, many colleges and universities have thriving cultural scenes right on campus, regardless of whether they're in an urban environment or a more secluded setting. For example, many schools have their own performing arts centers that not only provide a space for student productions, but also draw visiting artists and performance groups. Others have art museums with their own fine collections. Whatever culture might be found on a specific campus, though, will be found ten times over within a city. As a result, students who want an especially rich cultural life will often check out city schools.

For anyone attending a school in an urban area, there are going to be certain negatives that should be considered. Many students who haven't grown up in a city, but hope to go to college in one, have a fantasy image of what city life is like—constant excitement, hobnobbing with a sophisticated crowd, dancing the night away in chic clubs. They're in for a rude awakening—usually to the sound of a police siren or car horn—when they have to deal with the realities of big-city living. They haven't thought about such things as trying to study to the accompaniment of car horns and crowds or having to dodge panhandlers on the way to class. The level of noise and activity can be tiring, even overwhelming.

City schools are themselves chaotic places, where you'll have to fend for yourself to find your way. Don't expect buildings arranged on spacious quads with expansive lawns and carefully manicured gardens. Instead, many city colleges consist of high rises concentrated on a few city blocks, with a few benches or sculptures in between. At any city school, safety is going to be a concern. On campus, the schools usually make a big effort to protect students with their own security forces. While comforting, the extra security can sometimes make students feel as if they're living in a prison state. When students leave campus, they're on their own and have to play it safe and develop a street-smart attitude.

This may sound like a pretty bleak portrait of life at city schools. For many students, however, being able to draw on the many social and cultural resources of the city vastly outweighs the disadvantages. At rural and suburban campuses, you might have to wait for visiting performers to come to campus. At city schools, you just hop on public transportation or walk a few blocks to see theatre and dance performances, hear music groups and bands, or see major works of art. When you get tired of institutional food, you can choose from scores of restaurants and eateries, from fast food to various ethnic cuisines. If you're interested in sports, you can attend major league games and events. Rather than a social life centering on parties in the same locations—apartments, dorms, frat houses—you can go to bars, cafes and dance clubs of all kinds.

Studying in an urban environment can also enhance your education in many different ways. If you're studying art, for example, you don't have to stare at a picture in a textbook; you can head to a museum and look at actual paintings. If you're studying theatre or music, you can go to a play or concert. If you are preparing for a professional career, there are many opportunities in a city for internships and other work experiences, and you don't necessarily have to take a leave of absence from your own school.

All big schools, urban or otherwise, have their problems, including large and overcrowded classes, difficulty getting to interact closely with professors, and frustrating administrative bureaucracy. To succeed at large schools, you need to take the initiative and be aggressive in order to take advantage of academic opportunities. One good strategy is to get in the habit of asking lots of questions—from professors, fellow students, advisors, administrators, etc. You'll be surprised by how much you learn from talking to other people about things going on at your school—everything from the best courses and professors to where you can find the perfect cup of coffee. If you don't want to be treated like a number, don't let yourself be one. Go up to a professor after class and introduce yourself. Many professors will be happy to chat for a few minutes to get to know you.

The same strategies can help with forging friendships. Because urban schools don't usually have much of a central campus, there's no sense of real community. In order to feel at home, you need to find a niche. Chances are nobody is going to come knocking on your door asking to make friends or to join their club; but chances are also likely that there'll be no shortage of things to do and people to meet if you seek them out. One of the best things about most city schools is that they reflect the diverse populations of their cities in which many ethnic and cultural groups are represented. The student bodies at these schools, while not necessarily closely knit, will certainly be dynamic and interesting.

Even if you're a true culture vulture, you might wonder at times why you put up with all the noise and the crowds and the other problems of big city living. But then you'll go to some concert or club or museum, and it'll all be worth it.

BOSTON UNIVERSITY IN BOSTON, MASSACHUSETTS

Admissions Address: Office of Undergraduate Admissions, 121 Bay State Road, Boston, MA 02215
Phone: (617) 353-2300
Web Address: web.bu.edu/

If you want a school where people know your name, this ain't it. With about 30,000 students, Boston University can't offer the kind of intimate experience you'll find at many liberal arts colleges. What BU does offer, however, is something small rural colleges can't: the chance to study in what may be America's most dynamic college city.

Located directly on the Charles River in the historic Back Bay district, Boston University virtually blends into the city after which it is named. The T, perhaps the world's most user-friendly public transportation system, links the school to any of the city's social, cultural, and culinary attractions that form the basis of the BU student's social life: major historical sites, a thriving theater district, the Boston Symphony, the Museum of Fine Arts (with its superb collection of American art), ethnic food establishments of all kinds (from Chinatown to the cheap and tasty Italian eateries of the North End), popular music and comedy clubs, games at Fenway Park, and a dizzying selection of coffeehouses, cafes, and bookstore-cafes.

The largest school in the city, BU's extensive facilities and academic offerings bring thousands of students from across the country and

Boston University

🏛🏛🏛🏛
$$$$$
★★★

Setting: urban
# of Undergraduates: 14,609
Men: 42.9% **Women:** 57.1%
Tuition: $21,970
Room and Board: $7,570
# of Students Applied: 25,991
  Admitted: 13,835 Enrolled: 3,969
Required Admissions Test: Either SAT or ACT, TOEFL (for foreign students)
H.S. Rank, Top 10%: 55%
Top 25%: 88%
Top 50%: 99%
Avg. Score of Applicants
  Admitted: SAT Verbal: 631
  SAT Math: 630 ACT Comp.: 27
Average GPA of Applicants
  Admitted: 3.40

around the world to study within this quintessential collegiate city. Students can find almost any program of study they want in BU's ten undergraduate colleges, including programs in communications, education, fine arts, theater and music, engineering, management, and health care. The College of Liberal Arts has the largest enrollment; a liberal arts student tells us that the college is particularly good in the sciences, psychology, and international relations. BU's communications programs are reputedly excellent. Boston is also known for its combined BA and medical or dental degrees, which, although grueling, enable students to receive their degrees in record time (usually 7 years) without having to go through the labors of applying to medical schools. Admissions and requirements are different for each college, but all students take certain core courses, such as English composition. According to one student, the workload also varies significantly, depending on the department as well as the student's own commitment to their studies.

Within the university, you'll also find several innovative smaller programs. The College of General Studies helps prepare less-qualified high school graduates for college academics; many participants in the program transfer to other schools within BU at the end of the two-year program. The University Professors Program combines cross-disciplinary studies with individualized study.

BU's vast facilities and resources meet the needs of its large student body. The library system is one of the biggest and most extensive in the nation. Of course, as often happens, the bigger the school, the more red tape and bureaucratic headaches—both of which are common complaints among BU students. "After your first year, you learn to work through the quirks in the system," explains a junior who obviously hasn't let the bureaucracy beat him down. The housing on campus—for those who can get it—is decent, particularly in the smaller, renovated brownstones. The student residence halls have tight security, as befits an urban campus, which keeps them safe but can be a pain; freshmen and sophomores especially complain about the strict policies regarding after-hours visitors. After freshman year, it is possible to move to university-owned apartments that have fewer restrictions.

Just over half of the students live on campus. As a college town, Boston offers students plenty of living spaces, but not always of the best quality. Students need to watch out for overpriced dumps in bad areas. All freshmen are guaranteed housing, and most live in the 14-story Warren Tower, which houses more students than the entire populations of smaller liberal arts colleges. Although this environment does help freshmen meet loads of other students (individual floors become student communities), the massive tower doesn't create an especially cozy environment.

Although attending a large, urban university like BU does mean sacrificing a sense of togetherness, it has its social advantages. As one student remarked, "There's not a united student body because there are so many divergent interests and different types of people. As a result, BU offers nearly every activity under the sun. Best of all, many of these activities are linked to organizations at Boston's other colleges." On campus, students can choose from hundreds of activities, from cheering on Boston's powerhouse hockey team (1995 NCAA champions who made it to the final four in 1996) to joining a fraternity. BU's own acclaimed theater, dance, and music programs ensure that there are frequent professional-quality cultural events on campus. Beyond those options, a student told us, "BU definitely tries to use the city's vast cultural offerings to its advantage." Students like walking up and down fashionable Newbury Street, hanging out in the Boston Commons, exploring Cambridge's coffeehouses and cafes, pigging out on clam chowder and baked beans, among other things, at Faneuil Hall, and visiting friends at Boston's many other universities and colleges.

DEPAUL UNIVERSITY IN CHICAGO, ILLINOIS

Admissions Address: Admissions Office, 1 East Jackson Boulevard, Chicago, IL 60604-2287
Phone: (312) 362-8300 (800) 4-DEPAUL
Web Address: www.depaul.edu/

DePaul has two campuses, each in a distinctive and interesting section of Chicago and with its own specialized programs of study. DePaul is primarily a commuter school, although roughly 2,000 people live on campus and many more live in areas surrounding the campuses. The Loop Campus in downtown Chicago is home to the schools of commerce and computer science and caters primarily to the preprofessional set, particularly in business and prelaw. Students hoping to find professional careers upon graduation can take advantage of the school's location in downtown Chicago by participating in a number of work and internship opportunities.

Located in a more affluent region of Chicago, the Lincoln Park Campus is the home of the schools of arts and science, and theater and music, as well as the site of the residence halls. Students have great things to say about the neighborhood surrounding their campus, where there are "many young people around," as well as nice shops and cafes.

THE ROAD TO COLLEGE

DePaul University

$$$$
★★

Setting: Urban
# of Undergraduates: 6,436
Men: 42.5% **Women:** 57.5%
Tuition: $13,460
Room and Board: $5,980
# of Students Applied: 4,966
  Admitted: 3,890 **Enrolled:** 1,157
Required Admissions Test: either SAT or ACT
Lowest 25% of Freshmen Scored At or Below: SAT Verbal: 500 SAT Math: 490 ACT Comp.: 21
Highest 25% of Freshmen Scored At or Above: SAT Verbal: 570 SAT Math: 560 ACT Comp.: 27
H.S. Rank, Top 10%: 25%
Top 25%: 53%
Top 50%: 84%
Most Popular Majors (% of Student Body): Computer Science (5.3%), Accounting (5.2%), Psychology (4.2%), Communications (3.7%), Education (2.4%)

All students complete general requirements in natural and social science and math; English composition; world civilization; philosophy and religion; and art, music, and literature. Class sizes are kept pretty small, enabling students to interact closely with peers and professors. Teaching is highly valued at the school, taking precedence over professors' personal research. Students praise their teachers, who "communicate with the students on an individual basis." The school has consistently been making improvements in the form of renovations and expansions of its facilities. The recently completed library at Lincoln Park, with its spectacular three-story reading room, is one of several major improvements made in recent years. The drama department is one of the best in the country and makes use of the historic Blackstone Theatre.

DePaul ranks as the nation's second-largest Catholic school, and about half of the students are Catholic (perhaps only a quarter remain active Catholics, however). The school has a diverse student body in terms of culture and ethnicity, even though a majority come from Chicago and its suburbs. A sophomore told us that students are generally "urban-minded and laid-back." Those students who live on campus in DePaul's comfortable housing often form closely knit circles of friends. However, many students do not live on campus and there's less interaction between resident and communtor students. Extracurricular activities, clubs, and campus events may bring DePaul students together outside of classes, none more so than basketball games. In the past, students have taken great pride in their men's basketball team, the Blue Demons, and going to games has been a major form of social activity. Recent losing records, however, have diminished basketball's popularity.

For most students, the city of Chicago functions as the primary source of culture and entertainment. Chicago's eclectic range of architectural styles makes it a fascinating city in which to wander; if you walk up and down Michigan Avenue in the downtown area, you'll see not only major department stores and hotels, but several breathtaking skyscrapers and buildings. Chicago's hot theatre scene includes many of the most well-known theatres and companies in the nation, such as the Goodman Theater, which often produces major productions before they go to Broadway, the Steppenwolf Company, which has included such well-known actors as Laurie Metcalf and John Malkovich, and Chicago's famed Second City improv comedy troupe. For museums, there are the Fine Arts Institute, with its outstanding Impressionist collection, including Seurat's "Isle of La Grand Jatte," the Field Museum, with various cultural and natural history exhibits, and the hands-on exhibitions of the Museum of Science and Industry (make certain you check out the giant walk-through heart). Chicago also has a hopping nightlife, including cavernous bars and clubs lining Rush, Lincoln, and Halstead streets, favorite student hangouts. But more than anything, Chicago is famous for its hip blues clubs and deep-dish pizza, which is why it's such a great city for students.

EMORY UNIVERSITY IN ATLANTA, GEORGIA

Admissions Address: Admissions Office, Boisfeuillet Jones Center, Atlanta, GA 30322
Phone: (800) 727-6036
Web Address: www.cc.emory.edu/welcome.html

Emory is one of the top academic institutions in the Southeast; it's also located in one of the most highly praised cities in the region. Just about anyone who visits or lives in Atlanta raves about this friendly, easily manageable city. Located within the more conservative realm of the South, Atlanta has a youthful and progressive population that fosters the city's eclectic night life and hopping cultural scene. "The best thing about Emory," comments a student, "is its proximity to downtown Atlanta and yet its isolation from what would otherwise become a constant distraction."

Many Emory students are on a preprofessional track, particularly in prelaw and premed; Emory's programs in these fields are among its best, and Atlanta provides students with many internship opportunities. In addition to standard liberal arts programs, the school offers many special academic options, including several accelerated and dual degree programs For example, there's a dual engineering degree with Georgia Tech, and it's possible to obtain a bachelor's and master's degree in certain fields, like English, in four years.

Due to an enormous endowment the school receives from the Coca-Cola Co., Emory also offers superb resources and facilities, including cutting-edge science labs and equipment, the sleek George Woodruff Physical Education Center, and the ten-story Woodruff Library. The Michael C. Carlos Museum, right on the Emory campus, was designed by renowned architect Michael Graves, and it has an outstanding permanent collection of Egyptian, Greek, Roman, and pre-Columbian art and sculpture. Walking through the campus, you'll also see all kinds of construction as more improvements and expansions take hold. A new business school and a "virtual library" are currently underway.

Emory University

$$$$$
★★★

Setting: urban
# of Undergraduates: 5,799
Men: 44.1%   Women: 55.9%
Tuition: $19,870
Room and Board: $7,040
# of Students Applied: 10,040
   Admitted: 4,462   Enrolled: 1,180
Required Admissions Test: Either SAT or ACT
H.S. Rank, Top 10%: 82%
Top 25%: 98%
Top 50%: 100%
Avg. Score of Applicants
   Admitted: SAT Verbal: 620
   SAT Math: 630   ACT Comp.: 27
Average GPA of Applicants
   Admitted: 3.70
Most Popular Majors (% of Student Body): Biology (14.1%), Psychology (13.8%), Business (9.7%), Political Science (9.4%), Nursing (8.3%)

Emory's core requirements have recently changed and now include the following: seminars in writing; natural and mathematical sciences; social sciences; humanities; historical, cultural, and international perspectives; a language requirement, and phys ed.

The school attracts many big-name faculty members, partly because of the research opportunities it affords them. Nevertheless, professors are attentive to their teaching duties and their students. Students particularly get the chance to work closely with prominent senior faculty in the upper-level courses.

Unlike many of its Southern counterparts, Emory has a much more geographically mixed student population; only about half of the students hail from the South, as the school's reputation for academic excellence and appealing location attracts students from across the country and from more than 50 foreign countries. There's about a 20 percent minority population, and many students are concerned about fostering healthy relations between different groups. The Racial and Cultural Educational Source (RACES) is a student group that promotes racial awareness and multiculturalism.

On campus, Emory has its own fast-paced social scene, in large part sparked by the very popular Greek system. About 50 percent of students join fraternities or sororities, which host parties that are a central aspect of Emory social life. Extracurricular activities, clubs, and organizations run the gamut. The school regularly brings well-known guest speakers and performers to campus.

If campus events aren't enough, students can turn to the many cultural and social options offered by Atlanta. The city is spread out in many different, distinctive sections, each with its own character and social attractions. The Buckhead, Little Five Points, and Midtown sections all have bars and music clubs that are popular among students. Buckhead is the more collegiate area, where there's "bar after bar after bar, perfect for dancing and scamming," while the funkier Little Five Points and Midtown areas draw mixed crowds where you're more likely to find "a wide variety of quirky restaurants and hole-in-the-walls." For cultural attractions, there's the Woodruff Arts Center, a performing arts complex that includes the High Museum of Art, the ballet, opera, and symphony. Atlanta also has tons of "starving artists theaters." The enormous Fernbank Science center, a natural history museum, houses a planetarium and IMAX theater. For something a bit different, one student recommends a visit to the Center for Puppetry Art, where you can get a close look at some of the Muppets. Or you can check out the Coca-Cola Museum to get a look at such dinosaurs as New Coke, which lost miserably to Classic Coke when it was introduced about 10 years ago.

GEORGE WASHINGTON UNIVERSITY IN WASHINGTON, D.C.

Admissions Address: Admissions Office, 2121 I Street N.W., Washington, DC 20052
Phone: (202) 994-6040 (800) 447-3765
Web Address: www.gwu.edu/~go2gw

Like many city schools, George Washington does not have a central campus unless, of course, you take into account the city itself. With its historical and government buildings, museums, and monuments lined up along expansive malls and reflecting pools, the District is virtually a giant campus, and GW students make it home. They can research papers in the Library of Congress, sun themselves on the National Mall, and wave to their neighbor, the president. One student told us, "Our campus is five blocks from the Lincoln Memorial, so my friends and I sometimes go there to watch the sun rise over the Capitol. It is definitely cool."

Located near Foggy Bottom, GW has six undergraduate schools that each has its own admissions procedures and core requirements; all schools require that students take freshman composition. In the College of Arts and Sciences, students fulfill extensive general education requirements in the sciences and humanities that take up a substantial number of credits.

Located in the heart of the nation's capital, the school's location greatly enhances the educational experience at GW. As one political science major praised, "There are opportunities for the kinds of internships that I couldn't get anywhere else." Not surprisingly, a number of students are on a preprofessional track, heading for careers in medicine, law, business and, of course, politics. The school's politically oriented departments and programs—such as government, public policy, and international relations—are among its greatest assets, particularly because of the prestige and experience of the faculty. The professors are not only teachers of politics, they're political practitioners; your advisor may also be advising some of the most powerful people in government.

Students live in dorms, converted apartment houses and hotels around the city, and a few fraternities. Many residence halls have been recently

---

George Washington University

$$$$$
★★★

Setting: Urban
# of Undergraduates: 6,098
Men: 44.2% Women: 55.8%
Tuition: $20,370
Room and Board: $7,325
# of Students Applied: 10,356
    Admitted: 5,973 Enrolled: 1,657
Required Admissions Test: Either SAT or ACT
Recommended: SAT II
Lowest 25% of Freshmen Scored At or Below: SAT Verbal: 560 SAT Math: 550 ACT Comp.: 24
Highest 25% of Freshmen Scored At or Above: SAT Verbal: 660 SAT Math: 650 ACT Comp.: 29
H.S. Rank, Top 10%: 41%
Top 25%: 78%
Top 50%: 97%
Average GPA of Applicants Admitted: 3.55
Most Popular Majors: International Business, Business Administration, Biology

renovated, and they're clean and spacious. Most freshmen live in the large, noisy Thurston Hall, providing at least one central place where students can meet and hang out. About half the students move off campus, many to nearby housing. However, housing in the District can be very pricey.

GW has a reputation for being a major party school, in part because of rumors of a relatively light workload. One junior reacted by saying, "if it's a party school, we're still looking for the parties." Mention a light workload to some students, and they're liable to be overcome by hysterical fits of laughter. The workload is relative, depending upon the major or program and a student's own commitment. Like so many large universities, the educational experience at GW is what the individual student makes of it.

Like D.C. itself, the population of GW is an ethnically and culturally diverse one with a real international flavor. Students come from all over the United States and from about 100 foreign countries. However, as with many large, urban universities, students tend to form small, tight-knit groups. Some students do become involved with campus activities and organizations. Basketball games bring substantial numbers of students together, particularly since GW's team began making it to the NCAA Division I tournament. The Greek system is an active presence and draws large numbers of students. Frat parties, however, aren't the only game in town. Many students head for smaller parties in apartments, or out to the District's bars and clubs. The Georgetown section of the city is particularly known for its popular nighttime hangouts. Washington is also rich in cultural resources, from major performances and productions at the Kennedy Center to the many museums that line the National Mall. The National Gallery alone is big enough to keep you occupied for several weeks. Most of the museums and monuments in the city are free, which certainly makes students happy.

An undergraduate in his final year reflected on his experience at GW, stating, "lots of unpredictable stuff happens here, in terms of the activities you'll be invited to participate in, the internship and career opportunities that will pass your way, and the friends and relationships you'll inevitably make."

NEW YORK UNIVERSITY IN NEW YORK, NEW YORK

Admissions Address: Office of Undergraduate Admissions, 22 Washington Square, New York, NY 10011-9191
Phone: (212) 998-4500
Web Address: www.nyu.edu/

In March 1995, a front-page story in the *New York Times* noted that New York University, once considered by many applicants as a "safety" school, launched a successful campaign to make it comparable with the nation's top universities. With the $1 billion endowment it raised, NYU proceeded to attract top faculty from prestigious universities, expanded its facilities, including such additions as a neural science center and institute of math, raised its admissions standards, and built and renovated student residence halls and other academic departments.

Within its seven undergraduate schools, NYU offers many quality academic programs. Many students consider themselves prelaw, premedicine, and prebusiness majors, and departments within these fields are highly ranked nationally. The Tisch School of Art is one of the nation's most renowned schools of theater, dance, film, and television, and NYU's performing arts departments have recently been pumped with money. Graduates from the film school include Spike Lee, Oliver Stone, and Martin Scorsese, and actors and playwrights trained at NYU have been known to make it on the Great White Way. The Gallatin Division offers a unique program that involves individualized, independent study.

Class sizes and the quality of teaching and advising at NYU vary dramatically, often depending upon the school or department. While there are enormous lecture courses and professors who disappear once class ends, there are also smaller, primarily upper-division classes with professors who go out of their way to make themselves available to students. As at any large, urban school, students need to seek out opportunities. They'll especially need to be stout of heart to deal with NYU's infamous bureaucracy. The traditionally nightmarish process of getting classes has been improved somewhat by phone registration.

NYU doesn't have a campus so much as an enclave of buildings located within a concentrated area. Students cross busy Manhattan streets to get from one building to another. Washington Square Park lies at NYU's center and acts somewhat like a university quad. On a sunny day, you'll find plenty of NYU students hanging out in the park, as well as street musicians, vendors, and other assorted characters.

New York University

🏛🏛🏛🏛
$$$$$
★★★

Setting: Urban
# of Undergraduates: 14,177
Men: 42% Women: 58%
# of Students Applied: 18,986
Admitted: 8,262 Enrolled: 3,090
Required Admissions Test: Either SAT or ACT
Lowest 25% of Freshmen Scored At or Below: SAT Verbal: 600 SAT Math: 590 ACT Comp.: 27
Highest 25% of Freshmen Scored At or Above: SAT Verbal: 690 SAT Math: 690 ACT Comp.: 29
H.S. Rank, Top 10%: 60%
Top 25%: 94%
Top 50%: 99%
Avg. Score of Applicants Admitted: SAT Verbal: 640 SAT Math: 637 ACT Comp.: 28
Average GPA of Applicants Admitted: 3.40
Most Popular Majors (% of Student Body): Business (14%), Performing Arts (6%), Psychology (5%), Nursing (4%), Political Science (4%)

NYU's facilities range in quality, although more money is being put into improvements each year. Bobst Library, the main library with 14 floors, can be a little overwhelming to navigate but offers excellent resources and archives. Although NYU's intercollegiate teams have not traditionally been the school's strong point, its women's basketball team won the NCAA Division III title in 1997 and the Coles Sports Center has one of the nicest indoor pools in New York, as well as basketball and racquetball courts and a weight room. Enjoy the Center while you can, because membership to one of Manhattan's health clubs after you graduate will cost you more than a car.

Finding housing in New York City can be a nightmare; people aren't joking when they talk about scanning the obituaries in search of vacant apartments. Due to recent additions and renovations, NYU is able to offer students decent and affordable housing in prime locations. Still, a number of students head off-campus to apartments of their own, which vary in price and quality. A housing database accessible only to NYU students helps people locate off-campus deals.

The student population reflects the ethnic and cultural diversity of New York City and is one of the school's strongest assets. "NYU is like a Benetton ad, we're so diverse," a senior told us. The range of social and cultural activities students engage in is as diverse as the population. For most students New York City is the primary attraction. "I'm here because this is the most dynamic city on earth," proclaimed a happy graduating senior. "But I don't know how I ever learned to balance my studies with all that New York has offered me. I remember being forced into the dilemma, should I study or go out? many times during the past four years."

New York University lies in the heart of Greenwich Village, site of the city's funkier dance clubs, bars, cafes, and shops. Many hot NYU hangouts line Bleecker Street, just a few blocks south of Washington Square Park. SoHo, with its art galleries and hip boutiques, is within easy walking distance. When you consider the rest of the city, with its museums, restaurants, night spots, parks, and theaters, the social options become astronomical. The student activities board offers discount tickets to Broadway shows, Lincoln Center concerts, and major sporting events, although many events now appear on the school's database.

New York can be a tough place to live, requiring that you develop a tough skin and acquire a street-smart attitude (it can also be a nightmare for parents, constantly worried about their children in the Big Apple).

NYU students are aware that safety is a concern in a large city and that they have to be more on guard than they would in a rural locale. The constant activity, while exciting, can be disorienting and intimidating. Some students understandably have trouble making the adjustment to New York. Fortunately, NYU offers extensive, free counseling and support services to help along the way. And as the song goes, if you can make it in New York, you can make it anywhere.

UNIVERSITY OF PENNSYLVANIA IN PHILADELPHIA

Admissions Address: Admissions Office, 1 College Hall, Philadelphia, PA 19104-6376
Phone: (215) 898-7507
Web Address: www.upenn.edu/

"The stereotypical thing everyone says about Penn is that it's a rural campus in an urban area," says one recent graduate from the University of Pennsylvania. Penn, along with Columbia and Harvard, is an Ivy League school located in a major city and, therefore, boasts of the rich variety of cultural and social opportunities of an urban school. At the same time, the campus itself is a compact, student-friendly academic setting with many superb facilities.

Penn has four undergraduate colleges: the School of Nursing, the School of Engineering and Applied Sciences, the College of Arts and Sciences, and the Wharton School of Business. Wharton is indisputably the star and is generally considered one of the top business schools in the country, particularly known for its emphasis on financial analysis. Finance has the highest enrollment at Penn as a whole. Wharton is also highly selective and competitive. A junior at Wharton praised the high quality of its teaching and the many internship and career opportunities the school affords, especially because of the "great alumni network."

The College, as students refer to the School of Arts and Sciences, has the largest undergraduate enrollment and offers a variety of courses and programs. Among the most popular are English, history, and psychology. Due to Penn's excellent medical school and teaching hospital, many undergraduates also take up premedical sciences, such as biology.

Core requirements vary by school, but all students take some kind of basic curriculum with courses in areas such as the humanities and sciences, and demonstrating proficiency in writing and foreign language.

University of Pennsylvania

$$$$$
★★★★

Setting: Urban
# of Undergraduates: 9,921
Men: 57% **Women:** 43%
Tuition: $21,130
Room and Board: $6,966
# of Students Applied: 15,861
　Admitted: 4,776 **Enrolled:** 2,358
Required Admissions Test: Either SAT I and three SAT IIIs
Average Combined SAT: 1,381
H.S. Rank, Top 10%: 81%
Top 25%: 98%
Top 50%: 100%
Avg. Score of Applicants
　Admitted: SAT Verbal: 596
　SAT Math: 677 ACT Comp.: 28

With a large student population, Penn has certain problems typical of big schools, such as overcrowded classes and problems registering—especially during students' first two years. The introductory classes push through hundreds of undergrads each term, rendering professor-student interactions few and far between. Most students, however, praise the social opportunities they enjoy as a result of the large student body.

Just off the campus, the West Philadelphia section is a rundown area that is high in crime. The campus itself is self contained and certainly collegiate in appearance, with academic buildings separated by grass and trees, especially along Locust Walk, the central campus throughway. The ivy-covered College Hall, the main campus building where you'll find the admissions office and other administrative offices, is one of the older buildings on campus. The Main Library, identified by the sculpture of a giant button in front, is a popular meeting site for students ("I'll see you at the Button"). Wharton is actually two buildings that look like one. Dietrich Hall, a later addition to the school, wraps around the original Steinberg Hall. A great deal of money was recently put into the Lauder Institute, a center for business seminars that draws high-powered executives from around the world. Houston Hall is the student union, where you'll find a food court, video arcade, lounges, meeting rooms, and a stage.

Most freshmen are housed in the Quad, divided into three different sections that enclose grassy areas perfect for Frisbee, football, and the occasional party. There are a lot of freshmen in one place, which makes the quads pretty noisy and highly social. Many upperclassmen move into one of the High Rises, described as "definitely apartment-type living, with more space but fewer social opportunities than in the dorms." The High Rises contain suite arrangements with kitchens and private bathrooms. Many upperclassmen also move to fraternities or off-campus apartments.

Students come from all 50 states and more than 100 foreign countries. Minority students make up about 30 percent of the students, with a particularly large population of Asian American students. "We're primarily a liberal, politically correct campus," says a Penn junior, adding that "we were the first Ivy League school to have a female president."

Students enjoy many activities on their campus. The Greek system is an active one, with about 30 percent of the student body joining. There are even two coed fraternities, one a business professional society. The school's hundreds of clubs and organizations include many professional

Cultural Meccas

and honors societies, as well as several culturally oriented groups. Among the various student music and performance groups, Mask and Wig, an all-male comedy troupe, is particularly well known and is considered a Penn institution.

Several intercollegiate sports teams are good, but football, a frequent contender for Ivy League champion, is far and away the school's pride and joy, followed by basketball and wrestling. Franklin Field, where Penn football games are waged, is one of the oldest stadiums in the country. There, the Quakers are cheered on by crowds of exceptionally supportive and enthusiastic student fans.

Traditional campus events include Hey Day, a celebration on the last day of class when juniors become the kings of the school at a large party with music and partying and games. "The juniors march together down Locust walk with hats and canes," a student describes. "After they are declared seniors at the quad, they tap each others canes like mad swordfighters and bite chunks out of each others' hats."

Spring Fling is the biggest event of the year—in fact, one of the biggest parties on the East Coast—essentially a four-day bash on the Quad, with usually famous bands, carnival booths, and various food stands.

Students also head to local spots near campus (although the bar scene has really been affected by the drinking laws, which are seriously enforced). Smoky Joe's, known as the "Pennstitution," is a college bar tradition. Students also take a subway, bus, or cab to other parts of Philadelphia. South Street is lined with funky cafes, bars, shops, and clubs. Going to comedy clubs is especially popular. Philadelphia also has a rich cultural scene: the Philadelphia Orchestra, several art museums and galleries, including the wonderful Philadelphia Museum of Art and the Barnes Foundation, and events at the Annenburg Center, which features major dance, music, and theatre performances. By the time they graduate, most Penn students have discovered that there's much more to Philly than the Liberty Bell, cream cheese, and cheesesteak.

UNIVERSITY OF PITTSBURGH IN PITTSBURGH, PENNSYLVANIA

Admissions Address: Office of Admissions and Financial Aid, Second Floor Bruce Hall, Pittsburgh, PA 15260
Phone: (412) 624-PITT
Web Address: www.pitt.edu/

University of Pittsburgh

🏛🏛🏛🏛🏛
$$$
★★

Setting: Urban
# of Undergraduates: 12,757
Men: 47.6% Women: 52.4
In-State Tuition: $5,416
Out-of-State Tuition: $11,776
Room and Board: $4,964
# of Students Applied: 9,455
  Admitted: 7,505   Enrolled: 2,650
Required Admissions Test: Either SAT or ACT
Lowest 25% of Freshmen Scored At or Below: SAT Verbal: 500 SAT Math: 500 ACT Comp.: 21
Highest 25% of Freshmen Scored At or Above: SAT Verbal: 610 SAT Math: 610 ACT Comp.: 27
H.S. Rank, Top 10%: 23%
Top 25%: 53%
Top 50%: 89%
Avg. Score of Applicants Admitted: SAT Verbal: 564 SAT Math: 565 ACT Comp.: 24
Most Popular Majors (% of Student Body): Engineering (8%), Business (4%), Psychology (4%), Communication (3%), Nursing (3%)

Pittsburgh, and maybe it's just a problem of how the word sounds, continues to make many outsiders wince. The city seems to conjure up images of an industrial wasteland with ashes falling from the sky as if in *The Great Gatsby*. But how wrong that image is: When people come to Pittsburgh for the first time, they are amazed at how pleasant the city has become, with friendly residents, surrounding mountains, and clean water. It also boasts a flourishing cultural scene, with upscale shopping districts, museums and galleries, an excellent symphony and opera, and a decent nightlife.

The University of Pittsburgh campus, located on a hill in the Oakland district and aligning the beautiful, 456-acre Schenley Park, is itself a scenic addition to the city. Easily accessible to the city's cultural, social, and sporting activities via a free shuttle service, Pitt is well placed to benefit from Pittsburgh's many possibilities.

Pitt offers a wide range of academic programs and is particularly known for its programs in engineering and health-related sciences. The school's strongest programs and best facilities are those that prepare students for professional careers, and a majority of the students consider themselves preprofessionals. Premed students, for example, are able to observe and study at the university's acclaimed medical center. A new undergraduate School of Business continues to attract more and more students. The College of Arts and Sciences has several excellent departments, including history, philosophy (ranked #1 in the country), and international relations. The prestigious Honors College offers top students the opportunity to study in a more intimate, intense academic environment, with only 10 people in a class.

As a large university, Pitt presents its challenges for undergraduates, including large classes and limited interaction with professors. Intro classes may take 100 to 200 people; upper divisions are thankfully smaller. Students who take the initiative and seek out opportunities, however, can receive an excellent undergraduate education. In fact, an impressive number of Pitt graduates earn Rhodes and Marshall scholarships. There are many special academic options available at Pitt, including opportunities for independent study and research, extensive study-abroad programs, and the unique Semester at Sea, which combines world travel and course work aboard a ship. Although students from all over the country line up to do Semester at Sea, Pitt students get some preferential treatment since their university is in charge; a few full scholarships (i.e., free round-the-world cruise) are available only to Pittsters.

One of the benefits of attending a large university is that students can take advantage of its extensive facilities. Pittsburgh already has plenty, and more are being built or renovated. Because of the low tuition for state residents, about 90 percent of the Pitt students come from Pennsylvania. However, more students from other states and foreign countries have enrolled in recent years. Because of its large enrollment and urban setting, there's not a real campus community, especially since most nonfreshmen don't live on campus. Students tend to hang out in small, isolated groups depending on common interests or backgrounds. The primary social attractions on campus are fraternity parties and sports. The Greek system is active, but it's not the primary social outlet on campus. Pitt has a long history of devotion to its basketball and football teams; while the teams have lost some of their past glory, students' enthusiasm remains high.

Students feel that the University of Pittsburgh enjoys a great urban setting, a diverse campus with an approximately 20 percent minority population, and strong academics. Opportunities for internships abound in the city, and a placement office helps numerous students land jobs right after graduation. "I think more Pitt students land jobs right out of college than at most other institutions," explained a student about to embark on his career.

UNIVERSITY OF SOUTHERN CALIFORNIA
IN LOS ANGELES, CALIFORNIA

Admissions Address: Admission Office, University Park Campus, Los Angeles, CA 90089-0911
Phone: (213) 740-1111
Web Address: www.usc.edu/

A recent international relations graduate reflected on his experience at Southern California, saying, "USC really offered me the college experience I wanted: the opportunity to study in Los Angeles with its beautiful weather and nearby beaches, along with a strong academic program and an intense social scene." Indeed, USC—or the University of Spoiled Children, as it's sometimes referred to as—attracts many people because

University of Southern California

$$$$$
★★

Setting: Urban
# of Undergraduates: 13,716
Tuition: $19,140
Room and Board: $6,632
# of Students Applied: 12,790
  Admitted: 9,193 **Enrolled:** 2,843
Required Admissions Test: Either SAT or ACT
Lowest 25% of Freshmen Scored At or Below: SAT Verbal: 520 SAT Math: 530 ACT Comp.: 22
Highest 25% of Freshmen Scored At or Above: SAT Verbal: 640 SAT Math: 670 ACT Comp.: 29
H.S. Rank, Top 10%: 43%
Top 25%: 72%
Top 50%: 93%
Avg. Score of Applicants Admitted: SAT Verbal: 579 SAT Math: 608 ACT Comp.: 25
Average GPA of Applicants Admitted: 3.56
Most Popular Majors (% of Student Body): Business (25%), Social Science (12%), Engineering (11%), Natural Science (10%), Humanities (5%)

of its prime location. Once known as a huge party school with mediocre academics, most of USC's programs have improved tremendously, making the school more competitive. Its film school is usually considered the best in the country.

As you might expect, movies are a large part of Los Angeles culture, and many Trojans take part in the industry in some way—making movies, writing movies, talking about movies, or just plain going to movies. But LA also has many other impressive cultural options for USC students, including fine art institutions, such as the Getty Collection, the Los Angeles County Museum of Art, and the Museum of Contemporary Art, several important theaters, including the Mark Taper Forum (which has premiered many major American productions), a symphony, opera, and ballet. USC students also take advantage of the city's diverse night life, ranging from bars and music clubs of all kinds to dance clubs catering to the superchic. And of course the nearby beaches offer year-round surfing, tanning, and people watching.

LA's nonstop activity may be distracting, but students do get around to class. The school's specialties lie in the preprofessional fields, and most students are well on the way to specific careers. Many of those who graduate attain prestige and success in a variety of fields; USC alumni range from professional sports superstars and Olympic athletes to corporate CEOs to movie moguls and Oscar winners (USC's alumni network is huge). Programs in the schools of business and engineering are considered excellent. Many of the traditional liberal arts departments are also good, including political science and the natural sciences.

As you might expect, given its location in Movieland, USC programs in film and television are particularly famous and extremely competitive. Graduates from the program include big names in entertainment, such as director George Lucas. In addition to faculty members who are themselves experienced professionals, students get the opportunity to hear a number of prominent guest lecturers and speakers currently working in the movie biz. As you walk through the campus, you'll pass buildings named after the likes of Johnny Carson, Steven Spielberg, and Lucas. Programs in drama, music, and journalism are also highly rated.

While admissions procedures and certain requirements vary by program, all students must fulfill extensive general education requirements. Including courses in several broad academic areas, the general requirements ensure students receive a basic liberal arts education before pursuing a specialty. Some students, to satisfy the general education requirements, enroll in a special honors program called the Thematic Option, an interdisciplinary approach to required material with a heavy emphasis on writing. While grueling, the Thematic Option provides students with an outstanding academic experience.

For a major research institution of its size, USC manages to keep many nonintroductory classes below 30 students. Professors are also reportedly highly accessible, although students might have to take the initiative in seeking them out. As a junior told us, "once you reach upper division courses, class sizes drop dramatically and it becomes much easier to get to know your professors."

While accessible to all parts of Los Angeles, USC sits in the South Central section, an area high in crime—students are encouraged to be extremely careful in that neighborhood. The university maintains tight security on campus and does an impressive job at keeping the students safe. The self-contained campus has enough trees and ivy-covered academic buildings to provide it with a collegiate atmosphere that sets it apart from the surrounding region. Many students live on campus, and the dormitories range from basic double-room housing to nicer student apartments that upperclassmen vie for.

Although a substantial number of students come from California, the rest come from all across the country and from more than 100 foreign countries. There's no tuition break for in-state students, which may be why USC has a reputation for attracting the children of the rich and famous. In actuality, USC is diverse in many respects. About half the student body is white, and Asian American, Hispanic, and African American students, as well as international students, are fairly well represented.

Because USC is a large school, it's easy for students to feel isolated or lost. However, many are able to find extracurricular activities and social groups that provide a smaller community within the larger school. Most USC students enjoy a fun and varied social life. Over 20 percent of the student body joins one of the school's 26 fraternities or 12 sororities. While this is a large number of students, it doesn't dominate the social scene. One student told us that "a lot of people complain about the Greek system ruling the social life, but it's not true. One of the best things about the school is the diversity of the student population in terms of their interests." There are literally hundreds of clubs, organizations, and activities.

If you watch the crowds of student fans who attend Trojan football games, especially if they make it to the Rose Bowl, you'll see how all these students, despite their differences, are Trojan warriors at heart. Trojan football is a central part of USC's identity, and many long-standing school traditions revolve around it, including a week-long pep rally to precede each year's battle against their archrival, the UCLA Bruins. The Notre Dame game receives similar attention. USC's exceptional athletic facilities, many of which were used during the 1984 Olympic games (like the pool at the Lyon Recreational Center), make intercollegiate and intramural sports and recreational activities tremendously popular.

While campus-oriented social opportunities abound, they don't compare with all that awaits students in Los Angeles and the surrounding areas. For those with transportation, beaches, mountains, deserts, and parks are all within driving distance. Many students head out clubbing at Hollywood and Los Angeles night spots. Melrose Avenue remains a popular hangout for students, and not just because of a certain popular television show. For all those that head west to experience Hollywood, USC is an excellent introduction to the fascinating, if troubled, society surrounding it.

VANDERBILT UNIVERSITY IN NASHVILLE, TENNESSEE

Admissions Address: Admissions Office, 2305 West End Avenue, Nashville, TN 37203
Phone: (615) 322-2561
Web Address: www.vanderbilt.edu

"Vanderbilt is a small, conservative Southern school with many students from the North," assessed a Vanderbilt undergraduate. "The curriculum and academics are excellent, but the social scene isn't for everyone."

Academically, Vanderbilt offers a number of quality programs and departments. There are four undergraduate schools: arts and sciences, engineering, music, and education and human development. Preprofessional programs are particularly popular among undergraduates, especially in premed, biology, and engineering. The core curriculum includes required courses in broad major areas, such as natural and social sciences, humanities, and history. While some introductory courses may be large, most classes are seminar size, especially at the higher levels. Professors are known to be casual, friendly, and easily approached.

CULTURAL MECCAS

The secluded campus, with its lush foliage, gardens, and lawns, has more of a community environment than most urban campuses. Most students live in the school's small but comfortable housing, available in a number of styles and arrangements. Only seniors may live off campus. The students tend to be conservative in their politics and values. A number come from the South, but there is a large percentage from Northeastern states too.

Because about half the students go Greek, the social life centers mainly on the fraternities and sororities, which host all kinds of parties and special events that are sometimes open to the entire school. "It's a very image-conscious place," admitted one sorority girl. Those who don't rush fraternities or sororities might easily feel left out unless they make an effort to create their own social lives. There are other options available on campus, including several clubs, community service and charitable organizations, extracurricular activities, and intramural sports. Vanderbilt's intercollegiate sports teams— particularly men's and women's basketball teams, which vie for spots in the NCAA Sweet 16— draw student fans and contribute to the sense of school spirit.

Vanderbilt students have tons of live music venues practically on their doorstep. They can hear live music just about any night of the week, thanks to Nashville's hundreds of live-music spots. Of course, country and western and bluegrass are the most prominent musical selections, but there's much more to Nashville than country crooners; decent rock and alternative music venues and a range of bars, clubs, and restaurants are also easily found in the city.

While enjoying the nightlife of Nashville, Vanderbilt students make use of a beautiful campus that's set off from the rest of the city and has a laid-back social scene all its own. In fact, the students and city folk seem quite removed from one another in social terms. "They see us as rich, sloppy drunks," asserted one student, "and we see them as rather backward."

Vanderbilt University

$$$$$
★★★

Setting: Urban
# of Undergraduates: 5,748
Men: 51.7% Women: 48.3%
Tuition: $20,900
Room and Board: $7,430
# of Students Applied: 8,667
  Admitted: 5,200 Enrolled: 1,545
Required Admissions Test: Either SAT or ACT
Lowest 25% of Freshmen Scored At or Below: SAT Verbal: 590 SAT Math: 610 ACT Comp.: 26
Highest 25% of Freshmen Scored At or Above: SAT Verbal: 680 SAT Math: 700 ACT Comp.: 30
H.S. Rank, Top 10%: 62%
Top 25%: 89%
Top 50%: 99%
Avg. Score of Applicants Admitted: SAT Verbal: 637 SAT Math: 660 ACT Comp.: 28
Average GPA of Applicants Admitted: 3.50
Most Popular Majors (% of Student Body): Human Development and Family Studies (11%), Psychology (11%), Economics (10%), English (9%), Political Science (7%)

ALSO, CHECK OUT THESE SCHOOLS:

Barnard College
University of California—Los Angeles
California Institute of Technology
Carnegie Mellon University
Catholic University of America
University of Chicago

The Road to College

Columbia University
Cooper Union
CUNY—Brooklyn College
CUNY—Hunter College
CUNY—Queens College
Emerson College
Emory College
Eugene Lang College
Georgetown University
Georgia Institute of Technology
Harvard University
University of Houston
Howard University
Johns Hopkins University
Juilliard School
Lewis and Clark College
Macalester College
Massachusetts Institute of Technology
Morehouse College
Occidental College
University of Pennsylvania
Reed College
Rice University
Southern Methodist University
SUNY—Buffalo
Tulane University
Vanderbilt University
Washington University

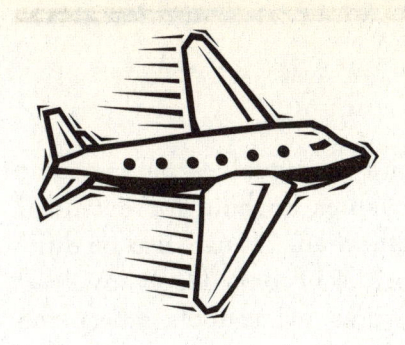

Travel Agencies

The opportunity to study abroad means more than a chance to eat foreign food and go sightseeing. As many schools now recognize, study abroad can be a formidable component in a student's college education. Speaking and reading a foreign language is the most effective way for a person to develop fluency in that language, and there's no better way to learn about a foreign culture than from the inside. Away from the familiar surroundings of your own campus, you're driven to act more independently and, in the process, you gain greater knowledge, confidence, and maturity.

For these reasons, most every college and university now makes it possible for students to study abroad in some capacity. The ones we've listed here especially encourage study abroad and make it particularly easy for you to do so, which is why a majority of the student population at these schools study abroad at some point.

Many schools maintain strong affiliations with sister schools in other countries, and some even have their own campuses and departments abroad. That means you don't have to go through tedious application and transfer procedures when you study abroad, and you have the security of knowing the credit you receive abroad will be transferred without a problem. These schools might help you find a place to live, sometimes in a residence hall, sometimes with a foreign family. Many have special courses or programs to help you prepare for the experience of going abroad. In addition to being able to enroll in a foreign university for a semester, many schools offer other study-abroad opportunities, such as special courses or professor-led field trips during the intercession and summer sessions.

Leaving your own campus for a semester or a year involves making some sacrifices. Putting friendships and relationships on hold for extended periods of time can make it hard to maintain them. It can also be difficult, even impossible, to hold major positions or become deeply involved in certain clubs and extracurricular activities. At schools where the majority of the students study abroad, it might be easier to grapple with some of these problems because your peers will be more understanding of the situation. But with so many students away, the social life at these campuses will inevitably be scattered.

Living in a foreign country where you're noticeably different from most everyone else can be intimidating. If you're shy, overly self-conscious, or tend to be uncomfortable about not fitting in, you may not have a positive experience. Study abroad means giving up the comforts of home to learn the customs and manners of a new place, an adjustment some students are unable or unwilling to make. But, as those who have studied abroad will attest, you wind up learning about much more than customs and cuisine—you learn about yourself.

Dartmouth College

$$$$$
★★★★★

Setting: Rural
# of Undergraduates: 4,250
Men: 53% Women: 47%
Tuition: $21,846
Room and Board: $6,282
# of Students Applied: 11,398
   Admitted: 2,273 Enrolled: 1,095
Required Admissions Test: Either SAT I or ACT; three SAT IIs
H.S. Rank, Top 10%: 91%
Top 25%: 98%
Top 50%: 100%
Avg. Score of Applicants
   Admitted: SAT Verbal: 640
   SAT Math: 700

DARTMOUTH COLLEGE IN HANOVER, NEW HAMPSHIRE

Admissions Address: Office of Undergraduate Admissions, 6016 McNutt Hall, Hanover, NH 03755
Phone: (603) 246-2875
Web Address: www.dartmouth.edu/

When you hear about Dartmouth's D Plan, it's not a reference to the average grades or some fabulous meal program. The Dartmouth Plan is an innovative academic arrangement whereby the year is divided into four ten-week terms. Students are required to take courses during three of those terms, but generally they get to choose which ones; everyone must remain on campus during the summer after the sophomore year, but most students don't mind. The summer term brings an almost camplike atmosphere to the school, as studying is combined with sun worshipping, swimming, and generally living out-of-doors most of the time. This flexible academic schedule also makes it easier for students to take part-time jobs or internships, travel abroad in off-season, or just relax when they feel like it. A history major reflected on the merits and shortcomings of the D Plan: "It makes it a lot easier to get important internships since you're not forced to compete with all the other college students in summer. It can also fracture relationships since your friends might leave in the middle of the school year to do an internship or pursue something else."

TRAVEL AGENCIES

Unlike some large research universities, Dartmouth emphasizes undergrad education—the College is the focal point of the institution (yet there are noteworthy grad programs in medicine and the sciences, business, and engineering). This is not a school where the big-name professors are sequestered far from any actual students. Even intro courses are often taught by faculty stars. Although profs are engaged in their own research, they are committed to their teaching and put their students first. So Dartmouth students generally receive individualized attention from faculty, many of whom came to the school because they actually like teaching at the college level. Dartmouth's rural, small-town location also helps out here too; since many faculty live in or near Hanover, they're not in a frenzy to high-tail it off-campus at the end of the day. They're accessible, easily found during office hours, and usually very willing to chat.

The distribution requirements include four classes each in natural sciences, social sciences, and humanities, at least one course in a non-Western culture, and demonstrating writing and foreign language proficiency. First-year students choose from a selection of freshman seminars that focus on writing. Dartmouth's many highly touted departments include English, government, history, and political science. The foreign language study program, which includes study abroad, is very popular: "a painless way to knock out your foreign language requirement," according to a junior. In conjunction with the foreign language study program, Dartmouth offers its students a plethora of study-abroad programs, including cultural and language-oriented ones, in countries around the world.

While Dartmouth has its fair share of traditions and historical prestige, it has demonstrated its commitment to the computer age by requiring all students to have computers. The school held up its end of the bargain by connecting all dormitory rooms, as well as academic rooms and centers around campus, to the Dartmouth computer network. Students take advantage of this, not only to send one another messages but to trade class notes, receive assignments, and find academic sources and materials. "People use E-mail much more than phones here," asserted a nightly hacker.

The picturesque Dartmouth campus is surrounded by gorgeous New Hampshire countryside. Many students are attracted by the lure of outdoors activities—hiking, camping, and canoeing—in addition to winter sports. Warm weather aficionados take note though: the New Hampshire winter is long and cold. Most students take advantage of outdoor sports available to them. Dartmouth owns a nearby skiway for downhill skiing, and many students are avid skiers. Ski lessons can even be taken to fulfill phys ed requirements. The Winter Carnival is a popular social event enlivening the campus during February, and students' extracurricular activities don't drop off during the winter months, an indication of how devoted they are to maintaining an active social scene.

The dormitories are arranged in several clusters around the campus; most are comfortable and roomy. There's a variety of dining halls around campus serving different kinds of food in different arrangements, from buffet-style to late-night dining. Housing is limited, which may be one reason Greek life is so popular. Almost half the men and more than a third of the women enter the Greek system, which still plays a significant role even for those students who don't join houses (you can't join until your sophomore year anyway, and non-Greeks are allowed to attend parties). The administration has taken some pains in recent years to get houses to tone down their rowdier behavior, though, and the college has also sought to provide social alternatives for students. There are varied cultural events in the college's Hopkins Center and elsewhere on campus, as well as countless extracurricular activities and clubs.

The dominance of the fraternities on campus contributes to the image of Dartmouth as an "old boys" school for "Joe College" types. The ultraconservative *Dartmouth Review* still seeks to bedevil the administration for being a "liberal conspiracy," and is determined to undermine the college's hoary traditions. Yet the *Review*'s time has passed, and while a number of students may still fit the conservative profile of yesteryear, Dartmouth is trying hard to change its image. Some years ago, the school's decision to change the mascot from the Indian to the Big Green made headlines, creating a controversy between different factions; the incident, while confirming the continued presence of the "old boys," also demonstrated that there are more than a few students with other views. As one undergraduate commented, "the school is much less of an old boys network than it once was. Today, our conservative history is probably our biggest impediment."

About one quarter of the Dartmouth population is made up of minorities, including one of the largest Native American student populations in the country. Students who steer clear of the old boy network can, with a little perseverance, find and befriend those with similar interests and backgrounds. Still, Dartmouth is not a place where everyone will necessarily have an easy time and feel comfortable.

Another major part of student life at Dartmouth is athletics; Dartmouth has some of the best varsity teams, men's and women's, in the Ivy League. The football team, for example, has won the Ivy League Championship several times and went undefeated in 1996. Games are well attended and are social events in their own right, with rowdy fans flocking to the stadium and transforming games into loud parties.

KALAMAZOO COLLEGE IN KALAMAZOO, MICHIGAN

Admissions Address: Admissions Office, 1200 Academy Street, Kalamazoo, MI 49006-3295
Phone: (616) 337-7166 (800) 253-3602
Web Address: www.kzoo.edu/

Kalamazoo does more than encourage students to study abroad; it virtually requires it. The school's innovative curriculum, known as the K Plan, is designed to combine classroom learning with real-world experiences, including study abroad. Almost all Kalamazoo students devote a portion of their junior year to study in one of more than 30 countries. Due to a special endowment, they usually don't have to pay any more than they would to remain at Kalamazoo.

In addition to studying abroad, students gain further real-world experience by devoting part of their sophomore year (usually the summer after) to Career Development Internships. Working closely with school advisors, students select a specific internship that will help them learn more about a career they find interesting. The required Senior Individualized Project provides students with another opportunity to work independently and immerse themselves in an area of interest. Again with the help of faculty advisors, students complete a project of their own choosing, from a thesis paper to scientific research to completion of a creative work.

Although students at Kalamazoo spend a great deal of their time outside the classroom, they also receive a solid liberal arts background through their course work. The distribution requirements are particularly widespread, covering social science, natural science, computer science and math, art and literature, and proficiency in writing and foreign language. Students are also required to pass a written comprehensive examination in their majors. All these requirements mean that students' four years are pretty well mapped out. The K Plan, therefore, balances opportunity to experiment and explore through various off-campus activities with the benefit of set structural guidelines.

Kalamazoo College

$$$$$

Setting: Urban
# of Undergraduates: 1,302
Men: 41.9% Women: 58.1%
Tuition: $17,976
Room and Board: $5,565
# of Students Applied: 1,247
    Admitted: 1,170 Enrolled: 361
Required Admissions Test: Either SAT or ACT
Lowest 25% of Freshmen Scored At or Below: SAT Verbal: 573
    SAT Math: 561 ACT Comp.: 24
Highest 25% of Freshmen Scored At or Above: SAT Verbal: 677 SAT Math: 682
    ACT Comp.: 29
H.S. Rank, Top 10%: 43%
Top 25%: 77%
Top 50%: 95%
Avg. Score of Applicants Admitted: SAT Verbal: 614
    SAT Math: 622 ACT Comp.: 27
Average GPA of Applicants Admitted: 3.59
Most Popular Majors (% of Student Body): Biology (15%), Economics (12%), English (9%), Health Science (9%), Psychology (9%)

A Kalamazoo student told us that, in addition to the K Plan, many students like the academic choices they find. Sciences, particularly biology majors, are particularly strong, although many other departments, like International and Area Studies, have large enrollments. Due to the Career Internship opportunity, many students have already decided on their futures. The internship and study-abroad experiences Kalamazoo students put on their résumés often impress prospective employers.

Kalamazoo is on the quarter system, which enables the students to balance out study abroad and internships with their classroom work. It also means, as a freshman was quick to point out, that "we have to cover a semester's worth of work in ten weeks." Most students, we hear, study "about six hours a day." Yet a full schedule has three classes rather than the four typical at most colleges, easing the study burden somewhat. Students forge relationships with their professors, who serve as counselors and advisors on special projects and in helping students find internships. "Professors are very involved in student lives. I've already been invited to dinner five times with different professors," a freshman told us.

Facilities at the small, handsome campus range in quality. A student praised the dormitories but criticized the lack of computers and limited sports facilities. Almost all students live on campus in one of six dorms, most of which are being wired to connect rooms with the campus computer network. Students are supposed to reapply for housing every quarter, but those who "squat" simply stay on. While on campus, the full dining plan is required; the cuisine and decor of the dining halls often attempts to prepare students for the international flavors that await them. A student warned that when you add in the costs of the required campus housing and dining to the tuition, Kalamazoo is "a very, very expensive" school. Luckily, it also seems very generous with its scholarship money.

The student population is already tiny, and even smaller when you consider the numbers studying abroad or completing internships each semester. As a result of all the moving around students do, maintaining long-lasting, steady friendships becomes difficult. The social scene, a student tells us, is fractured. Most people, she said, become "seriously involved" with extracurricular activities or sports. Kalamazoo has excellent music programs, and its choir is remarkably good for a school of its size.

There are no fraternities or sororities, so most parties spring up in people's rooms. Some larger events—such as Monte Carlo night and the

Day of Gracious Living, a day devoted to being outside and enjoying the spring weather—are aimed at the entire student body. A number of themed residences, including an Asian house, Women's Resources Center, and Peace House substitute for frats and sororities and host numerous social activities. Sports at Kalamazoo College, while not its strong point, are reportedly getting better, particularly in men's football and basketball and women's soccer. While the on-campus social scene might be somewhat limited, students look forward to the many experiences and adventures awaiting them during their quarters off campus. Some also visit the few bars, clubs, and movie theaters in Kalamazoo, and top bands like Counting Crows occasionally hold concerts at the city's Wings Stadium.

LEWIS AND CLARK COLLEGE IN PORTLAND, OREGON

Admissions Address: Office of Admissions, 0615 S.W. Palatine Hill Road, Portland, OR 97219-7899
Phone: (503) 768-7040 (800) 444-4111
Web Address: www.lclark.edu

Given the school's name, it's probably not surprising that opportunities to go off and explore the world are such a central part of the Lewis and Clark experience. With one of the oldest and largest study-abroad programs in the country, Lewis and Clark makes it easy and affordable for students to study in a number of foreign countries. Over the past 35 years, Lewis and Clark students have studied in well over 61 countries, from England and France to parts of India, Zimbabwe, Ecuador, and China. Between 15 and 17 programs are offered annually, with a focus on developing countries. Students can choose between a language-intensive program and a country/culture study. The school foots the bill for travel expenses so students can study overseas for almost the same cost as remaining on campus.

Lewis and Clark's focus on international interests extends well beyond these study-abroad options. The school's international affairs department is one of the best around, particularly known for hosting its renowned annual conference. Many students take up serious foreign language study that extends well beyond learning how to say "Good morning" and "What time is it?" International topics and foreign-language proficiency are both required parts of the curriculum.

While on their own turf, Lewis and Clark students receive a fine liberal arts education within a pleasant campus setting. The school has many

---

Lewis and Clark College

$$$$$
★★

Setting: Suburban
# of Undergraduates: 1,816
Men: 43.6% **Women:** 56.4%
Tuition: $18,350
Room and Board: $5,770
# of Students Applied: 3,291
   Admitted: 2,242 **Enrolled:** 450
Required Admissions Test: Either SAT or ACT
Lowest 25% of Freshmen Scored At or Below: SAT Verbal: 580 SAT Math: 560 ACT Comp.: 24
Highest 25% of Freshmen Scored At or Above: SAT Verbal: 680 SAT Math: 660 ACT Comp.: 29
H.S. Rank, Top 10%: 38%
Top 25%: 69%
Top 50%: 91%
Average GPA of Applicants Admitted: 3.20
Most Popular Majors (% of Student Body): International Affairs (10%), Psychology (8%), Biology (8%), English (8%), Sociology/Anthropology (7%)

strong departments, including English, anthropology, history, and gender studies. The small undergraduate population allows students to work closely with one another and form relationships with professors.

A former estate, the Lewis and Clark campus has a clean, stately design, its buildings carefully arranged among elegant formal gardens and cobblestone paths. As it is located in the Pacific Northwest, the school is surrounded by breathtaking natural scenery, including views of Mt. Hood and Mt. Saint Helens. The setting makes the school an ideal spot for enjoying outdoor sports, such as hiking, climbing, camping, skiing, and kayaking. The College Outdoor program organizes excursions throughout the school year.

The student population is geographically diverse, attracting a number of students from foreign countries. However, there's not a substantial minority population, although both students and the administration would like it to become more ethnically diverse. The small campus environment does foster a sense of community further enhanced by students' common interests and shared experiences. A sophomore comments that, "students here are pretty laid-back and easy to meet. There's not much competition for grades; rather, people seem self-motivated." The two-year residence requirement facilitates friendships as well.

In addition to outdoor sports and recreation, students enjoy all kinds of campus extracurricular activities and social events. There's a strong network of clubs, sponsored by student government. The social scene tends to be casual and low key. Students go to small parties and gatherings in dorm rooms or off-campus apartments. Many head to downtown Portland, easily accessible via car or public transit. Portland is a friendly city with nice restaurants, shops, coffeehouses, parks, and pedestrian malls, and an underground music scene that is coming to rival Seattle's.

Students at Lewis and Clark, following in the footsteps of their famous namesakes, are true explorers—and they find their adventures in their challenging academic programs and beautiful natural surroundings, as well as in exotic, faraway places.

ST. OLAF COLLEGE IN NORTHFIELD, MINNESOTA

Admissions Address: Admissions Office, 1520 St. Olaf Avenue, Northfield, MN 55057-1098
Phone: (507) 646-3025 (800) 800-3025
Web Address: www.stolaf.edu

Well over half the students at St. Olaf study abroad at some time during their four years. Global Semester, one of the college's most popular programs, allows students to visit 10 countries in five months. Each year, 25 selected students travel with professors to Asia, the Middle East, and parts of Europe and take classes along the way. While this time away provides a needed break from the bitter Minnesota winters, it should not be viewed as a mass exodus from St. Olaf. The college's location, gorgeous campus, and rewarding liberal arts program alone make it a real find; the chance to study abroad is a great additional opportunity.

St. Olaf registers as a Lutheran-affiliated school, and the denomination's influence is evident in many specific ways. Students must take several religious courses as part of their core curriculum, and many other courses draw on religious perspectives. There are also some rigid guidelines regarding student life, including strict policies against alcohol and drug use and regulations governing visitors of the opposite sex after hours. The high percentage of Lutheran students (about 50 percent) does, however, create a close community, one in which most people treat one another with kindness and respect.

The distribution requirements can take up to two years to fulfill and include courses in such broad areas as fine arts, natural science and math, history, philosophy, literature, social science, cross-cultural studies, English composition, and foreign language. St. Olaf has notable offerings in many different traditional liberal arts areas, such as biology, chemistry, and economics, as well as acclaimed music, dance, and fine arts programs. In addition to the two yearly semesters, students must take one class each January called an "interim." They use this time to delve deeper into a topic or to try an elective; one student spent her interim in the Caribbean studying regional literature.

There are also several innovative programs available to qualified students. The two-year Great Conversation program is an in-depth exploration of great works of literature and philosophy. Students in the Paracollege design their own program of study and work closely with faculty in small seminars and tutorials; they receive lengthy personal evaluations rather than letter grades. Most teachers at St. Olaf know their students by name. Their support helps students through the somewhat grueling academic requirements and heavy workload.

St. Olaf College

$$$$$
★★

Setting: Small Town
# of Undergraduates: 2,854
Men: 41.4% **Women:** 58.6%
Tuition: $16,500
Room and Board: $4,020
# of Students Applied: 2,332
   Admitted: 1,804   Enrolled: 777
Required Admissions Test: SAT or ACT
Lowest 25% of Freshmen Scored At or Below: SAT Verbal: 550 SAT Math: 550   ACT Comp.: 23
Highest 25% of Freshmen Scored At or Above: SAT Verbal: 670   SAT Math: 670 ACT Comp.: 30
H.S. Rank, Top 10%: 37%
Top 50%: 96%
Avg. Score of Applicants Admitted: SAT Verbal: 610   SAT Math: 620   ACT Comp.: 26
Average GPA of Applicants Admitted: 3.60
Most Popular Majors (% of Student Body): Biology (14.88%), Psychology (11.04%), Economics (10.74%), English (9.05%), Mathematics (8.13%)

Housing on campus is spacious and comfortable, which is fortunate because most students live on campus and, come winter, can expect to spend a lot of time indoors. In addition to standard housing, a number of foreign language houses are ideal places to prepare for study abroad. "Honor houses" have also been established for students involved with volunteer projects in the community.

On campus, there's not much of a party scene; when there are parties, they will usually be small, low-key affairs held in dorm rooms. Students do become deeply involved in a number of extracurricular activities and organizations, and activism is big here (especially volunteer work). The student activities board arranges special events on campus, from dances to visiting lecturers and performers. A $26 million student center called the College Commons is being built, and will even have a movie theater. Live bands, music groups, and theater and dance productions provide constant on-campus entertainment. Intercollegiate and intramural sports are both favorite pastimes. Hockey games draw a decent crowd of student fans. Students take advantage of the school's location and the long winter to enjoy outdoor sports like skiing, sledding, skating, and broomball.

St. Olaf is in a rural location, so the entertainment options are limited. Northfield is a small, country town that has some popular student hangouts but not much else to bring students off campus. Students sometimes head to their neighbor, Carleton College, for more varied social activity. Only seniors are allowed to have cars, although the Twin Cities of Minneapolis and St. Paul can be reached in half an hour by bus. And of course study abroad—like one long, major road trip—satisfies most students' wanderlust.

Also, Check Out These Schools:

Amherst College
Barnard College
Bates College
Boston University
Bucknell University
University of California—Davis
University of California—San Diego
University of California—Santa Cruz
Carleton College
Claremont McKenna College

Travel Agencies

Colby College
Colgate University
College of William and Mary
Colorado College
University of Colorado — Boulder
Davidson College
Duke University
Earlham College
Franklin and Marshall College
Grinnell College
Hamilton College
Hobart and William Smith Colleges
University of Illinois — Urbana/Champaign
Johns Hopkins University
Kenyon College
Lafayette College
Macalester College
University of Michigan — Ann Arbor
Middlebury College
New York University
University of Pennsylvania
St. John's College
Sarah Lawrence College
Smith College
Southern Methodist University
Stanford University
Sweet Briar College
Tufts University
Union College
Vanderbilt University
Vassar College
Wabash College
Washington and Lee University
Washington University
Wellesley College

Global Villages

In recent years, many American colleges and universities have added courses and programs in non-Western cultures and/or ethnic studies. This reflects an understanding, after years of approaching academic material from the same point of view, that examining something from a single perspective is rather limiting. It's like looking only at a small square taken from a much larger, much more interesting picture—looking only at the Mona Lisa's hair, for example, without ever getting to see her smile or her face.

What holds true for academic study is equally true for the social environment. Many schools have attempted to create academic communities in which students from different backgrounds can interact and, therefore, learn from one another. Other people certainly have a great deal to teach us, not only about their own lives, backgrounds, and experiences, but about ourselves as well. You frequently hear college graduates remarking, "I learned just as much from other people I met as I did in my classes."

It makes sense that the more kinds of people there are to meet, the more you might learn. Global Villages are schools where people from a variety of backgrounds meet and mingle. These schools have taken active measures to recruit students from different cultural and ethnic groups and to foster interaction among students. Many schools, for example, might have a Dean of Multicultural Relations or Dean of Minority Affairs, who work full time to create a comfortable campus environment in which all students feel at home.

The social scenes at such schools will often reflect the dynamic and diverse nature of the student body. Many cultural and ethnic groups will form their own clubs or organizations which host various political and social events, including inviting guest speakers, hosting open conferences or forums, and throwing parties. These groups greatly enhance the campus social scene, adding a variety of social options and opportunities for meeting people. But for students within these groups, they have an important political role as well. They ensure that their group's presence on campus is noticeable, that their voices are heard in campus affairs, and that the interests and needs of those students are protected.

At some schools, while different cultural groups might form and be significant in number, they don't necessarily mix with one another. At other schools, though, efforts are made to foster intercultural interaction through various social events, conferences, forums and at some, in a common multicultural center or dormitory. Certain schools also attract students who are generally open to and interested in sharing experiences with many different people.

College is unique in that it's one of the few times in life when you're thrown together with all kinds of people who, despite their individual differences, are essentially in the same boat as you. Everyone is hoping to meet people and to make friends. Take advantage of the situation. Meeting people within a Global Village, you will constantly be fascinated, even amazed, by what you learn.

GEORGETOWN UNIVERSITY IN WASHINGTON, D.C.

Admissions Address: Office of Undergraduate Admissions, 103 White-Gravenor, 37th and O St Northwest, Washington, DC 20057-1002
Phone: (202) 687-3600 (202) 687-5055
Web Address: www.georgetown.edu/

Georgetown University, one of the nation's oldest and most well-known academic institutions, has a distinctive international focus. About 10 percent of the students are foreign nationals originating from more than 100 countries and many of the school's most highly rated academic programs have an international emphasis.

International studies is the most popular major, followed by government—not surprising given the opportunities offered by the university's location. The Capitol offers innumerable study and internship opportunities in these fields, enabling students to experience government and politics in action (indeed, some get so caught up in "Potomac Fever" that it detracts from their studies). Georgetown's esteemed faculty includes politicians, political advisors, journalists, and ambassadors.

GLOBAL VILLAGES

There are four undergraduate schools at Georgetown—Arts and Sciences, Business Administration, Nursing, and Foreign Service—each with its own admissions standards. Language and Linguistics is a separate faculty under the Arts and Sciences school. Georgetown's world-famous School of Foreign Service is particularly competitive. Combining study of history, politics, economics, and foreign language, the school prepares diplomatic hopefuls and others for overseas careers. Arts and Sciences is also highly competitive, with many outstanding departments, including psychology, English, history, and premedicine. Even the business school has an international focus and includes programs in global economics.

You have to list one school on your Georgetown application, which means you won't have much opportunity to try various courses before choosing a major. While entering, students need to be set on some specific career or academic path, since transferring between schools is possible after the first year but discouraged. One student told us that a problem with Georgetown is the manner in which students are divided by concentration, creating a "real rift" between those with professional versus academic aspirations. The university bureaucracy is another big minus, we are told.

Specific core requirements differ by school, but all students take basic liberal arts courses as well as English, theology, and philosophy. Special academic opportunities include cross-registration at the many schools in the Washington Consortium, which includes Catholic, American, and Howard, self-designed majors, and accelerated, five-year, combined B.S./M.S., B.A./M.A., or M.B.A. degrees. About 30 percent of the student body takes advantage of Georgetown's far-reaching study-abroad program in over 20 countries around the world (Languages and Linguistics students usually study abroad at some point).

Undergraduates have a great deal of interaction with the faculty, even with the big names. Professors teach most of the classes, and students report that their profs make themselves readily available for one-on-one advising and conversation. "Even in the bigger classes, professors get to know each of us by name. They really work hard to help us," one student remarked.

Georgetown was founded in 1789 and is the oldest Roman Catholic academic institution in the United States. It continues to be affiliated with the Jesuit tradition of the Church, embracing a holistic educational philosophy. The academic requirements include theological studies and classes in ethics, and the school has a high number of Jesuits on faculty.

Georgetown University

$$$$$

Setting: Urban
# of Undergraduates: 6,051
Men: 48% **Women:** 52%
Tuition: $21,405
Room and Board: $7,765
# of Students Applied: 13,010
  Admitted: 2,992 **Enrolled:** 1,415
Required Admissions Test: Either SAT or ACT
Lowest 25% of Freshmen Scored At or Below: SAT Verbal: 620 SAT Math: 610 ACT Comp.: 26
Highest 25% of Freshmen Scored At or Above: SAT Verbal: 720 SAT Math: 710 ACT Comp.: 31
H.S. Rank, Top 10%: 79%
Top 25%: 95%
Top 50%: 99%
Avg. Score of Applicants Admitted: SAT Verbal: 610 SAT Math: 670 ACT Comp.: 29
Most Popular Majors (% of Student Body): International Politics (10%), Government (8.9%), English (8%), Finance (6.8%), Psychology (6.7%)

The Road to College

About 55 percent of the students are Catholic, which means there are many who are not, and you'll actually find a healthy mixture of religious faiths in the student body. At times, the church's doctrines have led to clashes with students, including a long court bout over whether or not the gay student group could be officially recognized by the school; the students won the right to exist as an official school club (a pro-choice group did not, however, earn that same right).

Georgetown students come from all 50 states, many from wealthy backgrounds. The majority seem conservative politically, but viewpoints do run the gamut from right to left. Students are generally highly intelligent, extremely motivated, and determined to succeed in whatever field, academic or professional, they're immersed in. The student population, in addition to the high percentage of foreign nationals, is diverse in other ways: 7 percent are African American, 8 percent Asian American, and 6 percent Hispanic.

Students are drawn just as much to the university's ideal location as to its excellent academic programs. An upscale, residential neighborhood with Old World charm, Georgetown has escaped the urban blight of the rest of Washington, D.C. In addition to its charming brownstones and cobblestone streets housing executives and members of congress, Georgetown's M and Wisconsin streets boast fashionable shops, restaurants, bars, and clubs—all within easy walking distance for students. Back on campus, the university has a historic look to it. It's heavy on the Gothic gray stone edifices, with more modern buildings here and there.

Even if it didn't enjoy such a wonderful location, there would be no shortage of things to do on campus. In fact, a number of students report that the variety of activities at the school is its best asset. There's a club or organization for just about every culture, activity, and professional and political interest, from an Intercultural Relations Club to the many student service groups organized by the Volunteer and Public Service Center. The modern Leavey Center is a huge student union and conference facility that is used as a home base by over 100 clubs.

There's no Greek system at Georgetown, but there are plenty of ways to have a good time. "*Playboy* ranked us the best party school in the nation five years ago. People work hard, but they also play hard," one student told us. Students hang out and socialize in dorm rooms, off-campus apartments, or local bars. The Georgetown sports teams are famous for throwing parties. Students also attend the occasional large block party and semiformal or formal, including the superposh Annual Diplomatic Ball.

Ever since a young basketball hotshot named Patrick Ewing began to show off his moves for the Georgetown Hoyas, athletics at Georgetown have become more and more of a beloved schoolwide obsession. The basketball and football teams are fanatically followed; games usually turn into social events, with rowdy cheering in the stands as well as rowdy pregame and postgame parties. Most students use the Yates Recreational Complex, an enormous underground athletic facility with a swimming pool, track, racquetball and squash courts, basketball and tennis courts, and weight machines.

Those are just a few of the things to do on campus. Just off campus, there's all of Georgetown, and beyond that, the exciting national capital—and global village—of Washington, D.C.

PITZER COLLEGE IN CLAREMONT, CALIFORNIA

Admissions Address: Admissions Office, 1050 North Mills Avenue, Claremont, CA 91711
Phone: (909) 621-8129 (909) 621-8000
Web Address: www.pitzer.edu/admission/admisform/html

Pitzer College offers an alternative education in an open, free-spirited academic environment. A progressive, friendly student body and faculty create a community in which students from divergent backgrounds freely exchange ideas and opinions—and where such exchanges are considered integral parts of students' educations. As a graduating senior points out, "this is a place for alternative thinkers—if not when they first arrive here, then definitely by the time they leave."

With around 800 students, Pitzer is an intimate environment in which students receive tremendous individualized attention and where all faces are familiar ones. But it's also a part of the Claremont College system (along with Pomona, Scripps, Harvey Mudd, and Claremont McKenna), which greatly expands the college's resources, facilities, and academic and social options.

Begun in 1963 as an alternative, all-female school, Pitzer went coed in the 1970s. The school has maintained its primary emphasis on social and behavioral sciences, which remain its strongest departments; but many departments in the humanities are also excellent. Majors in psychology, sociology, anthropology, and political sciences are its main attractions. Other highly rated fields include the humanities, arts, economics, and history. Most courses stress environmental awareness in their curriculums.

Pitzer College

🏛

$$$$$

★★

Setting: Suburban
# of Undergraduates: 782
Men: 43.4% **Women:** 56.6%
Tuition: $19,360
Room and Board: $7,606
# of Students Applied: 1,416
   Admitted: 1,082 **Enrolled:** 869
Required Admissions Test: Either SAT or ACT
Recommended: SAT II
Lowest 25% of Freshmen Scored At or Below: SAT Verbal: 599 SAT Math: 599 ACT Comp.: 23
Highest 25% of Freshmen Scored At or Above: SAT Verbal: 600 SAT Math: 600 ACT Comp.: 24
H.S. Rank, Top 10%: 30%
Top 25%: 54%
Top 50%: 83%
Avg. Score of Applicants Admitted: SAT Verbal: 599 SAT Math: 597 ACT Comp.: 25
Average GPA of Applicants Admitted: 3.33
Most Popular Majors (% of Student Body): Psychology (20%), Sociology (14%), Art (12%), Political Studies (10%), English (7%)

More than half of Pitzer graduates go on to professional or graduate school.

Pitzer's educational philosophy provides students with choice and independence. They are given almost total responsibility over the direction of their own educations. Since general requirements are slim, with basic classes in science, art, math, and writing, students enjoy more credits to play around with. They can design their own majors and conduct independent projects and research. Pitzer's academic offerings include study abroad and a program in international and intercultural studies.

The small, seminar-like classes are akin to intellectual investigations in which students and faculty together probe a topic from various viewpoints and approaches. Professors, who teach all the classes, are generally on friendly terms with their students and constantly challenge them to examine and rethink their assumptions. They are also considered a close part of the campus community and become involved in many events and activities.

The Pitzer campus, like the other Claremont colleges, is California in look and feel—comfortable and easy to get around, with plenty of grass for lying out and enjoying the sunshine and palm trees. There's even a swimming pool known as a daytime party spot among students. Despite the limited size of the campus, students can freely use the other Claremont campuses, including athletic facilities, libraries, and state-of-the-art science facilities.

The student body is the most ethnically diverse of the Claremont colleges, including about 40 percent minority students (13 percent Hispanic, 12 percent Asian American, 6 percent African American, and 5 percent foreign national). About 40 percent of the students are from out of state, primarily from the Northeast. A huge international program attracts many foreign students. The gay and lesbian population is open and accepted.

Since its founding, Pitzer has developed a reputation as a hippie haven, an image today's students are sick of hearing about. While far fewer flower children and Deadheads wage naked protests on the grounds, the students continue to be very liberal and activist. Concern about racism, sexism, homophobia, and the environment are shared by many. Pitzer students value and respect one another's individuality, creating an open and broad-minded environment in which students give free voice to their beliefs (so long as they're politically correct ones, we are told). "You need to be very tolerant here," advises a sophomore.

Students like their studies but don't stress out about them. Their laid-back attitudes contribute to the casual campus social scene. Rather than going to huge bashes, they hang out in smaller groups around campus, in noisy dorm rooms, or in the student union, called the Gold Center. Smoking is reportedly very prevalent. The Grove House, with a restaurant and space for live entertainment, is another popular campus hang-out for coffee stops, poetry readings, and drum circles. Students can always go to the other Claremont colleges for bigger parties and social events.

Pitzer students can join clubs and organizations with students from all five Claremont schools. Cultural and ethnic organizations enjoy greater popularity than those concerned with politics (one student lamented a trend towards political apathy on campus). Road trips to all parts of California, from a major city to a quiet rural area or beach, are popular weekend options. You'll need a car, or at least a friend that owns one.

Students seem to create good times for themselves all year long; some even attend classes in pajamas. Yet the big Pitzer social event is the Kahoutek festival, named after a comet that was supposed to destroy the earth but failed to do so. The weekend-long event with its live bands, international foods, and displays by local artists has been characterized as "like Woodstock meets Lollapalooza." Maybe that's representative of the Pitzer experience as a whole.

RUTGERS UNIVERSITY (THE STATE UNIVERSITY OF NEW JERSEY) IN NEW BRUNSWICK

Admissions Address: University Undergraduate Admissions, P.O. Box 2101, New Brunswick, NJ 08903-2101
Phone: (732) 445-3770 (732) 932-INFO
Web Address: www.rutgers.edu/ugadmissions

While Rutgers has about 30,000 students, it avoids the impersonality typical of large institutions with its system of separate campuses. "Within your own college and campus, Rutgers has the feeling of a small school," commented a new student. The university's smaller liberal arts colleges are located in Camden and Newark, but its four major campuses are in the New Brunswick area. These include various professional schools—such as engineering, nursing, pharmacy, and the arts—as well as several liberal arts colleges: Douglass (for women only), Cook (specializing in agricultural and environmental sciences), Rutgers, and Livingston. Each college has its own appearance, from the stately older

The Road to College

Rutgers U/ Rutgers College

$$

★★★

Setting: Suburban
# of Undergraduates: 9,931
Men: 48.5% **Women:** 51.5
In-State Tuition: $4,028
Out-of-State Tuition: $8,200
Room and Board: $5,134
# of Students Applied: 16,683
   Admitted: 8,711 **Enrolled:** 2,273
Required Admissions Test: Either SAT or ACT
Lowest 25% of Freshmen Scored At or Below: SAT Verbal: 530 SAT Math: 540
Highest 25% of Freshmen Scored At or Above: SAT Verbal: 640 SAT Math: 660
H.S. Rank, Top 10%: 35%
Top 25%: 80%
Top 50%: 98%
Avg. Score of Applicants Admitted: SAT Verbal: 584 SAT Math: 602
Most Popular Majors (% of Student Body): Psychology (14%), Political Science (8%), Biological Sciences (8%), English (7%), Econmics (6%)

buildings of Rutgers College, the oldest school in the system, to the more modern, recently constructed Busch. The schools also differ in admissions standards and core requirements, but students can freely enroll in courses at all of them. Together, the schools offer more than 100 programs for undergraduates. They are connected by a shuttle bus, which makes taking advantages of all of Rutgers facilities and resources much easier. Some students complain that they spend too much time shuttling between campuses, however, and that the buses often become jam-packed.

Just as there are all kinds of colleges and programs at Rutgers, there are all types of students who can lay claim to the Rutgers sweatshirt. The school's low tuition for state residents primarily attracts those from New Jersey, who account for 85 percent of the population. But New Jersey is itself a diverse state and the student body reflects this mixture, with many different cultures, ethnic groups, socioeconomic groups, religions, and regions represented. About 40 percent of the student body is made up of minority students (15 percent Asian American, 11 percent African American, 9 percent Hispanic, 2 percent foreign). Students are reportedly tolerant and respectful of various views.

While the colleges help break down the larger university, Rutgers remains a big place. Lower-level classes can number several hundred students, which makes getting close attention from professors nearly impossible. However, upper-level classes might have as few as 10 to 15 students. Because of the large enrollment, getting into certain courses can take some perseverance. The bureaucratic procedures are tedious, if not downright infuriating. Telephone registration has reportedly made things somewhat easier, but there are still some bugs that need to be worked out of the system. Many students wish they could talk to an actual human being during the angstful registration process.

Only about half of the students live on campus. Although that does mean a large percentage commute and therefore, may take off right after classes, there are still several thousand students who rely on the campus for their social lives. They can find a wealth of social activities, all of which help break down the bigger university into smaller, more community-like circles. For example, students from the same colleges live together in the same dorms, and each college also has its own student center, providing prime hang out space. Off-campus parties, especially in houses off College Avenue, draw a lot of students as well.

344

GLOBAL VILLAGES

The 200 clubs and organizations at Rutgers run the gamut of political, cultural, religious, professional, and social interests. There are several large coalitions for various minority groups, each of which might have smaller student groups within it. These organizations include the Rutgers Asian American Coalition for Equality, the Paul Robeson Club (an active African American group), and the Latino Student Council.

Other components of the social scene include the Greek system and athletics. Fraternities and sororities draw about 7 percent of the men and 3 percent of the women and supply a steady stream of parties and social events. Many of Rutgers' Big East teams, particularly in football, men's and women's basketball, men's and women's soccer, field hockey, and tennis, draw loyal fans. Two major spring festivals, Ag Field Day and Rutgers Fest, boost the school's social morale as university-wide parties with live music, lots of food, and plenty of debauchery.

New Brunswick, after a major clean up and renewal phase, now offers some nice shops, restaurants, and other forms of entertainment, although there are still some seedier neighborhoods. If students want a break from their own campus, New York and Philly are both easy road trips, each only about an hour away by train. Students don't overlook options in their own state, from concert and sporting events at the Meadowlands to the beaches of the Jersey Shore, just to name a few. Rutgers has the academic and social options to meet the interests of about 30,000 students, although within your own college you may forget there are that many fellow Rutgers students wandering about.

TEMPLE UNIVERSITY IN PHILADELPHIA, PENNSYLVANIA

Admissions Address: Undergraduate Admissions, 1801 N. Broad Street, Philadelphia, PA 19122
Phone: (215) 204-7200
Web Address: www.temple.edu/

As the founders of the City of Brotherly Love would no doubt approve, students at Temple University report how people from all geographic and cultural backgrounds become part of a generally friendly and easy-going student body. Temple's diverse student population includes about 20 percent African American, 10 percent Asian American, and a small percentage of Hispanic students, as well as students from 60 foreign countries. All 50 states are represented as well. As a Temple junior told us, "What I like about Temple is that it has the opportunities of a big university but the feel of a small college. It's very easy to meet people here."

Temple University

$$$
★★

Setting: Urban
# of Undergraduates: 14,417
Men: 44.1% **Women:** 55.9
In-State Tuition: $5,628
Out-of-State Tuition: $10,510
Room and Board: $5,712
# of Students Applied: 9,419
  Admitted: 5,961 **Enrolled:** 2,321
Required Admissions Test: Either SAT or ACT
Lowest 25% of Freshmen Scored At or Below: SAT Verbal: 429 SAT Math: 488
Highest 25% of Freshmen Scored At or Above: SAT Verbal: 552 SAT Math: 641
H.S. Rank, Top 10%: 19%
Top 25%: 43%
Top 50%: 79%
Avg. Score of Applicants Admitted: SAT Verbal: 500 SAT Math: 492
Most Popular Majors (% of Student Body): Elementary Education (6%), Psychology (6%), Business Administration (5%), Accounting (4%), Biology (3%)

Students aren't shy about saying hello or sparking conversations with others in class or around the campus, we hear.

Many students are drawn to Temple by its reasonable tuition, especially Pennsylvanians. Tuition is exceptionally low for in-state students, and they account for about 80 percent of the student body. Temple offers an impressive variety of academic programs and research facilities, with preprofessional fields accounting for the highest undergraduate enrollments. There are 11 undergraduate schools, including highly rated programs in business and communications. The school's African American studies program is considered excellent, and there are many popular course offerings in Asian and Latin American studies as well.

"Teachers make us feel like we're people, not statistics. They're always willing to get to know us and to help us meet other students," a junior told us. She pointed out, though, that as the school hires more part-time professors, the quality of the teaching is being adversely affected. The core curriculum includes English composition, the arts, foreign language, math, science, and technology, and courses in such interesting areas as intellectual heritage, American culture, race and racism, and the individual and society.

Many Temple students commute—only about 10 percent live in campus housing—so the social life doesn't center on the campus, and the student community is a fractured one. As one student told us, "at 8 P.M. the campus is barren." There are certain social venues, though, that enable students to meet and interact. The Student Activity Center functions as a social home base, providing a much-needed central location for students to hang out over snacks and coffee, as well as a meeting space for various student organizations. Fraternities and sororities draw about 3 percent of the students, and for these students Greek life functions as a kind of community within the larger university. In addition to hosting parties and special events, many houses are committed to community service in the city. The school's clubs and organizations include several major cultural groups, including the African American Student Union, and student associations for Hispanic, Caribbean, Korean, and Chinese students. Nothing, though, galvanizes student spirit for the school as much as its strong sports teams in football and its NCAA Division I basketball team.

Although the main campus lies about a mile north of downtown Philadelphia, the schools within the university are spread out across seven campuses, many accessible by a free shuttle bus. Those studying premed or prenursing, for example, will move between classes on the main campus and classes at the health and sciences school, about 10 minutes away. The neighborhood surrounding the main campus is run down and raises concerns about safety, but the college itself has tight security. Other parts of Philadelphia offer many social and cultural options, from going to museums, concerts, plays, and sporting events to hanging out in the funky bars and cafes along South Street.

UNIVERSITY OF HOUSTON IN HOUSTON, TEXAS

Admissions Address: Admissions Office, 129 Ezekiel W. Cullen Building, Houston, TX 77204-2161
Phone: (713) 743-1010 (800) 741-4449
Web Address: www.uh.edu

Deep in the heart of Texas, the University of Houston offers numerous academic programs to its undergraduates at low tuition. UH boasts many highly rated programs, including business, chemical engineering, art and music, and hotel and restaurant management. The science programs benefit from an esteemed faculty of researchers and many new, modern facilities.

Required courses include English, social science, natural science, history, math, cultural heritage, and physical education. The workload at Houston is demanding, and students receive solid educations. Class size—which can number in the hundreds, especially in introductory levels—gets much smaller as you specialize and move on to higher levels. Professors teach many courses, impressive for a school of this size, although the larger lectures might break down into sections led by TAs. Students often complain about the difficulty of getting into classes, including the required ones, and are advised to plan and register early (students approaching graduation sometimes get held back when they're unable to enter a required class). The honors program offers highly qualified students study in a more intimate setting with greater individualized attention.

The Houston campus, while big, enjoys a nice, open layout. Most buildings are relatively new and, therefore, in good condition. While some buildings are standard academic affairs, there are some that are more impressive, including the stunning architecture building.

Native Texans comprise the majority of the student body. This includes a 44 percent minority population, and students generally get along rather

---

University of Houston

$$

Setting: Urban
# of Undergraduates: 14,817
Men: 47% Women: 53
In-State Tuition: $1,020
Out-of-State Tuition: $7,440
Room and Board: $4,405
# of Students Applied: 6,584
  Admitted: 4,070 Enrolled: 2,433
Required Admissions Test: Either SAT or ACT
Lowest 25% of Freshmen Scored At or Below: SAT Verbal: 420 SAT Math: 450 ACT Comp.: 19
Highest 25% of Freshmen Scored At or Above: SAT Verbal: 540 SAT Math: 570 ACT Comp.: 23
H.S. Rank, Top 10%: 21%
Top 25%: 47%
Top 50%: 78%
Avg. Score of Applicants Admitted: SAT Verbal: 487 SAT Math: 513 ACT Comp.: 22
Average GPA of Applicants Admitted: 3.00
Most Popular Majors (% of Student Body): Business Administration (12.4%), Education (8.6%), Engineering (7.6%), Biosciences (7.5%), Psychology (5.3%)

well, and there's little tension between groups. Many students are slightly older than average college ages and attend part time.

Only about 10 percent of UH students actually live on campus. The social scene, therefore, isn't centered on campus; it's split into various factions and social venues. Students living in the dorms have an easier time making friends with fellow students. "There's a very limited social scene for commuters," comments one resident. Becoming involved with a club or activity is another way to meet people and have some form of social life, and with 200 possibilities to choose from, finding one you like shouldn't be a problem. The school's many extracurricular activities include a TV and radio station, student government, political and professional clubs, student performance groups, and intramural sports. About 4 percent of the students belong to the Greek system; that's not a large percentage, but the houses manage to hold many parties attended by large numbers of students.

The campus's many lawns and grassy areas make great spots for hanging out and chatting, as does the student center and various small snack bars and eateries. Students like their school's accessibility to the substantial cultural and social offerings of Houston, but it's a spread-out city, and having access to a car is necessary to enjoy parts of it. Houston has a fantastic art scene, including the Museum of Fine Arts, the Contemporary Museum of Art, and a gorgeous sculpture garden, as well as many smaller galleries and museums, while interesting shops and restaurants are clustered in the hip downtown area. Many head to Richmond Street, a strip of trendy clubs and bars.

Also, Check Out These Schools:

Antioch College
Bennington College
Brown University
Bryn Mawr College
University of California—Berkeley
University of California—Davis
University of California—Santa Cruz
Colorado College
Cornell University
CUNY—Brooklyn College
CUNY—Hunter College
CUNY—Queens College

GLOBAL VILLAGES

Earlham College
Eugene Lang College
Evergreen State College
George Washington University
Hampshire College
University of Hawaii—Manoa
Howard University
Kalamazoo College
Lewis and Clark College
New College of the University of South Florida
Oberlin College
Occidental College
Sarah Lawrence College
Stanford University
SUNY—Stony Brook
Syracuse University
Temple University
Tufts University
Wellesley College
Wesleyan University

Alternative Havens

For all their differences in terms of location, students, facilities, and faculty, most U.S. colleges share ideas about the basic shape of education. In general, they follow a standard recipe for a higher-level education: equal parts core and major requirements, accented with exams and papers, sprinkled with a senior thesis or study abroad. The schools listed in this chapter—having initiated progressive, nontraditional academic programs—have thrown out that recipe entirely. In some cases, they've thrown out the cookbook as well! Some have gotten rid of things like grades, exams, and requirements; others have completely restructured the school year, omitting set course sequences and semesters. Some don't bother with any curriculum at all.

In each case, the rationale behind these innovations is that students receive a more valuable, meaningful education. At an Alternative Haven college, students become engaged in the pursuit of knowledge for its own sake—without the institutional structures and restrictions that can often bog them down. While students at other schools might soon forget what they've learned after exam week, students at these colleges become so immersed in their chosen studies that they remain an ingrained part of them. Students develop their own critical abilities so that they can tackle virtually any subject and apply what they learn from one area to another.

Right now, you're probably thinking, "No grades? No exams? No requirements? Where do I sign up?" You should know that in almost every case, these progressive academic approaches make more demands on students than the traditional ones. No grades doesn't mean there aren't evaluations, and no requirements doesn't mean there's no work. As students are responsible for a large part of their own educations, they have to do even more work to make certain they get it. They need to arrive in class not only having read the assignment, but ready to raise questions and make contributions to class discussions. Very often, they complement their course work with lengthy papers or independent research projects that can take the better part of an academic year to complete. As part of their studies, students might also meet directly with faculty members, making it impossible to slink down behind someone else when asked a question.

Students who go to Alternative Havens, though, usually thrive in this kind of scholarly atmosphere. They work hard at their studies because they like what they're studying. Most students at these colleges aren't necessarily thinking of a professional career, at least not yet. They're interested in expanding their knowledge in various scholarly fields and disciplines.

These students, much like the progressive academic philosophies at their colleges, can't be neatly categorized according to set definitions and types. They are nonconformists, accustomed to doing their own thing. They often describe themselves as people who didn't fit in with any crowd in high school. They value individuality—in themselves and others. For that reason, the student bodies tend to be much more tolerant and open to different ideas and experiences. There's little, if any, discrimination against minority groups, and gay and lesbian students are often openly accepted. Students tend to be politically active and leftist. Politically correct ideals and values are alive and well at these schools.

Socially, the kinds of activities that draw large crowds of similar students at other colleges and breed school spirit—things like fraternity parties and team sports—don't hold much appeal. Students are more likely to hang out in small groups or attend informal get-togethers than huge parties. Extracurricular and social activities, though, reflect the students' divergent interests and experiences, running the gamut from the popular to the more bizarre.

Having academic freedom and independence requires tremendous self-discipline and motivation, and some students might feel lost without a set structure to keep them on track. Many of the schools we've listed have very high drop-out rates after the first year. For these reasons, the schools listed in this chapter particularly require a great deal of thought and investigation before one decides to enroll. If you are interested in a school listed here, it's probably a good idea to go visit and talk with some students to try to get a sense of whether it's the place for you.

For now, get ready to take a walk on the academic wild side. You'll be surprised at just how different a college education can be.

ALTERNATIVE HAVENS

ANTIOCH COLLEGE IN YELLOW SPRINGS, OHIO

Admissions Address: Admissions Office, 795 Livermore Street, Yellow Springs, OH 45387
Phone: (513) 767-6400 (800) 543-9436
Web Address: antioch-college.edu/

For many students, the experience of graduating from college and entering the work force is akin to being hit on the head with an anvil. They suddenly realize that in their insular, protected collegiate environment, they haven't been prepared at all for life and work in the real world. Students at Antioch, though, have been in the real world all along. Antioch's co-op program requires students to fulfill five internships before they graduate. They study for several months on campus, then take off to work in some field of interest, for which they receive college credit. The student's advisor will help in the selection of a co-op, which doesn't necessarily have to be job related. For example, students might conduct volunteer work or study abroad.

When on campus, students become deeply immersed in their studies. There are few core requirements, allowing them room in their schedules to experiment with different subjects. Emphasis is placed on reading original texts, which students are asked to analyze and deconstruct. An advantage to Antioch's small population is that classes are relatively small and professors get to know students well. Instead of grades, students receive extensive evaluations directly from their professors.

Undergraduates describe the workload at Antioch as "heavy," although it has eased up somewhat since the college switched from a trimester to semester system. The internship requirements force students to become independent quickly. As one student explained, "application to the co-op department compels us to lead creative lifestyles, since we must learn to succeed in big city environments where we do our internships. Students become more motivated, too, once they find out what awaits them after graduation."

Although located in a rural region, many Antioch students have good things to say about Yellow Springs, a town with a "real granola" population that includes vegetarian eateries, health food stores, folk art galleries, New Age shops and boutiques, and Birkenstocks galore. Many students are themselves nature lovers, and the campus itself has enough open spaces, fresh air, and expansive woods to keep them happy. The Glen Helen Woods that surround Antioch contain numerous paths for biking, rollerblading, walking, and jogging.

Antioch College

$$$$$
★★

Setting: Small town
# of Undergraduates: 547
Men: 38.9% Women: 61.4%
Tuition: $16,812
Room and Board: $3,998
# of Students Applied: 468
   Admitted: 376 Enrolled: 154
Required Admissions Test: none
Recommended: SAT, ACT
**Lowest 25% of Freshmen Scored
   At or Below:** SAT Verbal: 550
   SAT Math: 480 ACT Comp.: 22
**Highest 25% of Freshmen
   Scored At or Above:** SAT
   Verbal: 670 SAT Math: 600
   ACT Comp.: 28
H.S. Rank, Top 10%: 17%
Top 25%: 44%
**Avg. Score of Applicants
   Admitted:** SAT Verbal: 520
   SAT Math: 540 ACT Comp.:
   25.3
**Average GPA of Applicants
   Admitted:** 3.10
**Most Popular Majors (% of
   Student Body):** Art (17%),
   Sciences (16%), Social Sciences
   (15%), Literature and Creative
   Writing (13%), Communications
   (6%)

With so many students leaving campus for their internships, there's inevitably a certain amount of instability in the college's social scene. But as one student told us, "There's a specific effort among students to create a sense of community," made easier by the school's small size. Students tend to socialize at intimate get-togethers and informal parties rather than at huge bashes, although many people can be seen celebrating their freedom and youth on the campus's various open spaces. Also, students often become committed to one of the school's clubs and organizations, many of which are politically oriented.

The student population tends to be, as one student told us, "pretty radical." One form of the school's radical politics sparked a nationwide controversy. Antioch initiated a sexual consent policy, according to which students must receive verbal consent prior to any form of sexual interaction, that led to debates at colleges across the country regarding sex on campus. The point is to promote open dialogue between people, reducing the threat of sexual harassment and sexism. For most Antioch students, causing a ruckus is nothing new. People who enroll here expect to challenge popular ideas and break out of social constraints. As one told us, "We tend to be out on the edge of what's acceptable and what isn't." For students who have also been living on the edge, Antioch offers the educational and real-world experiences to set them on the path to post-graduation success.

BENNINGTON COLLEGE IN BENNINGTON, VERMONT

Admissions Address: Admissions Office, Route 67A, Bennington, VT 05201
Phone: (802) 442-5401, (800) 833-6845
Web Address: www.bennington.edu/

A Bennington freshman told us she likes the school because "students have the freedom to explore their interests with guidance from caring professors." Working closely with advisors, with whom they meet on a regular basis, students map out their academic programs according to their own interests. They can immerse themselves in a single field, say biology or drama, or dabble in several, no matter how strange the combination. Having tossed out traditional grading policies and final examinations, Bennington encourages its students to learn for the sake of learning.

The distribution requirements aren't at all limiting. Students take four courses in seven broad areas, and at least one year of coursework beyond

ALTERNATIVE HAVENS

the introductory level in three disciplines. Therefore, they enjoy great freedom to test out various fields. They are also encouraged to combine theory with practice in their work. For example, while studying literature, students might write their own stories, or while studying drama they will act in plays. Bennington's well known and highly touted fine arts programs make their headquarters in the massive Visual and Performing Arts Center.

Because Bennington is such a small school, fewer courses are offered than at other liberal arts colleges. However, the classes that are on schedule leave the students feeling like experts. Classes remain very small, usually between 5 and 20 students. Undergrads receive undivided attention from their professors and get to know each one personally. Instead of letter grades, they receive in-depth written evaluations from their teachers. Students often follow up their interest in a subject by working in small tutorials and seminars.

Many people are scared away by Bennington's exorbitant tuition, which may be why the school has a reputation as a haven for elitist rich kids. Many students, though, receive some form of financial aid, especially Native Americans and those from overseas. The tuition is spent on the college and the students in noticeable ways. For example, the faculty-student ratio is exceptionally low, and students receive extensive guidance and advising throughout their educations. Additionally, the school invests heavily in its facilities, so students get to use resources and equipment in stellar condition.

The pretty Bennington campus is surrounded by miles of Vermont woods and countryside. Most students live on campus in one of 15 coed houses. Each house has its own personality and serves as a focal point for socializing. Another facet of the school's permissiveness is its roommates policy; students of the opposite sex can share rooms if they both request it.

Because they're given so much freedom, Bennington students must be extremely self-motivated to complete their academic programs. The school attracts individuals who are independent, individualistic, and proud of it. The social scene at Bennington reflects the diversity of the students' experiences and interests. There are no fraternities and no intercollegiate sporting events. Even though there are several campus-wide social events a year, students tend to hang out more in small circles, often with their housemates or with those who share similar interests. Most people know each other at least by face, and younger students speak of getting a lot of support from upperclassmen.

Bennington College

$$$$$
★★

Setting: Rural
# of Undergraduates: 289
Men: 33.9% Women: 66.1%
Tuition: $26,400
# of Students Applied: 541
   Admitted: 385   Enrolled: 119
Required Admissions Test: Either SAT or ACT
Lowest 25% of Freshmen Scored At or Below: SAT Verbal: 463 SAT Math: 436   ACT Comp.: 26
Highest 25% of Freshmen Scored At or Above: SAT Verbal: 657   SAT Math: 703   ACT Comp.: 32
H.S. Rank, Top 10%: 40%
Top 25%: 67%
Top 50%: 91%
Avg. Score of Applicants Admitted: SAT Verbal: 572   SAT Math: 609   ACT Comp.: 26
Average GPA of Applicants Admitted: 3.46
Most Popular Majors (% of Student Body):
   Interdisciplinary (25%), Visual Arts (22%), Literature (17%), Thematic (14%), Drama (10%)

The town of Bennington doesn't offer much in the way of social activities, other than a few coffeehouses and restaurants, and the nearest cities are pretty far away. Although students venture off-campus for such outdoor sports as hiking, skiing, and canoeing, the social life is centered on campus. Fortunately, with all the talented student performers, there's always a decent concert, play, or dance performance on campus.

COLORADO COLLEGE IN COLORADO SPRINGS, COLORADO

Admissions Address: Admissions Office, 14 East Cache La Poudre Street, Colorado Springs, CO 80903-3298
Phone: (719) 389-6344 (800) 542-7214
Web Address: www.cc.colorado.edu/

Colorado College

$$$$$
★★★

Setting: Urban
# of Undergraduates: 1,963
Men: 46.9% **Women:** 53.1%
Tuition: $19,026
Room and Board: $5,100
# of Students Applied: 3,426
  Admitted: 2,051 **Enrolled:** 593
Required Admissions Test: Either SAT or ACT
Lowest 25% of Freshmen Scored At or Below: SAT Verbal: 580 SAT Math: 580 ACT Comp.: 25
Highest 25% of Freshmen Scored At or Above: SAT Verbal: 680 SAT Math: 680 ACT Comp.: 30
H.S. Rank, Top 10%: 43%
Top 25%: 80%
Top 50%: 99%
Avg. Score of Applicants Admitted: SAT Verbal: 626 SAT Math: 630 ACT Comp.: 27
Most Popular Majors (% of Student Body): Biology (12.5%), English (13%), Psychology (8.2%), Economics (8.2%), History (7%)

The educational philosophy at Colorado College takes the idea of an academic concentration to extremes. With Colorado's Block Plan, students take just one course at a time. Before you rush to apply because it sounds so easy, consider that students remain in that course all day for about three and a half weeks. Some of the more complex courses might carry over to the next session. A Colorado student told us that "the work is intense," but the benefit is that "you get completely absorbed in what you are studying, and you become close friends with your professor and peers since you're with them so often." Another student cautioned that a drawback to the block plan is limited long-term retention, since the material is learned in such a short period of time. "You either love the block plan or hate it," he went on to say.

In this intensive academic environment, where class size is limited to 25 people, there's a special kind of bonding that takes place between students and faculty. Students rave about their caring teachers, who often give out their home phone numbers. To help break up the monotony of the classroom setting, many professors take their classes out for breakfast or lunch, one student told us. Several Colorado courses include field trips; subjects such as environmental studies and geology take advantage of the college's natural surroundings, but other classes travel to more exotic locations around the world.

The general requirements include blocks in natural science, Western civilization, and non-Western civilization. Students also have the option to head off-campus for blocks; they can study abroad or become involved in a brief internship. Colorado College has another location at the Baca campus, as well as a mountain cabin where outdoor classes, especially in field studies, are often held.

At the end of each block, students are given a four-day break to take a breather before the next one. Many take the time to travel to visit friends at other schools or go home. Others take advantage of the outdoor activities offered by the school's Rocky Mountain location. Skiing, mountain climbing, hiking, and camping are favorite sports for Colorado students.

The social scene at Colorado College flourishes, even in the midst of the cold of winter. Student-sponsored dances, parties, and festivals keep campus life happening. People also check bulletin boards for dorm parties and off-campus bashes. The Greek system here remains more active in hosting philanthropic events than parties. When students want a quick getaway, Denver lies about an hour away and offers more options for food, music, shopping, and culture. Colorado Springs, unfortunately, doesn't have much for students.

While the student body is largely homogenous, increasing the school's diversity is a concern shared by the administration and students alike. "Most of us are upper-middle class and white," commented a junior. "Despite our homogeneity, we are very open-minded—after all, granolas, hippies, and preppy alternative thinkers live together in relative harmony." Colorado College is a liberal school, despite its location in one of America's most conservative bastions. A significant number of students work in community-service programs or join politically oriented organizations or clubs. They voice their concerns about a host of topical issues, including, as one student told us, concerns about their own apathy.

Colorado may not be the place for those who believe that variety is the spice of life. Yet for those who love the block plan and appreciate the school's eclectic members, this is the best place in the world to study.

EUGENE LANG COLLEGE IN NEW YORK, NEW YORK

Admissions Address: Admissions Office, 65 West 11th Street, New York, NY 10011
Phone: (212) 229-5665
Web Address: www.newschool.edu

Although Eugene Lang College has an undergraduate enrollment of fewer than 400, its connection to other entities makes it seem much larger. Lang is the undergraduate college of the prestigious New School for

Eugene Lang College

$$$$$
★★

Setting: Urban
# of Undergraduates: 369
Men: 34.4% Women: 65.6%
Tuition: $17,560
Room and Board: $8,555
# of Students Applied: 398
　Admitted: 275　Enrolled: 80
Required Admissions Test: Either SAT or ACT
Lowest 25% of Freshmen Scored At or Below: SAT Verbal: 570
　SAT Math: 470
Highest 25% of Freshmen Scored At or Above: SAT Verbal: 673　SAT Math: 633
H.S. Rank, Top 10%: 48%
Top 25%: 79%
Top 50%: 97%
Avg. Score of Applicants Admitted: SAT Verbal: 610　SAT Math: 540　ACT Comp.: 27
Average GPA of Applicants Admitted: 3.30

Social Research. After their first year, Lang students are able to enroll in courses at the New School's graduate facility, which attracts an esteemed faculty of international renown. Students can also take courses and enroll at other New York City schools, such as the Parsons School of Design and Cooper Union.

At Lang, students have complete control over their educational programs. There are no required courses; instead, students design their program within one of five broad interdisciplinary concentrations in the social sciences and humanities with the help of an advisor. Central to the Lang educational experience are the small seminars in which students study. With only 400 undergraduates, there's no need for large courses and lectures. Most classes have fewer than 15 students, creating an open intellectual atmosphere in which students test out and question themselves and one another. The seminars also enable students and the faculty to get to know each another, fostering an easygoing familiarity among the campus population. "I'm on a first-name basis with teachers and members of the administration," said a transfer student. "I love being able to ask for help so easily and having teachers care about what I think."

First-year students are guaranteed housing and tend to hang out together in dorms. Once students move off campus, though, they are likely to form their own social circles. While there are no sports facilities and limited campus social activity, the students consider all of Greenwich Village their greater campus. The Village is the home of New York's funkier shops, restaurants, bars, and night spots. And when you add in the rest of the city, Lang students have endless social and cultural opportunities. Both academically and socially, Lang is for students who want the freedom and choices to shape their own experiences.

EVERGREEN STATE COLLEGE IN OLYMPIA, WASHINGTON

Admissions Address: Admissions Office, 2700 Evergreen Parkway NW, Olympia, WA 98505
Phone: (360) 866-6000, ext. 6170
Web Address: www.evergreen.edu/

Evergreen abandoned the traditional college curriculum, asking its students to follow an interdisciplinary approach to higher education. Rather than fulfilling distribution requirements followed by concentrated study within a major, students pursue a single "program" each term. Each program centers on some broad topic that is investigated from several academic approaches. Students follow one program per quarter, and the manner of study is diverse, combining lectures, discussion seminars, workshops, and hands-on experiences such as labs, studios, and independent research projects. The programs are usually team taught by several professors, who represent different academic disciplines.

Under this innovative system, students learn how to connect issues and ideas across fields and disciplines. Courses are not isolated topics one forgets from semester to semester, but interrelated subjects that form part of a bigger picture. Students graduate with the ability to discern between the diverse and often conflicting values involved in an issue, and their sense of perspective gives them an important advantage.

Since Evergreen students work closely with other students and teachers in the same program, they form particularly close relationships. "Students and professors are on a first-name basis," a senior told us. "We often have dinners together." Rather than grades, students receive evaluations that they respond to and discuss with their teachers.

The academic year is divided into quarters, and most programs last one or two quarters. "Students can choose how much they want to put into their program. The more motivated they are, the more they will learn and understand," a junior told us. In general, students become deeply involved with their studies, especially once they appreciate the interrelatedness of their topics.

Evergreen students are known as "Greeners," a designation that draws on much more than the school's name. The campus is surrounded by acres of Washington woods and is accessible to undeveloped Pacific beaches. Evergreen residents can walk to Puget Sound. In addition to providing a serene, natural setting, the location is ideal for outdoor sports of all kinds, from hiking to sailing. Among the school's largely liberal population, concern with the environment is one of the hot political issues, along with gay rights, women's rights, and multiculturalism.

Because Evergreen is a publicly funded college, Washington natives account for about 75 percent of the students. However, the school's non-traditional academic approach attracts many out-of-staters. The quality of the academics and facilities makes the price, for in- or out-of-state residents, a reasonably good bargain. The students and the administration hope to increase the number of minority students.

Evergreen State College

$$
★

Setting: Rural
# of Undergraduates: 3,020
Men: 42.6% **Women:** 57.4
In-State Tuition: $2,346
Out-of-State Tuition: $8,295
Room and Board: $4,470
# of Students Applied: 1,892
    Admitted: 1,587   **Enrolled:** 558
Required Admissions Test: Either SAT or ACT
Lowest 25% of Freshmen Scored At or Below: SAT Verbal: 540 SAT Math: 490   ACT Comp.: 21
Highest 25% of Freshmen Scored At or Above: SAT Verbal: 650   SAT Math: 610 ACT Comp.: 26.4
Avg. Score of Applicants Admitted: SAT Verbal: 594 SAT Math: 546   ACT Comp.: 23.7
Average GPA of Applicants Admitted: 3.13

The open-minded nature of the academic programs carries over to the social environment at the school. There's little tension among students from different backgrounds and lifestyles. The gay and lesbian population is visible and accepted. In general, Greeners are open to and respectful of all kinds of viewpoints, yet eager to question one another and themselves.

The social atmosphere is "pretty mellow," according to an Evergreen senior. Students attend movies or campus cultural events or hang out in dorm rooms, apartments, and coffeehouses. A student points out that Olympia, like Seattle a few years ago, has a thriving underground music scene.

While words like interdisciplinary and multicultural have become highly publicized catch phrases in college brochures, these concepts are as firmly rooted to Evergreen as the Washington fir trees that grace the campus.

NEW COLLEGE OF THE UNIVERSITY OF SOUTH FLORIDA IN SARASOTA, FLORIDA

Admissions Address: Admissions Office, 5700 North Tamiami Trail, Sarasota, FL 34243-2197
Phone: (941) 359-4629
Web Address: www.sar.usf.edu/nc

The New College of the University of South Florida is an experiment set apart from the main U.S.F. campus. Instead of a set curriculum with required courses, students here work closely with faculty advisors to plan a schedule suited to their personal interests. Each semester, students work out a "contract" with their faculty advisor that outlines their academic program and goals for that term. The result, a freshman says, is a "free, nonjudgmental atmosphere where creativity thrives."

Although students do eventually concentrate in a single field, they have room in their schedules to test out different subjects that interest them. In addition to the standard course offerings, students can design their own area of study in a private or small group tutorial with a professor. A separate January term, required three out of the four years, provides extra time for work on independent studies and special projects. Students don't receive letter grades, just a designation of Satisfactory or Unsatisfactory and detailed personal evaluations from their teachers. The combination of small classes, tutorials, and extensive advising means

---

New College of the Univ. of South Florida

$$
★★★

Setting: Suburban
# of Undergraduates: 596
Men: 45.8% Women: 54.2%
In-State Tuition: $2,167
Out-of-State Tuition: $8,461
Room and Board: $4,018
# of Students Applied: 650
  Admitted: 346 Enrolled: 187
Required Admissions Test: Either SAT or ACT
Recommended: None
Lowest 25% of Freshmen Scored At or Below: SAT Verbal: 640
  SAT Math: 600 ACT Comp.: 27
Highest 25% of Freshmen Scored At or Above: SAT Verbal: 740 SAT Math: 700
  ACT Comp.: 32
H.S. Rank, Top 10%: 64%
Top 25%: 93%
Top 50%: 100%
Avg. Score of Applicants Admitted: SAT Verbal: 690
  SAT Math: 649 ACT Comp.: 29
Average GPA of Applicants Admitted: 3.90
Most Popular Majors (% of Student Body): Anthropology (9.5%), Psychology (8.7%), Literature (6.5%), Biology (6.1%), Psychology (6.1%)

that students get to know most teachers personally.

The school's low tuition, especially for Florida residents, draws many to the school (some people have complained that low tuition translates to mediocre facilities). Because the curriculum is rather unstructured, students need a good deal of self-motivation to succeed here. The benefit of this unstructured system is that students can follow their own curiosity and pursue it as far as they want.

Undergraduates comment that academics at New College are rigorous and things can get stressful. The social life allows them a break, however, centering on parties known as "Walls" held outside the central courtyard. They also find some relief in the sub-tropical Florida climate, and relaxing under a palm tree has been known to calm a nerve or two. Just as they can determine their own academic programs, students here can also create their own clubs and activities. The freedom and choice given to them makes New College, as one student raved, "a creative, liberating place to be."

ST. JOHN'S COLLEGE IN ANNAPOLIS, MARYLAND, AND SANTA FE, NEW MEXICO

Admissions Address: Admissions Office, P.O. Box 2800, Annapolis, MD 21404
Phone: (800) 727-9328
Web Address: www.sjca.edu

St. John's offers one of the most innovative, and yet traditional, curriculums of any North American college. The decision to have students focus on the great ancient works—those books that influenced so much of modern thought—sounds vaguely like a *Dead Poets Society* for the entire student body. Indeed, undergraduates at both the Maryland and New Mexico campuses refer to St. John's as a very special society.

At a time when study of the canon has been de-emphasized at most campuses, St. John's students spend their four years scrutinizing the great works of Western civilization, from ancient Greece through the 20th century. The somewhat complicated curriculum is carefully mapped out to include the study of math, sciences, literature, philosophy, music, and foreign language (Greek and French only). For each subject, students go directly to the original source, reading the words of such great thinkers as Plato, Euclid, Freud, and Newton rather than having their ideas transmitted via textbooks and lecturers. Many students become so

St. John's College

$$$$$

Setting: Urban
# of Undergraduates: 438
Men: 56.8% Women: 43.2%
Tuition: $19,846
Room and Board: $5,950
# of Students Applied: 338
   Admitted: 292   Enrolled: 112
Required Admissions Test: None
Lowest 25% of Freshmen Scored
   At or Below: SAT Verbal: 610
   SAT Math: 540
Highest 25% of Freshmen
   Scored At or Above: SAT
   Verbal: 710   SAT Math: 670
H.S. Rank, Top 10%: 40%
Most Popular Majors (% of
   Student Body): Liberal Arts
   (100%)

---

engaged in the books that they spend their evenings talking about them in social settings, we are told. One sophomore reflected her enthusiasm by saying, "It's so exciting to see the historical process in the making as we read these original sources. The difficulty, sometimes, is pretending we don't know what the outcome of an idea is."

Classes are conducted as small, discussion-oriented tutorials during which everyone delves directly into the texts. The tutors, as the professors are called, ask leading questions to facilitate discussion rather than lecturing. Because the tutorials and seminars are so dependent upon discussion, students do extensive reading in preparation, and attendance is a must. "Our tutors give us a great deal of respect by valuing our ideas and encouraging us to speak out. We show our respect for them by studying hard and keeping prepared," commented a junior. Rather than traditional written examinations, students complete papers that they present and discuss in class. St. John's students don't receive grades but meet directly with their tutors for evaluation of their work.

Another unusual facet of St. John's is its dual location; although they share the same curriculum, the Santa Fe and Annapolis campuses are different in style and climate. The 35-acre Annapolis campus has an Old World academic appearance, largely because it actually is old; most of its brick buildings date to the late 1800s. The school has modernized some residence halls and academic buildings. The campus's proximity to Washington, D.C. makes trips to the nation's capital a popular activity. The 250-acre Santa Fe campus, on the other hand, opened in 1964. It's much more modern and has a distinctive Southwestern flavor, from its architectural style to its spectacular mountain and desert views. While students revile the food at both campuses, they like the closeness engendered by the compact campus arrangements.

The general atmosphere at both Annapolis and Santa Fe is that of a tight intellectual community, where you'll find students and tutors deeply engaged in scholarly discussions, inside and outside the classroom. At the same time, students find time to enjoy extracurricular and social activities, including campus-wide "waltzes" and parties. While both campuses sponsor occasional parties, alcohol is restricted to dorm rooms for those over 21. Students at the Santa Fe campus enjoy barhopping in their adobe town on weekends.

St. John's is not for everyone. The direct mode of inquiry at the college means long hours spent hitting the books; students must be willing to struggle with extremely difficult texts. Those who wish to study something other than the great works of Western Civilization will not want to apply here—student programs are predetermined until their fourth year. Even after beginning their study at St. John's, a high number of students choose not to continue. But those who do stick it out emerge as true scholars, receiving an impressive educational background while exercising and strengthening their critical abilities.

SARAH LAWRENCE COLLEGE IN BRONXVILLE, NEW YORK

Admissions Address: Admissions Office, One Mead Way, Bronxville, NY 10708
Phone: (914) 395-2510 (800) 888-2858
Web Address: www.slc.edu

The academic programs and general environment at Sarah Lawrence allow creativity and imagination to flourish. For each course, students are required to complete a substantial independent project. What form that project takes, though, is largely up to the student and can range from traditional papers to creative works. Students take only three courses a semester to provide them with the extra time necessary for work on their projects. Throughout the semester, students meet regularly with their professors in a series of one-on-one tutorial-like sessions during which they discuss their progress.

For a school whose students receive so much academic freedom, Sarah Lawrence also provides its students with an exceptional amount of advice and support from their teachers. Before registering for a course, students meet with the professor to discuss whether or not it will be appropriate for them. Students also take freshman seminars, during which they have weekly one-on-one sessions with the professor. This professor also functions as the student's academic advisor—or "don," as they're known at Sarah Lawrence—who provides guidance and structure within the somewhat structureless environment. Grades are de-emphasized to enable students to explore and experiment in a noncompetitive environment. Although grades are kept on file and can be viewed upon request, they're not considered as important to students as the detailed evaluations on their work they receive from their teachers.

The general requirements, which are relatively easy to fulfill, include one course in three areas chosen from humanities, creative and performing arts, social sciences and history, and natural sciences and math. The flexibility of the curriculum, as well as the emphasis on independent work,

---

Sarah Lawrence College

$$$$$
★★★

Setting: Suburban
# of Undergraduates: 994
Men: 25.1% Women: 74.9%
Tuition: $21,450
Room and Board: $6,902
# of Students Applied: 1,717
  Admitted: 920 Enrolled: 296
Required Admissions Test: Either SAT or ACT
Lowest 25% of Freshmen Scored At or Below: SAT Verbal: 580
  SAT Math: 520 ACT Comp.: 24
Highest 25% of Freshmen Scored At or Above: SAT Verbal: 690 SAT Math: 630
  ACT Comp.: 28
H.S. Rank, Top 10%: 35%
Top 25%: 63%
Top 50%: 92%
Avg. Score of Applicants Admitted: SAT Verbal: 640
  SAT Math: 570 ACT Comp.: 26
Average GPA of Applicants Admitted: 3.31
Most Popular Majors: Writing, Theater, Dance, Music, Psychology, Literature, Visual Arts

appeals to students working in the arts (dance, theater, and music), which are Sarah Lawrence's most popular and most acclaimed departments.

The school is known to attract an artsy, cosmopolitan student body. The men and women of Sarah Lawrence tend to be intelligent and highly creative, politically liberal, and personally nonconformist. A student we spoke with said, "I don't think I'm very representative of the student body here. But then again, nobody is representative of it. We're a diverse bunch." The campus social life reflects the eclectic tastes of the students. Students can go to any number of dance and theatre performances, attend poetry readings or concerts, or hang out at the campus pub or in dorm rooms. While freshmen live in dormitories, older students live in spacious college-owned houses on a street adjoining campus.

Students love their compact 40-acre campus, with its immaculate landscaping, grassy hills, and charming Tudor architecture. They also love that it's only a 30-minute train ride from New York City. The school itself is located in Bronxville, an upscale suburb that has some nice eateries and expensive boutiques but not much that appeals to students. When students head off-campus it's usually to Manhattan, where they can find the cultural and artistic venues, and funky bars and clubs, that are suited to their cosmopolitan tastes.

Also, Check Out These Schools:

Brown University
University of California—Santa Cruz
College of the Atlantic
Cooper Union
Hobart and William Smith Colleges
Kalamazoo College
Kenyon College
Lewis and Clark College
Oberlin College
Pitzer College
Reed College
Rhode Island School of Design
Sarah Lawrence College
Wesleyan University

Scenic Routes

After hours spent cooped up in some classroom, lab, or—heaven forbid—the library, you may find yourself desperate to get out into the fresh air. At city schools, fresh air may not be easy to come by. But at the schools listed in this chapter, you'll find fresh air in abundance.

Located in some of the most beautiful parts of the country, these schools are surrounded by breathtaking natural scenery. Their locations make these schools ideal places for participating in a number of outdoor sports. You can go jogging, biking, or take walks in a serene and scenic setting. Some schools are in prime spots for enjoying winter sports, such as skiing and skating, while others are located in warmer climates where you can go sailing and swimming year-round. Some are close to national parks and mountain ranges, where you can go climbing, camping, hiking, and white-water rafting in spectacular settings. And there are even colleges where it's possible to participate in all these activities.

To help you enjoy the great outdoors, these schools often have superb athletic and recreational facilities. Outdoor clubs at these schools will often organize trips for students throughout the year. Many schools offer wilderness and outdoor adventure programs lasting up to several weeks. Outdoor expeditions might even be an optional part of freshman orientation or a field trip for a class.

Academically, these schools also benefit from their locations. They excel in academic programs in fields that draw on the natural surroundings, such as environmental studies, natural resources, geology, oceanography, forestry, agriculture, and wildlife studies.

Then there are the emotional benefits. With the great outdoors serving as the natural backdrop for these campuses, they're among the most scenic in the country. You'll be able to work and study in a serene environment that's perfectly suited for deep contemplation.

Students who are drawn to these schools, not surprisingly, often consider themselves nature lovers and fit the "granola" stereotype, right down to their Birkenstocks. Protecting the environment is a major concern shared by these students, who become involved with politically oriented action groups related to the issue.

Some of these schools are in pretty remote and isolated regions, which is where, after all, you're most likely to find undeveloped nature at its finest. If you consider attending one of these schools, you should investigate whether there's enough activity on campus to keep you busy when you're not studying or on nature hikes. Many schools are accessible both to nature and to cities, enabling students to get a "culture fix" when they want it.

One drawback to going to any of these schools is that, if you're indeed an outdoor sports lover, you'll be tempted to blow off all your work to go have fun. After all, you'll have access to activities that most people only get to do when on vacation. You might find your skiing and surfing skills improving while your grades are slipping. With a little discipline, though, you can manage to do both. Think of heading to the slopes or the surf as a well-deserved reward for the work you accomplish.

ARIZONA STATE UNIVERSITY IN TEMPE, ARIZONA

Admissions Address: Admissions Office, 795 Livermore Street, Yellow Springs, OH 45387
Phone: (513) 767-6400 (800) 543-9436
Web Address: antioch-college.edu/

"I think we have one of the sunniest campuses in the country," an Arizona State student told us. Considering the school is located smack in the middle of the Southwestern sunbelt, ASU should have plenty of sun. Students looking to enjoy outdoor recreation will certainly find it on Arizona State's "country club" campus. The temperate weather and excellent sport and recreational facilities make outdoor activities—from golfing and tennis to swimming and suntanning—possible year-round.

There's also no shortage of academic offerings, either. The nine undergraduate schools include education, social work, nursing, architecture, arts and sciences, as well as the highly acclaimed programs in engineer-

SCENIC ROUTES

ing and fine arts that lead to 86 undergraduate programs. General requirements include courses in literacy and critical inquiry, humanities and fine arts, social and behavioral sciences, natural sciences, global awareness, and cultural diversity. The workload, a student tells us "is moderate," requiring about two hours of study time a day. ASU also has a prestigious Honors College, which provides about 1,000 qualified students with a more intensive and challenging academic experience.

With a total enrollment of about 40,000 students, of whom about 24,000 are undergraduates, ASU does have problems typically found at large schools. Classes at introductory levels can be huge, and more popular courses may be difficult to get into. Telephone registration has made registering for courses a bit less frustrating, but there are still miles of red tape students need to cut through.

Despite the school's size, a student tells us that "for the most part, the professors are really good and seem to care about the students' well being." Students also benefit from the school's resources and facilities, which are generally excellent, particularly for programs in the sciences, engineering, and performing arts.

The campus itself is fantastic, consisting of contemporary buildings surrounded by a surprising number of trees and flowers, despite the arid climate and high temperatures. Housing can be extremely tough to get, forcing most students to find off-campus apartments or move into fraternity houses. The on-campus dining offers a variety of options and types of cuisine of a quality much better, we hear, than standard college fare.

About 70 percent of the students come from Arizona, drawn by the school's low tuition and extensive academic offerings. There's already a fair-sized minority population, and the administration has recently taken specific measures to promote even greater diversity on campus.

ASU has a reputation for being a party school, and indeed, those looking for parties won't have to search far. A good time can be found at fraternities and sororities, as well as in student's dorm rooms and apartments. There's much more to the social life than partying, though. As an ASU senior told us, "A lot of people have the image of ASU as just a party school, but there are a lot of great things going on here aside from that." There are a dizzying number of clubs, organizations, and extracurricular activities. Almost all students become deeply involved in some activity outside of their classes.

Arizona State University / Main Campus

🏛🏛🏛🏛
$$
★★

Setting: Urban
# of Undergraduates: 24,159
Men: 49.4% **Women:** 50.6%
In-State Tuition: $1,940
Out-of-State Tuition: $8,308
Room and Board: $4,287
# of Students Applied: 14,374
  Admitted: 11,224 **Enrolled:** 4,245
Required Admissions Test: Either SAT I or ACT
Lowest 25% of Freshmen Scored At or Below: SAT Verbal: 480 SAT Math: 490 ACT Comp.: 20
Highest 25% of Freshmen Scored At or Above: SAT Verbal: 600 SAT Math: 600 ACT Comp.: 26
H.S. Rank, Top 10%: 24%
Top 25%: 49%
Top 50%: 82%
Avg. Score of Applicants Admitted: SAT Verbal: 540 SAT Math: 544 ACT Comp.: 23
Average GPA of Applicants Admitted: 3.20

Most ASU students are major sports fanatics. They'll show up in large numbers to cheer on their Division I teams, the Red Devils, at football and basketball games. They'll also use the school's many recreational facilities to participate in intramural sports of all kinds.

The school's locale provides even more social activities. A student praised Tempe as a "college town with lots of clubs and bars. There are also a lot of local bands that play around here." The nearby city of Phoenix offers more entertainment and culture. Having a car is a big help when it comes to exploring some of the surrounding areas. Fortunately, there's no shortage of parking.

The offerings provided by the ASU campus, facilities, and location manage to pull off a seemingly impossible feat: making it possible for almost every one of the many students to find some activity they enjoy.

UNIVERSITY OF ALASKA IN FAIRBANKS, ALASKA

Admissions Address: Admissions Office, 2nd Floor Signers, P.O. Box 757480, Fairbanks, AK 99775
Phone: (907) 474-7500
Web Address: www.uaf.edu

When many nonnative Alaskans head north for college, they envision themselves befriending eccentric but warmhearted locals and studying by the glow of the Northern Lights. Not prepared for the realities of long, dark, subzero winters, a large percentage drop out. Those who truly love the outdoors, though, will not be disappointed: The campus of the University of Alaska, overlooking the city of Fairbanks, is surrounded by the stunning wilderness of the Last Frontier.

This is the place to go to enjoy winter sports of all kinds, from ice skating to ice climbing and from skiing to snowshoeing. "Our favorite sport here is dogsled racing," a sophomore told us. "There's a big competition called the Yukon Quest. Part of the trail for the race goes right through Fairbanks." Hockey is their leading intercollegiate sport, competing in Division I, and attending games is a major form of entertainment for students. The hockey team was recently admitted to the Central Collegiate Hockey Association, promising more intense and competitive games. Basketball is a favorite spectator and participant sport as well; one freshman said that students play for hours at a stretch.

In terms of academics, many UAF programs—particularly those related

SCENIC ROUTES

to the Alaskan environment and local wildlife—draw on the location. The general education requirements include courses in English, oral communication, library skills, natural science, math, social science, and humanities. Students praise the "one-on-one contact" they receive from professors and counselors. One student said biology is the of the biggest majors, and a new, state-of-the-art natural science facility offers expanded opportunities.

In addition to taking advantage of the spectacular natural surroundings, students enjoy a number of campus activities and social events, including movies, dances, student performances and concerts, and several extracurricular activities and clubs. We're told there is a relaxed social life, between hanging out in the main student center or attending small, informal parties at dorm rooms and apartments. A program to renovate all residence halls will be completed by 1999, and all classrooms and dorms are being networked. The university recently completed a student recreation center that offers a multitude of activities including a climbing wall, aerobics areas, and a full-size indoor track.

The majority of the student body is from Alaska, although students do come from other parts of the country, primarily the Northwest. There's also a large percentage of Native American and Eskimo students. The students are generally a closely knit and friendly bunch, which is a comfort that helps get everyone through the winter. The extreme cold, relative isolation, and darkness of winter can be trying. One student told us that by the time she walks the three minutes it takes to get from her dorm to her classes, her breath is already frozen to her face! But if you do go to the University of Alaska, you're rewarded with spectacular wilderness views and the unique chance to live in our northernmost state.

University of Alaska / Fairbanks

$$
★★

Setting: Suburban
# of Undergraduates: 3,675
Men: 49.6% **Women:** 50.4
In-State Tuition: $2,160
Out-of-State Tuition: $6,480
Room and Board: $3,790
# of Students Applied: 1,460
  Admitted: 1,147 **Enrolled:** 667
Required Admissions Test: Either SAT or ACT
H.S. Rank, Top 10%: 5%
Top 25%: 15%
Top 50%: 42%
Avg. Score of Applicants Admitted: SAT Verbal: 457
  SAT Math: 486 ACT Comp.: 20
Average GPA of Applicants Admitted: 2.95
Most Popular Majors (% of Student Body): Education (3.4%), Business Administration (2.9%), Biology Sciences (2.5%), Civil Engineering (1.4%), English (1.2%)

UNIVERSITY OF COLORADO—BOULDER

Admissions Address: Admissions Office, Administrative Center, 125 Regent Drive, Boulder, CO 80309-0030
Phone: (303) 492-6301
Web Address: www.colorado.edu/

When people talk about the most scenic locations in the United States, the Rocky Mountains are right up there with the Grand Canyon and Mount Rushmore. Well, there's no college located in the Canyon, but there is one at the foot of the Rockies. Students at the University of Colorado at Boulder are surrounded by breathtaking mountain views that many people see only on postcards.

369

University of Colorado/Boulder

$$

★★

Setting: Urban
# of Undergraduates: 18,039
Men: 52.1% Women: 47.9%
In-State Tuition: $2,369
Out-of-State Tuition: $13,914
Room and Board: $4,370
# of Students Applied: 14,850
  Admitted: 11,860 Enrolled: 3,952
Required Admissions Test: Either SAT or ACT
Lowest 25% of Freshmen Scored At or Below: SAT Verbal: 530 SAT Math: 540 ACT Comp.: 23
Highest 25% of Freshmen Scored At or Above: SAT Verbal: 630 SAT Math: 640 ACT Comp.: 28
H.S. Rank, Top 10%: 25%
Top 25%: 59%
Top 50%: 93%
Most Popular Majors (% of Student Body): Psychology (6%), Environmental Biology (5%), Molecular Biology (4%), Kinesiology (4%), English (3%)

As you might guess, UC's location, accessible to some of the best skiing in the country, is a major draw. UC students love to ski, and they ski often, taking advantage of student discounts at nearby ski resorts. Skiing and snowboarding, however, aren't the only outdoor activities popular at UC. Hiking, rock climbing, jogging, biking, and mountain biking are all popular UC student pastimes.

With more than 25,000 students, UC is obviously a pretty big university. Then again, the west is big sky country and the number of academic offerings reflect the school's size. There are several undergraduate schools including business, engineering and applied science, environmental design, music, and arts and sciences. Among undergraduates, the preprofessional programs and departments have large enrollments and are among the school's best offerings, particularly in business, engineering, and premed sciences. Although each school has its own admissions and distribution requirements, general requirements include writing and foreign-language proficiency, as well as courses that demonstrate critical thinking and cultural diversity.

UC students must wrangle with the typical challenges of attending a large school, including administrative procedures that can be trying, to say the least. Many classes, particularly at the introductory levels, will be large and crowded, but they usually break into smaller sections, labs, or study groups corralled by teaching assistants. Professors have to divide their attention among so many students that they may not know everyone by name. Students who make it a point to seek out and get to know their teachers usually find them helpful and friendly.

Fortunately, the breathtaking environment and chance for physical activity alleviates much of the stress associated with attending a big school. The UC campus is considered one of the most gorgeous in the country, and not only because of the natural backdrop. The 600-acre campus is encircled by stunning scenery, and its pleasing layout and architecture contribute to its overall beauty.

When nature fails to provide stress relief, students have a more direct approach. One student told us that on the night before finals begin, "everyone hangs out their windows yelling and banging on pots and pans. We're just letting off steam before the more intense work begins."

As a research-oriented institution, UC provides its students and faculty with high-quality facilities and equipment, particularly in the science-related fields. Other major facilities on campus include an enormous student center and athletic complex with an indoor pool, ice rink, and tennis and racquetball courts. The dormitories range in size and quality, the most recent and reportedly the most accommodating being Kitteridge Dormitory. Many students move off campus after their first year.

More than half the student body is from Colorado, taking advantage of the exceptionally low tuition. The outdoor opportunities, academic programs, and idyllic campus make the school attractive to plenty of out-of-state residents as well, despite having to pay a more hefty tuition. The remainder of the students hail from California and the East Coast.

The student body includes a 15 percent minority population. Students lean heavily to the left and are vocal about their political views and beliefs, especially when it comes to environmental issues. Most students share a common love of the outdoors that also makes them a generally friendly and cohesive group. "I think we're all a bunch of granolas," one student reported, "though some more obviously than others."

Physical activities and outdoor sports are unquestionably the focus of most students' lives outside the classroom. Students can join any number of clubs whose members share an interest in a particular activity. Intramural and intercollegiate sports are very popular. Students pack UC's stadium for football games, especially against main rival Nebraska.

UC students enjoy an active social life. Almost 20 percent of the students go Greek, which makes the fraternity and sorority presence strong enough to provide social events and parties, but not so big that it completely takes over the campus. In addition to Greek-sponsored events, there are often more intimate parties held in rooms or off-campus apartments. The school's many clubs and organizations provide smaller social circles. A sophomore told us, "I was homesick when I started out here, but I joined a club and it's great. I have met a lot of people who share my interests. Some of the older students were very helpful to me."

Boulder is an ideal college town, with a pedestrian strip lined with trendy cafes, shops, restaurants, and bars that support an active local music scene. Each year the town and the UC campus both host a number of cultural events, festivals, and conferences.

UC students are blessed in more ways than one with their school's location. They live close to nature, but by no means are they isolated.

Boulder is a city, and Denver is an easy 30-minute trip away. Students can get all the big-city culture and excitement they want without having to sacrifice peace, quiet, or freshly packed powder.

UNIVERSITY OF HAWAII IN MANOA

Admissions Address: Admissions Office, 2600 Campus Road, Room 001, Honolulu, HI 96822-9978
Phone: (808) 948-8975
Web Address: www.hawaii.edu/uhinfo.html

Located within miles of the famed surfing beaches of Waikiki, the University of Hawaii at Manoa offers the recreational activities of a vacation resort, and in large quantities. Most students attending the school, though, are Hawaiian residents and not mainlanders looking for a four-year vacation.

The high cost of living and expensive flights back and forth to the continent keep the out-of-state student population at a minimum. Those who do hail from the other 49 states usually come for specific programs that draw on the school's location, such as marine biology, tropical agriculture, Asian and Pacific studies, and tourist-related management. "That, and the great beaches," said one mainland junior.

As the major research institution of the University of Hawaii system, the Manoa campus offers many academic programs in its 13 undergraduate schools, including programs in business, education, engineering, health science, architecture, and physical science. While students do enjoy their tropical campus and the sport and recreational activities it affords, the workload isn't necessarily all paradise. There are stiff, general-education requirements that can take up to two years to fulfill. Students are required to take courses in expository writing, math, world civilization, arts and humanities, natural and social sciences, and a foreign language.

The facilities on the campus vary significantly in quality, although the school does seem to be making some improvements. The university's housing tries to accommodate many students and can be very crowded. The Towers are large and in good condition, but the rooms themselves aren't terribly spacious. Many students search for off-campus housing which, while available, can be very pricey in a tourist-trade city.

However, the athletic facilities are exceptional and, not surprisingly, athletics are a major part of student life. The intercollegiate games are usu-

---

University of Hawaii / Manoa

$$
★★

Setting: Urban
# of Undergraduates: 10,098
Men: 45.4% **Women:** 54.6%
In-State Tuition: $2,832
Out-of-State Tuition: $9,312
Room and Board: $4,528
# of Students Applied: 4,094
  Admitted: 2,640 **Enrolled:** 1,437
Required Admissions Test: Either SAT or ACT
Recommended: SAT
Lowest 25% of Freshmen Scored At or Below: SAT Verbal: 470 SAT Math: 510
Highest 25% of Freshmen Scored At or Above: SAT Verbal: 580 SAT Math: 610
H.S. Rank, Top 10%: 34%
Top 25%: 68%
Top 50%: 92%
Avg. Score of Applicants Admitted: SAT Verbal: 518 SAT Math: 566
Average GPA of Applicants Admitted: 3.30
Most Popular Majors (% of Student Body): Psychology (4%), Elementary Education (3%), Secondary Education (2%), Civil Engineering (2%), General Business (2%)

ally well attended, especially football games waged against archrival Brigham Young. The school's baseball, basketball, football, swimming, and volleyball teams have all done well and draw respectable crowds. The general atmosphere of the school is friendly and relaxed, as befits a tropical paradise. One student summed up the attitude of her fellow classmates: "I can't imagine a friendlier group of people."

A substantial majority of the students are of Asian descent; white students account for less than 25 percent. Other than major games and the Hawaiian music festival, most social activities don't draw huge crowds. Instead, students go to some fraternity parties and small dorm or apartment parties or head to popular off-campus hangouts. They also can take advantage of the entertainment offerings of Honolulu.

And yes, a number close their books and head for the surf.

UNIVERSITY OF MIAMI IN CORAL GABLES, FLORIDA

Admissions Address: Office of Admission, P.O. Box 248025, Coral Gables, FL 33124-4616
Phone: (305) 284-4323 (305) 284-2211
Web Address: www.ashe.miami.edu

When you look at pictures in the University of Miami brochure—Mediterranean-style buildings around a picturesque lake, palm trees swaying in the wind—you might mistake it for Club Med. Of course, not every day at the University of Miami is as picture perfect as the ones depicted in the brochure, (hence the school team, the Hurricanes) but you'll get more chances to do your impersonation of a NASA solar panel here than, say, Beantown.

Yet there's more to the University of Miami than Florida sunshine. Miami offers a variety of academic programs, from one of the most renowned marine biology programs in the country to an esteemed music department. The school excels in preprofessional areas that are most popular with undergraduates. There are also noteworthy special academic options, including several dual-degree programs for selected students in such fields as law, business, medicine, and engineering; an honors program in which 1,800 qualified students study in a more intimate academic environment; and an extensive study-abroad program. The importance of academics is growing here. One student told us, "There really isn't a 'party school' mentality. I think the caliber of students they're attracting is much better. I don't think of this as 'Suntan U' anymore."

University of Miami

$$$$$
★★★

Setting: Suburban
# of Undergraduates: 7,359
Tuition: $18,220
Room and Board: $7,101
# of Students Applied: 10,112
   Admitted: 6,107   Enrolled: 1,708
Required Admissions Test: SAT I or ACT
Lowest 25% of Freshmen Scored At or Below: SAT Verbal: 510 SAT Math: 510   ACT Comp.: 21
Highest 25% of Freshmen Scored At or Above: SAT Verbal: 620   SAT Math: 630   ACT Comp.: 27
H.S. Rank, Top 10%: 42%
Top 25%: 71%
Top 50%: 93%
Average GPA of Applicants Admitted: 3.70
Most Popular Majors (% of Student Body): Business Administration (8.4%), Biology (5.5%), Psychology (3.94%), Business Management (2.29%), Accounting (1.55%)

The requirements differ according to the student's school as well as his or her chosen major. Most students are required to take courses in writing, natural and social science, history, humanities, and a foreign language. Generally, the workload for courses is heavy enough to prevent students from becoming complete beach bums. Serious about their studies and their future careers, most students put in a decent amount of study time per week.

As a large research university, Miami does have some of the problems typical of big schools, including large lecture courses and professors who are more interested in their research than their students. Many of these problems, however, aren't as bad as at some of the more enormous universities. In fact, most courses at Miami will have fewer than 25 students, who are then able to receive more individual attention from the professor. Students also benefit from the school's many quality facilities and resources. Due to fundraising drives and substantial donations, the school has been able to invest in expanding and improving the campus facilities. An upper-level student said, "for the most part you're able to talk to professors. You'll find some that really care about students—especially business professors. They'll share their real-world business experiences with you." The same student said her impression of the college of arts and sciences professors were that they were more concerned with publishing.

The unique housing system also helps the university feel more like a small college. Students live in one of five residential colleges, each housing a senior faculty member. Each college forms its own community hosting social, cultural, and educational programs and events. Although the college housing system is praised by students, many do eventually move off campus as quality housing is readily found in surrounding areas.

Miami also has a diverse student body. The substantial international and minority population, making up almost half the student body, includes a large Hispanic population. Although more than half the students are from Florida, the rest come from all parts of the country and from over 100 foreign countries. Several organizations and events are devoted to fostering cross-cultural encounters, including a week-long international festival.

Miami students enjoy a social life that draws on many of the school's assets. Sports are extremely popular, both to play and to watch. When you hear students talking about the "Canes," they don't mean sugar cane, candy canes, or dancing with Fred Astaire, but the Hurricanes, the name of their sports teams. To begin with, all native Floridians are born with football in their veins. While this may make circulation difficult, it also makes them more and more ravenous for college ball as they progress through the education system. Miami's Hurricanes won the national championship several times, and students are rabidly devoted followers, filling the stands of the Orange Bowl to cheer and show their school spirit, especially for the big rival game against Florida State. Miami has several successful intercollegiate teams, including the men's baseball team recent winners of the College World Series and women's basketball. One student tells us tennis is also very popular now.

On campus, there's no shortage of spots to hang out and relax, from the school's student center—complete with bowling alley, pool tables, and Ping-Pong—to the campus pub, known as the Rathskeller. Then there's the outdoor pool, perfect for suntanning, swimming and—for some—studying.

The Greek system, while not the only form of social activity, contributes to the school's social scene; about 10–15 percent of the students go Greek, so it doesn't dominate the social scene. Greek week games are fun and well attended, according to one frat member.

The school's location also makes a number of excellent off-campus attractions available to students, although having a car makes them much more accessible. Beach lovers can easily get to some of Florida's finest sands. The city of Miami has all the cultural and social offerings of a major city, including restaurants, music clubs, and stores. Students also have easy access to the funky Coconut Grove and affluent South Beach areas. As for crime worries, several students told us that while the city itself may be bad, the area around the school is pretty safe, requiring only the amount of vigilance necessary in any other American suburb.

While their friends at other schools hope to squeeze in a chance to do some tanning, swimming, and pool lounging during their spring break, University of Miami students have the chance to make every week like spring break. Miami students work hard and receive a strong education, but if you can study outside under a palm tree as easily as in the library, why not?

UNIVERSITY OF PUGET SOUND IN TACOMA, WASHINGTON

Admissions Address: Admissions Office, 1500 North Warner Street, Tacoma, WA 98416-0062
Phone: (206) 756-3211 (800) 396-7191
Web Address: www.ups.edu

University of Puget Sound

$$$$$

Setting: Urban
# of Undergraduates: 2,675
Men: 42.2% Women: 57.8%
Tuition: $17,450
Room and Board: $4,720
# of Students Applied: 4,112
   Admitted: 3,204 Enrolled: 658
Required Admissions Test: Either SAT I or ACT
Lowest 25% of Freshmen Scored At or Below: SAT Verbal: 550 SAT Math: 540 ACT Comp.: 24
Highest 25% of Freshmen Scored At or Above: SAT Verbal: 650 SAT Math: 650 ACT Comp.: 28
H.S. Rank, Top 10%: 44%
Top 25%: 76%
Top 50%: 97%
Avg. Score of Applicants Admitted: SAT Verbal: 607 SAT Math: 604 ACT Comp.: 26
Average GPA of Applicants Admitted: 3.55
Most Popular Majors (% of Student Body): Business (15%), English (11%), Humanities (18%), Biological Sciences (13%), Psychology (9%)

Located directly between the mountains and ocean, the forest and the coastline, the University of Puget Sound is in a perfect spot for taking advantage of the diverse activities made possible by the natural beauty of Washington State. UPS students can head for the Puget Sound for such activities as windsurfing, water skiing, and sailing. They can also trek in the opposite direction, toward the majestic Mt. Rainier Park and surrounding areas that are ideal for hiking, climbing, camping, and observing wildlife.

In addition to providing an abundance of outdoor activities, the surroundings make the UPS campus, with its panoramic views of distant natural scenery, one of the most picturesque in the country. Don't think nature is only to be found off in the great wide-open; the campus itself has expanses of green and areas laden with Washington firs.

One of the best experiences UPS students have is the freshman orientation "passages" week, when they are trundled off en masse to campgrounds on the Olympic Peninsula. "It was great," one student said; "The best friends I have here are the ones I met that week."

If the weather or schedules don't permit outdoor activities, students can amuse themselves on the climbing wall, amongst other features, in the Outdoor Adventure Residence Hall.

UPS is one of the strongest liberal arts schools in the Pacific Northwest. It has highly regarded programs in many academic fields, particularly in the sciences. All students receive solid liberal arts backgrounds beginning with a stiff core curriculum. Students are required to take courses in written and oral communication, mathematical reasoning, historical perspectives, humanistic perspectives, comparative values, international studies, fine arts, science in context, and natural world studies. There are also several special academic options, including a highly selective honors program, and opportunities to study abroad. Administrators see the school as a great stepping stone into the Pacific Rim business community, and have structured programs to take advantage of the growing international economy in Washington State.

"The workload is very challenging. We all study quite a bit here," a student told us. Class sizes are small, and students need to be prepared to participate; you never know when you might be called on by name. The small classes also mean that most professors are able to get to know their students individually. Students we spoke to praised the faculty for being not only available but also "open, friendly, and easy to talk to."

While facilities vary in quality, they're improving significantly as the school continues to invest its endowment in renovation and construction. Recent improvements have included additions to the science facilities (including a unique paleomagnetic animal physiology lab), and expansion and renovation of performance spaces for the music and theatre programs (including a 500-seat concert hall); major additions and improvements are also underway for the sports facilities.

First-year students are required to live on campus in dorms that, typical of the freshman experience, are noisy and crowded. Upperclassmen have more options, including moving into a university-owned house with a group of friends. Many of the houses center on themes, including four foreign-language houses, as well as several for students with common interests. Groups of students can apply to start new theme houses.

One student told us that the best thing about the school is that "everyone is very open to new things and taking risks. This creates a very comfortable community." For a long time, UPS students have had the reputation of being mostly wealthy and conservative. One liberal student told us that this image stems from "some very vocal, very conservative students who make a ruckus." The same student pointed out the presence of a strong coalition of Asian, Black, and Hispanic students, and other efforts being made to increase the diversity of the student body. One student told us "I think we come from all around the country."

On campus, students enjoy a number of events, including student performances, concerts, and theatre productions. The university's student-run radio station is also very popular.

Greek life is an important part of the social scene on campus and draws more than one-third of the students. Other campus social events include dance formals and an extravagant Homecoming festival. A student told us that beyond the Greek system, the social life centers on Seattle, only about half an hour away. Seattle has a number of social and cultural options, including a thriving music scene and, of course, more coffee shops than you could shake a cinnamon stick at.

THE ROAD TO COLLEGE

UNIVERSITY OF VERMONT IN BURLINGTON, VERMONT

Admissions Address: Admissions Office, 194 South Prospect Street, Burlington, VT 05401-3596
Phone: (802) 656-3370
Web Address: www.uvm.edu/

University of Vermont

$$$

Setting: Suburban
# of Undergraduates: 6,945
Men: 46% **Women:** 54%
In-State Tuition: $6,732
Out-of-State Tuition: $16,824
Room and Board: $4,706
# of Students Applied: 8,578
   Admitted: 6,469 **Enrolled:** 1,799
Required Admissions Test: Either SAT or ACT
Lowest 25% of Freshmen Scored At or Below: SAT Verbal: 520 SAT Math: 510
Highest 25% of Freshmen Scored At or Above: SAT Verbal: 610 SAT Math: 610
H.S. Rank, Top 10%: 15%
Top 25%: 49%
Top 50%: 90%
Avg. Score of Applicants Admitted: SAT Verbal: 579 SAT Math: 583
Most Popular Majors (% of Student Body): Business Administration (9%), Biology (6%), Psychology (6%), English (5%), Political Science (4%)

The University of Vermont has a reputation for being one of the biggest party schools in the country. There's no doubt that UVM students know how to have a good time, but their fun isn't found only at keg parties. With such natural scenery as the Green Mountains, Lake Champlain, and major ski resorts including Stowe and Sugarbush nearby, Vermont is a haven of outdoor activities of all kinds.

In addition to the superb skiing, students enjoy sports such as climbing, hiking, mountain biking, rafting, and kayaking, just to name a few. At the same time, Burlington is a small city high in New England charm as well as culture and entertainment. Students can frequent a number of bars, restaurants, galleries, shops, dance clubs, and movie theatres. A sophomore summed it up by saying, "It's great. I can go skiing all weekend and still be at school when I have to."

UVM's eight undergraduate colleges include agriculture and life sciences, business, health, education, engineering and math, natural resources, and arts and sciences. Requirements vary by school. Arts and sciences, the largest school at UVM, has a core curriculum including study in humanities, natural and social sciences, and courses in non-European culture.

Preprofessional majors, such as business, management and premedicine, all have large enrollments. UVM's strongest programs are generally considered to be in the sciences and environmental fields, which benefit from the surrounding natural resources and wildlife. In addition to these academic programs, interest in nature and the environment at UVM is evident in other ways. A number of students are nature buffs who make the environment a major political issue. There's a large, active student organization devoted to the protection of the environment, as well as a special-interest house for students who share these concerns.

UVM has an innovative academic program called the Living Learning Center that combines course work with field trips and independent study. Groups of students with common interests share suites, study together, and help one another with independent projects.

UVM is a medium-sized, research-oriented university. That means it's large enough to have some of the typical problems plaguing big schools—such as overcrowded classes, problems getting into select courses, messy registration procedures, and miles of red tape for any administrative request—yet small enough to be more manageable than schools with enrollments in the tens of thousands.

While UVM has made efforts to promote ethnic and cultural diversity, the student body remains predominantly white. Many students come from the Northeast. While not ethnically diverse, the student body is diverse in other ways; the school's location, facilities, and social life attract an interesting mixture of hippies, granolas, nature lovers, and jocks. While stricter drinking laws have tamed the wild party scene, parties can still be found in abundance at UVM, including the massive event that is UVM's Oktoberfest weekend. Fraternities and sororities account for much of the social activity, hosting parties not only for their own members but some open to all students.

Unlike at some other reputed party schools, however, the Greeks don't dominate the party scene at UVM. Students converge in dorm rooms, apartments, and off-campus hangouts. There are many school-sponsored social events and activities, including movies, concerts, and plays, as well as special social events. Keeping with current university trends, UVM recently installed a climbing wall in their university center. Also, oddly enough, one of the most popular hangouts on campus is a center called "the Wall." A bonus found only at UVM is the Club Cabin, a mountain getaway owned by the university that is available to students and student clubs for retreats, getaways, or for use as a jumping-off point for additional ski slopes.

In addition to parties, students are also interested in athletics. All UVM students have a physical education requirement but are hardly pressed for ways to fulfill it. Intercollegiate and intramural sports are both popular. Although there's no football team, the hockey team more than makes up for it; the well-attended hockey games provide a forum for UVM students to express their school spirit—loudly.

It's telling that well over half the UVM students are from out of state and are willing to pay the higher tuition for nonnatives. With strong academic programs in a variety of fields, gorgeous natural surroundings, and plenty of opportunities for socializing and skiing, UVM has a lot that makes it appealing.

ALSO, CHECK OUT THESE SCHOOLS:

Bates College
Bennington College
Bowdoin College
Brigham Young University
University of California—Davis
University of California—Los Angeles
University of California—San Diego
University of California—Santa Barbara
University of California—Santa Cruz
Colby College
Colgate University
College of the Atlantic
Colorado College
Dartmouth College
Evergreen State College
Hampshire College
Lewis and Clark College
Middlebury College
University of Oregon
Pennsylvania State University
University of Puget Sound
Reed College
St. John's College (NM)
University of Southern California
Sweet Briar College
University of Washington

Serious Fun

When you hear about party schools with notorious reputations, certain images come to mind: drunken orgies that last all week long. Students regaining consciousness wearing other people's underwear. Groups streaking across the central quad in the middle of winter. Outrageous fraternity pranks involving livestock.

In contrast to these popular images of wild times on campus, the reality is that schools are employing strict alcohol-enforcement policies. Increased awareness of the health risks involved with alcohol and drugs has also led many students to find other forms of social activity. But a February 1996 survey by the American Medical association found that the level of drinking prevalent among young adults is very high. The AMA found that one in five 18- to 30-year-olds regularly engage in "binge" drinking (more than four drinks in one session for women, or five for men).

Many schools continue to have crazed social scenes where, as students told us, "the weekend lasts all week long." Students at these schools told us that the alcohol policies don't prevent students from drinking, especially at off-campus parties and events. But they also told us that there's little pressure to drink, and many students choose to abstain. Because of a generally festive social atmosphere at these schools, you can enjoy just as fun and frenzied a social life without necessarily drinking heavily.

The social focal point of many party schools is an active Greek system that sometimes draws more than half the student body. Fraternities and sororities provide members with a close group of friends and an instantaneous social life. As one student said of his fraternity, "One of the best things about it is that it gives you a family away from home." Members regularly participate in a number of social events, such as movie nights, pub nights, barbecues, and semiformal and formal dances. In addition to hosting smaller, invitation-only parties, most houses also throw large, open parties, where you'll find dancing, music, and crowds of students singing "Burning Down the House" and "Louie, Louie." Of course, joining a fraternity or sorority provides members with more than just the chance to party all the time. Sometimes, joining a fraternity or sorority also means you get a decent place to live and an above-average dining plan. Houses also offer you a chance to become involved in house activities, from intramural sports to house government to community service and volunteer work. When you graduate, you become part of a strong alumni network whose members help one another with their careers and social advancement throughout their lives.

Each fraternity and sorority tends to have its own personality and reputation that you'll quickly pick up once you arrive on campus. During a rush period, you can visit various houses to find one where you think you'll fit in. Then it's up to the members of the house to decide whether or not to invite you to pledge. Sometimes the competition to get into more popular houses can be tough.

At schools with active Greek systems there's often a great deal of pressure to join a house. Students who don't rush or don't get into a house might feel like outsiders, unless they become involved in some other social activity or organization. If you are considering a school with a strong Greek presence but don't want to rush yourself, you might want to investigate the other social options available. Many students who choose not to pledge often feel they benefit from the Greek presence at their schools because they can attend a number of large parties.

Another major form of social life at these schools centers on intercollegiate sporting events. Many well-known party schools have powerhouse sports teams that are strongly followed by student fans. Games are attended by most of the student body and therefore become parties in their own right. Students will get together before the game at tailgate parties and at post-game celebrations. Partying reaches a peak at Homecoming, when games are against arch-rivals or involve championship titles.

The social scene at some party schools draws heavily on the surrounding areas. When schools are located in or near major cities that have a thriving night life, students can head off-campus in search of clubs, bars, and hangouts.

SERIOUS FUN

But it's not just fraternities or sports or the night life that make a school a party school. More than anything, it depends on the students themselves. These are schools where, quite simply, students generally like to have a good time. They find ways to have fun practically anywhere at anytime. Just about every spot on campus, from grassy quads to dorm rooms to library study areas, becomes a social hangout.

With so many social temptations, it can be all too easy to forget that you're supposed to be getting an education. Many of these schools earned a reputation in the past because of supposedly easy workloads that gave students plenty of time for partying. In an effort to become more competitive, however, most of these schools have since revamped their academic programs. Out went many of the fluff courses and easy-grading policies, and in came stiff course requirements and tougher admissions standards. These schools now offer exceptional academic programs, superb facilities, and renowned faculties.

As a result, you can receive a solid education at these schools, although it may not be easy. With all those social distractions and temptations it can be hard to focus on work and studying. Both the social life and academic experience will truly be what you make of it. The students we spoke to told us that some students blow off work or take easy "gut" courses so they can party all the time, while others slave away, at least during the week, and wait until the weekends to party. "It's a question of having the weekend start Monday night or Thursday night," a student told us. Either way, though, you do get a weekend. And if you go to one of these schools, you're guaranteed it will be an eventful one.

LEHIGH UNIVERSITY IN BETHLEHEM, PENNSYLVANIA

Admissions Address: Admissions Office, 27 Memorial Drive West, Bethlehem, PA 18015-3094
Phone: (610) 758-3100
Web Address: www.lehigh.edu/

Lehigh must be doing something right. A high percentage of graduating students go on to law and medical schools or pursue other successful careers. Just ask Lee Iacocca, one Lehigh graduate who managed to do okay for himself.

"In general, our partying doesn't take away from studying and class time," a Lehigh junior told us. "We work pretty hard," said another, "but with that we earn the right to enjoy ourselves too."

383

Lehigh University

$$$$$
★★★

Setting: Urban
# of Undergraduates: 4,232
Men: 62.2% **Women:** 37.8%
Tuition: $21,350
Room and Board: $6,220
# of Students Applied: 7,178
   Admitted: 3,899 **Enrolled:** 1,101
Required Admissions Test: Either SAT or ACT
Recommended: Either
Lowest 25% of Freshmen Scored At or Below: SAT Verbal: 546 SAT Math: 579
Highest 25% of Freshmen Scored At or Above: SAT Verbal: 632 SAT Math: 671
H.S. Rank, Top 10%: 43%
Top 25%: 78%
Top 50%: 98%
Avg. Score of Applicants Admitted: SAT Verbal: 590 SAT Math: 625
Most Popular Majors (% of Student Body): Mechanical Engineering (5.2%), Civil Engineering (4%), Industrial Engineering (3.8%), Finance (3.6%), Psychology (2.9%)

When they're not enjoying their school's busy party scene, Lehigh students are immersed in a varied and intense academic program. Lehigh's particular strengths are the School of Engineering and Applied Science and the School of Business and Economics. The College of Arts and Science is the largest undergraduate school and has several notable departments, including architecture, biology, government, English, and psychology. Each school has its own requirements. The study time depends on the department and major, but many students have heavy workloads, especially in engineering courses.

Lehigh is Lafayette's archrival, and like most nemeses, the two are more similar than either would like to admit. Both offer strong academics and major party scenes in scenic Pennsylvania settings. However, there are significant differences as well. Unlike Lafayette, Lehigh has a few graduate schools. Undergraduates benefit from access to these facilities, and qualified students can enroll in accelerated graduate degree programs. Lehigh also has a larger student enrollment. As a result, some introductory classes can have several hundred students that break down in weekly discussion sections led by graduate students. Upper-level courses are significantly smaller.

The expansive, 1,600-acre campus is situated on the side of a hill, providing both a view as well as a serious aerobic workout for any student trekking from classes to dormitories. The style of campus buildings varies from traditional ivy-covered to institutional, to contemporary structures.

We heard no complaints about the housing (outside of the usual freshman song of "small, cramped, noisy"). The housing differs in arrangement, including a few residential colleges, a number of special-interest theme houses, and school-owned apartments. No quiet little town, Bethlehem is an industrial city that doesn't offer much to attract students. One student told us his main complaint about the school was that it was difficult to get to Philadelphia without a car because of the lack of public transportation.

The Lehigh student body is largely white, wealthy, and conservative. Men outnumber women about two to one. Students primarily come from the Northeast. Their strong sense of school spirit helps create a family-like student body in which everyone works together and plays together. As one student told us, "the best thing about the school is the people. The faculty and the students are down-to-earth and genuine."

At this social campus, Lehigh students like to hang out and relax just about everywhere, from their dormitories to fraternities to their dry campus pub. About one-third of the students join the 28 fraternities and 8 sororities, and the Greeks make certain there's no shortage of parties. On campus, alcohol policies are strict and the administration's efforts to control the party scene have been a major issue, so most parties are held off campus. One student said they understand the administration's concern, but they want to enjoy their college fun while it lasts.

If they're worn out from parties, students can attend many other campus events, including movies, live music, comedians, and cultural events, or become involved in one of the many clubs and organizations. Intramural and intercollegiate sports are both popular. Most Lehigh games are attended by raucous fans. If you really want to see Lehigh school pride in full force, check out the annual "big football game" against Lafayette.

SOUTHERN METHODIST UNIVERSITY IN DALLAS, TEXAS

Admissions Address: Admissions Office, Dallas, TX 75275-0296
Phone: (214) 768-2058 (800) 323-0672
Web Address: www.smu.edu

According to one graduate, the Southern Methodist University campus is "a jewel in the midst of Dallas," and not only because of its beautiful, traditionally collegiate campus. The rich variety of academic programs, from a top-ranked business school to an acclaimed theater and art school, combine with a thriving student social scene to make SMU a real gem. A junior told us, "this is a real friendly campus. People are genuinely concerned with your well-being—that's the faculty, staff and other students. It makes college a real good experience."

SMU has four undergraduate schools: the school of business and management, engineering and applied science, humanities and science, and fine art. Many students are on a preprofessional track, and the undergraduate schools offer strong programs in several areas that prepare students for career success, particularly in the highly rated school of business and management. Considered one of the best schools in the country for performing and theater arts, the Meadows School of Art utilizes first-rate facilities, including The Bob Hope Theater, the Greer Garson Theater, and an art museum that boasts a fine collection of Goya's works. The school counts many well-known artists, performers, and theater

Southern Methodist University

$$$$$
★

Setting: Urban
# of Undergraduates: 5,006
Men: 46.7% **Women:** 53.3%
Tuition: $16,790
Room and Board: $6,109
# of Students Applied: 3,924
   Admitted: 3,514 **Enrolled:** 1,218
Required Admissions Test: Either SAT or ACT
H.S. Rank, Top 10%: 35%
Top 25%: 71%
Top 50%: 89%
Avg. Score of Applicants
   Admitted: SAT Verbal: 510–630
   SAT Math: 520–640   ACT Comp.: 21–27
Average GPA of Applicants
   Admitted: 3.20
Most Popular Majors: Business, Finance, Psychology, Advertising, Political Science

practitioners among its alumni, including Academy Award winner Kathy Bates and Pulitzer Prize–winning playwright Beth Henley. The English, history, natural sciences, and psychology departments at Dedman College, the liberal arts school, are also excellent.

SMU's curriculum is designed to accommodate students' individual interests within structural guidelines. Students take specific classes, such as writing seminars and courses in race, ethnicity, and gender, as well as longer sequences in their chosen disciplines. Most students are required to include a liberal arts minor in addition to their major field of study. There are several special academic options available to qualified students, including dual degrees, interdisciplinary majors, self-designed majors, study abroad, and even field work at the school's New Mexico campus. Dallas offers students many opportunities to gain work experiences and find internships.

As SMU is not a terribly large university, students are able to interact a great deal with their professors. "Students and professors have a real one-on-one relationship here, which makes SMU a better learning environment," a junior told us. Small classes and a low student-faculty ratio enable students to receive a great deal of attention from their professors. Some introductory classes are large, but most classes have fewer than 30 people.

So . . . what about the partying? One student said "this school is not just partying, but that's a lot of it. This place has definitely been four years of nonstop fun. " Another student told us that partying does distract many students from studying. Those who put the work in, however, do receive an excellent education and still manage to enjoy a healthy social life.

Students have good things to say about their pretty, tree-lined campus, with its primarily Georgian and Jeffersonian architecture, "reminiscent of Monticello." One student raved, "The architecture and the layout of the campus are just beautiful." Students are fortunate that SMU invests a lot of its endowment into the school, both in maintaining the immaculate campus and facilities as well as constructing various additions. All freshmen live on campus in dormitories, many with a festive atmosphere, while upperclassmen usually move off campus to fraternity or sorority houses or apartment complexes. The school is located in an affluent suburb, so housing can be expensive.

SMU, as its name indicates, was founded by the Methodist Church. However, the school is open today to all religions and creeds, and only a small percentage of the students are practicing Methodists. The school has taken steps to increase its ethnic diversity, and now claims a minority undergraduate population of slightly less than 20 percent. About half of the students are native Texans; the rest come from the other 49 as well as several foreign countries.

Students say more of their classmates are conservative, although not necessarily politically vocal or active. Many students come from wealthy families and some do flaunt their money, from their clothes to their sports cars. But the student body is not nearly as snobby and elitist as their reputation may indicate. The campus has a generally friendly and casual social environment, where people still smile and greet one another on the way to classes.

Although the campus is strictly dry, as a student reports, that "doesn't affect the amount of partying at all." There's no shortage of social activity. The Greek system is an active presence, with about one-third of the student body joining 15 fraternities and 11 sororities. The enormous colonial mansions that line fraternity row are known for their blowout parties that draw large crowds of students.

Beyond fraternity events, students have numerous social opportunities including over 150 extracurricular activities and organizations. There are tons of student hangouts on campus and in the surrounding areas, from the sleek student center to favorite pizza and fast-food joints. The university's program committee also provides on-campus entertainment, from movies to visits by popular rock bands, while the performing arts departments produce first-rate plays and performances on campus.

Attending SMU Mustang sporting events is also extremely popular. Recovering after some lean years, SMU's Mustang football team is gaining popularity again and earning the strong support they've always enjoyed. Games, which themselves are major happenings, still draw crowds of rowdy fans to cheer their school. Basketball and swimming, both men's and women's, are some of SMU's highly rated sports teams.

As if all that weren't enough, nearby downtown Dallas has a slew of popular clubs, hangouts, and a thriving music scene, not to mention a fine cultural and art scene.

TULANE UNIVERSITY IN NEW ORLEANS, LOUISIANA

Admissions Address: Office of Undergraduate Admission, 210 Gibson Hall, 6823 Saint Charles Avenue, New Orleans, LA 70118
Phone: (504) 865-5731
Web Address: www.tulane.edu/Admission/

Tulane University

$$$$$
★★

Setting: Urban
# of Undergraduates: 4,952
Men: 50.3% Women: 49.7%
Tuition: $22,066
Room and Board: $6,600
# of Students Applied: 8,385
    Admitted: 6,410 Enrolled: 1,409
Required Admissions Test: Either SAT or ACT
Lowest 25% of Freshmen Scored
    At or Below: SAT Verbal: 600
    SAT Math: 590 ACT Comp.: 26
Highest 25% of Freshmen
    Scored At or Above: SAT
    Verbal: 700 SAT Math: 690
    ACT Comp.: 31
H.S. Rank, Top 10%: 56%
Top 25%: 79%
Top 50%: 99%
Avg. Score of Applicants
    Admitted: SAT Verbal: 651
    SAT Math: 638 ACT Comp.: 29
Most Popular Majors (% of
    Student Body): Engineering
    (16.23%), Business (11.76%),
    Biology (8.6%), Psychology
    (7.19%), English (5.6%)

Plenty of schools are known as party schools, but how many are located in one of the party capitals of the world? Known for hot Cajun food and even hotter jazz clubs, New Orleans is a city where people play all day and all night all year long, leading up to that granddaddy of all parties, Mardi Gras. Given that, as one student told us, "New Orleans is a great city, and Tulane is in the heart of it," it's really no surprise that most Tulane students rave about their social lives.

Students may come for the social scene, but the school is also a highly respected academic and research institution. Due to its many strong academic programs and superb facilities, Tulane is considered one of the top universities in the South. Undergraduate programs in preprofessional fields are particularly good and benefit from their association with Tulane's graduate schools. The traditional liberal arts departments are excellent, as are more unusual programs, such as environmental sciences and political economy. Tulane's Latin American studies program is one of the largest and most renowned in the country.

The undergraduate schools include the recently completed A. B. Freeman School of Business and the schools of architecture and engineering. There are two schools for arts and sciences: the College of Arts and Sciences for men and Newcomb College for women. The schools are essentially the same, and men and women take their classes together. Only the administration buildings and governing bodies are separate.

The core curriculum for liberal arts students includes courses in humanities, fine arts, social sciences, natural sciences, and math and includes requirements for demonstrating proficiency in writing and foreign languages. Courses in Western and non-Western civilization are also required. The credit system was recently restructured to induce students to study more.

Tulane offers interested and qualified students a number of special academic options, including study abroad, accelerated degrees in medicine, law and business, self-designed majors, and an acclaimed honors program. Students can also cross-register at such nearby schools as Loyola and Xavier.

The campus, while located in an urban setting, is itself charmingly picturesque, with several sprawling grassy areas neatly bordered by colorful flower gardens and stylish Victorian homes. In recent years, the school has devoted substantial amounts of funding to making improvements around the campus, including multimillion-dollar renovations of the residence halls and numerous additions, including state-of-the-art computer and scientific research facilities, a performing arts center, an art gallery, an environmental science building, and athletic and recreational facilities.

The student body has a total minority population of about 20 percent, including a 6 percent population of African American students. Many students come from the South, although the school also attracts healthy numbers from the Northeast. All 50 states, as well as several foreign countries, are represented.

Not all Tulane students party every night, although there are certainly those who try. Many students take their studies very seriously. A freshman told us that "it's everyone's individual choice whether they want to party or study; there are definitely students who should probably be studying more."

There is no doubt, though, that Tulane is a very socially oriented campus. Just about everywhere you go, you'll see students hanging out and socializing—from the university center, with its large game room and pub, to the library, which is reportedly not only a popular hangout but also an infamous pick-up spot. Many of the dorms themselves are social meccas, particularly those arranged as suites with common social areas. A number of upperclassmen move off campus to nearby apartments.

While the city of New Orleans is under federal pressure to crack down on underage college drinking, students tell us if they can't get served at bars they can always find parties. Once of age, students can take advantage of the open container law and get drinks in "go-cups" on Bourbon Street; however a freshman told us that alcohol regulations in New Orleans appear relatively lax and that many students regardless of age head to nearby bars or clubs for fun.

In addition to the infinite social offerings of New Orleans, Tulane has its own thriving social scene. About 25 percent of the students pledge fraternities or sororities. Students report that parties thrown by the Greek system, some trying to rival Mardi Gras celebrations in their extravagance, are very well attended. "On Fridays, we have TGIF parties, with live bands. Everyone goes to the quad to hang out," a student said. All Tulane schools get Mardi Gras off (so they can go party), but one student told us it would probably be better policy to have the next day off, so they can all recover.

But students are also quick to point out that there is much more to Tulane than partying. "There is a lot of opportunity here. There are so many extracurricular activities and clubs you can get involved with," we heard. Tulane students can choose from a variety of campus organizations and activities, from participating in volunteer groups to attending movies, concerts, and comedy shows on campus. Another student said "we do our fair share of partying here, and then some, but we know the limits, I think we know when to get down to work. There's a mix between partying and getting the homework done."

Sports are also big at Tulane. Its basketball team has frequently made it to the NCAA tournament in recent years. Tulane also has many other excellent intercollegiate teams, including football, tennis, volleyball, and baseball. Needless to say, students take their sports seriously. Basketball and football games draw large crowds of zealous student fans, many of whom have camped out overnight to get tickets. As one sophomore observed, "We get dressed up to go to the games. Some guys wear a jacket and tie."

It's telling that classes at Tulane are canceled every year so that students can enjoy the annual Mardi Gras celebration in New Orleans. This is a school where students can and many do study hard, but there's always a time to stop work, kick back, and enjoy.

UNIVERSITY OF CALIFORNIA/SANTA BARBARA

Admissions Address: Admissions Office, University of California, Santa Barbara, CA 93106
Phone: (805) 893-2485
Web Address: www.ucsb.edu/

Time to study. Make certain that you bring your books, paper, pen . . . and don't forget your suntan lotion. Suntan lotion?! Sound like a dream come true? Well, if your campus is on a beach, there's not much stopping you from studying by the surf. There's also nothing stopping you from swimming, surfing, playing volleyball, and working on your tan all year long.

SERIOUS FUN

For UC—Santa Barbara students, this dream is a reality. While their friends in the Northeast are freezing their butts off, UCSB students enjoy their own beautiful beach. That may be why UCSB students also enjoy a social scene that is described by some as "busy" and "chaotic."

Many students, though, expressed concern that UCSB's reputation as a party school eclipses the school's other offerings, particularly in various academic fields. As part of the acclaimed University of California system, Santa Barbara maintains high academic standards. As a student told us, "There are a lot of people who've worked hard to get in and continue to work hard once they get here."

Santa Barbara offers students a wide scope of quality academic programs as well as many superb facilities and resources. Utilizing cutting-edge facilities, the science and technology departments, particularly in physics, biology, chemistry, and engineering are among UCSB's best. Marine biology is particularly strong, not surprising given the school's ocean-front property. In the humanities, English and history are among the school's many fine departments. Requirements vary by college but usually include humanities, art and literature, social science, natural science, English, writing, and a university-wide required ethnic studies course. UCSB also offers an extensive study-abroad program, with programs at more than 100 foreign universities.

As a medium-sized research institution, UCSB is more manageable than most larger universities but still poses certain challenges for undergraduates. Getting into certain courses can be tough, and classes at the introductory levels are large. Receiving individual attention from professors, especially from those who are focused primarily upon their own research, can be difficult. Aggressive undergraduates who track down and meet with professors, however, will usually find them quite willing to offer advice and even a friendly word or two. Additionally, students occasionally get to work with professors on sophisticated research projects. "I like all my professors," said one student, "but sometimes it is hard to see them with my and their schedules to consider."

UCSB is on a quarterly system, which means that exams and deadlines come up frequently—much more frequently than most students would like. While the workload can be heavy, the amount of studying required largely depends on individual student commitment. One student told us, "You can easily remove yourself from the party scene. But there are also people who party a lot and just do enough work to get by."

University of California / Santa Barbara

🏛🏛🏛🏛
$$$$$
★★

Setting: Suburban
# of Undergraduates: 16,281
Men: 46.6% **Women:** 53.4
In-State Tuition: $0 (plus fees)
Out-of-State Tuition: $8,394
Room and Board: $6,131
# of Students Applied: 19,232
   Admitted: 14,958 **Enrolled:** 3,464
Required Admissions Test: Either SAT I or ACT, SAT II
Lowest 25% of Freshmen Scored At or Below: SAT Verbal: 500 SAT Math: 520
Highest 25% of Freshmen Scored At or Above: SAT Verbal: 600 SAT Math: 620
Top 25%: 100%
Avg. Score of Applicants Admitted: SAT Verbal: 549 SAT Math: 569
Average GPA of Applicants Admitted: 3.52
Most Popular Majors: Business, Economics, Biological Sciences, Psychology, Communication, Sociology

Most of the student body are native Californians; minority students, primarily Hispanic and Asian Americans, make up a large portion of the student population. Students are generally laid-back and very socially oriented, although much of the socializing and partying take place in cliques rather than large, open parties. A student told us "people just start getting together and when more people show up, it's a party." Students report that while it's difficult for minors to buy alcohol, it's not that hard for them to drink it if they want to at off-campus keg parties.

UCSB might be a party school, but the parties aren't necessarily found in the same place. Most of the partying takes place off campus but is entirely open to students living on campus as well. Many students live in large apartment complexes in nearby Isla Vista, where the social atmosphere is like living in Animal House without having to wear Greek letters. In this party haven, there will always be something going on any given night of the week. Halloween night, though, is the major party night of the year and draws thousands of costumed visitors. Fraternities and sororities, while not necessarily the only game in town, do throw a number of their own parties and special events. In addition to attending parties, students also frequent a number of local bars and clubs.

Sports and athletics of all kinds are also favorite activities. UCSB intercollegiate teams compete in the NCAA Division I. Some of its strongest teams are in basketball, water polo, baseball, and volleyball.

With distractions like parties, sun, and the beach, it's easy to turn your college years into a long vacation. But, as one student told us, most people tend to confine their partying to weekends—which usually begin Thursday nights—enabling them to achieve a balance between academics and fun. UCSB has both in large amounts.

UNIVERSITY OF FLORIDA IN GAINESVILLE

Admissions Address: Admissions Office, 201 Criser Hall P.O. Box 114000, Gainesville, FL 32611-4000
Phone: (352) 392-3261 (352) 392-4000
Web Address: www.ufl.edu/

Like their archrival in football, Florida State, students at the University of Florida enjoy all kinds of fun in the sun, from a major party scene to the fanatical following of their football team. The variety of academic and social offerings reflects the school's size, with a total student population of nearly 30,000 students.

SERIOUS FUN

At this large school, pride in the school's team manages to unite almost the entire student body. Students flock to the 85,000-seat stadium to cheer on Gator football, which in past years has played in top bowl games like the Sugar Bowl. Game days start out with tailgate parties, and the festivities carry right over to the stands and to postgame parties. Thousands come to the school's Homecoming extravaganza, the highlight being the Gator Growl, a pep-rally spectacle that rivals Vegas glitz. basketball has the next most fanatical following.

As with schools everywhere, the social scene at UF has been affected by the crackdown on underage drinking. While the school may not be as wild as in previous years, students still know how to have a good time. "There are parties every weekend, and there's always something going on during the week. It's an exciting social scene here," a sophomore told us. He went on to explain that the lure of partying can make it difficult to study. "Sometimes when I have tests and I know I should be studying, I'll go out partying because there's always a lot going on," he said. Another said, "Hey, why not party all the time? This is a great place, its a lot of fun, and I'm only going through college once."

For students who manage to avoid temptations and seriously hit the books from time to time, it is possible to receive a strong education at the university, which offers countless majors and fields of study. And the low tuition makes it a great bargain, especially for Florida residents.

With 14 undergraduate schools, including schools of communication and journalism, engineering, education, and liberal arts, the University of Florida offers an enormous number of major and degree programs. Preprofessional and career-oriented majors are among the school's most popular and strongest, particularly programs in business, journalism, communications, engineering, and premed. There are many special academic options available as well, including internships, study abroad in more than 30 countries, and an honors program.

While requirements vary by major, for most students the first two years are devoted to general education courses in a variety of basic academic areas, including history, philosophy, cultural diversity, social sciences, math, physical and biological sciences, literature, and composition. "I learned a lot in courses I thought I would never have a use for," one student said.

As with any large, research-oriented university, undergraduates have to fend for themselves as they grapple with large lecture courses and

---

University of Florida

🏛🏛🏛🏛
$$
★★★

Setting: Suburban
# of Undergraduates: 26,663
Men: 50.5% Women: 49.5
In-State Tuition: $1,793
Out-of-State Tuition: $7,038
Room and Board: $4,500
# of Students Applied: 12,901
   Admitted: 7,588   Enrolled: 3,318
Required Admissions Test: Either SAT or ACT
H.S. Rank, Top 10%: 60%
Top 25%: 89%
Top 50%: 99%
Avg. Score of Applicants
   Admitted: SAT Verbal: 615
   SAT Math: 630   ACT Comp.: 27
Average GPA of Applicants
   Admitted: 3.85
Most Popular Majors: Psychology, Finance, English, Advertising, Elementary Teacher Education

393

bureaucratic procedures that border on nightmarish. With so many students, it makes it difficult for professors to provide much individual attention, but students who seek them out during office hours will usually find them helpful.

There are many advantages, though, to the university's large size, including the variety of courses that enable students to find just about any topic they want. The positive side of being a major research university is the availability of high-quality resources and facilities for undergraduates.

The large, 2,000-acre campus, while located in the midst of lush Floridian foliage, actually looks like a small, quaint city. In recent years, the school has made many improvements to the campus facilities, constructing new buildings and renovating old ones. However, the institution of state budget cuts makes it unclear whether such improvements will continue.

While housing is guaranteed for freshmen, most students live off-campus, some commuting from home, some moving to fraternity and sorority houses, and many relocating in affordable off-campus student housing in nearby apartment buildings.

With the super-low tuition for Florida residents, the grand majority of the student body comes from within the state. The male to female ratio is roughly equal. There is a small population of foreign students (approximately 2,000), and the remainder of the population is comprised of students from the other 49 states. Minority students make up more than one-quarter of the student body, split equally between African, Asian, and Hispanic Americans—a large number in terms of actual students. With about just under 30,000 undergraduates, the student body represents a variety of backgrounds, cultures, experiences, and political views.

The social scene, while an active one, is as mixed as the student population. About 15 percent of the students join 29 fraternities and 18 sororities, and Greek life provides plenty of social opportunities. The Greeks don't make up the majority of the student body, and there are other ways to have fun at UF. Students can find parties most any time, particularly at off-campus sites. The campus itself is ripe with places to socialize and hang out, including the enormous student center. The city of Gainesville has many cultural and social offerings that appeal to students, from a number of bars and clubs to shops, restaurants, and theaters.

In addition to basketball and football, UF has many powerhouse teams, including women's gymnastics and tennis, men's golf, and both men's and women's swimming. "Believe it or not," one student told us, "we've really gotten into tennis here" (we think it's a Florida thing). Most students participate in the school's intramural program, which includes a healthy selection of popular sports. The sunny weather combined with the school's extensive athletic and recreation facilities make it possible for students to enjoy just about any sport or activity year-round. Well, almost every activity—you may have to go somewhere else for your cross-country skiing.

Also Check Out These Schools:

Arizona State University
Boston University
Bucknell University
University of California—Los Angeles
University of California—Santa Cruz
Colgate University
University of Colorado—Boulder
University of Connecticut
Dartmouth College
Denison University
Duke University
Emory University
Florida State University
Hamilton College
Hobart and William Smith Colleges
University of Illinois—Urbana-Champaign
University of Massachusetts—Amherst
University of Miami (FL)
University of the South
Vanderbilt University
University of Vermont
University of Virginia

Go State!

Make no mistake about it: These schools are large. Even at a middle-sized state school, going to class as a freshman can sometimes feel like marching with an army across a campus that's a small country in its own right. As with any category of schools, there are positives and negatives to attending a big state college or university. Fortunately, though, the opportunities for students at these schools also tend to be very, very big.

First and foremost of these big breaks is the price tag: Tuition at a state school for students who live in the same state is, comparatively, dirt cheap. Funding allocated from state taxes and federal land and sea grants dramatically lessens the need for financial aid and helps to ensure modern and well-maintained research facilities. For the same reason, you can also count on well-stocked libraries and an abundance of resources that most private colleges or universities would be hard pressed to acquire without making tuitions go ballistic. If sheer breadth of selection is what you most desire in a college—be it in courses of study, sports to play, or extracurricular activities to enjoy—this kind of school is what you need.

Of course, the drawbacks are legend: large classes, overworked and impersonal advisors, and perhaps a feeling of being lost that never fully dissipates until you don the graduation gown. Faculty can be elusive, although sometimes they'll be so impressed by your efforts to track them down that you'll get all the attention you want and more. That's why students who do well at these schools are often driven individuals who aren't afraid to make themselves known in a crowd and show initiative in seeking out what they want. Fear not, though, if you're uncertain of what you'd like to do when you grow up. Big state schools generally offer a selection of courses and majors that is second to none in sheer comprehensiveness. Picking and choosing what works for you is what these colleges are all about.

Well-financed and successful sports programs are often a hallmark of the larger state universities, which naturally have a broader selection of recruits to choose from and extensive scouting efforts. There's usually no shortage of extracurricular activities either, with Greeks running amok (sometimes literally) and a plethora of clubs catering to any interest, no matter how obscure. And the students you interact with on campus will certainly not be the cookie-cutter, homogeneous bunch that makes many smaller schools so bland. There are no shortages of interesting, diverse opportunities on these campuses, and students who have been there awhile say that they've discovered a wealth of new meaning to the phrase, living large.

LOUISIANA STATE UNIVERSITY AND A&M COLLEGE IN BATON ROUGE

Admissions Address: Admissions Office, 110 Thomas Boyd Hall, Baton Rouge, LA 70803
Phone: (504) 388-1175 (504) 388-3202
Web Address: www.lsu.edu/

Louisiana State University and A&M College

$$

Setting: Urban
# of Undergraduates: 17,901
Men: 50% Women: 50
In-State Tuition: $2,687
Out-of-State Tuition: $5,987
Room and Board: $3,570
# of Students Applied: 7,908
    Admitted: 6,401   Enrolled: 4,025
Required Admissions Test: Either SAT or ACT
Recommended: ACT
H.S. Rank, Top 10%: 26%
Top 25%: 51%
Top 50%: 79%
Avg. Score of Applicants
    Admitted: ACT Comp.: 23.14
Average GPA of Applicants
    Admitted: 3.09
Most Popular Majors (% of Student Body): General Studies (7.1%), Psychology (6.2%), Accounting (5.6%), Political Science (4%), English (3.9%)

Whether it's the location, the gardenlike campus, or the variety and excellence of the programs offered, it seems like everyone we talked to from LSU was completely in love with their school. In spite of its large size, students say they all feel like they are very much a part of a small community.

"I've lived my whole life in Louisiana and I really wanted to go to school out of state. I never wanted to come here," said one senior, "But I came because it was a cheap, in-state school, and I ended up loving it!"

Nearly 90 percent of the undergrads hail from the Sportsman's Paradise (according to Louisiana license plates), attracted by the low in-state tuition, diverse program offerings, and attractive setting. "this is a very lush, green area. There's flowers blooming all the time, its like we're living in the garden of Eden," said one student. Of the remaining 10 percent of the students that aren't from Louisiana, 1,500 hail from foreign countries. Men and women are equally represented, and the total minority population peaks at under 15 percent.

What started as a southern plantation, is now a "self-contained city within a city." The campus offers a variety of attractive buildings including the original homestead, Italian-Victorian houses, and state-of the art research and library facilities. The garden theme was echoed by most students who know the campus as a "botanist's joy," and even Louisiana natives are impressed by the continual beauty of their surroundings here.

LSU is both the Land Grant and Sea Grant college for the state, as well as being designated a major research institution, so students are assured of up-to-date and well-funded technical programs. Agricultural programs benefit from comprehensive herbariums and arboretums as well as the Burden Research Plantation. In all, LSU has 14 undergraduate colleges, enabling students to earn bachelor's degrees in more than 75 specific fields.

While engineering attracts its share of students (don't forget, the petroleum industry is very big in the delta region), the most popular program is the general college, where students are allowed to design their own major and incorporate three different minors into their custom-built program. Known on campus for its intensive guidance and excellent turnout, one student said the general major is such a choice selection because it draws instructors from all of the other LSU programs.

Despite its size, students report being able to reach their professors easily when they need them. "The professors are wonderful," our senior said, "I'd heard that I wasn't going to be on a first-name basis with them, but that's not true." Students who do well are eligible for the Honors College, an intensive program that offers small classes and great research opportunities to hard-working undergrads. Once past the intro courses, students can expect to be taught by professors in 15–30 person classes.

"It is a big school—oftentimes freshman can feel lost or disoriented, but people get into social groups fairly quickly," a sophomore told us. "The university has programs to get people integrated right away. Its big here, but the people are friendly." Another student told us freshman have many events organized to help ease them into college life.

Housing takes a variety of forms, from dormitories to theme houses to frat halls, but in order to get their choice picks students must register one year in advance. There are 24 fraternities and 14 sororities at LSU. The Greek council allows quite a long rush period so students can take their time and choose a Greek house that's right for them. If students aren't into the Greek scene, they can join any of the 250 clubs, activities, or intramural sports on campus as well. The Greek system at LSU prides itself on things other than partying as well, specifically numerous fundraising. Top on this list is the "Taste of the Tiger," a Greek cook-off with all proceeds going to charity.

It would be an understatement to say LSU students can take advantage of an active social life. As one student told us, "When one magazine profiled the top 10 party schools in the country, they left out LSU because they said the profile included only amateur partiers." Major-league partying takes on many forms at LSU. The Greek system certainly accounts for much of the revelry, but students congregate in dorms, lawns, or halls to have fun. Off campus, "Tiger Town" is the bar and club strip in Baton Rouge that caters to LSU students. Another student told us that when they want a different party scene, New Orleans's Bourbon Street is only an hour and a half away. "We can study till eight or nine and still get there when things are just warming up," one senior told us.

Even though its a big party school, another student said, "There's such a wide variety of students that there's something for everyone to do. It's good because it's so big; everyone is able to find their own niche."

When they're not partying or studying, LSU students follow their school's Division I football team or the Division III baseball team, or occupy themselves with any of six museums or galleries on campus.

Size seems to work for LSU, as there is something for everyone here, and most students are very satisfied with their future alma mater.

UNIVERSITY OF GEORGIA/ATHENS

Admissions Address: Admissions Office, Terrell Hall, Athens, GA 30602
Phone: (709) 542-2112
Web Address: www.uga.edu/

There are always certain aspects of state schools that, no matter what else they offer, you're going to have to deal with. Most have huge campuses with huge enrollments, and most require that you do the work needed to keep from getting lost. Some, though, are top-notch learning institutions. The University of Georgia is all of these things. And if you can handle the challenges, the University has a lot to offer, including a first-rate education and a lot of ways to make you feel like you're at a small school rather than a degree factory.

First of all, it could be free. Students who live in Georgia and maintain a B average through high school can attend state schools tuition free and receive $100 per semester to help with the cost of books. While room and board are yours to pay for, it is still one of the best educational values to

Go State!

be found. Funded by the Georgia lottery, this financial aid program makes it possible for the school to open its doors to any qualified Georgia student. Like most state schools, Georgia is dependent to some degree on funding from the state. However, gifts from foundations and wealthy alumni also make up a large part of Georgia's budget, so they are somewhat protected from any rumblings in the statehouse to raise tuition or cut programs.

Georgia—Athens, the school's main campus, is 605 acres and 313 buildings big. Its academic offerings are equally large. You can choose from 171 different majors at Georgia. General business is the largest major, followed by psychology, English, biology, studio art, political science, and accounting. Georgia also has two very popular preprofessional programs: premed, which is four years, and prejournalism, a two-year program after which you apply to the well-respected School of Journalism for another two years to receiver your bachelor's degree.

The faculty is top-notch, with many Pulitzer Prize and National Science Award winners on staff. There is no distinction between graduate and undergraduate faculty at Georgia, so the A-level profs are as likely to be found in your junior and senior classes as they are among graduate courses. Classes in your major are small and are kept that way by the administration. Your introductory classes will be another matter. Some freshman classes can number over 300 students, and when classes get that large, they are often broken into two or three sections and taught by graduate TAs. While the professor remains in charge, your contact with him or her can be limited.

Most students find their professors friendly and "as accessible as they can be." In a school with over 20,000 undergraduates, professors can't offer the same time to students that they can at smaller schools, but they do their best. All the profs have office hours, and they're good about keeping them. The problem comes when you have class when they're in their office. You can make an appointment with professors easily enough, though. But the situation is typical of student-faculty relations. "Most students here really like their teachers," said one student, "but you have to make the effort. There are just too many people for the professors to follow you around." All the students we spoke to agreed, and one even went so far as to say, "You can turn the situation to your advantage, because you are really forced to take responsibility for yourself and your needs. It can be great growing experience."

The same can be said for student-advisor relationships. "Some students

---

University of Georgia

$$

★★★

Setting: Suburban
# of Undergraduates: 20,317
Men: 45.4% **Women:** 54.6%
In-State Tuition: $2,115
Out-of-State Tuition: $7,296
Room and Board: $4,045
# of Students Applied: 13,309
  Admitted: 7,428 **Enrolled:** 3,249
Required Admissions Test: Either SAT or ACT
Recommended: SAT
Lowest 25% of Freshmen Scored At or Below: SAT Verbal: 560 SAT Math: 550
Highest 25% of Freshmen Scored At or Above: SAT Verbal: 650 SAT Math: 650
Avg. Score of Applicants Admitted: SAT Verbal: 596 SAT Math: 587
Average GPA of Applicants Admitted: 3.55
Most Popular Majors (% of Student Body): Psychology (4.2%), English (4.2%), Finance (3.8%), Early Childhood Education (3.4%), Political Science (3.1%)

get really tight with their advisors; many advisors keep in touch with their students after graduation," one student said. "But it's up to the student. There are a certain number of meetings you are required to have with your advisor to make sure you're completing your degree requirements, but after that you're on your own." All agreed, though, that advisors were there when you needed them and as often as you needed them. "You have to take the lead. You have to make yourself known to your advisor. They will be responsive, helpful, and compassionate, but the community is so big that they can't go looking after all the students they're assigned to." Some students know and love their advisors, others don't even know their advisor's name.

Georgia also maintains a renowned honors program. Although usually only about 10 percent or less of incoming freshmen are admitted to the program, it helps make the school smaller for those in the program. "My introductory classes mostly had about 20 people," said one student in the program, "while my roommate's had over 100." Students in the honors program also work more closely with professors and advisors than do other students. "I've received more individual attention here than I would have received at any of the other schools I applied to," said one junior in the program.

Those not in the honors program have many other ways to make the place seem smaller. There are more than 400 different clubs and organizations on campus, and that can often be the springboard to falling into a comfortable place at Georgia. "Your smaller niche of friends will come from your involvement with the clubs," said one student. Again, you have to take the initiative. While this might not be the place for the extremely introverted, it does offer various opportunities to make student feel like they can make a home in Athens.

Speaking of Athens, while those who live there bristle at its description as a "college town," it is the social center of campus. Athens is actually a small, safe city whose downtown directly adjoins campus. Consequently, it is the social center of the school. "We're much more likely to go walk downtown on a Friday night than go prowling the dorms or frats looking for parties," said one student. Athens was ground zero for the alt-rock scene (a few years ago, bands such as the B-52s, the Georgia Satellites, and R.E.M. called it home) and as a result you can go into town and see a different live band any night of the week. There are also cafes, shops, restaurants, and coffeehouses. More than one student listed the relationship with Athens as their favorite thing about the school (though more than one listed the parking as their pet peeve), and while the citizens of Athens will remind you that there is more to the city than the college, they enjoy having the students around, and many businesses and shops cater to their needs.

With so much going on just outside the gates, the actual campus is pretty quiet. About one-quarter of the undergraduates are Greeks, and while that's a fairly large proportion, there is not a strong division between them and the rest of the student body. "Once we're in town, there's no distinction," said one student. The school did just finish construction on a 400,000 square foot athletic center and a state-of-the-art performing arts center.

The student body is friendly and diverse. "Remember, this is a state school," said one student. Georgia—Athens draws students from downtown Atlanta and rural Georgia, so there is a pretty good mix of white and African American, rich and poor, urban and country students. They tend to be middle-of-the-road politically, and while one student said Athens has seen "every march known to man," students tend to be pretty laid-back.

With its friendly student body, myriad organizations, and top-notch academics, Georgia—Athens offers much to counter the sting of big state schools. "The opportunities are there, if you want them," said one student. "If you're willing to go get them, you can't do better."

UNIVERSITY OF MARYLAND/COLLEGE PARK

Admissions Address: Admissions Office, Mitchell Building, College Park, MD 20742-5235
Phone: (301) 314-8385
Web Address: www.umcp.umd.edu/

If you are looking for a large school with a diverse and fun student body close to, but not immediately in a culturally attractive city, look no further than UMD. Maryland students seem to have all the advantages of a large school with few of the drawbacks.

With 13 colleges and 97 undergraduate programs, UMD students have many options open to them. The school has done its best to banish symptoms that plague other large schools, including huge classes and distant professors. Freshman begin with a First Year Focus program, a curricular buffet similar to other universities freshman programs. Course Clusters are also available freshman year, offering a limited-enrollment

University of Maryland / College Park

$$
★★
$$

Setting: Urban
# of Undergraduates: 20,995
Men: 51.2% Women: 48.8%
In-State Tuition: $3,744
Out-of-State Tuition: $4,873
Room and Board: $5,442
# of Students Applied: 17,046
  Admitted: 10,457 Enrolled: 3,638
Required Admissions Test: Either SAT or ACT
Lowest 25% of Freshmen Scored At or Below: SAT Verbal: 540 SAT Math: 550
Highest 25% of Freshmen Scored At or Above: SAT Verbal: 640 SAT Math: 660
H.S. Rank, Top 10%: 26%
Top 25%: 61%
Top 50%: 92%
Average GPA of Applicants Admitted: 3.45
Most Popular Majors (% of Student Body): Computer Science (5%), Psychology (4.1%), Criminology (4%), Biological Sciences (3.7%), General Business (3.6%)

"academic road map" to guide students with life and career choices. College Park Scholars are academic achievers whose academic programs are coordinated, and who live together in selected residence halls equipped with computer and classroom space for a closer learning and living experience. Finally, the Gemstone Students are a group drawn from engineering, business, and humanities schools to team up in a four-year research oriented program involving social and technological concerns. A recent and timely project was on privacy issues and intellectual property on the Internet.

Even without the special programs, students claim professors are accessible. "I've been really happy with all my professors," said one junior English major, "all my classes at this level are small. Intro classes in the first two years are large, but they have discussion sessions, and those are very helpful." College Park's computerized, automated telephone registration makes getting the classes they want relatively easy for students.

UMD's most popular programs are Computer Science, Psychology, Criminology, Biology, and Business. Three quarters of the undergraduate population come from Maryland; the remainder migrate mostly from the East Coast, primarily Virginia, the District of Columbia, New York, New Jersey, and Pennsylvania. The school boasts a phenomenal 38 percent minority population and has a nearly equal men-to-women ratio.

Attending a large school in a metropolitan area does not phase most UMD students. "I wanted to go to a big school," said a student; "you can make a new life if you want to. This seems like the opposite of everything you hear about a big state school because my classes aren't that big and everyone is friendly and very close." Another student said, "Anyone who comes here and wants to make the most of it, can. The opportunities are all here. The academic and social programs offer a lot of good experience." Many students, even those from out of state, stay in the MD/VA/DC area after they graduate. "It's a really cool place to live," said one junior; "I did an internship on the Hill this summer, and I'd come out of work and say, 'I live here!'"

"I was initially attracted by the campus," one sophomore told us; "it's beautiful; it looks like a gameboard." With an endorsement like that, we know that UMD's suburban setting is pleasing to its students. Pretty as it may be, only 36 percent of undergraduates live on campus (housing is guaranteed for freshman). Dorms, while livable, are small—but off-campus accommodations are easy to find. Shared homes and Greek houses off campus are popular. The same student told us, "Dorms can become a subculture. People don't have to leave—they cocoon themselves, but when they move off campus things change—they discover the area and themselves."

The area does have a lot to offer. The cultural powerhouse that is Washington, DC is a metro ride away, including monuments, museums, trendy shopping sections, and fine dining. Baltimore is little more than a half-hour north, and Annapolis is an hour east. Bethesda, less than 10 minutes' ride away, is known in the Washington area for its wonderful selection of restaurants and bars, and in College Park plenty of establishments cater to the UMD crowd—Terrapin Station and Santa Fe Café are names we've heard repeatedly from students. Students can take the university shuttles for safety or convenience around campus or to the nearby metro stop, which makes having a car on campus unnecessary.

Once known primarily as a party school, UMD is participating in the national collegiate trend to cut down on underage drinking. As part of that effort, UMD is building the Maryland Center for the Performing Arts, which, in addition to teaching facilities, will provide a variety of student entertainment options. For students who want to stay in their rooms, UMD considers itself the pioneer of college Internet connections. Currently the school has over 31,000 E-mail accounts, many connected through fiber-optic networks. Every student residential room is wired.

The 23 fraternities and 15 sororities draw 15–20 percent of the students, though many students attend Greek-sponsored parties. The Greek scene isn't the biggest draw on campus, but intramural and varsity sports may be. A 240,000 square-foot campus recreation center will open this year, giving students access to gyms, racquetball, and indoor running tracks. UMD's teams are the Terrapins, and they have an active and enthusiastic following. Men's basketball, men's and women's lacrosse, and men's soccer have all been top contenders in the past few years and consistently draw standing-room-only crowds. "Our basketball is the greatest. There's no question about it," said one energetic supporter who said he and friends regularly paint their faces for home games.

With such all-around enthusiastic endorsements, it's clear UMD students are very happy with their school. And they should be; UMD offers students an attractive and enjoyable campus life to nourish them while they study hard in demanding programs that will fuel future careers.

UNIVERSITY OF MINNESOTA/TWIN CITIES

Admissions Address: Office of Admissions, 240 Williamson Hall, 231 Pillsbury Drive, Minneapolis, MN 55455
Phone: (612) 625-2008 (800) 752-1000
Web Address: admissions.tc.umn.edu

University of Minnesota / Twin Cities

🏛🏛🏛🏛
$$
★★★

Setting: Urban
# of Undergraduates: 19,689
Men: 49.4% Women: 50.6
In-State Tuition: $4,090
Out-of-State Tuition: $10,327
Room and Board: $4,056
# of Students Applied: 13,914
  Admitted: 7,637 Enrolled: 4,279
Required Admissions Test: Either SAT or ACT
Recommended: ACT
H.S. Rank, Top 10%: 27%
Top 25%: 59%
Top 50%: 84%
Avg. Score of Applicants Admitted: SAT Verbal: 484
  SAT Math: 568   ACT Comp.: 25
Most Popular Majors (% of Student Body): Psychology (3%), Mechanical Engineering (2%), Business (2%), History (1%), Biology (1%)

Students at Minnesota may be at the highest risk of being lost in the fog of the big-school syndrome, but most students seem to at least fare well if not thrive in a metropolitan environment that threatens to swallow up lesser folk. "When I first got here it was a really, really big place," said one student. "If you don't know where you're going, its a very large space, but you do figure it out by the end of the first term." She went on to tell us that "socializing can be hard. You don't meet the same people twice, and some people can be very cliquish."

Known as a "classic Big-Ten Campus," Twin Cities is the largest of the four University of Minnesota schools. Its 24,000 undergraduates can choose from 19 colleges to advance their education. The school offers 125 majors in just about everything, from Accounting to Wood and Paper Science. With such a large population Twin Cities has a viable minority population, made up mostly of Asian Americans and African Americans. There are 2,500 international students in the undergraduate body.

One student said the computer and information system is a real boon, offering everything from online counseling to electronic personal organizers custom-made for each student. The university network also allows online registration, which, can still be a real headache. "Computer information services can be overloaded. I don't think there's good enough computer service for all of us," one student said.

For such a large school, housing details at the home of the Golden Gophers are ironed out consistently and with few complaints. If they register by a certain date, students are guaranteed housing; as a result, most students stay in university housing throughout their college lives. Life in the dorms is "OK, mostly," said one student, "but often loud."

As with many other large state schools, freshman can expect a lot of large, 100-plus lecture classes taught by teaching assistants. One student told us that by sophomore year intro classes weed out a lot of people, so students can expect classes to thin out. She pointed out that professors tended to be very accessible, many of which were very concerned more about teaching than research. The student added that " TAs can be just as helpful because they've been in your shoes and can communicate ideas better a lot of the time."

With three-quarters of its students in-state residents, most of the Twin Cities undergraduate population is used to the long, cold midwest winters. Still, one student told us, "there's not a lot to do here in the winter." Twin Cities has a roughly equal representation of men and women. The ethnic population accounts for less than 10 percent of the student body; most are Asian American. An activity that draws students, townspeople, and tourists to the Twin Cities area is the annual St. Paul Winter Festival, famous for its ice sculptures.

Right in the middle of Minneapolis, with St. Paul hardly a stone's throw away, UM—Twin Cities does offer access to the social highlights of Minnesota's best cities. There are plenty of museums, concerts, and theaters around town to entertain students. Coffee houses and dance clubs are popular amongst undergrads as well. One student said, "I chose to come here because I like what large cities have to offer. There are all types of people, and they are usually more open-minded in a big city." Accessibility to off-campus activities is good; students don't have to travel far, and University and public transportation bring events even closer.

Sports are a big draw at Twin Cities. Hockey and basketball are Division I teams, and though students have to pay for admission to the games, special package deals are available. There are 11 men's and women's intercollegiate teams in the Big Ten Conference. The hockey team is part of the Western Collegiate Hockey Association, and the basketball teams belong to the NCAA, so games are usually competitive and almost always attract a crowd. There are plenty of opportunities for intramural sports as well at Twin Cities.

UNIVERSITY OF MISSOURI/COLUMBIA

Admissions Address: Admissions Office, 230 Jesse Hall, Columbia, MO 65211
Phone: (573) 882-7786 (800) 225-6075
Web Address: www.missouri.edu/regwww/

The University of Missouri at Columbia was the first state university west of the Mississippi River. In 1839 it blazed a trail of higher education accessible to all, and in the 1990s it strives to continue that mission.

Students report that the most remarkable thing about Missouri-Columbia is, despite the fact that it has over 20,000 students (about 16,000 of them undergraduates) the place is "friendly and open," says

University of Missouri/Columbia

$$

★

Setting: Small town
# of Undergraduates: 15,651
Men: 47.4% **Women:** 52.6%
In-State Tuition: $3,744
Out-of-State Tuition: $11,187
Room and Board: $4,080
# of Students Applied: 8,406
  Admitted: 7,595 **Enrolled:** 3,737
Required Admissions Test: ACT or SAT
Lowest 25% of Freshmen Scored At or Below: ACT Comp.: 23
Highest 25% of Freshmen Scored At or Above: ACT Comp.: 29
Average Score of Applicants Accepted: ACT Comp. 25.3
H.S. Rank, Top 10%: 33%
Top 25%: 64%
Top 50%: 91%
Most Popular Majors (% of Student Body): Business (12%), Social Science (9%), Engineering (8.7%), Education (6.9%)

one student. "I say hello to a dozen people every time I walk across the campus. It really doesn't feel that huge at all."

Missouri/Columbia has six undergraduate colleges: the College of Agriculture, Food, and Natural Resources; the College of Arts and Sciences; the College of Business Administration; the College of Engineering; the College of Human Environmental Sciences; and the School of Journalism. Journalism is by far the most popular major on the campus, as Missouri-Columbia is home to the acclaimed University of Missouri School of Journalism, but English and the business majors are also popular. Since Missouri has its own School of Medicine and School of Law, premed and prelaw programs are also popular. There are also many interdisciplinary majors available, and students, working with their advisors, can design their own program across departments or even across schools. With six schools, the course selection is huge.

Freshman classes are big—one student reported an average of 150 students in her first-term classes—but they whittle down to about 30 students per class by sophomore year and into the teens by junior and senior years. The accessibility of your professors can vary widely; though students report that faculty get more attentive the further up into your major you go—you could be lost in the shuffle early if you don't make yourself known. Most students say that the faculty all post office hours and keep them, and are also very willing and eager to make appointments outside their office hours to suit students schedules.

One unusual aspect of Missouri/Columbia students report is, unlike most other schools, you are more likely to find your classes taught by graduate assistants or TAs as you work your way up. "When you get into your major, the school likes to keep groups small. So if there are too many people in your class, the professor will break the class into smaller groups and have the TAs run the group." It can be a fifty-fifty split on classes taught by faculty and classes taught by TAs, another student reports.

Needless to say, with a school this size some guidance is needed to find your way though the woods. Missouri/Columbia places a high value on student-advisor relationships, and all the students we talked to raved about their advisors, not only about their patience and accessibility, but how much they cared about them. "It's really needed with so many courses to choose from," said one student. Another said, "my advisor seems to be always available when I need him."

While Missouri/Columbia obviously has some of the challenges big state schools are known for, they also have one of the biggest advantages: price. Missouri residents pay about $3,700 per year, and even nonresidents can attend for about $10,000. The nonresident tag may not seem like a bargain, but for the opportunities available, it is a value. Furthermore, three out of four Missouri students receive some form of financial aid.

All first-year students are required to live on campus, after that the percentage of students living on campus goes down, as both off-campus housing in Columbia and the Greek system are available. Most students report the dorms are safe, clean, and fun; a few considered them the center of social life at Missouri/Columbia. "There are always meetings and things going on in the dorms, not to mention parties and get-togethers," said one student. Another raved about the number of programs run by Residential Life. "We have discussion groups, get-to-know-your-neighbor groups, floor meetings, and mixers. It helps make the place smaller, and really builds a community."

The Missouri/Columbia student body is a diverse one, both racially and economically. "There are a lot of working-class students here," reported one student. "Being a state school with great programs, it draws a whole mix of students." Students also mix and mingle with each other freely, we hear. "There's no self-segregation," said one student. "We all have stuff in common, we're all in this together."

As mentioned, social life centers around the dorms and the Greeks, and on Friday and Saturday night you won't have to look too hard to find a party. The one place there is some division is between the Greeks and the non-Greeks. "Most Greek parties are open to all," said one student, "but there isn't a lot of association between the Greeks and the dorms." Still, students say that those living in the dorms are always "having people over" and there's always something to do.

Those tired of the party scene can take advantage of the concerts and shows on campus, or head into Columbia, which, by all reports, is very student-friendly. While it is a thriving city in its own right and probably can't be called a college town, Columbia does have lots of bars, restaurants, shops, and clubs, many of which offer student discounts. "The students and the people in town like each other, there's an easy interaction," said one student. Sports are also huge at Missouri/Columbia, as the school belongs to the powerful Big 12 conference and fields a number of powerful teams, including football and men's and women's basketball.

Missouri/Columbia is a big state school that feels like a small, friendly college. The value is undeniable; the programs are solid and, in many cases, excellent. "I love this place," said one student. "It feels so friendly and open, it really provides a place to relax, open your mind, and get a great education."

UNIVERSITY OF OREGON IN EUGENE, OREGON

Admissions Address: Admissions Office, 240 Oregon Hall, Eugene, OR 97403
Phone: (541) 346-3201 (800) 232-3825
Web Address: www.uoregon.edu

University of Oregon

$$

Setting: Urban
# of Undergraduates: 12,008
Men: 47.4% Women: 52.6
In-State Tuition: $3,646
Out-of-State Tuition: $12,014
Room and Board: $4,776
# of Students Applied: 8,361
   Admitted: 7,515 Enrolled: 2,576
Required Admissions Test: either SAT or ACT
Lowest 25% of Freshmen Scored At or Below: SAT Verbal: 500 SAT Math: 490
Highest 25% of Freshmen Scored At or Above: SAT Verbal: 610 SAT Math: 610
H.S. Rank, Top 10%: 25%
Top 25%: 43%
Top 50%: 58%
Average GPA of Applicants Admitted: 3.31
Most Popular Majors (% of Student Body): Business (12%), Architecture & Allied Arts (8%), Psychology (7%), Journalism (6%), English (5%)

If you can navigate the rain, the rain, and the rain, the University of Oregon is a fascinating place to go to school, mostly because of its solid academic credentials and outspoken and interesting student body.

There are seven undergraduate school at Oregon; the College of Arts and Sciences is the most popular, followed by the School of Business Administration, the School of Architecture and Allied Arts, and the School of Journalism. Add to this the interdisciplinary studies available, and it is easy to see that there's something for everyone here. While business administration is the most popular major (followed by psychology, biology, English, and prejournalism), it is the choice of less than 10 percent of the students, which indicates the amount of individuality students put into their studies. "If you know what you want and you can put together the program, you can study it here at Oregon," said one student. Another added, "The advisors are fantastic." Advisors work with their students to see that their study courses comprise as much of their interests as possible, and when necessary, help them assemble their own. "There is so much here to choose from," a student told us, " that it would be a waste to not take advantage of as much of it as you can."

With about 13,000 undergraduates, the school is large by most standards, yet not as large as other state schools around the country. This helps keep the community feeling tight and faculty accessible, within means. "You won't find the same small-town feeling like you would at Reed or Amherst," said one student, "but you get to know a lot of people here quickly. That includes faculty." Most go the distance to make themselves accessible, giving out office and home phone numbers as well as E-mail addresses. "I've never had a hard time tracking a prof down," said one student. "Most of the time they're really glad you came to them if you have a problem of some sort."

Oregon's student body is a fascinating lot. About 40 percent are nonresidents (very high for a state school) and nearly 10 percent are from overseas. This group draws from 95 different countries, many from Asia. There's also some diversity ethnically: minorities make up nearly 13 percent of the student body, though Asian-Americans make up a disproportionate amount of that percentage. Still, this is one of the most diverse student bodies you'll find at a state school.

It's also one of the most outspoken. The daily student newspaper, the Oregon Daily Emerald, is independent of the University and not afraid to take on issues uncomfortable to the administration (tuition hikes, faculty salaries, and deals with the food service are just a few) as well as national issues. The school is more left than right, from all reports, though the conservatives make their voices heard as well. The two ongoing concerns of Oregon's students seem to be the environment and state funding of their school. Green isn't just the school team's color here, it's an attitude. "We're lucky to be going to school in one of the most beautiful regions in the country," one student said, "and students here, whether they're from Oregon or not, tend to get very protective of it." Environmental protests are pretty common, especially against logging concerns and for endangered trees and animals.

Student are even more vocal on the subject of their school's funding. Oregon students' tuition and resources are at the whims of the state legislature, which, unlike their neighbors to the north and south, is not afraid to target the state universities when it comes time to trim the budget. "The school went through something like this in the early '90s," said one student. "The legislature passed a budget-cutting bill that raised tuition and forced the school to drop many good programs. It took years for the school to recover. This year, they tried to do it again. The students banded together and reminded the legislature what it cost them the last time they tried this, and it worked. They left us alone." This is a student body not afraid to speak its mind.

As mentioned, Oregon can be a beautiful, fascinating, mind-opening place, if you can work around the rain. "It's my one complaint about the place, and of course no one can do anything about it," said one student. Another added, "even if you're from Oregon, sometimes it's a little much to take." Most student, though, adjust, at least that's what we hear.

Oregon has a sense of community and students there enjoy not only their school, but being students. Many big state schools can feel like degree factories, but Oregon is definitely different. "We love this place," said one student. "Sometimes it makes us mad, but that's only because we care about it so much." "This is a great place to grow," said another. "You'll not only push yourself to the limit, you'll feel like you're a part of something bigger—not just the university, but the whole world around you."

UNIVERSITY OF TENNESSEE/KNOXVILLE

Admissions Address: Admissions Office, 320 Student Services Building, Knoxville, TN 37996-0200
Phone: (423) 974-2184 (800) 221-8657
Web Address: www.utk.eu

University of Tennessee/Knoxville

$$

Setting: urban
# of Undergraduates: 16,005
Men: 51.1% **Women:** 48.9%
In-State Tuition: $2,220
Out-of-State Tuition: $6,556
Room and Board: $3,620
# of Students Applied: 8,630
    Admitted: 6,438 **Enrolled:** 3,692
Required Admissions Test: either SAT or ACT
Lowest 25% of Freshmen Scored At or Below: SAT Verbal: 500 SAT Math: 490 ACT Comp.: 21
Highest 25% of Freshmen Scored At or Above: SAT Verbal: 620 SAT Math: 620 ACT Comp.: 27
H.S. Rank, Top 10%: 22%
Top 25%: 52%
Top 50%: 82%
Avg. Score of Applicants Admitted: SAT Verbal: 558 SAT Math: 554 ACT Comp.: 24
Average GPA of Applicants Admitted: 3.24
Most Popular Majors (% of Student Body): Business and Marketing (15%), Social Sciences and History (12%), Engineering (11%), Psychology (7%), Agriculture (7%)

Land Grant colleges that are large research universities seem to be good indicators of large schools that do well by their students—and the University of Tennessee at Knoxville is no exception.

With almost 19,000 undergraduates, Knoxville is a large school, but students reported they feel like they're part of a community while still reaping the benefits of an excellent, well-funded education. There is roughly an even distribution of men and women at Knoxville, and the school has what seems to be an average minority population of just under 10 percent. A recent administrative program was initiated to enhance the undergraduate minority population, and Knoxville stands out as a national leader in African American undergraduate, graduate, and professional scholarships and incentives. More than 85 percent of the undergraduate body is drawn from Tennessee, many attracted by the state's scholarship program.

There are more than 300 majors in 15 colleges to choose from at Knoxville, but business administration, engineering, psychology, and education are the most popular. Special science and technology programs, such as the Science Alliance Partnership with the Oak Ridge National Laboratory, give Knoxville students special opportunities to advance at a state school. Other ground-breaking programs include waste management, materials processing, and veterinary medicine. The state and federal funds available draw a significant number of well-known researchers to Knoxville's campus. However, a high student-to-faculty ratio and a concentration on research are signs that undergrads will have to deal with teaching assistants and lines outside their professor's doors throughout the first half of their college careers.

The school does its best to make connections for its students too. Recently Knoxville announced a research project with Tennessee-based

GO STATE!

Saturn Corporation and Sun Microsystems Computer Company. With corporate interaction like that, many Knoxville students can take advantage of experience gained and networks woven upon graduation.

The size of the school is taken in stride by most students. "I came from a very small high school, so coming to a school of this size, you only get lost if you let yourself. If you go to class and don't talk to teachers, you'll just be a number. If you talk with your professors and become involve, then you're not gonna be a number; teachers will get to know you," one junior told us. This can-do attitude is pervasive among Knoxville students, most of whom feel right at home in a large-school environment.

The campus mixes traditional southern architecture with modern, high-tech buildings without looking incongruous. The grounds are reported to be well maintained, and with the beautiful Tennessee countryside as a backdrop, students are apt to burst out into song with "The hills are alive with the sound of music" as easily as with "Rocky Top," the school fight song.

Housing is not a problem in the Knoxville area. Freshmen must live either on campus or with a relative in town. We're told that as students advance, they tend to move off campus; one sophomore cited cramped and noisy dorms as the cause. Approximately 85 percent of the freshman live on campus, but only 35 percent of all undergraduates live on campus. Most seek inexpensive housing in Knoxville or move into their fraternity or sorority buildings.

The Greek system has a strong presence on campus, and is responsible not only for the majority of the partying, but also welcoming the students to campus. "I thought I'd be lost here, but when I joined my sorority I got to be part of a big family," one student said. There are 25 fraternities and 19 sororities on campus, and just under 20 percent of the students are active members. Non-Greek students attend open parties when they occur.

Students sing the school's fight song vibrantly and with little provocation at every sporting event and most parties. Football and women's basketball are the most popular sports, and have been national title contenders for several years now; their games are always packed. Knoxville now boasts "the largest on-campus stadium in the United States" for over 100,000 fans, ensuring students will always be able to get to see the game. A full range of intramural sports are offered as well, and many students take advantage of them year-round.

The University of Tennessee at Knoxville seems to have it all—good academics, nice campus and town, promising career programs; Tennessee residents and out-of-state students alike graduate satisfied with their choice of schools.

UNIVERSITY OF WASHINGTON IN SEATTLE, WASHINGTON

Admissions Address: Admissions Office, Mail Box 355840, 1400 North East Campus Parkway, Seattle, WA 98195
Phone: (206) 593-9686
Web Address: www.washington.edu

University of Washington

$$
★★

Setting: Urban
# of Undergraduates: 20,876
Men: 49.5% **Women:** 50.5%
In-State Tuition: $3,250
Out-of-State Tuition: $9,866
Room and Board: $5,418
# of Students Applied: 12,874
  Admitted: 8,819 **Enrolled:** 4,036
Required Admissions Test: either SAT or ACT
Lowest 25% of Freshmen Scored At or Below: SAT Verbal: 500 SAT Math: 520 ACT Comp.: 22
Highest 25% of Freshmen Scored At or Above: SAT Verbal: 620 SAT Math: 640 ACT Comp.: 27
H.S. Rank, Top 10%: 37%
Top 25%: 70%
Top 50%: 98%
Average GPA of Applicants Admitted: 3.61
Most Popular Majors (% of Student Body): Business Administration (7.6%), Psychology (6.8%), English (5.8%), Political Science (4.9%), Accounting (3.6%)

"This is a self-service university. It is its greatest strength and its biggest problem. No one will bring what you need to you, you have to go and get it. But if you do go and get it, nothing or no one will stand in your way, and the rewards will be huge." This was how one Washington senior described the University he loved.

The University of Washington is a school of around 35,000 students, 703 acres, 220 buildings, and sixteen major schools and colleges. No matter how you slice it, it is big. It's also not for everyone, since you should have a pretty good idea what you want and what you're getting into when you walk in the door. But if you do know these things, and are ready and willing to look and work for them, you'll find top-notch academics, extraordinary opportunities, a great city to go to school in, small classes (relatively), a widely diverse student body, and 300 different organizations to make the place seem a little smaller.

About two-thirds of the undergrads at UW are in the College of Arts and Sciences, with another sizeable number in the School of Business Administration. UW has no set "core curriculum" but there are departmental requirements. Students must take courses in social science, natural science, and the humanities, but within those areas there are hundreds of applicable choices. Again, if you know what you want and don't mind sorting it out and making choices, you're bound to find something to your liking. The most popular majors are also the strongest ones at UW: biology, business administration, accounting, English, psychology, and zoology. Interdisciplinary majors are also popular; with this many courses to choose from, enterprising students can design some unique majors. Some interdisciplinary majors include regional studies, Asian studies, and communications and environmental planning.

With as many undergraduates as UW has, it is remarkable that class sizes generally stay pretty small. While there are large freshman lecture classes, the average class size is about 39 students, and in many cases, it is much smaller. UW has a freshman seminar program, which offers first-year students a chance to take courses with professors who volunteer to teach them in a small seminar setting. In the past, freshman seminar classes have included Chinese democratization, ethical issues in public education, and new and emerging diseases.

Despite the size, the faculty is reported to be very accessible, thanks in large part to the campus E-mail system, which connects the whole campus. "Everyone is on the system," said one student. "You drop an E-mail to a professor, and he's back to you within 24 hours, if not sooner. It's the best way to drop a question or set up an appointment." Most students reported that the faculty was friendly, approachable, and caring. About 75 percent of the classes are taught by the profs, the rest by either non-permanent faculty or TAs.

Washington has a very diverse and interesting student body for a state school. To begin with, the average age of undergraduates is 28. "A lot of the undergraduates are adults coming back to school," said one student. "Rather than drawing away, it truly enhances the experience." Needless to say, this makes for a great deal of economic diversity among the student body. "You love to hear students' experiences because they are so different," one student said. "It makes for a real feeling of community." There's a high percentage of minorities among the student body, but it's misleading: While about a quarter of the students are Asian Americans, only 4 percent are African American, and 2 percent are international students. Most students report that they would like to see a more racially diverse student body, but since nine out of 10 UW students are from Washington, the student body is always going to demographically resemble the state.

Most of the students live off campus after their freshman year. By all reports, the dormitories are quite beautiful, with each room equipped with cable television and computer network hookups. The food plans, it seems, are the problem. At least one student called the on-campus food plans, which involve laying out money at the beginning of the semester and being issued a debit card, as "a rip-off." Another student explained that once you're locked into the plan, the quality of the food goes way down while food not covered by the plan—which costs extra—is better. "It gets frustrating," said one student. Fraternities and sororities are an alternative that about 15 percent of students take, although all the frat houses are off campus, too. While the Greeks throw many parties ("we have some Animal Houses here" said one student) most students say that they are not a real campus force. "I don't see a lot of Greek letter sweaters around campus," said one student. According to most students, they move off-campus because they get fed up.

However, off campus is Seattle, by all accounts a great city, with many opportunities for young people. The whole coffee bar craze started here in Seattle, as did grunge rock. Any night of the week students take the quick trip into downtown Seattle to hit the clubs, as well as the bars and cafes. Ninety percent of students are Washington residents, most choose to stay in Seattle after graduation.

UW has both the best and most challenging aspects a large state school can offer. More than one student we spoke with said that UW offered them their only chance to go to college, and a reputable college at that. With the Washington state legislature committed to UW's funding and offering of financial aid, UW could be the best deal in the state for Washington residents.

UNIVERSITY OF WISCONSIN/MADISON

Admissions Address: Admissions Office, 750 University Avenue, Madison, WI 53706
Phone: (608) 262-3961
Web Address: jumpgate.acadsvcs.wisc.edu/admissions/

Most state schools end up looking pretty much like the state they are in, since the tuition and fees for residents of the state are so much better than out-of-state residents. While Wisconsin residents get a discount if they go to Wisconsin, tuition and fees are still kept low enough for out-of-state residents to allow a student body that has one-third from out-of-state as well as representatives of 132 different countries. It also has terrific academics, Big Ten sports, and—for the Midwest—a moderate climate.

Wisconsin has eight undergraduate colleges: the College of Agricultural and Life Sciences, the School of Business, the School of Education, the College of Engineering, the School of Human Ecology, the College of Letters and Science, the School of Nursing, and the School of Pharmacy. There are also undergraduate courses available at the Medical School that can lead to certification as a physician's assistant. The College of Letters and Science is the most popular with undergraduates, followed by the School of Business. Altogether, there are 140 undergraduate majors available.

Most classes are taught by the professors; the students we spoke with said that maybe one class in ten is taught by the TAs, and most of these are freshman level. Freshmen are assigned an advisor when they enter, and they can keep their advisor for all four years, or they can change their advisor when they move into their major. Students say if you have a good general idea of what area you want to move into (business, the arts, media, etc.) you can do pretty well. "I met my advisor my first week here," said one student, "and in the time I've been here we've gotten pretty tight." "With so much to choose from here," said another, "it's real important you have an advisor you feel comfortable with. That's why so many of us hit it off with our advisors well." "They really care," said a third student. This attitude carries to the faculty as well. "Even though there are a lot of students here, there are many ways the focus is made smaller," said one student, "and this helps the profs get to know us a little more than you would think at a school this size." The profs are accessible, with many giving out either home phone numbers or beeper numbers where students can reach them late at night or during a busy day.

One reason Wisconsin is able to draw a more diverse student body than most other large state campuses is that housing is guaranteed for anyone who requests it. The dorms are a center of campus social life, with parties and get-togethers the primary source or weekend fun. Less than 10 percent of students go Greek, while they don't dominate the social scene, "they're there" said one student. They also host many parties that are open to the entire campus.

While the student body is diverse in that a good number come from out-of-state, there is also a range economically and politically. There are students here from well-to-do backgrounds who come for the top-notch programs, and students from working-class families taking advantage of the educational value. While you will meet students from all over the world at Wisconsin, there is still a small minority community. Some folks in the administration we talked to said, "we're working on that." Financial aid and recruiting are where they are putting their efforts. Still, one student wonders why, if Wisconsin can draw students from all over the globe, "why they can't draw more students from downtown Milwaukee."

Students are vocal politically. Wisconsin boasts two daily papers, unusual for any school, with one leaning to the left and one to the right. While the school has been "traditionally liberal," there are many conservative voices, we hear. Wisconsin students are not afraid to express themselves, but as one student told us, "there's no real tension. We're all about as good at listening as we are at talking, and we like to do that a lot."

University of Wisconsin/Madison

🏛🏛🏛🏛🏛
$$
★★

Setting: urban
# of Undergraduates: 26,910
Men: 47.6% **Women:** 52.4
In-State Tuition: $3,180
Out-of-State Tuition: $10,750
Room and Board: $4,860
# of Students Applied: 15,250
  Admitted: 11,886 **Enrolled:** 5,455
Required Admissions Test: either SAT or ACT
Lowest 25% of Freshmen Scored At or Below: SAT Verbal: 520 SAT Math: 550 ACT Comp.: 24
Highest 25% of Freshmen Scored At or Above: SAT Verbal: 650 SAT Math: 670 ACT Comp.: 29
H.S. Rank, Top 10%: 43%
Top 25%: 85%
Top 50%: 99%
Avg. Score of Applicants Admitted: SAT Verbal: 610 SAT Math: 620 ACT Comp.: 26
Average GPA of Applicants Admitted: 3.68
Most Popular Majors (% of Student Body): Chemical Engineering (2%), Electrical Engineering (2%), English (2%), Mechanical Engineering (2%), Kinesiology (1.5%)

There are over 600 student organizations on campus, and new ones are popping up all the time. If groups are not your thing, and the dorm and frat scene are boring, you can also head into Madison, as many students do. While not a college town by any means, students are warmly welcomed into the city, and many restaurants and shops offer student discounts. "Folks here are very friendly," said one student. Many others report that going into Madison offers a break from the campus scene. "It's nice to get out and get some air," said one.

Wisconsin sports are huge, particularly the football team, the men's and women's basketball teams, and the hockey team. Wisconsin is a Big Ten power, and the annual game against archrival Minnesota is the campus event of the fall. In the winter, the hockey team steps to center stage, and their games draw regularly large crowds. Even though it is in the upper Midwest, the climate is not severe, and the winters not unbearably long. "This isn't Minnesota," said one student showing some school and state pride.

Wisconsin has a myriad of opportunities available to its students, both in and out of the classroom. With its diverse student body, the school takes on the feel of a smaller private university rather than a large state institution. And that feeling transcends other aspects of academic and campus life. "It's comfy here, it's home. There may be more undergraduates on campus than people in my hometown, but everyone's attitude helps to make it easier to get your arms around," said one student.

Sports Powerhouses

Nothing sparks school spirit as much as intercollegiate sports, which may be why athletics have long been a major part of higher education. Go to a game at any school with a powerhouse team, and you'll see students from all walks of life become a single entity of screaming fans. These students gain a tremendous pride in their school that lasts throughout their lives. Who hasn't seen some sedate, older relative launch into the old college cheer at the mere mention of his or her alma mater?

Most schools have some kind of sports and athletic program. The ones we've selected for this chapter, though, are those that have longstanding, solid reputations in their particular sport or sports. They are also schools at which athletics—whether playing on some intercollegiate or intramural team or just attending games—functions as a major part of student life. That's not to say that these schools offer strong sports and nothing else. Their strengths extend well beyond the playing field, as many of these schools also boast exceptional academics, faculties, and facilities.

Competition to play on the teams at these top-rated schools is often intense. If you're an average athlete set on playing a varsity sport, you may want to consider schools with less competitive athletic programs where you'll actually get to play rather than warm the bench. On the other hand, if you're an exceptional athlete, you may already have heard from many schools hoping to win you over. Many of these schools heavily recruit top high school athletes. Just keep in mind that scandals in recent years over recruiting have affected certain schools, placing some of them on probation. In general, these schools offer substantial athletic scholarships of various amounts and types. If you excel at any sport, you may have a decent chance at getting some kind of aid.

Students who don't play on varsity teams benefit from their school's sports programs in a number of ways. Athletic and recreational facilities at these schools are usually in prime condition and will certainly exceed the typical college fieldhouse in range. From popular intramural programs to physical education courses, many students participate in an impressive variety of sports and activities at these schools.

The presence of a powerhouse team generally means a more active social scene on campus. Student sports fans get the chance to attend games played by the nation's top college teams, with the added thrill of having a personal stake in the outcome. The games themselves will be the focus of an entire day or weekend or, in some cases, a whole week's worth of special social activities, some as crazed as the wildest of fraternity parties—from pregame tailgate parties to pep rallies to Homecoming parades. The enthusiasm and pride students generate for their school at games carry over to other facets of campus life. When you scream your heart out for your school, you can't help but feel good about it.

FLORIDA STATE UNIVERSITY IN TALLAHASSEE, FLORIDA

Admissions Address: Office of Admissions, A2500 University Center, Tallahassee, FL 32306-1009
Phone: (904) 644-6200
Web Address: admissions.fsu.edu

There are as many ways to have fun in the Florida sun at FSU as there are students. As one student explained, "We've got a very strong Greek system, so there are usually quite a few parties every weekend. If you're not into the party scene, there is also a big alternative band scene and several local bars. But in the fall, the party scene relies heavily on football."

FSU's powerhouse football team, the Seminoles, have been appearing in the Top Ten rankings for the last several years. The atmosphere at home games is that of a blowout party with about 20,000 of your closest friends. Just about everybody goes to the home games, and students show their school spirit in the form of deafening cheers and various sports-centered traditions. Games against archrival University of Florida bring their enthusiasm, and partying, to extreme levels. FSU students have been known to have pep rallies lasting over a week!

Besides football, FSU has many strong intercollegiate teams including men's basketball and baseball and women's softball, volleyball, swimming, and new soccer team. All students can take advantage of FSU's

Sports Powerhouses

extensive sporting and recreational facilities, which include a new health and fitness center with an indoor pool and new exercise equipment. The school's location makes a number of outdoor sports easily accessible, particularly water sports at nearby lakes.

But FSU students get much more than the chance to watch great teams. There are 14 undergraduate schools, enabling students to study in hundreds of fields. Many students are on a preprofessional track, for which FSU boasts some of its strongest academics, particularly in the business school. The natural sciences are also good and utilize high-quality facilities. Theatre, music, dance, and performing and fine arts are also well regarded. The core curriculum includes courses in social and natural sciences, math, history, English, and fine or performing arts. As the school is located in the state capital, a number of work experiences and internships are available, particularly in politics and government.

Just like at other schools with active social scenes, it's possible to apply yourself and get an excellent education at FSU, but it takes discipline to fend off the social temptations. Students are also faced with other obstacles stemming from FSU's size. Some classes number hundreds of students, and more popular or required classes are sometimes difficult to get into. Students need to make the initial effort in seeking out help, guidance, and opportunities from their professors.

In an attempt to address concerns about overcrowding, the administration has implemented a "Take 15" campaign to encourage students to take more academic units in an attempt to free up class space sooner for others. But, as one junior told us, "a lot of students are upset about the campaign because so many of us have to work while we're in school. I'd like to take 15 units but I just can't." One student pointed out that budget cuts have also affected the quality of the education. On the bright side, tuition is still exceptionally low for both Florida residents and out-of-staters.

About 80 percent of the students come from Florida. The rest come from all over the United States and more than 100 foreign countries. The minority population makes up about 5 percent of the student body, which represents a significant number given the large student enrollment. Southern hospitality seems to thrive here; students are generally friendly and courteous to one another.

Although there is a large student population, the campus itself is rather compact and easily managed. A variety of styles of buildings, from Gothic academic structures to more modern edifices, are interspersed

Florida State University

$$
★★

Setting: Urban
# of Undergraduates: 19,874
Men: 45% Women: 55%
In-State Tuition: $1,882
Out-of-State Tuition: $7,127
Room and Board: $4,897
# of Students Applied: 16,593
    Admitted: 12,200   Enrolled: 4,053
Required Admissions Test: Either SAT or ACT
Lowest 25% of Freshmen Scored At or Below: SAT Verbal: 510   SAT Math: 510   ACT Comp.: 21
Highest 25% of Freshmen Scored At or Above: SAT Verbal: 610   SAT Math: 610   ACT Comp.: 26
H.S. Rank, Top 10%: 47%
Top 25%: 72%
Top 50%: 95%
Avg. Score of Applicants Admitted: SAT Verbal: 565   SAT Math: 560   ACT Comp.: 23
Average GPA of Applicants Admitted: 3.40
Most Popular Majors (% of Student Body): Biology (7%), Criminal Justice (6%), Psychology (5%), English (4%), Political Science (3%)

amidst tree-lined patches of green. Campus housing varies in quality to the point where some dorms have air conditioning and others don't. Most upperclassmen move into affordable housing located off campus. Those who have to commute to the campus often opt for the bus because finding parking on campus can be a nightmare.

The Greek system draws around 20 percent of the student body, who can choose from over 25 fraternities and 19 sororities. With an undergraduate enrollment of over 20,000 students, that adds up to a significant number of students, but not enough to dominate the social scene and create pressure to join. In fact, there are over 300 clubs and organizations on campus that run the gamut of interests. At the same time, the city of Tallahassee offers alternative social opportunities, although some students complain about the lack of cultural events that one might find in a larger city.

FSU offers students a huge, vibrant campus, great sports teams, fantastic weather, and an active social scene. But as one student advises: "Don't be scared away by the football and party rep. It's got good academics and arts programs as well." For a full-on university experience at a surprisingly affordable price, FSU is well worth checking out.

INDIANA UNIVERSITY/BLOOMINGTON

Admissions Address: Office of Admissions, 300 North Jordan Avenue, Bloomington, IN 47405-7700
Phone: (812) 855-0661
Web Address: www.indiana.edu/~iuadmit

Indiana is practically the national shrine to basketball. In the midst of Hoosierland, Indiana University faculty and students, along with several thousand other fans, follow their school's basketball season with reverence and passion while paying homage to Bob Knight, one of the kings of college basketball, at his home court.

Believe it or not, there's more to IU than powerhouse basketball. IU, one of the largest universities in the region, offers many impressive academic programs—several considered tops in the country—as well as exceptional facilities, a renowned faculty, and one of the most appealing collegiate settings in the nation.

SPORTS POWERHOUSES

IU's 12 undergraduate schools provide about 20,000 undergraduates with hundreds of different majors and programs of study, including education, health, nursing, social work, environmental affairs, and arts and sciences. The undergraduate business, music, and journalism programs are considered among the best in the country. The education program benefits from the recent addition of the Center for Excellence in Education. Many departments are excellent, including biology, chemistry, foreign languages, history, and international studies, just to name a few.

In addition to its standard offerings, IU has a number of special academic options, including dual majors, interdisciplinary programs, opportunities for independent research, study abroad, and an honors program in which students study in smaller seminars. Requirements vary by school, but most have stiff general education requirements in broad liberal arts areas including arts and humanities, social sciences, natural sciences, history and math, foreign language, and writing.

With a population akin to that of a small city, IU is an enormous research institution. The size has its advantages, particularly in the variety of academic and social offerings, as well as the number of high-quality facilities available to students and faculty. Yet students have to be prepared to take the bad with the good, including class sizes that can number in the hundreds, limited interaction with professors, difficulty getting courses, and tedious registration procedures. As with all large schools, it's important to learn some aggressive maneuvers in order to successfully grapple with these challenges. Students who seek out professors for advice will usually find they get the help they need.

While they're dealing with some of these more headache-inducing problems, IU students at least have the benefit of being on a campus that seems designed to suit their every academic and social need. Considered one of the most scenic in the nation, IU's immaculate campus combines lush natural foliage with beautiful landscaping, and features academic structures that range from the Gothic to the contemporary. The impressive facilities include an art museum designed by I. M. Pei, an enormous library system, and a student center that's the largest in the nation. In recent years, the school has been renovating many old facilities while adding new ones. While dormitories vary in style and age, most students get the on-campus housing they want. Many upperclassmen opt to move off campus where they have access to affordable housing.

For Indiana residents, the tuition is an incredibly good bargain. About 70 percent of the students are Indiana natives while the rest, many

---

Indiana University / Bloomington

$$
★★

Setting: Suburban
# of Undergraduates: 24,034
Men: 45% **Women:** 55
In-State Tuition: $3,320
Out-of-State Tuition: $10,868
Room and Board: $4,284
# of Students Applied: 16,725
   Admitted: 14,516   **Enrolled:** 4,862
Required Admissions Test: Either SAT or ACT
H.S. Rank, Top 10%: 22%
Top 25%: 56%
Top 50%: 94%
Avg. Score of Applicants
   Admitted: SAT Verbal: 546
   SAT Math: 554   ACT Comp.: 24
Most Popular Majors (% of Student Body): Business (17.7%), Education (14.9%), Biology (7.5%), Environmental Studies (6.4), Psychology (6.4)

drawn by the school's renowned academics and athletics, come from all 50 states and more than 100 foreign countries. There are so many students at IU that virtually every type of student is represented. With about a 10 percent minority population, however, the student body is fairly homogeneous in terms of race. IU's administration is quick to point out that this figure is still considerably higher than the state average.

Most students are conservative, politically and socially. Some students report that many groups splinter off, and there's no sense of community. The school is taking measures to foster intercultural relations and ease any tensions between groups.

Students enjoy about as many social opportunities as they do academic ones. There's an active party scene that includes attending off-campus apartment parties, hanging out in local bars, and going to fraternity and sorority parties. Greeks attract about 25 percent of the students, who can choose from over 30 fraternities and over 18 sororities, many with their own beautiful mansionlike houses. Despite the large number of chapters, going Greek is still highly competitive and inevitably leaves many disappointed. Those who don't find alternative social options might feel left out.

For those who want them, there are many other activities and social opportunities, including hundreds and hundreds of clubs and organizations. The campus has a number of entertainment venues, including movie screenings and concerts. The prestigious music school provides concerts and performances of the highest quality.

The town of Bloomington receives raves from students. It caters primarily to the IU population, and students frequently venture off campus to the large variety of local eateries, shops, music venues, and general hangouts. The natural surroundings, with lakes and woods in abundance, are ideal for a number of outdoor sports and field trips.

Then, of course, there's that frenzied affair known as basketball season. Believe it or not, though, there are other sports besides basketball to be enjoyed at Indiana. The school's many other powerhouse teams include soccer, swimming, and men's and women's track and tennis. Football games also draw large crowds, especially the annual contest against rival Purdue. IU students are able to use the school's superb athletic facilities, which include a new recreation and aquatic center, for a number of intramural sports and other activities. Particularly well known, thanks to the movie *Breaking Away*, is the Little 500, a marathon bicycle race that is one of the most famous collegiate sporting events in the country.

SPORTS POWERHOUSES

SYRACUSE UNIVERSITY IN SYRACUSE, NEW YORK

Admissions Address: Admissions Office, 201 Tolley Administration Building, Syracuse, NY 13244
Phone: (315) 443-3611
Web Address: www.syr.edu/

"Sports rule," at Syracuse University, according to one student. "They bring the campus together," figuratively and literally. Just check out the hordes who crowd the cavernous Carrier Dome to cheer on the Orangemen at intercollegiate events. Basketball games are the main attraction, with football a close second. Men's lacrosse is a national power that has won a record six NCAA championships, including the 1995 crown. Go to just about any intercollegiate game, and you'll see Syracuse's large student body become a single, screaming mass of fans. "People who aren't even sports fans are sports fans when Syracuse is doing well," says one senior.

A large institution, Syracuse offers a wide range of academic programs; many of the strongest and most popular programs serve as preparation for specific professions and careers. The 11 undergraduate schools include architecture, engineering, management, and visual and performing arts. SU is particularly known for its prestigious S. I. Newhouse School of Communications, considered one of the best communications programs in the nation. The College of Arts and Sciences is the largest school and has many strong programs, particularly those in the natural sciences. The many special academic options at SU include an acclaimed honors program in which students study in a more intimate and intense academic setting, as well as extensive study-abroad offerings.

Undergraduates benefit from Syracuse's graduate schools in many ways. They can use high-quality, state-of-the-art resources and facilities and have the chance to study with the schools' prestigious faculty members. Undergraduates can also take courses in the graduate schools, including the renowned Maxwell School of Citizenship and Public Affairs.

The admissions procedures and core requirements vary by school. Most schools require that students take courses in several academic areas, such as social science, natural science, math, humanities, writing, and foreign language.

The amount of studying varies significantly from student to student. SU is a place where those who put in the effort can receive a strong education, but it's possible to take a lighter load, a student told us.

Syracuse University

$$$$
★★

Setting: Urban
# of Undergraduates: 10,002
Men: 49% Women: 51%
Tuition: $16,710
Room and Board: $7,220
# of Students Applied: 10,149
    Admitted: 6,670 Enrolled: 2,409
Required Admissions Test: Either SAT or ACT
Lowest 25% of Freshmen Scored At or Below: SAT Verbal: 450 SAT Math: 520
Highest 25% of Freshmen Scored At or Above: SAT Verbal: 570 SAT Math: 650
H.S. Rank, Top 10%: 33%
Top 25%: 77%
Top 50%: 95%
Avg. Score of Applicants Admitted: SAT Verbal: 505 SAT Math: 580

425

There's no question that Syracuse is a big university, and students will feel it. Many classes, especially at introductory levels, are huge, sometimes numbering hundreds of students. These classes do break down into weekly discussion sections, usually led by TAs. When it comes to more personal interaction with professors, students often have to pursue the faculty in order to get attention. A student did praise teachers for their efforts to get to know their students: "There's a lot of personal attention paid to students by faculty. You're not just a number." Negotiating the tricky bureaucracy at Syracuse also presents its challenges.

These problems may be waning, though, as the school has adopted a new mission statement that includes a concerted effort to change undergraduate education at Syracuse. The goal: "to become a student-oriented research university." Related initiatives include working to lower the student-faculty ratio, decrease TA teaching duties, increase undergraduate involvement in faculty research, and encourage senior faculty to bring their research into undergraduate classrooms. Regardless of these efforts, a junior explains "the thing is that everyone takes the huge classes at some point but you leave those behind when you progress in your major. I tend to get lost in the bigger lecture classes and do a lot better in the small classes but, in the end, it's all up to what you want to do."

The Syracuse campus is scenic and not too difficult to manage, given its large size. Because it's located on the side of a hill, just getting to class can provide a good leg workout. The campus features many modern structures as well as a number of older buildings officially listed as Historic Places. The impressive Quad is the major focus of campus, surrounded by most of the school's academic buildings. There are several renovation projects currently underway, and many of the dorms and science facilities have recently received improvements.

Syracuse has a reputation for being a real party school, although, according to one student, the administration is trying to crack down on this facet of student life with regulations limiting the number of people allowed in frat houses and related measures. Roughly a quarter of the school joins the 23 fraternities and 19 sororities and with so many houses, there's one that's right for almost everyone. For parties, students head to fraternity or sorority events or go to off-campus apartments. There's also a thriving bar scene on nearby Marshall Street and some popular clubs farther away from campus, several of which host 18-and-over nights so underclassmen can attend.

In addition to parties and bars, there are plenty of other social and extracurricular options, including about 300 activities and clubs. With a top communications school on campus, it's not surprising that the radio station and newspaper are both excellent. And due to the top-notch visual and performing arts schools, there are frequent student performances. Also, the Carrier Dome provides more than a great sports venue; major rock groups often make the Dome a stopping point on their tours—a very cool bonus.

The minority student population at Syracuse makes up about one-fifth of the student body. One student complains that the student body splits itself into different groups, sometimes along ethnic and cultural lines. As for politics, another student says "there's a wide range of political views. Although most students don't generally classify themselves as liberal or conservative, people definitely speak their minds."

While no one could argue that Syracuse's weather isn't "really harsh," one student echoes Neitzsche in pointing out that "it makes you stronger." And that's the type of perspective Syracuse students seem to have. The benefits of going to school here far outweigh the downsides. To use another student's extreme example, even if you couldn't care less about Syracuse athletics, "the sports notoriety gives us a national reputation that helps with job hunting later on."

UNIVERSITY OF CALIFORNIA IN LOS ANGELES

With a total student population of about 30,000, UCLA is itself the size of a small city and has the social offerings to match, including a performance space that draws top touring companies, cafes and restaurants, galleries and museums, not to mention the greater opportunities afforded by its Los Angeles location. But no description of UCLA would be complete without mention of its famed sports teams. The Bruins are perennial contenders for a multitude of NCAA championships. One student summarized the school's proud athletic history and sports powerhouse status quite simply: "We're UCLA."

UCLA's most notable teams are its championship basketball and football teams, both of which have turned out countless professional stars. Other highly rated sports are track and field, tennis, baseball, gymnastics, waterpolo, and both men's and women's volleyball. UCLA students are proud supporters of their Bruins, and attending games is a major social

University of California/Los Angeles

$$

Setting: Urban
# of Undergraduates: 22,468
Men: 47.9% **Women:** 52.1
In-State Tuition: $0 (plus fees)
Out-of-State Tuition: $8,394
Room and Board: $6,181
# of Students Applied: 28,075
  Admitted: 10,911 **Enrolled:** 3,821
Required Admissions Test: Either SAT or ACT; SAT II (three subject tests)
Lowest 25% of Freshmen Scored At or Below: SAT Verbal: 550 SAT Math: 580 ACT Comp.: 22
Highest 25% of Freshmen Scored At or Above: SAT Verbal: 660 SAT Math: 700 ACT Comp.: 28
H.S. Rank, Top 10%: 97%
Avg. Score of Applicants Admitted: SAT Verbal: 629 SAT Math: 659
Average GPA of Applicants Admitted: 4.08
Most Popular Majors (% of Student Body): Biology (9%), Psychology (9%), Economics (9%), Political Science (6%), Chemistry (5%)

event, especially those played against archrival USC. One student fan confided that he believed his intense dislike of USC "anchors" him. Most students don't confine themselves to the stands, though. UCLA has enough sports teams, intramural events, and recreational activities for virtually everyone to become involved in something.

The academic offerings at UCLA rival the social ones in diversity and number. The enormous UCLA campus is split into two distinct areas that reflect its diverse strengths; the North campus is home mainly to the liberal arts, while the South campus houses the sciences. Not many schools have such high-quality academic programs in such completely different fields. For example, the science and engineering programs at UCLA are excellent, but so are the famed film, theater, and performing arts divisions. Although each school and program has its own requirements, general education requirements ensure that all students receive a solid liberal arts education.

While the variety of academic and social offerings draws many students to the school, there are also the typical problems and hassles of any large university: huge lecture classes, professors who need to be chased down for advice, problems getting into more popular classes, and miles and miles of red tape. But the enterprising and aggressive student can find ways around many of these problems, particularly by seeking out professors for guidance when it's needed.

Although located in an urban environment, UCLA is not a typical urban campus. It has its own beautifully landscaped campus clearly set off from the other parts of the city. The Westwood area that surrounds campus is home to numerous shops, restaurants, and movie theaters and resembles a typical college town despite the Los Angeles mailing address.

Having such a large student population, almost every type of student is represented. UCLA has a diverse student population on almost every level; liberal and conservative factions, gays and lesbians, fraternity devotees and independents, various cultural and ethnic populations are all a part of the mix. This diversity means almost anyone can find a group with which they feel comfortable. At the same time, many students choose to remain within their chosen niche, which means there is no real sense of a cohesive UCLA community.

The academic year is divided into quarters, which creates some stress for students as exams and papers roll around more frequently than with the semester calendar. At the same time, UCLA students know how to enjoy their free time. UCLA has a reputation for being a real party school, in large part due to the enormous Greek system; there are more than 34 national fraternities and 21 national sororities, and almost all host large parties and social events throughout the year. Those who don't join don't feel left out, as there's no shortage of other parties and social events. There's also a huge number of extracurricular activities, clubs, and organizations to choose from.

As if all that weren't enough, there's the entire Los Angeles area with its rich and varied cultural and social offerings. East Coasters love to characterize their West Coast counterparts as suntanned health fanatics obsessed with movies and unable to get anywhere unless by car. To some extent, some of these LA stereotypes apply to the UCLA population. To enjoy the many offerings in the expansive city, not to mention going to the beach or skiing in the mountains, having a car is essential; unfortunately for UCLA students, having a car can also be a royal pain given the nightmarish parking situation.

Whether you're looking for a great education, an active social life, a rock-solid sports program, or just some truly unbelievable weather, it's hard to go wrong with UCLA.

UNIVERSITY OF CONNECTICUT IN STORRS

Admissions Address: Admissions Office, 2131 Hillside Road, Storrs, CT 06269-3088
Phone: (860) 486-3137
Web Address: www.uconn.edu/

When asked to comment on his school's athletic environment, one student summed things up well: "Sports scene? Well, it's UConn."

With both men's and women's basketball teams in regular contention for the NCAA championship, UConn students are understandably enthusiastic about supporting their Huskies. Crowds of student fans flock to the Gampel Pavilion, the university's sports center, to scream their lungs out for their school's team. Football season gets things started each year, and the annual game against archrival Yale is a season highlight. Although basketball has long been UConn's number-one sport, many other intercollegiate sports teams are also considered powerhouses, including men's football, field hockey, and baseball, and men's and women's soccer. And if they're not watching a sport, chances are UConn students are playing one as part of UConn's extensive intramural program.

University of Connecticut

$$
Setting: Rural
# of Undergraduates: 10,360
Men: 49% Women: 51%
In-State Tuition: $4,158
Out-of-State Tuition: $12,676
Room and Board: $5,462
# of Students Applied: 10,183
   Admitted: 6,806   Enrolled: 2,166
Required Admissions Test: Either SAT or ACT
Lowest 25% of Freshmen Scored At or Below: SAT Verbal: 500 SAT Math: 500
Highest 25% of Freshmen Scored At or Above: SAT Verbal: 600   SAT Math: 600
H.S. Rank, Top 10%: 23%
Top 25%: 59%
Top 50%: 95%
Avg. Score of Applicants Admitted: SAT Verbal: 553 SAT Math: 559
Most Popular Majors (% of Student Body): Business (13%), Engineering (8%), Psychology (5%), Biological Sciences (4%), Education (3%)

Students are also fans of the wide range of academic offerings. UConn is a large university with ten undergraduate schools, so there's no shortage of major and course options. Engineering and business programs both draw large percentages of students. Because the school was originally founded as an agricultural college, the agricultural program is a UConn mainstay. In the College of Liberal Arts, English, psychology, economics, history, and political science are all popular programs of study. One student told us that the theater program, after having been significantly developed in recent years, is also strong.

The core curriculum includes broad requirements in fields including math, literature and the arts, philosophical and ethical analysis, social science, science and technology, foreign language, expository writing, and culture and modern society.

With an enrollment of over 10,000 undergraduates, it's inevitable that there will be problems getting into certain courses and that required classes will be large. Still, many classes have only 20 to 30 people. When it comes to advising, professors generally need to be sought out. Students who make it a point to go to see professors during office hours or after class will usually find them very approachable. "Overall, our professors are excellent," a sophomore told us.

While academic programs receive praise from students, the facilities get less positive reviews. "The dorms are much too small and there's no variety. A lot of the facilities need renovation right now. That's our biggest weakness." Due to budget cuts, it's not certain if major renovations will in fact happen. However, the tuition remains very low for in-state residents.

Most students are Connecticut residents. Minority students make up a relatively small percentage of the student body but out of a total enrollment larger than 11,000, that percentage translates into a visible number. "This is actually a very diverse student body," a student told us.

UConn is in a pretty rural area surrounded by woods and fields, but not much else. The school's setting, according to one sophomore, is "peaceful and relaxing," while another student referred to it as "going to school on a farm." Out of some necessity, students create an active social scene themselves. The dorms function as mini social units and each dorm has its unique character; this helps students form smaller communities of friends within the larger university. Many have their own teams for intramural events and host special functions and socials.

The student union, with its pool tables and video games, is a popular place to hang out. About 10 percent of the students join fraternities or sororities, which frequently throw parties and socials. There are also parties off-campus at student apartments and houses. Several major, campus-wide social events throughout the year attract students in large numbers. One student told us, "Spring Weekend is a big party tradition. There are cookouts, a fair, and parties everywhere."

The nearby town of Storrs offers few diversions, mostly in the form of a few local bars and hangouts; we hear that Thursday's dollar draft night is a particular favorite among students. For a temporary break from Storrs and the campus, Boston and New York are each less than three hours away by train. "It's helpful to have a car," one student advises. "There is mass transportation, but it's a pain." To get farther away, UConn offers study-abroad opportunities in more than 25 countries. And, of course, students can follow the Huskies to out-of-town championship tournaments.

UNIVERSITY OF NOTRE DAME IN SOUTH BEND, INDIANA

Admissions Address: Admissions Office, 113 Main Building, Notre Dame, IN 46556
Phone: (219) 631-5000
Web Address: www.nd.edu/

"Every football weekend is like homecoming weekend," a proud Notre Dame graduate told us. With its long history of championships, Notre Dame has become practically synonymous with college football. For each game, "scores and scores of alumni and families" flock to the stadium, where "you'll see everyone wearing the school colors." Almost the entire student body crowds the student section to cheer loudly and proudly for the Fighting Irish. Football games at Notre Dame are at the center of many social events and campus traditions, including tailgate parties before the game, a cross-campus victory parade behind the marching band after a win, traditional school cheers—including, we hear, "handwaving to the 1812 overture"—and the antics of the Leprechaun, the school's mascot. Then there's "Touchdown Jesus," depicted an enormous mosaic alongside the 12-story library that, with his hands raised to the heavens, indeed looks as if he's signaling a score for the Fighting Irish.

University of Notre Dame

$$$$$
★★★

Setting: Urban
# of Undergraduates: 7,859
Men: 61% Women: 39%
Tuition: $19,000
Room and Board: $4,850
# of Students Applied: 9,400
  Admitted: 3,700 Enrolled: 1,885
Required Admissions Test: Either SAT or ACT
H.S. Rank, Top 10%: 80%
Top 25%: 97%
Top 50%: 99%
Avg. Score of Applicants
  Admitted: SAT Verbal: 590
  SAT Math: 670 ACT Comp.: 29

Football isn't the only thing treated with reverence at Notre Dame. Because it's a Catholic university, religion influences the academics and social atmosphere in many ways. A majority of the students are Catholic, and a number consider themselves fairly religious. And "lots of people attend Sunday evening mass in the dorms," according to one student. As part of Notre Dame's required courses, students take about two years of philosophy and theology.

One student we interviewed told us that many feel the school's policies, which accord with the doctrines of the church, can "limit growth." He pointed out, as an example, how it took the university a long time to officially recognize the gay and lesbian student group. Likewise, some students are down on the strict regulations, known as "parietals," that control the visiting hours in student dorms for members of the opposite sex. Other students argue, however, that many students are themselves very supportive of such school policies.

Notre Dame offers a number of outstanding academic programs in its four undergraduate colleges: engineering, science, business, and arts and sciences. Even though one student told us, "It seems like everyone's major is accounting," the school of arts and letters is the largest school and has a number of strong departments. The basic curriculum includes courses in sciences, humanities, history, math, writing, and philosophy, as well as theology. The First Year of Studies functions as a supportive and helpful transition period for first-year students. All first year courses are mapped out and include a number of these core requirements.

Notre Dame students receive guidance and support from faculty and professors in large amounts. "Professors take time out to talk to you," a student praised.

The Notre Dame campus, graced by two lakes right on campus, revolves around the impressive gold-domed administration building. As one student described the campus, which she called "spectacular, especially in the fall," the architecture includes "very old brick, ivy-covered buildings" as well as "newer buildings that were built to look like the old ones, except they haven't gotten the ivy to hang just right yet." The campus also has a grotto, modeled on Lourdes Cathedral, where Mass is sometimes held.

About 85 percent of the students are Caucasian, which makes for a fairly homogeneous student body. Most students lean to the right, politically and socially, although there are a fair number of liberals. With the football season sparking school spirit, the student body is pretty tight. "One of the best things here is the sense of community. It's a relatively small campus, so there's a real sense of community," a junior told us.

In terms of location, the Notre Dame campus is fairly isolated. South Bend "isn't exactly Chicago" in terms of entertainment options, and the bitter winter weather can force students to stay close to campus. As a result, the social life is limited to the campus, where it centers on the dormitories. All dorms are single sex and mix all four years of students together. The dorm system resembles the college system at other universities, with students tending to live in the same dorm their entire on-campus lives, which produces a strong community atmosphere. Although a number of seniors do move off campus in order to escape some of the regulations, the majority remain on campus all four years. Many dorms sponsor special social events, such as Screw Your Roommate dances during which people set their roommates up with dates. Even so, a student told us "this isn't a real dating school. People mostly hang out with groups of friends."

One student summed up Notre Dame social life like this: "Freshmen go to the dorm parties. Sophomores begin throwing the parties. And juniors start hitting the off-campus bars." In addition to the dorm-sponsored parties, many students head to off-campus parties or to local bars. Others go to the on-campus Senior Bar, which has dry nights for under-aged students. A number of campus clubs and organizations are also popular, especially those involving community service and volunteer work, which is highly encouraged.

Even at the close of football season, sports remain a major part of student life. Notre Dame has extensive athletic and recreational facilities, including a "huge new complex that's got just about everything," a student told us. Many of Notre Dame's varsity teams have stellar records, including men's and women's track. "Interhall" sporting events of all kinds waged between dorm teams are also extremely popular. In the spring, when the last mounds of snow have melted away, there's the week-long Festival that includes such sporting events as chariot races through the mud, and "Bookstore Basketball," a nonvarsity basketball tournament in which anyone and everyone can participate. Apparently, many do; the event attracts about 700 teams.

At Notre Dame, people are serious about their studies. They're also serious about their partying. Many students are serious about their religion. And of course, everyone's serious about football. "Everyone goes to the football games. Even if you don't know what a first down is, you go for the social scene," comments a junior. This powerful mix makes Notre Dame an attractive choice for many.

UNIVERSITY OF MASSACHUSETTS/AMHERST

Admissions Address: University Admissions Center, Whitmore Building, Amherst, MA 01003-0120
Phone: (413) 545-0222
Web Address: www.umass.edu

"You can be interested in anything, and UMass will have something to offer you!" says one junior currently studying communications at the University of Massachusetts—Amherst. The large student body, with a large diversity of interests, is involved in hundreds of activities and enjoys a fast-paced, party-filled social life. But most have one thing in common, says this student: "Everyone is into athletics."

UMass has come to be identified with Midnight Madness, the all-night festivities surrounding the first official night of basketball practice that epitomizes the enthusiasm for college basketball. Students flock to the 10,000-seat Mullen Center to support their beloved basketball team, which has risen to become a contender for the NCAA championship.

It seems as if everyone at UMass either watches a sport or plays one. The athletic facilities are tremendous, including acres of outdoor athletic fields, a 20,000-seat stadium, several pools, tennis and racquetball courts, an indoor track, weight rooms and exercise areas, and two ice rinks. But then again, many things at UMass are on a grand scale, including its 1,400-acre campus. For example, the school boasts the largest library system of any public school in the Northeast.

UMass's undergraduate schools include humanities and fine arts, social and behavioral science, natural sciences and mathematics, education, management, engineering, food and natural resources, health sciences, nursing, public health, and hotel management. As one student comments, UMass's size provides "more of an opportunity to take such a wide variety of classes." Many students are on a preprofessional track, particularly in business, communications, and engineering, which are all considered strong and have large enrollments.

General education requirements for all students include courses in writing, the social world (which includes courses in literature, fine arts, his-

SPORTS POWERHOUSES

tory, and social sciences), the biological and physical world (more focused on natural sciences), and mathematics and analytical reasoning.

Students can also take advantage of special academic opportunities. Through a program called the Bachelor's Degree with Individual Concentration, for example, students are free to develop their own curricula. The University Without Walls program allows students to earn credit for real-world and work experiences.

The numerous academic offerings at UMass are further supplemented by the school's participation in the Five College Consortium, which includes the reputable New England schools of Smith, Mt. Holyoke, Hampshire, and Amherst College. Students can take up to two courses a semester at these other schools at no extra charge.

Due to UMass's size, classes will often be huge, numbering into the hundreds, and tend to be lecture oriented. It's obviously no easy feat to get to know professors, and students must take the initiative. Still, students report a number of professors make themselves accessible and are helpful and friendly when students encounter them.

The housing system at UMass is—surprise—expansive and considered to be one of the largest in the nation. It has to be, because students are required to live on campus for the first two years. The 45 or so residence halls are divided into five areas that differ in atmosphere, from more sedate and study-oriented housing close to the academic buildings to the louder, super-social Southwest area, popular among freshmen. Most rooms are standard college doubles.

About 70 percent of the students are from Massachusetts, and the tuition is substantially less for them than for out-of-staters. Much of the rest of the student body comes from the northeast including other parts of New England, New York, and New Jersey. The minority population is around 15 percent. Students report, though, that the student body is diverse in many ways, particularly in the range of personalities, experiences, and interests.

While UMass is no longer as wild as when it was commonly known as "Zoo Mass," there's still no shortage of partying. "The social scene is great. There are a lot of off-campus parties and there's a bar scene," a student describes. The town of Amherst is quintessentially New England, quiet and quaint, and has some good bars and restaurants. "Tons of people go "uptown," as student rather facetiously refer to Amherst.

UMass / Amherst

$$
★★

Setting: Suburban
# of Undergraduates: 17,386
Men: 52% Women: 48%
In-State Tuition: $3,328
Out-of-State Tuition: $3,390
# of Students Applied: 17,705
  Admitted: 13,164 Enrolled: 3,985
Required Admissions Test: Either SAT or ACT
Lowest 25% of Freshmen Scored At or Below: SAT Verbal: 500 SAT Math: 510
Highest 25% of Freshmen Scored At or Above: SAT Verbal: 610 SAT Math: 610
H.S. Rank, Top 10%: 12%
Top 25%: 38%
Top 50%: 78%
Avg. Score of Applicants Admitted: SAT Verbal: 567 SAT Math: 573
Average GPA of Applicants Admitted: 2.97
Most Popular Majors (% of Student Body): Psychology (8%), Communication (6%), Hotel, Restaurant & Travel Administration (6%), Political Science (4%), English (4%)

435

Many students remain on campus taking advantage of the opportunities to be found there. The Greeks account for some of the social life but are in no way the majority, as only about seven percent of the men and five percent of the women rush. "We're considered a dry campus, but I don't think the drinking age affects the amount of drinking. Some people party seven nights a week. As students mature, they learn how to balance the studying and partying," a student says.

Of course, there are always other options. "You don't have to worry about the Zoo Mass rep," a senior told us. Another student concurs: "Even if you are not into the party scene and drinking, there is always something else to do." UMass's 250 activities and clubs run the gamut, including art, theater and music groups, volunteer organizations, an active student government, various professional societies, many cultural and ethnic organizations and centers, and the Daily Collegian, which has the largest circulation of any college newspaper in the Northeast. There's always some visiting speaker or performer on campus. Major bands perform at the annual Spring Concert, a day-long musical festival/party.

Although Zoo Mass may no longer accurately describe UMass, students are so busy with all the activities, sports, and socializing that they don't feel the need to uphold the partying tradition.

VILLANOVA UNIVERSITY IN VILLANOVA, PENNSYLVANIA

Admissions Address: Admissions Office, 800 Lancaster Avenue, Villanova, PA 19085-1672
Phone: (610) 519-4000 (800) 338-7927
Web Address: www.vill.edu

Because Villanova is located in a wealthy, quiet suburb of Philadelphia, students turn to campus sports to provide much of the action. When it comes to the basketball court, they get it in abundance. NCAA tournament regulars since their 1985 championship win, Wildcat basketball is a major component of Villanova. As befits the Wildcats, the Villanova students are wildly supportive of their school teams. In addition to basketball, both men's and women's track are successful teams and have nurtured a number of Olympic medal winners. Villanova's huge sports complex allows all students to take part in a number of athletic and recreational activities.

Villanova is a Roman Catholic school, although it welcomes all faiths, and the influence of the church is evident in many ways. Most students are

SPORTS POWERHOUSES

Catholic, and church services are well attended. As part of their core curriculum, students take religion and philosophy courses. The school is run according to church doctrines, which strictly regulate alcohol and drug policies as well as limit the hours for student visitors of the opposite sex.

Many students are already set on a career path, and preprofessional programs are among the school's strongest. Graduates of the business-oriented College of Commerce and Finance, if they don't go directly into business, often get accepted at top business and law schools. The other three undergraduate schools are the colleges of engineering, nursing, and arts and sciences. Many of the liberal arts departments, including political science, English, and psychology, are considered good. All students receive a broad background through Villanova's general education requirements which, in addition to religious studies, include courses in the humanities—literature, foreign language, philosophy, religious studies, history, and social sciences—and the sciences—biology, chemistry, computer science, astronomy, and physics.

'Nova's size allows students to study in small and intimate academic settings. A "really big" introductory class generally has fewer than 100 students. This allows for a great deal of interaction with peers and professors, and students describe the atmosphere as decidedly uncompetitive. One student praises the school's size in this way: "it's not too small but it's small enough to participate in activities. Everyone has an opportunity to get involved." The student body also enjoys a sense of community that is only increased by their enthusiasm for their teams. "The entire school is community oriented. It's very friendly and supportive."

In an attempt to foster an even greater sense of community, the school is implementing a program called The Villanova Experience in which first year students take classes and participate in special activities with others from their dorms and sometimes from their halls. There has also been discussion of expanding this program to include second-year students.

The student body is socioeconomically and ethnically homogeneous, with a small minority population. Most students, while not very outspoken politically, consider themselves conservative. The dorms are generally in good condition, but there aren't enough of them to go around. Although students generally like the campus, describing it as beautiful, many upperclassmen opt for off-campus housing, which is not especially easy to find or affordable in this wealthy suburb.

Villanova University

$$$$$
★★

Setting: Suburban
# of Undergraduates: 6,341
Men: 49.4% **Women:** 50.6%
Tuition: $18,370–$19,140
Room and Board: $7,260
# of Students Applied: 9,247
  Admitted: 6,013 **Enrolled:** 1,588
Required Admissions Test: Either SAT or ACT
Lowest 25% of Freshmen Scored At or Below: SAT Verbal: 560 SAT Math: 580
Highest 25% of Freshmen Scored At or Above: SAT Verbal: 650 SAT Math: 690
H.S. Rank, Top 10%: 36%
Top 25%: 63%
Top 50%: 93%
Avg. Score of Applicants Admitted: SAT Verbal: 620 SAT Math: 645
Average GPA of Applicants Admitted: 3.58
Most Popular Majors: Business, Engineering, Nursing, Political Science, Psychology

The social life for students consists of hanging out in the dorms and at the huge student center, or attending parties in off-campus houses. "A lot of people drink here," says one sophomore. "It's a big activity." The Greek system draws large numbers of students—about 35 percent of the men and almost half the women—and keeps up a steady stream of parties for students. There's also a bar scene in Villanova, but bars are very strict about not serving minors. In fact, the entire suburb polices student activities to an extreme degree that causes some dissatisfaction.

Students also get involved in a number of popular clubs and extracurricular activities. And the campus is "big on community service," according to one student. "For example, Villanova has the largest Habitat for Humanity chapter of any university in the country." Philadelphia is a quick-and-easy train ride away and provides many more social offerings. Many students also visit friends at nearby colleges.

While sports at Villanova are big—"everybody loves basketball"—and the academics are well respected, the primary draw for many is the friendly, laid-back environment. As one student admits, "the social life might not be as good as at other schools but the sense of community here more than makes up for it."

Also, Check Out These Schools:

Arizona State University
Birmingham—Southern College
Boston College
Boston University
Brigham Young University
University of California—Berkeley
University of California—Los Angeles
Carleton College
Colby College
Colgate University
College of the Holy Cross
University of Colorado—Boulder
Colorado College
Dartmouth College
Duke University
Florida State University
Georgetown University
Georgia Institute of Technology
Gustavus Adolphus College
Hampden-Sydney College

SPORTS POWERHOUSES

Hobart and William Smith College
University of Illinois — Urbana/Champaign
University of Iowa
University of Miami
University of Michigan — Ann Arbor
University of North Carolina — Chapel Hill
Ohio State University
Pennsylvania State University
University of Pittsburgh
Rutgers University — New Brunswick
University of Southern California
Southern Methodist University
Stanford University
Temple University
University of Texas — Austin
Texas A&M University
Tulane University
University of Vermont
University of Virginia
Wabash College
Wake Forest University
Williams College
Wofford College

SPORTS EXTRA

The Big Rivalries

Here are some athletic conferences and their members:

The Atlantic Coast Conference (ACC)
Clemson University
Duke University
Florida State University
Georgia Institute of Technology
University of Maryland/College Park
University of North Carolina/Chapel Hill
North Carolina State University
University of Virginia
Wake Forest University

The Big Sky Conference
California State—Northridge
California State—Sacramento
Eastern Washington University
Idaho State University
Portland State University
University of Montana
Montana State University
Northern Arizona University
Weber State University

The Big Ten
University of Illinois/Urbana-Champaign
Indiana University
University of Iowa
University of Michigan
Michigan State University
University of Minnesota-Twin Cities
Northwestern University
Ohio State University
Pennsylvania State University
Purdue University
University of Wisconsin/Madison

The Big West Conference
Boise State University
California Polytechnic SLO
University of California/Irvine
University of California/Santa Barbara
California State University/Fullerton
California State University/Long Beach
University of Nevada/Las Vegas
University of Nevada/Reno
New Mexico State University
University of North Texas
University of the Pacific
Utah State University

The Ivy League
Brown University
Columbia University
Cornell University
Dartmouth College
Harvard University
University of Pennsylvania
Princeton University
Yale University

Mid-Eastern Athletic Conference
Bethune-Cookman College
Coppin State College
Delaware State University
Florida A&M University
Hampton University
Howard University
University of Maryland/Eastern Shore
Morgan State University
North Carolina A&T State University
South Carolina State University

The Missouri Valley Conference
Bradley University
Creighton University
Drake University
University of Evansville
Illinois State University
Indiana State University
University of Northern Iowa
Southern Illinois University
Southwest Missouri State University
Wichita State University

America East Conference
Boston University
University of Delaware
Drexel University
University of Hartford
Hofstra University
University of Maine/Orono
University of New Hampshire
Northeastern University
Towson State University
University of Vermont

The Pacific Ten Conference
University of Arizona
Arizona State University
University of California/Berkeley
University of California/Los Angeles
University of Oregon
Oregon State University
University of Southern California
Stanford University
University of Washington
Washington State University

The Southeastern Conference (SEC)
University of Alabama
University of Arkansas
Auburn University
University of Florida
University of Georgia
University of Kentucky
Louisiana State University
University of Mississippi
Mississippi State University
University of South Carolina
University of Tennessee
Vanderbilt University

University Athletic Association
Brandeis University
Carnegie Mellon University
Case Western Reserve University
University of Chicago
Emory University
Johns Hopkins University
New York University
University of Rochester
Washington University

The Big East
Boston College
Connecticut
Georgetown
Miami
Notre Dame
Pittsburgh
Providence
Rutgers
Seton Hall
St. John's
Syracuse
Villanova
West Virginia

Hoop It Up

Here are the "Sweet 16" of the 1997 NCAA Division I men's basketball tournament:

Arizona
California
Chattanooga
Clemson
Iowa State
Kansas
Kentucky
Louisville
Minnesota
North Carolina
Providence
St. Joseph's
Stanford University
Texas
UCLA
Utah

North Carolina, Arizona, Minnesota, and Kentucky made it to the Final Four. In the sensational championship game, Arizona (which was ranked only fourth in its conference) defeated Kentucky in overtime by the score of 84–79.

Here's the "Sweet 16" of the 1997 NCAA Division I women's basketball tournament:

Alabama
Colorado
Connecticut
Florida
George Washington
Georgia
Illinois
Louisiana Tech
Louisiana State University
Notre Dame
North Carolina
Old Dominion
Stanford
Tennessee
Vanderbilt
Virginia

Notre Dame, Tennessee, Old Dominion, and Stanford made it to the Final Four. In the finals, Tennessee won the national title by defeating Old Dominion by the score of 68–59.

It's a Whole New Bowl Game

Here are the results of some of the 1996–97 college football bowl games.

Aloha Bowl:	Navy 42, California 38
Alamo Bowl:	Iowa 27, Texas Tech 0
Sugar Bowl:	Florida 52, Florida State 20
Sun Bowl:	Stanford 38, Michigan State 0
Holiday Bowl:	Colorado 33, Washington 21
Citrus Bowl:	Tennessee 48, Northwestern 28
Cotton Bowl:	BYU 19, Kansas State 15
Fiesta Bowl:	Penn State 38, Texas 15
Orange Bowl:	Nebraska 41, Virginia Tech 21
Rose Bowl:	Ohio State 20, Arizona State 17

ADMISSIONS

R. Fred Zuker

"Son, your mother and I have reviewed your prospects for college and we've decided to abandon the idea and sell you off for medical experiments."

Applying to College

Many high school students think that applying for admission to colleges—particularly the most competitive ones—is much like taking a chance at the lottery. They believe that decisions are made arbitrarily. A student once asked me whether admissions officers used the "stair-step approach" to make their admissions decisions. That is, do they take a stack of applications and throw them down the stairs, admitting students whose applications land on the first step, wait-listing the ones that land on the second step, and rejecting the rest?

Viewed from the outside, selective colleges may appear to make admission decisions without any apparent logic. College applicants, however, only see the admissions process from a very limited perspective. They don't see the full range of ability that exists in the entire applicant pool. You may be one of the best students in your school, but when you apply to a competitive college, you're up against many other applicants who are equally qualified, and the college has only a limited number of spaces in its freshman class.

But don't despair. Take heart that there is a form of logic to the process. Each college and university has an admissions system, and they all work fairly well. Admissions officers really want to make the best fit between applicants and their institution. To do that, they sift through all the material that you and other applicants provide, make evaluations, and decide. Their job is to take the information from you and give it a fair review.

Your job is to decide how you're going to present yourself to the readers of your application file. That's the part of the process you control. Maximizing every part of the application process to cast yourself in a positive light will give you the best chance to stand apart from the competition. To accomplish this goal, you must have a strategy. You must be aware of your strengths and prepare your applications in a way that focuses attention on your strongest qualities. That's what this section will

In the Same Boat

You're not alone. Thousands of people are applying to colleges along with you. Many share your fears and concerns about the admissions process.

help you do. You'll learn the ins and outs of when to apply, how to apply, how to sell yourself, and how to make your final decision.

DON'T LET IT GET YOU DOWN

The whole getting-into-college process is quite formidable and can, at times, be tough to handle. Recent research I conducted with high school seniors confirms what counselors, teachers, and parents have known for a long time: Senior year of high school is a time of intense stress. The level of stress was high in both fall and spring semesters, but the fall semester had a slight edge. Considering all the things that you have to do as a senior—plus the effect of test-taking, college visits, and filling out applications—and it's easy to see why the fall is a difficult time.

If you find yourself getting snowed under by all the demands on your time and your energy, find a way to slow down, let some things go (preferably not your studies), and protect your health. Some stress is unavoidable, but if you find that you're having difficulty functioning as you do normally, then it's time to seek some professional assistance. You may only need help putting together a workable schedule or getting some tutoring assistance to make it through the first grading periods. The main thing is to keep the communication lines open with your counselor and your parents. They can't help if they don't know there's a problem.

HELP YOURSELF

When you feel stressed out, it's never a mistake to ask for help. The only mistake is to wait too long and, in the meantime, get into even greater difficulties.

A WORD TO PARENTS

The college admissions process responds best to students and families who realize that this is a great time for students to exercise decision-making skills and develop perseverance that will stand them in good stead later. The parent's role is to help the student by being supportive and respectful of the student's ownership of the process.

Parents are often called upon to manage some of the logistical matters of the process, including arranging for travel and coordinating such admission-related activities as test preparation, test taking, and making appointments. But there's another element that's an important part of parent involvement: giving your son or daughter the benefit of your wisdom and experience. As long as you're not trying to live vicariously through the success of your daughter or son, it's fine to help her or him aspire to the most competitive colleges in reach. Simply remember that your role is in support of the main character in this drama—the student applicant.

Stress Alert

In one study on stress, female high school students reported higher levels of stress than their male counterparts.

INTRODUCTION

The transition to college is a true rite of passage in American culture, and it can be an experience that is productive and meaningful to all involved. If you need help sorting out any of these issues, contact a college admissions officer with your questions. They want you to succeed just as much as you do. And remember to look for the humorous and lively parts of the process. Taken too seriously, anything can become a burden. This is one activity that should invigorate the student. After all, it's a time of self-exploration and growth, and there's nothing more exciting than that.

When to Apply

The admissions process can be long and involved, but there are things you can do to avoid the last-minute crunch. Ideally, you should begin thinking about college as early as your junior year. The first thing you should do is go to your guidance office in September of your junior year and do the following:

- Ask for the PSAT Registration Booklet
- Talk with your guidance counselor about planning for college
- Start thinking about the qualities you want in your ideal college

Once you've taken these initial steps, you'll want to start planning your application schedule. The application process requires that you compile loads of information about yourself, fill out a lot of forms, and meet rigid deadlines. You'll have to get organized to make sure you know all the important dates and to avoid missing any deadlines.

TIMING

Timing is everything in the college admissions process. You face deadlines for taking standardized tests, deadlines for submitting your admission applications, deadlines for financial aid applications, and deadlines for returning all of the other bits and pieces to the admissions office. Colleges also have deadlines—for sending decision letters and notices for financial aid and scholarships. Keep in mind that each step in the process takes time and that there's often a lot of waiting between steps. And remember the most important piec of advice: Never, ever, miss a deadline.

EARLY DECISION

Early decision plans are designed for students who have evaluated their college choices at an early date, have determined which school is their

Pencil Me In

Get yourself a calendar, preferably one of those 18-month numbers with a page for every day so you can jot down all the requirements for the college admission process, starting as early as spring of your junior year. Give yourself at least two weeks notice before each deadline to get things done.

It's Early at the Top

The most selective colleges are awarding an increasing number of the seats in their freshman classes to applicants who apply by November. By mid-December of 1995, Harvard had accepted enough students to fill 60% of its entering class, Princeton had admitted 49%, and many other top schools were above one-third.

Source: *The New York Times*

Advantages of Early Decision

- You don't have to wait around so long to find out if you're in
- You don't spend time and money filing a lot of applications
- You have more time to plan how to pay for college

Disadvantages of Early Decision

- If accepted, you're obliged to attend
- You may discover a more suitable college later
- The earliness of the deadline may force you to submit a less-polished application, unless you begin planning your application extra early

first choice, and want to settle their college decision relatively early in their senior year of high school. The rule for early decision is simple: Use it only if you're certain of the college that you want to attend. If you decide to apply for early decision, you should understand that you're entering a binding agreement with the college. If you're admitted, you'll attend and pay your non-refundable commitment deposit up front. Therefore, if you're not absolutely certain that you want to attend a particular college, you may be able to opt for early admission (you find out early, but it's nonbinding) or regular decision.

Some colleges will say that you have a better chance of admission if you apply using early decision, but it really depends upon the applicant pool and how selective the college is overall. Don't count on early decision to increase your chances of admission greatly, but if you're sure that this college is the one, it won't hurt your chances if you let them know that you care enough to make this early commitment.

A couple of caveats: If you think your senior grades or SAT/ACT scores from your senior year will help your case, early decision or early admission probably isn't for you. If financial aid is a major consideration, you'll only be able to get an estimate of your likely financial aid package—rather than a firm offer—if you apply for early decision. Keep these factors in mind when you make the decision.

THE APPLICATION SCHEDULE

Many students wonder when to begin the college admissions process in earnest. You should begin as early as fall of your junior year. It's the most important year academically because it's the last complete year that the colleges will have to evaluate. Junior year is also the time to start preparing for the SAT I and II and/or the ACT. If you're already a senior, don't despair. Although you can't change your junior grades, you still have enough time to make sure your application stands out from the crowd.

Applications for admission generally don't appear until the summer between your junior and senior year. If you checked the box on the PSAT registration materials to enter in the Student Search Service, colleges all over the country will send you their promotional materials in an effort to recruit you. Keep in mind that this type of popularity is fleeting and that you must separate the information you need about a college from the hype in its catalog.

Once you know which colleges or universities you want to consider, make sure you're on their mailing lists. You can do this by returning the

When To Apply

cards you receive from Student Search mailings, filling out the response cards at college fairs, or by writing a letter to the colleges you're considering. Use the sample expression-of-interest letter below as a guide.

Sample Expression-of-Interest Letter

June 30, 1997
College of Michoice
100 Old Main
Michoice, MI 00000

To Whom It May Concern:
I will graduate from Central High School in June 1997, and I am interested in possibly attending your institution. Please send me all pertinent information so that I can apply for admission, financial aid, and scholarships.
I am particularly interested in your departments of underwater weaving and extraterrestrial real estate management. I would also appreciate information on your hackeysack team and your student-operated radio station.

Thank you for your assistance.
Sincerely,

Angela Chase
101 Plaza del Flannel
Catalano, CA 90210

The Three Flavors Of Admission

Early decision: You find out early, and you must attend.

Early admission: You find out early, but you can choose not to attend.

Regular admission: You find out later, and you can choose whether to attend.

Avoid the Crunch

One of the greatest pitfalls encountered by students in the application process is procrastination—putting off the applications until the last minute. You can avoid this trap by setting up a calendar with all of the deadlines for each college you intend to apply to. Your 18-month calendar will help you with this, but you should put all the dates on a single piece of paper, so you see exactly how big the job is.

Your calendar should highlight dates for getting the recommendations from counselors and teachers that you will need. Remember: The most popular teachers will be swamped with requests. A high school biology teacher once told me that he was asked to write more than 50 recom-

The Road to College

To Avoid Catastrophe:

- Plan ahead.
- Spread out your work.
- Give yourself plenty of time to complete each facet of the application.
- Don't wait until the last minute.

mendations one year. Don't be number 50! (We'll look more closely at recommendations in a later chapter.)

Your calendar should also include the big events for you in high school, such as deadlines for activities in which you are involved, final exams, and family trips to visit colleges. You'll have to work your college application schedule around these dates, but don't use your activities as an excuse to miss those application deadlines.

That should answer most of your questions about when to apply. The main things to remember are: Get organized and don't procrastinate. Use the Application Flowchart Worksheet on the following page to help you organize your application schedule and keep track of all the deadlines. If you need additional copies, detach the copy of the Applications Flowchart Worksheet in the Forms and Worksheet section in the back of the book and photocopy as many as you need.

What's Next?

Now that you've decided when to apply—and you already decided where to apply after reading through the Selection section—your next step is to apply to the colleges you've chosen. Often, filling out applications isn't a breeze because various college applications ask different questions and require different things of you. In the next chapter, "How to Apply," we'll show you how to devise an application strategy that will enable you to present yourself in the best possible light.

WHEN TO APPLY

APPLICATIONS FLOWCHART WORKSHEET

Official Deadlines	College A	College B	College C
Preliminary application deadline			
Application deadline			
College financial aid application deadline			
National financial aid application forms deadline			
Candidate notification date			
Candidate reply date			
Personal Timetable			
Application completed and mailed			
Application acknowledgment received			
High school record form and counselor recommendation form delivered to guidance counselor			
Forms mailed			
First recommendation form delivered to _____ (name)			
Form mailed			
Second recommendation form delivered to _____ (name)			
Form mailed			
Midyear school report form delivered to guidance counselor			
Form mailed			
SAT I/SAT II/ACT scores requested to be sent to college			
Institutional financial aid form completed and mailed			

"No, I haven't heard from A&M yet, but Caitlin over there got accepted early-decision at Rice."

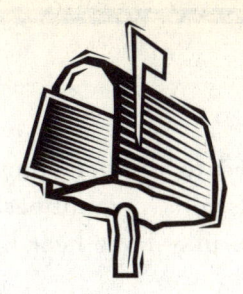

How to Apply

Once you start receiving applications, you'll quickly notice one thing: Almost none of them are exactly alike. Some may require no essays or recommendations; others might require two or more of each. Some have very detailed forms requiring extensive background information; others are satisfied with just your name and address and very little else.

Despite these differences, most applications follow a general pattern with variations on the same kinds of questions. So read this chapter with the understanding that, although not all of it is relevant to all parts of every application, these guidelines will be valuable for just about any college application you'll encounter.

DEVELOPING YOUR APPLICATION STRATEGY

The first part of your application strategy should be to aim high. But before you can determine what is an appropriate range of college competitiveness for you, you need to have a firm grasp of how the colleges will review your application. College admissions committees will consider your academic record as the primary factor in determining your admissibility. They will scrutinize the following parts of your academic record:

- **Courses.** The more demanding your academic program, the higher your evaluation will be in this area.

- **Grades.** The committee will consider how well you've done in the context of the norms for your school. If you're attending a very competitive high school and you've done well, that will be more impressive than an equally strong showing at a less demanding school.

- **Standardized Test Scores.** SAT, ACT, and other standardized test

What They Want
Colleges want you to show them why they should accept you. Taken together, the elements of your application should accomplish this task.

scores are a nationally normed measure designed to predict your first-year performance in college. College admissions committees give them a lot of weight—but, despite what you may have heard, not as much as your courses and grades.

- **Counselor/Teacher Recommendations.** Competitive colleges, particularly the smaller ones, put a good deal of weight on teacher recommendations. That's why you should choose your recommendation writers carefully.

As for other admissions criteria, private college admissions committees are much more interested in extracurriculars and personal qualities than are public universities. Private colleges will review the contributions you've made to your school and community. They'll also consider your writing skills, which will be reflected in your essays, and what other people think of you as a person, as evidenced by the recommendations you receive from teachers and counselors. Personal interviews with admissions staff or alumni will also contribute to their impression of you as a person.

Nonacademic factors are important, particularly for the private institutions, but they don't make up for a less-than-outstanding academic record. In a competitive admissions environment, you'll need all of these factors working for you in order to be successful.

How Competitive Are You?

You can use the scale on the next page to give yourself a rating—much like an admissions committee will do when they review your credentials. You'll need to be honest with yourself in evaluating where your high school career would be ranked in the various categories.

This rating system does not take into account a wide swing in one category or another. In general, if you're strong in GPA and courses and weak in standardized scores, you can consider yourself a bit stronger than your point total indicates. The most competitive colleges, however, require successful candidates to be superior in all aspects of their applications.

Top Of The Charts

Scoring high on standardized tests will help you get into the college of your choice. Preparation is the key to success on the SAT, ACT, and other tests.

How Do You Measure Up?

Put your SAT or ACT score and GPA alongside the median numbers of the schools that interest you. The comparison will give you a good idea of where you stand, but remember that many schools don't just look at their applicants' numbers.

COMPETITIVENESS SCALE

GPA of 3.75–4.00	= 5 points
GPA of 3.50–3.74	= 4 points
GPA of 3.00–3.49	= 3 points
GPA of 2.75–2.99	= 2 points
GPA of 2.50–2.74	= 1 point

Note: The Grade Point Averages (GPAs) are considered unweighted even though most colleges will give you extra credit for Advanced Placement or International Baccalaureate grades.

SAT I of 1300–1600 (ACT Comp. 30–36)	= 5 points
SAT I of 1200–1290 (ACT Comp. 27–29)	= 4 points
SAT I of 1100–1190 (ACT Comp. 24–26)	= 3 points
SAT I of 1000–1090 (ACT Comp. 22–23)	= 2 points
SAT I of 900–990 (ACT Comp. 19–21)	= 1 point

If you have a record of outstanding extracurricular achievement—such as all-state orchestra, student body leadership, other local, regional, or national recognition for citizenship, leadership, or academic achievement—*and* you feel your recommendations will be outstanding, give yourself another *3 points*.

Or: If your extracurriculars are solid, but not at the highest leadership or recognition level, and you feel your recommendations will be very positive, give yourself another *2 points*.

Or: If your extracurriculars are limited to participation—but little leadership—in a relatively narrow range of activities and your recommendations will be good, give yourself another *1 point*.

If you are part of an underrepresented ethnic minority group (African American, Latino, Native American, etcetera), give yourself another *2 points*.

If your mother or father attended the college you're considering, give yourself another *1 point*.

The maximum number of points you could get is 16 (although very few people will actually get the full 16 points). Add your point total and see where you are on the following scale:

11 to 16 Points = You have a shot at the most competitive colleges in the country. There is no guarantee that you'll be admitted, but it does mean that an application to this level of institution is warranted.

7 to 10 Points = While you would have only a long-shot at the most competitive colleges, you would be a good candidate at the second-tier (less competitive, but well respected) colleges in America.

6 Points or Below = You will be competitive at colleges that are less selective but still are looking for good students.

THE ROAD TO COLLEGE

Traffic Jam

Here are a dozen schools that receive more than 15,000 applications each year:

- Boston University
- University of California-Berkeley
- University of California-Los Angeles
- University of California-San Diego
- Cornell University
- Indiana University
- University of Michigan
- Ohio State University
- Penn State University
- Purdue University
- Rutgers-New Brunswick
- University of Virginia

A Basic Application Strategy

- Apply to at least two "safety" schools.
- Apply to a few "wishful thinking" schools.
- Apply to several schools between these extremes.

Choosing Your Colleges

You may be wondering how many colleges you should include on your applications list. There's no magic number. The length of your list depends upon your range of interests and the kind of institution you want. If size, geographic location, and academic program are not limiting factors, your list may include institutions from all over the country and would be longer than the list of someone who wants to stay close to home and attend a state institution.

But no matter how many schools you apply to, you want to ensure that you'll be receiving a good number of those big, fat envelopes full of information for admitted students. These envelopes always contain a letter that has the word "congratulations" written somewhere in the text. Those are the letters you want. Not those skinny No. 10 envelopes that usually contain the word *unfortunately* somewhere in the text. The Three-Tier approach to choosing your colleges, described below, will guarantee that at least some of your envelopes will be of the large variety.

In the Selection section of this book, you went through the process of determining which colleges offer what you want. The Three-Tier approach allows you to use that information to make sense out of the selection process as it relates to your academic and extracurricular record. Use the Application List in this chapter to list the schools to which you plan to apply.

Tier One: This group of colleges will include your longshots. Aiming high is okay. In fact, it's desirable. If you don't receive at least one rejection letter, it probably means you didn't aim high enough. (You probably should apply to two to five institutions in this category.)

Tier Two: These institutions provide all the things you are looking for in a college but are less selective than the Tier-One places. They'll give you a better chance for admission but are still selective. (You should probably apply to two to five institutions in this category.)

Tier Three: These colleges also meet nearly all your requirements, but they are virtually certain to offer you admission based on what you know about your academic record and their admitted student profile. Some students make the mistake of paying too little attention to this group of colleges. Choose them carefully and do as good a job completing the applications as you do with your Tier-One colleges, because you may actually have to attend one of these colleges if your Tier-One and Tier-Two choices don't work out. (You should apply to at least two institutions in this category.)

If you are applying to a public university system—such as the University of California or the University of North Carolina—remember that campuses within those systems have different levels of selectivity for both in-state and out-of-state applicants. Moreover, some universities may have a variety of campuses fitting into all three tiers of selectivity. Don't limit your applications to only the most selective campus if you think your chances for admission there are small. Place the various campuses in the appropriate tiers to maximize your chances for admission.

Go for It!

Apply to a few schools that seem just beyond your reach. You might be pleasantly surprised!

MAKING THE GRADE WITHOUT TAKING THE TEST

About 30 colleges no longer require standardized test scores for admission, including:

Bard College
Bates College
Bowdoin College
Goddard College
Hampshire College
St. John's College

Note: You should go ahead and take the SAT or ACT anyway. Even at these schools, submitting a strong test score will improve your chances of admission.

APPLICATION LIST

Break down your list of schools into the three tiers as discussed in this chapter. The number of schools on each list depends on your individual circumstances.

Tier One: "Wishful Thinking" Schools

1. _____
2. _____
3. _____
4. _____
5. _____

Tier Two: "In Between" Schools

1. _____
2. _____
3. _____
4. _____
5. _____

Tier Three: "Safety" Schools

1. _____
2. _____
3. _____
4. _____
5. _____

UNDERSTANDING THE APPLICATION EVALUATION PROCESS

At this point, you're probably asking yourself: How do colleges determine which students to admit? College admissions procedures vary according to the type of institution. Public universities tend to use a formula-based approach. Your GPA and SAT I, ACT, and SAT II scores are combined to give you a selection score or academic number, and this number will be used to determine your admissibility. For example, several of the University of California campuses use the following formula to divide their applicant pools:

GPA × 1,000 (Maximum 4,000) + SAT I score (Maximum 1,600) + SAT II score (Maximum 2,400) = selection score (Maximum 8,000)

The campuses using this system will compute this number for all the applicants and draw a line at a certain score. All those above the line are admitted; all those below the line are denied.

This formula system has come under attack, however, because it uses the SAT scores inappropriately and makes hard distinctions on factors that are difficult to compare. The GPA component, for example, varies in meaning according to the difficulty of the courses taken by the student and the relative competitiveness of the school. In other words, a student at a very demanding high school who chooses the most challenging courses and earns a 3.5 GPA will be at a distinct disadvantage when compared to a student at a less demanding high school who takes only the minimum level of courses and earns a higher GPA. The system does give some extra consideration to students who elect honors and AP-type courses by adding points through a 5.0 scale (A = 5, B = 4, and so forth) or by adding a "plus" for a strong program of study. These formulaic systems give relatively little weight to extracurricular and personal factors. Ethnicity and personal hardships do figure into an adjustment to the academic scale at many schools, but they do little to offset the very strong emphasis on the objective criteria.

As we said, private colleges and universities tend to give much greater weight to extracurricular and personal factors in the evaluation process. When applying to these colleges, it's more important for you to concentrate on the subjective portions of your application such as your essays and the recommendation writers you choose.

Number Crunch

Some colleges will decide which students to admit merely by using a formula that combines each applicant's SAT/ACT score and GPA. More weight will be given to your GPA than your standardized test scores.

Yields

Check out the yields at these colleges:

U.S. Naval Academy	81%
Princeton	57%
Birmingham-Southern	49%
Indiana	44%
Michigan	39%
Pomona	35%
UCLA	34%
SUNY-Binghamton	29%
Washington University	25%
Bucknell	22%

The Waiting Game

Colleges put some applicants on a waiting list just in case they've underestimated the number of admitted students who actually decide to enroll. They use wait-listed students to fill up any empty slots in the incoming class.

Deciding on the Numbers

Every year admissions deans or directors are given an enrollment target by their presidents or chancellors. College administrators determine these numbers by looking at the budget and tuition revenue and projecting how many tuition dollars the institution will need in order to function. Enrollment targets are less critical for public universities because they receive enrollment-based revenue streams from state government, but the principle is still the same. In either case, the admissions office is charged with generating enough applications to allow them to choose the class they want, with the kind of academic credentials that will keep the faculty happy and with enough diversity and talent to satisfy all the other interests represented in the campus community. Not an easy job!

Once the applications are in, the dean or director must decide how many of these applicants to admit. To do this, he or she must predict what hundreds of 18-year-olds will do about their college careers. The deans use sophisticated statistical information about the applicant pool that's based on gender, geographic location, academic ability, financial need, desired majors, and other factors. These statistics give them a clue about what will happen if they admit various numbers of students.

This process is imprecise, at best, so admissions officers hedge their bets by "overbooking." If the college's goal is a freshman class of 500 students, the admissions dean may decide to admit 1,000 students, which means she is betting on a "yield" of 50 percent. You may think that a 50 percent rate of acceptance of offers for admission is low. In fact, it's quite high. Harvard University, for example, has a yield of about 70 percent. Looked at another way, 30 percent of the students admitted to Harvard end up going somewhere else. The highest yields in the land are at the military service academies, which makes sense when you consider all the obstacles that an applicant to West Point, Annapolis, or the Air Force Academy must negotiate in order to gain admission.

Admissions officers further protect themselves by assigning a number of applicants to the waiting list. The waiting list doesn't protect applicants. It gives the college some insurance in case they have miscalculated the yield (in other words, if fewer admittees accept their offers of admission than they had anticipated).

The evaluation process itself involves a review of your credentials and the assignment of some rating. This is done in a variety of ways, such as by the numerical formula described above. Private colleges are more likely to assign an evaluation to both academic and nonacademic factors.

Once these ratings, or readings, have been done, the usual practice is for the top 20 percent of the pool to be admitted outright. The bottom 20 percent of the pool will be set aside for those dreaded skinny envelope letters.

This leaves the remaining 60 percent of the applicant pool. This group is sometimes referred to as the muddy, or murky, middle. The freshman class is rounded out with this group of applicants. The admissions committee will spend most of its time discussing these applicants, poring over their letters of recommendation, essays, counselor comments, and the other factors that they will throw into the acceptance mix.

You should know that you'll be considered, in most cases, with other applicants from your high school. The committee does this to make sure that there's some consistency of decisions within the applicant group from the same school. They may decide to deny the valedictorian and admit someone just barely in the top half of the class, provided that person can reverse jam a basketball. But the committee certainly wants your high school to know that they are making that kind of decision, and may contact your school to let the counselor know what's happening.

Many college admissions offices will contact their "feeder" high schools before the decisions go out to alert the counselors if there's an apparent inconsistency in the decisions or if it has been a particularly difficult year for the high school. Also, the counselor may be able to help the admissions officer sort out some of the more difficult decisions and also soften the blow for the students who are going to be getting bad news.

The Committee

College admissions committees are usually made up of members of the admissions staff, faculty, students, alumni, and occasionally guests, such as high school counselors. Some colleges hire "readers" who just do the first readings of applications. These people may be members of the campus community, such as faculty spouses or retirees from the faculty or staff. Ordinarily, readers aren't members of the actual committee. In some cases, the professional admissions officers are not voting members of the committee or they have a combined vote. The dean or director of admissions usually chairs the committee, but not always. There may also be a faculty chair, particularly at small colleges where admissions decisions are seen as much more important to the faculty.

The professional admissions officers are often young, and many are recent graduates of the institution they represent. They tend to be "people persons" and enjoy meeting the public and talking about their insti-

Committee Composition

The typical admissions committee has several different types of members, including admissions office staff, faculty members, current students, and alumni.

A Rose By Any Other Name...

In California there were so many regional reps from eastern and midwestern schools that they decided to form their own organization, the California Regional Admissions Personnel. The group's acronym proved a bit too embarrassing, and they reorganized under a different name.

tution. Some large offices have regional directors who are responsible for a particular part of the country. They will be the first reader on the applications from their region and often will make a presentation on the applicants to the full committee. They'll also make recommendations on the decisions and answer any questions the other committee members may have about the applicants from their region.

There are also "regional reps" who live in the region they represent but return to the campus during file-reading time, for decision making, and for training in the fall. You may find the regional reps visiting your school if you live on the opposite coast from the college or university you're considering. It's well worth your time to meet these reps; they may be the persons ultimately making the case for your admission before the full committee.

Many colleges include other members of the community on the admissions committee. Faculty representatives, student representatives, and an alumni representative will often have seats on a committee. Some offices invite local high school guidance counselors to participate in the evaluation phase of the process. Because there's such diversity on any admissions committee, there's no way to tailor your application to appeal to one segment or another. I remember that one of the strongest admissions committees I served on consisted of some members who loved music and the arts but weren't interested in athletics. But there were also at least two former varsity athletes on the committee, and one member who had a comprehensive collection of early country and western music recordings. The faculty members tended to focus on their areas of expertise, but they also had a variety of personal interests that figured into their evaluations of the applicants. However, you can be sure that all members of the committee—no matter how different from each other—will be literate, sophisticated, humane, and intensely interested in everything about you that might reflect on your potential as a member of their community.

Timing Again

College admissions officers are on a schedule that has definite seasons. In the fall they're on the road visiting high schools, attending college fairs, and appearing at college nights—sometimes in drafty gyms and crowded lunch rooms—as the guests of the school guidance counselors.

Early Birds

The advantages of submitting your application early include:

- You have time to correct any problems or omissions
- Admissions officers will be fresher and less harried when they read your application
- You have time to set up an interview, if required
- You won't have to rush to meet any deadlines

In the winter they're busy reading applications. The file-reading season is the most intense time of the year because the admissions office is facing deadlines just as the applicants were when filling out their application forms.

There's no disadvantage to sending your application right at the deadline, but there are pluses if you get your application in early:

- If any component of your application is missing, you'll have time to get it in before it's too late.

- Admissions officers become weary as the file-reading season wears on; the files that are complete and ready to be read early in the process may be reviewed more carefully when the staff is not at the edge of exhaustion.

- Some institutions, including Harvard and Radcliffe, like all applicants to have an interview with a staff member or a local alumnus. The earlier your application is received, the sooner the college can contact you about an interview.

- If you get your applications completed and sent well in advance of the deadline, you avoid the stress of squeezing everything into the last minute.

APPLICATION TYPES AND SPECIAL APPLICATION PROGRAMS

The conventional application comes in a packet that includes the application, detailed instructions and, in some cases, a separate institutional financial aid application. This conventional application will describe the notification options the college offers, such as early decision, early action, rolling admissions, and regular decision. The deadline dates will be clearly stated along with the testing requirements and the last test date that can be used for consideration in that admissions cycle (usually the last test for Fall admission is in January for the SAT I and II or February for the ACT.)

Don't forget to read the instructions and other material in the application completely before you begin to fill out the forms. It's amazing how many students forget the simplest elements of the process, such as enclosing the check for the processing fee or signing the application. These oversights will, at best, slow down the processing of your application, and they may even stop it altogether until the problem has been resolved.

Always Read The Instructions

Before you start filling out an application, make sure you know exactly what the application asks you to submit. Double-check that each element is enclosed in the envelope before you mail it.

You'll find the last word on the requirements for admission right there in the instructions for this year's application. Don't rely on what the college required last year or what one of the big, fat reference books in your school's library or counselor's office says. Fee amounts, deadlines, test requirements, and essay questions are only some of the items on college admission applications that are subject to change every year.

Preliminary or Part I Applications

Several selective private and public colleges and universities use a two-part application process. The Part I form usually consists of questions of a demographic type: name, address, high school, and so forth. This information is used to open your application file and is requested earlier than the Part II forms. Forms for Part II usually consist of sections on activities, secondary school report form, counselor and teacher recommendation forms, and the essay questions. Be mindful of the deadlines on this type of application because the Part I forms often must be received before the Part II forms will be processed. Most institutions using this type of form require that the application processing fee be submitted with Part I. This fee is usually nonrefundable, even if you decide not to complete Part II.

The Common Application

The Common Application has been in existence for many years. It offers one standard form that's used by a great many private colleges and universities. Let's take a look at how it works. The applicant completes the form as thoughtfully and carefully as possible and then makes photocopies, which can be sent to as many of the participating colleges as the applicant wishes. Copies may also be made of the School Report form and the Teacher Evaluation pages to cover the requirements of the individual colleges. Almost all the colleges subscribing to the Common Application require the School Report, but not all require Teacher Evaluations.

Some of the colleges that use the Common Application, particularly the more selective ones, will require additional information or writing samples. Some will send you a supplement with instructions on submitting other material. Each college has separate instructions about processing fees, deadlines, and other requirements. The Common Application also allows you to use a computer disk to complete the application, but the colleges vary in which computer software format they require: DOS for PC, Windows, or Macintosh. You may be asked to submit only a printout of the application, a disk only, or a printout and disk.

The Common Application saves a great deal of time for the applicant and for the college. Some colleges use it exclusively; others have their own

The Common Application

The National Association of Secondary School Principals prints and distributes the Common Application for participating colleges. The Common Application is available in early Fall. If you need one, ask your guidance counselor.

applications but will accept the Common Application. Members of the Common Application organization "encourage its use and all give equal consideration to the Common Application and the college's own form." Remember that this form should be completed very carefully. Some applicants have added colleges as "backups" with the Common Application and dashed off their essays without too much thought. That does not serve the student well and only adds to the processing burden of the colleges. Make the effort to thoughtfully fill out the Common Application well. It will save you time and give you some excellent college choices.

Computer-Supported Applications

The latest wrinkle in the world of college admission applications is the use of the computer-generated application on a disk. As we've just seen, the Common Application allows the use of computer disks to create an application. But some colleges and universities now have additional computer-assisted options for their applicants. Some of the more popular of these alternatives include:

The Collegescape site on the World Wide Web (www.collegescape.com) allows students to apply to upwards of 200 colleges, including MIT and Harvard, gratis. Students can identify schools of a given size, location, and tuition using the site's College/Student Matchmaker and research colleges by perusing school profiles. Everything is handled online—there are no CD-ROMs, diskettes, or software downloads. To date, 55 colleges and universities like this form of application so much that they've waived application fees for students applying through this site.

Also on the Web is CollegeEdge (www.collegeedge.com), which lets applicants fill out and submit online applications for approximately 200 colleges. This site even checks each application for missing or out-of-range data. Participating colleges receive submitted applications instantly and can browse them directly via a secure Intranet. This system is free, but schools still charge their normal application fees.

If you have access to a computer with a CD-ROM drive, it's a good idea to check out *Apply! '98*, a free CD-ROM you can use to simplify the application process. Using *Apply!*, you can generate a suggested list of colleges by matching your personal criteria and preferences with a database of over 1,400 colleges, conduct an on-line financial need interview, search through 180,000 scholarships to find appropriate matches, visit colleges on the Internet (the Internet Explorer browser, which allows you to access the Web, is included on the CD), and apply to hundreds of colleges and universities nationwide.

Brave New World

You may be able to apply to college using the latest computer technologies. One of the most popular programs is CollegeLink, with 740 subscribers, including:

- Boston U
- Dartmouth U
- Emory U
- Johns Hopkins U
- U of Maryland
- MIT
- Penn State
- U of South Carolina
- Southern Methodist U

The CD-ROM contains more than 500 school applications that are exact duplicates of the colleges' own forms. You simply fill in the form on screen, print out a completed copy, and submit it to the college, either electronically or through the mail. The information you use to complete an application is automatically saved, allowing the computer to fill in the appropriate fields on subsequent applications.

Apply! '98 is available on CD-ROM for both Macintosh and Windows and is free to students and high school counselors. The disc can be ordered by calling (203) 740-3404 or by visiting their website at http://www.weapply.com.

If you decide to take advantage of computer technology, remember to give yourself sufficient time to resolve any technical problems that might arise. Another tip: Avoid using disks that have been copied from an original. It's possible that some data elements will be lost. If you've borrowed a disk from another student, at least make sure that none of *their* data elements are still in the file. Some of the software programs make automatic entries in other places on the disk based on an entry in one element: Be sure that all those fields contain your data rather than the previous user's.

COLLEGE APPLICATION CHECKLIST

The following list of things to do with every application should be used with all the applications you submit. Not every application will require all these steps, but they're all worth considering for each one:

- ☐ Proofread your application to make sure you have completed all required items or put an "NA" (not applicable) in the appropriate places. **Make a photocopy of your applications**.
- ☐ Sign and date each application and sign recommendation forms if a waiver of your right to review the recommendation is requested.
- ☐ Submit printouts, or carefully typed-out applications only. Use black ink and definitely don't use pencil for anything.
- ☐ Make sure you enclose a check, money order, or fee-waiver request for the processing fee. Make sure it's for the proper amount and made out to the correct party, such as "The Regents of the University of California."
- ☐ Make a photocopy of your check and keep it in your admissions file.
- ☐ Submit your School Report (Recommendations) to your counselor. Make a note of the date for each of these forms you give to your counselor.
- ☐ Keep track of the Teacher Recommendation forms given to your recommendation writers. Keep careful records of who you ask to write recommendations for you and the date you made the request. Don't forget to give your recommendation writers a stamped, addressed envelope to send in the recommendation, or else a note telling them that you'll pick up the completed, signed and sealed recommendation to be included in your application packet. (See the Letters of Recommendation Organizer Worksheet on page NNN).
- ☐ Give a transcript (or School Report transcript) request to your counselor or registrar with a notation of the date it was requested.
- ☐ Ask for a mid-year School Report or transcript request covering your grades through the first trimester or semester of your senior year.
- ☐ Request SAT I, SAT II, or ACT score reports, if the official report is required. Some colleges will take scores from the transcript. Others require an official report from the Educational Testing Service (ETS) or ACT. Score Request Forms are available in your counselor's office.
- ☐ Enclose your essays. Carefully proofread for content, grammar, punctuation, spelling, etcetera. If you have printed out or typed your applications on separate pages, make sure your name and social security number are on each page. **Make photocopies of your essays.**
- ☐ Attach photographs, if requested. Photos are used to identify you as a person rather than just a set of numbers. Be sure your name and Social Security number are carefully printed on the back of each photo. No shots from kindergarten, please.
- ☐ Mail your applications using a U.S. Postal Service Certificate of Mailing. Get one of these from your post office for each of your applications. The cost is small, and the peace of mind is well worth it.

Sell Yourself

Try to create an image of yourself that will stick in the minds of admissions officers. Remember to:

- Present facts concisely
- Double-check to make sure facts don't conflict
- Exclude any useless, unnecessary facts

The Real You

Don't try to make yourself sound like someone you're not. Your application will sound forced, and admissions officers can detect most attempts at deception.

APPLICATION BASICS

One of the greatest fears applicants have about the admissions process is that the information they convey to the committee doesn't accurately reflect their true selves. Or that somehow the information provided will be misinterpreted by the readers, and the applicants' wonderful qualities won't be recognized. How do you avoid either of those possibilities? Here are some suggestions:

1. Be yourself. Application readers usually aren't looking for a specific type of student. Sure, if you're applying to Harvey Mudd or MIT, there will be a pretty strong emphasis on your ability in science and mathematics. But even in specialized places like those, they're still looking for balance—both among individual applicants and in the class as a whole. That means there's room for students who are more focused on a particular part of the academic spectrum. But there's also room for the "Renaissance man or woman" (One of the clichés recommendation writers often use: Avoid it in your essays. It's almost as bad as "She marches to the beat of a different drummer.").

Some application readers put great store in leadership ability among applicants. Other readers like seeing students who combine athletic and artistic qualities. All combinations of positive qualities will be valued. But you need to present yourself as who you are and what you have done and in a way that strongly emphasizes what contributions you will make to the campus.

2. Be positive. All aspects of your application should indicate that you're moving in a positive direction toward the realization of your academic goals. Even if you have endured great difficulties in your life, it's important to indicate how you've learned from those experiences and, as a result, are stronger and better able to face what lies ahead.

3. Use anecdotes. An anecdote is a brief account of an interesting or humorous incident. There's no better way to convey to a reader who you are than through the use of anecdotes. Begin right now to think about things that have happened in your life that will help your reader know you better and understand what you have to offer to their campus. These incidents don't have to be big, life-or-death kinds of things. They can be relatively mundane, but they should be meaningful to you and should illustrate some trait you possess or significant learning experience that you've had.

Many college applicants say their lives have been uninteresting, even boring, when it comes time for them to tell college admission officers why they're special. If you think for a moment about what you've done in high school, at home, or in your community, you're bound to find things that are interesting, even though on the surface they may appear commonplace. Here are several types of anecdotes that will get you thinking and that will keep application evaluators reading:

- **Your intellectual development.** Do you remember the first book you ever read? What was it and how did reading it make you feel? When was the first time you actually thought about thinking? Was it when you were watching television (unlikely), watching a movie, reading a book, talking with friends, or simply lying in bed pondering the day's events?

- **Significant people in your life.** Obviously there are your parents, but what about brothers or sisters, other relatives who have had a real impact on who you are, coaches, employers, someone who gave you a chance to show what you can do?

- **Influential teachers.** Almost every college-bound student I know has had at least one memorable teacher. What made that person unique? Was it personality, knowledge, caring, or all of these? What did they do in the classroom to grab your attention? Did they dress in costumes, dance, sing, make cookies, or have you teach the class?

- **Special hardships that you have overcome.** Has your family gone through a difficult time, such as separation, divorce, financial troubles, many relocations, illness, death, natural disasters, dislocations? If so, how have these things affected you and your development?

- **Community service.** Have you been a volunteer in your community, such as in church or temple programs, hospitals, nursing homes, tutoring programs, working with disadvantaged/low-income students? What have these kinds of activities meant to you?

- **Travel or living abroad.** Have you had any significant travel experiences or have you lived in another country? Have any of these experiences taught you something important about yourself or how you live?

Don't Be Just Another Face In The Crowd

In your application, focus on what you think makes you stand out, what makes you better prepared for college than other applicants. Accentuate your strong points.

Story Time

Using anecdotes in your essays is a good way to show the admissions committee who you really are.

- **Leadership.** Have you been in a position of leadership in which your participation made a difference? For example, have you revitalized a club that had ceased to function? One of my students was elected activities director of a nearly defunct science club and brought it back to life by programming such events as a school science fair, trips to a local amusement park for their science day, and visits by scientists and students from the local university.

- **Business/Job Experiences.** Have you had a job or formed a business that gave you insight into the world of work or how businesses are organized? Another student learned an important lesson in life by serving for two summers as a busboy at a popular restaurant. He developed immense respect for the busboys who were supporting their families through their work and putting themselves through college.

These are only a few examples of the types of anecdotes that might bring your application to life. Begin to keep a record of the things that might fall into this category. Ask your parents to help you remember stories from your earlier years that you may want to write about. This exercise will help you develop the focus that you'll need when you approach your applications. These types of incidents—and what you have learned from them—have helped form the kind of person you are. They will also be very handy when it comes time to write those application essays.

Different Strokes

Different colleges want different things from applicants. As you tackle each application, make sure you know exactly what it asks for.

COMPLETING THE APPLICATION

Keeping the three basics—be yourself, be positive, and use anecdotes—in mind, it's time to get down to filling out the application.

Read the Instructions Again

The most important advice about completing your applications is to read the instructions carefully before you begin. Do this early to be sure you know the deadlines and all application requirements, such as standardized tests, essays, and letters of recommendation. Be sure you do everything that the application asks you to do.

There Are No Trick Questions

College application questions tend to fall into categories, but none of them is a "trick" category. College admissions officers want the most accurate information about you that they can get. They aren't interested in making this process any more difficult than necessary. But admissions offices vary in the amount of information they need. You'll find that some applications consist of little more than questions about your name, address, and where you attended high school. Others, from the more competitive colleges, may ask for two creative essays, plus short essays on your activities, as well as teacher recommendations. Just keep in mind the different levels of information required by the types of colleges you're considering.

Tooting Your Own Horn

Many applicants are uncomfortable engaging in too much self-aggrandizement. In other words, they don't like bragging about themselves. As with most things in life, there's a continuum of self-described achievement. No one likes the person who's obnoxiously self-centered and self-promoting. On the other hand, college applications want you to divulge your strengths. If you don't provide the information on your accomplishments, the admissions committee won't have it. They're not mind-readers and need to hear from you about what you've done. Sure, your recommendation writers will provide good information about what you have done, but you are the final word on what your accomplishments have meant to you. View the application process as your opportunity to showcase what you've accomplished. You should do so with pride. Here are two simple rules to keep in mind:

1. **Limit your recitation of accomplishments to your high school years only.** The only exception is if what you're doing in high school goes back to beginnings in earlier years. Then a mention of how you began your interest in swimming, the violin, or journalism might be helpful.

2. **Pay particular attention to those activities that have been most meaningful to you.** Even if you weren't the class leader but were just involved in planning, say, a fund-raiser to help the homeless in your community, discuss what it meant to you. The committee will want to know about your activity and why it was important.

Typical application questions

The following questions may not all appear on every application that you complete, but they're likely to appear on some applications:

- **Personal information.** These questions ask for objective information—names, addresses, and the like. Make sure you use the same name throughout. That means don't use your nickname unless they ask for it with a "name you prefer to be called" question.

Self-Promotion

When discussing your accomplishments, clearly explain what you've done and what it has meant to you. But don't go overboard to the point that you sound arrogant.

- **Enrollment information.** These questions ask when you hope to start your college career—fall semester 1998, for example—and whether you're going to use any special admission options, such as early decision or early action.

- **Major or anticipated academic concentration.** Many students spend hours agonizing over this question. Some feel that the wrong choice here will jeopardize their chances for admission. If you're applying to a professional program—such as engineering, architecture, nursing, or business—your choice will make a difference in your admissibility. You'll be competing against students who consider themselves competitive for programs with high demand and relatively few spaces available. That means the requirements are going to be more stringent, the competition keener. If, on the other hand, you're looking for a good liberal arts and sciences program and you aren't sure about your major, that's okay. In some ways it's even preferred for you to indicate "undecided" as your major. Undecided, in fact, is one of the most popular major choices. Some large public universities will have a very competitive situation for such high-demand majors as computer science or psychology. Read the information in the application to determine if there are such popular majors. If there are, the best advice is to avoid citing a preference for one of these majors because it could affect your chances for admission. Going undeclared or undecided does not prevent you from choosing any major once you're enrolled, unless it is specifically stated that you can't apply for admission to such a major unless you indicate it on your application.

Don't worry too much about premed or prelaw majors. On most college campuses you can major in any area and still consider yourself to be premed or prelaw. Premedical students, however, must take a prescribed sequences of courses, including general and organic chemistry, biology with laboratory, physics, mathematics, and English. The medical college bulletins or your health sciences adviser can give you precise information on the requirements, including the tests you must take, such as the MCAT (Medical College Admissions Test), for medical school admission.

Prelaw students should choose a major they really enjoy because admission to law school is almost exclusively based on college GPA and LSAT (Law School Admissions Test) scores.

How To Apply

Your major matters relatively little, as long as you emerge from your course of study with good communication and logic skills.

Transfer students, on the other hand, must be much more careful about indicating a major on their application. If you're planning to transfer as an upper-division or junior-level student, that means you must have completed the lower-division prerequisites for your proposed major. Some majors have many more prerequisites than others. Upper-division transfers aren't usually allowed to apply as "undeclared" because they should have completed prerequisite requirements for a major during their first two years. These regulations vary quite a bit from institution to institution. Check with your transfer-student adviser at your college or at the college you're considering for transfer.

- **Residency information.** These questions help the college determine whether you're a resident of the state (for publicly supported institutions) and of the U.S. (for all institutions).

- **Language proficiency.** Some applications ask this question in order to determine your English ability. They may also ask whether English is your native language and whether you've taken the (TOEFL) Test of English as a Foreign Language.

- **Statistical information.** These questions, which are usually optional, ask about the applicant's ethnicity. Answering these questions doesn't have a negative effect on your chances for admission and may actually help if you're from an underrepresented ethnic group.

- **Income information.** This information should not affect your admission status because most colleges operate under what's referred to as the "need-blind" policy. This means that your financial aid status will have no effect on the committee's evaluation of your application.

- **Parents' level of education.** Some colleges will give preference to students who are in the first generation of persons from their family to attend college.

- **Parents' occupations.** If your family is of modest means and paying for your college education will be a challenge, this information may give your application special consideration.

Undecided?

Many college-bound students don't know what their major will be. If you're one of them, don't worry about indicating "undecided" as your major. In most instances, you really don't need to declare a specific major on your application.

THE ROAD TO COLLEGE

- **Institution outreach questions.** These questions ask how you found out about the college. They help the school fine-tune its recruitment activities.

- **Scholastic information.** You'll be asked to provide information about all your previous schooling through high school. They will ask if you've attended any other high schools or colleges, the dates of attendance, and any schooling you might have had outside the United States. Don't leave anything out. If it comes to light later that you failed to mention some part of your academic career, you might have a problem. If you're in doubt about this, ask your counselor.

- **Test information.** The colleges want to know what standardized tests you've taken, with the scores, and dates, and the dates of the tests you plan to take. Most require an official score report.

- **Academic record.** Many colleges ask you to submit official transcripts. But some colleges ask you to self-report your courses and grades and compute an academic GPA (grade point average). This self-reporting of grades and courses can be tricky, so read the instructions carefully and follow the rules to the letter. If your report contradicts your official transcript, your admission status could be in jeopardy. Don't complete these sections from memory. *Always work from your transcript to avoid potentially embarrassing or disastrous errors.*

- **Transfer academic record.** Transfer applicants may be asked to report all colleges they have attended and provide information about college courses and grades. Again, be sure to mention all institutions you've attended and all courses you've attempted. This information will be verified by official transcripts later. Here again, always use your transcript to complete this section. Don't work from memory.

- **Scholarships and financial aid.** A common application question asks whether you plan to apply for merit-based scholarships or need-based financial aid. You should always apply for the merit-based awards unless you're clearly not competitive for them. Applying for need-based financial aid should *not* affect your chances for admission. There's a continuing controversy in higher education, however, over the precise meaning of the term

Report Card

If an application asks you to report your own grades, get your official transcript from your guidance counselor. Reporting a wrong grade could be embarrassing, and it might even hurt your chances of admission.

"need-blind" admissions. As the term implies, if the college to which you're applying states that they are need-blind, it means that they're not influenced in their admissions decisions by the applicant's financial aid status. Many colleges, however, don't meet the full need of the students who apply and who have demonstrated financial need. Because of this, they tend to offer the best financial aid packages to the best students. All in all, this is sometimes referred to as "preferential packaging." In some cases, colleges simply run out of grant (gift) money and decide not to offer admission to marginal, high-need students. This is a hazy area in which ethics, institutional viability, truth in advertising, and recruitment pressures all collide. The best advice is that if you think you will qualify for need-based aid, you should plan to apply for it and not worry about the consequences. This means that you have to be careful about where you apply and be prepared to ask questions about financial aid policy and the number of applying students who receive financial aid.

- **Activities.** These questions often state that you should list only activities engaged in during the high school years. They are often broken down into in-school and out-of-school categories. In-school includes high school or college (for transfers) activities in which you have participated. You'll be asked to rank these activities in order of importance and specify which years you engaged in these activities and how much time per week was involved. Don't worry about absolute precision here. An estimate of the average time spent will suffice. You may also be asked about positions you held in these organizations or honors you might have won. The questions may also ask if you intend to continue these activities in college. If you're unsure of the answer to that question, answer "yes." Your answer is nonbinding and a "yes" will show that you're enthusiastic about contributing to your college community.

Some applications say that it's all right to attach additional sheets if your list of activities is too long. Other applications limit you to the space provided. If you're able to attach extra sheets and elect to do so, remember to use the same format as that of the application and avoid the tendency to pad the list. Keep it limited to the important activities and avoid causing the reader to "space out" over too many attached pages of accomplishments.

Activities Overload

Don't make the mistake of listing every possible activity you can think of. As with most things in life, quality is more important than quantity. And an admissions officer's eyes may well glaze over if you include a super-long list of activities.

Out-of-school activities include such things as after-school jobs, service organizations, religious activities, hobbies, or special interests you may have. You may be asked how long you have been involved in these activities and if you have held any positions of responsibility or have won any honors.

- **Honors and awards.** Some applications will ask you to list separately any honors or awards you've received. They will want the name of the award, a brief description, and the date you received it. Keep this list limited to the important awards in your life but don't neglect to mention things that may seem unimportant, such as promotions at your job and recognition for hours of volunteer service. These kinds of awards and recognition give the committee a glimpse into the kind of person you are.

- **Your signature.** You must sign the application in order for it to be processed. Your signature simply informs the college or university that you know that the information you have provided in the application is true. If it's later determined that you have misrepresented any information, your admission or enrollment may be rescinded.

Your Personal Data Sheet

A good way to organize your thinking for college is to compile a Personal Data Sheet (PDS), on which you can list all of your extracurricular activities, relevant dates of participation, and any honors or positions of leadership you won. You can divide the list into in-school, out-of-school, employment, and honors and awards. You can give this same form to your recommendation writers to remind them of your accomplishments. The PDS can also contain your name, address, phone number, GPA, and senior year courses. You might think of it as your high school resume. Follow the example on the next page.

WHAT'S NEXT?

Now that you've got a grip on applications basics, let's now turn to the part of the application where you can really give admissions officers a more complete picture of who you are—the essays.

WHOA!
Occasionally students get a bit overly enthusiastic about reporting their activities. Or, they may take the instructions too literally. As the applicant did a few years ago when, under the heading "Activity," she wrote "Horseback riding" and under "Positions Held" she wrote, "On top!"

How To Apply

PERSONAL DATA SHEET

NAME
(Social Security Number)
Address
Phone Number

High School ─────────────────────────────────

Academic GPA ─────────────────────────────────

Test Scores (Include your best SAT I and II and ACT scores and any Advanced Placement scores that you've received.) ─────────────────────────

Senior Year Courses ─────────────────────────────
───
───
───

Activities and Awards
(Include jobs, academic and nonacademic honors, and awards by year.)
SENIOR YEAR ─────────────────────────────────
───
───
───

JUNIOR YEAR ─────────────────────────────────
───
───
───

SOPHOMORE YEAR ─────────────────────────────
───
───
───

FRESHMAN YEAR ─────────────────────────────
───
───
───

Essays that Work

The part of the application process that applicants have the greatest control over—and that causes the greatest difficulty—is, without a doubt, the essay. Applicants are vexed by such concerns as: What do they want me to write? What makes a good essay? Why are these questions so lame? How important is this essay anyway? Is anyone really going to read it? These are important questions, so let's take a close look at each of them.

What Do They Want Me To Write?

The college application reader wants to read something that reflects who you are. These essay questions are often phrased as requests for "personal statements." Occasionally a college will actually ask for a personal statement and an essay. That means they want something about who you are, how you think, what has shaped your development. They don't want an academic exercise, although they will pay attention to how you express yourself in writing. A set of essay directions from one particular college application states: "The essay helps us to evaluate the way you reason and organize your thoughts as well as your writing style and expertise. Most importantly, it allows you to reveal a part of yourself that a transcript or counselor recommendation cannot. This is an opportunity to distinguish yourself from other applicants."

What Makes A Good Essay?

In general, colleges will evaluate the content and style of your essay. Their ultimate goal is to learn more about you. You can give them exactly what they want through the content of your essay and through the style of your writing. A good essay should quickly create an image of who you are and why you want to go to college.

The Write Stuff

Application essays should be viewed as an opportunity for you to show admissions officers what you're really made of.

How To Handle Specific-Question Essays

If an application asks you a specific question, answer the question clearly and concisely and don't stray from the topic at hand.

WHY ARE THESE QUESTIONS SO LAME?

College admissions officers spend a great deal of time trying to find questions that will give the applicant enough freedom to be creative but also enough structure to guide their work. That means there's a great variation in the questions you may encounter on your applications. Essay questions, however, tend to fall into eight broad categories:

1. **The "open door" question.** These questions give you total freedom in what you write. They will ask you to "tell us something about yourself that you think we should know but which is not reflected somewhere else in your application." The application for the University of Denver says, "Our Admission Committee wants to know what you are thinking, feeling, or laughing about. Provoke us. Amuse us. Educate us." These essays are a great opportunity to tell the Committee something about yourself that might have interfered with your education—a hardship or an illness, for example. This question is a good place to use your "basic essay," which we'll cover later in this chapter.

2. **The "why education and why here" question.** These questions seek to determine why you want a college education and why you have chosen that particular institution. Occasionally, a college will ask you what you hope to do with the education you'll receive at the institution. A firm rule for this type of question is be positive about the institution. College admissions professionals and faculty are proud of their institutions. They like to see that same appreciation mirrored in the thinking of the applicant. Don't go overboard with insincere praise but, whenever possible, do emphasize particular strengths of the college rather than just generalities. This means that you must know something about the institution. Scan their catalog and their viewbook—that colorful brochure full of photos of students at play, in laboratories, in residence halls, or in a class being held on a verdant lawn by a professor who's gesturing Socratically—to determine what is unusual, especially strong, or particularly pertinent to your interests. Write about those things.

3. **The "current event" question.** Some colleges will want you to comment on a current event or issue and ask your opinion about it, its outcome, and future implications of the event or issue. The most effective response to this type of question is almost always a personal one. If you can relate to an event of local, personal importance, your essay will have more impact than if you dis-

cuss the issue or event from a national or international perspective. However, if you're knowledgeable of events on the national or global stage and feel passionately about them, by all means go ahead and write about them. The personal perspective is always helpful, and it usually makes for more interesting reading as well.

4. **The "significant person" question.** You may be asked to describe a person who has had a significant influence on you. These questions give you a chance to talk about yourself and your relationships with siblings, parents, friends, teachers, coaches, and just about anyone else who has had an effect on your life. Remember to keep your response personal. Write about the effect that he or she had on you—not on the class, or the city, or the team. The person's impact may have gone way beyond you to many others, but the committee wants to know about your interaction with this person and what it meant to you.

5. **The "moment in your life" question.** These questions want you to describe a meaningful, embarrassing, or humorous moment in your life and its significance. Again, the more personal your response, the better. In writing this type of essay you should limit the description of the event to the essential facts and spend most of the allotted space writing about the significance of the event to you. That's what the reader really wants to know about. The reader also wants to know the outcome of events. So don't forget to tell them how the embarrassing moment turned out.

6. **Specific academic questions.** These questions are usually found on applications to specific programs, such as engineering, nursing, architecture, foreign service, and business programs. The questions are designed to determine whether you have been thoughtful in your selection of this field. Keep your response personal if you can. Use anecdotes from your exposure to—or experience with—the field. Let the reader know how important the specialized field of study is to you and how you hope eventually to use your studies to benefit your community as well as yourself.

7. **The "if you had been there" question.** These questions give you the chance to go back in history and be another person, interview a historical person, invent something, or take part in a historical event or, in some cases, a future one. This type of

Don't Leave 'Em Hanging

If you describe an event from your life in any of your essays, make sure you let the reader know how things turned out.

THE ROAD TO COLLEGE

The Mystery Of The Curious Jell-O Incident

When choosing a writing sample, make sure that teacher comments don't confuse the reader. One student, for example, submitted an English essay in which he states at one point, "I am not a violent person." In the margin his teacher had written, "Yes, but what about the Jell-O incident?" A comment like that may leave the reader wondering.

Essay No-Nos

1. Don't dwell on your weak points.
2. Don't employ dull chronological histories.
3. Don't disregard length limitations.
4. Don't lie in your essay—or in any part of your application.

question gives you the chance to talk about something of importance to you from the past or the future. You can be a bit expansive here and show something of your knowledge but, as always, keep it personal and don't try to be overly impressive with your knowledge of a historical period or person. Keep yourself in the writing, and you'll keep your reader there as well.

8. **The writing sample.** Some colleges may require that you submit a copy of a paper you've written for a class. Papers written for English or social science classes are considered most helpful, particularly if they include grades and teacher comments. Obviously, you want to choose a good example of your work here. Be sure to make a clear photocopy and put your name and social security number on each page.

HOW IMPORTANT IS THIS ESSAY ANYWAY?

Private colleges and universities tend to place more importance on essays than do public universities. There are some exceptions to this general rule, and you don't want to assume that no one will read your essay if you're writing it for a public institution. But because private institutions put more weight on the personal factors, the essay takes on greater importance for them. At such schools, a brilliant essay won't make up for serious academic shortcomings, but it will make a great deal of difference in a highly competitive admissions situation where all other factors are more or less equal. Remember: You want everything in your application working for you. The essays are a big part of what you control in this process and can leave a lasting positive impression on your readers.

IS ANYONE GOING TO READ IT ANYWAY?

There's a myth that at many large public universities the admissions staff simply checks to see if the required essay is there, but no one actually reads it. Although it's true that public universities tend to place less emphasis on the essays and other nonacademic criteria, it's not true that the essays are unimportant and won't be read. If your application is very strong or very weak academically, your essay may receive only a cursory glance. However, if you fall in the murky middle group of applicants at either a public or private institution, then the essay becomes much more important. It may make the difference between admission and rejection. It's much safer to assume that your essay will be read and that it will count in the final determination of your admissibility. This will keep you focused on writing the best essay possible.

THE FOUR CS OF COLLEGE APPLICATION ESSAY WRITING

If you want to write a distinctive essay, you should be:

1. **Creative.** Try to be creative, but be careful not to offend your reader. Avoid clichés and bromides. College admission officers hate them. Students who write in an engaging, interesting manner will be miles ahead of those who plod through a predictable writing exercise. Enliven your writing by using anecdotes, bits of dialogue, and humor. And don't forget to structure your essays effectively. The first and last paragraphs should be the most important ones in any essay that you write. Grab your reader's attention in the first paragraph with something that excites their curiosity, and then use the closing paragraph to tie your essay together and leave the reader with the desired impression.

2. **Concise.** The Harvard and Radcliffe bulletin encourages applicants to write concisely, saying, "The best essays are not necessarily long essays." Take this advice to heart. Use only as many words as you need to say what you want to say. College admission officers are very busy during the reading season. Long, tedious essays tend to make them impatient.

3. **Casual.** Your college essays aren't formal writing exercises. The tone should be casual but not chatty. A personal statement loses some of its vibrancy when the writing is too stiff and formal. Use language that's appropriate to the subject. And remember to avoid sesquipedalianism (the unnecessary use of big words).

4. **Careful.** Be sure your essays are grammatically correct, properly spelled, and appropriately punctuated. Don't rely exclusively on your word processor's spell-checking program. Remember that the computer doesn't know whether you've used the wrong word in those instances where the word is another correctly spelled word, such as "piers" for "peers." Your essays should be typed or printed out, if possible. As a last resort, you can handwrite your essay; colleges understand that some people don't have access to a computer or a typewriter. Make sure it's legible and use black ink, even if green ink is your favorite.

Use the Essay Writing Worksheet on the next page to plan, organize, and draft your essays.

How to Write A Distinctive Essay

- Create a quick image of who you are and why you want to go to college.
- Sell your image briefly and accurately.
- Include real-life examples to support your points.
- Make sure your enthusiasm shines through.

ESSAY WRITING WORKSHEET

Name of college: _____

Essay topic or question: _____

First thoughts about the topic: _____
_____

Possible responses or approaches: _____
_____
_____

Working title: _____

Outline of introduction: _____
_____
_____
_____
_____
_____

Middle paragraph: _____
_____
_____
_____
_____
_____

Conclusion: _____
_____
_____
_____
_____
_____

YOUR BASIC ESSAY

A good way to begin your serious essay writing is to compose a basic essay that can be used in a number of the categories mentioned above with little or no modification. Your basic essay should probably discuss the following topic: "Describe a personal experience that will tell the committee more about the person you are." Your response should be based on a personal anecdote—something that has happened to you.

Here are the elements of the basic essay:

- **Strong opening.** Make your first paragraph a grabber. Don't start with a recitation of facts about yourself unless they're facts that aren't found elsewhere in the application. For example, instead of saying, "I have a job as assistant manager at McDonalds." You could say, "What do you do when the number two french-fry vat is down, the drive-through window microphone is not working, and there is a potential confrontation between rival gangs in the parking lot? Answer: Call me, the assistant manager."

- **Strong closing.** Your basic essay—and all your essays—should leave readers with a clear sense of what you were trying to say. The last paragraph should tie the essay together and make it memorable. It should relate back to the opening paragraph, answering the questions of what happened and what the experience meant to you. In our example the writer might conclude, "We were able to bring another french-fry maker online. We found that the drive-through cord was unplugged. A call to 911, resulting in a police cruise-by, calmed things down in the parking lot. It was a typical day for me at McDonalds, but I loved it because it let me be a creative and caring leader for my staff and my customers at the same time. I plan to bring those same skills to college and develop them even further."

- **Title.** Always title your major essays so readers will be prepared for what they encounter. A title also allows you to set the tone for the essay from the beginning. Using our example again, you might call it, "My Experience as Assistant Manager at McDonalds," or "French Fries and Gang Fights: A Typical Day at McDonalds." Which do you think might attract more interest from a potential reader? The latter title gives the reader a taste of what you'll be saying in your essay and does so in a way that's at once arresting and ingenious.

THE SHORT-ANSWER ESSAY

Short-answer essay questions are usually specific to your extracurricular activities or academic interests. The committee wants to know something pretty specific, such as, "We are curious about your current academic interests and goals. Please discuss the subjects or areas that most interest you." You may be instructed to use the space available or attach extra pages if necessary. Writing these essays is definitely an opportunity to put into practice the adage "less is more." Answer the questions succinctly and directly. Don't hesitate to make your responses personal, but keep them brief. It isn't necessary to give titles to short-answer questions.

Computer Glitch

If you're using a word processor to write your essays and you've stated that "The University of Awesome Parties is definitely my first choice," be sure to change the school name if you recycle the same essay when you apply to the College of Serious Studying.

The Basics

Your basic essay—and all of your essays—should have a title, a strong opening, and a strong closing.

ESSAY TIPS

Here are some tips that will help you make sure your essays work:

- **Feedback.** It's okay—in fact, it's advisable—for you to ask your teacher, counselor, parents, or anyone else to discuss essay topics or read a rough draft of your essay and give you their impressions. As long as the thinking and writing is your own, seeking advice from others won't violate the spirit of the process.

- **Rough drafts.** Always write rough drafts of your essays, even the short-answer variety, and let them "cool off" for a day or two. Then go back and reread them to make sure that they say exactly what you want them to say.

- **Identify your essays.** If you're given a choice of options, be sure to indicate on your essays which question you're addressing. You may do this by writing or typing the question before you begin your essay, unless it takes up needed space. If this turns out to be the case, just list the number or letter that corresponds to the question or topic you're addressing.

- **Proofread.** "I always wanted to be a collage student and now I almost are one." This is an extreme example, but it gets across the point: Check and double-check your essays for grammatical and spelling errors before mailing them in. Proofread your essays by reading them backwards one word at a time. This will help you pick up any misspelled words. Then read the essays front to back for content. Check out the Proofreading Hit List on the next page for commonly misspelled words.

Essays That Work

Timing

Some colleges, like Harvard, tell you that you can send in your essays after you submit your application, to avoid missing the application deadline. This gives you some flexibility, but it's dangerous because it allows for more procrastination. Resolve that you'll have your essays ready with everything else that goes into your application packet when it is to be mailed.

Good Essays Don't Just Happen

Don't just dash off your essays. Write rough drafts. Reread them. Rethink them, if necessary. And revise them as needed.

PROOFREADING HIT LIST

Spellcheck and carefully proofread your application to catch misspellings and typos. Here are the most commonly misspelled words on applications:

Incorrect	Correct
alot	a lot
athelete	athlete
calculas	calculus
calender	calendar
candy stripper	candy striper
cirriculum	curriculum
colledge	college
compleat	complete
conncellor	counselor (or counsellor)
docter	doctor
eleminate	eliminate
excelerate	accelerate
lecrosse	lacrosse
medecine	medicine
metriculate	matriculate
oppertunity	opportunity
perspective	prospective (as in "prospective student")
persued	pursued
piers	peers
psycology	psychology
sensative	sensitive
seperate	separate
sponser	sponsor
studnet (most frequent typo)	student

Small Errors— Big Mistake

Once you've finished your essays, get other people to read them. Type your final drafts and proofread them carefully. Make sure it's perfect—that means no typos!

491

WHAT'S NEXT?

That's the scoop on essays. If you follow the advice in this chapter, you shouldn't have any problems writing effective essays that will make your application stand out from the crowd.

Let's now turn to another important component of your application that you can control—recommendations.

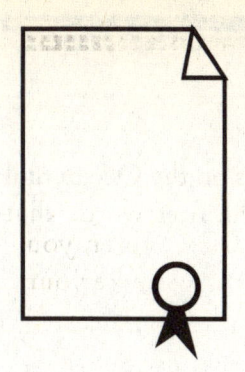

Recommendations

Not every college application asks you to submit recommendations. Public universities are less likely to ask you for recommendations than private schools are. The exceptions to this rule most often arise when public universities require recommendations for students seeking admission to a special program, such as an honors program, or for consideration in a scholarship competition. Private colleges and universities—again, in keeping with their stronger emphasis on the personal factors—are much more likely to require one, two, or, in some unusual cases, three recommendations.

TYPES OF RECOMMENDATIONS

Colleges will typically ask for two types of recommendations: the school report/college counselor recommendation and the teacher evaluation. Everybody has teachers, so the teacher evaluation should be no problem. Not everybody, however, has a college counselor at their high school. If your school doesn't have a counselor, you'll still need to have the school report completed by a school official. There's probably an assistant principal, registrar, or other person who takes care of this responsibility. This person will also have to see that an official transcript is either attached to the school report form or sent separately to the college or university admissions office. If you have no idea who that person will be in your school, ask one of your teachers.

CHOOSING YOUR RECOMMENDERS

There's an old saying in college admissions counseling: "When choosing your recommenders, make sure the people you choose like you." Sounds obvious, you may say, but after reading thousands of recommendations, I occasionally wonder how many students keep that admonition in mind. What's the best way to gauge how your teachers will respond to the questions on a teacher recommendation form? Simple. Ask yourself how your

A+ Recommender
The best recommendation writers will be those who:
- like you
- know you well enough to provide a credible opinion
- write well

teachers would respond to this question (which appears on the Occidental College teacher recommendation form): "What are the first words that come to mind to describe this applicant?"

Timing

It does make a difference when your recommendation writers taught you. More recent teachers tend to write the best recommendations, and some colleges even require that your recommenders be teachers who have taught you recently. One college application, for example, stipulates that recommendation writers must be "academic teachers who have taught you within the last two years."

School Reports

You may or may not know your counselor very well. You usually don't have any choice who that person will be. The best thing to do for your counselor recommendation is to make sure your counselor gets to know you before the recommendation has to be written. That doesn't mean showing up at the counselor's office the day before the recommendations are due and having a chat. It means talking with the counselor early in the application process and letting her or him know who you are. In large public schools that can be a challenge because the counselors are dealing with so many things in addition to college advising. The private school counselor has much more time to spend with each student because helping with the college admission process is a major focus of the private school counselor's job. Even in the private schools, however, it helps for students to make a point of interacting with the counselor. Familiarity with you and your situation will make their job easier and will result in a more accurate and helpful recommendation.

Who Writes the Best Recommendations?

Taciturn math and science faculty are typically more succinct and direct in their recommendations than are more loquacious English and social study teachers. Over 20 years of experience in reading recommendations has told me that science and math teachers tend to write shorter and less sophisticated recommendations. That's not necessarily bad for you, the applicant, but it's a tendency worth keeping in mind.

The ideal approach in choosing recommendation writers is to provide the application reader with a balance between math/science and English/social studies recommenders. They'll probably present different sides of your experience as a student and provide a valuable perspective on your academic strengths and, in some cases, shortcomings.

Schmooze Alarm

It pays to get to know your high school guidance counselor because they'll write the official school report or counselor recommendation that colleges require.

Balancing Act

Try to find recommenders from different parts of your life. Recommendations from people who know different things about you will draw a more complete picture of you.

PREPPING YOUR RECOMMENDERS

It's a good idea to identify in advance the teachers you think would make good recommendation writers. The qualities you should consider are:

- **Knowledge of you and your academic work.** If your teacher can speak to your qualities (assuming you possess them) of intellectual curiosity, perseverance, discipline, and so forth, it will serve you well.

- **Anecdotal observations.** Are there specific things you did in association with your teacher—such as helping with projects, conducting research, working as a lab assistant, and overcoming obstacles—that will sound really good in a recommendation? Admissions committees enjoy reading accounts of what students have actually done in class rather than just a collection of platitudes about a student's sterling character.

- **Knowledge of you in nonacademic capacities.** Teachers who have worked with you in clubs or other extracurricular activities are even better bets. They'll be able to talk not only about your academic prowess but also mention your qualities as a leader, team player, and organizer.

- **Evidence of good writing skill.** You probably already know who among your potential recommenders will write the best, most lucid, and most easily understood letters. You also probably know the teachers who will write one or two sentences with a scratchy ballpoint pen and let it go at that. Seek out the former and avoid the latter. In some cases you won't have a choice and can't avoid the teacher who hates writing recommendations. Some will warn you that they don't like writing recommendations. Take the warning seriously. Most teachers, however, recognize the importance of good recommendations and will do their best.

WHEN DO YOU ASK FOR A RECOMMENDATION?

You should allow your recommendation writers at least a month before the deadline for the submission of your admissions application. Make a note on your calendar with the names of your recommendation writers, the date you requested the recommendations, and the colleges for which you asked them to write recommendations. A gentle reminder a couple of weeks later is a good idea. Use the Letters of Recommendation Organizer on the next page to keep track of all your recommendations.

Was His Name Mr. Dumm?

If you choose your recommendation writers carefully, you'll avoid receiving a recommendation similar to the one where the teacher wrote, "Joe is an igma." (The admissions committee thought perhaps the teacher meant Joe was a member of a high school fraternity.) Not only did this teacher not write well, he also didn't seem to know the applicant very well.

THE ROAD TO COLLEGE

Make It Easy

What you should do to help your recommendation writers:

- Tell them early on about the deadline dates.
- Give them materials to help them write their recommendation.
- Provide all the forms that they'll need; stamped, addressed envelopes; and your home address and phone number.

WHAT TO GIVE RECOMMENDERS

Students are often confused about what materials or guidance they should give to their recommenders. Here's a list of the basics:

- **Any recommendation forms that are enclosed with your application.** If you're asking a person to write a recommendation and the college doesn't supply you with a recommendation form, give them a typed page that lists the colleges you would like them to contact and tell them what you need—a letter about your association with them or a testimonial to your particular abilities, for example.

- **Stamped, addressed envelope.** If you're asking your recommendation writers to send your recommendations directly to the college, you should provide the envelope and postage. This also makes it easier for your recommendation writers to get the recommendations done and in the mail on time. If you're going to send the letters yourself, tell your recommendation writers what time you'll pick up the recommendations.

- **Your Personal Data Sheet.** Your recommendation writers may know you very well, but don't count on them to remember all of your achievements. Your Personal Data Sheet will remind them of the things you have done in high school, making it easier for them to write a well-informed recommendation for you. The PDS will also answer the questions about you that may appear on the recommendation forms.

"Letters of Recommendation" Organizer

Name _____ Title _____
Business address _____
_____
Date recommendation requested _____
Date recommendation sent _____
Sent thank-you note _____ Notified of final outcome _____

Name _____ Title _____
Business address _____
_____
Date recommendation requested _____
Date recommendation sent _____
Sent thank-you note _____ Notified of final outcome _____

Name _____ Title _____
Business address _____
_____
Date recommendation requested _____
Date recommendation sent _____
Sent thank-you note _____ Notified of final outcome _____

Name _____ Title _____
Business address _____
_____
Date recommendation requested _____
Date recommendation sent _____
Sent thank-you note _____ Notified of final outcome _____

After you've completed this sheet, duplicate it and place a copy in the file folder of each school that you're applying to.

WHAT ABOUT THE CELEBRITY FACTOR?

Everyone would love to have a recommendation from a famous or prominent person. The rule here is to only ask for such letters if the person knows you well and can add something to your application that's not represented somewhere else. A well-known person who knows your family but doesn't know you is simply not a good recommendation writer. He or she can say nothing about you that will help the admissions committee—except, perhaps, about your blood lines. Once a colleague made the comment after reading a long, elaborate letter about an applicant's illustrious ancestors, "Too bad we can't admit him for breeding purposes."

Recommendations are used by admissions committees to fill in the gaps in your application that are not covered by grades, scores, and activities. Your recommenders are going to give your evaluators a glimpse of you from a different perspective.

Other Supporting Materials

Some colleges actually seek supporting material for admission to such programs as fine and performing arts. They will want to see examples of your work: slides, videotapes, and audio tapes. In that case, follow these suggestions:

1. **Never send anything that you want returned.** Admissions offices often don't have the time to return supporting materials. Even if they do have time, they'll only return material if you send a postage-paid return package for the material.

2. **Never send originals of works of art.** Instead, send high-quality slides, mounted on clear plastic carrying sheets that are clearly marked with identifying information and dates to help the committee know what they're considering.

3. **Submit videotapes and audio tapes that are of the highest quality possible.** I have listened to many audition-type tapes of good performances that were ruined by scratchiness and generally poor sound quality. The same is true of videotapes of performances or auditions. Try to arrange for someone knowledgeable to tape you. Bouncy, poorly lit, and inaudible videotapes don't help your cause.

4. **Make sure other materials are clearly marked.** Computer programs you have written, poetry, and screenplays should have your name, social security number, and identifying information attached.

The Applicant with Good Taste

Many years ago, the admissions office where I worked received a rather large package containing a dining-hall-type plastic tray with a plate, silverware, and plastic glass carefully glued on. In the middle of the plate was a typed note that said, "I want to go to Pomona College so badly that I can taste it!" We thought this was clever, and since the student was strong in every way, this added a bit of whimsy to his attractiveness. The applicant chose not to attend Pomona, however, which made me wonder if he had sent replicas of the Pomona tray to admissions offices all over the country.

Waive It Good-Bye

As a general rule, it's advisable to waive your right to read letters of recommendation. Admissions officers place greater trust in recommendations written in confidence.

AUDITIONS

Some schools may not be satisfied with tapes and may actually ask to see you perform. Be well prepared: Do your research on who will be evaluating your performance and what they will be observing. Remember that the audition might include an assessment not only of your talent but also of how you would fit into the group for which you're being evaluated. So be prepared for questions about your training, your leadership, and your desire to go on in a career. Have an artistic resume with you to present to your evaluators, even if you've already sent one to them.

DON'T FORGET THE CHOCOLATE CHIP COOKIES

I once said jokingly to a group of applicants that they should carefully limit any extra material they submit to the admissions office, with the exception of chocolate chip cookies, which should be sent directly to me. Within a few weeks I had received two shipments of chocolate chip cookies. The first part of my message to the students is worth remembering: Be careful about sending supplemental material to a college admission office. Never do it if the application instructions specifically say not to send such items.

WHAT'S NEXT?

At some schools, admissions committees provide applicants with an additional opportunity to make themselves stand out—beyond their recommendations and essays—through interviews. The next chapter, "Interviews and Campus Visits," will give you tips on how to do your best at admissions and scholarship interviews, and it will let you know what to look for when you visit college campuses.

Name-Dropping: Just Don't Do It

Years ago I received a letter of recommendation from a prominent television personality. The letter said:

To the Committee on Admission:

"Mr. McKay asked me to write a letter of recommendation for his son, Dylan. I told him I would do so. I know Mr. McKay and he is a fine man. I have never met his son. Here is the letter.

Sincerely."

It was clear the writer was uncomfortable with this assignment, and, rather than create a lot of meaningless copy about a person he did not know, he did as he said he would and wrote the letter but let the committee know that his offering was not to be taken seriously.

Interviews and Campus Visits

Like essays, interviews are chances to present your case directly to the admissions committee. The difference is that, in an interview, you're making contact with someone connected to the admissions office who may become your advocate when your application is reviewed. That's why you want to make the best possible impression you can.

Not every college requires, or even offers, an interview. If you're applying to a college that has a mandatory interview, make sure you schedule one. If you're applying to a college that offers an optional interview, you need to decide whether you want to take them up on their offer. It really depends on you. If the thought of a personal interview terrifies you—and you'd rather have your teeth drilled without painkillers than answer questions about yourself—you should probably skip the interview and let your application speak for itself. If your interpersonal skills are polished, however, you may want to consider arranging an interview, especially if your application could use a little extra boost.

A Little Extra Push
In a very competitive admissions situation, you want everything working in your favor, including your interview.

HOW IMPORTANT ARE PERSONAL INTERVIEWS?

A personal interview usually won't make or break your chances for admission. Like personal essays, however, interviews are important because they augment the admissions committee's knowledge about you as a person. Interviews may add some additional information about your academic interests, but the application will provide most of the facts the committee will use.

Some students are convinced that they can compensate for deficiencies in other parts of their application if they're able to "wow" someone in an interview. This isn't true, unfortunately, because the interviews are relatively less important than other parts of the application process. Most colleges feel they cannot put too much weight on interviews for two reasons: not all candidates will have the benefit of an interview, and inter-

Private Investigator

Private colleges and universities are more likely to offer or require interviews than public institutions.

views are merely shallow impressions of a person based on a 20- or 30-minute conversation. Other factors are regarded as much more reliable than interviews in determining a candidate's admissibility.

Private institutions—as you've probably guessed—are much more likely to offer individual interviews to prospective students than are their publicly supported counterparts. They do so because they want to make a good impression on you, just as you're trying to make a good impression on them. In other words, the interview is part of their recruitment program. They want you to feel good about your encounter with their campus.

Public universities are usually less interested in this recruitment aspect of the admissions process and instead focus more on the evaluation of objective data, such as courses, grades, and scores. Personal qualities that come through in an interview simply do not play as big a role in the public university evaluation process. That's not to say that, if you have an interview at a public university, you should assume it doesn't matter very much. You never know when the public university's decision might come down to a review of your file, so you want positive, rather than negative, comments from an interviewer in it. Also, some public universities will require interviews for certain selective scholarships. This type of interview is different from the admissions interview, and we'll discuss these scholarship interviews in depth later.

ARE ADMISSION INTERVIEWS REQUIRED?

Admission interviews are never required for the public universities. For most private colleges and universities, interviews are not required. Some of the more selective institutions, however, require either an interview on campus or with an alumni volunteer who lives near you.

ON-CAMPUS INTERVIEWS

Let's take a look at the things that you should expect to encounter at an on-campus interview:

Who Will Interview You?

Interviewers are most often members of the admissions office professional staff. You'll most likely be interviewed by an associate or assistant dean (or director), an admissions counselor, an admissions intern (usually a student who's been specially selected and trained for this purpose), or a member of the faculty or other staff person who conducts interviews for the admissions office. Don't be concerned if you're not interviewed by the dean (or director) of admissions. In many offices, they conduct relatively few interviews and are often too busy to do a good job anyway.

Most interviewers will write some comments about their meeting with you. Those comments will go in your application file and will be reviewed by the committee when your application is evaluated. Bring along a copy of your Personal Data Sheet to leave with the interviewers; it will help them remember who you are.

Arriving at the Interview

Private colleges take a great deal of pride in offering a warm welcome to the prospective student and her or his family. Admissions offices are usually cozy and well appointed, and interviews are conducted in private offices where there will be no interruptions.

When you get to the admissions office you'll usually check in with a receptionist, who may give you a form to complete with your name, address, and some questions about your academic record and extracurricular activities. Some admissions office waiting areas now have computers you can use to check the status of your application or to access a CD-ROM tour of the campus and the school's various departments and programs.

The admissions officer conducting the interview will come to the waiting area and introduce herself or himself to you and your parents, if they're with you, and escort you back to the office where the interview will take place. Most admissions officers prefer not to sit behind a large desk and stare at the interviewee across an expanse of oak. They would rather have a closer setting with you across a small table or some other more relaxed seating arrangement.

The Interview Itself

Most college admissions interviewers want you to do well in your interview. They will "structure" the interviews by giving you some idea of the kinds of questions they'll be asking—about your academic interests and extracurricular activities, for example—and give you a chance to ask them any questions you may have about their campus.

Interviews usually unfold into three segments: Icebreaking, Information Trading, and Closing. Let's take a look at each one:

- **Icebreaking.** The first few minutes of the interview are usually devoted to such pleasantries as the weather, your trip to the campus, or comments about the campus tour. This time will give you an opportunity to calm down and hear the sound of your voice in this new environment. The key is to be natural.

Interview Aid

Give your interviewer a copy of your Personal Data Sheet. It'll help him conduct the interview, and he can use it when he's writing up his interview report.

On Your Own

The interviewer will want to speak to you alone. Your parents, or whoever is with you, should remain in the waiting area or explore the campus on their own until your interview is over.

The Road to College

- **Information Trading.** Here the interviewer gets to the serious questions of the interview. He or she expects you to do the bulk of the talking. Most interviewers consider the interview a success if the interviewee has talked about 70 percent of the time.

- **Closing.** The interviewer will bring the interview to a close by asking whether you have any questions. It's a good idea to have one or two questions prepared, even if you know the answers, in order to appear engaged and interested. The interviewer may also tell you a little bit about what will happen during the rest of the admission process. The content of this section of the interview is determined by the time of year and the corresponding phase of the admission cycle of the admissions staff.

Typical Interview Questions

Below are some of the most often asked college admission interview questions. It's a good idea to have thought through your answers in advance.

1. Why are you interested in Nirvana State College?

2. What is your best academic subject and your worst?

3. Do you have a major in mind? If you answer "yes," the next question will be, "Why did you choose that major?"

4. How did you hear about Nirvana State?

5. What do you like to do when you aren't studying?

6. How would your friends describe you?

7. What books/movies have you read/seen lately?

Here are some tougher questions of a more specific nature:

1. Do you think your high school education has been relevant to today's competitive world?

2. Who has been the most influential person in your life, and in what way?

3. Describe an issue in your community that needs immediate attention. What would you recommend to improve the situation?

Don't Freak

Some nervousness is natural in an interview situation. Try to calm yourself during the icebreaking phase of the interview so you can think clearly when the interviewer starts asking the serious questions.

Loose Lips Sink Ships

When a dean of admissions asked an interviewee why he was interested in his college, the candidate replied enthusiastically, "I don't want a large college or a small college. I want a mediocre college just like yours."

4. What is your definition of leadership? How would you describe your leadership style?

5. If you were given a million dollars and told to spend it on a pressing societal problem, which would you choose and how would you spend the money?

6. If you could interview anyone living or dead, who would you choose and what would you ask them first?

7. What do you consider to be your greatest strength? Your greatest weakness?

When answering these and any other questions, be as direct as you can but don't answer in monosyllables. And don't answer any question with just a "yup" or a "nope." Be prepared for follow-up questions if you profess real interest in, or knowledge of, a particular topic. It's unimpressive if you mention that you're a great fan of Steven Spielberg films but don't know that he directed *Schindler's List* or *The Duel* (Spielberg's first film to receive critical acclaim). You're the interviewee and should do most of the talking, but don't go overboard in bragging about yourself. Be matter-of-fact about your accomplishments; the interviewer will recognize the level of your achievements.

What to Do with Your Parents

College admissions interviews are for you, the applicant. If your parents visit the campus with you, they may want to take the campus tour and ask plenty of questions. But when you go to the admissions office for your interview, you'll find that the admissions officer wants to talk with *you*. Some admissions officers will offer the parents a chance to ask questions after the personal interview, but rarely will an interview be conducted in the presence of parents. You may want to encourage your parents to spend some time exploring the campus on their own while you have your interview.

Scholarship Interviews

Interviews for scholarship selection are different from those strictly for admissions purposes. If you've been invited to an interview for a scholarship, you should be pleased. It means you have a good chance of being selected. Keep in mind that scholarship interviews are a key factor in determining whether you receive the scholarship (unlike admissions interviews, which usually don't have a major influence on whether you're admitted). Be prepared for challenging questions.

Interview Tips

- Practice with friends or family members beforehand.
- Dress appropriately.
- Arrive early.
- Be prepared to discuss the facts in your personal statement.
- Maintain eye contact.
- Don't fidget.
- Try not to speak too quickly.
- Use the interview to flesh out your application and to impress the interviewer.

Here are a few steps that you should take when preparing for scholarship interviews (or any interview, for that matter):

1. **Know what the committee wants.** If you're a candidate for a scholarship that rewards leadership, community service, or academic achievement, you can be sure that many questions will be related to your background in this area and what you'd hope to accomplish if given the opportunity afforded by the scholarship.

2. **Do your homework.** Learn as much about the scholarship as you can. Read everything you can find on the purpose of the scholarship, what the committee hopes winners will do with the award, past winners, and the composition of the selection committee. Also, review any paperwork you submitted, such as essays and the names of recommendation writers. Questions about these items may come up during the interview.

3. **Dress for success.** Scholarship interviews are almost always more formal than admissions office interviews. Assume that the interview situation calls for coat and tie or nice dress and be sure that what you wear is clean and neat. Scholarship interviews tend not to see the appeal of grungewear. Neither do admissions staff, for that matter.

4. **Arrive early.** Get directions to the interview location and give yourself plenty of time to find a parking place, get to the interview site, use the bathroom, and settle in. If you are asked to bring anything, be sure that you have it with you. Take care of as much of this the day before the interview as possible.

What to Do After Any Interview

Be sure to ask your interviewer for her or his business card. When you return home, write a thank-you letter. Here's a suggested format:

Date
Interviewer's Name and Title
College Address

Salutation:

Opening Paragraph: Thank your interviewer for their courtesy and interest and mention the date of your interview.

Middle Paragraph(s): Reconfirm your interest in the college, perhaps mentioning something that you learned about the campus during your visit.

If there is information you wish to add to your file, such as newly won honors or just-arrived grades or scores, you can include those here.

Closing Paragraph: Mention that you look forward to learning more about the college and attending in the fall. Suggest that you would be happy to provide any additional information if it is needed.

Sincerely,

(Signature)

Typed Name
Address
Phone Number

Alumni Interviews

Instead of on-campus interviews, many schools have their alumni interview applicants who live in their region. Your application instructions will tell you whether an alumni interview is required. If one is, the college will have the alumni representative in your area contact you. Alumni interviews are usually conducted in the offices of the alumni but may be done in a local restaurant, the home of the alumni volunteer, or even in your own home.

What to Expect from an Alumni Interview

The alumni who conduct these interviews are volunteers. They love their alma mater and want to share their enthusiasm with new generations of students. Remember that when you meet with the alums. They love to hear good things about their alma mater. Be positive and let them know how much you're interested in their college or university.

Alumni interviewers will contact you to set up an appointment. If they call you and you're no longer interested in the college, let the alumni interviewer know. If you're still interested in the college, the interviewer will schedule an appointment at a time and place that is mutually acceptable. Try to get the interview completed as early as possible to give the alumni interviewer plenty of time to complete the comment sheet and return it to the admissions office.

Alumni interviews will vary greatly in their level of formality. Assume the interview is just the same as a campus interview with a member of the admissions staff. Dress and act accordingly. It may be that you or your family know the interviewer. Even so, treat the interview as if it were your opportunity to meet for the first time a representative of the college or university the alumni interviewer represents. Ask your alumni interviewer for a business card. If they don't have one, make a note of their name, address, and phone number. You may want to call them later if you have more questions about the college.

Alumni Interview Follow-Up

Use the same guidelines that we suggested earlier for campus interview follow-up. Write a short thank-you note as soon after the interview as possible.

Campus Visits

A campus visit is the best way to see what a college is really like. Here are some common questions you might have (and answers) about visiting college campuses:

Alumni Interviews

Many of the colleges that require or offer interviews have alumni representatives interview students, especially those who live far away from the college.

When Should I Visit?
Campus visits are best made on a weekday during the regular academic year. College campuses undergo remarkable changes at about 3:00 P.M. on Fridays and don't return to normal until about the same time on Sunday afternoon. Weekend visits and visits during the summer are better than not visiting at all, but keep in mind that college life is different during the academic year.

How do I Arrange a Campus Visit?
Contact the Office of Admissions and let them know when you want to visit. Give them at least two weeks' notice. Avoid the last week of the term because that's when students will be taking exams and finishing term papers. College students tend to be somewhat surly during these times and may not make the best impression on a prospective student. The ideal plan is to visit one campus per day. If you must cover a number of colleges in a short time, give yourself no more than two campuses per day. Because of the travel time between campuses, that's pushing pretty hard, though. When you make the call to arrange your visits, note the phone number and name of the person with whom you speak. If you allow enough time, many admissions offices will send you travel, lodging, and parking information.

Where Can I Stay?
The best place to stay is in one of the residence halls (usually called dorms). Many campuses have overnight-stay programs for prospective students. These programs may be called the Student Ambassadors, the Host Program, or something else, but the idea is usually the same—to match you with a student who will allow you to stay with them in a residence hall. Some campuses will also include meal coupons for prospective students. Make sure you find out if the food edible and dorm life tolerable. The admissions office will also encourage you to attend classes with your host and to tour the campus. Use the Campus Visit Reminders worksheet to help you plan your visit and the Campus Visit Notes sheet to record your visit. You'll find both sheets on the next two pages.

WHAT'S NEXT?
Everything in the preceding chapters should have helped you submit the best possible applications. In the next chapter, "How to Make Your Final Decision," we'll take a look at what you should do once acceptance letters start rolling in.

A Visit Is Worth a Thousand Pictures

The best way to find out what a college is really like—and to determine whether you'd fit in there—is to actually visit it.

Overnight Sensation

If a college you're visiting allows prospective students to spend a night in a residence hall, take them up on their offer.

THE ROAD TO COLLEGE

CAMPUS VISIT REMINDERS

Things to do:

❑ Call campus and make appointment: Phone # (_____) _____ – _____

Bring the following:

❑ Letter from campus confirming date, time, and location of your interview

❑ List of questions for your interview

❑ Copies of unofficial transcript

❑ Copy of Personal Data Sheet for each interview

❑ SAT I, SAT II, and ACT scores

❑ Samples of your work (if appropriate)

❑ Campus map

❑ Parking permit (if necessary)

❑ Airplane, train, or bus tickets (if necessary)

❑ Letter confirming overnight residence hall visit

❑ Confirmed reservations at local hotel (if you're not staying on campus)

❑ Interview clothes (clean)

❑ Copy of this book (or photocopy of this section)

❑ Money or traveler's checks

❑ Camera

INTERVIEWS AND CAMPUS VISITS

Campus Visit Notes

Name of college _____ Telephone _____

Travel instructions _____

Lodging _____ Telephone _____

Interview/date/time/location _____

Name of interviewer _____

Impression gained from interview _____

_____

_____

_____

Time of tour _____ Tour guide's name _____

Impression gained from tour _____

_____

_____

Places I would like to see again _____

_____

_____

Names of faculty, staff, or students met _____

_____

_____

Classes or other activities attended _____

_____

_____

Overnight visit date and time _____

Name of student host _____

General impression from visit _____

_____

_____

How to Make Your Final Decision

Having filled out your application, written your essays, gotten your recommendations, gone through interviews, and made campus visits, your next step is to sit back and wait for those fat envelopes we've been talking about throughout this section. If you followed our advice and maximized every part of your application, you can take a deep breath and rest assured that you presented yourself in the best light. But then you have to start focusing again once letters of acceptance begin to arrive in your mailbox.

THE COLLEGES GO RECRUITING AGAIN

Once you've collected all those fat envelopes, it's time for you to make the decision of which college to attend. You may be surprised to learn that the process has now taken a 180-degree turn since you filed your application: You're now in the position of making the colleges wait as they made you wait while they were reviewing your application.

The colleges that have offered you admission, however, aren't going to wait passively until you have decided. They're going to help you choose them. Colleges will inundate you with invitations to teas, receptions, campus "admission days," and other events designed with one purpose in mind—to convince you to accept their offer of admission.

It's particularly important for you to separate the important information you need from the hype of the recruitment "yield" programs (so called because the colleges want to increase the acceptance rate, or yield, of the students to whom they have offered admission).

This is also a time when you may receive direct phone calls from currently enrolled students, faculty, and local alumni. All these contacts can provide you with valuable information. To take best advantage of this

It Feels Good to Be Wanted

Once you've received a letter of acceptance from a college, it's likely that they'll call or write to convince you to enroll.

bounty of interest in your decision, you need to know what else can help you make the best choice.

Your Strategy for Making the Best Choice

The strategies that worked for you during the first part of the process can be helpful again now. Refer to the list of factors you were considering when you decided where you would apply for admission. See how well the colleges that have offered you admission meet those requirements. Resist the temptation to make a hasty decision until you know all of your options.

Campus Visits

The best way to make the final decision is to visit (or revisit) the campuses that are still in the running. As mentioned above, you may be invited to attend special on-campus events held in honor of newly admitted students. Keep in mind that these events are carefully orchestrated to make the most positive impression possible on you and your parents.

But if you look beneath the hype, these events can give you valuable insight into exactly what the campus culture and opportunities are like. By staying overnight in a residence hall, talking with students and faculty, reading the bulletin boards, and eating the food in the dining halls, you'll be able to tell if this is the place for you.

Waiting Out the Waiting List

In addition to overbooking their acceptances, colleges further protect themselves by placing a number of applicants on a waiting list. These students will be reevaluated if the admissions office determines they need to admit more students to fill the class.

If you find yourself on a college's waiting list, your best bet is to assume that you won't be admitted and protect yourself by accepting an offer of admission from one of your other choices. There's never a guarantee that you'll be admitted from a waiting list. The best you can do is let the admissions office know right away that you're still interested. A letter from you affirming your interest and adding any additional honors or other pertinent information that's not already in the file is a good idea.

If you're admitted from a waiting list and decide to accept the offer, be sure and let the interim college know that you'll be going somewhere else. That will give them time to take someone from their own waiting list to fill the slot you've vacated.

Make Sure You're Covered

If you're on a waiting list of a college that you really want to attend, don't convince yourself that you'll eventually get in. Let the admissions office know that you're still interested, but go ahead and send in your deposit at an interim school. That way, if your number-one college doesn't go through, you won't be left stranded.

Comparing the Colleges

Make copies of the College Comparison Worksheet, beginning on the next page. As you accumulate information and impressions about the colleges that you've applied to, fill in a worksheet for each school. These worksheets will help you compare the colleges and help you make a decision that you'll be happy with.

What's Next?

At this point, you've probably been admitted to several colleges and either selected the one that you want to attend or narrowed down the list to a few schools. In either case, financial aid is now an important consideration because you want to start thinking about how to pay for your education at your chosen school, or because you want to compare the financial aid offers of each college you're still considering. In the next section, we'll guide you through the challenging world of financial aid.

The Road to College

COLLEGE COMPARISON WORKSHEET

Name of College _____

Admissions

Special items to be submitted with application _____

Percent of applicants accepted _____

Tests required _____

Average test scores of applicants _____

Average high school GPA or class rank of applicants _____

Special admissions plans (rolling, early decision, advance placement) _____

Admission selectivity rating (most competitive, highly competitive, competitive) _____

Academic Life

Academic or career orientation _____

Majors of interest _____

Special programs (study abroad, internships, unusual degree programs) _____
_____

Individual or dual majors _____

Grading systems _____

Academic calendar _____

Student-faculty ratio/average class size _____

Faculty advising programs _____

Percent of faculty holding Ph.D. _____

Graduate schools or programs relevant to your interest _____

Student Body

Total enrollment _____

Undergraduate enrollment _____

Geographic area most students come from _____

Male-female ratio _____

HOW TO MAKE A FINAL DECISION

Ethnic/religious enrollment _____

Percent of commuters vs. campus residents _____

Percent of students who graduate _____

Percent who go on to graduate study _____

Campus Life

Distance from your home _____

Nearest major city _____

College setting _____

Facilities of interest to you _____

Athletics _____

Extracurricular groups _____

On-/off-campus housing _____

Board plans available _____

Regulations worth noting _____

Costs/Financial Aid

Application fee _____

Enrollment deposit _____

Tuition _____

Room and board _____

Traveling costs _____

Off-campus living, dorms, etcetera _____

Forms required for aid _____

Typical aid package _____

Sample on-campus jobs _____

Work-study programs available _____

College's estimated total budget _____

Percent of students receiving aid _____

Financial Aid

BY ALICE MURPHEY AND
THE STAFF OF KAPLAN EDUCATIONAL CENTERS

"Sheesh! If I'd known college was going to be this expensive, I wouldn't have read to you so much when you were young."

An Introduction to Financial Aid

In the two previous sections of this book, you determined what schools might be right for you and learned the most effective approaches to getting into them. Now we'll tackle the intimidating topic of how to pay for college once you're accepted. Because paying for college usually requires help in the form of financial aid, we'll give you an overview of the financial aid process and tips on how to optimize your financial aid package. This is very important information because the financial aid packages offered by colleges may turn out to be a major factor in deciding which school you ultimately attend.

Not long ago, the two most costly purchases in a person's life were a house and a car. Now, for most families, the cost of a college education has far surpassed that of a car. For some families, a child's education has replaced the family home as the single most expensive purchase they'll ever make. The total cost of attending many private, independent colleges already exceeds $100,000 for the four years, and by the year 2000 the total cost will likely be more than $150,000. Even at lower-cost, state-supported colleges, the four-year total can be staggering. Unless Bill Gates is your dad or Madonna's your mom, these numbers should quickly convince you of the importance of financial aid.

What Is Financial Aid?

Financial aid is money available from various sources that help students pay for college. It can help make even expensive colleges affordable for qualified students.

The Price Is Right

"There may be something rising faster than the price of going to college....The price of not going."
—*The Wall Street Journal*

Paying for College

Figuring out how to pay for college requires two initial steps. You must first calculate how much it will cost to get an education at the schools you're applying to. Many college-bound students think this is a breeze: You just add up the tuition, the cost of living in a dorm, and grub money—right? Guess again. There are many other expenses to consider, and virtually all of the expenses vary among individual students and among colleges. Only when you've determined how much your education will likely cost—based on the obvious and the hidden expenses—can you proceed to the next step and explore all the financial aid options. Make sure you know the landscape when you actually start applying for your fair share of financial aid.

So let's start with the first step—calculating the cost of your education.

How Much Will College Really Cost?

Most college catalogs list the required tuition and fees for each college included, plus an average cost of room and board. The tuition figures listed are usually fairly accurate, although prices do change quickly, and many additional fees may not be included in the published total. The room and board figure, moreover, can be way off, and many costs that you should consider often aren't even mentioned in the catalogs. To make an informed judgment about the cost of attending a particular school, therefore, you've got to take note of all of the major components of college costs:

Tuition

Tuition is the amount that a college charges you to attend classes. Some colleges have a flat tuition rate for all full-time students, regardless of how many credit hours you take. At other schools, the amount charged depends on how many credit hours you take. Such schools typically have

Digging For Gold

What's the best approach to financial aid? Simple: Research all the possibilities carefully and apply early.

Comparative Shopping

What would you rather spend $100,000 on?

o 112,359 bottles of Snapple Bali Blast

o 6,666 copies of No Doubt's "Tragic Kingdom" CD

o 2,327 pairs of Levi's SilverTab jeans

o 114 Pro-Flex 555 mountain bikes

o 1 four-year college education

a published per-credit fee. So, make sure you know exactly what your intended course of study would cost.

Required vs. Not-Required Fees
Some fees, such as registration and basic activities fees, are paid by all students, and other fees depend on the specific classes that you take. For example, science majors may have to pay a refundable glass breakage deposit of $50 to $100 per lab course. (Sure, you might get your money back, but it's really hard to make it through a lab without breaking a pipette or a petri dish.) Some colleges may have optional student services fees or a varying service fee depending upon whether you choose to participate in certain activities. If you decide to participate in intramurals, for example, you might have to pay a participation fee and buy a uniform.

Books and Supplies
Here again, the amount of money students spend will vary according to their major. For example, science textbooks can be extraordinarily expensive ($75 or more for some titles); other textbooks are usually cheaper, but an English literature course may require students to buy ten or more novels. Lab workbooks, photocopied articles, and study guides, meanwhile, don't always get figured in when colleges quote book costs. For these reasons, you should add 10 percent to 15 percent more to the figure the college provides, particularly if you'll be taking science or art courses.

Room and Board
Room expense depends upon whether a student lives in a dorm, apartment, group house, or a relative's home (just to name a few housing options). Dorm costs also vary depending on whether the accommodation is in a single, double, triple, or quad bedroom and on whether it's on- or off-campus. Many colleges, unfortunately, lump room and board charges together, which can be misleading. Board costs vary widely based on the meal plan that the student chooses (meal plans usually differ according to the number of meals per week—10-meal plans, 21-meal plans, etcetera), diet, the number of late-night snacks, and so forth. Remember: The school's estimated board cost will include only meal plans, not snacks, alcohol, or splurges. At many schools, meal plans aren't mandatory, and students often find that they can save money by preparing their own meals.

Transportation and Travel
The cost of commuting back and forth from the local residence to classes and the cost of getting to and from home during vacations and breaks

Fees

Fees are charges, usually small, that cover costs generally not associated with the student's course load, such as the cost of athletic activities, clubs, and special events.

can add up. Many factors will affect your transportation costs: the proximity of your residence to the college, the availability of public transportation, whether the college is clear across the country or near your parents' home, whether you go home once, twice, or a dozen times, and whether you're close enough to drive home. Keep these factors in mind when you calculate the costs of various colleges.

Personal Expenses
Personal expenses include such things as clothes, laundry, cleaning, toiletries, and entertainment. Each student will, of course, have different requirements in these areas. You know yourself better than anyone else, so you should be able to come up with your own estimate for this cost item.

Medical and Dental Expenses
You'll probably still be eligible to remain on your parents' health insurance while you're a student, even away from home, so you can assume that your insurance cost will be about the same as it is now. Don't discount a few extra expenses, though. If you're attending college away from your hometown, health care may be more expensive there than at home.

Miscellaneous Expenses
Miscellaneous expenses include such things as disabled-student expenses, summer programs, extra books or supplies, tutoring, club dues, fraternity and sorority dues, activity fees, and so forth. Use your best judgment when estimating these costs.

Cost Worksheet
Use the worksheet on the next page to total up the expenses that you'll likely incur in your first year of college. Here are estimates for each cost component:

- **Tuition:** Use the figure provided by the colleges you're considering (or from the profiles contained in this book)

- **Fees:** $100 is a good estimate of the costs of class or activity fees

- **Books and Supplies:** Figure about $300 a semester for a total of $600

- **Room and Board:** Use the amount provided by the college for standard on-campus dorm living and a three-a-day meal plan

The Road to College

- **Travel and Transportation:** For in-state (or equivalent distance) figure about $400; for out-of-state, figure about $1,000

- **Personal Expenses:** $1,500 is a good estimate for these costs

- **Medical and Dental Expenses:** $150 is a good estimate for dental, doctor, and prescription expenses

- **Miscellaneous Expenses:** Estimate your costs here if you plan to join a fraternity, sorority, or special club

Keep in mind that the preceding numbers are estimates. If you have special circumstances, adjust the numbers accordingly. Now, go ahead and fill in your own costs for each school that you're considering. You'll probably need more copies of this worksheet. There's a duplicate of this worksheet in the Forms and Worksheets section near the back of the book. Make as many photocopies as you need.

ESTIMATED FIRST-YEAR COLLEGE COSTS

Tuition	$
Fees	$
Books and Supplies	$
Room and Board	$
Transportation and Travel	$
Personal	$
Medical and Dental	$
Miscellaneous	$
Other	$
TOTAL	$

Now that you've totaled up the estimated costs, you're probably wondering whether you can afford to go to college. Don't despair. Many others have stood in your shoes, and they made it through just fine. So, let's take a close look at how students and their parents pay for a college education.

How Families Pay for College

Families get money to pay for college from three sources: past income, current income, or future income. Most families pay college costs from a combination of all three sources. Let's take a look at each one:

Past Income

A family's past income is reflected in their savings and investments. These assets provide families financial strength and the freedom that comes with it. The more savings they have, the more families are able to do what they want, including paying for college educations.

Current Income

The second way students and their families pay for a college education is out of their current income. Current income includes all wages, interest, and dividends on investments, and all other income, whether it's taxable or nontaxable or whether the family uses it for education purposes or not. Current income also includes financial aid in the form of scholarships and grants and any tuition benefits that the family or student may receive from an employer.

Future Earnings

The third way students and their families pay college costs is out of future earnings, through loans. Loans—whether they are for school, home mortgage, or credit card purchases—are simply ways people pay for things out of future income. Loans can be a reasonable way of paying later for something that you get now. And when the return you get is as great as the difference in salary between a college-educated person and one who does not go to college, it's also an attractive investment.

The Big Picture

When you think of financial aid, you probably think of money provided by the federal government to help pay for a college education. Although much of financial aid—more than $31 billion annually—does come from the federal government, $2.5 billion comes from state grant programs each year, and more than $8 billion annually comes from nongovernment sources—agencies, foundations, clubs, individuals who award private scholarships, and the colleges themselves.

Assets

Assets are financial holdings, such as checking and savings accounts, stocks, bonds, trusts and other securities, loan receivables, home and other real estate equity, business equipment, and business inventory.

Need-Based Aid

Need-based financial aid is given to students who are judged to be in financial need of assistance. This determination is based on the student's income and assets and his or her family's income and assets, as well as other factors. Most financial aid is need-based.

Some programs award aid based solely on the student's need; others are based solely on merit. There are also some programs based on a combination of need and merit. Under many scholarship programs, for example, selection of the recipient is based on merit, but the award amount will depend upon need.

You Don't Have to be a Genius to Get a Scholarship

Most colleges award at least some scholarships based on merit, but not everybody who gets one is a genius or star athlete. Yes, if a college is looking to recruit an exceptional athlete, musician, or physicist, it will offer that student thousands of grant dollars, or else a reduction in the amount of tuition charges, regardless of whether the student has demonstrated financial need. But some colleges—particularly colleges trying to maintain or increase their enrollment as well as the so-called second- or third-tier schools trying to improve their reputations—may award scholarships to students with grades or SAT/ACT scores that aren't beyond the stratosphere. In addition, many states award merit-based scholarships that require only decent grades, not financial need.

As part of meeting financial need, many schools award higher amounts of grant and scholarship money to students that they most want to attract. For example, a college seeking to increase the enrollment of women in its science programs may award entering female students more grant aid than entering male students. Similarly, a college wanting a more ethnically diverse student population may award larger amounts of grant aid to members of underrepresented ethnic groups. State-supported colleges, which generally have less flexibility in making merit-based awards, usually don't make these types of award decisions.

Gift Aid vs. Self-Help Aid

Financial aid programs also differ according to whether the money is a gift or merely aid that must be earned or paid back. Scholarships and grants are considered gift aid, whereas loans and work programs—the Federal Work-study program, for example—are self-help aid.

Most students pay for their schooling using a combination of gift aid, self-help aid, and family contribution. Naturally, you'll want to maximize the gift portion of the mix so that neither you nor your family will be saddled with debt and so that you don't have to work too many hours during school. After all, you'll want to concentrate on your classes, not on making money to pay for them.

Merit-Based Aid

Merit-based financial aid is awarded on the basis of personal achievements or individual characteristics of the recipients rather than on the basis of their financial need. It usually comes in the form of scholarships or grants.

Give It A Shot

If your grades and/or test scores are high or if you have a specific talent, you should think about a merit-based scholarship to help fund your college education. Even if your grades aren't spectacular, you may be surprised at how many colleges will offer merit scholarships as an enticement.

The most recent data available, which is for the 1993–94 academic year, show that more than 55 percent of all financial aid comes in the form of loans. Families are relying more and more on loans to fund college expenses, and these loans are being subsidized less and less by the federal government.

You and your parents should be careful to put the ratio of gift to self-help aid into perspective. Because college graduates earn much more even the first year out of school than do their colleagues who do not go to college, taking on a reasonable level of debt should not deter you from choosing an expensive college—if it's the right one for you.

Financial Aid Eligibility

Eligibility for need-based financial aid is determined by one of two "need-analysis" formulas that seek to measure a family's financial strength and ability to pay for college expenses.

Federal Methodology—A need-analysis procedure developed by Congress that's used to calculate Family Contribution.

Institutional Methodology—An alternate method of need-analysis used by individual colleges to calculate a Family Contribution to determine eligibility for institutional and non-federal aid.

Federal Methodology, a formula that is specified by law, takes into account many variables, including expenses over which a family has no discretion, such as taxes, employment expenses, and basic needs. There's also an allowance for your parents' saving for retirement that increases as they get older (in recognition that more of their assets should be available to them as they near retirement age).

Once your family's assets and income are totaled, these allowances are subtracted off the top, leaving an amount over which your family theoretically has discretion. Your family can use these resources to buy a car, home furnishings, a boat, whatever. Or, they could be saved for a rainy day. The members of the U.S. Congress, and probably most of us as well, believe that the primary responsibility for paying for college is with the parents and students themselves, to the extent they are able. That means that at least a portion of their savings and income should go toward paying educational expenses.

Earning Power

According to the *Statistical Handbook of Working America* (Gale Research, 1995), the average high school graduate earned $21,241 per year while the average college graduate earned $34,385 per year. If you measure the value of a college education in just these financial terms, you can see why people place such a high value on it—and why it may be worth taking on substantial debt to get.

Free Money

Grants and scholarships provide aid that doesn't have to be repaid. Some programs require recipients to maintain a certain grade point average or take certain courses.

State Scholarships

Many state-awarded merit-based scholarships—Cal Grants and Garden State Scholarships, for example—require only decent grades, not financial need.

FINANCIAL AID PROGRAMS

Now that you have a grip on the basics of financial aid, let's take a look at specific aid programs. There are a number of different programs that offer different types of aid. You should explore all of these programs to determine whether you qualify for aid. There are three major financial aid sources—colleges themselves, state governments, and the federal government—and three types of aid: grants and scholarships, loans, and work-study.

Institutional Grants and Scholarships

Most colleges offer some gift aid from their own resources—either merit- or need-based or both—which they may call either grants or scholarships. Institutional grants and scholarships can be very competitive, particularly if they're merit-based. So they may be awarded only to full-time students who apply by a published deadline, and more money may go to applicants with higher grades. To help offset their higher costs, private, high-cost colleges tend to have more gift aid available than low-cost, publicly supported colleges. Although some of the funds used by private colleges for gift aid come from their fundraising efforts, a great deal of the additional scholarship and grant money comes from the tuition that other students pay.

State Grants

All 50 states have grant programs, but students usually have to be a resident of the state awarding the grant to qualify. Most state programs also require that students attend a college in the state of residency. To get the address of the agency in your state that handles financial aid programs, check out the list in the Resources section near the back of the book.

Federal Pell Grant

The single largest grant program is the Federal Pell Grant, which in the 1995–96 academic year provided aid to more than 3.7 million students. The total spent was almost $5.7 billion, with an average award per student of about $1,500. The maximum award for the 1997–98 academic year is $2,700, and the amount students receive will depend on the cost of their school, their eligibility based on the need-analysis formula, and whether they attend full-time or part-time. Although millions of students receive Federal Pell Grants, most students from middle-income families don't qualify for them because their families' incomes are too high.

Federal Supplemental Educational Opportunity Grant (FSEOG)

This program—whose official title is a mouthful, for sure—is generally referred to just by its initials or by the term "Supplemental Grant." Colleges themselves award FSEOGs; because they must award these grants to the neediest students, the grants are mostly awarded to Federal Pell Grant recipients. The total available in 1993–94 was about $500 million, which went to fewer than one million students (an average of about $550 per student).

Other Federal Grants

There are a handful of other federal grants available in such programs as the Robert C. Byrd Honors Scholarship, science scholarships, nursing scholarships, and a few programs targeted to graduate students. These grants and scholarships, as indicated by their names, are specifically targeted and are generally merit-based. Although these are federal grants, state scholarship agencies choose the scholarship winners. For more information, contact your state financial aid agency.

LOAN PROGRAMS

The federal government sponsors several loan programs to help students pay college costs. The provisions of the various programs vary greatly, so make sure you know the differences.

Federal Perkins Loan

Eligibility for the Federal Perkins Loan program is based on student need. Each participating college has a pool of money from which they make these loans directly to students. The college decides the amount of the loan and who receives it. The interest on the loan—currently 5 percent—does not accrue while the student is in school, and repayment does not begin until six months after graduation. Not all Perkins Loans have to repaid. If, for example, you ultimately use your education to teach handicapped children, teach in a designated school that serves low-income students, or serve in selected specialties of the armed forces, VISTA, the Peace Corps, or certain Head Start programs, the loan will be canceled. The maximum award is $3,000 per year for undergraduates, but the average loan is about $1,350.

Loan Sharks

The interest rate on educational loans is usually lower than for other types of loans. For students who have no credit history, it's usually easier to get student loans than other kinds of loans.

Federal Perkins Loans

The Perkins Loan program is a federal financial aid program that consists of low-interest (5 percent) loans for students with exceptional financial need. Although the money comes from the federal government, the colleges themselves award Federal Perkins Loans.

Subsidized Loans

When a loan is subsidized, the borrower is not responsible for all of the interest payments. For Subsidized Federal Stafford Loans, for example, the government pays interest to the lender on behalf of the borrower while the student is in school and during approved grace periods.

Federal Stafford Loans

Under the Stafford Loan program, students can borrow money to attend school and the federal government will guarantee the loan in case of default. There are two types of Federal Stafford Loans—Subsidized (need-based) and Unsubsidized (not need-based).

Federal Family Education Loan Programs (FFELP)

Three loan programs for dependent students and their parents make up the Federal Family Educational Loan program: the Subsidized Federal Stafford Loan, the Unsubsidized Federal Stafford Loan, and the Federal PLUS Loan (Parent Loans to Undergraduate Students).

Subsidized Federal Stafford Loan

A Subsidized Federal Stafford Loan is a need-based loan made by a bank, savings and loan, credit union, or some other lender. Each college determines eligibility for this loan by using the need-analysis formula, and the college financial aid office must certify the student's eligibility on a loan application. First-year students can borrow up to $2,625 per year, sophomores up to $3,500, and juniors and seniors up to $5,500. The loan has a one-year adjustable interest rate set in June of each year based on the 91-day Treasury Bill rate plus 3.1 percent. The maximum rate is 8.25 percent; the 1996–97 rate will be 7.66 percent. Borrowers pay an origination and insurance fee totaling 4 percent, which are subtracted from the proceeds. As with the Perkins Loan, interest doesn't accrue while the borrower is in school, and repayment doesn't begin until six months after graduation. All cancellation and deferment terms are included in the loan's promissory note.

Unsubsidized Federal Stafford Loan

This program has basically the same terms as the Subsidized Federal Stafford Loan except that eligibility is not based on need, and interest accrues even while the borrower is in school. Although students may choose to defer any payments while still in school, interest will accrue; therefore, when repayment begins, they will owe considerably more than the amount they first borrowed. For that reason, the Unsubsidized Federal Stafford Loan program is considered the least attractive federal student loan program.

Federal PLUS Loan

The Federal PLUS program is an unsubsidized, non-need based loan program for parents of undergraduate students. The interest rate is set once a year in June. The 1995–96 rate was 8.98 and will be 8.72 percent through June 1997. Eligibility is not based on need and repayment begins 60 days after the money is loaned. There's no annual limit on the amount borrowed; parents can borrow up to the cost of education at the college, minus any financial aid the student receives, including loans. As with the Federal Stafford Loan, fees totaling 4 percent are subtracted from the proceeds. A lender will check credit records to see whether the student's parents have a bad credit history. If so, they may have problems qualifying for the loan.

William D. Ford Federal Direct Loan

Not every college, however, participates in the Federal Family Education Loan program that we just discussed. Some opt for the Federal Direct Loan program, which has terms similar to those of the Federal Stafford Loan program. The major difference is that under the Federal Direct Loan program, the U.S. Department of Education rather than a bank is the lender. There are subsidized, unsubsidized, and parent loans under the Federal Direct Loan program. The U.S. Department of Education believes that the Federal Direct Loan program will save taxpayers money and is encouraging colleges to sign up for it. Approximately 40 percent of all Federal Stafford loans certified in 1995–96 were done through the Federal Direct Loan Program.

Another big difference between the Federal Direct Loan and the Federal Stafford Loan is that the former offers additional repayment options. Direct Loan borrowers can repay their loans either with a fixed monthly payment over a period of 10 years, a lower fixed monthly payment for up to 30 years, a graduated repayment plan in which the amount changes, or an income-contingent plan in which they pay a percentage of their income. Federal regulations are pending which will make the repayment provisions for both programs the same.

WORK PROGRAMS

Many students work while they're in college to help pay expenses. Federal and state work-study programs provide funding for part-time jobs for students. These jobs range from working at the library check out desk and helping out at the school cafeteria to helping out individual professors. Many students who don't qualify for work-study programs find their own jobs—on campus or off campus.

Federal Work-Study Program (FWS)

The Federal Work-Study Program is a need-based program under which students are awarded an amount of money that they earn through employment. Many FWS jobs are right on campus, and FWS recipients work side-by-side with other student workers at the same rate of pay. The only difference is that a portion of the student's salary is paid through federal funds (for that reason, employers are often especially eager to hire FWS recipients). Eligibility for FWS is determined through the federal need-analysis formula. Each college, in turn, determines who receives FWS and in what amount.

Need Help?

To find out about how the KapLoan program can help you get information on financing your college education, call: 1-888-KAP-LOAN toll-free.

Federal Direct Student Loans

Under the Federal Direct Student Loan program, students can get federal loans directly from their colleges with funds provided by the U.S. Department of Education instead of a bank or other lender.

Work While You Study

A work-study job is often part of a student's financial aid package, and the jobs are usually on campus. The money earned is used to pay for tuition and other college costs.

State Work-Study Programs

A few states offer work-study programs that are similar to the Federal Work Study Program. You should check with your state agencies or the financial aid office at prospective colleges.

Part-Time Jobs

Although part-time jobs aren't a financial aid program in the traditional sense, many students help finance their education through part-time employment both on and off campus, and virtually every college offers part-time jobs to students. Part-time jobs are not need-based in the sense that no need analysis or financial aid application is necessary. How students present their need for the job to the prospective employer or to the job placement office staff that refers them, however, may go a long way toward their being hired.

WHAT'S NEXT?

Now that you know something about the major aid programs, let's see how you can get this money. The next chapter, "An Inside Look at the Financial Aid Application Process," will cover the nuts and bolts of applying for financial aid—getting the right forms, filling them out properly, and making sure you get the best aid package.

An Inside Look at the Financial Aid Application Process

Applying for financial aid always seems like a daunting prospect to families facing it for the first time. The forms seem to always be changing and each college seems to want you to provide something different. In this chapter, we will help you to navigate through the process.

First of all, there are two forms you need to become familiar with. The basic required form for all federal aid is called the Free Application for Federal Student Aid (FAFSA). This form must be filed by any student who wishes to be considered for the federal financial aid programs—a Federal Pell Grant, federal work-study, a Federal Perkins Loan, a Federal Stafford Loan, and the other federal programs that will be described in this chapter.

The other form you may need to file is called the CSS/Financial Aid PROFILE form. This form first became available in October 1995 when the College Scholarship Service (CSS) of the College Board developed a new application process, which is now used by many institutions. This process was designed to provide information to colleges that wanted more information (and earlier information) than the federal government was providing from the FAFSA. Usually, these colleges have their own funds to award and the PROFILE process gives them the additional information that they need for the award process.

In this chapter, we'll take you through every stage of the financial aid application processes—both the federal process and the institutional process used by some schools.

GETTING ON THE RIGHT TRACK

Which application process should you follow? Does the new process apply to your situation? The answers to these important questions

When It's Time to Change, You've Got to Rearrange

When you apply for institutional aid (funds controlled by the schools), you'll use the customized application called the Financial Aid PROFILE.

depend on whether you're applying to a college that uses only the FAFSA or a college that awards its own institutional aid using the new application.

All of the government programs require the Free Application for Federal Student Aid (FAFSA). Many of the schools' programs require the College Scholarship Service's (CSS's) new Financial Aid PROFILE. So, you'll either be completing just the FAFSA, just the PROFILE, or both.

Before we get into the financial aid application process, we need to point you in the right direction. You must first make two basic decisions:

Decision 1
Which colleges will you be applying to for admission and financial aid? As soon as you know that, you can start the financial aid process. Keep in mind that you can work on your financial aid applications at the same time you complete your admissions applications.

Decision 2
Will you be filling out the Financial Aid PROFILE (that is, do any of the schools you're applying to require it)? Or will you be filling out the FAFSA? This will determine, for our organizational purposes, which "track" you're on, as you'll see.

To find out which colleges do or don't want you to use the PROFILE, read the instructions included in the PROFILE Registration packet or check directly with the financial aid offices at the colleges. You can pick up a PROFILE registration packet in your high school guidance office.

So, what do you do at this point? Well, if the college is listed in the PROFILE Registration Form packet, you know the school wants it. If it's not listed, check all the literature you've received from that school to make sure they didn't change their requirements after the deadline to be included in the instruction booklet. And, of course, you could always call the college financial aid office just to make sure.

As a general rule, more of the private colleges, particularly those that have a significant amount of their own financial aid money, and fewer of the state-supported colleges, which often have limited financial aid resources, will want you to use the PROFILE. But that's not always the case, so double-check. In addition some, many private scholarship programs, such as the National Merit Scholarship Program, will require the PROFILE.

Federal Aid Vs. Institutional Aid

Federal aid, not surprisingly, refers to financial aid from government-sponsored programs. Institutional aid refers to aid from school-sponsored programs.

Like Clockwork

It's important that you submit required forms and appropriate documentation at the right time. Otherwise, you could miss out on essential aid.

Decision 3
Do all the colleges you've applied to want you to fill out the PROFILE? If yes, no problem. Just follow along Track A as the colleges prompt you (we'll get more into this later). However, if one or more of the schools don't subscribe to this new service, you also have to follow Track B.

TRACK A AND TRACK B

If all the schools you've applied to—or will apply to—use the Financial Aid PROFILE form, you're on Track A only.

If none of the schools you're interested in uses the Financial Aid PROFILE form, you're on Track B only.

If some of your schools require PROFILE and some don't, you're on Track A *and* Track B.

Here's the outline of Tracks A and B. Notice that the two tracks merge at Step 3.

TRACK A
1. Fill out PROFILE registration.
2. Complete/submit PROFILE.

TRACK B
1. Pick up FAFSA.
2. Complete/submit FAFSA.

3. Review acknowledgment letter.
4. Verify reported income.
5. Examine your award letter.
6. Compare financial aid packages.

TRACK A

This track is for students applying to at least one college that requires the PROFILE.

Step 1: Fill out the PROFILE Registration

The PROFILE Registration is a one-page form that initiates the financial aid process. You provide some basic information, and CSS generates your own customized financial aid application. Many schools use the PROFILE form specifically for their early decision candidates.

PROFILE Registration Form

On your PROFILE Registration, you'll list all the schools you've applied to that require you to use the PROFILE service (list only those schools that want the PROFILE). Send this registration form to CSS in the envelope provided, making sure you've included the required payment.

Making Tracks

TRACK A: At least one of your schools requires the PROFILE.

TRACK B: None of your schools require the PROFILE.

The Road to College

OFA: Our Favorite Acronyms

CSS: College Scholarship Service, the arm of the College Board that handles financial aid and processes the Financial Aid PROFILE.

FAFSA: The Free Application for Federal Student Aid, the federal financial aid application that establishes eligibility for all federal programs, including loan programs, and for some institutional aid.

Step 2: Complete and Submit the Financial Aid PROFILE

A few weeks after submitting the registration form, you'll receive in the mail a customized financial aid application called the Financial Aid PROFILE. With this form you'll be able to apply for institutional aid at the colleges you've designated. These colleges will get the information you've reported and also be able to estimate your eligibility for federal aid. If eligible, you'll eventually have to fill out the official federal application, the FAFSA, in order to receive federal aid.

The Financial Aid PROFILE is customized for you, your family, and the schools you've designated. It includes questions that every applicant for financial aid has to fill out, questions that only the colleges you've designated want you to fill out, and relevant supplemental forms. A personalized cover letter will instruct you what to do and tell you about deadlines and requirements for the colleges you designated on the PROFILE Registration Form.

The PROFILE Application for Institutional Aid

In addition to the cover letter, your customized PROFILE packet will include your financial aid application for institutional aid at the colleges you've designated. The first and second pages of the application will collect student information, the second and third will ask for parent information, and the third and fourth pages will seek more detailed information.

When a College Wants More Information

In addition to the cover letter and the customized application, the PROFILE packet will include additional questions colleges want addressed in order to award their own funds. There will also be codes to tell you which colleges want which questions answered.

If you're only on Track A, you can skip ahead to Step 3.

Track B

This track is for students applying to schools that don't use the PRO-FILE.

Step 1: Pick up a Free Application for Federal Student Aid (FAFSA)

If none of the colleges that you're applying to uses the PROFILE, you initiate the financial aid application process using the FAFSA. This is the form that every financial aid applicant must eventually fill out to establish eligibility for federal aid and, for schools not using the PROFILE, for institutional and state aid as well. The form is available in November or December from your guidance office. You cannot complete it in until after January 1st.

The FAFSA is the only form allowed to establish eligibility for federal financial aid programs, which include the Federal Pell Grant, Federal Supplemental Educational Opportunity Grant (FSEOG), Federal Work Study, Federal Perkins Loan, Federal Stafford Loan, and Federal Direct Loan programs. The FAFSA is also used by many state agencies and colleges to award their own funds.

FAFSA

On the following pages you'll find a blank copy of the four-page FAFSA for your perusal. We've placed additional blank forms in the Appendix, so you can start drafting your applications. You cannot submit these sample forms. You'll need to use original, current applications.

CyberFAFSA

The FAFSA express is an electronic version of the FAFSA form available from the federal government. This software program allows you to complete the FAFSA on your computer and electronically transmit your information to the federal processor by modem. You can also download the software from KapLoan's Web site (http://www.kaploan.com).

🚗 **THE ROAD TO COLLEGE**

Free Application for Federal Student Aid
1997–98 School Year

WARNING: If you purposely give false or misleading information on this form, you may be fined $10,000, sent to prison, or both.

"You" and "your" on this form always mean the student who wants aid.

Form Approved
OMB No. 1840-0110
App. Exp. 6/30/98

U.S. Department of Education
Student Financial Assistance Programs

Use dark ink. Make capital letters and numbers clear and legible.   **E X M 2 4**

Fill in ovals completely. Only one oval per question.   Correct ●   *Incorrect marks will be ignored.*   Incorrect ⊗ ✓

Section A: You (the student)

1–3. Your name
1. Last name
2. First name
3. M.I.

Your title (optional)   Mr. ○ 1   Miss, Mrs., or Ms. ○ 2

4–7. Your permanent mailing address *(All mail will be sent to this address. See Instructions, page 2 for state/country abbreviations.)*
4. Number and street (Include apt. no.)
5. City
6. State
7. ZIP code

8. Your social security number (SSN) *(Don't leave blank. See Instructions, page 2.)*

9. Your date of birth   Month Day Year   1 9

15–16. Are you a U.S. citizen? *(See Instructions, pages 2–3.)*
Yes, I am a U.S. citizen. ○ 1
No, but I am an eligible noncitizen. ○ 2
A
No, neither of the above. ○ 3

10. Your permanent home telephone number   Area code

17. As of today, are you married? *(Fill in only one oval.)*
I am not married. (I am single, widowed, or divorced.) ○ 1
I am married. ○ 2
I am separated from my spouse. ○ 3

11. Your state of legal residence   State

12. Date you became a legal resident of the state in question 11 *(See Instructions, page 2.)*   Month Day Year   1 9

18. Date you were married, separated, divorced, or widowed. If divorced, use date of divorce or separation, whichever is earlier. *(If never married, leave blank.)*   Month Year   1 9

13–14. Your driver's license number *(Include the state abbreviation. If you don't have a license, write in "None.")*
State   License number

19. Will you have your first bachelor's degree before July 1, 1997?   Yes ○ 1   No ○ 2

Section B: Education Background

20–21. Date that you (the student) received, or will receive, your high school diploma, either *(Enter one date. Leave blank if the question does not apply to you.)*
- by graduating from high school   **20.** Month Year 1 9
OR
- by earning a GED   **21.** Month Year 1 9

22–23. Highest educational level or grade level your father and your mother completed. *(Fill in one oval for each parent. See Instructions, page 3.)*

	22. Father	23. Mother
elementary school (K–8)	○ 1	○ 1
high school (9–12)	○ 2	○ 2
college or beyond	○ 3	○ 3
unknown	○ 4	○ 4

If you (and your family) have **unusual circumstances**, complete this form and then check with your financial aid administrator. Examples:
- tuition expenses at an elementary or secondary school,
- unusual medical or dental expenses not covered by insurance,
- a family member who recently became unemployed, or
- other unusual circumstances such as changes in income or assets that might affect your eligibility for student financial aid.

540

Section C: Your Plans *Answer these questions about your college plans.*

24–28. Your expected enrollment status for the 1997–98 school year
(See Instructions, page 3.)

School term	Full time	3/4 time	1/2 time	Less than 1/2 time	Not enrolled
24. Summer term '97	○ 1	○ 2	○ 3	○ 4	○ 5
25. Fall semester/qtr. '97	○ 1	○ 2	○ 3	○ 4	○ 5
26. Winter quarter '97-98	○ 1	○ 2	○ 3	○ 4	○ 5
27. Spring semester/qtr. '98	○ 1	○ 2	○ 3	○ 4	○ 5
28. Summer term '98	○ 1	○ 2	○ 3	○ 4	○ 5

29. Your course of study *(See Instructions for code, page 3.)* [Code]

30. College degree/certificate you expect to receive
(See Instructions for code, page 3.)

31. Date you expect to receive your degree/certificate [Month Day Year]

32. Your grade level during the 1997–98 school year *(Fill in only one.)*

- 1st yr./never attended college ○ 1
- 1st yr./attended college before ○ 2
- 2nd year/sophomore ○ 3
- 3rd year/junior ○ 4
- 4th year/senior ○ 5
- 5th year/other undergraduate ○ 6
- 1st year graduate/professional ○ 7
- 2nd year graduate/professional ○ 8
- 3rd year graduate/professional ○ 9
- Beyond 3rd year graduate/professional ○ 10

33–35. In addition to grants, what other types of financial aid are you (and your parents) interested in? *(See Instructions, page 3.)*

- **33.** Student employment   Yes ○ 1   No ○ 2
- **34.** Student loans   Yes ○ 1   No ○ 2
- **35.** Parent loans for students Yes ○ 1   No ○ 2

36. If you are (or were) in college, do you plan to attend **that same college** in 1997–98?
(If this doesn't apply to you, leave blank.)   Yes ○ 1   No ○ 2

37. For how many dependents will you (the student) pay child care or elder care expenses in 1997–98?

38–39. Veterans education benefits you expect to receive from July 1, 1997 through June 30, 1998

- **38.** Amount per month $_____.00
- **39.** Number of months

Section D: Student Status

40. Were you born **before** January 1, 1974? .... Yes ○ 1   No ○ 2

41. Are you a veteran of the U.S. Armed Forces? .... Yes ○ 1   No ○ 2

42. Will you be enrolled in a graduate or professional program (beyond a bachelor's degree) in 1997-98? .... Yes ○ 1   No ○ 2

43. Are you married?... Yes ○ 1   No ○ 2

44. Are you an orphan or a ward of the court, or **were** you a ward of the court until age 18? .... Yes ○ 1   No ○ 2

45. Do you have legal dependents (**other than a spouse**) that fit the definition in Instructions, page 4? .... Yes ○ 1   No ○ 2

If you answered **"Yes"** to **any** question in Section D, go to Section E and fill out **both the GRAY and the WHITE** areas on the rest of this form.

If you answered **"No"** to **every** question in Section D, go to Section E and fill out **both the GREEN and the WHITE** areas on the rest of this form.

Section E: Household Information

Remember:
At least one "Yes" answer in Section D means fill out the GRAY and WHITE areas.

All "No" answers in Section D means fill out the GREEN and WHITE areas.

STUDENT (& SPOUSE)

46. Number in your household in 1997–98
(Include yourself and your spouse. Do not include your children and other people unless they meet the definition in Instructions, page 4.)

47. Number of college students in household in 1997–98
(Of the number in 46, how many will be in college at least half-time in at least one term in an eligible program? Include yourself. See Instructions, page 4.)

PARENT(S)

48. Your parent(s)' **current** marital status:

- single ○ 1
- married ○ 2
- separated ○ 3
- divorced ○ 4
- widowed ○ 5

49. Your parent(s)' state of legal residence [State]

50. Date your parent(s) became legal resident(s) of the state in question 49 *(See Instructions, page 5.)* [Month Day Year] 1 9

51. Number in your parent(s)' household in 1997–98
(Include yourself and your parents. Do not include your parents' other children and other people unless they meet the definition in Instructions, page 5.)

52. Number of college students in household in 1997–98
(Of the number in 51, how many will be in college at least half-time in at least one term in an eligible program? Include yourself. See Instructions, page 5.)

Section F: 1996 Income, Earnings, and Benefits
You must see Instructions, pages 5 and 6, for information about tax forms and tax filing status, especially if you are estimating taxes or filing electronically or by telephone. These instructions will tell you what income and benefits should be reported in this section.

Page 3

STUDENT (& SPOUSE) *Everyone must fill out this column.*   **PARENT(S)**

The following 1996 U.S. income tax figures are from: **53.** *(Fill in one oval.)*   **65.** *(Fill in one oval.)*

- A—a completed 1996 IRS Form 1040A, 1040EZ, or 1040TEL .... ○ 1   A .... ○ 1
- B—a completed 1996 IRS Form 1040 .... ○ 2   B .... ○ 2
- C—an estimated 1996 IRS Form 1040A, 1040EZ, or 1040TEL .... ○ 3   C .... ○ 3
- D—an estimated 1996 IRS Form 1040 .... ○ 4   D .... ○ 4
- E—will not file a 1996 U.S. income tax return   *(Skip to question 57.)* ○ 5   E   *(Skip to 69.)* ○ 5

1996 Total number of exemptions (Form 1040–line 6d, or 1040A–line 6d; 1040EZ filers— *see Instructions, page 6.*)   **54.** _____   **66.** _____

1996 Adjusted Gross Income (AGI: Form 1040–line 31, 1040A–line 16, or 1040EZ–line 4— *see Instructions, page 6.*)   **55.** $ _____ .00   **67.** $ _____ .00

1996 U.S. income tax **paid** (Form 1040–line 44, 1040A–line 25, or 1040EZ–line 10)   **56.** $ _____ .00   **68.** $ _____ .00

TAX FILERS ONLY

1996 Income earned from work   (Student) **57.** $ _____ .00   (Father) **69.** $ _____ .00

1996 Income earned from work   (Spouse) **58.** $ _____ .00   (Mother) **70.** $ _____ .00

1996 Untaxed income and benefits (yearly totals only):

Earned Income Credit (Form 1040–line 54, Form 1040A–line 29c, or Form 1040EZ–line 8)   **59.** $ _____ .00   **71.** $ _____ .00

Untaxed Social Security Benefits   **60.** $ _____ .00   **72.** $ _____ .00

Aid to Families with Dependent Children (AFDC/ADC)   **61.** $ _____ .00   **73.** $ _____ .00

Child support received for all children   **62.** $ _____ .00   **74.** $ _____ .00

Other untaxed income and benefits from Worksheet #2, page 11   **63.** $ _____ .00   **75.** $ _____ .00

1996 Amount from Line 5, Worksheet #3, page 12 *(See Instructions.)*   **64.** $ _____ .00   **76.** $ _____ .00

Section G: Asset Information

ATTENTION!
Fill out Worksheet A or Worksheet B in Instructions, page 7. If you meet the tax filing and income conditions on Worksheets A and B, you do not have to complete Section G to apply for Federal student aid. Some states and colleges, however, require Section G information for their own aid programs. Check with your financial aid administrator and/or State Agency.

Age of your older parent   **84.** _____

STUDENT (& SPOUSE)   **PARENT(S)**

Cash, savings, and checking accounts   **77.** $ _____ .00   **85.** $ _____ .00

Other real estate and investments value *(Don't include the home.)*   **78.** $ _____ .00   **86.** $ _____ .00

Other real estate and investments debt *(Don't include the home.)*   **79.** $ _____ .00   **87.** $ _____ .00

Business value   **80.** $ _____ .00   **88.** $ _____ .00

Business debt   **81.** $ _____ .00   **89.** $ _____ .00

Investment farm value *(See Instructions, page 8.)* *(Don't include a family farm.)*   **82.** $ _____ .00   **90.** $ _____ .00

Investment farm debt *(See Instructions, page 8.)* *(Don't include a family farm.)*   **83.** $ _____ .00   **91.** $ _____ .00

THE FINANCIAL AID APPLICATION PROCESS

Section H: Releases and Signatures

Page 4

92–103. What college(s) do you plan to attend in 1997–98?
(Note: The colleges you list below will have access to your application information. See Instructions, page 8.)

Housing codes	1—on-campus	3—with parent(s)
	2—off-campus	4—with relative(s) other than parent(s)

	Title IV School Code	College Name	College Street Address and City	State	Housing Code
XX.	0 5 4 3 2 1	EXAMPLE UNIVERSITY	14930 NORTH SOMEWHERE BLVD. ANYWHERE CITY	S T	XX. 2
92.					93.
94.					95.
96.					97.
98.					99.
100.					101.
102.					103.

104. The U.S. Department of Education will send information from this form to your state financial aid agency and the state agencies of the colleges listed above so they can consider you for state aid. Answer **"No"** if you **don't** want information released to the state. *(See Instructions, page 9 and "Deadlines for State Student Aid," page 10.)* .... 104. No ○ 2

105. Males not yet registered for Selective Service (SS): Do you want SS to register you? *(See Instructions, page 9.)* .... 105. Yes ○ 1

106–107. Read, Sign, and Date Below

All of the information provided by me or any other person on this form is true and complete to the best of my knowledge. I understand that this application is being filed jointly by all signatories. If asked by an authorized official, I agree to give proof of the information that I have given on this form. I realize that this proof may include a copy of my U.S. or state income tax return. I also realize that if I do not give proof when asked, the student may be denied aid.

Statement of Educational Purpose. I certify that I will use any Federal Title IV, HEA funds I receive during the award year covered by this application solely for expenses related to my attendance at the institution of higher education that determined or certified my eligibility for those funds.

Certification Statement on Overpayments and Defaults. I understand that I may not receive any Federal Title IV, HEA funds if I owe an overpayment on any Title IV educational grant or loan or am in default on a Title IV educational loan unless I have made satisfactory arrangements to repay or otherwise resolve the overpayment or default. I also understand that I must notify my school if I do owe an overpayment or am in default.

Everyone whose information is given on this form should sign below. The student (and at least one parent, if parental information is given) must sign below or this form will be returned unprocessed.

106. Signatures *(Sign in the boxes below.)*

1. Student
2. Student's Spouse
3. Father/Stepfather
4. Mother/Stepmother

107. Date completed — Month | Day | Year 1997 ○ / 1998 ○

Section I: Preparer's Use Only

For preparers other than student, spouse, and parent(s). Student, spouse, and parent(s), sign in question 106.

Preparer's name (last, first, MI)

Firm name

Firm or preparer's address (street, city, state, ZIP)

108. Employer identification number (EIN)

OR

109. Preparer's social security number

Certification: All of the information on this form is true and complete to the best of my knowledge.

110. Preparer's signature — Date

School Use Only

D/O ○   Title IV Code

FAA Signature

MDE Use Only
Do not write in this box   Special handle

MAKE SURE THAT YOU HAVE COMPLETED, DATED, AND SIGNED THIS APPLICATION.
Mail the original application (NOT A PHOTOCOPY) to: Federal Student Aid Programs, P.O. Box 4008, Mt. Vernon, IL 62864-8608

543

THE ROAD TO COLLEGE

Good Housekeeping

Fill out all financial aid forms neatly, accurately, and completely. Keep copies of everything that you mail out and record when you sent in the forms.

Step 2: Complete and Submit Your FAFSA

The FAFSA asks questions about your family, the income and assets of you and your parents, and your college plans. It's relatively straightforward, but here are four important tips for completing the application:

- have your and your parents' financial records handy before you start

- complete only those sections you're required to complete

- double-and triple-check your responses for accuracy, especially your social security number

- make sure you and your parents sign and date the application

Step 3: Review Your Acknowledgment Letters

Here's where Tracks A and B merge, although there are still different requirements for federal and institutional funds.

A few weeks after you submit your PROFILE and/or FAFSA, you'll receive an acknowledgment letter in the mail, confirming the information you reported. If you only complete the FAFSA, the acknowledgment will take the form of a Student Aid Report (SAR). Review all the material to make sure that the information is accurate. If there are any errors, check the letter or report for details on how to submit the necessary corrections to the processor.

The Student Aid Report

After submitting the FAFSA, you'll receive a Student Aid Report (SAR). The SAR shows the information that was processed and indicates the amount of your expected Family Contribution. The SAR will be sent to the financial aid office of the schools you selected on the application.

The most important element of both your PROFILE acknowledgment letter and your SAR will be the calculated Family Contribution (FC). Family Contribution is the amount of money it's been determined that you and your family can pay. As such, the FC establishes your financial need and, therefore, your eligibility for federal programs. Although only the FAFSA leads to official results, the PROFILE will provide your college with enough information to estimate your federal eligibility. The colleges you designated on your application receive this information about your FC and use it to put together your total financial aid offer.

Step 4: Verify Your Reported Income

Often, you'll be asked to send a copy of both your and your parents' income tax return directly to the financial aid office at each college. These documents are used to verify the income reported on the application.

Some families must also send documents that verify the amount of untaxed income a family received, statements from banks and investment accounts that verify the amount of a family's assets, a supplemental form that details the assets and income from a farm or business, information from a divorced or separated parent, and any other documentation that a college financial aid office determines is required to verify the information reported on the application.

Step 5: Examine Your Financial Aid Award Letter

After your file is completed—and usually after you have been accepted for admission—the financial aid office of each college that has accepted you will put together your financial aid package. Colleges use your Family Contribution to determine your eligibility for financial aid. The family's financial need equals the total cost of attending that college minus the calculated Family Contribution. Because each school's total cost is different, a family's need for aid will be different at each school. In theory, the Family Contribution is supposed to remain the same regardless of where the student will be attending. In practice, however, the family contribution does differ quite significantly from school to school.

The Waiting Game

Presumably, if it appears that you'll be eligible for some federal aid, the school will eventually ask you to fill out a FAFSA. We suggest waiting until you've been told to fill it out, since some colleges may want you to wait until they are sure you'll be using the correct numbers.

FINANCIAL NEED FORMULA

Financial Need = Total Cost − Family Contribution

The amount of need-based financial aid that a student can receive	Tuition, Fees, Room, Board, Books, Etcetera	The amount of family financial resources that should be used to help pay for college costs, as determined by a need-analysis formula

The college will then send you an award letter that details your eligibility for specific financial aid programs. Most students are awarded aid from a combination of programs and from the different sources available to the college, hence the term "packaging."

The financial aid award letter will often tell you what aid you will receive if you attend that school, and how much you and your family will have to pay out of your own pocket. For first-year students, this letter is often sent with, or soon after, the letter of admission. Ideally, this package will supply the amount of money you need in order to pay for college, the

Verification

A process of review to determine the accuracy of the information on a student's financial aid application.

545

amount of money that you and your family can not afford to pay yourselves. Realistically, you may still have financial aid that's not with financial aid awards. You'll have to meet this "unmet need" by increasing your family contribution, taking out a larger loan, or working more hours than you originally planned.

A Word on Loan Applications
If you're awarded a Federal Stafford Loan, you'll also need to complete a loan application and a series of paperwork about the loan. After your college's financial aid office certifies that you're eligible, you or the financial aid office must forward your loan application to the lender of your choice. This lender can be your local bank, a national bank, savings and loan, credit union, or private organization. The financial aid office can often help you choose an appropriate lender.

If you've been awarded either a Federal Direct Loan or a Perkins Loan, the lender is either the federal government or the college itself, so you won't need to send your supplemental loan application to a bank.

Outside Scholarships
Outside scholarships that students obtain from their high school, local community organizations, service clubs, private companies, or any other sponsor not specifically connected with the college are tied into a student's financial aid package. If a student receives need-based aid and an outside scholarship, most colleges try first to use this additional scholarship to meet any unmet need that remains after financial aid has been awarded, and then reduce the loan or work portion of the package before reducing the grant portion.

Employee Tuition Benefits
A great deal of aid comes from tuition stipends that companies pay their employees for dependents attending college. This source accounts for a great deal of the money referred to when headlines say, "Millions in Financial Aid Go Unused." It goes unused because not every employee who has access to these funds has a child going to college. But millions of dollars do, in fact, go to students.

Step 6: Compare Your Financial Aid Packages
Colleges use different approaches to financial aid packaging in determining how much to award an eligible student from its financial aid programs (scholarships, grants, part-time jobs, and loans). Very few colleges, if any, offer only grants and scholarships in the financial aid awards that they offer students. As college costs have risen, students and

---

Package Deal

A financial aid package is the total amount of financial aid a student receives. Federal and nonfederal aid in the form of grants, loans, and work-study are combined in a "package" to help meet the student's need. Using available resources to give each student the best possible package of aid is one of the major responsibilities of a school's financial aid administrator.

Corporate Cash

Parents should check with their employers to determine whether they sponsor an employee tuition benefit program.

their families have found that they must rely more and more on loans to finance college expenses. Most colleges try to balance the amount of loan and work with grant aid so that no student is overburdened with debt after graduation.

Sample Financial Aid Packages

Here are sample aid packages that three different colleges might award a student with a calculated Family Contribution as shown. Note that the Family Contributions can be quite different—even for the same family. In this example, College 1 uses the Federal Methodology, College 2 uses the Institutional Methodology with a minimum student contribution, and College 3 uses the Institutional Methodology requiring a higher student contribution.

	College 1	College 2	College 3
Cost of Attendance	$12,100	$26,000	$28,900
Family Contribution	6,600	8,100	8,600
Need	**$5,500**	**$17,900**	**$20,300**
Award			
Institutional Grant	0	9,900	13,600
State Grant	2,000	0	4,000
Federal Stafford Loan	2,625	2,625	2,625
Federal Perkins Loan	0	1,500	0
Federal Work-Study	875	1,500	0
Federal PLUS	0	2,375	0
Unmet Need	**0**	**0**	**75**

Analysis of the Packages

The three colleges offered quite different packages to this student. When you analyze your own financial aid package, the key is to look at what the total cost will be to you and your family—the family and student contributions, all self-help awards (loans and work), and any unmet need.

In this example, College 1, a low-cost state college, used the Federal Methodology and awarded no institutional grant to the student. The total cost to the student's family will be the sum of $6,600 (Family Contribution), $2,625 (Stafford Loan), and $875 (Federal Work-Study), or a total of $10,200. The only "free money" in this package is the state grant.

Award Letter

The document by which a college notifies a student that he or she has qualified for financial aid is called an award letter. It usually gives information about the types and amounts of aid offered, specific program information, and the conditions that govern the award.

High-cost College 2, which uses the Institutional Methodology to award its aid, is an extremely competitive college that doesn't award any merit aid to its students. Despite the $9,900 need-based grant, the total cost to the family will be $16,100 (the sum of $8,100 family contribution, $2,625 Stafford Loan, $1,500 Federal Work-Study, $1,500 Federal Perkins Loan, and $2,375 Federal PLUS), which is $6,000 more than College 1. Because this college isn't located in the student's state of residence, the student isn't eligible for the state grant.

College 3 isn't quite as competitive as College 2, despite the higher cost, and it awards students different grant amounts based on the academic strength of the applicant. They want very much for this student to attend. As a result, they offered a very generous University Scholarship of $13,600, in addition to the state grant for which the student is eligible. Despite the highest cost, the family's total cost comes to $11,300, only $1,200 more than at the low-cost state college. If our student's academic strength was weaker, however, the University Scholarship offered would be reduced significantly.

In terms of total indebtedness, the student would end her first year owing just $2,625 at College 1, $4,125 at College 2 (and her parents $2,375 in PLUS loan), and just $2,625 at College 3. None of the three colleges listed left any sizable unmet need. If a student has an unmet need after all aid is awarded, that amount can either be earned, borrowed, or met by additional Family Contribution.

Which college should our student attend? Well, if the decision is based strictly on money, there's no question that College 1 would be less costly to the family, although College 3 is just slightly higher because the student's academic record makes her extremely attractive to College 3.

The biggest question that the student should ask is: Does a few thousand dollars a year make a difference? If she really loved College 2, or if it had the ideal program for her or was located in the place she most wanted to be, would a few thousand dollars make a long-term difference? Probably not.

When you total up your costs and compare financial aid packages, these are the same sorts of questions that you should ask yourself. When you start analyzing your own financial aid offers, check out the tip list on the next page.

❖ ❖ ❖ ❖

So, those are the major steps in the financial aid process. Keep in mind that you'll have deadlines for each of these steps, so you'll want to make sure that you stay on top of the due dates and make sure you get the paperwork in on time. Don't wait until a day or two before forms are due to begin filling them out. You might need information about your family's finances that isn't readily available. Use the timetable on page 551 as a general guide in planning your financial aid application schedule.

Tips for Comparing Financial Aid Awards

1. Don't assume the package that offers the highest amount of grant aid is the most attractive financial aid award. Instead, add up the total self-help aid offered. You may discover that you'll graduate from a high-cost college with less debt than if you graduate from a low-cost school.

2. Compare the unmet need and expected Family Contribution from each college. A college offering more grant aid, while expecting a greater Family Contribution, could be less attractive financially. Students who need to borrow funds to meet a high expected Family Contribution could graduate with more debt.

3. Make sure the budget used to determine your package is realistic. If it's low and will need to be increased to meet your actual expenses, chances are you'll have to borrow or earn more to meet that additional need.

4. Include travel expenses into your budget. If a college is located some distance from your home, your travel costs could be high, and a budget revision may be necessary to incorporate this additional expense.

5. Find out whether each scholarship you expect to receive from an outside source will have an adverse affect on the rest of your financial package. Also find out whether you can renew it after the first year.

6. Compare the terms of the different loans within your financial aid package. Borrowing a smaller amount from a loan program with less attractive terms could end up costing more than borrowing a larger amount from a loan program with more attractive terms.

7. Consider consolidating your loans. Borrowing smaller amounts from multiple loan programs can end up costing you more. Although you can sometimes combine payments by consolidating loans, the terms for a consolidated loan may end up being less attractive.

8. Find out if financial aid awards for continuing students remain consistent with first-year packages. Some colleges award more grant aid to freshman and increase the loan or work portion in the upper-class years.

9. Keep in mind that the short-term cost of a college education is only one criterion for choosing a college. If a school meets your educational needs, and you're convinced it can launch you to an exciting career, a significant up-front investment may turn out to be a bargain over the long run.

From the *College Planning Quarterly*, February 1994

Financial Aid Timetable

Early Fall
In late September of your senior year in high school, visit your guidance office and find out whether the college(s) you're applying to want you to fill out the PROFILE. If at least one college does, complete the PROFILE Registration and list the colleges you're applying to (only those requiring the PROFILE). Send the completed form to CSS along with the correct fee.

Late Fall/Early Winter
If you submitted the PROFILE Registration, you'll receive your customized Financial Aid PROFILE (usually a few weeks later). Read it carefully to find out when you're supposed to send it in. Complete it and send it in as instructed.

If none of the colleges you're applying to require the PROFILE, or if any of the colleges you're applying to tell you to do so, complete and submit the FAFSA—**after January 1st of your senior year, but before any college deadlines.** List on the FAFSA all colleges you will be applying to, regardless of whether they use the PROFILE or not. If all of the colleges you're applying to use the PROFILE, do not fill out the FAFSA until at least one college tells you to do so.

When you receive an acknowledgment from either or both of your financial aid applications (either the PROFILE, the FAFSA, or both), review the materials and make sure the information is accurate. If it's not, you'll have to make the necessary corrections, and both forms will provide instructions on how to do so.

Late Winter/Early Spring
If requested, send copies of your and your parents' income tax returns to each college you've applied to (college(s) may ask you to submit these materials sooner; follow their instructions). You may also have to send other verifying documents. If a college requests something, send it as soon as possible. Always keep a copy of everything you send.

During this time, you'll receive an award letter from each college, generally along with or soon after you receive your letter of admission. Compare award letters to make sure they reflect accurate information and to know how much you and your family are going to be expected to pay.

Send in your nonrefundable deposit, guaranteeing admission.

If required to do so, complete any and all paperwork for your student loan, parent loan, tuition payment plan, etcetera.

Finally, pay the tuition and fees as required by the college.

What Your Financial Aid Office Doesn't Want You To Know

Your financial aid package is often negotiable, and it's becoming more likely that after negotiation a college will enhance their original offer.

Negotiating Your Financial Aid Award

Much to the chagrin of college financial aid administrators, many families have turned to negotiating with financial aid administrators to improve the aid package they've been awarded. After all the policy decision-making and sweating over how to best use the limited funds they have available, administrators now must deal with families who are armed with financial aid awards from competing colleges and who want their offer sweetened.

Not only are more and more families asking for better offers, but more and more colleges are giving better offers, particularly to students with strong academic credentials. Some colleges, in fact, actually invite families to show a competing college's offer so they can try to meet or beat it. Although colleges don't guarantee that they'll change anything, the implication is clear: Feel free to negotiate! The college admitted you. They believe that you can succeed. The last thing that they want is to lose you without having the opportunity to change your financial aid award.

If a college is willing to offer a more competitive aid package, they'll let you know if you simply ask. If they don't negotiate, they'll let you know, and you can make an informed admission decision. With negotiating financial aid awards, there's no harm in asking, but you should be prepared to accept a "no."

A Negotiating Scenario

To give you an idea of how you can negotiate a higher financial aid package, here's a possible negotiating conversation:

Parent: *My daughter is very interested in attending your college. In fact, it's probably her number-one choice. But we have a little problem that I hope you can help with.*

FAA: *I'd be delighted to try.*

Parent: *There are a couple of things, actually. First, I'm a bit concerned about the Family Contribution that was calculated. I don't know how I can possibly come up with that amount. As it is, our income can barely meet our expenses. Is there anything you can do to lower that expected contribution?*

FAA: *First, why don't you review the numbers you reported on your application. If there are any errors, let us know and we'll recalculate. Second, if there are any unusually high expenses that aren't reflected in these numbers—high medical bills, for example—let us know. We may have some flexibility there. Third, as you know, you can always take out a PLUS loan to meet your family share.*

Parent: *Thanks. I'll let you know. But there's something else that bothers us. As I said, your school is probably my daughter's first choice, but frankly the financial aid award isn't as attractive as some others she's received. She's going to have to borrow an awful lot to make it through. Is there anything you can do to help her out?*

FAA: *Well, you know, we spend a great deal of time working up packaging guidelines for students. I'll be happy to review hers to make sure we didn't make any errors. Also, if there are any special expenses that she'll have that are not usually considered in our budgets, let me know so we can consider whether the budget we used for her is appropriate.*

Parent: *That'll be nice. But there's nothing unusual. We're just concerned that the two other colleges that have accepted her have made her significantly better offers in terms of how much she'll have to borrow or work. If it were just a few dollars difference, I wouldn't say anything. But these are pretty big differences. Big enough that we may have to recommend that she go to one of those other schools. Are you sure you can't do something?*

FAA: *Tell you what. Why don't you send me a copy of the offer letters from those other schools. I'll look at them and see what I can do. No guarantees, you understand. But we'd very much like your daughter to come here, so I promise I'll give her every possible consideration.*

Parent: *Thanks. That's all I can ask.*

MEETING YOUR SHARE OF EXPENSES

After the financial aid application and awarding processes are over, most families face the daunting task of having to come up with significant sums of money at the beginning of each term. Families who have the resources to pay—but cannot pay all at once without using all their assets or without experiencing severe cash-flow problems—have several options to help them overcome their difficulties. These methods include tuition payment plans, federal loans that are not based on need and are not subsidized, home equity loans, lines of credit, and private loans from banks and other lenders.

Tuition Payment Plans

Today, many schools offer extended payment plans to help families meet their expected contribution. These plans let families pay the tuition, fees, dormitory room, and food contract over time, rather than at the beginning of each term. A typical tuition payment plan will begin the May or June preceding enrollment and extend to February or March with 10 or

12 monthly payments rather than one large one in September and another large one in January. Families pay no interest. The only cost is a nominal fee to administer the program and, with some plans, a charge for life insurance on the unpaid balance.

Home Equity Lines of Credit

If your parents need to borrow, either to meet the other costs of education—books and supplies, transportation, and so forth—or to meet the entire family share, borrowing against the equity in their home can be an excellent source of income. A line of credit in which you can borrow as much as you need, rather than in one large sum all at once, is generally more appropriate. These lines of credit have the double advantage of usually being tax deductible and being the least expensive loans (that is, with the lowest interest rate and best terms available) because the lender has collateral against the money. A disadvantage of any home equity loan or line of credit, of course, is the possibility that a family unable to make the payments could lose their home.

Federal PLUS Loans

The Federal PLUS Loan is a non-need-based loan for parents of undergraduate students. Parents may borrow up to the entire cost of education, as determined by the college, minus the total financial aid eligibility, whether or not the aid is accepted. As we discussed earlier, the interest rate, based on the T-bill rate, is adjusted annually. The maximum interest rate is 9 percent; through June 1997, the rate will be 8.72%. Borrowers begin paying back the loan within 60 days of receipt of the funds, and the repayment period is up to 10 years, depending on the amount borrowed.

Private Loans

A number of loan options that are not government-backed also exist to help parents and student's offset the cost of a college education. Privately-sponsored loan programs have been around since the mid-1980s, when it became apparent that financial aid was not keeping up with tuition increases and that middle-income families needed more help than what was available. Ironically, some of these private loans are the lowest-cost loans available. The financial aid office at your college can help you locate these other sources.

Many of these organizations allow credit-worthy students and parents to borrow up to the total cost of education, less any financial aid received. They also allow up to 30 years to repay, which makes monthly payments more affordable. Most lenders offer competitive interest rates, low fees, and generous repayment terms. As a result, these privately funded loans

Talk With A Professional

If your parents are considering securing home equity lines of credit, refinancing their home mortgage, repositioning their assets, and obtaining loans against their life insurance policies or stock and bond portfolios, they shouldn't tackle these sorts of financing strategies without the assistance of a professional personal financial advisor.

are a popular and affordable alternative for many families. For example, Kaplan can help you find ways to pay for college through Kaploan, the Kaplan Student Loan Information Program. Through an association with one of the largest providers of federal student loans, the KapLoan program can provide you with information about the various types of loan programs available and offers a number of free services to help you complete the student loan process.

It's up to you and your family to decide which lender to use. The terms of private loans vary from lender to lender, so you should compare terms by reading all the fine print closely.

Borrowers Beware!

Before you or your parents take out any type of loan, be sure to ask the following kinds of questions:

1. What are the exact provisions of the loan?

2. What is the interest rate?

3. Exactly how much has to be paid in interest?

4. What will the monthly payments be?

5. When will the monthly payments begin?

6. How long will the monthly payments last?

7. What happens if you miss one of the monthly payments?

8. Is there a grace period for paying back the loan?

Consolidation

When a borrower has multiple loans, either from one lender or several, the monthly payment of each separate loan can sometimes add up to more than the monthly payment if all the loans were combined. The Federal Consolidation Loan Program was established to make it easier for students who have multiple loans or who have borrowed from more than one lender to pay back their loans. Under the terms of this program, Federal Stafford, Federal Direct, and Federal Perkins loans can be combined with one lender, one interest rate, and one monthly payment. You'll learn more about this possibility when you take out your first loan.

Money Management and Budgeting

Debt management has become an extremely hot topic in higher education. As you and your parents decide what is an appropriate amount to borrow to pay for college expenses, you should reevaluate your own estimate of your total costs, how much you and your family can contribute toward the college expenses, and the total financial aid package offered. The idea here is to limit the amount you and your parents have to borrow, to the extent practical. That may mean tightening your belts a little, working a few more hours than planned, or saving as much as possible from summer jobs. It may also mean evaluating how much is appropriate to borrow for your education.

Parent Borrowing: How Much Can They Afford?

When your parents are deciding how much they can afford to borrow to pay for your education, they should use the same criteria that lenders use when considering an applicant's ability to repay a loan. The total monthly payments for housing (mortgage and home equity loans) should be no more than about 28 percent of their gross monthly income. And the total payments for all other loans—including education loans, credit card payments, and all other installment loans (car, furniture, and so forth)—should not exceed 8 percent of their gross monthly income. So, adding these numbers, your total monthly payments for all loans should not be more than 36 percent of your gross monthly income.

Student Borrowing

For most students, it's generally smart to keep borrowing to a minimum, especially early in their education, because it's likely their total indebtedness will increase as they progress through their academic program. If you're planning to attend graduate or professional school, this may be especially important because there's little grant aid available for graduate students and most graduate students have to borrow significant amounts to complete their education.

Paying Back Your Student Loans

For the last several years, there's been a great deal of media attention centered on student loan defaulters, specifically, stories about how deadbeats don't pay back their student loans. It's especially attention grabbing when the defaulter is a doctor or lawyer. Loan defaults are certainly a problem that costs taxpayers millions of dollars each year. But the truth is, most borrowers—about 85 percent—do pay back their loans, and the majority of student loan defaulters are people who are in financial difficulty and unable to pay.

Pay Back

Failure to repay a student loan can ruin your credit rating and make your finances much more difficult in the future. This is a good reason to consider a college's graduation and job placement rates when you choose a school.

When a loan is not repaid, lenders have a number of steps they can take to get back their money, including law suits, garnishing wages, and even holding funds from income tax refunds. If a lender has to resort to these options to get their money back from you, it will seriously hurt your credit rating. That means you'll be unable to borrow money for any other purpose, such as buying a car, getting a credit card, or qualifying for a home loan. Morality aside, it's clearly not a good financial idea for borrowers to default on their loans. If you experience financial difficulty, don't just stop making the payment. The best step will be to stay in contact with the lender. Very often you can work out a way to make some payments and keep your credit record clean. Of course, the best thing you can do is try to limit the amount of money you borrow in the first place.

Parting Words

Choosing and paying for college has certainly become complex. Even the process of applying for financial aid, once fairly straightforward, has become rather tedious and full of inconsistencies. Students who apply to a number of comparably priced colleges often receive a vastly different financial aid award from each. As a result, college costs and financial aid are quickly becoming two of the most important factors students and families consider when choosing colleges. When students apply to a number of colleges, they generally include one "safety" school, that is, one they are pretty sure will accept them. Now, many students regularly include a financial safety school, one they know that they can afford.

It's easy to see why college costs and financial aid awards can affect a student's college choice. But students and families should keep in mind that any one particular college is not appropriate for everyone and that the bottom line cost is only one of the criteria. Rather, it's essential to focus on what has influenced your choice of college up to this point in the decision, namely, the quality of the education, curriculum, student-faculty ratio, location, size, proximity to home, extracurricular activities, and social and cultural opportunities.

While the cost is a real concern for most families, an investment in higher education is an investment for a lifetime. A wise choice will return far more than just the dollar value of the initial investment. A college education will be the foundation for a lifetime of learning, personal growth, and friendships well beyond graduation. Make sure you're making a sound investment.

A Lifetime Investment

You don't have to settle. Yes, a college's cost is probably going to be a factor in your decision. But it doesn't have to be the deciding factor.

"Honey, are you all right in there? Should I call 911?"

ACCESSIBLE ACADEMICS

Especially for Persons with Disabilities

YES YOU CAN!

During the height of the "Great Depression," a bright, ambitious young man named Bob sought to attend college. Bob wanted to go to an urban, hometown school with a reputation as one of the best universities in the country. He was an excellent candidate for admission. His performance in high school had been stellar; in fact, his application was so impressive that the university offered him, sight unseen, a full academic scholarship for his four years at the school. All the necessary pieces were in place for Bob to embark on an outstanding academic career.

There was only one problem—Bob was a student with a disability. He had muscular dystrophy, and he had to use a wheelchair. When he showed up on campus for the first time, an embarrassed and dismayed admissions officer explained that the university had not realized Bob used a wheelchair when they admitted him and awarded him a scholarship. The admissions officer maintained that under the circumstances, the university would have to rescind its scholarship offer because, given the limited resources of the university, "It would be unfair to waste a scholarship on someone confined to a wheelchair." The loss of his scholarship wasn't Bob's only problem. As he explored the campus for the first time, he realized that most of the buildings in which his classes were to be held were not wheelchair accessible.

Undaunted, Bob looked for ways to keep his dreams of college, a career, and independence alive. He managed to find a night job that would pay for his education, and enlisted the help of local firefighters, who acted as his personal assistants and carried him up flights of steps so he could attend classes in inaccessible buildings. As a result of his resourcefulness and perseverance, Bob was able to graduate with honors, go on to graduate from law school, and ultimately wind up serving as vice president of a major airline.

The First

In 1950, the University of Illinois established a program to assist disabled World War II veterans, most of whom used wheelchairs, to return to college. This program, the first of its kind, was successful in removing architectural barriers on campus and creating a rich college life for students with disabilities, including wheelchair sports teams and a fraternity for wheelchair users.

The Road to College

For every person like Bob who was able to call upon his or her inner and community resources to successfully attend college, there were literally thousands of people with disabilities who were denied the opportunity because of barriers and institutionalized discrimination. Fortunately, times are changing. Because of the efforts of trailblazing advocates like Bob and civil rights legislation like Section #504 of the 1973 Rehabilitation Act and the Americans with Disabilities Act, people with disabilities are attending colleges and universities in unprecedented numbers. Today's group of college students with disabilities is more independent and knowledgeable about their rights than any previous generation. This section is designed to help educate students with disabilities about their rights and opportunities as they choose a college and university, and in doing so, assist them in joining the new generation of empowered college students with disabilities.

Voices of Independence

Success through college can be measured in very tangible ways; grade-point averages, degrees and honors awarded, admission to graduate schools, and highly paying jobs upon graduation are all concrete indicators of growth and success in college. However, college students with disabilities achieve a less tangible success that cannot be measured by such objective criteria and yet has as significant an impact on the lives of students with disabilities as any academic honor or achievement. For many students with disabilities, college represents liberation: liberation from the notion that they are somehow intrinsically "bound" by limitations of a disability, and liberation from society's preconceived notions of what the lives of people with disabilities must be like.

Living and learning in an environment that is often far more accessible and accepting of differences than most settings they will encounter in the "real world," students with disabilities are often able to attend college and meet other people like themselves. They arrive at a new, empowered, proud understanding of what it means to be a person with a disability. This new understanding prepares students with disabilities for a lifetime of success and adds momentum to a growing movement of people with disabilities who are remaking everyday life in their own image.

For many students with disabilities, the college experience offers the opportunity to transcend traditional notions of limitations and capabilities. Here's the experience of Norman S., a wheelchair-using college senior majoring in accounting and information systems:

A Rich Culture

For students with and without disabilities, college is often their first introduction to the richness of disability culture, an alternative, proud, empowering way of experiencing disability flourishing on college campuses across the nation.

> When I entered college, I felt very unsure about myself... very insecure about my ability to succeed. After only a few years in school, I achieved success in the classroom and made a lot of friends on campus—friends who accept and like me for who I am. I think the experience has changed my whole outlook. I feel a lot more confident about my abilities, a lot more confident that people will like me for who I am. It's also made me more independent. Because I was forced to use city buses to travel to school, I now travel all over without feeling afraid. If something goes wrong, I know in my heart that I'm resourceful enough to work it out.

College often represents one of the first opportunities for students with disabilities to advocate for themselves. This introduction to self-advocacy is described by Lisa N., a junior with a learning disability majoring in education:

> When I was in high school, everything I needed was taken care of for me by my parents or my teachers. Special test arrangements were made for me; applications were filled out for me. Suddenly, you're in college and expected to do things for yourself. At first, I wasn't ready to accept the responsibility and I just shut down. I cried a lot and had a really hard time. At a certain point, I just decided that enough was enough and decided to take things into my own hands. I got help in learning how to ask for things on my own through the Disabled Students Services Office. Now I know my rights and always ask for the accommodations I need. I still feel a little queasy asking a professor for the help I need. But after I ask and get the help, I feel so much better about myself!

Aside from building better advocates, the college experience helps to build well-rounded individuals. This personal growth through college is articulated by Alexandra S., a wheelchair user who is a sociology major:

> On one of my first days on campus, a friend from high school invited me to come to the Disabled Student Union. This group planned events with a lot of other student clubs on campus. Within a few months, I was the most "involved" person on campus. I was on every campus committee. I ran for student government. Before this whole experience, I was scared to death of speaking in public. Now I can sit in front of a room full of strangers and talk about a campus event without even thinking about it. I've met a lot of friends here that I know I'll have for the rest of my life.

For students with and without disabilities alike, college represents a journey of self-discovery and self-acceptance. For some, like Thomas S., a 24-year-old anthropology major, this is more important than the courses themselves:

> When I was first learned I was HIV-positive, my whole world turned upside-down. At that point, in the larger scheme of things, school seemed relatively unimportant to me. The campus seemed like a very cold, empty place; I felt very alone there. I was going to quit when I met a guy from the Gay and Lesbian Union who encouraged me to stay and get involved. I hooked up with a community support group—people who were really living with HIV and AIDS and they helped me to feel less alone, less afraid. I'm still not so into my studies, but I am really into college. I'm involved in politics on campus and in the community. I'm really committed to educating people . . . and that's what college is supposed to be about.

Above all, college gives students with disabilities a prevailing sense of empowerment. Darryl K., a student who is blind, sums it up well:

> One night I went to a restaurant off campus with some friends and the management gave me a hard time about eating there with my guide dog. My friends told me to let the whole thing go, but it made me really angry. The next day, I told some friends who were disabled about what happened and they all got angry. So the next night, we made reservations and four of us had dinner there—all of us with guide dogs! I was a little nervous at first, but that whole experience was such a rush! I think it created a stronger bond between me and my friends. I feel that same bond with all people with disabilities. After experiences like the night in the restaurant, I feel like I can change the world . . . well, at least my little part of it. That's why I'm going into law. I want to make a difference in the lives of others . . . to help people make a change.

STUDENTS WITH DISABILITIES IN HIGHER EDUCATION

Who are students with disabilities? They comprise one of the fastest growing populations among U.S. college students, as the percentage of freshmen reporting having a disability has tripled since the late 1970s. With this growth has come a change in the composition of the population of students with disabilities, as in the nineties, for the first time, college students are more likely to have hidden disabilities—like HIV or AIDS, psychiatric disabilities, or learning disabilities—than apparent ones. Today's college students with disabilities are part of a generation of people who are transforming the way we think about disability on and off campus.

According to the Americans with Disabilities Act, you are an individual

Oh, Canada

Colleges and universities in Canada also take steps to provide students with disabilities equal access to their facilities, programs, and curriculum. However, while higher education in the United States is characterized by both public and private colleges, Canadian colleges are all public schools. Thus, in contrast to the United States, where the quality and scope of services provided to students with disabilities varies greatly from school to school, Canadian colleges and universities offer services to students with disabilities that are fairly uniform, according to one Canadian school's director of services for students with disabilities.

with a disability if, for example, you have a physical or mental impairment that substantially limits one or more of your major life activities, like performing personal care activities, walking, seeing, learning, working, etcetera.

Applying a similar definition, about 9 percent of each freshman class typically describes themselves as having a disability. These students represent a socially, culturally, and ethnically diverse group. While students with disabilities as a group generally mirror the characteristics of the larger population of college students, there are some notable statistics:

- College students with disabilities are slightly more likely to be male (52 percent) than female (46 percent).

- Male students with disabilities are more likely than female students to be Caucasian.

- Students with disabilities were slightly more likely to come from low-income families than were students without disabilities.

TYPES OF DISABILITY AMONG FULL-TIME COLLEGE FRESHMEN WITH DISABILITIES— 1994*

Disability	Percentage
Learning	32.2
Partially Sighted or Blind	21.9
Health Related	16.4
Orthopedic	10.2
Hearing	9.7
Speech	3.3
Other	18.8

*Cathy Henderson, College Freshmen with Disabilities: A Triennial Statistical Profile (Washington, D.C.: HEATH Resource Center, American Council of Education, 1995).

A Growing Force

The percentage of college freshmen reporting a disability has tripled since the 1970s.

While students who comprise this population are individuals with a range of different disabilities, almost one-third were students with learning disabilities—the fastest growing group among students with disabil-

THE ROAD TO COLLEGE

Not Just Slow Learners

The fastest growing group among college students with disabilities is the population of students with learning disabilities. Once stigmatized as slow learners or underachievers, these students are now recognized as having disabilities that significantly affect their ability to learn. Specific learning disabilities exist in individuals with average to superior intelligence, adequate sensory and motor systems, and in adequate learning opportunities. Learning disabilities vary in the ways they manifest themselves and in their degree of severity, include difficulty with tasks in which reading is an essential component (dyslexia), difficulty with the physical act of writing (dysgraphia), difficulty with calculations or the rapid processing of math facts (dyscalcula), and difficulty concentrating and being prone to easy distraction (attention deficits). With the proper documentation of these learning disabilities, students are entitled to reasonable accommodations in the college setting.

ities. These students are more independent, more conscious of their rights, and more proud of their identities than any other generation of students with disabilities.

Disability Basics*

Before we explore in depth the issues of selecting a college for students with disabilities, here are some key terms you should know:

Americans with Disabilities Act (ADA) of 1990. The ADA is a civil rights law that prohibits discrimination against people with disabilities in most aspects of American life, including employment and access to facilities, goods, and services offered in most places providing services to the public, including colleges and universities. It provides that any otherwise qualified student with a disability should have equal access to all programs, facilities, services, and curricula offered by colleges and universities.

Reasonable Accommodations. The ADA provides that the necessary "reasonable accommodations" should be afforded to students with disabilities so that they may have equal access to college and university programs and facilities. "Reasonable accommodations" are modifications in programs, policies, facilities, and services that provide such equal access. Depending on the student's individual situation, examples of reasonable accommodations in higher education may include moving classes to buildings accessible to a wheelchair user, providing course materials in large print or Braille for students who are blind or visually impaired, administering exams in a modified format (extended time, quiet, proctored setting, etcetera) for students with learning disabilities, hiring sign language interpreters for students who are deaf. Colleges and universities are not required to provide such accommodations when the provision of these accommodations poses an "undue burden" to the institution or poses a "direct threat" to the health and safety of others.

Undue Burden. A college or university can, for example, deny the request of a student with a disability for a reasonable accommodation when provision of this accommodation represents an undue financial or administrative burden or undermines the essential integrity of a particular activity. In determining what may be an "undue burden," a college or university should consider the resources of the institution as well as the resources of the particular program or department.

---

*The information contained in this chapter is intended only as a brief summary of some of the major points relating to the ADA. What an institution may provide as a "reasonable accommodation" under the ADA may vary widely depending on the specific institution and/or facility as well as on the specific needs of the student involved. Students should contact school officials and/or an attorney for information regarding their particular situation. Nothing contained herein is intended (nor should it be relied upon) as legal advice.

Qualified Individual. Under the ADA, a "qualified individual" with a disability is one who is able to meet the performance standards or requirements of a particular program with or without reasonable accommodations. While colleges and universities should provide the accommodations necessary to allow students with disabilities to meet program requirement, the ADA does not require that they alter essential program requirements for students with disabilities.

Rehabilitation Act. Signed into law in 1973, the Rehabilitation Act represents the first piece of comprehensive civil rights legislation ever enacted for people with disabilities. Section #504, the antidiscrimination portion of this act, states that "no otherwise qualified handicapped individual shall, solely by reason of his handicap, be excluded from participation in, be denied the benefits of, or be subjected to discrimination under any program or activity receiving federal financial assistance." Title I of this act authorizes the existence and regulates the operation of State Vocational Rehabilitation agencies which often providing funding and support to college students with disabilities.

IEP. The Individuals with Disabilities Education Act (IDEA) provides that elementary and secondary students with disabilities, their parents, teachers, and school professionals should work together to develop an individualized education plan (IEP) that specifies action steps and goals to ensure equal access and opportunity to education for these students. IEP's can serve as a valuable resource to prospective college students as they seek to define their accommodation needs.

How the ADA Can Help

Because of their protection under Titles II and III of the Americans with Disabilities Act of 1990 and Section #504 of the 1973 Rehabilitation Act, otherwise qualified college students with disabilities should expect the following:

1. Equal access and opportunity to programs, facilities, and curriculum offered by a college or university

2. Reasonable accommodations to facilitate equal access and opportunity to participate fully in all aspects of college life

3. Auxiliary aids and services to facilitate equal access and opportunity to programs, facilities, and curricula, including (depending on the accommodation needs related to particular disabili

ties) qualified readers, note-takers, and sign language interpreters

4. Reasonable academic adjustments, which may include such items as testing in a modified, accommodative setting, and course materials and exams available in alternative, accessible formats

5. The right to file a legal complaint at any point during the complaint process

Do Your Homework

The key to making the right decisions when choosing a college or university is making sure that you're prepared. This preparation means you've taken all the steps necessary to gain access to the key resources you need to make important decisions about college. It also means acquiring the information necessary to ask the right questions and make informed choices.

While "doing your homework" is important for anyone choosing a college, it's particularly critical for students with disabilities—they have a unique set of logistics to work out related to their disabilities. For many students with disabilities, getting ready for college means far more than just deciding, "I want to go." College readiness involves making sure that you have access to essential resources in and out of school that will make the application process and college experience accessible to you as a person with a disability. Answers to the following questions will help assess your readiness for college.

Beyond Basket Weaving: Are You Academically Prepared?

Many high school students with disabilities, particularly those enrolled in special education units, find that they're not prepared for college because they were not encouraged to take core college preparatory courses. You may have significant gaps to fill before you explore majors and fulfill college degree requirements if you haven't taken more advanced math and writing courses in high school. High school students with disabilities must meet with high school college advisors to guarantee that the courses they're taking will properly prepare them for college.

The Paperchase: Is Your Documentation in Order?

If you have a disability, you'll want to be eligible for reasonable academ-

The Cradle

During the 1960s, a handful of students with severe disabilities led by Ed Roberts began a movement to gain equal access to all aspects of college life at the University of California at Berkeley. Through their advocacy efforts, they secured a federal grant to start the Physically Disabled Students Program, a program run by and for people with disabilities. Through this program, people with disabilities helped each other to obtain the support services necessary to live independently on and off campus. The ideas of self-direction and independence that drove this movement formed the ideological foundations of the Independent Living Movement, an international movement of individuals with disabilities and community-based advocacy organizations.

ic adjustments. Most colleges require some kind of formal documentation of your disability so they can define the set of accommodations that will maximize your educational opportunities. Before applying to college, it's generally a good idea to meet with a certified professional (doctors, psychologists, learning disability specialists, audiologists, etcetera) in order to determine how your disability might affect you in the college setting. Besides getting the documentation that you'll need for reasonable accommodations and support services, it's also a good idea to work with professionals to develop a profile of your accommodation needs. Students registered in special education programs can use their IEPs (individualized educational plans) to help develop this "accommodation profile."

SAT + ACT − ADA = Trouble: Are You Taking Exams Under Modified Conditions?

Many students with disabilities are not aware that under the Americans with Disabilities Act, they may be entitled to take standardized tests, like the SAT and ACT exams, in modified, accessible formats and settings. While many students with disabilities are able to take these tests under standard conditions, others, because of the nature of their disabilities, would benefit from taking the exam in an accommodative setting. Students who require reasonable accommodations for the SAT or ACT (extended time, a reader or writer, exam in an accessible format, etcetera) must request these accommodations from either the Educational Testing Services (ETS) or American College Testing (ACT) by their required deadlines. If you think you require accommodations, contact ETS or ACT a few months before the scheduled exam dates so that the necessary arrangements can be made for you.

Get Down with APC: Are You Taking Advanced Placement Courses?

Advanced placement courses can be your best friends. Aside from strengthening any application to college, receiving Advanced Placement credit for college can give you the flexibility to take slightly reduced course loads in your freshman year. Reducing your course load can ease some of the pressure during a year that will be filled with changes and adjustments.

The Bottom Line: How Will You Pay Your Way?

Most students with disabilities are at a distinct disadvantage as they try to fund their college education. Many students without disabilities are

Higher Ed... Higher Tech

The growth in assistive technology during the past decade has helped to usher in a new era of access for people with disabilities on college campuses. Students with disabilities should play an active role in developing a profile of their assistive technology needs jointly with experienced disability professionals (assistive technology specialists, physical and occupational therapists, mobility trainers, learning disability specialists, vocational rehabilitation counselors, special educators, college coordinators of services for students with disabilities, etcetera). It's also helpful to get input from other people with disabilities with similar needs.

The Road to College

able to save money for college by working at part-time jobs, either while going to school or during the summer, or by having a college fund set up for them by their families. Often though, students with disabilities don't have these options because setting up savings accounts often renders them ineligible for key disability benefits, such as SSI and Medicaid, which provide many students with foundations for independent living.

Working while attending school is difficult for any college student, but it's particularly hard for college students with disabilities. College students typically find part-time work in the service industry. These jobs are often labor intensive and involve a significant manual labor component that would be difficult to perform for many individuals with physical disabilities. In addition, most students with disabilities are never able to construct a completely accessible living and learning environment, so it often takes them longer to perform independent living and school-related tasks than the average college student. It's tough to work while you're in college because a job will cut into the time you'll need for daily living tasks and your studies.

While students with disabilities are confronted with barriers that limit their funding options for higher education, there are a host of college funding opportunities available. A little planning, creativity, and self-advocacy can go a long way in paying for a college education. Here are four funding options you and your family should explore.

Financial Aid. Students with disabilities should check out the funding options available to other college students. Because students with disabilities tend to be overrepresented among people from low-income families, many students with disabilities will be eligible for PELL and Federal Supplemental Educational Opportunity awards. Students with disabilities should also consider applying for Federal Work-Study Programs, as well as Perkins, Stafford, and Federal Direct Loan Programs.

Scholarships. A host of competitive scholarships are also available to students with disabilities, including scholarship and grant programs that target individuals with specific disabilities. For example, the President's Committee on Employment of People with Disabilities, in conjunction with the Nordstrom Corporation, annually awards competitive college scholarships to students with disabilities. Similarly, the National Federation for the Blind offers scholarships to outstanding students who are blind or have visual impairments. Some colleges and universities— Arizona State University, Hofstra University, University of Illinois at

---

Train and Maintain

When assessing your assistive technology needs, factor in the availability of training and technical assistance necessary to properly and fully address these needs. This technical assistance may be available through the vendors through which the technologies are purchased, Offices of Services for Students with Disabilities, academic computing centers, campus telecommunications centers, consultants hired through state vocational rehabilitation agencies, regional technical assistance projects established by the Tech Act, and peers with disabilities who have utilized the technologies.

Champaign-Urbana, just to name a few—offer college- and university-based scholarships for students with disabilities. Contact the admissions office of schools you are considering to learn if they offer any such scholarships.

Vocational Rehabilitation. State vocational rehabilitation programs for individuals with disabilities are valuable sources of college funding. Title I of the Rehabilitation Act mandates that each state offer vocational rehabilitation (VR) services to individuals with disabilities to assist them in living productive, independent, self-directed lives; to convert them from tax consumers to taxpayers. Thousands of individuals with disabilities have been able to utilize state VR programs to acquire funding for higher education.

Your ability to get a state VR system to subsidize the cost of your college education and related aids and services will largely depend upon your skills as an assertive self-advocate. The Rehabilitation Act requires that an individual with a disability must jointly develop an Individualized Written Rehabilitation Plan (IWRP) with his or her VR counselor. This plan specifies the vocational goal, the training and/or education needed to achieve this goal, and what can be expected of both the individual and the VR agency in achieving this goal. If students seeks the VR agency to sponsor their college educations, they should develop a vocational goal that can be attained only through higher education. For example, if you seek sponsorship for a bachelor's degree in computer science, it is not sufficient to specify your vocational goal as a "career in computer programming." A VR agency may argue that this same goal can be attained through training at a technical institute and refuse to sponsor your education at a four-year college. If the IWRP is developed in a way that necessitates a college degree, students with disabilities may be able to get the VR agency to contribute towards the cost of tuition, books, transportation, assistive technology, auxiliary aids and services, personal assistance services, and other expenses.

PASS. Many students with disabilities have been able to gain valuable work experience, maintain their disability benefits, and earn money for college by developing a PASS Plan. As a work incentive for recipients of SSDI and SSI, the Social Security Act created the opportunity for recipients to develop Plans to Achieve Self-Support (PASS). These plans allow individuals with disabilities to establish savings accounts to finance things that would ultimately allow them to move off benefits and become self-sufficient. They can then work and deposit all their work-related income into their PASS account. The accumulated funds in a PASS

Chart Your Course
To maximize your chances of getting adequate VR funds, make sure your IWRP states goals that can be attained only through higher education.

account would not affect eligibility for benefits (i.e., Medicaid, Medicare, SSI, SSDI). People with disabilities have used PASS accounts to fund the purchase of assistive technologies, adaptive transportation (modified van, etcetera), start-up fees for small businesses, as well as college educations.

To Tell or Not to Tell

Filling out admissions applications can be a tedious, nerve-racking experience for all students. For students with disabilities, the application process is complicated by a big choice: whether or not to disclose a disability. Will disclosing your disability improve or harm your chances of acceptance? The following represent key features of most application processes. Consider them as opportunities for disclosure and chances to convey a richer sense of what you have to offer as an applicant.

High School Transcripts. For students with disabilities concerned about disclosure, high school transcripts may be more than a mere summary of academic history. They offer clues ("Special Education" indicated in course descriptions and course codes) to admissions officers that a student has a disability. If you're concerned with confidentiality, meet with your college counselor to see if anything can be done to purge your transcript of any references to disability.

Taking the SAT and ACT. If you take college admissions tests under nonstandard conditions, your grade report will indicate those special conditions. Because most requests for exam administration under these conditions are disability related, advocates for people with disabilities have argued that the label "nonstandard" on an exam report can be interpreted by admissions officers as a code for "disability." This is something to keep in mind when requesting testing accommodations through a testing service.

Letters of Recommendation. Letters of recommendation give admissions officers a more complete sense of who an applicant is. Strong recommendations from faculty help to demonstrate to admissions officers that a given applicant will fare well at their institution. They can be a real help to students with disabilities if their high school grades were hurt by barriers encountered in the classroom. If you are concerned about the disclosure of your disability, you should speak with your recommenders to ensure that they disclose only personal information that you're comfortable with.

Interviews and Personal Statements. Interviews and personal statements let admissions officers evaluate applicants more holistically. If you're comfortable disclosing your disability, interviews and personal statements give a rich sense of what you could offer to a college, and may give you the chance to fully explain poorer academic performances brought on by the failure to be reasonably accommodated.

Narrowing Your Choice of Schools

Students with disabilities should make a list of key factors to consider when narrowing their choice of schools. Besides the factors covered in this book that pertain to all students, here are some issues of particular relevance to students with disabilities.

Big Pond or Little Pond?

Your choice of the size of school you'd like to attend will be affected by several factors, including individual personality and economics. However, there are some distinct advantages and disadvantages to big and small schools as they relate to the experience of students with disabilities. Smaller schools offer the advantage of smaller class sizes and more individualized instruction—settings in which it is often much easier to provide for the highly individualized accommodation needs of students with disabilities. However, smaller schools are less conducive to student anonymity, so it's often more difficult to preserve your confidentiality as a student with a disability. Bigger schools usually offer greater diversity and the opportunity for you to blend into the fabric of campus life. They often offer greater opportunity for students with disabilities to meet other students like themselves. While bigger schools usually have greater resources to provide reasonable accommodations, larger campuses can also be more impersonal and bureaucratic, have larger class sizes, and offer less individualized attention than smaller schools.

Sunbelt or Snowbelt?

Many students with disabilities are attracted by the prestige and tradition of some schools in the northeast and midwest. Once they move on campus, they also find that states in these regions may offer a comparatively higher rate of disability benefits than many southern and western states. But be cautious—"snowbelt" schools are also characterized by traits that hurt their accessibility to students with disabilities.

Many older schools in the northeast and midwest feature campus buildings constructed during a time when access for people with disabilities was an afterthought—if thought of at all. These schools are frequently situated in cold and snowy climates and on hilly terrain that tend to undermine access for individuals with physical disabilities. Colleges and

A Historic University

In 1864, Congress created the Columbia Institute for the Deaf and Blind in Washington, D.C., which was later renamed Gallaudet University. Originally conceived of as a school to train teachers for people who are deaf, Gallaudet was the first school of higher learning for the deaf. Gallaudet now educates hundreds of deaf college students each year and has emerged as a cultural center for the deaf community where American Sign Language, the official language of the American deaf community, flourishes.

universities in the south and west are located in states that usually offer lower rates of disability benefits and are less likely than schools in the northeast and midwest to be situated in cities with accessible mass transportation. But consider the pluses: Schools in the south and west are more likely to have newer, more accessible facilities, and are situated in places that are warm, flat, and dry, which facilitates access for people with physical disabilities.

Public or Private?

Both public and private schools have characteristics that enhance and limit access for students with disabilities. Public schools are typically cheaper to attend than private schools, so funding agencies (vocational rehabilitation agencies, the Veterans Administration, etcetera) are more apt to pick up the tab for tuition at these schools than at private schools. Because all public schools have had to comply with federal laws guaranteeing access and opportunity for students with disabilities since 1973, they may have more highly developed mechanisms for accommodating students with disabilities than private schools.

Public colleges are often part of larger college and university systems, and the resources of the entire system must be taken into consideration when assessing the appropriateness of the cost of a request for a reasonable accommodation at any one of the member colleges. Public colleges often have a higher threshold for establishing "undue financial burden" of these accommodations than do private schools. However, public schools often lack the resources and prestige enjoyed by many private schools. In fact, the superior resources of some private colleges have enabled these schools to develop some of the best programs and facilities accessible to students with disabilities in the country.

Residential or Commuter Schools?

If you have a disability, there are different advantages to going away to school or staying home and commuting to college. Going away to school and living in a dormitory setting offers the chance for independence and autonomy in a generally supportive environment. By living away from home in a college dorm, you'll have the opportunity to develop key independent living and self-advocacy skills that will serve you well for the rest of your lives. Dorming at school offers many long-term benefits, but the transition from home life to dorm life can be especially disruptive for students with disabilities. If you dorm, you'll have to work out the logistics of personal care and accessible housing along with managing the lifestyle changes experienced by all new college students. Coping every day with these life-altering changes can initially be very stressful. On the

The Junior College Alternative

Junior colleges offer a handful of distinct advantages for students with disabilities, including:

- lower cost
- greater likelihood of State Vocational Rehabilitation subsidy
- strong vocational emphasis
- easier academic and social transition

other hand, commuter schools offer the advantage of allowing you to draw upon an extensive support network you may already have in place, in a familiar setting, to successfully meet the changes and challenges of college life. However, choosing a commuter school in a familiar environment can sometimes foster dependence and stifle personal growth. And it's sometimes a formidable challenge to students with disabilities to negotiate largely inaccessible transportation options to commute between home and school.

Two- or Four-Year Colleges?

When prospective students think about attending college, they often think in terms of enrolling in a four-year college. However, it might be unnecessary to spend at least four years at a senior college when a junior college can meet your needs. Thousands of students with disabilities choose to continue their education by attending junior colleges. In fact, a higher percentage of students with disabilities attend junior colleges than senior colleges.

Senior colleges are typically more prestigious than junior colleges, and offer students more broadly based education. However, junior colleges also offer some distinct advantages over senior colleges for students with disabilities. They are usually cheaper and near communities in which people with disabilities live. Also, because they tend to be more vocationally oriented than senior colleges, it is often easier for students with disabilities to get State Vocational Rehabilitation systems to subsidize their education at junior colleges. For students with disabilities who do not feel as though they were adequately prepared for the rigors of a senior college, junior colleges offer the opportunity to shore up academic weaknesses and to ease the academic and social transition from high school to college. For students who see college as a vehicle for getting a job, junior colleges often offer a strong vocational emphasis and train students in ways that make them qualified for competitive employment opportunities, many of which are available in their own communities.

ASSESSING ACCESSIBILITY

Once you've narrowed the field and have a short list of colleges you're really interested in, you'll have to make some real choices. But before doing that, there's more work to be done. Here are the main factors to consider in judging how accessible the colleges on your short list will really be.

Get The Lowdown

Try to talk with students with and without disabilities at the schools you're considering. They can give you a great sense of how accessible a college is, as well as how welcoming it is to students with disabilities.

Ramps, Raised Dots, and TTYs: Physical Access

You have a disability, and you're on your way to attending a four-year college or university. The architectural and technological accessibility of a campus will be a major factor in your decision to attend a specific school. The following questions will help you evaluate the physical accessibility of a school.

1. What is the campus terrain like? Is it hilly or flat?

2. What is the campus infrastructure like? Are the walkways and roads well paved, or are they littered with cracks and potholes?

3. Do all the sidewalks have curb cuts?

4. Are all campus buildings accessible to students with mobility-related disabilities? If not, what is the college policy regarding moving classes and other activities to accessible sites to accommodate students with disabilities?

5. Are the public bathrooms wheelchair accessible?

6. Are nonacademic facilities (dorms, dining facilities, athletic and recreational centers, theaters, etcetera) accessible to students with disabilities?

7. Are there sufficient signs to indicate the location of accessible facilities, and is this signage available in accessible formats (i.e., Braille)?

8. Are the assistive technologies that you will need available?

9. Are the academic computing facilities accessible to people with disabilities?

10. If you are driving to school, is parking available to students with disabilities?

11. Are campus shuttle buses accessible to people with disabilities?

Get with the Program: Programmatic Access

For all students with disabilities, but particularly for students with learning disabilities, the program accessibility of colleges and universities will significantly impact their choice of schools. When assessing the programmatic access of colleges, keep the following questions in mind:

1. Does the faculty make course syllabi available to students in advance? The early availability of syllabi is critical to obtaining course reading materials in accessible formats.

2. How supportive is the institution of the modification of curriculum, the modification of core requirements, and the administration of exams in alternative formats to accommodate students with disabilities?

3. What is the college policy on providing reader, note taker, and interpreter services?

4. How supportive is the college of a student's right to tape classes as a reasonable accommodation for a disability?

5. Are course materials available in accessible formats?

6. What are the college policies on incompletes, leaves of absence, and independent study?

Office of Services for Students with Disabilities

Effective services and accommodations for students with disabilities on campus is usually an indicator of a high quality Office of Services for Students with Disabilities. Answers to the following questions serve as good indicators of the quality of services provided through such offices on college campuses:

1. Is there an actual office that coordinates the provision of reasonable accommodations and support services to students with disabilities, or does this responsibility fall to a person or office that has additional responsibilities?

2. Does the office offer liaison services to faculty, staff, and administration?

3. Does the office assist students with identification to faculty?

4. What types of counseling services does the office provide?
   - Academic advisement
   - Personal counseling

Go the Distance

Several institutions offer distance learning programs through which students with disabilities are able to earn degrees from home. Two of the more innovative programs are the Homebound Programs at Queensborough Community College and Queens College of the City University of New York. Designed for students with more significant levels of physical disabilities, these Homebound Programs allow people whose disabilities preclude class attendance to participate via telecommunications technologies. Classes are held in classrooms equipped with two-way speakerphones, and course materials are shuttled between students' homes and campus via mail, fax, electronic mail, and visits from support staff, who also administer exams to students in their homes. Through these programs, dozens of students with disabilities in the New York metropolitan area have been able to earn associate and bachelor degrees.

- Peer counseling
- Vocational counseling
- Diagnostic assessment for students with learning disabilities
- Compensatory and remedial skill development for students with learning disabilities
- Benefits counseling
- Independent living counseling

5. Does the office offer specialized tutoring?

6. Does the office offer priority accommodative preregistration?

Student Life: Are You Invited to the Party?

While access to academic life is critical, access and opportunity to participate in all aspects of student life is equally important your ability to derive full benefit from the college experience. Does the college you're interested in attending welcome students with disabilities to participate in student life? Answers to the following questions serve as good indicators of an institution's commitment to the full inclusion of students with disabilities into all aspects of campus life:

1. Is there an organization on campus run by and for students with disabilities? Such organizations help students with disabilities acquire self-advocacy skills and are often an important source of social change on campus.

2. Are students with disabilities well represented in other student organizations and programs?

3. Are students with disabilities represented in student government?

4. Are there athletic teams for students with disabilities?

The Campus Visit

The old saying is true: You'll never know where you're going till you get there. No telephone conversation with a college admissions officer or coordinator of services for students with disabilities or student services brochure can take the place of a single campus visit. The visit will give you a good feel for a college's attitude and approach towards students with disabilities. It can help you find out a college's culture regarding the accommodation and inclusion of students with disabilities. The following tips will determine how accessible and welcoming a campus is for students with disabilities:

Neon Wheelchairs

Once stigma symbols, assistive technologies now offer students with disabilities opportunities to express their individuality and pride in their identity as people with disabilities. According to Rory Cooper, "every wheelchair makes a personal statement, so choosing a wheelchair should reflect not only your physical needs but also your personality and lifestyle."* Students zooming across campus in eye-popping neon wheelchairs are now a feature of life on college campuses. Similarly, as text-to-speech technologies evolve and become more sophisticated, they can be tailored to reflect individual identities. The voice output from such technologies, once very mechanical and without a semblance of warmth, is now available in different tones, timbers, and octaves to better reflect individual personalities.

*Rory Cooper, "The Basics: Choosing a Manual Wheelchair" in New Mobility, Volume VII, Number 22, pp. 58–59.

ACCESSIBLE ACADEMICS

1. See how easy it is to navigate at the school. Explore the campus. Check for barriers. Try assistive technologies—get a sense of the technologies a school has to offer and how this inventory matches up with your accommodation needs.

2. Meet with the person on campus who coordinates services for students with disabilities. Get a sense of what services are available and how they are provided.

3. Meet with representatives of the academic departments in which you are interested and get a sense of their attitude towards accommodating students with disabilities.

4. Speak with the campus ADA compliance coordinator and get a sense of the college's policy for accommodating students with disabilities.

5. Ask to see the college's 504/ADA Transition Plan and its Annual Compliance Report. These self-assessments will give you a good sense of how effective a college is in accommodating students with disabilities and may alert you to campus barriers that may effect your decision to attend that particular school. These reports are public documents; anyone can ask to review them. They are typically housed in the office of services for students with disabilities, the school library, the student center, the affirmative action office, or the department of human resources.

6. Above all, speak with other students attending the college—talk to students with and without disabilities. This will give you a real sense of how accessible a campus is and how welcoming it is to students with disabilities.

TIME OUT: A MESSAGE TO PARENTS (AND STUDENTS)

This book is geared to students—and students will benefit from reading the following material. We wanted, however, to talk to parents directly about the college admissions process, so please share this section with a parent or guardian.

Even though your sincere expression of concern and offer of support to your kids in making decisions about college might cause you to be subjected to griping, don't be alarmed. It's understandable that you worry about your kids as they make one of the most important decisions of their lives. All parents worry about their kids making decisions about college;

The Parent Trap
Parents of students with disabilities—like all parents—worry about their children. While it's OK to be concerned about college decisions, try not to smother your child. Instead, express your concerns in ways that help him or her become more empowered and independent.

parents of students with disabilities are no different. Yet, students with disabilities confront a unique set of logistical challenges in choosing a school that can serve as additional sources of parental worry. It's okay to be concerned, but how you express that worry will determine whether or not you complicate your children's decisions, or help to empower them to make informed choices about their future.

Rather than expressing your worry by smothering and sheltering students with disabilities as they make choices about college, try to help them embrace challenges and uncertainty as opportunities for personal growth, for building a foundation for lives of independence, and for helping them to acquire more empowered, autonomous senses of self. Assisting your children in their college choices in this manner may also offer you the opportunity to transform your relationship with your children—from one in which your children are dependent upon you to one in which you foster their independence.

Confronting Myths about Disability

Many parental concerns about college choices are grounded in pervasive societal myths about the capabilities of people with disabilities. Parents or guardians of children with disabilities (particularly those adults who do not have disabilities themselves) live in a culture created by and for people without disabilities. Therefore, when kids with disabilities begin to strive for independence and try to make choices about college, adults are often confronted by their beliefs about disabilities, about what they think people with disabilities can accomplish, about how students may or may not be able to accomplish their goals, and about what the accomplishment of these goals represents. Parents may find themselves struggling to sort out myths about disability from reality as they go through the college admissions experience with their children.

The following represent some common myths about disability that parents or guardians may encounter when accompanying students with disabilities through the college admissions process.

The Myth of Incompetence. We have been socialized to believe that people with disabilities are somehow generally less viable, less capable than people without disabilities. As a result, we tend to have lower expectations for people with disabilities and hold them to a lower level of performance than people without disabilities. This has implications for the self-conceptions and performance of students with disabilities as the internalization of these lower expectations results in a self-fulfilling prophecy, with students' performances failing to reach the level of the students' full potential. It's very important for parents to destroy the myth of incompetence. Please assume that students with disabilities who meet standards for college admission; belong in college, and expect these students to succeed until proven otherwise.

The Myth of Helplessness. Our culture teaches us to assume that people with disabilities are perpetually dependent and in need of help from others at all times. This myth is particularly seductive for the parents or guardians of children with disabilities. However, with the development of independence-fostering assistive technologies and personal assistance services, there is less reason than ever before to assume that people with disabilities are in need of help. It's very important for parents to destroy the myth of helplessness. Sort out the help that is necessary for students to become more independent from the help that is not needed. Unneeded or unwanted assistance can cause unnecessary feelings of dependence among students with disabilities and can cause them to resent their well-meaning parents.

The Myth of Fragility. A common belief in our culture is that people with disabilities are somehow more physically and emotionally fragile than people who do not have disabilities. Because of this belief, we often treat people with disabilities as though they need to be shielded from potential harm and disappointment. Applying to college is a generally exciting and ultimately gratifying experience, but, at times, it can be nerve-racking and fraught with disappointment. When assisting students with disabilities to confront and cope with college-related setbacks, don't try to protect them from disappointment for fear that they somehow can't handle it. All adversity offers the opportunity for growth and maturity. All students must learn how to handle anger, criticism, and failure so they can acquire resilience. Resilience and good coping skills will ultimately serve students with disabilities well as they confront the challenges of college and real life. No one should be denied these opportunities for growth, especially since it's only in contrast to disappointments during the college admissions process that ultimate successes become so rewarding.

Too Much Pressure

Don't treat children with disabilities as heroic. Doing so can suggest that there's more riding on going to college than getting an education.

The Myth of the Supercrip. People without disabilities often regard the most common achievements of people with disabilities as amazing, as sources of wonder; they assume that in order to possess the "courage" and resourcefulness to perform activities of daily living, people with disabilities must possess powers far beyond those of mortals! With this myth, it's easy to regard as heroic the decision of students with disabilities to attend college and pursue a degree. While it's certainly important

A Winning Team

The philosophy underlying intercollegiate wheelchair basketball, according to one coach of the sport at a school in Texas, is to "treat student-athletes with disabilities like able-bodied student-athletes." In its efforts to extend equal access to students with disabilities in all aspects of college life, that school offers full athletic scholarships to members of its wheelchair basketball team.

to be proud of your child's decision and to acknowledge that it takes courage for anyone to tackle the challenges and rigors of higher education, it's important not to view his or her decision and accomplishments as unique or requiring an inordinate amount of bravery. Tens of thousands of students with disabilities make the same choices and succeed in college each year.

It's very important for parents to destroy the myth of the "supercrip." To treat college students with disabilities as unique and heroic puts enormous pressure on them. It makes them feel as though there's more riding on their going to college than getting an education and laying the foundation for a life of independence. There are many ways of treating students with disabilities as different and separate from other students. One way is to stigmatize them and assume that they can't achieve in college; the other, equally harmful way is to put them on a pedestal.

Helping that Really Helps

If you take the time to understand the implications of disability myths, helping your kids may seem more complicated and foreign than ever before. If, at any particular moment, you're confused about whether or not the help you're providing is truly benefiting your child, ask yourself the following question: "Is what I am doing helping my child to become more independent and to make his or her own decisions?" If the answer to this question is yes, then take heart in knowing that you've helped to instill an empowered sense of self in your child.

Use your expertise as a parent or guardian to help prepare your children for an empowering experience during the college admissions process. Here are some positive ways to help.

Share your advocacy skills with your child. Often, students with disabilities have been able to achieve and be included in all aspects of their educational experience only because their parents were assertive advocates on their behalf. Use your advocacy experience to teach them to be assertive self-advocates.

Encourage students to learn more. Help students learn more about assistive technologies that could aid students in their learning and in becoming more independent, about their individual learning needs and styles, and about resources that could assist them in college.

Encourage students to learn about disability rights and independent living. Help your children understand a college's legal obligation to provide them equal access and opportunity. This will help them to develop empowered, autonomous senses of self.

Encourage students to participate in all aspects of student life. Participation in extracurricular activities can help students with disabilities build leadership and interpersonal skills that will serve them well in making the transition to college and, later, to the real world.

Resource Guide

Many of the resources listed in this guide were abstracted from the *HEATH National Resource Directory on Postsecondary Education and Disability*, 1996. This valuable resource represents a biennial selection of resources in the major areas of interest in the field of postsecondary education and disability. This directory can be purchased at cost from the HEATH Resource Center, One DuPont Circle, Suite 800, Washington DC 20036–1193, or call (800) 54–HEATH; TTY: (800) 54–HEATH.

ABLEDATA

8455 Colesville Road
Suite 935
Silver Spring, MD 20910-3319
Phone: (800) 227-0216
Fax: (301) 587-1967
TTY: (800) 227-0216

ABLEDATA is a database of information on more than 20,000 products and assistive technologies for people with disabilities.

ACT Test Administration

P.O. Box 4028
Iowa City, IA 52243-4028
Phone: (319) 337-1332
Fax: (319) 339-3020
TTY: (319) 337-1701

In order to take the ACT under modified conditions, call or write for a Request for Special Testing.

Association of Higher Education and Disability (AHEAD)

P.O. Box 21192
Columbus, OH 43221-0192
Phone: (614) 488-4972
Fax: (614) 488-1174
TTY: (614) 488-4972

An international, multicultural organization of professionals dedicated to the full integration and equal participation in higher education for persons with disabilities.

American Association for the Advancement of Science Project on Science, Technology, and Disability

1200 New York Ave N.W.
Washington, DC 20005
Phone: (202) 326-6630
Fax: (202) 371-9849
TTY: (202) 326-6630

An information center designed to facilitate the advancement of people with disabilities in the fields of science, math, and engineering.

Council for Exceptional Children

1920 Association Drive
Reston, VA 20191-1589
Phone: (703) 620-3660
Fax: (703) 264-9494
TTY: (703) 264-9446

An international professional organization dedicated to improving education for "exceptional" children, including students with disabilities.

Disability Rights Education and Defense Fund

2212 6th Street
Berkeley, CA 94710
Phone: (510) 644-2555
Fax: (510) 841-8645
TTY: (510) 644-2555

A national disability law and policy center offering education and training on disability rights and policy issues.

Distance Education and Training Council

1601 18th Street N.W.
Washington, DC 20009
Phone: (202) 234-5100
Fax: (202) 332-1386

A voluntary association of accredited distance learning schools offering both degree and non-degree programs.

Educational Testing Services SAT Special Services for Students with Disabilities

P.O. Box 6226
Princeton, NJ 08541-6226
Phone: (609) 771-7137
Fax: (609) 771-7681
TTY: (609) 882-4118

For information on modified testing for the SAT exams, call or write for Information for Students with Special Needs.

Federal Student Aid Information Center

Office of Student Financial Assistance
Postsecondary Education
U.S. Department of Education
Washington, DC 20202
Phone: (800) 433-3243
TTY: (800) 730-8913

The center is available to answer questions about federal student aid.

HEATH Resource Center National Clearinghouse on Postsecondary Education for Individuals with Disabilities

One DuPont Circle, Suite 800
Washington, DC 20036-1193
Phone: (800) 54-HEATH
TTY: (800) 54-HEATH

A national clearinghouse that operates under congressional legislative mandate to collect and disseminate information nationally about disability issues in postsecondary education.

National Council on Disability

1331 F Street N.W.
Suite 1050
Washington, DC 20004
Phone: (202) 272-2004
Fax: (202) 272-2002
TTY: (202) 272-2074
An independent federal agency that makes policy recommendations on issues affecting people with disabilities.

National Council on Independent Living

2111 Wilson Boulevard
Suite 405
Arlington, VA 22201
Phone: (703) 525-3406
Fax: (703) 525-3409
TTY: (703) 525-3407
A national association of independent living centers (community-based advocacy organizations run by and for people with disabilities) and supporters, it provides information about independent living and relevant legislation and offers referrals to local centers to consumers.

National Parent Network on Disabilities

1727 King Street
Suite 305
Alexandria, VA 22314-2836
Phone: (703) 684-6763
Fax: (703) 836-1232
TTY: (703) 684-6763
A nonprofit organization dedicated to improving the quality of lives of youth and adults with disabilities and their families.

National Rehabilitation Information Center

8455 Colesville Road
Suite 935
Silver Spring, MD 20910
Phone: (301) 588-9284
Fax: (301) 587-1967
TTY: (301) 587-1967
An information center that disseminates information on disability and rehabilitation, including vocational rehabilitation.

Office of the Americans with Disabilities Act Civil Rights Division

U.S. Department of Justice
P.O. Box 66738
Washington, DC 20035-6118
Phone: (800) 514-0301
TTY: (800) 514-0383
This office provides information on the ADA.

President's Committee on Employment of People with Disabilities

1331 F Street N.W.
Suite 300
Washington, DC 20004-1107
Phone: (202) 376-6200
Fax: (202) 376-6219
TTY: (202) 376-6205
A federal agency serving as a national source of information and assistance on issues related to the employment of people with disabilities.

Social Security Administration U.S. Department of Health and Human Services

Phone: (800) 772-1213
TTY: (800) 325-0778
The SSA provides information about federal disability benefits.

WORKSHEET FOR STUDENTS WITH DISABILITIES APPLYING TO COLLEGE

This worksheet can be used as a checklist for selecting and applying to colleges. Make photocopies of the worksheet, one for each school you'll be applying to, and use the data you gather to help you decide the best school for you.

Basic Prep

1. Have you met with your college advisor to determine if you have taken the following college preparatory courses?

College Prep Math Sequence	Yes ___ No ___
College Prep Writing Sequence	Yes ___ No ___
Sciences	Yes ___ No ___
Foreign Language	Yes ___ No ___

2. Do you have access to current documentation of your disability necessary to verify your eligibility for reasonable accommodations and to help you to define your accommodations profile?

   Yes ____   No ____

3. Utilizing your documentation, your insight into your disability, and the insight and expertise of your parents, teachers, and school disability professionals, make a list of ways in which your disability might affect your ability to succeed in college.

4. Utilizing your documentation, your insight into your disability, and the insight and experience of your parents, teachers, and school disability professionals, make a list of some of the reasonable accommodations that might help you to succeed in college.

5. Have you contacted the Educational Testing Service or ACT Test Administration Services about taking the SAT or ACT exams under modified, accommodative conditions?

   Yes ____   No ____

The Road to College

6. Have you considered taking Advanced Placement courses in high school to lighten your freshman courseload and give you more flexibility in planning your college schedule?

    Yes ____   No ____

7. In seeking to pay for your college education, have you considered the following funding sources:

Pell grants	Yes ____	No ____
State financial aid programs	Yes ____	No ____
Federal Supplemental Educational Opportunity awards	Yes ____	No ____
Federal work-study programs	Yes ____	No ____
Perkins loan program	Yes ____	No ____
Stafford loan program	Yes ____	No ____
Federal direct loan programs	Yes ____	No ____
Vocational Rehabilitation sponsorship	Yes ____	No ____
Setting up a Plan to Achieve Self-Support	Yes ____	No ____

Your "Short List" — Narrowing Your Choice of Schools

1. Size of school: big ____   small ____
2. Region: "sunbelt" ____   "snowbelt" ____
3. Type of school: public ____ private ____ junior college ____ senior college ____
4. Living arrangements: at home ____   dormitory ____

The Campus Visit

1. Did you check the campus for apparent barriers?

    Yes ____   No ____

2. Did you ask what assistive technologies and auxiliary services are available to meet your accommodation needs?

    Yes ____   No ____

3. Did you meet with the individual or entity on campus designated to provide services to students with disabilities?

    Yes ____   No ____

4. Did you meet with representatives of the academic departments in which you would like to major and get a sense for these departments' attitudes toward accommodating students with disabilities?

    Yes ____   No ____

5. Did you speak with the campus 504/ADA Compliance Officer to get a sense of the college or university's policy regarding the reasonable accommodation of students with disabilities?

   Yes ____   No ____

6. Did you review the college or university's 504/ADA Transition Plan and Annual Compliance Reports?

   Yes ____   No ____

7. Did you speak with students with disabilities on the campus to learn what it is like to be a student with a disability on this campus?

   Yes ____   No ____

Disclosing Your Disability

1. Have you thought about how you feel about disclosing your disability in the admissions process?

2. Have you considered how your feelings about disclosing your disabilities relate to your
   High school transcripts? SAT and ACT test reports?
   Letters of recommendation? Interviews? Personal statements?

Assessing Services for Students with Disabilities

1. The name of the office that coordinates services for students with disabilities: _____.
   An individual in that office who will work with you to provide the services you need: _____.
   Another person or persons who have additional responsibilities in this area: _____.

2. Does the office offer liaison services to faculty, staff, and administration?

   Yes ____   No ____

3. Does the office assist students with identification to faculty?

   Yes ____   No ____

4. What types of counseling services does the office provide?

Academic advisement	Yes ____	No ____
Personal counseling	Yes ____	No ____
Peer counseling	Yes ____	No ____
Vocational counseling	Yes ____	No ____
Benefits counseling	Yes ____	No ____
Independent living counseling	Yes ____	No ____

If you are a student with a learning disability:

    Diagnostic assessment   Yes ___   No ___

    Compensatory and remedial skill development   Yes___   No___

5. Does the office offer specialized tutoring?

    Yes ___   No ___

6. Does the office offer priority accommodative preregistration?

    Yes ___   No ___

Student Life

1. Is there a campus organization for students with disabilities?

    Yes ___   No ___

2. Are students with disabilities well represented in other student organizations and programs?

    Yes ___   No ___

3. Are students with disabilities represented in student government?

    Yes ___   No ___

4. Are there athletic teams for students with physical disabilities?

    Yes ___   No ___

Asking the Right Questions

Key questions for people whose disabilities affect their mobility:

1. Are all campus buildings accessible? If not, what is the college policy on moving events in inaccessible buildings to accessible locations?

2. Are key points of campus access accessible (curb cuts on campus walkways, "handicapped" parking available, etcetera)?

3. Are dormitory facilities accessible?

4. Do you have access to accommodative, priority preregistration to ensure that your courses are scheduled in ways that allow you to get from one to another on time?

5. If you require personal assistance services on campus, how do you go about recruiting and paying for a personal assistant?

6. If there is a campus transportation system, is it accessible?

Key questions for students with learning disabilities:

1. What is the college policy on accommodative, modified testing (extended exam time, tests administered in alternative formats, etcetera)?

2. Are tutorial services available and what, if any, are the costs to you?

3. Are course materials (syllabi, books, handouts, etcetera) available to you in an accessible format (on audiotape, etcetera)?

4. Is someone available to assist you in identifying your needs to faculty?

5. Is academic advisement available?

Key questions for students who are blind or have visual impairments:

1. How are college materials (applications, forms, catalogues) and course materials (syllabi, books, handouts) made available to you in accessible formats?

2. How do you obtain the services of a reader?

3. How do you arrange for accommodative testing?

4. What assistive technologies are available to you on campus (Reading Edge machines, computers with the capacity for text-to-speech voice synthesis and text enlargement, braille printers, Visualtek machines, etcetera)?

5. Is there someone available to assist you with mobility training on campus?

6. What are the college policies on accommodating the use of guide dogs?

Key questions for students who are deaf or hard of hearing:

1. How do you arrange for interpreter services for both class and nonclass activities?

2. How do you arrange for notetakers for your classes?

3. Are assistive listening devices (infrared systems, "loop" systems, etcetera) available?

4. Is someone available to assist you in identifying your needs to faculty?

5. Are there TTYs available on campus?

Index of Schools Profiled

SCHOOLS PROFILED

Amherst College, 52
Antioch College, 353
Arizona State University, 366
Babson College, 274
Barnard College, 230
Bates College, 179
Bennington College, 354
Birmingham-Southern College, 258
Boston College, 292
Boston University, 305
Bowdoin College, 54
Brandeis University, 256
Brigham Young University, 294
Brown University, 77
Bryn Mawr College, 232
Bucknell University, 110
California Institute of Technology, 276
Carleton College, 56
Carnegie Mellon University, 278
Catholic University of America, 296
Claremont McKenna College, 112
Colby College, 114
Colgate University, 182
College of the Atlantic, 280
College of the Holy Cross, 298
College of William and Mary, 132
Colorado College, 356
Columbia University, 79
Connecticut College, 116
Cooper Union, 156
Cornell University, 82
CUNY/Brooklyn College, 160
CUNY/Hunter College, 160
CUNY/Queens College, 161
Dartmouth College, 326
Davidson College, 58
Denison University, 202

DePaul University, 307
Duke University, 85
Earlham College, 204
Emerson College, 281
Emory University, 309
Eugene Lang College, 357
Evergreen State College, 358
Fisk University, 246
Florida State University, 420
Franklin and Marshall College, 206
George Washington University, 311
Georgetown University, 338
Georgia Institute of Technology, 184
Gettysburg College, 118
Grinnell College, 60
Gustavus Adolphus College, 208
Hamilton College, 119
Hampden-Sydney College, 226
Hampshire College
Hampton University, 247
Harvard University, 88
Harvey Mudd College, 283
Haverford College, 61
Hobart and William Smith College, 229
Howard University, 249
Indiana University, 422
Johns Hopkins University, 259
Kalamazoo College, 329
Kenyon College, 121
Knox College, 209
Lafayette College
Lehigh University, 383
Lewis and Clark College, 331
Louisiana State University/Baton Rouge, 398
Macalester College, 211

Accessible Academics

Mary Washington College, 214
Massachusetts Institite of Technology, 92
Middlebury College, 65
Morehouse College, 251
Mount Holyoke College, 234
New College of the University of South Florida, 360
New York University, 313
Northwestern University, 185
Oberlin College, 67
Occidental College, 216
Ohio State University, 188
Pennsylvania State University, 190
Pitzer College, 341
Pomona College, 69
Princeton University, 94
Reed College, 122
Rhode Island School of Design, 286
Rhodes College, 124
Rice University, 135
Rutgers University, 343
Sarah Lawrence College, 363
Scripps College, 237
Skidmore College, 193
Smith College, 236
Southern Methodist University, 385
Southwestern University, 218
Spelman College, 252
St. John's College, 361
St. Olaf College, 333
Stanford University, 97
SUNY/Albany, 166
SUNY/Binghamton, 137
SUNY/Buffalo, 167
SUNY/Stony Brook, 168
Swarthmore College, 70
Sweet Briar College, 239
Syracuse University, 425
Temple University, 345

Texas Agricultural & Mechanical University, 170
The Juilliard School, 285
Trinity College, 220
Tufts University, 261
Tulane University, 388
Union College, 263
United States Air Force Academy, 162
United States Coast Guard Academy, 162
United States Military Academy, 162
United States Naval Academy, 162
University of Alaska/Fairbanks, 368
University of California/Berkeley, 139
University of California/Davis, 173
University of California/Los Angeles, 427
University of California/San Diego, 174
University of California/Santa Barbara, 390
University of California/Santa Cruz, 176
University of Chicago, 100
University of Colorado/Boulder, 369
University of Connecticut, 429
University of Florida, 392
University of Georgia/Athens, 400
University of Hawaii/Manoa, 372
University of Houston, 347
University of Illinois, 197
University of Iowa, 143
University of Maryland/College Park, 403
University of Massachusetts/Amherst, 435

University of Miami, 373
University of Michigan, 144
University of Minnesota/Twin Cities, 406
University of Missouri/Columbia
University of North Carolina/Chapel Hill, 147
University of Notre Dame, 431
University of Oregon, 410
University of Pennsylvania, 315
University of Pittsburgh, 318
University of Puget Sound, 376
University of South Florida
University of Southern California, 319
University of Tennessee/Knoxville, 412
University of Texas/Austin, 149
University of the South, 265
University of Vermont, 378
University of Virginia, 151
University of Washington, 414
University of Wisconsin/Madison, 416
Vanderbilt University, 322
Vassar College, 72
Villanova University, 436
Wabash College, 227
Wake Forest University, 195
Washington and Jefferson College, 267
Washington and Lee Univ., 126
Washington University, 268
Wellesley College, 240
Wesleyan University, 102
Williams College, 74
Wofford College, 222
Yale University, 105
Yeshiva University, 300

Notes

Notes

Notes

Notes

Notes

Notes

Financing college just got easier!

KapLoan, the Kaplan Student Loan Information Program,* can help you get information and advice on how to meet the cost of school.

Through an affiliation with one of the nation's largest providers of federal student loans, the KapLoan program can *direct students to the financing they need* to reach their educational goals.

The KapLoan program provides **free** *information and services to help you complete the financial aid process, including:*

Access to Student Loan Experts

- Available through the KapLoan **toll-free** hotline (1-888-KAP-LOAN) seven days a week, twelve hours a day.
- These experts can walk you through the financial aid process, answer questions, and even take student loan applications over the phone!

Application Editing

- A thorough review of your student loan application to aid in accuracy and help eliminate delays due to missing and/or incorrect information.

Credit Pre-Approval

- Notifies parents within 72 hours if they are likely to qualify for a student loan—even before they complete a loan application!

The Second Look

- This credit reevaluation program may assist parents in reversing a credit-denied status.

Call us TOLL-FREE today for more details!

KapLoan™

The Kaplan Student Loan Information Program

1-888-KAP-LOAN

http://www.kaploan.com

* Kaplan is not a lender and does not participate in determinations of loan eligibility. Telephone inquiries to 1–888–KAP–LOAN will be answered by representatives of a provider of federal and certain private educational loans.

about KAPLAN

come to us for the best prep

KAPLAN EDUCATIONAL CENTERS

"How can you help me?"

From childhood to adulthood, there are points in life when you need to reach an important goal. Whether you want an academic edge, a high score on a critical test, admission to a competitive college, funding for school, or career success, Kaplan is the best source to help get you there. One of the nation's premier educational companies, Kaplan has already helped millions of students get ahead through our legendary courses and expanding catalog of products and services.

"I have to ace this test!"

The world leader in test preparation, Kaplan will help you get a higher score on standardized tests such as the PSAT, SAT, and ACT for college, the LSAT, MCAT, GMAT, and GRE for graduate school, professional licensing exams for medicine, nursing, dentistry, and accounting, and specialized exams for international students and professionals.

Kaplan's courses are recognized worldwide for their high-quality instruction, state-of-the-art study tools and up-to-date, comprehensive information. Kaplan enrolls more than 150,000 students annually in its live courses at 1,200 locations worldwide.

"How can I pay my way?"

As the price of higher education continues to skyrocket, it's vital to get your share of financial aid and figure out how you're going to pay for school. Kaplan's financial aid resources simplify the often bewildering application process and show you how you can afford to attend the college or graduate school of your choice.

KapLoan*, The Kaplan Student Loan Information Program*, helps students get key information and advice about educational loans for college and graduate school. Through an affiliation with one of the nation's largest student loan providers, you can access valuable information and guidance on federally insured parent and student loans. Kaplan directs you to the financing you need to reach your educational goals.

"Can you help me find a good school?"

Kaplan offers expert advice on selecting a college, graduate school, or professional school. We can also show you how to maximize your chances of acceptance at the school of your choice.

"But then I have to get a great job!"

Whether you're a student or a grad, we can help you find a job that matches your interests. Kaplan can assist you by providing helpful assessment tests, job and employment data, recruiting services, and expert advice on how to land the right job. Our division, Crimson & Brown Associates, is the leading collegiate diversity recruiting firm helping top-tier companies attract hard-to-find candidates.

Kaplan has the tools!

For students of every age, Kaplan offers the best-written, easiest-to-use **books.** Our growing library of titles includes guides for academic enrichment, test preparation, school selection, admissions, financial aid, and career and life skills.

Kaplan sets the standard for educational **software** with award-winning, innovative products for building study skills, preparing for entrance exams, choosing and paying for a school, pursuing a career, and more.

Helpful **videos** demystify college admissions and the SAT by leading the viewer on entertaining and irreverent "road trips" across America. Hitch a ride with Kaplan's *Secrets to College Admission* and *Secrets to SAT Success.*

Kaplan offers a variety of services **online** through sites on the Internet and America Online. Students can access information on achieving acaemic goals; testing, admissions, and financial aid; careers; fun contests and special promotions; live events; bulletin boards; links to helpful sites; and plenty of downloadable files, games, and software. Kaplan Online is the ultimate student resource.

KAPLAN

KAPLAN

Want more information about our services, products, or the nearest Kaplan educational center?

HERE

Call our nationwide toll-free numbers:

1-800-KAP-TEST
(for information on our live courses, private tutoring and admissions consulting)

1-800-KAP-ITEM
(for information on our products)

1-888-KAP-LOAN*
(for information on student loans)

Connect with us in cyberspace:
On **AOL**, keyword **"Kaplan"**
On the Internet's World Wide Web, open **"http://www.kaplan.com"**
Via E-mail, **"info@kaplan.com"**

Write to:
**Kaplan Educational Centers
888 Seventh Avenue
New York, NY 10019**

Kaplan® is a registered trademark of Kaplan Educational Centers. All rights reserved.
On Campus™ is a trademark of Meetinghouse Technologies. All rights reserved.
* Kaplan is not a lender and does not participate in determinations of loan eligibility.

MINIMUM SYSTEM REQUIREMENTS*

	Windows®	Macintosh®
Operating System:	Windows 3.1, Windows 95	System 7.1
CPU Type and Speed:	486DX, 33 Mhz	68040, 25 Mhz
Hard Drive Space:	8 MB	12 MB
Memory:	8 MB	8 MB
Graphics:	640 X 480 X 256	640 X 480 X 256
CD-ROM Speed:	2X	2X
Audio:	16-bit Sound Blaster-compatible Speakers	Speakers recommended
Other:	Mouse, Modem	Modem

**The configuration above will allow you to run all the applications included on the Kaplan Get into College CD-ROM. The Digital Test Booklet, and CD Match will run independently on lesser configurations. Only the online service provider requires a modem.

INSTALLATION INSTRUCTIONS*

Windows® 3.1x
After inserting the CD-ROM in your drive, run "D:\setup31.exe" (where "D" is the letter of your CD-ROM drive) from the File menu of the Program Manager. Follow the directions on the screen.

Windows 95
After inserting the CD-ROM in your drive, double-click on "My Computer," then on your CD-ROM drive icon, and then on "setup95." Follow the directions on the screen.

NOTE: Windows 3.1x and Windows 95 Applications can be run independently by double-clicking on their respective executables (.exe files) in the Get into College folder. To run the Get into College intro video, QuickTime® for Windows must be installed. It has been included on the CD for your convenience.

Macintosh®
After inserting the CD-ROM in your drive, double-click on "My Computer," then on your CD-ROM drive icon, and then on "setup." Follow the directions on the screen.

NOTE: To run the Get into College intro video, QuickTime must be installed. It has been included on the CD for your convenience.

*Check the Readme file on the CD-ROM for any last-minute changes to the CD-ROM or its installation instructions.

SOFTWARE LICENSE/DISCLAIMER OF WARRANTIES

1. ACCEPTANCE. By using this compact disc you hereby accept the terms and provisions of this license and agree to be bound hereby.

2. OWNERSHIP. The software contained on these compact discs, all content, related documentation and fonts (collectively, the "Software") are all proprietary copyrighted materials owned by Kaplan Educational Centers, Inc. ("Kaplan") or its licensors.

3. LICENSE. You are granted a limited license to use the Software. This License allows you to use the Software on a single computer only. You may not copy, distribute, modify, network, rent, lease, loan, or create derivative works based upon the Software in whole or in part. The Software is intended for personal usage only. Your rights to use the Software shall terminate immediately without notice upon your failure to comply with any of the terms hereof.

4. RESTRICTIONS. The Software contains copyrighted material, trade secrets and other proprietary material. In order to protect them, and except as permitted by applicable legislation, you may not decompile, reverse engineer, disassemble or otherwise reduce the Software to human-perceivable form.

5. LIMITED WARRANTY; DISCLAIMER. Kaplan warrants the compact discs on which the Software is recorded to be free from defects in materials and workmanship under normal use for a period of ninety (90) days from the date of purchase as evidenced by a copy of the receipt. Kaplan's entire liability and your exclusive remedy will be replacement of the compact discs not meeting this warranty. The Software is provided "AS IS" and without warranty of any kind and Kaplan and Kaplan's licensors EXPRESSLY DISCLAIM ALL WARRANTIES, EXPRESS OR IMPLIED, INCLUDING THE IMPLIED WARRANTIES OF MERCHANTABILITY OR FITNESS FOR A PARTICULAR PURPOSE. FURTHERMORE, KAPLAN DOES NOT WARRANT THAT THE FUNCTIONS CONTAINED IN THE SOFTWARE WILL MEET YOUR REQUIREMENTS, OR THAT THE OPERATION OF THE SOFTWARE WILL BE UNINTERRUPTED OR ERROR-FREE, OR THAT DEFECTS IN THE SOFTWARE WILL BE CORRECTED. KAPLAN DOES NOT WARRANT OR MAKE ANY REPRESENTATIONS REGARDING THE USE OR THE RESULTS OF THE USE OF THE SOFTWARE IN TERMS OF THEIR CORRECTNESS, ACCURACY, RELIABILITY OR OTHERWISE. UNDER NO CIRCUMSTANCES, INCLUDING NEGLIGENCE, SHALL KAPLAN BE LIABLE FOR ANY DIRECT, INDIRECT, PUNITIVE, INCIDENTAL, SPECIAL OR CONSEQUENTIAL DAMAGES, INCLUDING, BUT NOT LIMITED TO, LOST PROFITS OR WAGES, IN CONNECTION WITH THE SOFTWARE EVEN IF KAPLAN HAS BEEN ADVISED OF THE POSSIBILITY OF SUCH DAMAGES. CERTAIN OF THE LIMITATIONS HEREIN PROVIDED MAY BE PRECLUDED BY LAW.

6. EXPORT LAW ASSURANCES. You agree and certify that you will not export the Software outside of the United States except as authorized and as permitted by the laws and regulations of the United States. If the Software has been rightfully obtained by you outside of the United States, you agree that you will not re-export the Software except as permitted by the laws and regulations of the United States and the laws and regulations of the jurisdiction in which you obtained the Software.

7. MISCELLANEOUS. This license represents the entire understanding of the parties, may only be modified in writing and shall be governed by the laws of the State of New York.

ACT, PSAT, and SAT are registered trademarks of their respective owners, who do not endorse or sponsor this product.

KapLoan™ is a trademark of Kaplan Educational Centers.

Kaplan Get into College CD-ROM, Copyright 1997, by Kaplan Educational Centers. All rights reserved.

Macintosh, QuickTime and the QuickTime logo are registered trademarks of Apple Computer, Inc. used under license.

Windows is a registered trademark of Microsoft Corporation.

If you need assistance with installation, need to request a replacement disk, or have any other software questions, call Kaplan at (970) 339-7142, Monday–Friday, 9 A.M. to 9 P.M.